APOLLOS OLD TESTAMENT
COMMENTARY

5

DEUTERONOMY

APOLLOS OLD TESTAMENT
COMMENTARY

5

DEUTERONOMY

Series Editors
David W. Baker and Gordon J. Wenham

J. G. McCONVILLE

IVP Academic
An imprint of InterVarsity Press
Downers Grove, Illinois

Apollos
Nottingham, England

InterVarsity Press, USA
P.O. Box 1400, Downers Grove, IL 60515-1426, USA
World Wide Web: www.ivpress.com
Email: email@ivpress.com

APOLLOS (an imprint of Inter-Varsity Press, England)
Norton Street, Nottingham NG7 3HR, England
Website: www.ivpbooks.com
Email: ivp@ivpbooks.com

InterVarsity Press®, USA, is the book-publishing division of InterVarsity Christian Fellowship/USA®, a movement of students and faculty active on campus at hundreds of universities, colleges and schools of nursing in the United States of America, and a member movement of the International Fellowship of Evangelical Students. For information about local and regional activities, write Public Relations Dept., InterVarsity Christian Fellowship/USA, 6400 Schroeder Rd., P.O. Box 7895, Madison, WI 53707-7895, or visit the IVCF website at <www. intervarsity.org>.

Inter-Varsity Press, England, is closely linked with the Universities and Colleges Christian Fellowship, a student movement connecting Christian Unions throughout Great Britain, and a member movement of the International Fellowship of Evangelical Students. Website: www.uccf.org.uk

USA ISBN 978-0-8308-2505-9
UK ISBN 978-0-85111-779-9

Set in Sabon 10/12pt
Typeset in Great Britain by CRB Associates, Reepham, Norfolk

Printed in the United States of America ∞

Library of Congress Cataloging-in-Publication Data

McConville, J. G. (J. Gordon)
    Deuteronomy/J. Gordon McConville.
        p. cm.—(Apollos Old Testament commentary)
    Includes bibliographical references and indexes.
    ISBN 0-8308-2505-3 (cloth: alk. paper)
    1. Bible O. T. Deuteronomy—Commentaries. I. Title. II. Series

BS1275.53 .M33 2002
222'.15077—dc22

                                                                2002027277

British Library Cataloguing in Publication Data

A catalogue record for this book is available from the British Library.

P	25	24	23	22	21	20	19	18	17	16	15	14	13	12	11	10	9	8	7
Y	28	27	26	25	24	23	22	21	20	19	18	17	16	15	14	13	12		

CONTENTS

To my mother, Betty McConville
and in memory of my father, Walter McConville
(1919–95)

EDITORS' PREFACE

The Apollos Old Testament Commentary takes its name from the Alexandrian Jewish Christian who was able to impart his great learning fervently and powerfully through his teaching (Acts 18:24–25). He ably applied his understanding of past events to his contemporary society. This series seeks to do the same, keeping one foot firmly planted in the universe of the original text and the other in that of the target audience, which consists of preachers, teachers and students of the Bible. The series editors have selected scholars who are adept in both areas, exhibiting scholarly excellence along with practical insight for application.

Translators need to be at home with the linguistic practices and semantic nuances of both the original and target languages in order to be able to transfer the full impact of the one into the other. Commentators, however, serve as interpreters of the text rather than simply as its translators. They also need to adopt a dual stance, though theirs needs to be even more solidly and diversely anchored than that of translators. On the one hand, they too must have the linguistic competence to produce their own excellent translations; they must, moreover, be fully conversant with the literary conventions, sociological and cultural practices, historical background and understanding and theological perspectives of those who produced the text as well as of those whom it concerned. On the other hand, they must also understand their own times and culture, and be able to see where relevance for the original audience is transferable to that of current readers. For this to be accomplished, it is necessary not only to interpret the text, but also to interpret the audience.

Traditionally, commentators have been content to highlight and expound the ancient text. More recently, the need for an anchor in the present day has also become more evident, and this series self-consciously adopts this approach, combining both. Each author analyses the original text through a new translation, textual notes and a discussion of the literary form, structure and background of the passage, as well as commenting on elements of its exegesis. A study of the passage's interpretational development in Scripture and the church concludes each section, serving to bring the passage home to the modern reader. What we intend, therefore, is to provide not only tools of excellence for the academy, but also tools of function for the pulpit.

David W. Baker
Gordon J. Wenham

AUTHOR'S PREFACE

It has been my privilege to be able to spend a lot of time with Deuteronomy over the years. Though one travels to other parts of the Old Testament in a teaching career, Deuteronomy is always somehow there, whether clad in the scholarly guise of the 'Deuteronomist' and 'Deuteronomistic' literature, or simply as the theological colossus that guards the entrance to Old Testament theology. So I am delighted to have been able to work on the present commentary, and to see it appear in the Apollos series.

I am most grateful to Professor Gordon Wenham, who was first my PhD supervisor and is now my colleague, for inviting me to contribute to the series. His friendship and encouragement over the years have been very important to me, as has his own scholarly work both on Deuteronomy and on other subjects. I have benefited greatly from his wisdom and guidance as I have worked on this volume. My thanks are also due to Professor David Baker, another friend and encourager, who, as co-editor of the series, has also made valuable comments on the manuscript.

Thanks are also due to my colleagues in Theology and Religious Studies at the University of Gloucestershire. Their willingness to cover various extra duties during a sabbatical term in 1998 made an important contribution to the advancement of the present work. And their collegiality in teaching and research continues to be enormously stimulating.

It is almost impossible to offer a commentary on Deuteronomy without mentioning Professor Norbert Lohfink. His contribution to Deuteronomy studies over several decades is prodigious. It has affected my thinking in too many ways to mention, even if the approach I adopt here is not quite the same as his. To a scholarly debt I add a personal one, because of his more than generous hospitality during a visit to the Philosophisch-Theologische Hochschule Sankt-Georgen, Frankfurt, in 1998.

Finally, I am grateful, too, to IVP for accepting the volume into the series, and especially to Philip Duce, who has given it careful and perceptive attention on the process towards publication.

J. G. McConville

ABBREVIATIONS

TEXTUAL

Aram.	Aramaic
BHS	K. Elliger and W. Rudolph (eds.), *Biblia Hebraica Stuttgartensia*, 2nd ed., Stuttgart: Deutsche Bibelstiftung, 1977
Dtr	the Deuteronomist
DtrH	the Deuteronomistic History (Joshua–Kings)
DtrN	the exilic 'nomistic' redaction of DtrH
Gk.	Greek
HB	Hebrew Bible
Hebr.	Hebrew
K	Kethibh (the written Hebrew text)
LXX	Septuagint
MS(S)	Manuscript(s)
MT	Masoretic Text
Q	Qere (the Hebrew text to be read out)
QL	Qumran literature
4QDeut(j, q)	fragmentary texts of Deuteronomy from Qumran
SamP	Samaritan Pentateuch
Syr	Syriac
Tg(s)	Targum(s)
TgJon	Targum Jonathan
Vg	Vulgate

HEBREW GRAMMAR

abs.	absolute	m.	masculine
def. art.	definite article	ni.	niphal
f.	feminine	pf.	perfect
hiph.	hiphil	pi.	piel
hith.	hithpael	pl.	plural
hoph.	hophal	prep.	preposition
imp.	imperative	ptc.	participle
impf.	imperfect	pu.	pual
inf.	infinitive	sg.	singular

MISCELLANEOUS

Akk.	Akkadian
ANE	Ancient Near East(ern)
AV	Authorized (King James) Version
BC	Book of the Covenant (Exod. 20:22 – 23:19)
cent(s).	century/ies
CH	Code of Hammurabi
ch(s).	chapter(s)
CL	Code of Lipit-Ishtar
EA	El Amarna tablets
ed(s).	edited by; editor(s); edition
esp.	especially
ET	English translation
EÜ	Einheitsübersetzung (German Bible translation, used in Braulik's commentary)
EVV	English versions
FS	*Festschrift*
HC	Holiness Code (Lev. 17 – 26)
HL	Hittite Laws
inc.	including
LE	Laws of Eshnunna
lit.	literally
MAL	Middle Assyrian Laws
mg.	margin
n(n).	note(s)
NIV	New International Version
NRSV	New Revised Standard Version
NT	New Testament
OT	Old Testament
p(p).	page(s)
REB	Revised English Version
rev.	revised (by)
RSV	Revised Standard Version
trans.	translated by
Ug.	Ugaritic
v(v).	verse(s)
VTE	Vassal Treaties of Esarhaddon

JOURNALS, REFERENCE WORKS, SERIES

AB	Anchor Bible
ABD	D. N. Freedman (ed.), *Anchor Bible Dictionary*, 6 vols., New York: Doubleday, 1992
ABR	*Australian Biblical Review*
AcT	*Acta theologica*
AfO	*Archiv für Orientforschung*
AJCL	*American Journal of Comparative Law*
AnBib	Analecta biblica
ANET	J. B. Pritchard (ed.), *Ancient Near Eastern Texts Relating to the Old Testament*, 3rd ed., Princeton: Princeton University Press, 1969
AOS	American Oriental Series
ASTI	*Annual of the Swedish Theological Institute*
ATANT	Abhandlungen zur Theologie des Alten und Neuen Testaments
AUSS	*Andrews University Seminary Studies*
BA	*Biblical Archaeologist*
BBB	Bonner biblische Beiträge
BEATAJ	Beiträge zur Erforschung des Alten Testaments und des antiken Judentum
BETL	Bibliotheca ephemeridum theologicarum lovaniensium
BHT	Beiträge zur historischen Theologie
BibInt	*Biblical Interpretation*
BibOr	Biblica et orientalia
BSac	*Bibliotheca sacra*
BK	*Bibel und Kirche*
BN	*Biblische Notizen*
BKAT	Biblischer Kommentar, Altes Testament
BTAT	Beiträge zur Theologie des Alten Testaments
BTB	*Biblical Theology Bulletin*
BVSAWL	Berichte über die Verhandlungen der sächsischen Akademie der Wissenschaften zu Leipzig
BWANT	Beiträge zur Wissenschaft vom Alten und Neuen Testament
BWAT	Beiträge zur Wissenschaft vom Alten Testament
BZ	*Biblische Zeitschrift*
BZAW	Beihefte zur Zeitschrift für die alttestamentliche Wissenschaft
CAD	I. I. Gelb et al. (eds.), *The Assyrian Dictionary of the Oriental Institute of the University of Chicago*, Chicago: Oriental Institute, 1964–
CBQ	*Catholic Biblical Quarterly*
ConBOT	Coniectanea biblica, Old Testament Series

CTA	A. Herdner (ed.), *Corpus des tablettes en cunéiformes alphabétiques découvertes à Ras Shamra-Ugarit de 1929 à 1939*, Paris: Geuthner, 1963
DBAT	*Dielheimer Blätter zum Alten Testament und seiner Rezeption in der Alten Kirche*
DSB	Daily Study Bible
EJT	*European Journal of Theology*
EstBíb	*Estudios bíblicos*
ETL	*Ephemerides theologicae lovanienses*
ETR	*Etudes théologiques et religieuses*
ETS	Erfurter theologische Studien
EvQ	*Evangelical Quarterly*
FAT	Forschungen zum Alten Testament
FRLANT	Forschungen zur Religion und Literatur des Alten und Neuen Testaments
FZPhTh	*Freiburger Zeitschrift für Philosophie und Theologie*
GKC	E. Kautzsch (ed.), *Gesenius' Hebrew Grammar* (rev. and trans. A. E. Cowley), Oxford: Clarendon, 1910
GTA	Göttinger theologische Arbeiten
HALAT	L. Koehler, W. Baumgartner and J. J. Stamm (eds.), *Hebräisches und aramäisches Lexikon zum Alten Testament*, 5 vols., 3rd ed., Leiden: Brill, 1967–95
HAR	*Hebrew Annual Review*
HAT	Handkommentar zum Alten Testament
HBS	Herder biblische Studien
HS	*Hebrew Studies*
HSM	Harvard Semitic Monographs
HSS	Harvard Semitic Studies
HTR	*Harvard Theological Review*
HUCA	*Hebrew Union College Annual*
ICC	International Critical Commentary
IDBSup	K. Crim (ed.), *Interpreter's Dictionary of the Bible, Supplementary Volume*, Nashville, TN: Abingdon, 1976
IEJ	*Israel Exploration Journal*
Int	*Interpretation*
IOS	*Israel Oriental Society*
IOSCS	International Organisation for Septuagint and Cognate Studies
ISBE	G. W. Bromiley (ed.), *International Standard Bible Encyclopedia*, 4 vols., 2nd ed., Grand Rapids, MI: Eerdmans, 1979–88
JAOS	*Journal of the American Oriental Society*
JBL	*Journal of Biblical Literature*
JBT	*Jahrbuch für biblische Theologie*
JCS	*Journal of Cuneiform Studies*

JJS	*Journal of Jewish Studies*
JNES	*Journal of Near Eastern Studies*
JPOS	*Journal of the Palestine Oriental Society*
JPSTC	Jewish Publication Society Torah Commentary
JQR	*Jewish Quarterly Review*
JRE	*Journal of Religious Ethics*
JSOT	*Journal for the Study of the Old Testament*
JSOTSup	Journal for the Study of the Old Testament, Supplement Series
JSS	*Journal of Semitic Studies*
LD	Lectio divina
NAC	New American Commentary
NCB	New Century Bible
NEchtB	Neue Echter Bibel
NIBCOT	New International Biblical Commentary on the Old Testament
NICOT	New International Commentary on the Old Testament
NIDOTTE	W. A. VanGemeren (ed.), *New International Dictionary of Old Testament Theology and Exegesis*, 5 vols., Grand Rapids, MI: Zondervan; Carlisle: Paternoster, 1997
NRTh	*La nouvelle revue théologique*
NTS	*New Testament Studies*
OBO	Orbis biblicus et orientalis
ÖBS	Österreichische biblische Studien
OBT	Overtures to Biblical Theology
OLA	Orientalia lovaniensia analecta
OTG	Old Testament Guides
OTL	Old Testament Library
OTS	Old Testament Studies
OtSt	*Oudtestamentische Studiën*
PEQ	*Palestine Exploration Quarterly*
RB	*Revue biblique*
RHR	*Revue de l'histoire des religions*
SANT	Studien zum Alten und Neuen Testament
SB	Sources bibliques
SBAB	Stuttgarter biblische Aufsatzbände
SBL	Society of Biblical Literature
SBLDS	Society of Biblical Literature Dissertation Series
SBLMS	Society of Biblical Literature Monograph Series
SBLSCS	Society of Biblical Literature Septuagint and Cognate Studies
SBLSP	Society of Biblical Literature Seminar Papers
SBT	Studies in Biblical Theology
SBTS	Sources for Biblical and Theological Study
Schol	*Scholastik*

ScrHier	Scripta hierosolymitana
SCSS	Septuagint and Cognate Studies Series
SEÅ	*Svensk exegetisk årsbok*
SFEG	Schriften der finnischen exegetischen Gesellschaft
SHANE	Studies in the History of the Ancient Near East
SJOT	*Scandinavian Journal of the Old Testament*
SOTSMS	Society for Old Testament Studies Monograph Series
SSN	Studia semitica neerlandica
StudBib	Studia biblica
TB	Theologische Bücherei
TDOT	G. J. Botterweck and H. Ringgren (eds.), *Theological Dictionary of the Old Testament*, 8 vols. (trans. J. T. Willis, G. W. Bromiley and D. E. Green), Grand Rapids, MI: Eerdmans, 1974– (ET of *ThWAT*)
Them	*Themelios*
TP	*Theologie und Philosophie*
ThQ	*Theologische Quartalschrift*
TS	*Theological Studies*
ThWAT	G. J. Botterweck and H. Ringgren (eds.), *Theologisches Wörterbuch zum Alten Testament*, Stuttgart: Kohlhammer, 1970–
TOTC	Tyndale Old Testament Commentaries
TynB	*Tyndale Bulletin*
UF	*Ugarit-Forschungen*
UT	C. H. Gordon, *Ugaritic Textbook*, Analecta orientalia 38; Rome: Pontifical Biblical Institute, 1965
VT	*Vetus Testamentum*
VTSup	Supplements to Vetus Testamentum
WBC	Word Biblical Commentary
WMANT	Wissenschaftliche Monographien zum Alten und Neuen Testament
WZUL	*Wissenschaftliche Zeitschrift Universität Leipzig*
ZA	Zeitschrift für Assyriologie
ZABR	*Zeitschrift für altorientalische und biblische Rechtsgeschichte*
ZAW	*Zeitschrift für die alttestamentliche Wissenschaft*
ZBK	Zürcher Bibelkommentare
ZKT	*Zeitschrift für katholische Theologie*
ZThK	*Zeitschrift für Theologie und Kirche*

INTRODUCTION

1. THE NAME OF THE BOOK

The name 'Deuteronomy' comes from the Greek translation (LXX) of Deut. 17:18, which misunderstands the phrase 'a copy of this law' as 'this second law' (*to deuteronomion touto*). The concept, however, was no doubt based on the observation that the book contained new laws besides those already met in Exodus–Numbers. The title in Hebrew is 'These are the words', which simply adopts the opening words of the book. This has the advantage of highlighting the importance of the words of Moses. Deuteronomy does not simply add new material to what was already known, but re-presents and inculcates the requirements of the covenant. Both these ancient titles make observations about the book that are reflected in modern interpretation, the former noticing the problem of the relationship between Deuteronomy and the rest of the Pentateuch, the latter focusing on its specific content.

2. ITS PLACE IN THE CANON

Deuteronomy is the fifth book of Moses, the last book of the Pentateuch. These are traditional designations, arising in the course of ancient interpretation. The term 'Pentateuch' is not biblical, but a word based on the Greek for 'five scrolls', and a product of the canonization of the books of the OT. The Hebrew word 'Torah', a key term in Deuteronomy, meaning 'law' or 'instruction', also came to refer to the books of Moses as part of the same canonizing process (though it took on other senses too). The association with Moses was the key factor in marking out this section of the Scriptures as a separate entity. References in the NT and in Jewish literature to 'the Law, the Prophets and the Writings' presuppose the threefold division of the canon that still obtains in the Hebrew Bible, where 'the Law' is the Torah in this narrow sense of the five books of Moses. The threefold division attributes a certain primacy to the Pentateuch (though there is no evidence that it actually acquired canonical status before the other divisions). In this context, Deuteronomy brings to a conclusion the story of the formative events of Israel's history with Yahweh. Its narrative of the death of Moses (Deut. 34) is important symbolically, marking as it does the end of the primary era in Israel's life, and the transition to the next phase.

Modern interpretation has seen the place of Deuteronomy in the canon as rather more complex, aware of its relation not only to the first four books of the Pentateuch but also to the books that follow it, namely Joshua, Judges, Samuel and Kings, called the 'Former Prophets' in Jewish tradition, or more generally the 'Historical Books'. (The book of Ruth is usually discounted for these purposes, being differently placed in the Jewish canon.) One approach to the organization of the OT is to include Joshua along with the books of Moses, resulting in a 'Hexateuch' ('six scrolls'), on the grounds that certain themes found in those books (including the gift of the land, prominent in Deuteronomy) are concluded there (von Rad 1966). In contrast, some have spoken of a 'Tetrateuch' ('four scrolls'), because of differences in style and content between Deuteronomy and the preceding books, and also because of its strong links with Joshua–Kings (Noth 1981). The modern discussion echoes the ancient one, in that it reflects on the one hand the continuity of Deuteronomy with the other books (in the significance attached to Moses, and in the Hexateuch theory), and the discontinuity (in the ancient idea of a 'second law' and in the Tetrateuch theory).

3. THE DISTINCTIVE FEATURES OF DEUTERONOMY

Deuteronomy is distinguished among the books of the OT in a number of ways. In the Pentateuch's basic narrative, stretching from the creation and the promise to the patriarchs in Genesis to the point at which the nation of Israel stands ready to take its promised land across the Jordan, Deuteronomy marks a pause. Its opening sentences (Deut. 1:1–5) follow directly from the final verse of Numbers (Num. 36:13), and prepare for an account of the words spoken by Moses to Israel there. The reader who is familiar with the story so far sees immediately that what is to come will have a certain resumptive character. This is because of the brief allusive recapitulation of the journey through the wilderness of Sinai, with only a few tantalizing geographical details. True to the announcement in the first verse, the book then consists largely of Moses' speeches, and the narrative as such hardly progresses. The end of the book is as definitely marked as the beginning, with its report of the death of Moses, which, given his prominence in the Pentateuchal story as a whole, is a clear point of closure. And in Joshua, the continuation expected at the end of Numbers now follows.

The book is also distinguished by internal features. It is couched in a recognizable sermonic style that makes heavy use of repetition and has distinctive vocabulary and phraseology (the classic account of it is in S. R. Driver 1895: lxxvii–lxxxviii; cf. Weinfeld 1972: 320–365). Prominent in this discourse, for example, are repeated references to the promise of the land that the people are about to enter, and exhortations to obey the commands of the covenant when they do so.

To style may be added structure. As is well known, the form of Deuteronomy bears a strong resemblance to that of an ancient treaty. The significance of this must be elaborated further in due course (see section 4.1 below). It is mentioned here simply to notice that it is one factor in identifying the book as somewhat self-standing. It has a recognizable beginning, middle and end, so to speak, according to a conventional contemporary pattern. The correspondence is not perfect, especially as regards the last six chapters of the book, and therefore this argument must be handled with care. The analogy with the treaty can be used only in conjunction with other observations as an argument for the independence of Deuteronomy (especially the unity given to the book by the speeches of Moses, and the closure effected by the account of his death).

Finally, Deuteronomy is marked out by its content. The framework of Moses' speeches revisits ground already familiar to the reader of the Pentateuch so far: the conquest of Transjordan (Deut. 2 – 3; cf. Num. 21:21–35), the giving of the Ten Commandments at Mt Sinai (here Horeb; 5:6–21; cf. Exod. 20:22 – 23:19), a series of laws that follow and elaborate these (Deut. 12 – 26; cf. Exod. 21 – 23), a commitment to keep the covenant (Deut. 26:17–19; cf. Exod. 19:8; 24:3, 7). Yet this is not just repetition. On the contrary, the topics in Exodus, Leviticus and Numbers to which Deuteronomy returns are dealt with in quite distinctive ways, as will be seen repeatedly in the commentary. In a certain sense, therefore, Deuteronomy deserves its misnomer 'second law'. The most celebrated difference between Deuteronomy and the laws in Exodus concerns the law of the place of worship, on which Deuteronomy apparently requires a single place (Deut. 12:5), while Exodus had allowed a plurality (Exod. 20:24). And the differences manifested in Deuteronomy appear to have certain consistent features, often emphasizing a more explicit concern for the welfare of the individual than corresponding laws in the other codes (cf., e.g., Deut. 15:12–18 with Exod. 21:2–6, and 'Comment' on the former).

The special character of Deuteronomy goes much deeper than mere humanitarianism, however. In its style, structure and content it constitutes a single harmonious concept, designed to organize the whole life of Israel under the authority of the one God Yahweh. The crucial theological category in Deuteronomy's programme was that of covenant, in which in turn Torah (law, instruction) is the regulating principle. Covenant, of course, is not unique to Deuteronomy; the whole Pentateuch may be said to be organized around the concept. However, it is in Deuteronomy that it takes the form of a model for the organization of the life of a people under God. Its closest parallels in the OT in this respect are found in the prophetic books, above all the eighth-century northern prophet Hosea, whose similarities of language and thought with Deuteronomy have been documented by Weinfeld (1972: 366–370). Hosea shares Deuteronomy's radical doctrine of loyalty to Yahweh alone, its hostility to the worship of other gods, its rooting of the relationship between Yahweh and Israel in deliverance from Egypt and the divine gift of land, its coolness towards the institution of monarchy, and its use of the concepts of covenant and Torah as fundamental ingredients of the relationship between God and people. There are, of course, idiomatic differences between Hosea and Deuteronomy (e.g. Hosea's development of the marriage metaphor for the loyalty of Yahweh to Israel, and its genre as prophetic critique, where Deuteronomy is programmatic). And regarding the prophets in general, comparison with Deuteronomy is complicated just because of idiomatic differences.

Even so, other shared features include the belief in the special election of Israel, and consequent responsibility to be God's people not in name only but in truth (Amos 3:2); punishment as a consequence of failure to keep the commitments implied in the relationship (Deut. 28; Hos. 4:1–3; Mic. 6:1–4; Is. 3:13–15; Jer. 2:4–13); and the possibility of repentance and restoration following the punishment (Deut. 30:1–10; Hos. 14; Amos 9:11–15; Is. 40; Jer. 30 – 33). Perhaps the most striking similarity between Deuteronomy and the prophets is the theology of the 'heart'. In the former this is best known in the exhortation called the 'Shema' (after its first word in Hebrew): 'Hear, Israel! ... you shall love the LORD your God with all your heart, with all your soul and with all your might' (6:4; cf. 10:12), but it occurs more widely and in key places. In the metaphor of a circumcision of the heart (10:16; 30:6) it has an express echo in Jer. 4:4, and in general comes close to the strong prophetic rejection of ritual actions that have no genuine corresponding devotion to God (e.g. Is. 1:10–17; Amos 5:21–24). In Deut. 30:1–10, in fact, the emphasis on obedience from the heart together with the need for the grace of God in restoring the covenantal relationship puts Deuteronomy close to the new-covenant theology of Jer. 31:31–34.

I have dwelt on Deuteronomy's relationship with the prophets at this early stage in order to try to orientate the book in the most appropriate way to the traditions of Israel. In doing so I have passed over many questions regarding the authorship and date not only of Deuteronomy but of the various parts of the prophetic books. I admit that the precise relationships of all these books to one another are not easy to describe. Yet I think that those strands in OT scholarship that have found an essential commonality between Deuteronomy and the prophets are on the right lines and that these similarities should be given priority when the former is located within Israelite theology and religion (von Rad 1929: 72–100, and cf. idem 1953: 23–27; Alt 1959). This is not to exclude relationships between Deuteronomy and other important parts of the OT, as we shall see (in section 6 below), or to suppose that the relationship between it and the prophetic books is a simple one. However, the comparison with the prophets suggests that Deuteronomy should be seen, in the context of the ancient world, as a radical blueprint for the life of a people, at the same time spiritual and political, and running counter to every other social-political-religious programme. It is the aim of the commentary to explain in what sense this is so.

In what remains of the Introduction, therefore, I offer a preliminary account of what makes Deuteronomy different. This involves a review of scholarly attempts to understand the book, followed by an explanation of the view taken in this commentary; some explanation of how it relates to other OT (and NT) literature, and a reflection on its enduring value. We begin, then, with an account of the critical readings of it.

4. THE CRITICAL INTERPRETATION OF DEUTERONOMY

4.1. Deuteronomy and Josiah's reform

Although it was observed already in ancient times that Moses himself was not likely to have written the parts of the book that spoke about him in the third person, especially the account of his death, Mosaic authorship began to be systematically questioned only in the modern period. W. M. L. de Wette (1805) suggested that Deuteronomy was not Mosaic, on the grounds that it differed in style and content from the preceding books (which he still regarded as Mosaic). This put on a new footing the old sense that the book was 'a second law', qualitatively different from the others. De Wette observed in passing that the reform of King Josiah (2 Kgs. 22 – 23) may have been an occasion of its authorship, because of the note there (22:8) that the 'book of the law' was found during the repairs to the temple. This observation became the central plank in the platform of the Pentateuchal analysis of J. Wellhausen (1885) that dominated OT scholarship for a century. It focused Deuteronomy research not on Israel's ancient origins but on the last half-century of the existence of the kingdom of Judah.

The classical critical account of Deuteronomy is well documented in introductions and commentaries (e.g. in Mayes 1994: 29–55; Tigay 1996: xix–xxvi). It is briefly as follows. The Pentateuchal literature derives from several distinct periods of Israel's history, and is composed from four source documents, J, E, D and P. The earliest writing is found in J and E (often regarded in practice as one, JE), which are from the monarchical time (10th–8th cents. BC). These documents contain the earliest theologizing about the origins of Israel, with the beginnings of covenantal and ethical thinking, the latter more developed in E than in J. It is in this context also that the earliest law code is found (Exod. 20:22 – 23:19, known to scholars as the 'Book of the Covenant' [BC]). Deuteronomy roughly corresponds to the source 'D', and is, as we have noted, the occasion or the product of the reform of religion documented in 2 Kgs. 22 – 23. The 'Book of the Law' was taken to be a form of Deuteronomy, in line with that book's own self-designation in closely similar terms (Deut. 28:58, 61; 31:26; cf. Josh. 1:8). (The chronology of the reform is given slightly differently in 2 Chr. 34 – 35, which suggests that it began in 628 BC, and the discovery of the Book of the Law merely gave it fresh impetus. Wellhausen set no store by Chronicles, but some later scholarship has regarded it as closer to the likely actuality than Kings, which has concentrated its account on the Book; Nicholson 1967: 8–11.)

On this view the main aim of Deuteronomy was to concentrate, or 'centralize', the worship of Yahweh in the Jerusalem temple, by abolishing and defiling all rival sanctuaries. A plurality of worship places had been the norm in the earlier period, as evidenced by the stories of Samuel (1 Sam. 9:14; 10:3) and Elijah (1 Kgs. 18), and by the law of worship in Exod. 20:24. The reform, as recorded in 1 Kgs. 22 – 23, implied that the worship in other sanctuaries was, or had become, untrue to Yahweh, whether because overtly dedicated to other gods or merely syncretistic. Indeed, the book signalled a new and heightened understanding of the covenant, intensifying the need for Israel's (or strictly Judah's) loyalty to Yahweh. It had other concerns too, notably the promotion of a spiritual and ethical concept of religion. Yet paradoxically it was also the beginning of priestly and bureaucratic control of religion, which was then continued in P (the exilic source that amplified the laws concerning worship, sacrifice and priesthood, notably in Leviticus).

The instrument of this 'centralization' was the law of the altar, the most important single element in the book according to this interpretation. The fullest formulation of this law is found in Deut. 12:5, and it recurs with variations throughout the law code in Deut. 12 – 26. In this formula 'the place' is regarded as a coded name for Jerusalem, left unnamed in order to maintain the authenticity of the Mosaic setting. (The interpretation of this formula is explained more fully in the 'Comment' on Deut. 12.)

Deuteronomy, in this reconstruction, is inseparable from a great reform of religion in the seventh century. This reform had a tremendous impact upon the life of ordinary Israelites. Accustomed to worshipping at their local sanctuaries, they suddenly had all this swept away. No longer could they sacrifice and feast at these sanctuaries; their priests were disqualified and the places themselves lay in ruins. Jerusalem, for some a long journey away, became the only recognized place of worship. One effect of the reform, therefore, was an actual reduction in the amount of cultic activity that took place, and many interpreters regard this as an intended consequence (the classic modern account in is Weinfeld 1972: 190; cf. Tigay 1996: xvii). Deuteronomy, it is held, promoted a kind of theology that diminished the influence of priests, and of 'sacral' religion in general, that is, religion as constituted by cultic and sacrificial performance.

Many features of Deuteronomy might be explained in this way. The permission of 'profane slaughter' in Deut. 12, for example, is not only a practical consequence of centralization, enabling meat to be eaten in homes throughout Judah, but may also have a strong ideological thrust, a challenge to the belief that meat might be slaughtered only by way of sacrificial offering. The tithe as a festive meal for the worshipper and household, and in the third year as a means of provision for the poor (14:22–29), seems deliberately to remove it from the perquisites of the Levites (Num. 18:21–25). The 'sabbatical' year, formerly a kind of taboo, a 'holiness' regulation allowing the land to 'rest' (Lev. 25:2–7; 26:34–35), is now strictly a social measure, an occasion for the release of debts (Deut. 15:1–11; Weinfeld 1991: 27–28). Slave release too loses its sacral aspect (Exod. 21:6, 'before God'), and also marks an advance in social thinking by treating women on a par with men (Deut. 15:12, 17). In Tigay's words, 'Deuteronomy's aim is to spiritualize religion by freeing it from excessive dependence on sacrifice and priesthood' (1996: xvii). This was the nature of what Wellhausen had identified as the D document in his JEDP analysis.

It will be useful at this point to pay further attention to the similarity between Deuteronomy and ANE political treaties, because this plays some part in all modern analyses of the book.

The covenantal structure of the book was observed by von Rad in his commentary (1966: 12), and attributed to its role as the liturgy of a cultic festival, without reference to data from the ANE. The importance of the form of second-millennium Hittite vassal treaties in particular was noticed by Kline (1963) and Kitchen (1966: 90–102). The main elements in the form are: 1. a preamble, announcing the treaty and those who are party to it; 2. a historical prologue, rehearsing the previous relations between the parties; 3. stipulations; 4. a deposition of the document for the purpose of periodic public reading; 5. witnesses, and 6. blessings and curses (Kitchen

1966: 92–93; cf. Wenham 1971c: 206–212). It can be slightly differently described, with a distinction made between general and specific stipulations, and less importance attached to the document clause (see Baltzer 1971: 10; Craigie 1976a: 22–23).

The form may be matched to Deuteronomy as follows: 1. preamble (1:1–5); 2. historical prologue (1:6 – 4:49); 3. general stipulations (5 – 11); 4. specific stipulations (12 – 26); 5. document clause (27:1–10; 31:9–29); 6. witnesses (32, note v. 1); 7. blessings and curses (27:12–26; 28). In any such matching of the treaty form to Deuteronomy, however, the caveat must be entered that a perfect match should not be expected, still less forced; that the form of Deuteronomy is influenced by law codes as well as treaties (its 'stipulations' are closer to laws than to treaty stipulations); and that the resemblance to treaty form is sometimes closer to Assyrian models, as for example, in the curse section in Deut. 28:15–68, which is in contrast exceedingly long by comparison with the Hittite treaties. In conclusion, therefore, Deuteronomy is independent and unique, simply drawing on known and available forms for its own purposes.

The first effect of the discovery of the treaty analogy, however, was to reopen the question of the book's dating. Kline, Kitchen (1966: 90–102) and Craigie believed that Deuteronomy was significantly closer in form to the Hittite treaties than to the Assyrian, especially because of the importance of the element that corresponded to the historical prologue, a feature that was peculiar to the Hittite treaties. They saw this as evidence for the second-millennium date of Deuteronomy. In the scholarly discussions that have ensued, the balance of opinion has come to favour the dependence of Deuteronomy on Assyrian treaties of the seventh century BC (Frankena 1965; Weinfeld 1972; Steymans 1995a). A factor in this has been certain close similarities between the curses in Deut. 28 and the Vassal Treaties of Esarhaddon (VTE; this issue is discussed in the commentary on Deut. 28). However, it is not possible, in my view, to settle the dating of Deuteronomy on the basis of the treaty analogies alone, or to explain them as the result of the exclusive influence of either the Hittite or the Assyrian types. It is best to think of Deuteronomy as drawing on the treaty tradition of the ANE rather freely. Weinfeld (1991), in practice, finds echoes of both Hittite and Assyrian treaties in his commentary. It is perhaps in this respect that the treaty form continues to affect the interpretation of Deuteronomy most strongly, that is, at the level of phraseology and concepts. An example is the insight that 'love' in the treaties is a way of expressing the loyalty of a vassal to the overlord (Moran 1963a; see on Deut. 7).

4.2. The reform as a royal programme

The postulate that Deuteronomy was the document at the heart of Josiah's reform has remained a cornerstone of criticism (e.g. Nicholson 1967;

Clements 1989). In modern scholarship this postulate has been developed in a number of important ways: first, Deuteronomy has been thought to have had a decisive influence on the development of covenant theology itself; and secondly, the book in its present form is held to be the product of a process of editorial and theological growth continuing into the exilic and post-exilic periods.

Since Perlitt's work (1969), it has been widely thought that Deuteronomy's theology of covenant and gift of land in particular were formed against the background of the crisis in Judah caused by the threat from Assyria in the seventh century BC: the idea of the land as divine gift arose precisely because of the possibility that it might be lost. The reform too is often seen as a response to Assyrian power in the area and its imposition of its religion (Nicholson 1967: 11; Lohfink 1987: 222–223, following Spieckermann's analysis, 1982). The classic analysis of Deuteronomy against an Assyrian background, however, is that of Weinfeld (1972, 1991).

At one level, Josiah's reform might be seen as an act of resurgent nationalism, encouraged by declining Assyrian power, and trading on ancient Israelite traditions. Weinfeld's thesis goes further, with a strong theory about the religious nature of the deuteronomic movement alongside its political occasion.

Pointing to similarities between Deuteronomy and features of the OT Wisdom literature, Weinfeld situates Deuteronomy in the royal scribal schools of the late Judean period. These schools corresponded, in his view, to the Assyrian scribal schools that produced and copied the Assyrian political treaties. In Judah, these scribes were not only political officials but also had a view of religion that contrasted with the sacral theology of the priests, and that might be found in Deuteronomy's well-known ethical and spiritual emphases and in its scant interest in sacrificial minutiae. For them the political and religious aspects of reform were inseparable.

The resulting synthesis proposes a radical reform of religion, which may be called 'secularizing' and 'demythologizing'. That is, Deuteronomy is said to reject elements in older religion that are held to be 'sacral', or mythological. In such religion, holiness has a tangible presence, which has to be handled carefully in suitable places, by prescribed means and specially authorized personnel. This explains the emphasis on sacrificial instruction and regulations governing the priesthood in the priestly literature (or P; that is, principally parts of Exodus and Leviticus). Deuteronomy sweeps all this away, bringing in a new and rational approach to religion, in which even the concept of God is revolutionized. On the grounds of the name formula in Deut. 12:5 and related texts, and the prayer of Solomon at the dedication of the temple (1 Kgs. 8, esp. vv. 27–30), Weinfeld (following von Rad 1953) argues that Deuteronomy promotes a purely spiritual view of God, in which he is not even present in the temple at Jerusalem, but merely leaves his 'name' there, as a kind of symbolic representation. It will be noticed, incidentally, that the relationship between Deuteronomy and P is quite differently understood compared with Wellhausen. P is no longer seen as a development from D, but as a concurrent, competitor ideology, continuous with the religion that Deuteronomy opposes.

Though the reform has this theological centre, critical of established religious institutions, it is nevertheless an establishment enterprise, promoting the authority of the royal and cultic synthesis in Jerusalem (just as the Assyrian scribal schools supported the Assyrian political establishment). Moses in Deuteronomy is, for Weinfeld (1972: 170–171), a 'quasi-regal' figure, which means that in his religious and civil power he stands for the Judean king, as does Joshua after him. Deuteronomy's theological radicalism is therefore put to the service of a retrenching central authority.

This direction has been taken further by B. Halpern, who associates the ideology of Deuteronomy with a revolution he attributes to King Hezekiah (Halpern & Hobson 1991: 21–27, 41–49). Using historical and archaeological evidence, Halpern argues that Hezekiah, faced with insistent Assyrian aggression, completely reorganized life in Judah. He denuded the countryside, leaving nothing in it for the ravages of the invader, concentrating the population instead in the capital, Jerusalem, and in other fortified cities. This produced, or completed, a social revolution, the final step in the transformation of Judah from a traditional, tribal society to a centralized bureaucratic state. In this scenario, as in Weinfeld's, Deuteronomy is seen as an instrument of the revolution, serving a 'statist' ideology (1991: 17).

Further analysis of these views, together with responses, may be found in the commentary (e.g. on Deut. 12). Preliminary observations on them are offered below in the conclusion to this section on critical interpretation.

4.3. The development of Old Testament religion

Interpretation of Deuteronomy has always been set in the context of an understanding of Israel's religious development, which itself is subject to change. In early criticism (Wellhausen, Driver), Deuteronomy's theology of covenant could be seen as an intensification of themes that were incipient in JE. Covenant in JE was related to the Davidic covenant, for which 2 Sam. 7 furnished direct evidence. This understanding was rooted in a concept of Israel's history whose framework was essentially derived from the biblical narrative. The brief dominance, in mid-century, of Noth's theory of the amphictyony (Noth 1930; 1960), with its affirmation of a united twelve-tribe Israel in a time before the monarchy, was the last flowering of this paradigm in critical scholarship.

Modern interpretation works with a quite different theory of Israel's history, in which the postulate of a united pre-monarchical Israel has been rejected, on the grounds that it was over-dependent on the biblical picture, and on the basis of new interpretations of available archaeological evidence (e.g. P. R. Davies 1993; Lemche 1988; T. L. Thompson 1992; Whitelam 1996). In this theory the concept of 'Israel' that emerges from the pages of the OT is entirely an invention of doctrinaire theology that arose as a result of the experience of the exile, and provided a historical justification for post-exilic monotheistic Judaism. In historical actuality, there was never a united Israel before the exile; the twelve-tribe picture is artificial; the religion of Judah's forebears was essentially the same as polytheistic Canaanite religion; aniconic monotheism arose as part of the new self-definition of exilic Judaism over against the traditional religious practices of the pre-exilic time (see the account and critique in Arnold 1999: esp. 395–396; J. S. Holladay 1987). On this view, the 'reforms' of Hezekiah and Josiah were not attempts to return to the old traditions but rather were the first decisive moves in separating Yahweh from the gods of Canaan.

It is at this point that archaeology makes a contribution to the analysis. At one time it seemed that archaeology offered no help to the study of reform in the late Judean period (N. Lohfink 1987: 210). This was because there is no clear evidence of widespread destruction at major sanctuary sites at this time (Arad and Beersheba notwithstanding; see Manor 1992; Manor & Herion 1992). Latterly, however, attention has focused on the sudden upsurge in the veneration of goddess figurines in the late seventh century (J. S. Holladay 1987: 274–278). These probably attest to the popular worship of the goddess Asherah, not in great sanctuaries but in domestic settings. The same kind of devotion no doubt lies behind the cult of the Queen of Heaven among the Judean exiles in Egypt in Jer. 44.

How then does Josiah's reform relate to this piety? One answer is that the sudden appearance of this kind of worship in the archaeological record signifies a return to popular religion, parallel to the aniconic deuteronomic reform. The former may then be seen as an unofficial religious reaction to the inroads of Asyrian religion, while the latter was an official, establishment reponse to the same threat (Levinson 1997: 63). The centralizing aspect of Josiah's reform, indeed, may have been provoked by the threat of the popular religion to the official line. (Otherwise it is not clear why a rejection of *Assyrian* religion in particular should prompt a centralizing policy; cf. N. Lohfink 1987: 223.)

Deuteronomy's covenantal theology is now widely seen as a product of the Josianic reform. Since L. Perlitt (1969), the conditional covenantal theology characteristic of Deuteronomy has been regarded as the invention of the deuteronomic movement, without strong antecedents in an earlier time. Not even Hosea could be cited as contrary evidence, since, in Perlitt's view, *tôrâ* and covenant there (Hos. 8:1) were deuteronomistic additions. Perlitt's analysis was widely accepted (e.g. by Nicholson 1986; Clements 1975). In Perlitt's understanding, the concept of a land given to a united Israel by Yahweh – the chief elements in deuteronomic theology – is a theological response to the loss of land, rather than the memory of a real charter in Israel's antiquity. All OT examples of this kind of theology, even if they purport to be early (such as the Decalogue), are in reality late and deuteronomistic.

While Perlitt's reconstruction came in advance of the most recent theories of the history of Israel, it is clear that it fits comfortably with them. Taken together, they add up to a formidable analysis. In it Deuteronomy has become a far more 'exilic' document than traditional criticism held it to be (N. Lohfink 1987: 209; Wellhausen [1889: 190–191] had also found exilic elements in the book, and there were voices in older literary criticism that thought it was entirely exilic; Hölscher 1922). Interpretation of Deuteronomy now regularly looks for its exilic or post-exilic audience as a key factor in its understanding. An effect of this is to regard Deuteronomy's vision of Israel as an independent political entity with a carefully articulated polity (political and social policy) as unrealistic and utopian (Perlitt 1994).

The exilic hypothesis has an obvious strength. The exile is the end-point of the trajectory in Deuteronomy, as is clear from the culmination of the catalogue of curses (Deut. 28:63–68), and the vision of a return to Yahweh after the exile (30:1–10). When this is recognized the book can be seen to offer a complete picture of the history of Israel, from the promise to the patriarchs (1:8) to the post-exilic restoration opening on to an indefinite future, full of the possibility of blessing.

It is scarcely possible, in the confines of a commentary, to engage fully with this new synthesis that dominates OT scholarship, since it involves a revision of virtually every dimension of OT study, history, literature, theology and hermeneutics (see Provan's [1995] hermeneutical critique of the new reconstructions of Israel's history). It is important, however, to demonstrate the interrelationship of these things. And the commentary's interpretation is based on a rather different synthesis, which will be explained below.

4.4. Deuteronomy as a literary tradition

Finally, in this review of modern study of Deuteronomy, the book in its existing form is widely regarded as the result a growing tradition. That is, the law code is seen as a mere nucleus, which became subject to various 'deuteronomic', 'deuteronomistic', and 'post-deuteronomistic' develop-ments. This concept is consistent with the previous point (the exilic tendency), and, like it, allows the book to relate not only to Josiah's reform but to later developments. The major stimulus to it in modern times came from Noth (1981), who argued that the law code of Deuteronomy had been used by the exilic deuteronomist as an introduction to the Deuteronomistic History (DtrH). This he accomplished by the addition of the historical sections at the beginning (Deut. 1 – 3) and the end (Deut. 31 – 34), finding these to be a distinct literary type, historical narrative, not law. They also typically used the plural form of second-person address, rather than the singular, which predominated in the laws. This criterion was adopted by a number of other scholars (e.g. Minette de Tillesse, Mittmann) in further refinements of the distinction between deuteronomic and deuteronomistic layers.

Differences of theological emphasis were also perceived, for example, on the topics of law and land, and perhaps especially in the theology of salvation: was the gift of the land an act of pure grace on the part of Yahweh, or did it require Israel's prior obedience to the Torah? Deut. 6:17–19 is an example of a text that is said to illustrate the latter tendency (see the 'Comment' there). Deuteronomy has thus been fully assimilated to a thesis that is influential also in the study of DtrH, according to which DtrH has passed through several redactorial hands, each having a distinct point of view on this topic (Smend 2000; Dietrich 1972). This illustrates how closely the study of the composition of the book is linked with an understanding of its theology and purpose. Provisionally it may be said that literary-theological analyses of the sort just described can foreclose the possibility that Deuteronomy exhibits a rhetorical method that stresses now one and now the other side of a theological coin.

The close link between literary and theological or ideological interpretation emerges also in the study of the literary origins and development of the law code. The similarities between Deut. 12 – 26 and the laws in BC (Exod. 20:22 – 23:19) have long been observed (S. R. Driver 1895: iii–x; von Rad 1966: 13), and remain the subject of analysis. In recent discussion the deuteronomic code has been traced not only to BC but also to Exod. 34:10–26, held to be an ancient 'Privilege Law' (that is, a law asserting the unique rights of Yahweh in Israel's worship; N. Lohfink 1991f: 173–177; 1976: 230). The possibility of tracing such links is contested by others, however, who stress the independence of the deuteronomic code (Levinson 1997: 8 and nn. 13, 14).

On another front, the relation of Deuteronomy to H (the 'Holiness Code', Lev. 17 – 26) is explored. Traditionally, H has been dated after Deuteronomy, but prior to P. H is distinguished from D partly on the grounds that it exhibits a different view of holiness. Lev. 17:2–7, for example, is widely held to abrogate Deuteronomy's innovation of secular slaughter of animals for food (Levinson 1997: 153–154). In contrast to P, H may be separate structurally, because Lev. 17 looks like the beginning of a new code, with its own altar law at its head. And it appears to address a people in the land, in a way that suits the pre-exilic period. Some modern work places P before H, however (Milgrom 1991; Knohl 1995; Joosten

1996). Braulik (1996) puts H before Deuteronomy on ideological grounds, the latter being no longer a law for the poor, but for an ideal society in which there are no more poor; he cites the law on taking interest, Deut. 23:20–21, as evidence. Other important works argue that H is simply part of P (Crüsemann 1996: 277–280; Blum 1990: 318–322). Weinfeld makes no distinction between them (1972: 190–243). The complicated relationship between these codes involves fundamental methodological questions, for it is clear that the entities cannot even be defined in an absolute way, but only in relation to each other. And various religio-historical scenarios can be postulated to explain them.

While the nature of the relationship between Deuteronomy and other law codes is difficult to decide with any certainty, it is clear that Deut. 12 – 26 has a high degree of internal organization (Otto 1994: 193–196; 1993b; and differently, Braulik 1993). The law code, therefore, is fully integrated into the larger book and its theology (regarding worship, ethics, and the nature of Yahweh). In its case also, any account of it must belong to a wider explanation of the setting and nature of the book. The methodological problem involved in such a task is to decide how the literary and the ideological studies relate to each other. In practice, neither can have priority. The interpreter has to adopt a total view of setting, subject-matter and purpose.

4.5. Conclusion

Since the critical interpretation of Deuteronomy is so diverse and complex, it is not possible to provide either a full account or a complete evaluation of it in this Introduction. In what follows I offer some critique of the view of Deuterononomy as a programme of the reform movement in the seventh century BC. I shall then go on to give an account of the setting of the book adopted in this commentary.

It is clear from the foregoing that Deuteronomy is no longer regarded in any simple way as the occasion or the product of Josiah's reform. The perceived association between the two remains in some form, but it is problematical. The question whether Deut. 12 – 18 must be understood against the background of Josiah's reform can be met only at the level of the strengths and weaknesses of the theory as a whole. Two factors may be noted here. First, while there is widespread agreement that the code and the reform are connected, the nature of the relationship between them is difficult to determine, and is in fact conceived in very different ways, as Tigay has catalogued (1996: 459–464). Notwithstanding the lines of interpretation described above, a number of questions remain unanswered. Did the centralization law refer first to Jerusalem (as most scholars, e.g. Clements 1989), or to another sanctuary (von Rad 1953: 38; Rowley 1967: 106; cf. McConville & Millar 1994: 117–118 and n. 87)? If it was

Jerusalem, what was its nature? Was it essentially religious (in circumscribing cultic religious practice) or political (a resurgence of nationalism)? In so far as it was political, was it a measure *of* the king and royal establishment (Weinfeld 1972: 158–171; Halpern & Hobson 1991) or *against* the king, by a reform party protesting against Hezekiah's paying of tribute to Assyria (cf. Crüsemann 1996: 212–224)? In so far as it was religious, does it enhance the authority of the Jerusalem priesthood, or is it 'secularizing' and 'demythologizing' (Weinfeld 1972: 190–243; von Rad 1953; Mettinger 1982)? Plainly the strong impulse to link the book and the reform has not resolved a wide range of historical questions.

The crucial role of interpretation of texts in all these decisions may be illustrated by the topic of 'name theology'. Weinfeld's belief that Deuteronomy has a distinct theology of the divine presence, based on texts concerning the 'name' of Yahweh, is open to serious question. The occurrence of the 'name' there has less to do with a 'spiritual', transcendent view of the divine nature and presence than with the contrast set up between the worship of Yahweh and the worship of other gods. The whole theory of a secularizing, demythologizing Deuteronomy is based, in my view, on doubtful premises such as this. (The quite disparate critiques of Milgrom [1973], Wilson [1995] and N. Lohfink [1995e; 1995d: 219–260] may be mentioned in support of the point.) The interpretation of the 'name' is considered fully in the 'Comment' on Deut. 12.

A point similar to the one just made concerns the tension in the idea of a reform that promotes the religious establishment of Jerusalem in the cause of a 'spiritual' religion. In one strand of interpretation (e.g. Welch 1924), Deuteronomy was thought to reflect 'northern', covenantal ideas like those of Hosea, which contrasted with the southern, cultic ideas based on the temple hierarchy, with its close monarchical associations. This led some scholars to defend the idea of Deuteronomy's promulgation in Jerusalem by suggesting an accommodation or compromise between the two types of ideology, reached when a host of 'covenantal' northerners poured into Judah as refugees from the Assyrian conquest of the kingdom of Israel in 722 BC (Nicholson 1967; cf. Clements 1965a). This resulted in the muting of a clear royal ideology. In this connection too, however, it is better to look for more active and positive reasons for Deuteronomy's coolness towards kings.

The reinterpretation of the reform as a measure against unofficial, private religion (noticed above), while it accounts for certain archaeological evidence, and some texts in Deuteronomy (Deut. 18:9–14; cf. 12:31), takes us some way from the thesis that Deuteronomy promotes a public centralizing reform.

It is often contended that the laws of Deuteronomy support the thesis that it is a centralizing document. A number of tradition-critical studies, based on this premiss, find a Josianic level in the law code, building on already existing legal material (e.g. Horst 1930; Merendino 1969; G. Seitz

1971; Rose 1975). This point of view depends to some extent on the contention that the law of the altar (Deut. 12:5, etc.) is a centralizing law, a contention that is contested in the commentary (the main reasons are given below). A further problem for the idea of a Josianic edition of the law is that centralization is not to be found in Deut. 19 – 25 (though this has to be demonstrated, and some have indeed found evidence of it, e.g. Gertz 1994; Otto 1998).

It is sometimes maintained, finally, that Deuteronomy presupposes a world that is more advanced than the world that appears from older writings. For example, the term *mišpāḥâ*, 'clan', which is frequent in Numbers, occurs only once in Deuteronomy (29:18[17]; Perlitt 1994: 194). Deuteronomy portrays Israel as a city culture, and refers to the people as 'Israel' or sometimes by its tribes. The absence of 'clans' is then interpreted as evidence that the old structure of Israel has changed. Once again, the point depends on how the texts are read. The frequent occurrences of *mišpāḥâ* in Numbers come in only a few specialized texts. Deuteronomy, by contrast, has theological reasons for depicting people as a unity. And its interest in cities belongs to its concept of a subdued land ('cities you did not build') and the expansion of its borders (12:20, etc.). Deuteronomy is about a united nation holding a land against outsiders. 'Clans' return to the Hexateuchal narrative in Joshua, when it comes to the specifics of the possession of territory (Josh. 13 – 21, *passim*). The interpretation of vocabulary patterns should not be undertaken in isolation from theological and contextual issues.

The various problems facing the thesis of a Josianic Deuteronomy raise again the issue of the relationship between Deuteronomy and the books of Kings, in which, of course, Josiah does organize a major public reform, and may have done so following a reading of Deuteronomy. On this a methodological point may be made.

The crucial premiss that the narrative of Josiah's reform gives the clue to the setting of Deuteronomy, though it has held sway from de Wette to the present, and been regarded by many scholars as the most assured result of modern critical study, is open to challenge. It is based on a logical fallacy. From the fact that Josiah apparently read Deuteronomy and acted on it, it is inferred that Deuteronomy prescribed precisely what Josiah did. The problem with this is that it pays insufficient attention to the separate agendas of each book. Features of Deuteronomy (especially the measures commanded in Deut. 12) are simply compared with features of the reforms as described in Kings, and the similarities discerned are made the key to interpretation. This, incidentally, is why there is no consensus on whether the programme of Deuteronomy belonged originally in the reform of Hezekiah or in that of Josiah.

I am arguing here that Deuteronomy should not be interpreted in isolation from the so-called Deuteronomistic History (DtrH). Admittedly, this is often attempted. The widely held theory of a major Josianic edition of DtrH (Cross 1973: 274–289; Nelson 1981; Knoppers 1993) is coherent with the view that there was also a major Josianic edition of Deuteronomy. The question is whether that theory offers the correct interpretation of either corpus. The strengths and weakesses of the theory are too complex to be rehearsed here. I have argued in a number of places (esp. McConville 1989) that the account of Josiah's reform must be understood in the context of the final form of the books of Kings (together with those who have argued for a single edition of these: Noth 1981; Hoffmann 1980; Hobbs 1985). In that context the celebration of the achievements of Josiah is muted by the swift reversal in Judah's fortunes immediately after him, and the rapid fall of the nation into defeat and exile. In my view DtrH is far from promoting the royal ideology, but rather shows that it led only to terrible failure.

However, even if one accepts the Josianic edition of DtrH, it does not follow that Deuteronomy must be attributed to the same source. The great problem for the idea that Deuteronomy is the document of a royal reform lies in the law of the king in Deut. 17:14–20. Because of this, Knoppers (1996), who accepts the theory of a Josianic edition of DtrH, finds a completely different point of view in Deuteronomy (cf. Levenson 1975). And Levinson rightly points out that this passage presents a real difficulty if one wants to make Josiah's reform the key to understanding Deuteronomy (1997: 153 n.). Deuteronomy's king is nothing like King Josiah. It follows that, while the author of Kings is undoubtedly influenced by Deuteronomy, there is no evidence in the specifically royal material in the two books for a major Josianic edition embracing them both.

5. A FRESH APPROACH TO DEUTERONOMY

The account given above shows the need for a comprehensive view of the setting and purpose of Deuteronomy to be developed. In what follows, I consider first the setting and ideology of the book, and second, the nature of the book itself.

5.1. Setting and ideology

An account of the setting and ideology of Deuteronomy needs to explain a number of features and to address certain issues. These include Deuteronomy's setting in religious history, its theology of covenant, the meaning of its regular formula concerning the 'chosen place' (Deut. 12:5, etc.), its attitude to non-Yahwistic religion, its own concept of the nature of religion, its 'polity', the function of the law code, its composition, and its relation to other books and religious phenomena, especially the prophets. Such an account cannot be done piecemeal, but rather by advancing a hypothesis that embraces all. The following is the hypothesis advanced and explored in the commentary.

Deuteronomy, or at least a form of it, is the document of a real political and religious constitution of Israel from the pre-monarchical period. (For a fuller statement of what follows see McConville 1998: 276–281, drawing partly on Halpern 1981b: 188–216.) The starting-point for this thesis is the laws governing administration in Deut. 16:18 – 18:22 (and 1:9–20). The initial advantage of beginning with these is that it locates the quest for the setting of Deuteronomy within the book itself, rather than outside it (in Kings). It is clear that Deuteronomy aims to circumscribe the powers of the king (17:14–20). It is not the king, but Yahweh, who has the power to give the land (16:18). The king, furthermore, has no essential place in the picture built up in Deut. 16:18 – 18:22, and may be appointed only at the request of the people (17:14–15; cf. 28:36). Unlike other ancient kings, he does not fight battles, maintain a harem, or even acquire wealth. He is no 'son' of God, as David is in the 'Zion' theology (Ps. 2:7); Israel itself has that role (Deut. 1:31), and the king is simply one among the 'brothers' in Israel.

The offices that are actually prescribed in Deut. 16:18 – 18:22 are those of judge, priest and prophet, in their separate roles (one may speak of a 'separation of powers'; N. Lohfink 1993b). But over all these is the people itself, addressed typically in the laws in the singular, 'thou'. This is Israel constituted as the assembly of Yahweh.

The programme of Deut. 16:18 – 18:22 is therefore in direct opposition to the prevalent ANE royal-cultic ideology, in which the king is chief executive in cult and political administration (Ahlström 1982: 1–25). Moses is precisely not a royal figure, but rather a prophetic one. It is as prophet that he is at the head of a succession in Israel (18:15), and is thus in line with the view of prophets in DtrH as those who oppose the royal abuse of power. His authority as prophet exceeds that of the other officials, including the king. It establishes the role of Torah in Israel, for which the people as such is responsible.

It is in this context that Deuteronomy is to be regarded as the 'Book of the Law (Torah)' (28:59). The prophetic authority of Moses as the spokesperson of Yahweh is carried into the life of the community by means of the book, deposited in the ark of the covenant and read formally in the assembly. The Book of the Torah is the means by which the rule of Yahweh, in his covenant with Israel, is expressed (cf. Clements 1989: 38).

In this covenant, religion and politics are one. Israel fulfils its political obligations by virtue of its loyalty to Yahweh, which has an integral social dimension. There is not only a theology of the gift of the land, but a vision, sketched in the laws, of how the land should be held. The laws bring the concept of the rule of Yahweh down to particular instances. In common with other ancient law codes the deuteronomic code is not comprehensive. It often addresses rather unusual cases, while omitting what might be regarded as basic issues. As a matter of history, it may be a representative case law. However, it has several important functions: it establishes the responsibility of the judges, themselves appointees of the assembly, for its implementation; it makes justice the essential principle of all administration (16:20); and it shows that the ultimate judge, and guarantor of justice even beyond the reach of the courts, is Yahweh himself (24:13, 15).

The religious dimension of Israel's responsibilities in the covenant is contained in the laws in Deut. 12 – 18. The place formula (Deut. 12:5, etc.) is at the heart of these. Far from requiring centralization in Jerusalem, however, with implications of a royal-cultic synthesis, its refusal to name any one place is no mere fiction (consistent with the Mosaic 'fiction'), but of the essence of the programme. Israel shall worship only Yahweh, not other gods, and they shall do so at his behest (his choosing). The altar law is to be understood in the context of a succession of 'places' of encounter with Yahweh – Horeb, Kadesh, Moab, Shechem, 'the place' itself (potentially in various, successive embodiments), exile, the land again. History does not end in a particular institutional configuration, but is in principle open. Deuteronomy's attitude to institutional worship is entirely consistent with that of the prophets.

Even so, the place formula is intended to be fulfilled in real religious-political arrangements. There will be actual places in actual times, and for these, Deuteronomy constructs a real political and religious programme. It does so in a way that challenges the political-religious programmes that were on offer elsewhere. In particular it explores the way in which the rule of God is expressed in the organization of a society. If the rule of gods in Assyria was expressed by means of a king who dominated every sphere of the nation's life, Yahweh in contrast was the one who gave land, upheld justice and conducted wars.

The above reconstruction is quite different from both the royal, 'statist' interpretation, and the exilic utopian one. It attempts to steer between this Scylla and that Charybdis.

It has in common with the 'statist' (royal, pro-Jerusalem) thesis that it finds a real religious and political programme in Deuteronomy. But far from promoting a royal reform, Deuteronomy stands on guard against any royal hegemony over the people of Yahweh on the model of ANE monarchies. In its tension with the kind of royal ideology that comes to expression in the Davidic dynasty, the essence of Deuteronomy's contribution to OT theology is typified by Solomon at the height of his power. In its orientation it plays its part in the contention over the nature of Israel around the inception of the monarchy. That there was such a contention is clear from texts like Judg. 8:23; 1 Sam. 8:5–8. The latter text is directly related to Deut. 17:14–15. It may therefore be seen as an exercise of the people's prerogative to appoint a king.

The story of 1 and 2 Samuel, however, shows how that decision took Israel inexorably into conflict with the structuring of the covenantal relationship as it is understood in Deuteronomy. The foundational narrative of the Davidic dynasty itself (2 Sam. 7) reflects this conflict, expressing a view at odds with the royal–cultic synthesis, in its insistence on the freedom of Yahweh and his refusal to have his history with Israel end in symbols of immoveable permanence (vv. 5–7). These characteristic elements in the theology of the OT are unlikely to have been exilic inventions. On the contrary, the capacity of Judaism to survive the demolition of the royal–cultic synthesis in 587 BC lies in the fact that the central ideas of Yahwism, which actually transcended the synthesis, were deeply embedded in the soil of Israelite religion. The only text that systematically develops these ideological traits is Deuteronomy, in the manner outlined above.

On the other hand, the reconstruction outlined has in common with the 'utopian' point of view that it leads into an open future, not married to any one religious-political framework. Though the religious-political ideology of Deuteronomy must be embodied in real arrangements in space and time – a fact that gives the book its sharp ethical thrust – the programme carries deeply within itself the capacity to critique such arrangements. It is even 'eschatological' in its figuration of an ideal society, characterized by unity, worship of Yahweh alone, and self-denying existence for the other. The genius of the book is to hold its hearers to practical obedience while proffering a vision that is never quite realized.

5.2. The thesis above may be retold as a 'story'

The concept of the book that has been advanced may be supported by conceiving it as a 'story'. At first glance, Deuteronomy has the appearance less of story than of law or preaching. However, it is cast in the form of a narrative, with all the components of plot, scene, character and dramatic tension. The reader of Deuteronomy is drawn into its world. In that world the people of Israel are pictured on their way from their origin, in the promise to Abraham that his descendants would possess a land (Deut. 1:8), to their destiny (restoration beyond exile; 30:1–10). Their immediate situation is outside the land, poised to enter it. In that pause, the possibility of divine blessing spread before them, lies the dramatic power of the book. Israel is in a moment of 'decision' (Millar 1994; 1998). Between their beginning and their end consists the immediate challenge to live in the promised land, according to the covenant with Yahweh (30:15–20).

The story may be conceived as a journey from place to place: from Egypt to Horeb, Kadesh to Moab, the land itself where the tribes gather at Shechem (Deut. 27), and the 'chosen place', into exile (28:63–68), and back to land (30:1–10). The heart of this journey narrative is in the capacity of Horeb, the archetypal place of decision, to be recreated in new places of encounter. The 'chosen place' is the first counterpoint to Horeb (see 'Comment' on Deut. 12). Left unnamed so as to be any place of realization of the covenant, it represents the challenge to Israel to live before Yahweh in the here and now. The second is Moab (though it is prior in a strict chronological sense). The function of the Moab covenant (so called at 29:1[28:69]) is hardly different, since 'Moab' is the place where Moses utters the repeated 'Today!', conveying the immediacy of the command and needed response. The idea of Deuteronomy as a narrative meets its limitation here, for its events are not simply retold out of interest in the past, but its times and places are 'pregnant', capable of being reborn continuously into the present. The Moab covenant may even be likened to the new covenant (Jer. 31:31–34), because, while maintaining the standards of Horeb/Sinai, it opens on to a future lying even beyond what should be the final defiance of that covenant, incurring its full sanctions (Deut. 28), and conceives of a new beginning, with a new enabling by Yahweh. This is more than covenant renewal; it is the establishment of a pattern of grace after failure that reaches all the way to the resurrection (cf. also N. Lohfink 1998).

Entailed in the approach to Deuteronomy offered here is an engagement with it as a unified concept. We shall return to the authorship question shortly. But its theological unity may be considered first in a strictly formal way. Critical scholarship following Noth has often set Deuteronomy's 'history' over against its 'law' (cf. Veijola 1993). That is, an original law book was given a historical dress that was alien to it. This polarization, I maintain, misses the force of the book. The 'history', identified by Noth in Deut. 1 – 3; 31 – 34, is more pervasive, as my account of the book as a narrative has attempted to show. And the 'law' is best seen as the moral-religious challenge that is presented in ever-changing historical moments. Nothing is more characteristic of Deuteronomy than the marriage of 'history' and 'law' into an urgent existential encounter. This is recognized in Weinfeld's commentary (1991: 14), in which he finds Deut. 1 – 3 to have much in common with the 'paranesis' (exhortation) of Deut. 5 – 28, thus calling into question its habitual designation as 'deuteronomistic', to distinguish it from the 'law'. The recognition is informed in part by the parallels between the form of Deuteronomy and ANE treaties and laws, in which a historical prologue precedes the stipulations (Hittite treaty) or the laws (e.g. Code of Hammurabi).

Deut. 1 – 3, therefore, is the necessary first episode of the story. It is a preliminary staging of the journey from Egypt, through wilderness, to land, and back into exile, matching the geographical progress and regress to covenant obedience and disobedience. It is the prerequisite of the covenant between Israel and Yahweh at Horeb (Deut. 4 – 5). The transgression of this covenant narrated in Deut. 9 – 10 echoes the pattern of failure in Deut. 1. In each case, however, the story goes on (much as the story of creation goes on after the flood; Gen. 6 – 9). The journey to land begun in Deut. 1 – 3 is dramatically resumed in 10:11, the sin with the golden calf put behind. This forward movement is put on pause for the lengthy spelling out of the laws and commands that would be the substance of covenantal life in the land (Deut. 12 – 25). Then follows the ratification of the Moab covenant (26:17–19), and the vision of the land is resumed with the command to renew the covenant in Shechem. The final chapters bring the narrative full circle, both picturing the people peacefully enjoying the plenty of Canaan (Deut. 33), and – paradoxically – projecting the faithful keeping of covenant into an undetermined future (esp. 30:1–10).

6. THE COMPOSITION OF DEUTERONOMY

The usual reconstructions of Deuteronomy's history are based on the belief that its two main horizons are the reforms of the seventh century BC and the exile. I have offered an alternative view of the origins of the book, and it follows that a corresponding account of its composition is needed. Up to now I have spoken as if the proclamation in the assembly and the book that took its place in the OT canon were one. Can the history of the composition and changing usage of Deuteronomy be traced?

There was no time at which Deuteronomy was not a book. That is, the history of its composition is not a transition from oral to written. The scenario outlined above entails that Deuteronomy as a book originated in its use in the assembly of Israel as the document of the constitution, not in deuteronomistic idealism. It was 'oral', therefore, in the sense that it was intended for spoken delivery, as its hortatory form makes clear. The assembly of Israel is the context that does best justice to Deuteronomy's character as both written document and spoken word. This concept lies behind the provisions in Deut. 31:9–29. As a book, it is kept beside the ark of the covenant as a witness to the status of Israel as the people of God. This can explain its narrative features as well as its character as Torah. Equally, as spoken word, it functions as exhortation, to ensure the people's loyalty. The spokenness of it also explains certain features. A case in point is the criterion of singular and plural second-person address, which has classically been used as a means of separating redactional layers in the book. In my view, the form of address is chosen simply for rhetorical reasons: the singular emphasizes Israel as a unity, the sovereign entity ultimately responsible for the administration of Torah; the plural is an arresting variation, focusing (paradoxically perhaps) on the responsibility of each individual to keep the covenant (McConville 2002b; *pace* Crüsemann 1996: 220).

In my view this picture is a valid alternative to the hypothesis that assigns the most typical deuteronomic language to the theorists of the reforms and the exile. It has its antecedents in the history of interpretation. Von Rad's belief that Deuteronomy originated in a cultic covenantal setting in northern Israel is not far removed from this.

There is no reason to suppose that the content of the book may not have changed over time. It is a fair question whether the document of the pre-monarchical constitution contained the vision of Israel's future beyond exile (4:29–31; 30:1–10), for example. It can well be argued that such a vision is implicit in the vision of Yahweh as the giver of land to a people that showed signs of disloyalty from the beginning (Deut. 9 – 10), and indeed it has points of contact with Hosea (cf. Hos. 14). However, arguments about dating tend to move in circles, and no account is offered here of a development in the writing of the book. This is not for lack of interest in historical interpretation, but from scepticism about the validity of criteria that are used. These usually depend on the concept that Deuteronomy manifests an evolution in terms of theological thinking and writing, tending to reject the picture of a pre-monarchical covenantal constitution, and to embody a move in the direction of doctrinaire nomism. The concept advocated here is quite different from this.

I have observed above that it is common to try to determine the relationship between the Book of the Covenant (BC) and the deutero-nomic code, and also to trace growth within the deuteronomic laws themselves. Here again, no special theory is advanced. The deuteronomic code is regarded neither as a simple development from BC, nor as a replacement of it. Neither do I take a view on the relative priority of D and the Holiness Code (H). The function of law codes as such in the ANE remains in itself a matter of debate. Those that we have are not complete systems of law, often focusing on unusual cases, and perhaps compilations reflecting on legal process as much as the stuff of the process itself (Boecker 1980: 55–56; Eichler 1987). In these circumstances it is precar-ious to draw firm connections between codes. In the commentary, the deuteronomic laws are regularly compared with those of BC and H. Indeed, it is sometimes supposed that the nub of a law depends on the points at which it differs from others. My assumption, however, is that no biblical law code was thought to be exclusive, but rather that the codes all operated in the public and intellectual world of Israel. The laws of Deuteronomy, therefore, as well as taking their place in the document of the constitution, will also have been a part of what was available to judges, local and central, as they considered cases brought before them.

It will be clear that the commentary, though it is critical of the consensus opinion, does not defend Mosaic authorship. The critique of the con-sensus has theological interpretation at its centre rather than primarily historical arguments. This is not to ignore the evidence brought to bear by conservative scholars (e.g. Kline 1963; Kitchen 1966; Merrill 1994; Millard 1972; Craigie 1976a; Wenham 1971c) that suggests that Deutero-nomy can fit the world of the second millennium. That evidence includes the similarity of Deuteronomy to the Hittite treaty form, many echoes of the thought of treaties and law codes, even the language of Deutero-nomy, so commonly claimed to be characteristic of seventh-century Judah.

In my view this kind of evidence broadly supports the relatively early date that I advocate. My interpretation of Deuteronomy is based on the assumption that the picture of Israel's ancient covenant with Yahweh is realistic (not only with Kline and others, but also, in general terms, with Day [1986b] and Andersen & Freedman [1980]). I have preferred, however, not to try to date the book exactly, but to look for the place that it had in the life of Israel. This approach gives the most satisfying answers, I think, to the special features of Deuteronomy (notably the laws), when compared with the other books of the Pentateuch.

A corollary of the position taken is that the interpretation of the book can be sought against the background of the changing scenes of Israel's life. If the core of the book is old, then it has a long history. The story of the discovery of the 'book of the law' (2 Kgs. 22:8) has a ring of authenticity, not only because it is not recorded in connection with any of the earlier reforms, even though the author of Kings understood history in the light of it, but also because its absence can explain, and be explained by, the course taken by the twin monarchies. In the days of its neglect it was perhaps remembered by prophets. Hosea's language and thought, as we saw above, are so close to Deuteronomy at points that the relationship between the two books is inevitably posed, and the direction of influence not easily established. The hypothesis advanced here finds echoes in Andersen and Freedman's understanding of that relationship rather than the more usual idea that Hosea is the precursor (Andersen & Freedman 1980: 53–54).

Finally, Deuteronomy becomes the canonical book *par excellence*. The idea of Deuteronomy as the initiator of 'book' religion is found already in Wellhausen (1885: 402). Critical scholarship often sees the rise of the canonical idea as inseparable from its composition in the late Judean period, that is, as a function of the loss of the emblems of statehood and a refuge in a religion of the book (cf. Rüterswörden 1987: 64, who says that only late editions of Deuteronomy see it as a written document). I suggest in contrast that the book of ancient Israel's constitution could by its nature produce the idea of canon (here with Kline 1972). The Torah taught by Moses takes on an authority equal to that of the words of Yahweh given at Sinai.

7. THE READING OF DEUTERONOMY

In this last section we consider the capacity of Deuteronomy to continue to be heard in faith communities. This might be called a 'canonical' interest, that is, the question how the finished book has meaning for readers of the Bible. The canonical approach to interpretation is a helpful perspective, as long as it does not exclude attention to the historical depth-dimension, or 'fix' its meaning once for all through the minds of the canonizers. We shall consider in turn 1. the capacity of Deuteronomy to speak to new audiences, 2. its main theological emphases, and 3. its contribution to biblical theology.

7.1. Deuteronomy and its audiences

Deuteronomy's ability to have new audiences is built into the book's self-understanding. This is because the re-realization of the Horeb covenant, the decisive moment in Israel's life with Yahweh, is central to it. The words of Moses spoken at Moab become the vehicle of the covenant, carrying it into the present and future life of the community. The key text for this is Deut. 5 – 6, in which Moses mediates between Yahweh and the people, and his words take on the authority of Yahweh's words at Horeb. But Moses' instruction at Moab is not an end in itself. Rather, Torah (5:1) can continue to be taught throughout the generations. This explains why Deuteronomy places such strong emphasis on the teaching of children (6:6–9), why it culminates with the deposition of the book of the law beside the ark of the covenant, to be read every seven years at the Feast of Tabernacles (31), and why Moses' 'Song' is given as a perpetual witness (32).

Indeed, Deuteronomy's reflection on the capacity of the words once spoken to have continuing validity is part of its very theology. It is an ideal example of a 'speech-act', that is, the spoken word producing an effect. Utterances do things between people in ways that do not always emerge from their surface meaning. ('Speech-act' theory is a development in linguistics that understands utterances as performances. Its classic formulation is that of J. L. Austin [1975], and modern advocates include Searle [1970], Vanhoozer [1994], Watson [1997] and Wolterstorff [1995].) One of the extensions of speech-act theory is from spoken word to written text, and the claim that utterances, when reduced to writing, can go on producing effects on ever new audiences (Watson 1997: 98–103; cf. Brueggemann 1997: 117–144; 721–725). It is easy to see how closely Deuteronomy's concept of its own role in the life of Israel corresponds to this understanding of how the word spoken and written can be authoritative. In theological terms, Deuteronomy makes a claim that God not only spoke, but goes on speaking by means of the teaching and interpretation of his word in believing communities. (Sonnet's recent thesis [1997] investigates the significance of Deuteronomy's self-presentation as a book about the writing of a book. In its interest in the transformation of Moses' speech into writing in tandem with Deuteronomy's momentum towards the land [e.g. p. 70], it shares some of the perspective of this commentary.)

To say that Deuteronomy (or any book) has the power to keep speaking to new audiences raises the question: how can it do so? Does it keep meaning the same thing? This is an important question preparatory to an assessment of its theological contribution. On the face of it, its impact on successive communities is bound to change with the changing circumstances in which it is heard. As the covenant document of the ancient Israelite assembly, it is a word that has the power to form a community, and contains the promise of life in the land continuing into an open future. As a part of the Scripture read by the exilic and post-exilic communities it testifies to the truth and justice of God, and to his mercy to a people that had proved unfaithful. This is what I mean by understanding the historical depth-dimension of reading the book. It is an important qualification of the ideal of finding the 'original' intention. Indeed, the modern kind of rhetorical criticism makes an important distinction in principle between 'historical situation' and 'rhetorical situation'. There are useful points on this in Malbon 1993. There is a danger of circularity in any quest for a book's 'situation': a situation is posited, then the book is read in its light, then the situation is refined in view of the book. Deuteronomy criticism, in my view, is a classic case of this. The rhetorical critic works more from within the text in order to try to clarify a 'rhetorical situation', which is defined in terms of the text's capacity to persuade. It is not, therefore, limited to one time and place. As readers, we are already in a succession of those who have read the book and applied it to themselves over generations.

One of the features of Deuteronomy that enable such rereadings is the availability of its *topoi* for metaphorical interpretation. Deut. 1 – 3 illustrates the point. As the commentary will show, the journey of Israel from Egypt via Horeb to the promised land readily becomes a metaphor for the life of faith (cf. N. Lohfink 1997a). This is not just the reader's fancy, for it is the illustrative power of this first narrative of the book that prepares and reinforces its main thrust: that a faithful Israel can enjoy the blessings that God offers it in the covenant, while an unfaithful Israel is condemned to return to the slavery from which it came. The capacity of Deuteronomy for metaphorical interpretation is both its potency and its danger, however. Responsible interpretation needs to seek ways of controlling it. There is a kind of 'typology' that translates the mandate for conquest into modern situations, as has been seen in our time in Israel and South Africa, though examples could be multiplied (N. Lohfink 1997b; Deist 1994). The necessary control on interpretation of Deuteronomy into new situations comes both from careful reading of the book itself and from considering its relation to other parts of the Bible (see the next two sections).

7.2. Deuteronomy and theology

Deuteronomy does not fall neatly into a single theological category. It is traditionally Torah, being one of the five books of Moses. As Torah it is close to wisdom, since both are interested in instruction, and the themes of law and wisdom often overlap (Braulik 1997: 225–271; Weinfeld 1991: 62–65). Yet, as we have noticed, it is also narrative, and has close affinities with the historical books Joshua–Kings. Equally, its central figure, Moses, is portrayed as the prophet *par excellence* (18:15), whose words are the word of God. All the canonical divisions of the OT are echoed in this sketch of the book's characteristics. Each of the theological genres says something about Deuteronomy's theology.

As Torah, it is authoritative instruction for Israel's life, bordering on law that can be pursued in the courts (in the nation's classical period). Its authority lies in its derivation from God himself. The laws of Deuteronomy enshrine principles that come from the nature of God: the duty owed to God by his human creatures in worship and obedience, the principles of justice, human dignity, the sanctity of life and retribution. As Torah, Deuteronomy aims to establish and form a people of God, that is, of one who can judge and sanction, bless and curse. In the context of the Pentateuch, Deuteronomy can be seen as the culmination, as the 'sanctions' of the Pentateuch (Watts 1995). It is as Torah that the book manifests its most characteristic formal features, its exhortations and sermonic style, insistent and urgent. The people of God should be, and can be, obedient (30:15–20), if only they will hear his voice.

Deuteronomy's character as law has regularly led to its being regarded as 'legalistic', critical scholarship owing an unfortunate debt to Luther in this respect. In modern times, the terms 'deuteronomic' and 'deutero-nomistic' have often been used pejoratively to suggest a simplistic theology of reward and punishment. The implication is always that the OT contains better forms of theology, such as those that emphasize promise and forgiveness or personal religion of the heart, or that see a place in God's plans for nations other than Israel. This does too little justice to the concept of Torah, as I have tried to explain it.

The aim of Torah is to create a righteous community. The issue of law and grace does come up, in the context of the people's failure to keep the covenant. This poses the question of moral capability, which is finally resolved theologically in a passage reminiscent of the new covenant of Jeremiah (Deut. 30:1–10; Jer. 31:31–34; 32:39–40). In both these places Yahweh enables the renewed people to be faithful, and faithfulness involves the keeping of Torah, or commandments (Deut. 30:8; Jer. 31:33). Torah is therefore not in tension with promise or forgiveness; rather, the latter come to fruition in the issue about the keeping of Torah. As for individual piety, the devotion of Israelites, both as a community and as individuals, is the aim of the book's exhortations to love the LORD from the heart (6:5; 10:12; 29:10–12[9–11]).

As wisdom, the book offers training in the right way to live, and in this respect is closer to Proverbs than to anything else. Like Proverbs, it is open to the objection of theological simplicity, appearing to offer material blessing in return for a good life. This is unfair to both books. The training of wisdom insists that what is right is also useful, because of the claim that there is order in the universe, moral as well as natural. Both books, in their separate ways, know that life cannot be reduced to simple equations, however; Deuteronomy's theology of mercy for an errant people is the clearest illustration of the point. And yet the claim about a divine order in the creation is still entered. And people are called to be trained in what is right, not merely to avoid retribution, but because a full and joyful human experience depends on the acknowledgment that life is a gift of God.

As prophecy, Deuteronomy sets before the people their moral failures, their capacity for unfaithfulness. The prophet calls the people back to their proper loyalty to Yahweh. This is the fundamental issue in the book, which in its entirety might be described as a discourse on the First Commandment, 'you shall have no other gods before me' (5:7). False prophets are those who entice the people away from Yahweh (Deut. 13); the true prophet is the one who speaks his words. The covenantal metaphor, which embraces the form of the whole book, expresses this exclusive claim on Israel's life. In this respect Deuteronomy is most like Hosea. The two books share the themes of the faithfulness of Yahweh to Israel, the faithfulness required of them in return, their fall into idolatry, a coolness towards monarchy, and a view of history in which idolatry leads to judgment, followed by forgiveness and restoration. (There are also important differences between them: Deuteronomy knows only 'other gods'; its polemic is against Canaanite religion, not baalism as such, or syncretistic Yahwism; Hosea uses the marriage metaphor to speak of faithfulness, while Deuteronomy uses the more straightforward language of covenant [incl. 'love']; Deuteronomy has no critique of Levitical priests, while the prophets do; Deuteronomy recalls no ideal period, as Hosea does; Deuteronomy anticipates Israel's history, while Hosea looks back on it; cf. Seifert 1996.) Even so, Deuteronomy's confrontation with the claims of other gods is the essential point in its prophetic character.

That critique of idolatry, furthermore, is a challenge to a culture or worldview, such that the book has rightly been called a cultural critique, or counter-culture (C. J. H. Wright 1990; and, differently, N. Lohfink 1977). That is, it stands against the political-religious synthesis found in societies in its world, in which tyrannical social structures were mirrored in polytheistic pantheons (Handy 1994). Deuteronomy redesigns the notions of God, people and king. The vision of a people in Deuteronomy is of a delivered people, on the verge of a land, a people consisting of 'resident aliens' (gērîm, 15:15), who go back into exile, and can come from it again. The origin in and possibility of exile is deep in Deuteronomy's concept. This affects its view of peoplehood and state fundamentally. It overwhelmingly affirms the individual, indeed the outsider; it is the opposite of totalitarian (despite Deut. 13, q.v.), rejecting the state as its own justification, as in Egypt and Canaan. In this respect it enables thinking about human worth within the political sphere, as well as the religious. Its vision for society, rooted as it is in a historical actuality that confronts other actualities, each being permanently possible, is what makes Deuteronomy prophetic. The whole is predicated on the axiom that Yahweh is God, Yahweh alone (6:4). The point is neither arithmetical nor sectarian. It is essentially about the nature of God, and what it means for life in human society.

7.3. Deuteronomy in biblical theology

Finally, we consider the theology of Deuteronomy as part of a biblical theology. In what way does it relate to other parts of the Bible, and what part can it play in theologizing that aims to be biblical? Is it true to speak of the 'limitations' of Deuteronomy (Goldingay 1987)? Or is it better to think of a kind of inner 'dialogue' with the rest of the OT and NT? In the previous section we saw that Deuteronomy partakes of some of the features of each of the canonical divisions of the OT. I now offer some pointers to an evaluation of the place of the book in biblical theology. This involves first some remarks about the relation of Deuteronomy to the priestly literature (P) and the so-called 'Zion' theology, and then a consideration of its relation to the NT.

7.3.1. Deuteronomy and the priestly literature

Deuteronomy's relation to the priestly literature has been one of the determining factors in its interpretation from Wellhausen to Weinfeld and the present day. Typically the relationship between the two has been seen as either developmental (P continues D's centralizing programme more rigorously) or competitive (P and D offer conflicting views of the world). In recent scholarship (as we saw above), the belief is gaining ground that P was prior to D on many matters on which each has something to say. Weinfeld documents these conveniently (Weinfeld 1991: 30–35), and shows significant differences between them.

However, as we also saw above, it is not clear that these are explicable as a 'desacralizing' programme of Deuteronomy's. The 'name' theology, in particular, should be thought to be concerned not with the nature of divine presence, but with the rights of Yahweh as opposed to other deities. And Deuteronomy shows a strong interest in holiness: the people of Israel is holy, while the other nations of the land are *ḥerem*, 'devoted to destruction'. That is, they are a kind of sacrifice to Yahweh, a 'negative holy', in an actual extension of the theology of holiness (compared with P), according to which the nations of the land are at the extreme negative end of a holiness spectrum, best illustrated in Deut. 20 (N. Lohfink 1995e;

cf. Houtman 1996). In comparing Deuteronomy and P, therefore, it is again misguided to think of a dissension between them over the holiness issue. Rather, a strong theology of holiness is in the thought world of each corpus. While P foregrounds the theology of presence, however, Deuteronomy is more concerned with the rival 'holiness' claims of Yahweh and the gods of the nations. The context of holiness language in Deuteronomy is its concept of Israel as counter-culture, which we observed above.

The relationship of the two blocks, P and D, within the Pentateuch still needs comment. Where the codes are thought to be in conflict, a process has to be assumed in which 'Codes criticizing previous laws, which they sought to replace, were combined with those laws into a single entity' (Crüsemann 1996: 329). The relation of D and P in particular is probably *the* central problem of Pentateuchal study, since each has a claim to be the final organizing voice. The claim of P lies in its combination of creation, promise, law and history, which produces the shape of the Pentateuch as we know it. D, on the other hand, is responsible for the idea of Torah, the only theological concept in the Pentateuch that expresses the union of law and history. Thus Blum, who argues that the final shape of the Pentateuch is priestly, says: 'The Priestly Pentateuch, indeed, is no Sinai-cultic lawgiving, with a relatively thin historical preamble, but the interpenetration of rich narrative and legal materials, that is best designated, with the tradition, as "Torah" ' (1990: 288, my translation; cf. Crüsemann 1996: 279–282). On this view P has incorporated D's concept, but widened it from a national to a whole-world (creational) horizon. (A similar view is taken by T. Römer [2000], who thinks the equation of 'the fathers' with the patriarchs is the work of a priestly redactor, and by Otto [1996], who sees Deut. 4 as a deliberate assimilation of the perspectives of the two blocks.) In my view it is unnecessary to deny a creational perspective to Deuteronomy.

Rather, the relation of Deuteronomy to P should be understood in the manner outlined above, that is, where P foregrounds the nature of the divine presence, while Deuteronomy locates Israel in a world environment. In this way it is Deuteronomy that most fully embraces the Pentateuchal nexus of creation, promise, history and law. (The arc from Gen. 1 to Deut. 4 is as important as any link of the former text to priestly sections of the Pentateuch.) Deuteronomy's elaboration of the concept of Torah is thus a suitable culmination of the Pentateuch.

7.3.2. *Deuteronomy and 'Zion'*

Along with the deuteronomic and priestly literature, one of the dominant voices in the OT is what is known as 'Zion' theology, that is, those books and traditions that celebrate Yahweh's choice of Jerusalem with its Davidic king, and his determination to defend it (Ollenburger 1987).

The leading examples are in the books of Psalms (e.g. Pss. 2; 46; 47; 76; 89:1–37; 110; 132) and Isaiah (e.g. 29:5–8; 31:4–5). It is immediately clear from this definition of Zion theology that it contrasts with the stance of Deuteronomy towards kingship and place of worship. Here is a block of material that not only exalts the Davidic king as God's chosen one, but contends that God is to be worshipped in a particular place, the temple at Jerusalem, which is the destination of his journey, or march, from Sinai (Ps. 68:17[18]). On the face of it, the Zion theology seems to have caved in to all the things that Deuteronomy resisted. In its celebration of Yahweh's 'holy hill', it takes on the hues of Canaanite worship, especially the worship of Baal on Mt Zaphon. Historically, David and Solomon may have incorporated aspects of the pre-Israelite Jebusite cult in their inauguration of the worship practices of the first temple. (For an account of the similarities between Canaan and the Jerusalem cult, see Clements 1965b; and note, for example, the depiction of the conflict between Yahweh and Baal as a rivalry between two mountains, Ps. 68:15–16[16–17] – where 'mountain of Bashan' is a term for Mt Zaphon.) The differences between Deuteronomy and Zion theology have been touched on already (in section 5.1 above) in the contrast we observed between the king law (Deut. 17:14–20) and the portrayal of Solomon in DtrH.

There are, of course, important similarities between the two blocks: the idea of the just rule of Yahweh in the world, demonstrated by his choice of Israel, both people and land; and the corollary of this, his victory and domination over other nations (Pss. 2; 46). The important difference between them might be expressed as the real and the ideal, or principle and practice. If Deuteronomy portrays what the chosen people of Yahweh ought to look like, the Zion theology reflects what it actually was or became. Canonically, the biblical story mediates between these different concepts of the polity of Israel under Yahweh in the books of Samuel and Kings (DtrH), where the permitting of both king and temple is seen as a compromise with the deuteronomic ideal. The history of Israel with Yahweh was the product of a host of events and encounters. Though there might always be judgment, repentance and renewal, there was in a sense no turning back once certain dice were cast. The assimilation of the Zion theology testifies to the realism of Yahweh's dealings with his people.

The point may be pursued by a comparison of Deuteronomy and Isaiah on the subject of the divine rule. Writing on Isaiah's concept of a society properly ordered under God, H. G. M. Williamson finds that the qualities essential to it are righteousness (*ṣedeq, ṣᵉdāqâ*), justice (*mišpāṭ*) and truth or faithfulness (*'emet, nᵉ'emān*; Williamson 1998: 243 and n.). In this respect, Isaiah is like Deuteronomy, which makes *ṣedeq* and *mišpāṭ* the foundation of proper administration of Israel, and the standard for its commerce (cf. Deut. 1:16; 16:18–20; 25:15). But Isaiah differs from Deuteronomy in that he has taken the Davidic king into his vision of an ideal Israel (esp. in 9:1–7[8:23b – 9:6]; 11:1–5; Williamson 1998: 254–264).

In biblical theology, this vision became the foundation of messianism, a thrust which cannot be found in Deuteronomy. The result of the adoption of the deuteronomic ideals (justice and righteousness) in a Davidic framework is to add a new voice to the OT's witness without silencing the other. The book of Isaiah, while it sets standards for practical policy, plays its part in the development of a biblical hope of the universal rule of God by means of the Messiah. The elect nation, Israel, becomes the 'servant of Yahweh', by which (or by whom) the light of salvation will come to the nations (Is. 49:1–6). Deuteronomy lacks this vision. It is this book, however, that keeps open the ideal of a society free from the temptations of absolute power. In both, the basic conditions for a faithful society, justice and righteousness, are maintained. Deuteronomy's lasting contribution is the regulation of all human authority by Torah.

7.3.3. Deuteronomy and the nations

The theology of Deuteronomy, as indeed that of Zion, poses one of the difficult questions of OT interpretation, namely the place of nations other than Israel. Deuteronomy conspicuously lacks the vision of those parts of the OT that foresee the salvation of the nations, or at least affirm Yahweh's interest in them (e.g. Gen. 12:3; Is. 40 – 55; Jonah). In contrast, as we have seen, Deuteronomy organizes the world of non-Israelite nations according to a holiness spectrum in which, at worst, they might be subject to the *ḥerem* (devotion to destruction). The picture is somewhat relieved by Deut. 2, in which Yahweh is the giver of land not to Israel only but to the other nations too (not unlike the idea in Amos 9:7). And there is certainly a concept of Yahweh's dealings with Israel as a demonstration to the world of what a society ought to be like (Deut. 4:6–8; cf. Millar 1998: 147–160).

The most positive approach to this issue, however, is to understand how Deuteronomy feeds into the theology of the more inclusive parts of the OT, and indeed the NT. The answer to this is implied in what has already been said about Deuteronomy's vision for a covenant society. Just as it stops short of a vision of a universal messianic kingdom, so it declines to develop the idea of universal salvation. Moreover, its blueprint for a nation under God is devised precisely by bringing it into contention with the rival blueprints associated with the religion and politics of Baal. The *ḥerem* is the stark expression of Deuteronomy's exhibition of society ordered as it ought to be. It can be regarded as symbolic of the conflict between order and chaos. The lasting contribution of the concept, however, is in its staging of the spiritual conflict that attends the attempt to establish justice and righteousness. Morality cannot be dissociated from an understanding of the nature of God.

7.3.4. *Deuteronomy in the NT and in theological interpretation*

The basis has been laid for a consideration of Deuteronomy's contribution to biblical theology on its widest plan. In itself, the book contains a paradox, between an open-ended vision of a perfectly ordered society under God and practical provisions that reckon with the imperfections of real people. This paradox carries over into an alignment of Deuteronomy in a biblical theology. In relation to the NT, the influence of Deuteronomy may be sought at the level of specific allusions, and also more generally.

It is possible to trace certain specific echoes of Deuteronomy in the NT (for the following interpretation of Luke, see G. Lohfink 1975: 17–32; 58–61). In Luke 1 – 2, the church is conceived as 'Israel', the people (*laos*) of God to whom Jesus has come. Acts 2 – 5 shows the apostles garnering the true 'Israel' out of the Jews, and only then beginning the Gentile mission. These indeed are causally connected; Israel is complete only when the Gentiles are brought in. In this context there are allusions to Deuteronomy. Acts 15:13–18, in its sketch of the story of Israel's salvation, refers to Deut. 14:2; 26:18–19, as well as to Exod. 19:5. Similarly, Acts 3:22–23 cites Moses' saying that Yahweh would raise up a prophet like him (Deut. 18:15, 18–19), a prophecy now applied to Jesus. The connection between ancient Israel and the universal church is established in the same passage by the reference to Abraham, who was sent first to 'you', that is, the Jews (Acts 3:26). And those (sc. among the Jews) who do not listen to the prophet (Jesus) will be rooted out of the people (another deuteronomic echo; Deut. 19:19; 21:9).

A further Christological application of Deuteronomy is made by Paul in Romans. For a discussion of his use of Deut. 30:11–14 in Rom. 10:1–5, see the commentary there. It seems that Paul's understanding of faith subsumes the keeping of the law, this having been achieved completely by Christ. It follows that this NT theology of salvation is filled with content drawn from the OT, not set against it.

The latter point leads into a reflection on the relevance of the OT law. The fulfilment of the Torah through the obedience of Christ could lead to the conclusion that it is, in consequence, no longer relevant. On the contrary, however, Christ's obedience to Torah confers validity on it. The point is analogous to the concept of the kingdom as 'now' and 'not yet'. The witness of the NT is that the kingdom of God will be established finally in a future time. Yet it is also present in the earthly presence of Jesus, and thus his church. The prophetic ministry of Jesus confronts the powers that be, and points to ways of understanding and leading them. N. T. Wright's description of what first-century Jews aspired to, as further interpreted by Jesus, is not unlike the programme of Deuteronomy (God as king, no foreign king, justice within society; N. T. Wright & Borg 1999: 31–37; N. T. Wright 1996: 651–652). In announcing the kingdom of

God, Jesus turned a searchlight on society as it was, not only Roman but also Jewish. And he did so by standing in the Israelite prophetic tradition, exposing the failures of people to live by the foundational covenantal principles of justice and righteousness.

For these reasons, it seems to me that the OT continues to be the primary source for thinking about the organization of human society. In a recent work, O. O'Donovan (1996) has sought to reclaim it for 'political theology'. At the heart of a subtle argument is the contention that the rule of God over the nations is revealed in the history of the one nation Israel, through which light comes to all. There is no simplistic translation of OT laws into modern times (in fact, the 'law', strictly defined, plays only a small role in the argument). Rather, the elements in God's rule, namely deliverance, judgment and possession, are found to be of universal validity, and realized decisively in the resurrection of Christ. (O'Donovan's discussion of Yahweh's rule in Israel centres on the role of the Davidic king, the deuteronomic law offering a positive picture of righteous kingship. In my view the king law is more critical, and I prefer to see Deuteronomy in the centre of the OT's portrayal of divine rule.)

The subordination of authority to law in Deuteronomy (where Torah is also the word of God spoken by the prophet Moses) is what gives the prophetic critique of the abuse of power its unique authority. This prophetic dimension is a key factor in any application of OT law to the modern world. The potency of Deuteronomy has rendered it capable of great abuse. Its use by white supremacists in South Africa to justify apartheid is well documented (Deist 1994).

Yet Deuteronomy has within it the key to a responsible interpretation. It consists in its refusal to identify its programme for a people under God once and for all with any particular institutional arrangement. This is the point of my dispute with the interpretations of the book that see it as in any sense an apologia for the Judean monarchy. In assigning final authority to the people as such, in charging them with the regulation of affairs by the Torah, and in setting the prophetic word over all other agencies, it precludes the use of religious authority to justify any *status quo*. The paradox of the book is that it aims to regulate the life of communities in reality, yet ever directs the attention of hearer and reader to an ideal that exposes the faults of the *status quo*. This is the lasting contribution of the book. It is capable of informing practical thinking about the organization of societies, while maintaining a vision of the kingdom of God. The kingdom is now and not yet. Or, differently, we 'seek the place that the LORD our God will choose, to put his name and make his habitation there' (Deut. 12:5).

8. THE FORM AND AIMS OF THIS COMMENTARY

The aims of the present commentary have been implied in all that has been said above. It will be clear that its first aim is to offer a theological interpretation of the text of Deuteronomy, in the context of the biblical canon. Historical issues are subordinated to this, with the proviso that interpretations are bound to pay attention to whatever can be known of the settings in which documents emerged. The dominant method employed in the commentary, however, is one that understands the book of Deuteronomy as a finished work. In this respect it is influenced by the canonical criticism of B. S. Childs. It has also drawn on the more linguistic approaches to meaning touched on above in relation to speech-act theory.

Above all, it is hoped that the commentary will prove useful in the interpretation of this important book of the OT. The format adopted is by now well established in other series (e.g. WBC). I have tried to shift the emphasis somewhat in the direction of the 'Explanation' section. All parts of the commentary are inevitably limited by space considerations. The 'Notes on the text' section, in particular, is plainly not exhaustive, but is intended to illustrate the interpretation offered.

TEXT AND COMMENTARY

DEUTERONOMY 1:1–46

Translation

[1]These are the words that Moses spoke to all Israel in the wilderness to the east of the River Jordan, in the Arabah. The place was opposite Suph, between Paran and Tophel, Laban, Hazeroth and Dizahab. [2]It takes eleven days to go from Horeb by way of Mt Seir to Kadesh-Barnea.

[3]In the fortieth year, on the first day of the eleventh month, Moses spoke to the people of Israel, according to all that the LORD had given him as commandment for them. [4]This was after he had defeated Sihon, the Amorite king who ruled in Heshbon, and Og the king of Bashan, who ruled in Ashtaroth and in Edrei.

[5]East of the Jordan, therefore, in the land of Moab, Moses began to explain this law, in the following way:

[6]The LORD our God said to us at Horeb: 'Now you have stayed long enough at this mountain. [7]Set out now, and travel till you come to the land of the Amorites, and to the territory of all its inhabitants in the Arabah, in the highlands and lower uplands, in the Negeb and the coastal plain, the land of the Canaanites, and Lebanon, as far as the great River, the Euphrates. [8]Look: I set the land before you; go and take possession of it. It is the land that the LORD swore to your forefathers Abraham, Isaac and Jacob to give to them and their descendants after them.'

⁹At that time I said to you: 'I cannot bear the burden of you alone. ¹⁰The LORD your God has increased your number, and here you are today, as many as the stars of the sky. ¹¹May the LORD, the God of your fathers, make you yet a thousand times greater in number and bless you, just as he promised you. ¹²Yet how can I bear alone your problems, your difficulties and disputes! ¹³Choose for yourselves wise, intelligent and experienced men, from all your tribes, and I will make them your leaders.' ¹⁴And you replied to me: 'What you propose to do is good.' ¹⁵So I took from among you wise and experienced men, and I made them your leaders: commanders of thousands, of hundreds, of fifties and of tens, and officers throughout your tribes. ¹⁶And I bound your judges at that time to hear cases between brothers, and to judge rightly, whether a man has a dispute with his brother, or with a resident non-Israelite. ¹⁷'Do not show bias in your judgment; hear the cases of great and small in just the same way, without fear of your fellow human beings, for the judgment is God's. But if a case is too hard for you, bring it to me and I will hear it.' ¹⁸And I gave you instructions at that time about everything that you should do.

¹⁹We travelled from Horeb and went through that vast and terrible wilderness, which you have seen, taking a route for the land of the Amorites, just as the LORD our God commanded us. And we arrived at Kadesh-Barnea. ²⁰I said to you: 'You have come to the land of the Amorite which the LORD our God is giving to us. ²¹See! The LORD your God has set the land before you. Go up and take possession of it, just as the LORD, the God of your forefathers, told you to. Do not be afraid or dismayed.'

²²Then all of you approached me and said: 'Let us send men ahead of us to explore the land for us, to bring back news about the way we should go and the cities we are coming to.' ²³This seemed good to me, so I took twelve men of you, one from each tribe. ²⁴So they set out to go up to the hill country, and came to the Valley of Eshcol, and explored it. ²⁵They took some of the fruit of the land, and brought it back to us, and also gave their report: 'The land that the LORD our God is giving us is good.'

²⁶But you would not go up. You rebelled against the command of the LORD your God. ²⁷You complained in your tents, and said: 'It is because the LORD hates us that he has brought us from the land of Egypt to give us over to the Amorites to destroy us! ²⁸Where are we to go up! Our brothers have dismayed us by saying: "The people are stronger and taller than us. The cities are huge, and fortified up to heaven. We even saw the Anakim there!"'

²⁹I said to you: 'Don't be terrified; don't be afraid of them! ³⁰The LORD your God, who goes ahead of you, will fight for you, just as he did for you in Egypt, before your very eyes; ³¹and also in the wilderness, where you have seen how the LORD your God carried you, as a father carries his son, all along your route, till you arrived at this place.' ³²For all that, you do not trust the LORD your God, ³³who went ahead of you on the way to search out a place for you to camp – in the fire by night and in the cloud by day, to show you the way that you should go.

³⁴When the LORD heard what you said he was angry and swore this oath: ³⁵'Not a single one of this wicked generation shall see this good land which I swore to give

to their forefathers. ³⁶I make an exception for Caleb, the son of Jephunneh; he shall see it. I shall give him and his sons after him the land that he has walked on, because he followed the LORD wholeheartedly.' ³⁷The LORD was angry even with me because of you, and said: 'You too shall not go in there. ³⁸Joshua, the son of Nun, your servant, will go. Encourage him, for he will bring Israel to its inheritance. ³⁹And as for your little ones, who you said would become a prey, your children, who this day do not know the difference between right and wrong, they will go in there. I will give the land to them, and they will take possession of it. ⁴⁰You, however, must set out and go back towards the wilderness, the way to the Reed Sea.'

⁴¹Then you answered me: 'We have sinned against the LORD. Let us indeed go and fight, as the LORD our God told us to.' And you all put on your weapons of war, and thought you would easily go up to the land. ⁴²But the LORD told me to say to you: 'You must not go up and fight, for I am not among you. If you do, you will be mown down by your enemies.' ⁴³I told you this, but you would not obey. Instead, you rebelled arrogantly against his command and went up to the land. ⁴⁴And the Amorites who lived in that hill country came out against you, and chased you just as bees do, and struck you down in Seir, as far as Hormah. ⁴⁵You returned and wept before the LORD. But he would not listen to your cries; he turned a deaf ear to you. ⁴⁶And so you stayed at Kadesh. Your stay was a long one.

Notes on the text

1. Two Hebrew MSS, LXX, Syr have w^e'$\bar{e}lleh$ ('and these') for MT '$\bar{e}lleh$ ('these', cf. 12:1). The addition may imply a connection with the preceding narrative (in Numbers). b^e'$\bar{e}ber$ $hayyard\bar{e}n$ means 'across the Jordan', from the standpoint of the speaker; this standpoint varies, as the respective contexts make clear, according to whether the speaker is the narrator (1:1, 5; 4:41, 46, 47, [49]), or Moses (3:20, 25; 11:30; cf. S. R. Driver 1895: xlii–xliii; Perlitt 1990: 10). The expression is sometimes translated 'Transjordan' (Craigie 1976a: 90), which seems to be favoured by 3:8, yet does not explain it in the other instances when it is used by Moses. A further possibility, 'in the region of the Jordan', can handle the latter objection, and is favoured by 4:29, where the term appears without the preposition b^e, and qualified by the adjective 'east'. The solution seems to be that if the meaning of the phrase is not clear from the context, it can be specified by a further term meaning 'east' or 'west'. (Cf. Josh. 5:1, 12:7; 1 Chr. 26:30. Num. 32:19 is a further comparable passage, where a specification in terms of standpoint ['across the Jordan and beyond'] is contrasted with a more strictly geographical specification ['across the Jordan to the east'].) It can in this sense be used as a geographical designation, but it can have different referents according to context. This also applies to 3:8, where the term is qualified by the following phrase, 'from the Wadi Arnon to Mt Hermon'. (The phrase 'el '$\bar{e}ber$ $b^e n\hat{e}$ $yi\acute{s}r\bar{a}$'$\bar{e}l$,

Josh. 22:11, is not precisely the same sort of usage, and is best rendered 'opposite the Israelite side' [REB].)

3. Some Hebrew MSS and some Greek versions read 'all the sons of Israel', conforming to v. 1, and in harmony with Deuteronomy's theological emphasis on the unity of the people.

4. One Hebrew MS, LXX, Vg, Syr read 'in Ashtaroth and in Edrei', conforming to Josh. 12:4; 13:12, 31. It seems then that both places are cities in which Og reigned, and that it is best to restore the 'and'.

5. *hô'îl*, 'he began': this verb is typically followed by another finite verb, not the infinitive (*HALAT* 2:365); here the 3 m. sg. pf. pi. *bē'ēr*, to 'explain', 'make clear' (or 'establish', see 'Comment'). The construction can express not only beginning, but also purpose, firm intention.

7. *har hā'emōrî*: 'the land of the Amorites'. The word translated 'land' is lit. 'mountain'; this, however, can have the simple sense of land or territory in Deuteronomy (cf. 3:25; 2:1–3). 'Amorites' is strictly a singular form, but here has a collective meaning. It is apparently connected with the Akkadian term Amurru, which in the second millennium could be used both to denote the land to the 'west', viz. Syria and Palestine in a general way, and as the name of a state in Syria. In first-millennium Assyria, the name was commonly used for Palestine. It is in this sense that it seems to be used here (cf. 1:19–20, 44). See further Gibson 1961.

8. While MT has 'Look!' in the singular, other MSS and versions (including SamP, QL, LXX, Syr) make it conform to the immediate context by putting it in the plural. However, sequences similar to the present one occur at 4:5; 11:26. These are perhaps not strictly examples of the alternation of singular and plural address in Deuteronomy, as the form *re'ēh* may rather be regarded as an interjection (but see note on v. 21).

natattî is perfect in form, but probably declarative in force ('I give').

nišba' yhwh, 'the LORD swore': SamP, LXX read *nišba'tî*, 'I swore', presumably on the grounds that Yahweh is speaking here. The change is probably unnecessary, as MT is simply making it quite clear that it is the LORD who is speaking. The form emphasizes, however, the close association of Moses' words and those of the LORD in Deuteronomy.

lāhem: one MS and SamP omit, perhaps finding the idea of the gift of the land to the patriarchs difficult. But the gift may be taken as being in principle to the patriarchs too (see 'Comment').

13. *wîdu'îm*: should perhaps be repointed as an active participle (cf. Eccles. 9:11), and hence, as there, 'experienced'; cf. Weinfeld 1991: 135.

15. MT's *'et rā'šê šibtêkem*, '(I took) the heads of your tribes', seems to anticipate unhelpfully *wā'ettēn 'ōtām rā'šîm 'alêkem*, 'I made them heads over you.' Read with LXX: 'I took from among you ... officers for your tribes.' LXX actually has 'officers as your judges': *tois kritais hymōn*, possibly influenced by v. 16. However, 'officers' are distinguished from 'judges' in 16:18, where both are appointed 'according to your tribes'.

16. Note the infinitive absolute, *šāmōaʿ*, used as imperative: 'hear!' (see GKC 113. 4. bb [a]; and cf. 16:1). SamP has imp. here.

21. 'Look!' is singular in MT, plural in LXX, Syr; cf. v. 8. Here, however, the number remains singular throughout the verse, in contrast to the surrounding material. The singular interjection may have occasioned one of those temporary changes in number that are a feature of deuteronomic discourse.

24. MT's 'it' is feminine, surprisingly, since the only nouns it could follow (*naḥal*, i.e. the valley of Eshcol, and *hār*, i.e. the hill country) are masculine. The pronoun presumably refers to 'the land' (*'ereṣ*, f.), as assumed in QL, Syr, Vg. This is in line with Num. 13:21, which records that the spies traversed the whole land. MT is probably to be retained although (or because) difficult.

25. LXX, Vg omit 'and also gave their report'. MT follows v. 22, and there is no compelling reason against it.

26. LXX, Syr, Vg have 'our God' for MT's 'your God'. Cf. vv. 30, 32, 33. MT is preferable in vv. 30, 33 for reasons of consistency within those verses, and probably therefore also in v. 26. There is a tendency to confusion on the point in the ancient versions, perhaps naturally; cf. also v. 28.

28. LXX has 'your brothers' for MT 'our brothers'; MT makes more sense. Some Hebrew MSS, LXX and SamP have 'greater in number' rather than 'taller'. This is an intelligible reading in view of 7:7; the relative fewness of Israel would be a natural ground for fear.

31. The change to the singular form of address in the first half of the verse seems to accompany the tender image of God carrying the people as a man does his son.

35. LXX omits 'this evil generation', which also has no counterpart in Num. 14:22–23. The phrase has therefore been interpreted as a gloss in MT, intended to avoid the impression that only the spies were referred to (S. R. Driver 1895: 25–26). If so, it is nevertheless consistent with the meaning of the context.

39. LXX omits 'as for your little ones … prey'. SamP omits 'who are still too young to know the difference between right and wrong'.

44. LXX, Syr, Vg have 'from Seir', which seems to be required for the sense.

45. LXX, Syr, SamP imply the reading *wattēšᵉḇû*, 'they sat', instead of MT *wattāšuḇû*, 'they returned'. The former may have been influenced by the same form in v. 46 (though see the collocation of 'sitting' and 'weeping' at Judg. 20:26, and Weinfeld 1991: 153).

46. 'Your stay was a long one': lit. 'many days, according to the days that you stayed (there)'. The latter clause virtually repeats the main statement, according to Hebrew idiom (cf. the divine name: 'I AM WHO I AM', Exod. 3:14). The phrase leaves the time unspecified; see 'Comment'.

Form and structure

Deuteronomy, though largely consisting of Moses' exhortation to Israel, is cast in a narrative framework. The opening words of the book (1:1) make an explicit link with the end of Numbers (Num. 36:13; see 'Notes on the text', above). The preaching of Moses is thus announced, but is first located both geographically and in the context of the story of Israel's deliverance from Egypt, which has been the dominant theme of Exodus–Numbers. The substance of Deut. 1 – 3 runs parallel to Num. 10 – 36, that is, it covers the time and events from Israel's departure from Mt Horeb (Deuteronomy's habitual name for Mt Sinai) to the time when the people stand in the plains of Moab, at the northern end of the Dead Sea and east of the Jordan, ready to occupy the promised land. Some of the land, indeed, namely the parts of Transjordan allocated to the tribes of Reuben, Gad and half of Manasseh, has already been occupied, admittedly after a false start. The theme of the book, therefore, namely the opportunity (and obligation) that lies before Israel to enter fully into the covenant blessings, is nicely reflected in the geographical setting. Israel is between the wilderness and Canaan, between the promise and its appropriation.

Formally, ch. 1 falls into four sections: 1. an itinerary from Horeb to the people's current location east of the Jordan (1–5); 2. a first exhortation to continue the journey into the promised land (6–8); 3. instructions for the routine legal regulation of the people's life (9–18); 4. a further command to go and take the land (19–21), followed by the narrative of the spies' expedition and the consequent failure of the people to take the land at the first attempt (22–46).

The arrangements for judging legal cases (9–18) seem to interrupt the narrative's progression (e.g. Plöger 1967: 13ff.; cf. Mittmann 1975: 24–33, 164). However, the parallel passage in Exod. 18:13–23 falls, as here, between the account of the exodus and the giving of the law at Sinai/Horeb. This may imply that a close connection is being stressed between the giving of the law and its implementation.

The 'shape' of the account is more complex than the superficial division into paragraphs that we have noted. The dominant motif of 'journey' provides a vantage-point for understanding the chapter. The book opens with a catalogue of places (1) and the parenthesis (2) concerning the length of the first stage of the journey, as far as Kadesh-Barnea. The places named in v. 1 echo place names on the route of the exodus (Num. 11:35; 12:16; 33:17–21). Thus while v. 1 looks at first glance like an indication of Moses' location, both verses actually stress that Moses and Israel are in the midst of a journey. (Mittmann [1975: 8] sees a tension between 'place' and 'route' in v. 1, and thinks the verse is composite; cf. S. R. Driver 1895: 2; Mayes 1994: 113. It is true that the syntax of v. 1, implying location, seems at odds with the sense, implying journey; but see 'Comment'.) The perspective looks beyond Kadesh to Moab (3–5), and on into the land itself (7–8). The point of view of the 'narrator' here and throughout the book is Moab, and it therefore already presupposes the action about to be described in chs. 1 – 3.

The journey motif is reinforced by the composition of the account. Among a number of verbs of motion (Plöger 1967: 19), three stand out as occurring at key moments, namely *pānâ*, 'turn', 'set out'; *nāśā'*, 'travel', and *'ālâ*, 'go up. Thus the first command to Israel in the book is, 'Set out and travel . . .' (7), that is, from Horeb to the land. The first response to the command is recorded in v. 19 with 'and we travelled'; the spies 'set out and went up' into the hill country (24); the people then 'would not go up' (26; cf. v. 28). In response, Yahweh tells them to 'set out, and travel' back in the direction from which they had come (40); and finally the people decide to 'go up' to the land in spite of this new command of Yahweh, and he again prohibits this (41b–42). The vocabulary thus sets up the theological issues, the relations between Israel and Yahweh being 'mapped', as it were, on a geographical canvas. Obedience is matched by progress; disobedience by retreat and failure.

Vocabulary aside, the shape of the chapter also marks the reversal in Israel's fortunes. Up to v. 25, there is progress towards the land (including the provision for life there, vv. 9–18), climaxing in the declaration by the spies that it is indeed a good land (25), a faithful acceptance of Yahweh's promise. Thereafter, however, the story is all retreat; the spies' faith is not echoed by Israel, and the land is (temporarily) lost. The language of the narrative, furthermore, belongs to the 'war of Yahweh', or 'holy war', according to which Yahweh conquers his enemies, in order to give the land to his own people. This, however, is put into reverse when the disobedient people is driven back by the Amorites and turns away from the land at Yahweh's command.

The standpoint of the narrative has been seen as pessimistic (contrast 1:32 with Exod. 14:30–31), anticipating the fall of Judah in 2 Kgs. 25, and thus exilic (Plöger 1967: 3; N. Lohfink 1960: 114ff.). The account is more open than this, however (see 'Explanation').

Deut. 1:9–18 has a close parallel in Exod. 18:13–27. There, the arrangements for administration are made before the events on Sinai, while here the timing is not precisely specified (merely, 'At that time', v. 9). Furthermore, the passage also echoes Num. 11:10–25, in which seventy elders are given 'some of the spirit that was on [Moses]' (25), in order to help him lead the people. The close connection here is in the phrase, 'I cannot bear the burden of you alone' (9; cf. Num. 11:14) (though the idea of Moses' endurance is present also at Exod. 18:23). While our passage is closer in content to Exod. 18:13–27 (the Numbers account having more to do with general spiritual oversight), it seems that Deuteronomy has collapsed the two other passages (one occurring just before the Sinai section, and one immediately after, in connection with the departure from the mountain) into one (here broadly with Mittmann [1975: 26–30], who rightly criticizes Plöger's idea of an independent narrative source underlying Deuteronomy). The use of the latter passage is appropriate for linking the idea of administration with the journey.

There are interesting connections between the measures taken here and the judicial reform of King Jehoshaphat recorded in 2 Chr. 19:5-11: the appointment of judges throughout Israel; the appeal to the principle that justice is not human but God's; the prohibition of showing partiality. These connections need not imply that the law dates from that reform (as Plöger on 16:19 [1967: 36-39], who thinks that as such it is an 'old' law remembered in a time of crisis). In some respects the laws here have parallels in the ANE (Weinfeld 1991: 140-141).

The account of the spies' mission (1:19-46) shows similarities with and differences from the account of the same in Num. 13 - 14. In traditional criticism, the latter is a composite of J and P, with P being responsible for the list of the spies' names, and the concept of one spy per tribe (Num. 13:1-16). Deuteronomy clearly knows the concept 'one from each tribe' (23), however, and the plainest reading of this is that it knows Num. 1 - 13 (P; cf. Weinfeld 1991: 143). Others have explained D's knowledge of P on this point by postulating a complicated literary history; Perlitt (1990: 97-98), for example, thinks that the spy tradition has been repeatedly worked over in the context of both P and D streams, which ultimately influence each other.

Comment

1:1-5

The opening verses of Deuteronomy resume the note struck in the final verse of Numbers (36:13), and are also echoed by Deut. 4:44-49; 12:1; 29:1[28:69]; 34:1-6. The passage shows a concentric pattern that highlights its theme (cf. Christensen 1991: 6):

A   These are the words that Moses spoke
B   East of the Jordan
C   Eleven days journey from Horeb
D   Moses spoke
C^1 After he had defeated Sihon
B^1 In the wilderness
A^1 Moses began to explain this law

The effect of this pattern is twofold: first, to splice the idea of word into that of geography and history – the word of God is spoken in and into Israel's historical experience with him; secondly, to create an equation between Moses' speech, God's commandment and the important idea of Torah.

The dominant idea in these verses is the words of God spoken through Moses. Indeed, the opening phrase, 'These are the words', is the name given to Deuteronomy in the Hebrew Bible. The words meant here are, in the first place, those that Moses is about to declare to Israel in Moab, in the three extensive speeches that compose the greatest part of Deuteronomy (1:6 – 4:40; 5:1 – 28:68; 29:1[28:69] – 30:20).

The words of Moses are immediately set in their historical and geographical context (1b–3a, 4). The data in the present verses emphasize that words of God are being spoken into a new, particular situation. Moses' speeches to Israel are located, loosely, 'east of the Jordan', or 'in the land of Moab' (1, 5; cf. 29:1[28:69]; see 'Notes on the text'). More precise data follow. The phrase 'in the wilderness' has no clear referent in Moab; it is further defined, however, by 'in the Arabah', indicating the gorge in which lie the lower Jordan valley and the Dead Sea, and which continues south to the Gulf of Aqaba and beyond. The other place names occasion some debate. Paran, Hazeroth and possibly Laban (= Libnah?) appear as staging-posts on Israel's exodus journey (Num. 10:12; 11:35; 12:16; 33:17, 20). If those places are actually meant here, the information is hard to understand as specifying a single location in Moab. It is possible that the similarity of these names to the locations on the exodus route is merely coincidental, and attempts have been made to identify certain names in our list with locations in the region of Moab, though without certainty (Noth 1981: 108–109; cf. Christensen 1991: 7; Perlitt 1990: 12–14). Probably, however, there is an actual reminiscence of the exodus journey, as is suggested also by the note in v. 2 (and perhaps by the term 'wilderness'). The 'present time' at Moab would thus be brought deliberately into connection with the various times and places along the way (see further 'Explanation').

The limits of the journey noted here (2) are Horeb and Kadesh-Barnea. Horeb is mentioned merely as the point of departure, though the note clearly anticipates the enormous importance the place will have in the book, as the place where the covenant was made with the generation before the one standing with Moses in Moab (5:2–3; 29:1[28:69]).

Kadesh-Barnea was the place in the wilderness of Paran (Num. 13:26), between the Sinai desert and the southern reaches of the Negev, where the Israelites camped during the period between the exodus and the entry to Canaan. The reference to the eleven days taken to reach it from Horeb is presumably a realistic detail, even though the precise location of Horeb is not known. In contrast, the forty years of v. 3 measure the long time from the exodus from Egypt to Israel's present position on the border of the promised land, because of the people's failure to enter it at the first opportunity due to their fear and lack of faith (Num. 13 – 14). It is assumed here that these events are known, though they will be rehearsed again in the present chapter as part of Moses' exhortation.

The precise detail ('on the first day in the eleventh month') seems to refer not only to the day on which Moses speaks, but also to the day of his death (32:48). It has been pointed out (van Goudoever 1985: 145–146) that, in the Israelite liturgical calandar, this is precisely two and a half months before the Passover. This may indicate that Moses' speeches are to be seen as a preparation for the first Passover that Israel would celebrate in the land (Josh. 5). In that passage, conquest and Passover are certainly closely connected. Here too, the idea would forge one more link between word and history in the present verses.

The allusion to Sihon and Og (see on 2:26 – 3:11, and cf. Num. 21:21–35) has the double function of reminding the Israelites that the conquest of the land has already begun in Transjordan, and of specifying again the exact setting of the speeches, thus creating a sense of expectation and significance.

Moses will speak 'according to all that Yahweh had given him as commandment for them' (3). This develops the idea of Moses' words in v. 1, and shows that what Moses will speak will come out of what has already passed between God and Israel on their journey to Moab, specifically echoing the covenant at Horeb, with its attendant laws (Exod. 20 – 23). The development continues when the preaching is also described as 'explaining this law (Torah)' (5). In Deuteronomy 'Torah' embraces both regulation (see 4:8, where Torah is an umbrella term covering individual laws) and instruction or exhortation. It is also closely associated with the covenant (see 5:1–2 for the close link between 'statutes and laws' and covenant; and 4:13 for covenant and the Ten Commandments; 31:9). Occurrences of the term in Deuteronomy fall predominantly in the opening and closing chapters (4:8, 44; 27:3, 8, 26; 28:58, 61; 29:21[20], 29[28]; 31:9, 11–12, 24, 26, 46; 33:4, 10; but see also 17:11, 18–19). These allusions show that the substance of the 'Torah' here is primarily Moses' preaching in Deuteronomy itself, which is finally written in a book that is understood as a covenant document to be read regularly on specified worship occasions (28:58; 31:9). It is not merely the preaching as such, however, but the preaching as set in the historical narrative of Israel's deliverance, and re-expressing the covenant at Horeb. This is clear from the sequel to 'These are the words ...' in a historical account (6ff.).

Verse 5 is resumptive, again bringing together both geography and the theme of God's word. That Moses 'explains' the law emphasizes the concern of Deuteronomy not merely to give information but to teach and persuade.

1:6–8

Moses' first speech (1:6 – 4:40) now begins. It immediately picks up the theme of God's word to Israel at Horeb from vv. 1–5 (6). It then proceeds (7–8) with God's command to Israel to occupy the land, whose parts are described, balanced by a reaffirmation of his ancient oath to Abraham, Isaac and Jacob, Israel's forefathers, or the 'patriarchs'.

It is immediately clear that the words of Moses will be in reality God's. The phrase 'the LORD our God' itself recalls the covenantal relationship already existing between God and Israel, and this is echoed by the reference now to Horeb. The word of God in question here, however, is a specific command, namely to leave Horeb, following the time the people had spent there, witnessing God's revelation of himself, hearing his commands and entering into covenant with him. In the Pentateuchal narrative, this is the subject matter of Exod. 19 – Num. 10 (see Num. 10:11–35 for the departure itself). The people have now stayed, or 'dwelt', long enough at Horeb. The command (which is echoed again at 2:3) shows that Horeb was not a final resting-place; rather, Israel must now move on, both physically and in terms of the covenant. This will become an important motif in the book.

When Moses says, 'The LORD our God said to us at Horeb' (6), this is not strictly factual, for by this time the vast majority of the generation that had actually stood at Horeb has passed away (see on 2:34–40). However, the new generation is often addressed as if it had stood itself at Horeb. This is a way of expressing the solidarity of Israel, and the need to re-enact the covenant in each generation (see further on 5:2–3).

The first reported command of God is now to move from Horeb and enter the land of Canaan (7). 'Set out now' is literally 'Turn', which carries the connotation of decision, a leaving behind and setting the face to the new destination. It occurs several times in this record of the journey from Horeb to Moab (chs. 1 – 3). As was shown above (on 1:1–46, 'Form and structure'), there is a moral dimension to this travelling, and the verb *pānâ* ('turn') itself partakes of this (cf. its use in 29:18[17]; 30:17; 31:18, 20).

The description of the land that lies before Israel broadly conforms to the outlines in Gen. 15:18–21; Deut. 11:24, though each of these differs in its details. This is the fullest. The 'land of the Amorites' is probably a general designation for the whole land. In my translation, correspondingly, 'Amorites' is understood as a name for the pre-Israelite peoples in general (cf. Gen. 15:16; Josh. 7:7; 10:5), though it can also be used for peoples in the eastern part of the territory described, including Transjordan (cf. 4; 7:1). The term 'its inhabitants' then stands in a kind of apposition to 'Amorites', but specifying those who live in the different parts of the land. The term 'Canaanites' seems here to refer to the peoples of the coastal area in particular (though in other texts it too can mean the pre-Israelite occupants of the land in general; S. R. Driver 1895: 11).

What follows then describes the land in detail. On the Arabah, see on v. 1. The word 'highlands' is again lit. 'mountain', but now in the specific sense of the central range running north to south, and comprising what would become Judah and Samaria. The 'lower uplands', or Shephelah, are the lower hills west of the Judean range, and running down to the coastal plain. The Negeb is the semi-desert area in southern Judah, and the coastal plain itself runs along the Mediterranean from the far south to the Carmel range in the north. The area described also includes Lebanon and territory running from the northern borders of Canaan as far as the Euphrates. The Euphrates is mentioned in all three texts named here, and this extent of the land was clearly regarded as ideal, though even under David it was scarcely possessed. (On the geography of ancient Israel see Rogerson 1985; Aharoni 1979.)

The area thus described is now called simply 'the land' (8). It is the land shown long ago to Abraham (Gen. 12:1), and given to him and his descendants by a promise that was repeated throughout the patriarchal narratives, to Isaac and Jacob as well as to Abraham (e.g. Gen. 13:17; 15:13–16; 26:2–3; 28:13, 15; see Clines 1989: 31–43). The appeal to that promise here is of central importance for Deuteronomy, which sees the imminent entry to the land of Canaan as its fulfilment (cf. 1:21; 6:3). The promise of land goes closely, of course, with that of descendants for Abraham (Gen. 12:2; 15:6). On this basis, the LORD says to the people that they themselves are the recipients of his ancient promise. When he refers to it as an oath, he stresses his irreversible commitment to it. The converse of this, however, is that the people must 'go and take possession of' the land. The verb 'take possession' is used frequently in Deuteronomy for Israel's entry to the land. It implies a certain right to it, by way of inheritance, though clearly it is a right that is contingent on God's gift. It also implies the need to dispossess the present inhabitants. The crucial point is, however, that the promise is received by active faith.

1:9–18

The need for organization of the tribes arose necessarily from the prospect of their movement on into the desert (Noth 1981: 15). The phrase 'At that time' (9) is somewhat general, recalling the whole period at Horeb. Moses' recognition that he could not 'bear' the people alone derives, as we have seen, from two accounts, in Exod. 18 and Num. 11. Moses' own initiation of the topic, namely the need of a system of administration for Israel, is closer to Numbers than to Exodus, where his father-in-law Jethro persuades him take the necessary measures (Exod. 18:14). Some commentators have supposed that the part of the non-Israelite Jethro has been deliberately suppressed here, because of the influence of later nationalistic, or 'Jewish', thought on Deuteronomy (Weinfeld 1991: 140). The reason rather is the sharp focus here on the relationship between Moses and the people, and the economical way of incorporating the existing, well-known traditions.

The phrase 'I cannot bear you alone', adopted from Num. 11:14, makes a rapid transition from the command to enter the promised land in vv. 6–8 to the topic of organization of the people. As such, it is presented not as a 'complaint' (thus rather differently from Num. 11), but as a consequence of the fulfilment of the promise. This connotation is reinforced by vv. 10–11. Verse 10 expressly recalls the promise that Abraham's descendants would be greatly multiplied (Gen. 15:5), and declares it to be already fulfilled. Thus, incidentally, the promise's elements of land and posterity are brought together in this connection. The thought is then carried further in verse 11 with the prayer that the increase and blessing would continue. Both the present fulfilment and the wish for the future are made dependent on the ancient promise ('just as he promised you'). This juxtaposition of 'already' and 'not yet' is typical of Deuteronomy's sense of a people always on the move, having received God's promises, and yet still moving into an open future with him.

Having established that the 'problem' is actually a function of blessing, Moses now spells it out further (12). In the phrase 'Your problems, burdens and disputes', only one of the words appears in Num. 11 (*maśśā'*, 'burden', Num. 11:17), and none of them in Exod. 18. At first glance, therefore, Deuteronomy stresses the problems of governing Israel by this increase in vocabulary (the noun *ṭorah*, here translated 'problem', occurs elsewhere only at Is. 1:14, where Israel's false worship is seen as a burden on God). The word 'dispute' (*rîḇ*), however, is also drawn from the wider narrative in Exodus, namely at Exod. 17:7, where it is used of the people's complaining about having been brought out of Egypt into the wilderness (interestingly, in close connection with the noun Massah, which resembles our *maśśā'* here). In our text the 'disputes' primarily refer to regular legal disputes; yet, by its use of language, the text may subtly recall Israel's basic stubbornness also, in keeping with an emphasis it will develop (cf. 9:6).

Moses now initiates the selection of leaders (13), calling on the people to do it, and indeed enlisting their support for the plan (14). This 'democratic' procedure, not reported in Exodus or Numbers, is consistent with Deuteronomy's emphasis on the responsibility of the people, as a unity, for its entire life before God (see below on 'brotherhood', 16). A further peculiarity of Deuteronomy is the criteria it requires for leadership, where the stress falls on wisdom. This seems to contrast with Exodus, which looks first for virtue (Exod. 18:21). Deuteronomy does sometimes use language that is close to 'wisdom' (cf. Deut. 4:6). The contrast between 'intellectual' and religious-moral qualities can be overdrawn, however. The wisdom advocated in Deuteronomy is closely related to the laws and teachings of God (4:5, 8). At its heart, furthermore, is an insistence on the wholeness of the human response required by God (6:4–5). Finally, the wisdom literature also places wisdom very close to the 'fear of the LORD' (Prov. 9:10). The requirement for leadership is above all in terms of character (hence 'experienced'; see 'Notes on the text').

The translation of v. 15 follows LXX. This is because MT ('I took the leaders of your tribes') poses the difficulty that the persons selected are here being made leaders, and therefore can scarcely be such at the outset (see 'Notes on the text'). The jurisdiction of the leaders is now further explained. The terms 'thousand', 'hundred', 'fifty' and 'ten' need not be taken as exact figures, but rather as relative sizes of units; 'thousand', indeed, can roughly correspond to 'clan' (Judg. 6:15; 1 Sam. 23:23; see de Vaux 1961: 216–217). More importantly, there is a fusion between judicial and military functions here (as also in Exod. 18:21, 25), and as occurred elsewhere in the ancient world (see Weinfeld 1991: 140–141; also 1977 on Hittite parallels to the present section). The term śār, 'leader', is used for 'official' in a broad sense in 1 Kgs. 4:2. (For other views of the relationship between judicial and military functions, see Bartlett 1969; Knierim 1961.)

The judges were to be assisted by 'officers'. Their role was apparently to communicate and implement decisions among the people (cf. Deut. 20:5, 8–9; Josh. 1:10; 3:2). Their organization according to tribes put them in a position to do this effectively.

The officials, introduced in v. 15 according to their different ranks, are now designated generally as 'judges' (16). As used in the book of Judges, the term means primarily a military deliverer, raised up for a crisis. Here, however, a regular judicial function is in view. (The two types of role seem to be combined in Samuel; 1 Sam. 7:15–17.) Moses binds the judges to perform their duties justly, perhaps in a formal ceremony involving an oath (Weinfeld 1991: 138). Their remit is to judge between 'your brothers', that is, Israelites (16). We have already observed Deuteronomy's understanding of the unity of the people before God. That understanding is now more fully characterized as a concept of the brotherhood of all members of the people – a frequently occurring idea, which lies behind much of the book's thought, and is conceived as a means of protecting the individual from the tyrannies of a hierarchical and oppressive society (cf. 15:7–18). The provision made does not rule out justice for the resident non-Israelite, however, whose needs are expressly catered for here and elsewhere in the book (cf. 14:29).

The heart of the judges' task is to hear cases and judge 'rightly', or with 'righteousness', as the related passage in 16:18–20 also strongly emphasizes. The idea implies both straight dealing and loyalty within a relationship. Judgment therefore should be according to the true merits of a case, and ordinary human compassion. This means that the judges must not be deterred from a decision by any consideration other than the truth. No preference is to be given to the prestigious or powerful. The stress on this recognizes the natural human fear of others who are powerful. To show bias, however, runs absolutely counter to the vision of Israel, and of society, that is offered in Deuteronomy, in which human beings are on an equal footing before God. This is why it is insisted that judgment belongs to God. Justice is not a commodity in the hands of those who can control it, but is in principle God's. The idea of Moses as a kind of Court of Appeal (17c) is related to this fundamental principle, for it symbolizes and guards the ultimate jurisdiction of God, which in turn is the only guarantee of a just society. Both the principle and the practice are reflected also in the reforming measures taken by King Jehoshaphat (2 Chr. 19:6, 8–11; cf. Prov. 16:33).

Finally, Moses shifts the focus from the judges to the whole people, recalling the obligations he laid on them 'at that time'. This seems to refer generally to the commands given at Horeb, rather than to the instructions for judicial administration in particular. The closure is intended to make explicit that the administrative arrangements just outlined are meant to implement the commands of God in Israel's daily life.

1:19–46

19–25. The new section takes up (19) from God's command in vv. 6–8 to continue the journey towards the land, designated here again as the 'land [lit. mountain] of the Amorites'. The actual progress recorded is that which was prepared for in v. 2, namely Horeb to the desert staging-post of Kadesh-Barnea. The wilderness between is portrayed as vast and life-threatening, perhaps to stress the faithfulness of God by way of encouragement to keep his commands. Kadesh, however, is only a halfway house. In a sense they have arrived at their destination ('you have come to the land of the Amorites', 20); and God 'is giving' it to them. The present tense of 'give' in v. 20 is reinforced by a past tense (21) which proclaims the gift an accomplished fact. In another sense they are merely on the threshold; the land has been set 'before you' (21b), and there remains the command to possess it (cf. 8). Possessing must be preceded by 'going up', that is, the actual approach and entry to the land, the act of faith itself. The verb is used several times in the present chapter, especially in vv. 21–28, or at the point of decision.

They are to possess it according to God's prior word to the forefathers (cf. 8), which thus takes on the character of command as well as promise. The command not to fear focuses on the moral and religious issue that now faces Israel. Possession will not follow automatically, but requires their faith, demonstrated in fearless action. (The same point was prominent in Numbers; Num. 14:9.)

The sequel (22–25) now takes up this very issue. The people take the initiative in a plan to send spies ahead to explore the land and bring back information about the journey before them and the land itself (22; the plan is more fully spelt out in Num. 13:17–20). It is stressed that the people as a whole make this move, and that it comes from them rather than from Moses. This differs from the account in Num. 13:1–3, where God himself initiates the spies' mission via Moses. It might be supposed that the people conceived the plan, and brought it to Moses who sought and gained sanction from God (so Craigie 1976: 101; Merrill 1994: 73). Yet it seems significant that Deuteronomy chooses to narrate the incident thus. Two features suggest that the people are being shown to have been blameworthy in their adoption of the plan. First, there is an irony in the words, 'Let us send men ahead of us', in an account that stresses that God himself goes 'ahead' of the people to prepare their way. This theme is developed in vv. 29–33, where the command not to fear is resumed (29), only to be met by the people's refusal (32), focused on their failure to believe that God went ahead of them into the land both to guide and to fight for them (cf. vv. 30, 33). Secondly, when Moses is refused permission to enter the land himself, there is reason to think that his role here in accepting the plan without demur (23) is regarded as culpable (see further on 3:26). Deuteronomy's narrative of the spies, therefore, is part of its exposition of the people's chronic failure to keep faith with God.

Moses' reply to the people, 'This seemed good to me' (23), carries an echo of their response to him in the matter of appointing judges (1:14). Together, the two phrases suggest a certain solidarity between Moses and people. Each suggestion, furthermore, is followed by a selection of representatives according to tribes (cf. v. 15; the similarity of language is close, especially when LXX 'from you' is followed in v. 15). The appointment of one spy per tribe follows Num. 13:2 (for the relationship of Deuteronomy to P at this point, see above, 'Form and structure'). Allusions to the tribal division of Israel are uncommon in Deuteronomy, ceding prominence to the stronger idea of the oneness of the people. But it is used here to establish the idea of proper representation of the people at important moments (as it is also in Josh. 3:12) – whether the decisions taken are for good or ill.

The spies' expedition to the land (lit. the hill country) takes them as far as the Wadi Eshcol, a fertile valley near Hebron, in what would become southern Judah (24). The name Eshcol means 'cluster', and is taken from the prodigious cluster of grapes which, according to Num. 13:23–24, the spies brought back. While the Numbers account relates how the spies travelled through the whole land (Num. 13:21), our passage limits itself to the excursion to the Eshcol valley; the pronoun 'it', however, is a veiled allusion to the land (see above, 'Notes on the text'), and the Wadi Eshcol, therefore, may be seen as representing it. (There may also be a suggestion, however, that the spies' mission has been truncated; the human endeavour has been necessarily limited.) The spies' report is entirely positive. In passing over the potentially frightening information conveyed by them according to Num. 13:28–29, Deuteronomy apparently wants to stress at this point that there are no grounds for the people not to go up into the land. The report that 'the land is good' is a kind of climax, which confronts the people with a decision.

26–28. In the fuller narrative in Num. 13:25 – 14:10, we read how the spies tell of the strength of the land, how the majority of them believe that the people could not take it (13:31), how they themselves took fright at the sight of the Anakim (13:33), and of the people's consequent plan to go back to Egypt, despite the wiser counsel of Caleb and Joshua (14:6–9). All of this is compressed here into the simple accusation that the people refused to obey God by going up, a refusal characterized as rebellion (26; cf. Num. 14:9; the verb in Deuteronomy is *mārâ*, in Numbers *mārad*).

The rebellious plan to return to Egypt is conveyed by the motif of murmuring (27; cf. Num. 14:2; again Deuteronomy uses its own verb). Here, however, the fearful and rebellious words are in the mouths of the people themselves. The declaration that God hates them is in direct contradiction of Deuteronomy's insistence that he has consistently acted out of love for them (Deut. 4:37; 7:8). It is a carefully directed complaint, for 'love' and 'hatred' belong to the language of covenant (Moran 1963a). The people are asserting that God never had any intention of bringing them into a covenantal relationship with himself when he brought them out of Egypt, but rather intended to destroy them. It is a statement of fundamental unbelief, made sharper by the use of the verb 'give', in the sense of 'give over to the enemy', when, on the contrary, the promised 'gift' of the land is a central plank in the promise.

The people's exclamation, 'Where are we to go up!' (28), with its use of the key word for the decision required of them, expresses their response, in their own mouths, to the exhortation of v. 21. It is a cry of despair and impotence that flies in the face of the promise. The terrifying prospect of facing the land's inhabitants is also conveyed through the people (28). What they say corresponds closely to what the spies had indeed said (the Canaanites are powerful and their cities well fortified, and there are giants; Num. 13:27–29). But Deuteronomy has allowed the words to come from the people themselves in order to stress their unbelief.

29–33. Moses exhorts them again not to fear, using a new, intense term for terror, which hints at the misplaced nature of the fear the people are feeling (29, cf. v. 21). His grounds are that 'the LORD your God goes ahead of you' (30). This looks like a direct response to the people's earlier demand: 'Let us send men ahead of us' (22). The proposed purpose of that expedition was to bring back knowledge of the land and of the route to it. Now we are shown emphatically that it is God himself who does these very things (31–33). The idea of guidance is prefaced, however, by the assertion that he will fight for his people (30). Here is the first direct statement in the book of God's Holy War (though cf. the parenthetical v. 4). That is, God himself appears as Warrior, the true victor over his people's enemies, who are at the same time his own enemies. God's capacity to wage war undergirds the central promise in Deuteronomy, and continues as a major theme into Joshua (cf. Longman & Reid 1995; and further bibliography in Merrill 1994: 78–79 n.). His war in the promised land is here seen as a continuation of the campaign begun in Egypt. Since the people have seen his victory there, they ought to believe that he can overcome again.

The theme of guidance is now elaborated, meeting the need timidly expressed in v. 22. God's care for his people along the route is couched in the intimate image of a man carrying his child (31; see 'Notes on the text'). He has borne the people thus through the dangers of the desert, 'till you arrived at this place'. The place in question is their current location of Moab. This, of course, is not the end of their journey. But God's capacity to bring them thus far is a paradigm of his power to do so again and again. (The metaphor of sonship recurs at 8:5 and 14:1 in 'election' contexts. There are echoes of wider ANE usage in Num. 21:29. Cf. also Jer. 3:4; Hos. 11:1.)

The theme is further developed in v. 33, where God is pictured going ahead searching out resting-places along the way. The use of the verb *tûr* ('search out') is striking. Its OT occurrences are concentrated largely in the narratives of Numbers, first in Num. 10:33, where the ark of the LORD is said to go ahead of the people to 'search out' resting-places for them. Thereafter it falls almost exclusively in the spy narrative of Num. 13 – 14 (12×), where it is by way of a keyword, referring to the activity of the spies themselves. Deuteronomy avoids the expression for the spies' activity, adopting it only for God's. It thus stands close to Num. 10:33 (notice the 'cloud' in the same context, 34); in relation to Num. 13 – 14, however, it makes the point, with some irony, that God alone went ahead of the people, and that this should have been sufficient for them. The 'cloud and the fire' recall the Exodus account of his leading in the desert (cf. Exod. 13:21–22). Here the memory of God's leading is more expressly directed at persuading the people to believe than in Exodus. The same concern explains the absence of reference to the ark (though it is important in Num. 10:33), and indeed the Jethro/Reuel connection (Num. 10:29–32), passed over here as it was in the recollection of Exod. 18 (Deut. 1:9–18, see above).

However, the pictures of leading in vv. 31, 33 are interrupted by a strong statement of Israel's unbelief (32). It is made in an uncompromising participial (present) form that confronts the present generation standing at Moab with their own faithlessness, thus refusing to allow the charge of unbelief to be attached to the previous generation only. God continues to challenge his people to faith now.

34–40. The next section concerns the question 'Who may enter the land?' God first responds in anger to the people's expression of unbelief (34, cf. vv. 27–28), swearing that 'this wicked generation' should not see the land (an oath that stands in ironic contrast to the ancient oath to the patriarchs, vv. 34–35). The logic of the Numbers narrative is thus preserved here, namely that the Horeb generation would not inherit the promise because of their unbelief, but that the next generation would do so. (See also 'Notes on the text'.) That concept stands side by side with the somewhat contrary thrust of Deuteronomy, namely that the generations are united in character (contrast 'the LORD heard what you said', v. 34). (The gift of the land, incidentally, can be expressed as a gift to the patriarchs, v. 35. This is another aspect of the unity of Israel; cf. 1:8, and 'Notes on the text' there and above.)

The exception made for Caleb is now related. The specific reasons for this are not given here, consistently with Deuteronomy's omission earlier of the details of the spies' report, in which (in the Numbers account) Caleb's faith had emerged. Here he is merely singled out in a general way for his wholehearted devotion to God. In this way the main lines of the Numbers account are adhered to once again, but subjected to the dominant concern to show that Israel was united in its faithlessness. (Num. 14:24 says that Caleb and his childen will 'possess the land'; Deuteronomy has passed over this too, perhaps because it might detract from its picture of the whole people at Moab about to do this.)

Moses, in contrast, will not see the land. No clear reason for this is given in Deuteronomy, beyond the tantalizing 'because of you'. The book of Numbers makes no mention of Moses' exclusion in its account of the spies' mission (Num. 13 – 14). It tells of it later in the context of Israel's approach to the land, after the enforced waiting period in the desert (Num. 20:10–13). The reason given there (12) is usually interpreted as implying arrogance on Moses' part (Wenham 1981: 150–151). Deuteronomy has presented the data characteristically. It has, first, compressed events (this is a more satisfactory way of looking at the text than to suppose that the incident in Num. 20 is not in view, because of the chronological difficulty; S. R. Driver 1895: 26–27; Craigie 1976a: 105). Nor is it necessary to suppose that Num. 20:12 is a later concept based on Ezekiel's doctrine of individual responsibility (Mayes 1979: 147; Weinfeld 1991: 150), for the reason given next. Taking its cue from Num. 14:30, which says that only Caleb and Joshua will enter the land, it goes immediately to the logical corollary of that, namely that Moses will not. (Aaron's exclusion along with Moses, Num. 20:12, is ignored here, presumably because of Deuteronomy's special interest in Moses.) Secondly, it preserves its picture of Moses as God's mouthpiece, and passes over specific guilt attaching to him (cf. above on 1:9–18, where he is exonerated from 'complaining', 9; *contra* Merrill 1994: 82–83). This leaves no very specific reason for the exclusion, beyond a kind of solidarity with the people, who have deserved it.

The exclusion of Moses gives rise to the designation of Joshua as his successor (38). The sudden mention of Joshua, now introduced as Moses' servant, makes little sense apart from a knowledge of the Numbers story. Yet, as with Caleb, his entrance is abrupt, and it is not said that he was one of the spies (cf. Num. 13:16). His appointment takes the shape here simply of a divine decision, consequent on Moses' exclusion. The chronology of

Numbers is once more compressed, as Joshua's appointment comes at the end of the desert period, not the beginning (Num. 27:15–18).

The logic governing exclusion and entry continues (39) with the assertion that the children of the Horeb generation will enter. The verse relays succinctly the content of Num. 14:31–35. The phrase 'your little ones who you said would become a prey' follows Num. 14:31 exactly. In our passage it lacks an antecedent (supplied in Numbers by Num. 14:3). It may be therefore that the phrase has been imported late from Num. 14:31 (see 'Notes on the text' on this and its absence from LXX). Yet Deuteronomy's treatment of the spies' story elsewhere includes details that presuppose the fuller account in Numbers, and the phrase may be an original part of its castigation of Israel's lack of faith.

The next generation is now characterized as not knowing the difference between right and wrong. That is, at this moment of decision ('today'), they are not yet morally responsible (cf. Is. 7:15). This is different from an assertion of innocence as such. They are, indeed, guiltless with respect to the failure to enter the land at the first command. They, therefore, become recipients of the promised gift of land, and will 'inherit' it. Their own tests of faith, however, are still to come.

The section ends with the logical conclusion of the disqualification of the Horeb generation, namely a command to 'set out and go' towards the desert, and the Reed Sea; that is, the way by which they had come. The language of the command is very similar to that in v. 7, yet the force of it is a grim parody of the former, where the land had lain open before them. Their way is no longer forward, but a retreat. For them, the door of opportunity is now closed.

41–46. The sense of irony and parody is now heightened by the people's belated attempt to go into the land (the account parallels Num. 14:39–45). Formally, the intention expressed in v. 41 looks entirely right. There is a confession of sin (the only one in Deuteronomy), and a resolution to 'go up' and fight in obedience to God's command. It is made clear, however, that this confession has no effect (cf. Jer. 3:22b–24), and that the new resolve does not come from obedience to God. (The point is stronger than in Numbers, for the prohibition that follows, reversing the original command [42], comes directly from God, rather than from Moses [cf. Num. 14:41–42].) The crucial development is that he is not 'among' them, literally, in their midst, an idea that is common and important in Exodus–Numbers, esp. Exod. 32 – 34 and Num. 14. The issue in each case is whether the LORD is among his people and therefore whether or not they can proceed towards the land (Exod. 33:3, 5; 34:9–10; cf. Exod. 17:7; Num. 14:14, 42[44]; and see Moberly 1983). Deuteronomy picks up this idea, specifically from Num. 14:42, 44, though without the imagery of camp, tabernacle and ark that prevails in the earlier narrative. (See also Deut. 6:15; 7:21; 23:14[15]; 31:17.)

The attempt to 'go up' without God is then characterized (43) as an act of great rebelliousness, by an accumulation of verbs: you did not obey (lit. hear, cf. 6:4); you rebelled (cf. v. 26); you acted arrogantly. Whereas before it was rebellion not to go up, it is now rebellion to go. The logic of the Holy War is also set in reverse, and the inhabitants of the land (the Amorites again being a general designation for these, contrast Num. 14:45) deliver a humiliating and costly repulse to Israel (44). Hormah was a Canaanite city in the Negev; the name, however, also carries an interesting and ironic echo of the idea of *ḥerem*, namely the ban of destruction to which Israel was to put the Canaanites (cf. 2:34; 3:6; 7:2). The motif of reversal continues (45) with the people's 'returning', and the twice repeated assertion that God did not 'hear' their cries of anguish, an echo of their refusal hitherto to hear him (43).

The long but unspecified period spent at Kadesh following the abortive attempt to take the land (46) is a return to what has already been designated a halfway house between Egypt and Canaan (2). The chronology is left somewhat open (lit. 'many days', though the phrase can equally mean 'years'). It is sometimes held that Deuteronomy's chronology regarding Kadesh is in tension with the data in Numbers, which speaks expressly of only one sojourn there (and which, it is said, JE dates early in the forty years and P dates late; Num. 13:26–27 JE; S. R. Driver 1895: 32–33; Budd 1984: 217). Deut. 2:1, indeed, seems to presuppose a long period of wandering in the area of Seir, in a passage that may take its cue from Num. 14:25. However, it is difficult to piece together a satisfactory chronology concerning Kadesh from any of the proposed sources (note the obscure datum in Num. 20:1). Deuteronomy obviously supposes that Israel came to Kadesh twice, before and after its failed attack on Canaan. (2:14 could refer to the first of these. S. R. Driver [1895: 32] thinks that a double visit may even be deduced from Numbers, though he does not think this solves the problem.) It is not very concerned otherwise with chronology. The importance of Kadesh is simply that it is not the land; Israel hovers between Egypt, the place of deliverance, and the land of promise yet to be fulfilled.

Explanation

1–5. The theme of the passage is the words of God to Israel through Moses, given at particular times and places. Thus the opening phrase, 'These are the words', unobtrusively introduces the most prominent idea in the book. The character of the word is gradually refined in these verses. It recurs as God's 'command' to his people through Moses (3), and finally as 'this law (Torah)' (5). The word is thus God's authoritative word, which in Deuteronomy will often be expressed in specific commands: the Decalogue itself (5:6–21), and the various laws of chs. 12 – 26. The specification of the word as Torah, however, suggests the purpose of instructing and guiding. The word of God, while often formally consisting of command and sanction, has the positive purpose of forming the people. This explains why so much of what God speaks through Moses in Deuteronomy will be in the form of exhortation.

The meaning of the word must also be fleshed out, however, by considering the data of time and place. The passage clearly locates the words of Moses within the history of God and his people since the encounter between them at Mt Horeb. The compressed, even cryptic, allusions to the journey to this point show that the story of Exodus–Numbers will be presupposed in what follows here. The effect of this is to establish a connection between the words of Moses that are here announced as imminent and the words of God that have already been given at Horeb, a connection that will be forged elsewhere in the book (5:2–3; 29:1[28:69]).

Nor is it simply that the words of Horeb are merely repeated or reinforced here. Rather, word, or Torah, is connected in a deep sense with the journey of Israel. The giving of Torah is cast in narrative form, such that history itself belongs to it. Law and history are not to be put apart in Deuteronomy. That is, the 'Torah' in Deuteronomy involves recalling God's deliverance of the people from Egypt, his guidance through the wilderness, a hint of their rebellion, which made an eleven-day journey take forty years, and at last the beginning of the conquest, the firstfruits of the promise of land (Gen. 12:1–3; Exod. 3:7–10) fulfilled in the defeat of Sihon and Og in Transjordan. Finally, it is essential to the concept of Deuteronomy that the encounter between God and Israel at Horeb was not final, but that there must be further encounters in Israel's history with him. The setting of the words in a journey expresses this, and the subtle fusion of the words once given and those about to be given reinforces it. The sense of expectation established in v. 1 is a permanent fact in Israel's moral and religious life. Knowing the word of God, it nevertheless always awaits it.

6–8. This important passage sets the present generation of Israel in its context, namely the history of God with his people. God's ancient oath to the patriarchs (or 'fathers') had led in time to the covenant with Israel at Horeb, and on into the present. There is thus a certain solidarity in Israel spanning the generations. The present generation is the 'seed' of Abraham, which is about to enter the land once promised to him.

However, the present moment is not an end but a beginning. The first command recorded in the book is to move away from Horeb into the land, a command that came to the generation before the present one, but has not yet been completely carried out, since the people still stand in Moab, outside the land. The ancient promise thus points still into the future with a command. This tension typifies the logic of Deuteronomy. It both affirms God's unqualified faithfulness to his promise, and poses the question whether and how far it can be realized, because it places Israel before the responsibility to 'go in and possess'. The reality of this ambivalence will be catalogued in the latter part of the present chapter.

9–18. In the account of the organization of the administration of Israel, Deuteronomy draws on existing accounts, but makes its own emphases. Brettler (1995: 66) notes a greater emphasis on Moses and on wisdom. The underlying idea, however, is God's blessing of Israel. Moses cannot 'bear' them alone because God is fulfilling his promise to Abraham to make them a great nation. Following on from v. 8, this passage thus brings together two great elements of the promise, namely land and numerical increase. This attitude to the people's growth is notably more positive than in Num. 11:11–17 (Brettler 1995: 69).

The nature of the organization is consistent with Deuteronomy's theology of the people. Its members are described as 'brothers'. Where translations obscure this (perhaps for reasons of inclusive language, as NRSV: 'members of your community', 16), something important is lost theologically. The idea of brotherhood has been construed somewhat negatively, as 'nationalism' (Mayes 1979: 124). Its real spirit, however, emerges clearly here, as a principle that guards the dignity and right treatment of each individual, in a world in which hierarchical and oppressive social structures were the order of the day. True, the idea is applied primarily within Israel. But this is not in principle exclusive, as the extension to the 'resident non-Israelite' shows. This openness modifies the strong military aspect of Deuteronomy. With this underlying idea, the judges are instructed to exercise their offices with righteousness, a concept that recognizes this equality in principle of all people. Furthermore, justice is ultimately God's, and those who judge (and, we may say, govern) bear a responsibility to him. Thus, the institution of a system of administration belongs to God's purpose of creating a people according to his own standards. The judging is to be seen as an application of the word or Torah of God to the people's daily life.

The positive light in which this provision is cast appears not only from the fact that Moses' declaration, 'I cannot bear you alone', is in thanksgiving more than in complaint, but also from the omission here of a direct reminiscence of the motif of grumbling or contention against God (differently from Num. 11). In Deuteronomy's organization of the material, that will follow the report of the spies.

19–46. The narrative of the spies conveys Deuteronomy's theology of history *in nuce*. It continues the movement of the 'journey' begun in the opening verses, and lets it function as a story of faith. The approach to the land takes the form of both command and promise; the task of 'going up' is both the challenge to faith and the prize. The topic of faith is at the heart of the passage. Crucial to the success of the enterprise is the presence of God with his people (42), or, in the journey idiom, going ahead of them (30–33). The destiny of Israel depends on their belief that this is the reality of their situation, a belief that must be given expression in action that carries risk and demands courage. The conflict set up by the need to enter the promised land is the classic conflict between faith and 'sight' (cf. Heb. 11:1–3). When the people rely on their own evaluation of circumstances, courage gives way.

The journey metaphor shows that the people have every reason to believe. The God who commands them to go up to the land is the one who has brought them out of Egypt, testifying there to his power dedicated to their salvation (30–31). They are therefore without excuse in their failure of faith. Their guilt is further emphasized by their perversion of God's good intentions for them into bad, his love into hate (27). Their fear is thus 'untrue' in the deepest sense, and an offence against God.

The characterization of the exodus generation as faithless is of great importance for the book's portrayal of Israel. Deuteronomy takes over from Numbers the basic structure of the 'spies' episode. That is, it explains the long delay in entering the land as arising from the guilt of the exodus generation, which is allowed (with a few exceptions) to die out without seeing it. However, there is a tension in our account between this structure and a perspective that begins to emerge strongly here, namely the solidarity of Israel in unfaithfulness. This is clear because Moses recalls the history of unfaithfulness in the context of an address to the new generation that stands at Horeb, as if that history were their very own. This is consistent with the view expressed elsewhere in the book that the people that is invited into covenant with God is deeply prone to unfaithfulness (Deut. 9:4–6).

The opening narrative, therefore, is no mere 'historical prologue', nor can its function be separated from that of the laws. It is rather an overture to the theology of the book. Its evocation of Israel in the wilderness has been called a typology of the centuries of Israel's sin (N. Lohfink 1998). The 'many days' of 1:45–46 have been taken as an indication of a long impending exile (in Babylon), even after the people's repentance (Wolff 1976: 100). However, the picture of Israel's condition is balanced and open, rather than pessimistic. Even in the wilderness Yahweh has been gracious (2:7). And the failure of faith and understanding shown here becomes the prelude to a story of success under God's guidance in Deut. 2 – 3. In the same way, the religious and moral poverty of Israel in the golden-calf episode, in which the people are characterized as habitually faithless (9:4–6, 22–24), leads directly into its final approach to the border of the land (10:11), which, in the concept of the book, they are about to enter (cf. N. Lohfink 1998). In this pattern of grace after failure lies the hope that Deuteronomy offers, in a theological 'illogicality' that resembles the new-covenant theology of Jer. 30 – 33.

Finally, the historical paradigm is no mere metaphor for the life of faith. Since Noth, Deut. 1:19–46 has been interpreted in the context of the exilic/ post-exilic community, and the problems arising from the loss of land. In Mayes' view (1979: 127), 'the present time of exile is the result of lack of faith and disobedience to the will of Yahweh. The promise of the land, which is a good land, remains in force, however, even if only for the next generation.' This is to make Deuteronomy's history a kind of paradigm for preaching, in the context of a spirituality informed by issues of faith and unbelief. It is true to say that in Deuteronomy history is written for its capacity to bear meaning afresh. However, the belief that it has no interest in history as such depends too heavily on the idea of an exilic setting.

DEUTERONOMY 2:1 – 3:7

Translation

[1]So we turned around and travelled back towards the wilderness by way of the Reed Sea, as the LORD had instructed me, going round the land of Seir for a long time. [2]Then the LORD said to me: [3]'You have been travelling around this area long enough; now turn to the north. [4]Give the people this command: "You are about to cross the border of your brothers the Edomites, who live in Seir. They will be afraid of you, yet you must be very careful [5]not to provoke hostilities with them, for I am not giving you as much as a foot's length of their land; I have given the land of Seir to the Edomites as their inheritance. [6]You may use money to purchase food from them to eat, and also buy water to drink from them with money. [7]For the LORD your God has blessed you in everything you have done. He has been watching over your journeying through this great wilderness these forty years; the LORD your God has been with you, and you have gone short of nothing."'' [8]So we passed on from our brothers the Edomites, who live in Seir, leaving behind the Arabah Road, and from Elath and from Ezion-Geber.

Then we turned and went on towards the wilderness of Moab. [9]Then the LORD said to me: 'Do not harass the Moabites or provoke hostilities with them, for I am not giving you any of their land as an inheritance, for I have given Ar to the descendants of Lot as an inheritance.' [10](In former times the Emim lived there, a people as strong and tall, and numerous, as the Anakim. [11]Like the Anakim they are also considered as Rephaim, but the Moabites call them Emim. [12]Formerly too the Horites lived in Seir, but the Edomites drove them out and destroyed them, and lived there in their place, just as Israel did in the land that the LORD gave them as their inheritance.)

[13]'Now make ready and cross the Wadi Zered.' So we crossed the Wadi Zered. [14]And the time we were on the road from Kadesh-Barnea until we crossed the Wadi Zered was thirty-eight years; in that time that whole generation of warriors died out from the camp, as the LORD had sworn they would. [15]Indeed the LORD turned against them, to root them out of the camp, until they had all perished.

[16]Now when the last of the warriors had died out from among the people, [17]the LORD said to me: [18]'Today you must cross the border of Moab, that is, Ar. [19]You will then be approaching the Ammonites. Do not harass them, or provoke them to hostilities, for I am not giving you any of the land of the Ammonites as an

inheritance; I have given it as an inheritance to the descendants of Lot.' [20](It also used to be considered a land of Rephaim. Rephaim lived there at one time, though the Ammonites called them Zamzummim. [21]They were a strong, tall and numerous people, like the Anakim. But the LORD destroyed them before the Ammonites, and they dispossessed them and lived there in their place, [22]just as he did for the Edomite inhabitants of Seir, when he destroyed the Horites before them so that they could live there in their place, as they do to this day. [23]And as for the Avvim, who lived in settlements in the region of Gaza, the Caphtorites, arriving from Caphtor, destroyed them and lived there in their place.)

[24]'Make ready to go and cross the Wadi Arnon. See, I have given the Amorite King Sihon of Heshbon, with all his land, into your hands. Begin to take your inheritance; provoke him to war. [25]This very day, I am beginning to put the fear of you on the nations under heaven; when they hear the rumour of you, they will tremble and be weak because of you.'

[26]I sent messengers from the wilderness of Kedemoth to Sihon King of Heshbon with terms of peace, as follows: [27]'Let me pass through your land by road; I will stick to the road, and not divert from it, to the right or the left. [28]You may sell me food and water to eat and drink; only let me march through, [29]just as the Edomite inhabitants of Seir did, and also the Moabite inhabitants of Ar, so that I may cross the Jordan and enter the land that the LORD our God is giving us.' [30]But Sihon, the king of Heshbon, refused to let us pass, for the LORD your God made him stubborn and defiant, in order to give him into your hands, as at this day.

[31]The LORD said to me: 'See, I have begun to give Sihon and his land over to you; begin to take his land as your inheritance.' [32]When Sihon and all his army came out to do battle with us at Jahaz, [33]the LORD our God gave us victory over him, and we struck him down, along with his sons and his whole army. [34]Then we took all his cities, and in each city we devoted men, women and children to destruction; we left not a single survivor. [35]We took the cattle as spoil for ourselves, however, as well as booty from the cities we had captured. [36]From Aroer, on the edge of the Wadi Arnon, and from the city in the wadi, all the way to Gilead, there was not a town that was too strong for us. The LORD our God gave everything over to us. [37]But you did not go near the land of the Ammonites, neither along the Wadi Jabbok, nor the cities of the hill country, so keeping the command of the LORD our God.

[3:1]Then we turned and went up the road to Bashan, and Og, king of Bashan, came out against us, with all his army, to do battle at Edrei. [2]The LORD said to me: 'Do not be afraid of him, for I have given him over to you, together with all his people and his land. You shall do to him as you did to Sihon, the Amorite king who reigned in Heshbon'. [3]And the LORD our God did also give Og, king of Bashan, and all his people over to us, and we struck them down until there was not a survivor left to him. [4]We took all his cities at that time; there was not a single town that we did not take from them, sixty cities, the whole region of Argob, the kingdom of Og in Bashan. [5]These were all cities fortified with high walls, gates and bars, besides a great many unwalled settlements. [6]We devoted them to destruction, just as we had done to Sihon, king of Heshbon, destroying every city, men, women and children. [7]But the cattle and the booty from the towns we kept for ourselves.

Notes on the text

2:1. 'Land': lit. 'hill country', Seir being mountainous.

3. 'Area': lit. 'hill country'.

4. 'Border': the word also means 'territory', as in 3:17. Here as at v. 18 it is hard to decide which is right. See 'Comment'.

'They will be afraid': Hebr. has, unusually, *waw* + impf. The imperfect is influenced by the preceding ptc. 'are about to cross, crossing'; it conveys present or imminent conditions, rather than a strict sequence. The suggestion of *BHS* (imp., as Josh. 24:14) implies a command to Israel to fear, and therefore to avoid provoking Edom. But MT is consistent with the context in which Yahweh is leading them to conquest (cf. v. 25).

5. *'al titgārû*, 'do not attack, provoke to hostility'; hith. *grh* (*HALAT* 2:194); cf. *gûr*.

LXX adds *polemon*, perhaps presupposing *milḥāmâ* as in v. 9; the same thing occurs in v. 19.

7. 'has been watching over your journeying': lit. 'knew', or better 'knows', since *yāda'* pf. often carries a present sense; the 'watching' is not past but continuing.

'great': LXX *kai tēn phoberan* presupposes *wᵉhannôrā'*, i.e. 'terrifying', as 1:19, rather than 'great' as MT here.

SamP harmonistically adds at this point Num. 20:14, 17–18, that is, the account of Israel's request to Edom to pass through its territory, which was refused.

8. *'from* our brothers the Edomites, who live in Seir, *leaving behind* the Arabah Road, and *from* Elath and *from* Ezion-Geber...' LXX has no counterpart to MT *mē-*, 'from', in the first two of the four expressions highlighted. LXX thus reads: '(we) went through our brothers' (territory), the sons of Esau, who live in Seir, *along* the Arabah Road, from Elath and Ezion-Geber'. LXX thus reports a passage through Edomite territory, following the shortest route to the next stage, the land of Moab, and this is in line with the narrative's supposition that the encounter with Edom met no resistance. MT is more coy. The threefold *mē-* is probably influenced by Num. 20:21: 'Israel departed from them (*mē'ālāyw*), leaving open the idea of a circuitous route as narrated in Numbers. It is not certain which text is original, but MT could be regarded as harmonistic.

11. 'are ... considered': impf. ni. *yēḥāšᵉbû* is taken here as having present force, as also *yiqrᵉ'û*, '(they) call (them)'.

12. The impf. *yîrāšûm*, 'drove them out'/'dispossessed them', is unexpected, especially as it is followed by *waw* consecutive + impf. *BHS* records no textual variants, however. S. R. Driver (1895: 37) suggests translating: 'they *proceeded* to possess them'.

14. 'in that time that whole generation of warriors died out', lit. 'until the completion of the whole generation', where *tōm*, 'completion', means in effect death. The same noun occurs, suffixed in the same sense, at the end of v. 15, and the verb *tāmam*, together with *lāmût*, 'to die', in v. 16.

15. 'To root them out of the camp', lit. 'to confuse them' (inf. qal, *hāmam*), that is, throw them into a panic so that they perish. The verb is used elsewhere of Yahweh's action in war (Exod. 14:24; Deut. 7:23).

23. *ḥªṣērîm*, 'villages', is taken by some ancient versions as a place name.

24. 'Make ready to go and cross', lit. 'Rise, go and cross', a series of imperatives; the doubled initial letter in *se'û*, 'go', is euphonic, that is, to help pronunciation.

'Begin to take your inheritance; provoke him to war': a further series of imperatives; 1. hiph. imp. *ḥālal*, 'begin'; 2. qal imp. *yāraš*, 'inherit' (variously *rāš* and *rēš* [cf. 1:21]; see also GKC 110h, and cf. v. 31); 3. hith. imp. *gārâ*, cf. above on v. 5.

31. 'begin to take his land as your inheritance', lit. 'begin! possess! to possess his land', which is awkward. The first two imperatives follow 2:24, while the following infinitive seems redundant. LXX has the infinitive *klēronomēsai* here. Either it simplifies MT, or it represents a Hebr. text that had the infinitive but not the preceding imperative.

33. 'his sons': the consonantal text suggests a singular, with a number of ancient versions. Analogy makes the plural likelier (cf. Num. 21:35).

34. 'in each city . . . men, women and children': lit. 'men, and the women and the children'. The first three words in Hebr. (*kol 'îr mᵉtîm*) can be read as 'every city of men', i.e. as to its male population', with Weinfeld 1991: 169; S. R. Driver 1895: 45. This may be intended to explain the imbalance between the lack of a definite article with the first of the three nouns while it accompanies the other two. However, despite this imbalance, 'men' can be taken as the first in a series of appositions, *kol 'îr* being translated simply as 'every city'. The list-like character of the three nouns is if anything stronger in 3:6, where the copula is missing from the second element, *hannāšîm*, 'the women'.

3:2. 'reigned': ptc. qal of *yšḇ*, 'sit, dwell'. It is translated 'reigned' because in the case of a king the 'sitting' implies a throne; the past tense follows the logic of the narrative.

3. 'till there was not a survivor left': the verb *hiš'îr* is odd following *ḇiltî*, which almost invariably precedes an infinitive construct (therefore *haš'îr* would be expected). The infinitive construct with *ḥireq* also occurs at 7:24; 28:48; Josh. 11:14. S. R. Driver (1895: 105) presumes a repeating error in MT at this point, but the form may be a genuine variant.

5. 'cities fortified with high walls, gates and bars': the syntax is loose, lit. 'fortified cities – high wall, doors and bar'; the singulars must be understood distributively.

6. 'destroying': *haḥªrēm* is inf. abs., introducing a clause that further specifies the corresponding finite verb (GKC 113h).

'men, women and children': cf. on 2:34.

Form and structure

Following the first failed attempt to enter the land of Canaan, and the resultant forty years of wandering in the wilderness, the story of the actual approach and entry now unfolds. It shares a basic pattern with the Numbers account (Num. 20 – 24): after the initial delay come the encounters with Edom and Moab, and the defeat of the Amorite Kings Sihon and Og in Transjordan. The narrative is distinctive, however. The encounters with Edom and Moab give no hint of the resistance offered by these according to Numbers (where Edom refuses to let Israel pass through its territory, Num. 20:14–21, and Moab hires the sorcerer Balaam to try to turn back the advancing horde, Num. 22 – 24). Furthermore, the account does not follow a realistic historical and geographical order, but rather a schematic one. This would necessitate the engagement with King Sihon at Heshbon *before* negotiating the Ammonite territory, and only then would the way lead on to the region occupied by King Og of Bashan. Rather, it follows a pattern that brings out a theological rationale: Edom, Moab and Ammon possess their territories by the gift of Yahweh, just as Israel will possess hers (2:1–23). The defeats of Sihon and Og (2:24 – 3:7) then take a more prominent position in the narrative than they do in Numbers (cf. Num. 21:21–35), becoming a kind of firstfruits of the dispossession of the inhabitants of the whole land, and a paradigm of the 'war of Yahweh' (or 'holy war'), in which his people utterly destroys his enemies (2:34; cf. Brettler 1995: 75–76).

There is a pattern in the five encounters in 2:1 – 3:7, with a total of five elements (though they do not all occur in each case): 1. Israel continues its journey; 2. Yahweh commands Moses regarding the people in question; 3. previous history of the region; 4. provision for the march; 5. Israel departs from the territory, or conquers and settles it (after Braulik 1986a: 29–30). The pattern is important for the theology of Deut. 1 – 3. (Christensen [1991: 39–40], in his rhetorical, or 'prosodic', analysis of Deuteronomy, sees 2:2–25 as the central part of Deut. 1 – 3.) The present passage in fact depicts the theology of land possession on a broad canvas. Israel's 'inheritance' of Canaan is only a part of Yahweh's distribution of territories to the nations. The criteria for his decisions are not absolutely clear. Edom, Moab and Ammon, to whom he has given their lands (2:5, 9, 19), are also related genealogically to Israel (in the latter cases as 'the sons of Lot', the nephew of Abraham, cf. Gen. 19:30–38). In the case of the Amorites, no such relationship is mentioned. In addition, however, they actively oppose the advance of Israel, which is evidently a justification for the wars conducted against them.

Comment

2:1–8a

1. The expression 'we turned around and travelled back' carries out the command in 1:40, after the abortive attempt to evade its consequences in the ill-judged attack on the Amorites (1:41–46). It exactly contrasts with the command in 1:7, which initiated the idea of movement into the land (cf. 1:24). The theme of the journey is thus resumed. But it is a journey in reverse, a consequence still of the first failure of faith (1:26–33). In what has been called an 'Anti-Exodus' (Moran 1963b), Israel faces the wilderness and Reed Sea, and thus Egypt itself, once more. The reference to words of Yahweh (lit. 'as Yahweh had said to me') recalls the promises in 1:8, 11, 21 (cf. 6:3, 19; 9:3), and is thus ironic in the present context, suggesting that the promise of land too is in reverse. The 'long time' (lit. 'many days') that Israel wandered in the region of Seir links with the same expression in 1:46, and refers to the same length of time, specified only in 2:14. Seir was the land to the south and east of Judah occupied by Edom (cf. Gen. 36:1–8), the subject of the next verses (2–8). The idea of wandering around it accentuates the fact that Israel is as yet homeless.

2–6. But now there is yet another decisive 'turn' (3): after the aimless wandering, the resumption of the journey towards the land. The 'turning' is followed by a 'going on', or 'crossing' ('*āḇar*) into the territory of Seir, or Edom (4). This verb is the most characteristic in the present chapter, occurring twelve times, and used to convey passing through or by other nations' territories, or over the gorges of Zered and Arnon (13, 24). It represents a progress that will ultimately lead into the promised land itself (with the 'crossing' of the Jordan, Josh. 1:2).

In the Numbers account, Israel asks the Edomites if they may follow the main route through their dangerous, ravine-riven land, by the so-called 'king's highway', a north–south route running somewhat to the east of the Arabah; they would make no territorial claim and pay their way. The Edomites refuse, and the Israelites have to take a longer, circuitous route (Num. 20:14–21). Nothing of this negotiation is conveyed here, neither the resistance nor the need to find an alternative route (see also below on v. 29). The close relationship of the two peoples ('your brothers', since the Edomite patriarch was Esau, brother of Jacob-Israel, Gen. 25:21–34) is picked up from Num. 20:14, as is the idea of peaceful passage (6). The only hint of a conflict is in v. 4, with its reference to the Edomites' fear at Israel's approach. This, however, is the occasion of a command not to make war on Edom, on the grounds that Yahweh has not given Israel the land that it occupies (5). The embargo is in direct contrast to the promise and command concerning the land of Canaan, including Transjordan. The rationale for this is important: Yahweh has given the land of Seir to Edom, just as he has given Canaan to Israel, as their 'inheritance'. The theology of

Yahweh's gift of land is thus set in a broad context; Yahweh has power far beyond Israel, and controls the destinies of the other nations also. The account of the encounter with Edom here is governed by this concept. Edom enjoys a special status in relation to Israel elsewhere in Deuteronomy also, there too on the grounds of close relationship (23:7–8). This is in contrast to parts of the OT in which it is depicted as one of Israel's worst enemies (Jer. 49:7–22; Obad.).

7–8a. The rationale for the peaceful negotiation with Edom continues with a statement about Yahweh's abundant care for his people (7). The period spent in the wilderness is specified as forty years (cf. Num. 14:33; cf. Deut. 1:3). The expression '[Yahweh] has blessed you in everything you have done' (lit. 'the work of your hand') recurs, with variations, several times in the book (14:29; 15:10; 16:15; 24:19; 30:9). In these cases the context is always the promise of reward in return for faithfulness to the covenant; 'the work of your hand' usually refers to the Israelites' regular labours in an agricultural context. The phrase is less transparent here. Indeed, the picture of Israel's progress to the land, including their long wilderness sojourn, has been one in which their needs have been met by Yahweh's special provision, as v. 7b makes clear (cf. 1:31). For this reason, Israel has no need to plunder its neigbours, and can afford to deal peaceably with Edom on its march to its land. (Verse 7 is sometimes taken to be secondary to the principal argument because of its change to the singular address [Mittmann 1975: 66]. However, that is to attach more weight to a strictly formal consideration than to the flow of the argument, which is consistent.)

The route taken is not clearly specified (8; contrast LXX, which implies a direct route through Edomite territory, in line with the tendency of the passage; see 'Notes on the text'). The directional data here are simply 'leaving behind', or 'away from'. Elath and Ezion-Geber are at the southern end, or beginning point, of the journey round Edom, and so are merely departure indicators. The phrase 'leaving behind the Arabah Road' is a possible hint that the best route was not taken (cf. Num. 20:21 and see 'Notes on the text'), yet it would not be inconsistent with taking the 'king's highway'. The phrase 'we passed on from our brothers the Edomites' is particularly opaque. The verb, however, is the one more usually translated as 'go over', in the sense of entering the land. The implication, therefore, is definitely of progress to that end, and a sense that Israel is now advancing inexorably under the powerful leadership of Yahweh.

2:8b–12

The new stage in the journey is again marked by 'we turned' (8b), even though this time there is no reverse, but a continuation. It is accompanied by '(we) went on', lit. 'crossed', the typical verb here for progress on the way (cf. v. 4). The approach to Moab, the land to the east of the Dead Sea (cf. 1:5), follows the same pattern as for Edom (see 'Form and structure'). Moab too is not to be drawn into hostilities (v. 9 corresponds to v. 5), nor does it stand in Israel's way. Its land has also been given to it by the sovereign Yahweh, as an 'inheritance'. The term 'inheritance' puts Moab's possession of 'Ar' (apparently a name for the land of Moab) on a par with Israel's of Canaan (explicitly so in v. 12b). The theology of Yahweh's gift is elaborated by the short pre-history in vv. 10–12. Just as Canaan had its prehistoric giant race, the Anakim (cf. 1:28), the land of Moab had its Emim (cf. Gen. 14:5), as indeed the land of Ammon had its own variety of giant, the Zamzummim (20). The term 'Rephaim' (also Gen. 14:5) is apparently a collective for all such primitive giant races. (In a number of OT texts the term has a different meaning, namely the dead, the inhabitants of the underworld, e.g. Ps. 88:11; Job 26:5; Is. 26:14. There may be a relationship between the two meanings, the reputation of the ancient heroes having been such that in a sense they lived on after their death. But the meanings may simply be separate. Ugaritic *rpum* may have a similar range of meanings, but does not shed further light on the present text. See further Brown 1997.)

The parenthesis now calls to the narrator's mind the Horites in Seir (12), though he has already dealt with Edom/Seir a few verses earlier; these occur with Rephaim and Emim also in Gen. 14:5–6. They are distinct from the Rephaim, however, and enter the OT story as a historical people (Gen. 34:2, LXX; Josh. 9:6–7, LXX). The Horites are sometimes identified with the mid-second-millennium people known as the Hurrians, but the identification is not certain.

Yahweh's sovereignty in the history and affairs of all these peoples explains why Israel is forbidden to lay claim to their territories. The same point is made by the omission here, as in the case of Edom, of any mention of the measures taken by Moab as reported in Numbers, where King Balak of Moab hired the sorcerer Balaam to invoke a curse on the people (Num. 22 – 24). Moab's historic enmity towards Israel is also known from the ninth-century Moabite Stone, on which King Mesha of Moab boasts of having broken free from King Ahab (cf. 2 Kgs. 3). Moab, together with Ammon, took advantage of Judah's weakness under pressure from the Babylonian Nebuchadrezzar on the eve of its exile (2 Kgs. 24:2). The hostility of these two is remembered more realistically in Deut. 23:3–6. Here, however, Deuteronomy emphasizes, not that Moab poses no threat to Israel, but rather that Israel need pose none to Moab, because that is no part of Yahweh's purpose.

2:13–15

The Wadi Zered is a gorge flowing from east to west into the Arabah south of the Dead Sea, and marking the northern boundary of Edom and the southern extent of Moab. The crossing is accorded some significance by the twofold repetition of the term 'cross' (13), and by the immediately following retrospect on the thirty-eight-year period in the wilderness (14–15). The oath referred to is recorded in Num. 14:21–23, and its effect in Num. 14:16, 35. The figure of thirty-eight years, rather than the forty years mentioned in v. 7, presumably allows for time taken to reach Horeb from Egypt (cf. Num. 1:1; 9:1) and hence to Kadesh-Barnea (Num. 10:11 – 12:16). The dying out of the wilderness generation is portrayed as Yahweh's warlike action against them, completing the reversal of fortunes that had befallen Israel in the failed attack on the land in Deut. 1 (see 'Notes on the text'). The inclusion of the retrospect at this point indicates, however, that the waiting period is now over; the march on the land has begun.

2:16–23

16–18. The passage through Moab is to happen 'Today' (18). The term is frequent in Deuteronomy in exhortation, to mark a time of decision or opportunity (e.g. 4:8; 5:1; 26:17–18; 27:9). This is the sense here, as in v. 25 (rather than specifying how long the journey through Moab would take). The point is that the time has come for the next stage of the journey. This is properly continued with the crossing of the Arnon gorge (24), the northern border of Moab, flowing from the east into the Dead Sea. First, however, there is a digression concerning the Ammonites (19–21).

19–23. The kingdom of Ammon lay to the north of Moab and somewhat to the east. There is no record in Numbers of a special encounter with this people, and indeed their territory was not directly in Israel's path. (The Ammonites are mentioned in Numbers in the context of the attack on Sihon, whose land Israel took 'as far as to the Ammonites, for the boundary of the Ammonites was strong'; Num. 21:24.) Israel passed close to the Ammonites' territory, therefore, and might have been tempted to do battle, but are here deterred from doing so. The account at this point follows the pattern set by the encounters with Edom and Moab and is introduced for the same theological reasons. Ammon is closely linked with Moab, not only in origins (Gen. 19:36–38), but also in hostility to Israel (as we have just seen). Its distinctive breed of prehistoric giants is called here Zamzummim (presumably the same as the Zuzim, Gen. 14:5). On the Ammonites' possession of their land, Deuteronomy is explicit that Yahweh himself drove out these ancient inhabitants in their favour. The statement is stronger than in the other similar instances in the chapter (5, 10–12). And this tendency to be more explicit on the point seems to have attracted a further comment on the Edomites, clarifying that the same was true of them (22, cf. vv. 5b, 12), just in case the point was not already clear! They, in fact, return to the argument, out of place, for the second time (cf. v. 12), probably as a device to help stress the theme of Yahweh's power to give land.

Finally (23), a new act of dispossession is mentioned, namely that of the Avvim, the original inhabitants of the southern coastal area of Canaan (cf. Josh. 13:3) by the Caphtorites. The Caphtorites, Caphtor being an old name for Crete, are better known in the Bible as the Philistines. They appear in a context similar to this in Amos 9:7, where the prophet shows that Yahweh has been sovereign in the lives of nations other than Israel. The placement of the present note here is striking because their land was on the sea coast of Canaan, as is clear from the mention of Gaza here, an area given to Israel according to Deut. 1:7. It is presumably significant, therefore, that their expulsion of predecessors is told as a bare fact, in contrast with the theological elaboration in the previous two verses regarding Ammon and Edom. In the deuteronomic vision, the 'Caphtorites' will have to yield in time to Israel.

2:24–30

24–25. The crossing of the Arnon gorge marks the entry of Israel into the promised land, or at least the part of it in Transjordan. The command to attack Sihon of Heshbon reverses the tendency in the march so far, in which Israel has not been allowed to attack its neighbour nations (1–23), with the specific command to provoke Sihon to war (24). It also continues the command first given in 1:21, in which Moses said that Yahweh had given the land into Israel's hand. Here that promise is focused on Sihon's kingdom. Now for the first time Israel is to 'begin to possess' the land (see 'Notes on the text'), in accordance with the deuteronomic concept that the promised land includes the Transjordanian part formerly controlled by Sihon and Og (see on 3:8–17).

The command is reinforced, not merely by an exhortation not to fear (as 1:21), but by the assurance that Yahweh has actually caused all nations to fear Israel (25). This recalls Moab's terror of its advance reported in Num. 22:3. The expression is hyperbolic, but aims to show that the people need have no fear, because Yahweh is sovereign. What is command in v. 24 is promise in v. 25, for there Yahweh declares that he will 'begin' to 'give' fear on all nations. The 'beginning' and 'giving' anticipate v. 31, where the giving is predicated directly of the land of Sihon. The nations' fear also accompanied Israel's crossing the Jordan at its entry to the land west of the river (Josh. 4:24; 5:1).

26. Heshbon was formerly a Moabite city, roughly due east of Jerusalem and the northern end of the Dead Sea, but by now in the hands of the Amorite King Sihon (Num. 21:26; it would in later times revert to Moab, cf. Is. 16:8–9). Israel's approach to Sihon follows the pattern established in the chapter so far, though events are narrated in more detail. Messengers are sent from Kedemoth, a town later identified as one of the Levitical cities in the territory of Reuben (Josh. 13:18; cf. 21:37). Moses himself is identified as the sender, as opposed to 'Israel' in Num. 21:21, in line with the heightened emphasis on Moses' authority in Deuteronomy, and possibly drawing out what was assumed to be implicit in Numbers (Brettler 1995: 73; and cf. Num. 20:14). The 'terms (lit. "words") of peace' (26) represent a conventional diplomatic opening, which implies the possibility of war (cf. Deut. 20:10). They are therefore a challenge to Sihon to submit to Israel's, and Yahweh's, terms – though Moses knows, as we do, that he will not. This is the first case in the present chapter in which the words to be used in the encounter are articulated (27–29), in a style that recalls Num. 20 – 21; hitherto in Deut. 2 the encounters are merely narrated. The narrative style signals in this way that this occasion will be different.

27–30. The message to Sihon is heightened in comparison with Num. 21:22, with a demand to be allowed to purchase food and drink (cf. Num. 20:19), an allusion to the compliance of Edom and Moab, and a declaration that Yahweh has given Israel the land beyond the Jordan. Edom and Moab had not in fact complied with Israel (Num. 20:14–21; 22 – 24); the claim that they did may be simply the rhetoric of war, aiming to bring pressure to bear. The unwillingness of Sihon (lit. 'the LORD your God hardened his spirit'), an additional explanation compared with Num. 21:23, recalls that of Pharaoh to release Israel from Egypt in the first stage of their journey (cf. esp. Exod. 10:27, which also has the parallel 'he refused', or 'he was not willing', as here). The point of the parallel with the exodus is to show that the conquest of the promised land continues the history of deliverance that began there. No human power can stand against Yahweh's will to save his people. (On 'this day', 30, cf. on v. 18.)

2:31–37

31–33. The command and promise of Yahweh in vv. 24–25 now become an accomplished fact (31). The 'giving over' of Sihon and his lands means Yahweh's decision to defeat him in his 'holy war'. Even so, this decision of Yahweh must be matched by Israel's faith and obedience to begin to inherit the land; the challenge is the same as in 1:8, and this time it must be met successfully. The defeat of Sihon is complete, the mention of 'his sons' (33; not in Num. 21, and see 'Notes on the text') denoting the extinction of his dynasty.

34–35. The razing of Heshbon (2:34–35) is the first instance in Deuteronomy of the *ḥerem*, or 'devotion to destruction' (a concept that is not used of the wars with Sihon and Og in Num. 21). Its application here, and in 3:6–7, is in line with the designation of this part of

Transjordan as part of the promised land. It is for this reason that the war against it is conducted, not as ordinary war, but as 'Yahweh war', or 'holy war', a distinction spelt out in Deut. 20:10–15, 16–18. The 'devotion to destruction', in religious history, means putting to death every living creature (in this case humans only) as a kind of sacrifice to Yahweh, on the grounds that the land belongs to his 'holy sphere', and is given only to those whom he has designated 'holy'. The underlying concept is that whatever is not 'holy' cannot come into Yahweh's presence. Conversely, the killing, as in sacrifice, is a kind of assimilation into the holy sphere, a making 'holy'. The same ideas are found in the book of Joshua, where the destruction of Jericho, the first city to fall to Israel after it has crossed the Jordan, is the classic case of the 'devotion to destruction' (Josh. 6; in that case cattle were included in the decree, v. 21; but cf. the relaxation of this for Ai, Josh. 8:2). The idea was not confined to Israel, but is found, for example, in the inscription on the Moabite Stone, in which King Mesha boasts that he subjected the city of Nebo to the *ḥerem*, in that case a 'devotion', or sacrifice, to the god Chemosh.

The 'holiness' theology that issues in the 'devotion to destruction' is elaborated at length in Deut. 7. There it is clear that Deuteronomy regards it as in some sense ideal, since it accepts an accommodation between the real and ideal (see on 7:2–3). It is often regarded by commentators as wholly ideal, a traditional concept preserved in Deuteronomy as a metaphor, in affirmation of the need for rigorous separation from Canaanite religion (Moberly 1999: 133–137; see further 'Explanation').

36–37. The land won is now described (36), in a manner that reminds the reader of accounts in Joshua (cf. Josh. 10:40–43). The note that no city was too great for Israel to take recalls their fear at the size of the Canaanite cities when they failed to take the land at first (1:28). In the event, such fears proved groundless, because nothing could withstand Yahweh in his war. And finally, the distinction between what was permitted to be taken and what was not, or between Yahweh's 'holy' land and land that he disposed of otherwise (the land of Ammon, in this case), is reaffirmed (37).

3:1–7

The conquest of King Og follows the pattern of the preceding narrative, here too elevated into a 'war of Yahweh', in an elaboration of the briefer Numbers account (Num. 21:33–35). The 'turning and going up' fits the narrative's pattern of the journey into the land (cf. 1:24 for the combination of 'turning' and 'going up'). Bashan was the land east of the Sea of Galilee and north of the River Yarmuk (thus much farther north than Heshbon), renowned in the OT for its wealth and fertility (cf. Deut. 32:14; Amos 4:1), as well as high-quality oak forest (Is. 2:13). Edrei was a city at its southern boundary (cf. 3:10). Yahweh's words to Moses (3:2) recall his exhortation prior to the engagement with Sihon (2:25); oddly there is no mention here of Og's sons, though these are known in Num. 21:35. The account of the victory follows the pattern found there too (Deut. 3:3–4, 6–7; cf. 2:33–35). Again, the extent of the region taken is specified, in accordance with the status of this land as 'holy land', which Israel is taking as part of its inheritance (3:4b). The region specified is large, the Argob being the eastern area of Bashan, as far as the desert. The allusion to the strength of the cities (5) makes the same point as 2:36b.

Explanation

This long section continues the 'geography' of faith that had begun in Deut. 1. Israel's progress and regress visualize their faith and lack of faith, most vividly in 2:1, as in 1:40, where they turn to go back to the desert, in the direction of Egypt (in an 'Anti-Exodus', Moran 1963b). The characteristic vocabulary of this geography is turning, journeying, crossing (e.g. vv. 1, 8). A major turning-point occurs between Deut. 1 and Deut. 2. The dominant movement is now forward, and the taking of the land is about to begin. One writer holds that the Edomite encounter is shaped by Deuteronomy's concept that Kadesh represents a time of disobedience and failure, while the post-Kadesh period is a time of spiritual progression (Glatt-Giladi 1997). This is true, as long as it is recognized that there is a tension between the two directions as perpetual possibilities. The distinction between the former failure and the new opportunity of success is also expressed by the dying out of the first generation and the forty-year waiting period (14–15; cf. 1:35). This is in remarkable contrast to the concept in 5:2–3, which fuses the Horeb generation with that of the exodus. The rationale in each case is theological. Here the more realistic chronology is part of the graphic symbolism of faith: those who cannot grasp the promise by faith will not receive it; those who can will. The issue is no longer whether the Israelites will enter the land, but that they should recognize the land as the gift of Yahweh as they enter it.

The careful distinction between land that is given to them and land that is not is part of this theme. The prohibition of their trespassing on territories given by Yahweh to other peoples is carefully crafted (to the extent that their resistance to Israel's progress reported elsewhere is passed over as unhelpful to the present purpose). This is, first of all, a function of the theology of holiness in Deuteronomy. As Israel is 'holy' (7:6), so by inference is its land, and this puts a clean distinction between Israel and other nations, and between its land and their lands (cf. N. Lohfink 1995e: 106). The 'devotion to destruction' (*ḥerem*) of the Amorite kings and their peoples is part of this picture, a topic that is quite explicit here in contrast to the parallel account in Num. 21. The application of the *ḥerem* to these peoples is consistent with the more rigorous view of the status of Transjordan in Deuteronomy than in Numbers, namely that it was fully a part of the promised land.

The holiness of people and land is thus announced as an important theme in Deuteronomy. In contrast to the widely held opinion that the book 'desacralizes' the life of Israel, compared with other theological traditions in the OT (Weinfeld 1972: 191–243), it intensifies the holiness theme by extending it to all of the people's life (N. Lohfink 1995e: 105–106; cf. 1995d: 219–260). The other nations, therefore, are not simply not-Israel, but represent the 'negative holy', an 'abomination to Yahweh' (7:25–26).

The *herem* in Deuteronomy is realistic in the sense that wars waged as acts of devotion to a god were understood as carrying out *herem*. However, a close reading of the narrative of conquest in Joshua suggests that it was not properly implemented, since the Canaanite peoples remained alongside Israel in the land (e.g. Josh. 15:63; 16:10). The command in 7:2a to destroy the seven nations of the land, furthermore, is followed by more practical ones, not to make treaties with them or intermarry (7:2b–4; see 'Comment' there). The function of the *herem* texts is to exhort the Israelites to regard the other nations of the land as beyond the pale, to be kept radically outside their lives. To put it otherwise, the *herem* draws a 'culture map' in which Israel occupies a different religious and social space (Nelson 1997: 53; following Schäfer-Lichtenberger 1994). This is not far from C. J. H. Wright's (1990) concept of Deuteronomy as a critique of Canaanite culture. N. Lohfink (1995e) has a similar view, although he thinks that the *herem* theology is based on an actual memory of conquest, which the reading of the Torah in Israel activates.

There is, moreover, a somewhat contrary tendency in Deut. 2. The distinction between land given to Israel and land expressly barred to it declares Yahweh's sovereignty in the affairs of all nations, an implication of the deuteronomic assertions of his supremacy in heaven and earth (as in 4:19; 32:8–9). The universal interest of Yahweh in the nations at large is less developed in Deuteronomy than in some other parts of the OT (such as Jonah; Is. 2:2–4; 49:5–6; Pss. 67; 87). But it is fundamental to its theology of his choice of Israel, which is thus put in a universal context (see further on 32:8–9; 33:2–3, on this point, and also the 'Explanation' of Deut. 7, for a further reflection on the election of Israel in relation to God's universal purpose).

The prohibition of other peoples' lands requires Israel to receive the land he has chosen for them as a gift. The clean distinction between land granted and land withheld has moral implications, similar to those expressed differently in Deut. 1 – Israel may take only what is given, and take it by faith, in Yahweh's own time. This means that the gift of land is ultimately ethical, not cultic. That is, boundaries are not set in stone for ever. That will be one of the major thrusts of the book as it unfolds. (The qualifications around election will emerge from a careful reading of Deut. 7.) In other OT literature the same is true for the nations that are favoured here (note esp. Amos 1 – 2; Obad.; Jer. 48; 49:1–22). Yet even so, Yahweh may finally save (Jer. 49:6; Amos 9:12). Yahweh's will to save will ultimately overflow national boundaries (see on 33:3, though it is admittedly a difficult text).

DEUTERONOMY 3:8–29

Translation

[8]So we took the land at that time from the two Amorite kings who lived in Transjordan, from the Wadi Arnon as far as Mt Hermon. [9](The Sidonians call Hermon Sirion; the Amorites call it Senir.) [10]We took all the cities of the tableland, all of Gilead and Bashan as far as Salcah and Edrei, the cities of the kingdom of Og in Bashan. [11](For Og king of Bashan was the last survivor of the Rephaim. His bed, which is made of iron, can still be seen in the Ammonite city of Rabbah; it is nine cubits long and four cubits wide, by the common cubit.)

[12]This is the land that we took possession of at that time: the territory from Aroer on the edge of the Wadi Arnon and half of the hill country of Gilead, together with its towns, I gave to the tribes of Reuben and Gad. [13]The rest of Gilead, together with all of Bashan, the kingdom of Og, that is, all the region of the Argob, I gave to the half-tribe of Manasseh. (Bashan used to be called a land of Rephaim. [14]Jair the son of Manasseh took the whole region of the Argob as far as the border of the Geshurites and the Maacathites; and he named them – that is, Bashan – after himself, the Settlements of Jair, and they are so called to this day.) [15]To Machir I gave Gilead. [16]But I gave to the tribes of Reuben and Gad the territory from Gilead as far as the Wadi Arnon (the middle of the wadi is the border) and to the Jabbok, the wadi that borders the territory of the Ammonites. [17]Their territory also included the Arabah, that is, the Jordan valley, from Kinnereth to the Sea of the Arabah, the Dead Sea, with the lower slopes of Pisgah on the east.

[18]At that time I gave you the following instructions: 'The LORD your God has given you this land to possess. Now all you fighting men shall cross at the head of your fellow Israelites, equipped for war! [19]However, your wives and children and your cattle (I know that you have much cattle) shall remain in the cities I have given you. [20]This you must do until the LORD your God has given rest to your brothers also, just like you, and they too possess the land the LORD your God is giving them, across the Jordan; then you may all return to the inheritance I have given you.'

[21]I also gave instructions to Joshua at that time: 'You have seen with your own eyes all that the LORD your God did to these two kings; the LORD will do the same to all the kingdoms to which you are going, over there. [22]Do not be afraid; for the LORD your God is fighting for you.'

²³I prayed to the LORD at that time as follows: ²⁴'O LORD, my lord, you have begun to show your servant your greatness and your mighty power, for what god is there in heaven or on earth who can do such deeds and feats as you? ²⁵Now I implore you, let me see the good land that lies across the Jordan, that beautiful hill country, and Lebanon.'

²⁶But the LORD was angry with me because of you, and he would not hear me. Instead he said to me: 'That is enough. Do not speak to me again about this. ²⁷Go to the top of Mt Pisgah and look to the west, north, south and east. So you will see with your eyes. But you shall not go across the Jordan. ²⁸Rather, give instructions to Joshua, and encourage and strengthen him. For he is to go over at the head of this people, and it is he who will enable them to possess the land that you will see.' ²⁹So we remained at the valley opposite Beth-Peor.

Notes on the text

11. *ḥlh*: this is read as *haʾlōʾ* in MT, and assumed to be so in other MSS and ancient versions. The sentence is strictly in the form of a question: 'Og's bedstead, is it not in Rabbah...?'

12. 'on the edge of the Wadi Arnon': the word 'edge' (*śᵉp̄at*) is not in MT here, but is in 2:36; 4:48, and is found in this verse in SamP, LXX and other MSS and versions.

Form and structure

The progress of Israel towards the land now achieves its first goal with the taking of the parts of Transjordan described here. The bulk of the passage specifies the parts of Transjordan that belong to the promised land. In the whole of Deuteronomy, this section most resembles the narrative of land distribution in Josh. 13 – 19. In Josh. 13, Joshua expressly prefaces the distribution of land west of the Jordan by recapitulating Moses' allocation of the territories in question here. Moses, like Joshua, 'gives' the land, thus taking plenipotentiary powers, rather like an ANE monarch, in whose gift lay the domains he conquered. The close description of boundaries, as in Josh. 13 – 19, is of the essence of the 'giving', for in this way the claim to ownership is made good, so as to be beyond dispute.

The similarity between Moses' actions and Joshua's is recognized in the passage, with the charge to the latter (21–22, 28). Joshua's actual commissioning will be narrated near the end of Deuteronomy (31:14–15, 23). Both in this chapter and in that context the theme is closely linked with Moses' death (3:23–28; 31:1–3; 34:5–8, 9).

A noteworthy feature of the passage is the series of interjections into the speech of Moses. Some of them help to describe the land clearly. More importantly, however, they introduce a voice other than that of Moses, namely the narrator's. This feature has been explored as a literary device, with the suggestion that the narrator has greater authority in the discourse than does Moses (Polzin 1980). The point may be put differently. The narrator's voice has the effect of putting the possession of Transjordan on a broad canvas, historically and geographically. The perspective is from a time later than Moses (note 'to this day', 14). In a sense the narratorial intrusions increase the significance of Moses' conquest, because they anchor it in a world of other, normal, historical processes. However, they also put his work in historical perspective, suggesting that the life of Israel must continue after him. In this sense the rhetorical feature complements the theme of his death and the succession of Joshua.

This section brings the 'historical prologue' of the book to its climax, and at the same time prepares for the instructional discourses to come. This climax is only a beginning. And the words of Moses, the substance of the discourse, will have their main effect after he has gone. The nearest counterpart to this in Deuteronomy is the Blessing of Moses (Deut. 33), which also reviews tribal lands, both east and west of Jordan, albeit in a quite different format, and (crucially) in Moses' anticipation only, as far as the western land is concerned.

Comment

3:8–11

8–10. The opening description is resumptive, referring back to the conquest narratives of 2:26 – 3:7, and giving the southern and northern limits of the territory taken. Mt Hermon appears for the first time as the northern marker (as in 4:48; Josh. 12:1); it is celebrated elsewhere in the OT both for its natural greatness and for its capacity to stand representatively for far-flung places (Pss. 42:6[7]; 89:12[13]; Song 4:8). A first interjection by the narrator shows Hermon to be a reference point for other nations (9). The Sidonians, in the north-west, and the Amorites, inhabitants of Canaan (1:7), use names for Mt Hermon (actually an extensive mountainous area), or the Anti-Lebanon, that are also known not only in the OT (Ps. 29:6) but in Ugaritic and Assyrian writings (Weinfeld 1991: 183). The area delimited in v. 8 is then described more fully in v. 10. The tableland (the 'Mishor', cf. Josh. 13:9) is the southernmost section, directly west of the Dead Sea, from the Arnon to the Jabbok (Ammon lying to the east, cf. 2:19). Gilead is the more rugged next stage, lying between the Jabbok and the Yarmuk, and Bashan is the northernmost area, stretching from the Yarmuk to Hermon. (The terms vary slightly within the OT, and the names may have been used differently at different times; cf. Rogerson 1985: 204.) This tripartite division of Israelite Transjordan also underlies the provision of cities of refuge in that region (cf. 4:43). Edrei marks a southern boundary of Bashan, somewhat to the east on the Yarmuk; Salcah is another boundary town, farther east.

11. A second interjection notes the legendary greatness of King Og, the last of the ancient hero figures known as the Rephaim (cf. 2:11). His 'bedstead' may be a sarcophagus, and the note that it was of iron probably derives from an early period, since this would be taken for granted in the Iron Age (Millard 1988; Weinfeld 1991: 185). The length was about 4×2 metres. The monument to the hero king's memory ironically becomes an eloquent witness to the power of Yahweh over all such giants (cf. 1:28).

12–17. The narrative now moves to the distribution of the land to the Transjordanian tribes (cf. Num. 32:28–42). Reuben and Gad share the southern half, comprising what was called the tableland in v. 10 and half of Gilead (presumably the western half), while the half-tribe of Manasseh receives the rest of Gilead and all Bashan. Above the Jabbok, Gad and Reuben's land extended in a narrow strip along the Jordan valley (the Arabah) as far as the Sea of Galilee (Kinnereth, v. 17; see Rogerson 1985: 29), Manasseh bounding it on the east.

The boundaries between Gad and Reuben, recorded in Josh. 13:15–28, are not specified here. This silence may point to Gad's effective absorption of the other in time. Dibon and Aroer, assigned to Reuben in Josh. 13:15–17, are said to have been rebuilt by Gad in Num. 32:34 (see also on Deut. 33:6, 20–21). Jair and Machir, two heroes of Manasseh, are also named in Num. 32:40–41. Jair (14) is remembered as a judge in Gilead (Judg. 10:3–5), where his cities, Havvoth-Jair, are also named (though the extent of his territory appears greater in the present text; for the Argob, see 3:4). Machir (15) became an established name for the Manassite people of Gilead (cf. Judg. 5:14).

The phrase 'to this day' (14; cf. 2:22) is significant, pointing to an indefinite future as the frame of the events being narrated. Once again, the narrator's note puts the occupation of the land on a broad historical canvas. In this case the details drawn from a relatively long period of Israel's settlement are preceded by another allusion to the Rephaim (13b), making the point that Yahweh governs the history of this place now.

3:18–22

18–20. Moses now directly addresses the Transjordanians. The settlement of Reuben and Gad is described at length in Num. 32, where it originates in their request to stay in the rich Transjordanian pasturelands. Moses agrees, on condition that they participate in the full conquest. The scenario is abbreviated here, but the same concern is expressed. The Transjordanians have already attained the 'rest' that remains the goal for all Israel, and indeed have 'inherited' their share in the promised land (cf. 12:9–10). 'Rest' and 'inheritance' are closely associated both here and in

12:9–10; possession is not only occupation but secure tenure. And the two terms have the effect of including the areas of Transjordan in question within the borders of the true promised land. (This is more clearly so than in Num. 32:6–15, where Moses is angry with Reuben and Gad, and compares them with the spies who discouraged Israel from going into the land; cf. Millar 1994: 30; von Waldow 1974: 498.)

21–22. Moses' charge to Joshua follows the concept in 1:37–38 that Moses himself would not enter the land, but that Joshua would lead the tribes into it. In language resembling the depiction of the deliverance from Egypt, where the people in general are reminded that they themselves witnessed Yahweh's power (4:34; 6:22), the victories over Sihon and Og now become evidence to Joshua personally that Yahweh will do likewise for him in Canaan. The command not to fear, otherwise given to the people on the grounds that Yahweh will fight for them (1:21, 29–30) is also given to him personally. The charge to Joshua sums up the theology of this chapter, and gives a perspective to the whole book; as Yahweh has done, so he will do. The succession of Joshua, introduced now, is thus integral to the theme; Moses has begun the conquest, Joshua will continue it. Faith in Yahweh's future deliverance is possible because of what he has so far done.

3:23–29

The final section elaborates the point in vv. 21–22. Moses, the great intercessor (cf. 9:25–29), on this occasion prays on his own behalf. The prayer is based on Yahweh's unique power (cf. 4:32–35; 32:39), and on Moses' own participation in the events by which he has shown it. Yet it presupposes too his knowledge that Yahweh has already decreed his exclusion from the land (1:37). In spite of this, he expresses with great emotion, on this occasion only, his desire to cross the Jordan and see the land. But he immediately adds the reason for his exclusion, in the same terms as in 1:37. And Yahweh's answer puts an end to the plea. The sentence is mitigated by the promise that he will indeed see the land, but only from outside it (27), which he will eventually do just before he dies (34:1–4). Instead of leading the people into the land himself, he must pass the torch to Joshua (28), whom he is to encourage and strengthen (cf. 31:23; Josh. 1:9). The themes of Moses' exclusion, his vision of the land and Joshua's succession come together here, as they do in Deut. 31 – 34. In his preparation of Joshua, Moses will have an active role in the conquest of Canaan. But it is one that involves the acceptance of his own exclusion. His leadership of Israel to this point is for their benefit, as his exclusion has somehow been on their account.

From the immediate past and the imminent future, the narrative comes back to the present in Moab (29), where Moses is ready to give his last exhortations to Israel (cf. 1:1–5; 4:45–49).

Explanation

The account of the distribution of land in Transjordan has several theological functions. First, it expresses the unity of Israel. The natural boundary of the River Jordan had the capacity to divide Israel, making Reuben, Gad and half-Manasseh most vulerable to being isolated. The concern of Moses here is borne out in Josh. 22, which reports a dispute between the Transjordanians and the remainder of Israel over an altar the former built at the Jordan (Josh. 22:10). The Joshua account, like Num. 22, suggests that the land east of the Jordan could be thought of as having a somewhat secondary status (note Josh. 22:9, 19). The building of the altar led to the suspicion that the Transjordanians were beginning to worship separately, and therefore in effect to secede from Israel (Josh. 22:16). The matter was resolved when the altar was explained as being, on the contrary, a safeguard against their exclusion, precisely on the grounds that their land was not properly Israelite (24–25). Even so, out of this debate emerges the strong connection in deuteronomic thought between the unity of Israel, its land and its adherence to the one God Yahweh.

Secondly, the interjections in the account put the conquest in the framework of a long history. This confirms Yahweh's claim to be the one who alone has the right and the power to dispose of land. The pretensions and reputations of legendary figures such as King Og fall before him. Yahweh has given land to Edom, Moab and Ammon (Deut. 2:1–23), as well as to Israel, but he opposes those who place their own claims in opposition to his. The long historical perspective of the interjections also serves to show the continuing process of taking the land. The notes about Jair and Machir, which do not fit neatly into the account if it is regarded as a single event, signal that the occupation of the land continues to be an obligation upon Israel, in spite of this 'gift' by Moses. This fits entirely with the broader theology of the book, in which the land given must also be taken by faith.

The historical frame of the account has both past and future dimensions. In that context Moses represents the past and Joshua the future. The succession of Joshua to Moses is crucial to the concept of Deuteronomy. The whole book is positioned at a crossroads. Geographically, the desert is behind and the land ahead; temporally, the possession of the land has begun but is largely still to be accomplished. What lies ahead must be shouldered by Israel without Moses. He will bequeath them in due course his teaching of the law. Already he has bequeathed them their first experience of the fulfilment of God's promise. They cannot always depend on him, however; they will have to find God faithful by taking the risks of faith on their own account. The passing of responsibility to Joshua betokens this need for Israel to accept the challenge. (This is elaborated in Deut. 31 – 34.)

Moses' prayer has similarities with Jesus' prayer in Gethsemane; both are prayers that reveal the heart, though the head knows the answer already. It need not be asked whether Moses thought Yahweh might relent; the importance of the prayer is that it measures the cost of his obedience to his calling. When Moses accepts that he may not again be his own advocate, and that he will not enter the land, we know that his service is disinterested. If the Satan had asked of Moses as he did of Job: 'Does he serve God for nothing?' (Job 1:9), this might have been the answer. Like the perplexed psalmist, Moses might have said: 'But for me, it is good to be near God' (Ps. 73:28). Moses' acceptance of the decree that he should not enjoy the benefits of the land is remarkable in the context of the covenant theology of Deuteronomy, in which blessing is the expected counterpart of faithfulness. It is one of the sharpest proofs that deuteronomic theology does not involve mechanical rewards and punishments.

DEUTERONOMY 4:1–49

Translation

[1]Now, Israel, listen to the statutes and laws I am about to teach you to do, so that you might have life, and come in and possess the land the LORD the God of your forefathers is giving you. [2]You must not add to the word that I am commanding you, or take anything away from it; rather, you must keep the commandments of the LORD your God, which I lay upon you. [3]You have seen with your own eyes what the LORD did at Baal-Peor; the LORD your God destroyed from among you every individual who went over to the worship of the Baal of Peor. [4]You, however, who have adhered to the LORD your God, are all alive today. [5]See, I now teach you statutes and laws, as the LORD my God has commanded me, for you to keep in the land you are about to enter and possess. [6]And you must indeed keep them carefully, for that will show your wisdom and understanding in the eyes of the peoples, who, when they hear of all these statutes, will say: 'This great nation is indeed a wise and understanding people'. [7]For what great nation is there that has a god so close to it as the LORD our God is whenever we call on him? [8]And what great nation has statutes and laws that are as righteous as this whole body of law that I am setting before you today?

[9]But be extremely careful to guard yourselves from forgetting the things you have seen with your own eyes, or from letting them slip from your minds as long as you live. And make them known to your children, and to their children. [10]Do not forget the day when I stood in the presence of the LORD your God at Horeb, and he said to me: 'Call the people before me in assembly; I want to let them hear my words, so that they may learn to revere me as long as they live on the earth, and to teach their children to do the same.' [11]So you approached and stood at the foot of the mountain; the mountain was ablaze with flame reaching to heaven itself; there was darkness, thick, cloudy gloom. [12]Then the LORD spoke to you from the

heart of the fire; you heard the sound of words, but saw no form; there was just a voice. [13]And he declared to you his covenant, which he was requiring you to keep, the Ten Commandments; then he wrote these on two stone tablets. [14]And me he commanded, at that time, to teach you statutes and laws which you are to keep in the land you are going over there to possess.

[15]Now, because you saw no form on the day when the LORD spoke to you at Horeb, from the heart of the fire, you must guard yourselves carefully [16]from corrupting yourselves by making an idol, or any kind of image, whether male or female in form, [17]or the form of any beast on the earth or the form of any winged bird that flies in the air, [18]or the form of any creature that crawls on the ground, or the form of any fish that swims in the waters beneath the earth. [19]Guard yourselves too from looking heavenwards and, when you see the sun, moon and stars, the whole host of heaven, being tempted into bowing and worshipping them; these things the LORD your God has allotted to all the peoples under heaven. [20]You, however, the LORD took and led out of the iron-smelting furnace, Egypt, so that as a people you might be his own inheritance, as you are today.

[21]But the LORD was angry with me on your account, and swore that I would not cross the Jordan or go into the good land that the LORD your God is giving you as an inheritance. [22]For I shall die in this land; I shall not cross the Jordan. But you will go over and make that good land your possession. [23]Be careful not to forget the covenant of the LORD your God, which he has made with you, by making for yourselves an image in any form, a thing that the LORD your God has forbidden you to do. [24]For the LORD your God is a consuming fire, a jealous God.

[25]When you have had children and grandchildren, and have lived in the land for a long time, should you become corrupt and make any images in any form, and anger the LORD your God by acting wickedly in his eyes, [26]I call heaven and earth to witness against you today that you will certainly perish quickly out of the land you are about to cross the Jordan to possess. You will not enjoy a long period in it; you will be totally destroyed. [27]The LORD will scatter you among the peoples; and you will be left few in number among the nations to which the LORD will drive you. [28]There you will worship gods that are made by human hands, gods of wood and stone that neither see nor hear, and neither eat nor smell. [29]If from there you seek the LORD your God, and search after him with all your heart and being, you will find him. [30]When you are in distress and all these ills befall you in days to come, you will return to the LORD your God, and hear his voice. [31]For the LORD your God is a compassionate God; he will neither abandon you nor destroy you, or indeed forget the covenant he made by oath with your forefathers.

[32]Think now about former times, before your own day, indeed ever since God created humanity on the earth, and from one end of heaven to the other; has such a thing ever happened, or been heard of? [33]Has a people ever heard the voice of a god speaking from the heart of the fire, as you did, and lived? [34]Or has any god attempted to come and take a nation for himself from among another nation, by trials, by signs and wonderful deeds, by making war, with strong hand and arm stretched out, and with great terrors – as the LORD your God did for you, before your very eyes in Egypt? [35]These things he showed you so that you might know

that the LORD alone is God; there is no other besides him. ³⁶From heaven he caused you to hear his voice, to discipline you, and on earth he showed you his great fire, and you heard him speak from the heart of it. ³⁷Because he loved your forefathers and chose their descendants after them, he brought you out of Egypt by his own Presence, and by his great strength, ³⁸to drive out before you nations that were greater and stronger than you, and to bring you into their land and give it to you as an inheritance, as it is today. ³⁹So you should acknowledge today, and take it to heart, that the LORD is God in heaven above and on earth below; there is no other. ⁴⁰And you must keep his statutes and commandments with which I am charging you today, so that it may go well with you and your descendants after you, and so that you remain long in the land the LORD your God is giving you in perpetuity.

⁴¹At that time Moses set apart three cities in the east, in Transjordan, ⁴²so that anyone who killed another unintentionally, having had no enmity with that person in the past, might take refuge there; he could take refuge in any of these cities and live. ⁴³They were Bezer, in the wilderness, in the plain belonging to the Reubenites; Ramoth-Gilead, which belonged to Gad, and Golan, a city of Manasseh in Bashan.

⁴⁴This is the body of law that Moses presented to the Israelites. ⁴⁵These are the precepts, statutes and laws that Moses pronounced before the people of Israel after they came out of Egypt. ⁴⁶He did so in Transjordan, in the valley opposite Beth-Peor, the territory of Sihon the Amorite king who had reigned in Heshbon, and whom Moses and Israel had defeated on their march from Egypt. ⁴⁷They took over his land and also that of Og, king of Bashan – two Amorite kings, therefore, to the east in Transjordan – ⁴⁸from Aroer on the edge of the Wadi Arnon to Mt Sirion (that is, Hermon), ⁴⁹and all the Arabah east of the Jordan, as far south as the Dead Sea and including the lower slopes of Mt Pisgah.

Notes on the text

1. 'about to teach': lit. 'am teaching'; LXX adds 'today', conforming to similar passages (cf. 5:1).

3. 'seen with your own eyes': lit. 'your eyes are those that see/saw' (Weinfeld 1991: 195); the participle with definite article is the complement of 'your eyes'.

5. SamP harmonizes the singular verb r^e'$\bar{e}h$, 'see!', to the surrounding plural. But the singular is used here for arresting effect, as in 1:8.

'for you to keep': Hebr. lacks 'for you', but the sense suggests it.

6. 'that will show': lit. 'that will be'.

8. 'body of law' is $t\hat{o}r\hat{a}$, which is here the entirety of Moses' teaching.

10. 'Do not forget': these words are not in Hebr., but they indicate that the whole verse is in apposition to 'the things you have seen' in v. 9.

'Call ... in assembly': the verb is linked to the noun $q\bar{a}h\bar{a}l$, 'assembly' (Deut. 23:1[2]).

11. 'darkness, thick, cloudy gloom': lit. 'darkness, cloud, thick cloud'.

15. 'On the day when': *yôm*, 'day', is here in the construct state, governing a whole clause (GKC 130d).

22. 'shall die ... shall not cross': participles, giving a sense of inevitability.

26. 'quickly'; the adverb is missing from some forms of LXX; cf. 9:3, 16. It may have puzzled LXX for reasons noted in the 'Comment'.

29. 'If ... you seek': the plural is isolated in the context. It is possible that the final *mēm* is a dittography with the initial *mēm* of the following word; but see 'Comment'.

30. 'When you are in distress': for this construction (prep. *b^e* with def. art., noun *ṣar* and *l^e* following) cf. Hos. 5:1; Is. 25:4; Ps. 107:6, 13, 19, 28. Here it functions effectively as a conditional or temporal clause, parallel to the following *waw* consecutive + perfect. The phrase is placed in SamP at the end of v. 29.

32. 'happened': *hyh*, ni. has this sense (*HALAT* 1:234).

37. 'his own Presence': lit. 'his face'. The same noun is frequent in the prepositional form *'lipnê'*, 'before', 'in the presence of' (cf. 1:45; 12:7). Here the noun virtually stands for the person of Yahweh (cf. LXX *autos*, 'he himself').

41. 'At that time': *'oz* + impf. signifies action that occurred during the period indicated by the context (GKC 107c).

43. 'They were' is not in Hebr.; the names in v. 43 are in apposition to 'three cities' in v. 41.

Form and structure

Placed between the historical retrospect (chs. 1 – 3) and the proclamation of the Decalogue (ch. 5), which in turn stands at the head of the long section of laws and commandments (chs. 5 – 26), Deut. 4 does not easily fit into patterns suggested by law code or treaty. The main part of it, however (4:1–40), is integrated into Moses' first speech. It is linked to the historical retrospect by the reference to Beth-Peor (3:29) in 4:3–4, and to the ban on Moses' entry to the land (3:23–28) in 4:21–22. And, with its long reflection on obedience to the covenant law and the prohibition of idol-worship, it anticipates the fuller account of the law-giving at Horeb in ch. 5.

We have seen in our study of Deut. 1 – 3 that a clean distinction between history and law is impossible in Deuteronomy; the history is at the same time paranesis. The focus now shifts to commandment. Yet the concept of a journey of Israel, prominent in Deut. 1 – 3, is also present here. The chapter's reflection on the relationship between the law first given at Horeb and all of Israel's subsequent life prepares for Deuteronomy's account in ch. 5 and beyond.

The chapter forms a unity. The address to Israel is sometimes in the singular (4:9–10, 19, 29–40) but predominantly in the plural, and the changes have been thought to indicate different redactional layers. The picture is not simple, however, and there are several 'rogue' singulars or plurals in contexts that are mainly the converse (1, 3, 5, 21, 23, 25, 29; these include the 'Shema', 'Hear!', in v. 1, and a similar apostrophe, 'See!', v. 5). They tend, moreover, to occur at the beginning and end of lines, possibly therefore serving a rhetorical purpose; at other times they simply reflect a tendency to mobility in style.

The change of number is in any case not a definitive criterion for some scholars. Mittmann (1975: 170–174) distinguished two *plural* layers (PL1 and PL2), on the basis of theological criteria; the second layer was held to elaborate the idea of Moses' *teaching* of the law. However, the close relationship between the law and its teaching is at the heart of the chapter's purpose. Knapp (1987: 30) distinguished layers that related to law (esp. vv. 1–14) and one that focused on the prohibition of images (15–18; Mittmann incorporated the latter in his PL2). These, however, are together associated with another important uniting theme of the chapter, that of the divine presence.

By contrast, the unity of 4:1–40 has been maintained by a number of scholars both because of its consistent theme of the law (Mayes 1979: 148–149) and for formal reasons (Braulik 1986a: 38–39). Braulik finds a threefold division, like that of a law code (prelude, 1–8; core of the law, 9–31; epilogue, 32–40). The middle section in turn resembles the form of a treaty: 10–14, prologue; 15–19, 23–24, the central stipulations; 25–31, curse and blessing. The chapter thus has features of both law and covenant. The covenantal dimension corresponds to a historical element, which has a broad sweep, from the far past to the far future (25–31, 32–35). And the chapter thus synthesizes history and paranesis.

The following analysis partly adopts that of Braulik. However, it includes vv. 41–49 because these passages, though they fall outside Moses' first speech, bind the chapter into the themes of history and journey. They also frame Deut. 1 – 4, however, by formally echoing the third-person introduction at 1:1–5. Deut. 4:44–49 is so similar in content to 1:1–5 that it has been thought 'superfluous' (S. R. Driver 1895: 79–80). It is better to think of the repetition as an 'inclusio', however; that is, a rhetorical device to indicate the closure of a section of the discourse. Lundbom (1996), in arguing this, notes an inversion of key words and phrases in this passage by comparison with 1:1–5. It follows that Deut. 1 – 4 as a whole is the first rhetorical unit in the book, serving as the prologue to the rest of it. It follows too that it is unnecessary to identify in 4:44–45 two separate introductions to originally separate speeches within chs. 5 – 11, addressing Israel respectively in the singular and plural (Steuernagel 1900: 20–21).

1–8	Commands; God's nearness by virtue of these; their revelation in history (Egypt, Peor)
9–14	The encounter: vision and word

15–24 Worship God alone; prohibition of idols, because 'you saw no form when the LORD spoke to you out of the fire'
25–31 Curse and blessing; the issue of idolatry
32–40 God is near, on earth, though he dwells in heaven
41–49 Resumption of the journey theme: the word embedded in history

The chapter has structural relationships beyond its immediate literary environment. The call to heed the 'statutes and laws' that Moses is proclaiming is echoed in 5:1; 11:32; 12:1; 26:18, that is, at key points of transition. The motif of 'dread' (*môrā'*, 4:34) has a somewhat similar distribution (11:25; 26:8; 34:12). There are further affinities with ch. 12: the call to obey, the concern to teach future generations, the opposition to idolatry, and – as we shall see – the theme of the divine presence with Israel. There are also important echoes in 4:25–31 of 30:1–10, each passage anticipating not only the exile but God's mercy in that event.

The chapter, therefore, can be seen as an anticipation, or even a summation, of the scope and themes of the whole book. It is widely dated to the exile, because of the knowledge of that event in 4:25–31, and associated with a stream of deuteronomistic redaction that also includes Deut. 30:1–10; 1 Kgs. 8:46–53 and Jeremiah's new-covenant theology (Wolff 1976). The late dating has also been supported by the comparison of themes of 4:32–40 with those of Isaiah 40 – 55.

Comment

4:1–4

1–2. Moses turns to the immediate setting, the plains of Moab, and signals his change of theme with the words: 'Now, Israel', and an exhortation to listen to God's commands. The words are similar to 6:4, 'Hear, O Israel', the well-known 'Shema' adopted in Jewish liturgy. In that case the 'Shema' (meaning 'Hear') demands attention prior to the statement of Yahweh's oneness. Here it calls for obedience to commands. To 'hear' can be to 'listen', 'heed', 'obey' (cf. 4:30; 11:13; 26:17; 30:2, 8, 10, 20). What must be heard can be either the voice of Yahweh or his commandments.

The commands that Moses refers to are designated by the phrase 'statutes and laws' (*ḥuqqîm ûmišpāṭîm*), a frequent expression in Deuteronomy, meaning the subject-matter of what Moses is about to promulgate. The various expressions for 'law' in Deuteronomy can have a number of different meanings: individual commands; the Decalogue; the whole body of law in the book; and last but not least the continuing application of the laws, here embodied in Moses' teaching. The 'statutes and laws' sometimes stand alongside another word for law, as in 4:45 (*'ēdōṯ*); 5:31; 7:11

(*miṣwâ*); in these cases they refer to individual commands. At other times, as here, and notably at points of transition, namely 5:1; 11:32; 12:1; 26:18, they stand for the body of law as propounded in Deut. 5 – 26 (with Braulik 1970).

The term *ḥuqqîm* has connotations of the inscribing of a law permanently. *mišpāṭîm* recalls the decision of a court, the verdict or judgment that follows a legal case. It can also mean an established precedent, and thus imply an appeal to a proper authority. It is not clear how far these connotations survive in a fixed phrase like this (cf. 1 Sam. 30:25; Josh. 24:25). The parallel texts, however, suggest that the phrase implies not only the giving of the laws, but their permanent establishment by a proper authority. Deut. 5:31 and 6:1 know that the laws about to be promulgated must be mediated to future generations. The expression there also points to the fact that 'most law in Israel will be mediated through constituted authorities' (N. Lohfink 1989: 8). It is appropriate, therefore, to an address that extends the laws once given at Horeb to the people's entire future life. As such, it embraces the Decalogue, the further laws, and Moses' preaching; 'the writer is forging a link between what happened at Horeb and the events in progress at Moab' (Millar 1994: 40), and indeed beyond.

Moses 'teaches' these statutes and laws, a frequent participial form in Deuteronomy, referring to the addresses he is giving or about to give. It embraces both the laws and their ongoing interpretation. In his teaching of the laws, Moses is authorizing all future due interpretation and application of law in Israel.

The logic of v. 1 appears to be that possession of the land depends on prior obedience to the laws, and some have thought this to be a mark of later layers of the book (Perlitt 1983: 54–55; N. Lohfink 1981: 98), as opposed to passages that make the giving of the land primary and the demand for obedience a consequence (e.g. 7:6–11). The rhetoric of Deuteronomy, however, cannot be broken up in this way into concepts that are at odds with each other. It has a dynamic in which gift of land and duty of obedience are interdependent. The priority can be expressed formally either way, and is a matter of rhetorical style. The converse of the order in v. 1 is found in vv. 5–6.

Notwithstanding the provision for interpretation of the law, the law itself is to be respected in its integrity, in a standard formula protecting legal authority (2). The term *dābār*, 'word', stands here for the whole law (i.e. all the laws in chs. 5 – 26). The same thought occurs in 12:32[13:1]. (Cf. also 30:14.)

3–4. A motive for obedience is drawn from the narrative told in Num. 25, and only hinted at in 3:29. It is a first assertion in this chapter that obedience to law is at the same time a matter of loyalty to Yahweh. The expression 'adhered to' is frequent in Deuteronomy, both reinforcing the call to obey (cf. 11:22; 30:20) and requiring faithfulness to Yahweh as oppposed to other gods (13:4[5]).

The tense in these verses is the participial present (lit. 'your eyes are those that see ... but you are adhering'), both making the events at Peor somewhat immediate, and showing that the need to keep covenant is always a matter of present decision. This is reinforced by the word 'today', here used to recall the judgment on the Peor generation (cf. v. 8).

4:5–8

5. The tense of 'teach' here is perfect, and could indicate an activity already completed. That would go against the drift of the context, however, which is specified by the 'today' in v. 8. This is one of the most characteristic expressions of deuteronomic preaching, used to express the urgency of present decision (von Rad 1966: 28–30). It is especially significant in the present chapter, which will make the Horeb encounter the ground of an appeal to the Moab generation and to all future generations (cf. 4:20, 26, 32, 38–40). It comes also in 5:1–2, where again the depiction of the Horeb encounter as a present event is the topic.

The exhortation is now put in the context of the entry to the land; the tense is again a participle, indicating that the possession is imminent. This is consistent with the picture in Deut. 1 – 3, where the issue of whether Israel would enter was settled.

6–8. The laws given to Israel are now put in an international context, and seen as the 'wisdom' of Israel. The vocabulary ('wisdom and understanding') is drawn from the 'wisdom' sphere of thought, found both in the OT (notably in Proverbs, Job and Ecclesiastes) and in a range of ANE literature. Law and wisdom were separate, though related, phenomena in early Israel (cf. the triad of the priest and law, the wise and counsel, and the prophet and word, in Jer. 18:18). A full equation of wisdom and Torah is not made until the second-century BC Wisdom of Sirach (e.g. Sirach 24:23).

The point here is not to make such a systematic equation between law and wisdom, but rather to demonstrate the uniqueness of Israel in its world. The 'peoples' are presumably not those that Israel is about to drive out of their homes in Canaan, but nations more generally in the ancient world. They themselves become witnesses to the greatness of Yahweh and what he has done for his people. The point is sharp, because in the ancient world nations were accustomed to think, and prove, that they had superior gods and divinely appointed institutions. The repeated 'what great nation ... ?' (7–8) – echoing the phrase 'This great nation' applied by the other peoples to Israel (6) – directs attention to just such claims. And the terms in which Israel's statutes and laws are described in vv. 6, 8 (wise, righteous) specifically echo claims made for King Hammurabi, the great Babylonian lawgiver of the early second millennium BC, in his law code (CH). Kings, in their wisdom, made just laws (see CH 1:30–31; 4:9–10;

24:1–5, 26–31). This text therefore opposes the claims of kings in the ancient world, consistently with the programme for an Israelite constitution in 16:18 – 18:22, in which the king plays a minor, even dispensable part (see on 17:14–20). Only the Torah given by God is wisdom and righteousness in Israel, and it is the people as a whole that is made wise and righteous by it.

Closely bound to the excellence of the laws of Israel is the nearness of its God (4:7). 'Whenever we call on him' suggests prayer in time of need or crisis (cf. 1 Kgs. 8:52; Ps. 145:18–19), and in Deuteronomy this may hint at the deliverance from Egypt (cf. Exod. 2:23). The link between exodus, divine presence and law lies at the heart of Deuteronomy (cf. 5:4–6, 7–21). It is taken further in the next passage.

4:9–14

The next paragraph, which resembles the prologue of a treaty (see 'Form and structure'), recalls the formative encounter between Yahweh and Israel at Mt Horeb. The fullest account of this comes in Exod. 19 – 24, and Deut. 5 will return to the theme. These verses, indeed, compress the content of 5:22–33.

9. Verse 9 introduces an important formula in Deuteronomy: 'Be extremely careful to guard yourselves from forgetting.' The verb is literally 'keep yourselves', the same verb that is used for keeping the commandments (e.g. 4:2, 6, 40). Here it is turned directly on to the person addressed (cf. 4:15, 23). A stronger translation of the line would be: 'Be extremely careful to guard your *souls* from forgetting', as the word *nepeš* sometimes bears this strong sense, and Deuteronomy typically calls on its hearers not merely to obey God's words, but to do so with all their being (cf. 6:5: 'with heart, soul [*nepeš*] and might'). A theme is struck here, therefore, that goes to the heart of Deuteronomy's ethic, and indeed of its analysis of Israel's condition. Obedience to God is not a matter of external observance, but of the mind and will. However, Israel is prone to forget God and his commandments (cf. 8:11–20), and therefore must be vigilant in its moral and religious life.

10. Moses recalls how he 'stood in the presence of the LORD' (or simply 'before the LORD'). This is the first of a number of similar texts. Levi stands 'before the LORD' in the regular worship (10:8; 18:7); the Moab generation stands 'before the LORD' (29:14); and Israel worships 'before the LORD' at the sanctuary (12:7, etc.; 31:11–13). The concept of the divine presence is therefore of great importance in Deuteronomy. However, in this case it is Moses alone who stands before Yahweh, because the present context stresses his role as mediator between Yahweh and Israel. The point is clearer in 5:23–27, which seems to be presupposed here. Deuteronomy emphasizes that Israel meets God primarily by means of his word, and to that end this passage will mitigate the idea of the vision of God, and highlight the role of Moses, the 'teacher' of the word. Moses therefore gathers Israel as an 'assembly' of Yahweh, the first use of this expression in the book (here it a verbal, as in 31:12, 28; elsewhere it is the noun, *qāhāl*: 9:10; 10:4; 18:16; 23 [6×]; 31:30). It signifies Israel formally gathered as the people of Yahweh, in his presence and subject to his word.

11–14. Most of the content of 5:22–33 is told briefly here. In Exodus, the mountain is covered with cloud, and with smoke from the fire in which Yahweh had descended on it (Exod. 19:9, 16–18). Deuteronomy adds the detail that Yahweh spoke 'from the heart of the fire' (12; 5:24), and also stresses that the Israelites 'saw no form; there was just a voice'. This does not mean that Yahweh is not really present, though it has been taken as evidence that Deuteronomy thinks of Yahweh as present only in heaven. Invisibility does not mean absence (I. Wilson 1995: 45–53). The expression 'before the LORD', here and elsewhere, strongly suggests otherwise. The present chapter elsewhere affirms both God's transcendence and his immanence (cf. v. 36; cf. v. 7 for Yahweh's 'nearness' to Israel).

Finally, the Horeb covenant is here equated with the 'Ten Commandments' (13; cf. 9:9–11, 15; 10:8). (This reference to the Ten Commandments might, of course, assume familiarity with Exod. 20:3–17. The term itself is used in Exod. 34:28, where it *may* relate directly to Exod. 34:17–26; in Deuteronomy, however, it plainly refers to the Decalogue, since that is what follows in ch. 5.) Covenant as Decalogue is only one angle on the topic in the book, and balanced here in v. 31 by the idea of covenant as oath to the patriarchs. But there is a special reason for the identification of covenant and Decalogue in this context.

Deut. 4:13–14 distinguishes between the Decalogue and other laws, the former representing the covenant at Horeb, and the latter presented in the context of Moses' teaching. This is different from Exodus, where the Book of the Covenant (Exod. 20:22 – 23:19) seems to be part of the covenant at Sinai itself. Deuteronomy's re-presentation is due to its contention that the covenant at Horeb is made new in each generation by its teaching and interpretation. The separation between the Decalogue and other laws, therefore, is part of the same picture as the insistence that the people saw no form, but heard only a voice, namely an insistence on the primacy of the word in Israel's relationship with Yahweh.

A further element in this picture emerges here (throughout vv. 9–14), namely the unity of the generations of Israel. It is striking that the generation listening to Moses' speeches in Moab is addressed as if it had itself experienced the exodus from Egypt. (The singular address in vv. 9–10 lends some emphasis to this new idea; the prevailing plural is resumed in v. 11, however.) This concept is in contrast to that found in chs. 1 – 3, where it was stressed that the Horeb generation could not see the land because of its disobedience to the first command to go into it (1:35–36; 2:16–18; cf. Judg. 2:10; cf. Weinfeld 1991: 203). That distinction between the generations was natural in the context of a historical reminiscence that had behind it the strong tradition found in Numbers. Here, however, we have the dominant view in Deuteronomy, which stresses that all generations of Israel are as one (cf. 5:2–5). The solidarity of Israel stretches both backwards and forwards, to the Horeb event on the one hand, and to succeeding generations on the other ('to your children, and to their children', v. 9). The Horeb event thus becomes a model for all time of Israel's position before God, at the place of decision (cf. Millar 1994: 32–49). And by this means the teaching of Moses can be extended to Israel in all generations.

In Deuteronomy Horeb appears almost exclusively in the framework of the book, not in the law code (1; 4; 5; 9:8; 18:16; 28:69). This led Perlitt to think that Deuteronomy plays down its significance. There is no reason to think as he does, however, that 'Horeb' is a deliberate de-localization of Sinai, an indeterminate 'desert place', purged of old Edomite associations (Deut. 33:2; Perlitt 1977). Horeb is indeed Sinai, and a crucial place in the journey of Israel. Its significance in Deuteronomy, however, depends on the relations that this encounter has with all the others (noted a moment ago). This paradigm encounter affirms that Israel did once meet Yahweh in a way that was decisive for its life, and therefore that it can and must go on doing so. The most important parallel with the meeting here is in Deut. 12:7 and similar texts; the single formative encounter at Horeb is translated by this analogy into Israel's continuing life, into an indefinite future (see further on ch. 12). This point is consistent with the portrayal of Moses here primarily as a teacher, and the insistence on teaching future generations the meaning of the events the present Israel has seen.

The question of what Israel actually *saw* at Horeb is shrouded in some of the mystery of the event itself. Deut. 4:12 seems to contrast with 5:24 (see 'Comment' there). The two passages belong within a larger picture of the elusiveness of the vision of God (cf. Exod. 24:9–11; 33:17–23). It is not quite true to say that Deuteronomy represents a shift from vision to word in its concept of the divine presence. Rather, word and actual encounter with Yahweh belong inseparably together.

4:15–24

15–19. The solemn exhortation to 'guard the soul from forgetting' now heralds the second of the chapter's 'twin peaks', the prohibition of making images. That prohibition is best known in the OT from the Decalogue (Deut. 5:8–9; Exod. 20:4–5). Here it anticipates that commandment, and also grounds it in the fact that Israel did not see the form of God at Horeb, the emphasis falling again on God's speech out of the fire. It is further grounded, however, in the creation, with echoes of Genesis. The portrayal of idolatry as 'corruption' recalls the 'corruption' of humanity

(Gen. 6:11–12) that leads to the destruction by the flood. The word for 'destruction' (Gen. 6:17) is a form of the same word as 'corruption'. And Deut. 4 has an echo of the same wordplay ('corruption' in vv. 16, 25; destruction' in v. 31). Thereafter, the development of the prohibition of image-making closely follows Gen. 1:14–27, with a reversal of the order of creation there: images of male or female; animals on the earth; birds in the sky; creeping things; fish; the sun, moon and stars. The creation of human beings in the image of God is not directly mentioned, but is strongly suggested in v. 16. This sophisticated allusion to Gen. 1:6 (described by Fishbane as a case of 'aggadic exegetical adaptation'; 1985: 321–322 and n. 19) brings its theology, according to which humanity is the only 'image' of God, to bear on an ancient world in which all kinds of images were an everyday fact of life, often depicting gods in the form of creatures, and in which the sun, moon and stars were also worshipped. It is clear from the OT that Israel frequently fell prey to such worship (e.g. 2 Kgs. 21:3, 5; 23:4–5; Jer. 19:13). And Deuteronomy uncompromisingly opposes it (cf. 7:1–5; 12:2–4).

Deut. 4:19 is surprising in view of Deuteronomy's emphasis on the oneness of God (6:4), for it seems to say that the sun, moon and stars have been assigned to the other nations for their worship. The term *ḥālaq*, 'allotted', balances *naḥ*ᵃ*lâ*, 'inheritance', used of Israel in v. 20. The same pair is used together in Deut. 32:9, both referring to Israel as Yahweh's special people. That passage (32:8–9) is similar in thought to this one, with the phrase 'sons of God' apparently referring to deities (see the translation there, following Qumran and LXX, with NRSV and NIV mg.). The idea that other nations were thought to have their particular deities, the 'sons of God / the gods', can be found elsewhere in the OT and other Jewish literature (Ps. 82; Dan. 10; *Jubilees* 15:31–32). Deuteronomy may give formal assent to this, as an extension of God's allocation to the nations of their territories (2:9, 19). More probably it is meant to contrast with the statement of Israel's special status in the next verse. It may even imply criticism; the 'exegesis' of Gen. 1:14–27 in vv. 16–19 supports this view, because that text also implies criticism of ANE polytheism.

20–21. Verses 20–24 now reinforce the exhortation in v. 15 to keep faithful to the God Israel met at Horeb. Verse 20 begins with an emphasis on 'you', in contrast to the other nations (19); while they are given over to the worship of the sun, moon and stars, Yahweh took Israel out of Egypt to be his own inheritance. The figure of the 'iron-smelting furnace' occurs also in 1 Kgs. 8:51; Jer. 11:4, perhaps recalling the hard labour in the burning heat of the day. Israel is Yahweh's 'inheritance' mainly in the framework (cf. 9:26, 29; cf. 32:8–9; Jer. 10:16; in the law code the term mainly refers to the *land* as *Israel's* inheritance, given by Yahweh; e.g. 12:9; 15:4; 19:10). The thought is close to that of Israel's 'sonship' of Yahweh (1:31; 8:5; 14:1; 32:6; cf. C. J. H. Wright 1996: 52), since it is sons who inherit in the OT world. It is close too to the 'treasured possession' of 7:6; 26:18; cf. Exod. 19:5. Yahweh has a special relationship with Israel, distinguishing it from all other nations.

The passage unexpectedly returns in v. 21 to the prohibition of Moses' entry into the land (cf. 1:37–38; 3:23–28). The link is the theme of inheritance, however, standing in the emphatic final position in the verse. The special people belongs in a land of its own (21); here the land as Israel's inheritance (typical of the law code) is brought in to balance the idea of Israel as Yahweh's inheritance. And it is into this 'inheritance' that Moses may not go.

22–24. The ban on Moses may be understood as cautionary; as he failed to inherit, so they might cease to enjoy the inheritance, if they prove unfaithful to the covenant, an allusion to the Ten Commandments, v. 13 (22–23). The warning fuses together the twin themes of Deut. 4 (covenant and idolatry) as closely as anywhere (*pace* Knapp 1987: 88; cf. the link between the tablets of the law and presence in 9:8–21). The closing motive clause (24) resumes the image of fire from the Horeb theophany, now applying it to God himself, and linking it with his 'jealousy', that is, his intolerance of the worship of other gods (cf. 5:9). Here too, therefore, the substance of covenant commitment is allegiance to Yahweh alone.

4:25–31

25. Moses' address now contemplates the long future. This passage corresponds to the commands to teach future generations the covenant (4:9; 6:7); it also illustrates the solidarity of Israel in all generations assumed here and elsewhere (4:9; 5:2–3). The Israel of the future can also be taken into the 'you' form of address, and be supposed to have stood in principle at Horeb. The case of a future generation's sinning is now contemplated, and the sin is in terms of idolatry (25; 'an image in any form' is the same phrase as in v. 23, and an abbreviated allusion to vv. 16–18). Idolatry above all is the evil that 'angers' Yahweh (cf. 9:18 for the same phrase, used there of the most famous idol of all, the golden calf; and 32:16, 21; 2 Kgs. 17:11, 17; 21:6; 22:17; Jer. 11:17).

26–28. These verses read like the curses of a covenant. Moses calls the heavens and earth to be the covenant witnesses. (Witnesses to covenants in the ANE were typically gods; in Deuteronomy, however, for obvious reasons, Yahweh turns to his own creation to perform this role; cf. 30:19; 31:28; 32:1; cf. Is. 1:2.) The curse is uncompromising, framed in v. 26 by two verbs reinforced by infinitive absolutes (and rendered by adverbs in the translation: 'certainly perish ... be totally destroyed'). The curse takes the extreme form, removal from the land, the undoing of the chief covenant blessing (hence the repetition in the verse of the formula of land gift). The swiftness of the punishment seems at odds with the story of Israel as it unfolds in the books of Kings, where generations of covenant-breaking, specifically by the worship of other gods, are passed over before the axe finally falls (but see 'Notes on the text'). The point may be the certainty of the judgment, rather than its immediacy. Rhetorically, however, it is suitable as a negation of continuance, one of the central features of the blessing.

Verses 27–28 threaten exile from the land. In the light of the story told in Joshua–Kings, this is bound to be read as an announcement of the Assyrian and Babylonian captivities (more particularly the latter because of vv. 29–31). Exile in itself, however, was a common threat in ANE treaties, and a frequent device of great powers to calm potential disturbance in far-flung territories. The specific echoes of these verses are with the story of Abraham and the patriarchs, where the promise of land was associated with that of increase of numbers (Gen. 12:1–3; 15:5–6, 7; cf. Deut. 1:8). The twin threat of scattering among the nations and reduction to a tiny number is the negation of that promise. The origin of Abraham in Mesopotamia, a place where other gods were worshipped (and the place of ultimate exile), is another echo here (cf. Gen. 15:7; Josh. 24:2). The passage does not specify the Babylonian exile, however; indeed, Deuteronomy does not use the term for 'exile' (in this sense) that is commonly found in Kings and Jeremiah to refer to the captivities in Assyria and Babylon (*glh*, e.g. 2 Kgs. 18:11; 24:14; Jer. 29:14; 39:9), or the related *gôlâ*, 'exiles' (Jer. 29:1). Here and at 28:37 it uses a general word for 'lead away' (*nhg*). The culmination of the punishment of exile is a return of the people to their own idolatrous roots, condemned to hope in gods that cannot deliver. The critique of other gods as those who are made by human hands of wood and stone and cannot see or hear is a prophetic theme (cf. Hos. 4:12; Jer. 2:27; 3:9; Is. 37:19; 44:9–20); the addition of 'neither eat nor smell' is a jibe about popular conceptions about deity among the other nations.

29–31. It is best to take vv. 29–31 as the completion of the thought in vv. 25–28. The syntax of 'you will look to' (*waw* + pf.) places it in a sequence of such forms beginning in v. 27. The isolated plural form of address, however, is an arresting rhetorical feature, indicating a significant new turn in the argument. The 'seeking' of Yahweh by Israel is not merely the next in a series of events, to be taken for granted; the conditionality is clear from the continuation: 'If ... you ... search after him with all your heart and being' (for this phrase, see 'Comment' on 6:5). Verses 29–30 consist of two 'if ... then ...' sentences; the first promises that they will find God when they search after him (29); the second also implies a condition ('in distress'), and culminates in returning and obedience (hearing). The two are in parallel; the 'finding' is tantamount to returning and obeying. And, while the 'hearing' is primarily obedience (cf. 'Hear his voice', 4:30; 26:17; 30:2, 8, 10, 20), the returning and hearing are more than a mere return to obedience, but are themselves blessing; since the punishment of exile involved the worship of gods that could not hear, this renewed 'hearing' of God's voice is a return to life itself. The passage then affirms that the punishment of exile need not be the end of the relationship between Yahweh and Israel; rather, his mercy continues. (The phrase 'in days to come', v. 30, lit. 'the end of the days', does not mean the end of time, but some later period, specified only by the context; cf. 31:29.)

There is no explicit hope of return to land, however (as in 1 Kgs. 8:46–53; v. 34 in that place is not a case of such hope, but only of restoration after defeat in battle). 'Returning' to the LORD probably means 'repenting' here, as it frequently does in the prophets (Hos. 6:1; Jer. 3:22; 4:1; and cf. Judg. 2:19; 8:33; 1 Sam. 7:3; 1 Kgs. 9:6; 2 Kgs. 17:13; 23:25–26). In both Hosea and Jeremiah, however, the theme comes to embrace the idea of return to the land following exile, though repentance is subsumed within this returning (Hos. 14; Jer. 31:17–18, 21). And while Deut. 4:29–31 is most like 1 Kgs. 8:46–53, the similar Deut. 30:1–10 stands closer to Hosea and Jeremiah, because there the hope of return to land is explicit (see also the 'Explanation' of that passage). (Wolff [1976] argued that Deut. 4:25–31; 30:1–10; 1 Kgs. 8:46–53 belonged to a second exilic deuteronomist. But this fails to see the important differences between these passages, and the trajectories of the theme within the books concerned; cf. also Mayes 1979: 367–368, N. Lohfink 1965a; and McConville 2000a.)

Verse 31 provides the ground for the promise in v. 30. The word 'compassionate' speaks of a deep emotional attachment, which, when all else is done, predisposes Yahweh to mercy. It occurs in contexts in which anger and punishment might be expected, but in which mercy has the final say. (The classic text is Exod. 34:6, which reaffirms Yahweh's love for Israel after the great apostasy of the golden calf, Exod. 32; cf. also Joel 2:13.) Though Israel may become 'corrupt' (šḥt) Yahweh will not 'destroy' (šḥt); though Israel may 'forget the covenant' (4:23), Yahweh will never do so. Moreover, the covenant is characterized as that which goes back to the patriarchal promise, a commitment to his people that pre-dates and takes priority over that of Horeb and the Mosaic preaching (cf. 'Explanation').

4:32–40

This final part of Moses' first address is a climactic grounding of the argument so far, adopting the device of the rhetorical question. The topics of exodus and Horeb, the twin themes of the entire argument from 1:1 to this point, are recalled twice in vv. 33–38 (in the order Horeb–exodus), the second being in each case a development of the first (cf. vv. 33 and 36; 34 and 37–38). The argument is prefaced (32) by putting the events in the context of a vast history; and it is concluded by resuming the appeal for faithfulness to the one God and obedience to the laws and commandments (39–40).

32. The historical context embraces the history of the world since creation, strictly since the *day* of creation, thus neatly bracketing all history between that day and 'today', v. 40. The word *bārā'*, 'create', is used only here in Deuteronomy–Kings, being more characteristic of Genesis (Gen. 1:1 – 2:4; 5; 6:7) and Is. 40 – 55. It is accompanied by *'ādām*, 'man, humanity', also rare in Deuteronomy (4:28; 5:24; 8:3; 20:19; 32:8), and at home in Genesis and Is. 40 – 55. The heaven–earth dimension, also indebted to Gen. 1, puts the salvation of Israel in a cosmic setting as well as in that of eternity, and foreshadows the important statement in v. 36 (see below). (The text closest to the present one is Is. 45:12: *bārā'*, *'ādām*, *šāmayim*, 'heavens'. However, the combination of *bārā'* and *'ādām*, together with *rûaḥ*, 'spirit', is found also at Amos 4:13).

33. This verse recalls vv. 12, 15, but adds the phrase 'and lived?', anticipating 5:24–27. The concept that no-one could see God and live is well known in the OT (though often in practice negated: Exod. 24:9–11; Judg. 13:22; Is. 6:5). Here (as in 5:24b) it is modified in accordance with the emphasis on hearing in this account of the Horeb event.

34. The uniqueness of Yahweh's deliverance is now described in a concatenation of terms for his great acts in saving Israel from Egypt. The 'signs and wonders' referred in Exodus to the miracles performed by Moses before Pharaoh (sign: Exod. 4:9; 7:3, cf. Num. 14:11; wonder: Exod. 4:21; 7:3, 9; 11:9–10). Apart from Exod. 7:9 the terms appear separately, but referring to the same acts (stopping short of the Passover and exodus themselves). Deuteronomy typically combines the two terms into a set phrase, as here (7:19; 26:8; 34:11; cf. 28:46). Here it adds 'trials' (*massōt*) (otherwise only at 7:19; 29:3[2]), corresponding to the verb 'attempted' (*nissâ*), suggesting the daring of invading the territory of another people (and therefore of its god). The mention of war apparently characterizes the conflict with Egypt as an act of war, conducted by Yahweh as the Divine Warrior, though it may also embrace conflicts on the way to the brink of the promised land, including victories over the Transjordanian kings (2:26 – 3:7). The 'strong hand and arm stretched out' becomes a stereotypical phrase in Deuteronomy, denoting God's powerful acts (cf. 5:15; 7:19; 9:29; 11:2; 26:8). In Exodus, the outstretched hand belongs to Moses, but it heralds the signs by which Yahweh demonstrates his authority and power (Exod. 10:12–13, 21–22). Deuteronomy transfers the figure to Yahweh himself (cf. Is. 5:25; 9:11, 16, 20). The list of terms for Yahweh's acts concludes with 'terrors' (*môrā'*, cf. 11:25; 26:8; 34:12; cf. Jer. 32:21), always qualified as 'great', and expressing the terror that fell on the other nations because they knew that Yahweh was with his people (cf. Num. 22 – 24; Josh. 2:9).

35. The point of this circumstantial description of Yahweh's unequalled power is made explicit in v. 35. It anticipates the First Commandment (5:6–7), which demands exclusive loyalty to Yahweh on the grounds of his deliverance of Israel from Egypt (as here). This is an even stronger statement of his uniqueness, however, since it says categorically that there are no other gods (not simply that they shall not worship other gods).

36. We noticed a moment ago that vv. 33–34 are expanded in vv. 36–38, where the rhetorical questions of the former are now answered by firm statements ('he caused you to hear ... he caused you to see', v. 36, cf. v. 35). In v. 36 Yahweh's power is again put in the context of all creation (cf. v. 32). 'Heaven' and 'earth' are in a parallelistic balance. It is misguided to ask whether the voice of God is really coming from heaven (36a) or from the midst of the fire on earth (33, 36b). The passage expresses the fact that Yahweh's presence on earth is not lessened by his dwelling in heaven, or his transcendence compromised by his appearance on earth. As the one God, he both fills the heavens and acts in specific events on earth.

37–38. The passage now returns to the evocation of deliverance, with the first assertion in the book that Yahweh has chosen his people. This has been implicit in the narrative of deliverance, in Yahweh's taking to himself 'a people from the midst of a people' (34). But now for the first time this act is given a theological name and content. Yahweh's choice of Israel means in practice his ability to deliver them from powerful enemies (38; cf. 7:7, where their smallness is stressed in the same connection; also 7:1; 9:1–3). The choice of Israel is in parallel with God's love, here applied first to the forefathers (cf. 10:15), but evidently for the sake of the generations to follow (cf. 7:6–13). There is at the same time a striking reference to the person of Yahweh, in the expression (lit.) 'by his face' (see 'Notes on the text'). This too seems to emphasize the close relationship between Yahweh and Israel as a whole. Deuteronomy's application of election to the people is consistent with its 'democratizing' tendency. In the Zion theology of the Psalms, election is applied to Judah, Zion and the Davidic line (Pss. 78:67–72; 132:13). Deuteronomy, however, takes a quite different view of kingship, and makes the people itself the supreme political entity (see further on Deut. 17:14–20). In this respect (as in others) it resembles Is. 40 – 55 (41:9; 43:10; 44:1–2 [with Shema]; cf. Is. 14:1; Ps. 33:12; 135:4).

39–40. Verse 39 takes up again the theme of the uniqueness of God (from v. 35), now reinforcing it with an appeal to 'take it to heart', that is, to give themselves over to believing it and behaving accordingly. The intimate connection between the uniqueness of God and his power in both heaven and earth appears again (cf. v. 36). The section closes with a renewed appeal for obedience to the laws and commandments (40), echoing v. 1, with its reference to Moses' present teaching (here 'commanding'), reinforced by the word 'today' (see above on v. 8), and holding out the prospect of long life in the land (cf. also v. 9). The phrase 'that it might go well with you' is echoed in the Fifth Commandment (5:16) and elsewhere (5:29; 6:3, 18; 12:25, 28; 22:7; cf. Jer. 7:23), and is part of Deuteronomy's vocabulary of blessing in the land (cf. 'a good land', *'ereṣ ṭôḇâ*, 8:7).

4:41–49

41–43. Moses' first speech now ends, and the chapter closes with two short passages that serve to set the preaching again in its historical context. The provision of cities of refuge (41–43) anticipates the more extensive regulation about these in 19:1–13 (see on that passage for a fuller explanation of the rationale behind such cities, and procedures for determining guilt or innocence). In essence, they provide a place of escape for the accidental homicide, who is subject to the tribal custom of blood vengeance, which might be exacted before a proper trial can determine whether the killing was intentional. Here as in 19:4 the phrase 'having had no enmity with that person in the past' signifies *prima-facie* evidence that the killing was unintentional. This first requirement regarding cities of refuge corresponds to the narrative of progress towards occupation of the land. As Moses and the people stand in Moab they have already subdued the Transjordanian territories of Kings Sihon and Og, and distributed land to two and a half tribes (2:26 – 3:17). The need for such cities is already established, therefore. The further regulation expands the same provision into the main part of the land west of the Jordan, and allows for yet further expansion, and more cities, in the future (19:1–3, 8–9). The cities mentioned here (43) are named again in Josh. 20:8, in the passage where Joshua commands the enforcement of the provision.

44–49. Verses 44–49 correspond to 1:1–5, with its summary account of Moses' preaching 'beyond the Jordan'. The structural similarities between the two passages have been noted above ('Form and structure'). The renewed allusion to the victories over Sihon and Og shows that the first four chapters take as their main theme the beginning of the conquest, the subduing of Transjordan being a kind of firstfruits. The vocabulary of law is again predominant, with 'Torah' as a general term for the whole law (44; cf. 1:5), and other terms referring to specific stipulations (44; cf. *dᵉbārîm*, 1:1). Only the term *ᶜēdōt* (translated above as 'precepts', 44) is new here. A plural form, it occurs only three times in Deuteronomy (45; 6:17, 20), being more at home in the Psalms (frequently in Ps. 119). It is probably related to the singular form *ᶜēdût*, which refers in Exodus to the tablets of the law kept in the ark (Exod. 25:16), and occurs frequently in that book in the expression 'ark of the covenant' (Exod. 25:22; N. Lohfink 1991a: 86 nn. 3, 5). It may have the same meaning in 2 Kgs. 11:12. The plural in Ps. 119 and Deuteronomy, where it is aligned with other expressions for 'law', is a more general designation for laws (for Braulik [1986a: 63–64] it is the whole law, paranesis and code). It is not clear why it occurs so infrequently in Deuteronomy (see N. Lohfink 1991a for a tradition-critical explanation).

Explanation

Deut. 4 expounds some of the central themes of the book. At its heart is the presence of God by means of his word. Word is systematically highlighted here in comparison with Exod. 19. Yahweh's presence to Israel is primarily by means of his word. The encounter between God and Israel at Horeb is the foundational speech of God to his people. His speech at Horeb, 'from the heart of the fire' (12, 33), is the dynamic event that gives rise to everything else. Word and event are not separate here (cf. Rendtorff 1993: 117); rather, the God who speaks is the God who has brought Israel out of slavery in Egypt, as the juxtaposition of vv. 33 and 34 shows. The scope of the chapter goes from the distant past (32) to the indefinite future (25–31, 40). God is in control of all time, and Israel knows him through his acts, interpreted in word-encounter (cf. Seeligmann 1977: 444). In this fusion of speech and act Deuteronomy is close to Is. 40 – 55, in which God shows his divine power by declaring beforehand that he would deliver his exiled people from Babylon (Is. 41:26–27; 43:9, 12).

Closely related to this theology of history is the assertion that Yahweh alone is God (35b, perhaps an even stronger statement of Yahweh's uniqueness than 5:7). It is because of his unique power that he can act in history, in a sweep that goes from the creation of the whole world, heaven and earth (36; cf. 4:19), to the salvation of Israel, past and future. Here too is an echo of the logic of Is. 40 – 55, in which God's power in history is an effect of his uniqueness and of the emptiness of the claims of other gods (Is. 43:10–14; 44:9–20; 46:1–2).

This theology of history also explains the hostility to the claims of other gods and the worship of idols. The complex idea of God who makes himself known at Horeb by his word, who reigns in heaven and on earth, sovereign over time and space, cannot be depicted in an image. The rejection of image-worship is as much about the way in which God is conceived as about the claims of other gods (15–19). Just as God may not be imaged, neither may he be identified with the sun, the moon and the stars. This, however, does not mean that he is not present. The rejection of images is a rejection only of one mode of realizing the presence of God. For the OT, that means of declaring the divine immanence is dangerous, reducing God, making him available to human ways and means. Representation also forces a depiction in terms of gender, and therefore naturally carries a connotation of sexual potency. It is a short step from this to the attempt to procure the favour of god or goddess by fertility rituals. Rather, God is one, free and sovereign, and can be known only by his own decision to speak to the people of his choice.

The choice of his word as the manner of his presence in Israel affects the way in which God relates to Israel in their regular worship. Central to this is the Torah, the teaching of his laws. The primary speech-act of God is not left in the past as a single event, but is made present by its representation in the laws and instruction given by Moses. Furthermore, the making present of the word of God through Moses' speech at Moab is not an end in itself, but rather shows how it may become continuously present in Israel. In fact, the death of Moses in Moab, before entering the land, is a crucial part of this picture. It is the teaching of the covenant as bequeathed to Israel by Moses that will go with the people into the land (Olson 1994). The essence of the Moab covenant is to assert that the decisive encounter with God can be continuously repeated. This repetition can take several forms, including the teaching of children by parents (6:6–9), and the work of prophets in succession to Moses (18:15–18). But it is also embodied in the visible life of Israel as a worshipping assembly (31:9–13). This passage gives the clue to the understanding of the 'place that the LORD will choose' (31:11; cf. 12:5), namely as the place in which Israel stands again before God as they once did at Horeb. The place is not named, for there is no limit in time or space on the future meetings of God and Israel.

In this chapter God is in all time and all space. There are creative tensions here. The unlimited God, who cannot be imaged, or reduced even to the sun, moon and stars, may yet be present to his people. But what of that other tension, between God's choice of one people, Israel, and his attitude to a world of nations? Is the universality of God turned to their benefit? A hint of their interest in the purposes of God comes in their admiration of Israel's wise and righteous law (6–8). The term *ṣaddîq* is normally used of persons (Weinfeld 1991: 195). Here 'righteousness' is embodied in the revelation of God given to Israel. This sharpens the tension in election to its extreme point. For the setting of 'righteousness' as the standard for God's people embeds a condition in their being chosen, and postulates a people of God that Israel in the event will not be. Yet the image remains. The implications of this are left to be developed elsewhere. Is. 61 depicts the display of the 'righteousness' (*ṣᵉdāqâ*) of God before the nations (61:10–11). The trajectory continues into the NT, where the 'righteousness' (*dikaiosynē*) of God is revealed in Christ (Rom. 3:21–22; N. T. Wright 1991). God's righteousness is saving (cf. also Ps. 143:1).

Deut. 4 reveals only a part of this trajectory. But it affirms an element that is never lost in the biblical story of salvation, namely that 'salvation is of the Jews' (John 4:22). This is not a sectarian or exclusivist point. Rather, it affirms that God's presence in the world has real coefficients in space and time. The contribution of Deut. 4 is to show that God's coming once does not exclude other comings, but is rather their prerequisite. A further feature of the chapter touches on this, namely the priority of the patriarchs over Moses (37), anticipating Paul in Galatians 3. While the focus in Deuteronomy is certainly on Moses and Israel, the origin of the story of salvation in the promises to Abraham (as also in Gen. 12:3) becomes a ground for their eventual extension to the Gentiles.

Finally, in its reflection on wrath and mercy (29–31), Deuteronomy is very close to the most profound message of the prophets (Hos. 11:8–9;

14). In its call for repentance followed by the possibility of return to land, Deuteronomy is entirely 'prophetic' (cf. 30:1–10).

DEUTERONOMY 5:1–33

Translation

¹Moses convened all Israel, and said to them:

Listen, Israel, to the laws and statutes I am pronouncing in your hearing this day. Learn them and be careful to keep them. ²The Lord our God made a covenant with us at Horeb. ³It was not with our forefathers that the Lord made this covenant, but with us, all of us who are alive here today. ⁴Face to face he spoke with you at the mountain, from the midst of the fire. ⁵(I stood between the Lord and you then, to declare the Lord's words to you, for you were afraid, and did not want to go close to the mountain.) He said:

⁶'I am the Lord your God, who brought you out of the land of Egypt, the house of slavery. ⁷You shall have no other gods in my Presence. ⁸You shall not make for yourselves an image in any form, whether in the sky above or on the earth below or in the sea. ⁹You shall not bow to it or worship it, for I, the Lord your God, am a jealous God, punishing the sin of those who turn against me as far as the third and fourth generations, ¹⁰but showing faithful love to thousands of those who love me and keep my commands. ¹¹You shall not use the name of the Lord in empty worship, for the Lord will not regard anyone who does so as innocent. ¹²Observe the Sabbath day and keep it holy, as the Lord your God has commanded you. ¹³You shall work and do all your tasks in six days, ¹⁴but the seventh day is a Sabbath to the Lord your God. You shall not do any work on that day, not you or your son or daughter, or your servant or your maidservant, or your ox or your ass, or any domesticated animal, or the non-Israelite foreigner who lives among you; this is so that your servant and maidservant might rest, just as you do. ¹⁵Remember that you were slaves in Egypt, and the Lord your God brought you out of there with his strong hand and mighty arm; it is for this reason that the Lord your God has commanded you to keep the Sabbath day.

¹⁶'Hold your father and mother in honour, as the Lord your God has commanded you, so that you may prolong your life and enjoy the good of the land the Lord your God is giving you. ¹⁷You shall not murder; ¹⁸you shall not commit adultery; ¹⁹you shall not steal; ²⁰you shall not be a false witness concerning your neighbour; ²¹you shall not desire your neighbour's wife, nor shall you covet his house or field or servant or maidservant or ox or ass or anything that is his.'

²²These words the Lord spoke aloud to your whole assembly at the mountain, out of the fire, the cloud and the darkness. Then he said no more, but he wrote the words on two stone tablets, which he gave to me. ²³But when you heard the voice coming from the darkness, and the mountain was ablaze with fire, you came to me, all the leaders and elders of your tribes, and said: ²⁴'Truly, the Lord our God has

shown us his glory and greatness, and we have heard his voice from the fire this day; we have seen God speak with man, and he has lived. [25]But now, why should we die! For this great fire will consume us if we hear the voice of the LORD our God any longer, and we shall die! [26]For who is there of all humanity who has heard the voice of a living god speaking out of a fire, as we have, and lived? [27]You go near, and listen to all that the LORD our God will say; then tell us everything that the LORD our God tells you, and we will listen and obey.'

[28]The LORD listened to what you said when you spoke to me, and the LORD said to me: 'I have heard what this people said when they spoke to you, and what they say is good. [29]I wish they might always have a heart like this, to revere me and keep all my commands always, so that it may go well with them and their children for ever! [30]Go and tell them to go back to their tents. [31]You, however, are to stand here with me. I will tell you all the commandment, the laws and statutes, which you are to teach them, so that they keep them in the land I am giving them as an inheritance.'

[32]So you must be careful to do everything the LORD your God has commanded you; do not deviate either to the left or to the right. [33]Live your lives completely in the way that the LORD your God has commanded you, and you will live and have well-being and remain long in the land you are about to occupy.

Notes on the text

8. *pesel kol-tᵉmûnâ*, lit. 'an image *of* any form', where the phrase is taken as construct; or it could be read appositionally 'an image, (that is) any form'; other MSS and versions (including QL, SamP) have 'an image *and* any form', as Exod. 20:4. The first option is taken here (slightly varied in the translation), for reasons given in the 'Comment'.

12. *ka'ᵃšer ṣiwwᵉkā yhwh*, 'as the LORD your God has commanded you' (cf. v. 16). B. Lang (1998) suggests that this phrase, on the basis of a parallel in a Hebrew ostracon, is not a reference to a past command, but should be translated: 'Thus Yahweh your God commands you', referring to the following commands. However, the reference to past words of Yahweh, in the form *ka'ᵃšer* + verb in pf., is part of a pattern in Deuteronomy (cf. 18:2). Furthermore, in v. 16 Lang's translation works badly with the following *lᵉma'an* ('in order that') and is better taken as a parenthesis, in the traditional way.

16. See note on v. 12.

23. 'the darkness'; LXX has 'fire', harmonizing to 4:12 (5:22).

24. The impf. *yᵉdabbēr* is here taken as referring to the past, as is the following *wāḥāy* (*w* + pf., *waw*-consecutive), against NIV, NRSV, though with Braulik 1986a: 53, as this makes better sense with the following phrase.

26. 'The voice of the living God' might equally be 'the voice of a living god', as the phrase is indefinite. QL makes it definite, perhaps in the name of orthodoxy. But an indefinite sense fits well with the rhetorical question, which implies that this is a *kind* of thing that is otherwise unknown. Consequently 'a fire' is the natural sense, though the word *'ēš*, fire, has the def. art.

27. On *'att*, 'thou', as a masculine form see S. R. Driver 1895: 87, and GKC 32 R.4). The word should probably be vocalized with final *â* (cf. SamP).

30. 'have well-being': lit. 'it will go well', the word *ṭôḇ* probably being in this case a form of the verb *ṭôḇ* (3 m.s. pf. qal, following *waw-consecutive*).

31. 'all the commandment, the laws and statutes'. MT inserts 'and' between 'commandment' and 'laws and statutes', with 7:11. However, 6:1 (MT) puts 'the commandment' (*hammiṣwâ*) in apposition to 'the laws and the statutes', thus making it, not a separate entity, but an umbrella term. SamP follows this pattern in 5:31; 7:11 also. LXX in contrast supplies 'and' in all three texts. Both SamP and LXX have rationalized an incongruity, albeit in opposite ways. The translation here follows SamP, for reasons given in the 'Comment'.

Form and structure

With ch. 5 we come to a major new section of the book, on some accounts the beginning of the original law book. For N. Lohfink (1963), it is the beginning of the *Hauptgebot* (Principal Law), namely Deut. 5 – 11. As it begins, the preliminary narratives are complete (4:41–49 finally settling the Transjordanian material). And the new development in subject-matter is matched formally by the beginning of Moses' second speech. This is not a clean break from the narratives, however. Noth's distinction between law and history has been somewhat overtaken by successors (though see Veijola 1993). One aspect of this is the tendency of tradition criticism to identify Deuteronomistic strands in chs. 5 – 11 continuing from chs. 1 – 3, partly on the basis of the continuing appearance of second-person plural address (Minette de Tillesse 1962; Mittmann 1975). Theologically too, however, the law–history division has been undermined by the analogy between Deuteronomy and the forms of treaties and law codes in the ANE (see also 'Explanation' on ch. 1, above).

Moses' second speech opens in this chapter with the fullest account of the central event in Deuteronomy, the giving of the law on Mt Horeb. This has been anticipated, as we have seen, in ch. 4. But now the idea of the word of God to Israel gains its fullest definition, describing the relation-ship between that event and the regular teaching of Torah in Israel. At the heart of the passage is the Decalogue itself, also familiar from Exod. 21:2–17. The argument in ch. 5 must be taken closely with ch. 6 (cf. N. Lohfink 1963: 290–291). Beyond that it also introduces a train of thought on the place of the Torah in Israel's life that continues up to ch. 11. The present chapter may be analysed as follows:

1–5   Prologue to the Decalogue
6–21   The Decalogue
22–31   Moses as mediator
32–33   Further exhortation to obey

This structure already makes clear that the concern of the passage is not only with law itself, but with its reception and transmission. The prologue establishes the identity of the covenant partner (Israel as constituted at Horeb; see 'Comment'), a theme taken up again after the report of the Decalogue in v. 22 (with the 'assembly'). It also highlights the role of Moses as mediator of the law, initially in vv. 4–5, then fully in vv. 23–31.

The passage establishes the primacy of the Decalogue itself in the laws contained in Deuteronomy. It is these ten commands alone that are written on the two stone tablets (22), where they are called 'these words' (cf. the 'ten words', 4:13). It is clear, therefore, that (again as in 4:13) the Ten Commandments are for Deuteronomy the substance of the Horeb covenant. Ch. 5 opens, however, with a call to heed the more general 'laws and statutes' (5:1), and this anticipates 5:32 – 6:3, which leads into the laws and exhortations that follow. By this means a close link is established between the Decalogue and the Mosaic preaching. This linkage is designed to give authority to the teaching and practice of law in Israel through Moses' successors. It is thus associated conceptually with Deut. 1:9–18 and 16:18 – 18:22. In the latter, this chapter is recalled expressly in connection with the promise of successors of Moses in the prophetic role of conveying the words of God to Israel (18:15–18; cf. 5:23–26).

It follows that the Decalogue is 'law' in a sense that needs careful definition, and that might differ from the way in which we understand that concept. This may be supported initially by noticing that the commandments contain a variety of material, from terse prohibitions (e.g. 'you shall not murder', 17) to explanation (the Sabbath grounded in the exodus, 15), and motivation ('so that you might prolong your life and enjoy the good of the land', 16). The last command (21) goes beyond the sort of behaviour that can be regulated in any court to the seat of all action, the heart.

This does not mean that the commands are not 'laws'. Israelites might not have distinguished clearly between command and law, since, for them, laws were rooted in the commands of God. So if someone was charged with murder he would be accused on the basis of the command, even though other laws might well be brought in to help specify the nature of the case and the gravity of the crime. Judges who tried cases would consider them in the light of a legal tradition. They would not be bound by written statute in the same way as modern law. This is why a set of commands like the Decalogue can function actually as law, yet also have aspects (explanation, motivation) that do not fit our conceptions of what a law should look like.

However, law in Israel is close to wisdom; that is, it is an intellectual activity that requires weighing the merits of cases in the light of a body of knowledge. (Keeping God's commands is called 'your wisdom' in 4:6.) It is also associated with that other great theological concept, 'righteousness' ($s^e\underline{d}\bar{a}q\hat{a}$), that is, God's right ordering of all things (see 6:25). The Decalogue, therefore, is a summary transformation of God's creative ordering of the world into commands for living for the people he has redeemed from slavery in Egypt. It may be that the order of the commands reflects a sense of their relative importance, since breach of the first six (7–17) normally led to the death penalty (see Wenham 1978: 29).

While the tenfold nature of the Decalogue has always been agreed in theological tradition, because of the phrase 'the ten words' in Deut. 4:13, the way in which the ten are made up has varied. Jewish tradition considered the LORD's opening statement, here in 5:6, as the first of the ten, and then combined the prohibition in v. 7 with the command not to make images (8–10). The usual Roman Catholic division takes vv. 7–10 as the first of the ten, and regards v. 6 not as a command but as a preamble. It is like the Jewish division, therefore, in combining vv. 7–10, but it makes up the number ten by counting each of the two commands not to covet (21). Reformed interpretation leaves v. 6 out of account (like the Roman Catholic in this respect), but finds two commands in v. 7 and vv. 8–10, and does not divide v. 21. (See accounts in Cole 1973: 152; Cassuto 1967: 251–252.) The last of these is followed here. In its favour is the fact that v. 6 is not strictly a command (although it may be read as implying one), and analogies with ANE law codes suggest that the self-introduction stands aside from the laws themselves. Verse 21 is taken as one because of its unity of theme. (Admittedly this is stronger in Exodus, where the same verb is repeated, while Deuteronomy uses two different verbs.) On a strict count of commands, however, the division into two is also valid.

The Decalogue exhibits certain differences from the form in which it appears in Exodus.

12. 'Observe' [not remember] the Sabbath day . . . as the LORD your God has commanded you' (see 'Notes on the text'). This fits with Deuteronomy's usage ('observe' or 'keep' is a common word of exhortation), presupposes the already existing form of the Decalogue, and shows that this is a conscious re-presentation.

14. The clauses concerning rest on the Sabbath are more expansive in Deuteronomy, specifying the ox and the ass as well as referring generally to cattle, and adding a clause to make it quite clear that the provision of rest applies to the servants.

15. The Sabbath command is motivated by the memory of Israel's slavery in Egypt, in contrast to its grounding in God's creation rest (Exod. 20:11). It thus, alone of the commandments, echoes the introduction to the Decalogue (6), which led Braulik to see it as its centre, reflecting its new prominence in the exile (Braulik 1986a: 51; cf. N. Lohfink 1965b).

16. The fifth command, like the fourth, recalls that it has been given before: 'as the LORD your God has commanded you'. It adds the typically deuteronomic 'and that it may go well with you' (or as translated here: 'that you may ... enjoy the good of the land') to the promise of long life found in Exodus. By means of the same insertion it also separates the promise of long life from its direct association with the land (contrast Exod. 20:12: 'that you may live long in the land.'). It is not clear whether it thus anticipates a life of Israel outside the land. More probably it is simply a case of expansionist deuteronomic style.

17–21. The sixth to tenth commands are linked by 'and', tending to make them a coherent block, rather than separate commands. (This is reflected in the alternative numbering for these and subsequent verses preserved in brackets in *BHS*; some editions of the OT follow the lower numbering, resulting in a three-verse discrepancy between versions of this chapter.)

21. The wife is here placed first (not second, after 'house', as in Exodus), and distinguished from everything else that might be coveted by the use of a separate word, and the position of the command in a separate clause.

Who is addressed by the 'thou' of the Decalogue? The propertied male, who has land, slaves and cattle, and who is active in cult and law? (So Braulik 1986a: 50; cf. Cazelles 1985, who thinks this generally for Deuteronomy.) It is true that the 'thou' shifts between a collective address and the individual, perhaps tending especially here to the latter; however, the collective is to the fore in 'your stranger' and 'your gates'. The Decalogue address does not support a social structure in which a particular class has special rights or responsibilities; this would be against the spirit of Deuteronomy. Where the individual is in view, even this should be subordinated to the concept of the brotherhood/sisterhood of all Israelites, as expressed in several laws (e.g. 15:12–18; 17:14–18; see also McConville 2002b).

Mention may be made at this point of the view of Kaufman (1978–9) and Braulik (1993) that the laws in chs. 12 – 26 follow the order of the Decalogue. The significance of the claim is to strengthen the observation that the Decalogue occupies a prominent place in Deuteronomy; indeed, that the book has to a large extent been organized around it. It is convenient to signal this thesis here, as I shall refer to it from time to time in the chapters that follow. In my view it has some cogency, even if it is not wholly convincing at every point. The correspondences found by Kaufman and Braulik may be set out thus:

Kaufman			*Braulik* (with 'transitional passages')	
1–2	12:1–31	Worship	1–2	12:2 – 13:19
3	13:1 – 14:27	Name of God	3	14:1–21

4	14:28 – 16:17	Sabbath	4	14:22 – 16:17	
5	16:18 – 18:22	Authority	5	16:18 – 18:22	
6	19:1 – 22:8	Homicide	6	19:1–23	Preserving life
7	22:9 – 23:19	Adultery	7	22:13 – 23:14	Sexuality
8	23:20 – 24:7	Theft	8	24:8 – 25:4	Property
9	24:8 – 25:4	False charges	9/10	25:5–16	Coveting
10	25:5–16	Coveting			

Comment

5:1–5

1. Moses' second address is introduced with a reference to 'all Israel', which recalls the first introduction in 1:1. His actual words begin with the typical call to 'hear' or 'obey' the commands about to be given (cf. 4:1; 6:4; the opening command is in the singular address of that formula, while the continuation adopts the plural). On 'laws and statutes', see on 4:1 (and above on 'Form and structure'). It is best to take these 'laws and statutes' as having a general reference to the laws in Deuteronomy, above and beyond the Decalogue, because they belong to what Moses is teaching 'today', i.e. on the plains of Moab (1), rather than to the words once heard on Horeb. There is an echo of Moses' 'teaching' (4:1, 5) in the 'learning' now required of Israel (the same verb, *lmd*, is used of both). The law as understood in Deuteronomy is not simply prohibition, but precept, a training in right living.

2–3. With v. 2 the focus turns sharply to Horeb. Moses now includes himself in the memory, referring not to 'you', but to 'us'. The emphasis here, however, falls on 'the LORD our God', by virtue of its initial place in the sentence, to show that Moses' authority derives only from him, and from the covenant at Horeb. The expression is *kārat bᵉrît*, literally he 'cut a covenant', the standard OT expression. The term 'covenant' has various referents in Deuteronomy. We have met it as an oath to the patriarchs (4:31), where 'covenant' signifies essentially promise. That aspect of deuteronomic covenant gains further development in ch. 7. The term will be used in due course of the covenant at Moab, a kind of renewal of the one at Horeb (29:1[28:69]). The present chapter, however, is the main text for covenant as implying binding stipulations. In the deuteronomic concept the oath and the binding requirement are not at odds, but combined. This is achieved by the rhetorical structure of the book, in which this portrayal of the Horeb event has been carefully prepared for by the narrative of exodus and initiated conquest (chs. 1 – 4). The oath to the patriarchs is in the background of this section (see 6:3b), and the journey framework is also manifest at points (5:31 – 6:1).

If the role of Yahweh is highlighted in v. 2, the phrase 'with us' is also significant, and this is resumed and extended in v. 3. The insistence that this covenant was made 'not with your fathers' is surprising in view of what has just been said. The first issue here is the identity of the 'fathers'. We saw (above) that on the broadest canvas of the book the 'fathers' have been specified as the patriarchs, Abraham, Isaac and Jacob (see above on 1:8, and T. Römer 2000). These three are also in view in 6:3. An understanding of the 'fathers' here as the patriarchs would make sense: though they received the promise, they did not themselves enter into the covenant. However, it seems that the concept is used somewhat flexibly in the book. In some contexts it directs the audience to past generations generally, just as references to 'your children' direct it forward. In such cases it belongs to that strand of deuteronomic rhetoric that emphasizes the immediate responsibility of the present generation. This is one of those cases. The force of the command to the present (Moab) generation depends not on a contrast with the patriarchs, to whom the promise was first given, but rather on a contrast with the generation that actually stood at Horeb.

In this lies the effectiveness of the assertion that the Horeb covenant was made with 'all of us who are alive here today'. The concept is in stark contrast with the narrative in Deut. 1 – 3, which insists, in common with Num. 14:20–35, that the generation that stood at Sinai-Horeb would not enter the land, as punishment for its failure to take it at God's command in the first instance; only their children would see it (1:34–40). The word 'alive' occupies the stressed final position in the sentence, thus, if anything, exaggerating the contrast. Yet the author of this text is scarcely unaware of the memory contained in those passages. Rather, we have here the clearest expression in Deuteronomy of one of its main contentions, namely that Israel in all its generations stands in principle once again at Horeb, confronted with the covenant commands as if about to be given for the first time (see also on Deut. 4:9–14).

4–5. The speech of Yahweh to Israel is now recalled. On his speaking 'from the midst of the fire' (4) see above on 4:12. Here as in Deut. 4 (and more explicitly than in Exodus, e.g. 20:18) Yahweh is said to have spoken directly to Israel. This is now boldly affirmed by placing Israel 'face to face' with Yahweh. The statement is remarkable in view of the OT's hesitation elsewhere to allow the direct vision of God (see Exod. 33:20), and the concern in Exodus to shroud the presence of God in smoke (Exod. 19:18) and to stress Moses' mediatorial role. It is the more remarkable because in v. 4 there is a change from the inclusive 'we' of vv. 2–3 back to to the second-person (plural) address, so that the encounter with Israel as such is stressed. This then goes further than Exod. 33:11, where Moses' intimacy with God, in similar terms, is his particular privilege. In fact, it seems to do so quite deliberately.

This intimate vision is curiously undercut in the next verse, however, with its parenthetical reminder that Moses did in fact mediate between

Israel and Yahweh, for the reason given in Exodus, namely that Israel feared to hear God directly (Exod. 20:18). Verse 5 appears on the face of it to contradict v. 4, and indeed v. 22 (see below), and a late correction to the thought expressed in those places (Mayes 1979: 166; Mittmann 1975: 132). Two balancing points may be made, however. First, statements of the direct vision of God in the OT are mitigated in other places too (with Exod. 33:11; cf. Exod. 33:17–23; cf. Exod. 24:9–11, followed by 24:12–18). Secondly, Deuteronomy appears to maintain a balance between God's direct communication of the Decalogue to Israel and the need for Moses' mediation of the subsequent laws. The same tension appears in 5:22–27, where some explanation is offered (see below on those verses).

Finally, it is better to see the changes of person in these verses (1–5) as having a rhetorical purpose than to explain them as a string of afterthoughts and contradictions (*contra* Mittmann 1975: 132–133). There is a certain symmetry in the progression from the initial 'I–you' address (1) through 'we' (2–3), to 'you' (4), and back to 'I–you' (5). And this effectively highlights the important theological issues of the chapter at its outset (the immediacy of the present generation's responsibility, yet the crucial role of Moses, and hence of the Torah, in its mediation).

5:6–21

6. The Decalogue (see also remarks under 'Form and structure' for the special features of Deuteronomy's Decalogue) is not a universal 'pure' ethic, but is conditioned by its historical setting, namely Israel's deliverance from Egypt into a new kind of life and relationships. (Braulik [1986a: 49–50] explains all ten commands as expressions of this 'freedom'.) The law arises in the relationship with Yahweh. His recollection here of his deliverance of Israel has echoes of his decisive self-introduction to Moses before the events of exodus and Sinai (Exod. 3:12). The 'house of slavery' is literally 'house of slaves'. It might refer not only to the Israelites' particular condition there, but to the nature of the Egyptian state as, by its constitution, enslaving.

The point of this introduction is not merely to identify Yahweh, but precisely to establish a relationship between Israel's experience of deliverance and the obligations that would now be imposed. The juxtaposition of Egypt, 'the house of slaves', and the laws given by Yahweh, shows strikingly that this law will not be enslaving, because of the nature of its giver as a deliverer from slavery.

7. The traditional translation of v. 7 (the First Commandment) as 'you shall have no other gods before me' was misleading, because it suggested precedence in rank or importance. The phrase means literally 'upon my face', or, as translated here, 'in my Presence'. The command excludes the worship of other gods alongside Yahweh, since syncretism (the mixing of religions) was a feature of the biblical world. Israel would, from time to time, worship other gods, such as Baal, as well as Yahweh. The specific imagery of Yahweh's 'face' may be illustrated from an inscription found at Kuntillet 'Ajrud (or Horvat Teman), late ninth to early eighth centuries, in eastern Sinai, which refers to 'Yahweh and his Asherah' (see Hess 1991), reflecting a belief then in that place (or among its pilgrims) that Yahweh had a goddess consort, Asherah, just as the powerful Canaanite deities (El and Baal) had. It is possible that in certain unorthodox Yahweh sanctuaries images or cultic pillars were erected to both Yahweh and another god or gods/goddesses. This illustrates the force of 'in my Presence'; there could be no physical symbol of another deity in the sanctuary of Yahweh. The point is also illustrated by the story of the Philistine god Dagon, who could not endure the Presence of Yahweh, symbolized by the captured ark of the covenant, and whose image was toppled and broken by it (1 Sam. 5:1–5).

8–10. The Second Commandment forbids the making of any image (*pesel*, cf. 4:15–19). This goes a step further than the first command, because it is concerned not only with whom to worship, but with the manner of doing so. The 'image' that is forbidden here is specifically an image of God (or a god/goddess) – the command does not prohibit art as such, therefore – and might be made from wood, stone or metal (cf. 2 Kgs. 21:7; Jer. 10:14; Is. 40:19–20). It was common in the ancient world to depict gods and goddesses by using animal shapes. The bull is widespread in Canaanite iconography, but horse figurines also are known in Judah, and in Egypt a wide range of animals was used to represent deity. The command in v. 8 clearly aims at the whole gamut of animal representation resorted to by the religious imagination of its world (cf. 4:17–18). This includes human forms too, of course, and indeed a large number of anthropoid figurines have been excavated in Judah, mostly female, and with a concentration in the Jerusalem area. (See Introduction for the relationship of this to theories about the centralization of worship.)

The word translated here as 'form' seems to be somewhat abstract in its meaning ('image *of* any form'; contrast Exod. 20:4: '[no] image *or any* form'; see also 'Notes on the text'). The abstract nuance may be influenced by the use of the same word in 4:15 in connection with the appearance of Yahweh (even though, of course, he was *not* seen in that place). It may also serve the purpose, more pointedly than the Exodus phrase, of indicating all manner of representation of the deity. The same purpose underlies the tripartite description of the creation (8b).

Many of the figurines discovered in Judah show evidence of having been deliberately destroyed, perhaps in Josiah's reform, and therefore reflecting Deuteronomy's hostility to images (Ben-Tor 1992: 361–362).

The commandment goes on to make clear that Yahweh will regard any worship of images as by definition false, a turning away from him. The first two commands thus prove to be closely related: any 'image' of a deity is in the nature of the case falsely 'in Yahweh's Presence'. The concept of his 'jealousy' now expresses his intolerance of such worship. The adjective *qannā'* occurs only six times in the OT (Exod. 20:5; 34:14 [2×]; Deut. 4:24; 5:9), five of them in the phrase *'ēl qannā'*, 'a jealous God', and the other in a combination with 'Yahweh' (Exod. 34:14). It clusters, therefore, around forms of the Decalogue and related texts, and indeed in connection with the fundamental embargo on the worship of rival gods. Jealousy in the OT is an active quality, a passionate loyalty, best illustrated among human beings by Phineas, the instrument of God's wrath against idolaters among his people (Num. 25), and turned by God himself into judgment for the same sin of unfaithfulness (Deut. 32:21).

This fundamental command is accompanied by a specific threat. The meaning of the punishment 'as far as the third and fourth generations' has been taken to mean that God's wrath actually falls on the three following generations because of the sin of the idolater. The story of the condemnation of Achan's whole family for his trespass on the things dedicated to God (Josh. 7) should probably not be used to interpret this command, however, since it belongs specifically to the realm of the 'ban' (see on 2:34), and implies that the family members were all directly affected by the mishandling of those holy things. Other biblical passages expressly repudiate the unjust victimization of the son for the sin of the father (Deut. 24:16; Ezek 18). The closest approximation to the principle of an extended, and thus undeserved, retribution comes in the books of Kings, where God's judgment falls on Judah in spite of Josiah's reform and because of the sins of his grandfather, Manasseh (2 Kgs. 23:26–27). Even there, however, the fate decreed for Judah gains confirmation in the evil of the kings who followed Josiah, so that those who fell to Babylon are shown to have actually participated in the guilt. There is therefore no clear biblical example of a punishment deliberately exacted because of the sins of a previous generation. The best understanding of the statement in the present verse is, then, that the idolater's sin will have effects that will rebound upon ensuing generations; and perhaps even that he himself, though he live to see the fourth generation (the presumed upper limit of a lifespan), will never be free from the consequences of his deeds. The context of multi-generational households should be borne in mind, since the fortunes of the individual and the group would hang together to a greater extent than in modern western societies. The counterpart in v. 10 ('thousands of those who love me and keep my commands') assumes that those who enjoy God's 'faithful love' do so because of their own righteousness. 'Faithful love' here stands for the well-known Hebrew word *ḥeseḏ*, often 'steadfast love', that is, God's faithfulness to his covenant commitment, the primary and essential quality of the covenant relationship. The imbalance between the fourth generation and 'a thousand generations' is a striking affirmation that mercy finally outweighs judgment. This is expressed further in Deut. 7:9, in the context of

Yahweh's choice of Israel and his attachment to them into an indefinite future.

11. The Third Commandment continues to develop the prohibition of false worship. The plain meaning of the word *šāw* is emptiness, or falseness (cf. v. 20, concerning 'false witness'; and Is. 59:4, where it parallels *tōhû*, 'emptiness'). 'Lifting up the name of Yahweh to emptiness' (to translate the phrase literally) probably means using it in the context of the worship of other gods, or perhaps simply in a false, manipulative way. A sanction is attached here too. 'The LORD will not regard ... as innocent' is a curious negative, but appropriate perhaps to the false quest for security (or 'innocence') that characterizes the calculating worshipper. (For a similar juxtaposition of words and ideas see Ps. 24:3-4, where the context is true worship, and the qualification is innocence, qualified as 'not lifting up *one's soul* to emptiness'.)

12-15. The Fourth Commandment, concerning the Sabbath day, is treated like a festival to be 'observed' (see 'Form and structure'). This is in line with the strong association here between Sabbath observance and deliverance from Egypt into the promised land. It is in contrast to the motivation for keeping the command in Exodus, which bases it on God's rest following the six days of creation (Exod. 20:11; see 'Form and structure'). The Sabbath command heads the festival calendar in Lev. 23 (Lev. 23:3), and establishes a pattern for the feasts (23:24, 32, 36, 39). And the theology of exodus and occupation of land informs the whole calendar (23:10, 42-43). The Sabbath idea further undergirds the institution of Jubilee (Lev. 25; note the Sabbath *year*, 25:4), which is based on the concept of freedom (25:10), understood as a restoration of the whole society to its ideal condition as a community established by the saving act of God into justice and blessing. The Sabbath command in Deuteronomy also enshrines such a concept of society. We have observed ('Form and structure') that it insists, more than does the book of Exodus, on the inclusion of all Israelites in the Sabbath 'rest'. It thus participates in Deuteronomy's memory of Egypt and its 'eschatological' thrust towards the ideal of a society enjoying freedom under the rule of God.

The basis of the deuteronomic command in the exodus ('slave in Egypt' recalling v. 6) does not negate or invalidate the basis of the command in creation in the book of Exodus (20:11); rather, Deuteronomy twice expressly recalls that the command is already known, presumably from that book. Its new interpretation represents an extension of the potential significance of the law.

16. The Fifth Commandment moves into the realm of the social order. Respect for parents includes the obedience of children, the most obvious modern inference from this command. In Israel, however, the requirement of obedience lasted beyond childhood, to the point where young people had to answer for their failings in this regard before the representatives of the whole community (Deut. 21:18-21). Honouring parents extended to the sort of lifelong respect accorded to father and mother that is evident in a number of OT narratives, such as the Genesis narratives about Jacob and Joseph (even if this respect was sometimes honoured in the breach, Gen. 27!). Probably it ultimately involved caring for parents into old age, when the parents were no longer economically active themselves, as may be inferred from Jesus' interpretation of the command in Mark 7:10–13. Such honouring was symbolic of respect for the whole social organization. Descriptions of the social hierarchy in Israel begin with the smallest unit, the *bêt-'āb*, or 'house of the father', move up to the *mišpāḥâ*, or kinship group, a clustering of families in an area or a group of villages, and culminate with the tribe (de Vaux 1961: 3–9; see also Josh. 7:14–18). The integration of the family into the larger social – and thus legal – entity is sharply illustrated by the movement from parental to civic authority in 21:18–21. The close connection between these spheres of authority explains why some writers, who think the commands in the Decalogue are expanded systematically in the further legislation in Deuteronomy, see the counterpart of this command in the administrative laws of 16:18 – 18:22 (Braulik 1993; Kaufman 1978–9; see above on 'Form and structure').

17. The elaborated commands in the first part of the Decalogue now give way to a series of short prohibitions (17–21), joined, as we noted, by 'and', thus conveying a sense of coherent consequentiality, and building up a total picture of the standards to be observed in the covenant community. The killing outlawed here is murder. The term used, *rāṣaḥ*, has a broader range than murder, and can include accidental killing (cf. 19:4; Num. 35:11). It always refers to the killing of one human being by another (or others), and is not used in judicial or military contexts. It is best to translate it 'murder', therefore, since judicial and military killing is not in view, and accidental killing cannot be meant, in the nature of the case (Zimmerli 1978: 134–135). The command corresponds to a concern to promote the life and well-being of other members of the covenant community, as its ramifications in the code (e.g. 22:1–4) make plain.

18. The law against adultery addresses not only sexual relations between people married to others, but also extramarital relations, rape and prohibited unions (22:9–30). Its orientation, according to the conventions of its time and place, is masculine: adultery seems to be primarily an offence committed by a man with another man's wife (22:22), although both are held responsible and pay the penalty. A woman, furthermore, is more vulnerable to legal process than a man because of her need to protect her virginity (22:13–19). However, this command too may be turned from a simple prohibition into a concern for the well-being of the other. It has close affinities with the Fifth Commandment (honouring parents) and is informed by a concern to maintain the social fabric.

19. The seriousness of the offence of theft must be understood in the context of a poor society, where property is both limited and a necessary means to survival. This prohibition too has its obverse in the requirement laid on people to protect the property of others (22:1–4). Its elaborations in the code show that its concern is not a doctrine of the sanctity of private property, but rather that the substance of the economy should be used responsibly for the good of the whole community (23:19–20, 24–25; 24:10–15, 19–22). The right of the individual, or family unit, to possess the means of their livelihood is a part of that concern.

20. The Ninth Commandment illustrates clearly that the Decalogue aims at sustaining the life of the community. It is not a direct and general prohibition of lying, but concerns false charges brought against one's 'neighbour', that is, another member of the covenant comunity. By the same token, this command shows that the Decalogue as a whole has a connection with the legal system. Its standards imply not only the need to develop a sophisticated statute book, such as the deuteronomic code itself, but also the means of investigation and enforcement (best illustrated in 19:4–13), which in turn require integrity and trustworthiness in the whole community. This command, therefore, is an essential part of the whole structure of the legal-ethical system. False charges brought in court may relate, of course, to any of the offences so far dealt with, and thus threaten the accused with extreme penalties, including death. (The OT has an account of the murderous intent that might motivate false charges: the story of Naboth, 2 Kgs. 21.) In the code, the safety of evidence is protected by the need to have more than one witness (17:6; 19:15), by the psychologically potent requirement that, after a person's conviction of a capital offence, the witnesses initiate the punishment (17:7), and by the subjection of false witnesses to the penalty appropriate to the crime of which they accused another (19:16–21) – the context, in Deuteronomy, of the 'law of talion'.

21. The Tenth Commandment is like the Ninth in that it embraces a number of the foregoing, and, even more than the Ninth, operates at the level of the desire of the heart. The wrong desire to have another's wife or property may easily be a prelude to adultery, theft or murder. This command shows that the Decalogue is not itself statute pure and simple, since the sin of 'coveting', though it may be guessed at by others, can hardly lead directly to conviction in court. It has something in common, therefore, with the 'love' commandment (Lev. 19:18b), and indeed with the great ethical texts of the OT, such as Job 31. It has been linked interestingly to the law of levirate marriage (25:5–10; see above on Kaufman and Braulik), which exposes the selfish motive, and which attracts no legal penalty, only popular disgust.

The command in Deuteronomy differs from that in Exodus by putting the desire to have a married woman in pride of place, and using a different word for this (ḥāmad) from that which is used for other objects of false desire ('iwwâ; ḥāmad is used throughout in the Exodus form). This word (*ḥāmad*) often connotes a strong, craving desire that leads quickly to wrong action (Deut. 7:25; Josh. 7:21); in at least one other place the desire is sexual (Prov. 6:25). Deuteronomy's distinction between the married woman and other objects of desire is in line with its tendency to show concern for the standing and the rights of women. The other verb (in its hithpael, or reflexive, form) can also imply a strong desire. The selection of two different verbs is probably not to be explained by different degrees of intensity, but by the intention to mark out the adulterous desire as different in kind.

5:22–33

The background passage in Exodus is Exod. 19:18–21. The issue in both these texts is the people's need of a mediator between them and God because of the danger to them of experiencing God's presence directly. In Exodus, Moses takes the role of mediator from the start. He alone penetrates the smoke that envelops the mountain, protecting the people from the vision of God. And the impression is that God also *speaks* to Moses alone (God answers *Moses* in thunder, 19:19). How far the people actually see and hear what passes between God and Moses remains slightly obscure in Exod. 20:18, where the literal reading of MT is somewhat illogical, namely that they 'see' the thunder and lightning and the sound of the trumpet. (SamP rationalizes this, spelling out that the people 'heard' the thunder and 'saw' the lightning.) We may surmise that the people actually hear the Ten Commandments (from the fact that Moses has descended the mountain at 19:25, and that he appears expressly as a mediator of God's words to the people for the first time at 21:1). But Exodus is not explicit on this, and we might deduce the opposite from 20:19, which could be taken to include the Decalogue in that which the people do not want to hear.

22. In Deuteronomy, in contrast, all is specified. Central to its picture is the pronouncement of the Decalogue before the whole 'assembly'. This term is important in the context. It is the whole community of Israel, gathered for worship; that is, in its most characteristic expression as the people of God standing in his presence. It appears six times in Deut. 23, in a passage that defines who in practice may be counted as members of this people so defined. But it is this present gathering that constitutes the 'assembly' *par excellence*, and other texts refer back to the occasion simply as 'the day of the assembly' (9:10; 10:4; 18:16). This implies that it was a defining moment in Israel's becoming God's people. (Exodus knows this too, but handles it differently, with its account of the covenantal ceremony in Exod. 24, absent from Deuteronomy; conversely, Exodus has no equivalent of Deuteronomy's use of *qāhāl* in the sense found here.) Deuteronomy's picture has the effect of showing that the whole people is directly involved in the reception of the Decalogue as the basic conditions of the covenant.

23–26. It is the 'assembly', therefore, that confesses, 'we have heard his voice from the fire' (24; cf. 4:11–12). There is a bolder statement than in Exodus of what they have seen, namely 'his glory and greatness' (24). A clear distinction is then made between this universal hearing of the Decalogue and the further laws that follow. The clean break between the two categories of God's speech is signalled by the phrase 'then he said [or added] no more' (22, recalling 4:2). The shift from the obscurity in Exodus to the clarity in Deuteronomy is facilitated by the use of the word *qôl* in both places, in the former meaning 'thunder' (19:19; 20:18), but here neatly adapted to its common sense of 'voice' (23).

There is a further development of the whole people's direct exposure to God's presence in v. 24, with its exclamation that they have 'seen God speak with man, and he has lived' (cf. v. 26). This is a variation on the well-known theme in the OT that the vision of God brings death, which finds its most direct statement in Exod. 33:20, where God responds to Moses' request to show him his 'glory' (33:18). The basic elements of that statement ('man ... see ... God ... live') are all present in Deut. 5:24, but in such a way as not to oppose it directly: they have seen not *God* but only *that God has spoken*. In this way the text remains faithful to its concept that God has revealed himself to the people in *word*. Nevertheless, even this encounter with God is close enough to the aweful vision to inspire fear in the people and their wish to avoid further exposure to the danger. This explains the apparent *non sequitur* between v. 24 and v. 25 ('we have seen God speak ... and ... lived', followed by 'now, why should we die!'), and the connection is spelt out in v. 26. Verses 23–26 are thus an elaborated version of vv. 4–5. The longer passage can be read as an explanation of the tension in those verses (which we noticed above).

27. The conclusion of the logic of vv. 23–26 is the request that Moses himself should hear God's further words on their behalf (27). The distinction between the Decalogue and the laws still to be given is again maintained, in this case by the use of the imperfects *yo'mār*, 'will say', and *yᵉdabbēr*, 'will tell' (translated here 'tells'). In that context the people commit themselves to keeping the covenant, in a declaration that is parallel to Exod. 19:8; 24:3, 7 in that more extended report of the actual covenant ceremony.

5:28–33

28–30. The people's words are now met by a response from Yahweh. He acknowledges their commitment (28, without a parallel in Exodus), which interestingly attributes 'speech' to Israel (five occurrences of *dābār* or *dibber*), and 'hearing' (twice) to Yahweh, in a neat inversion of the more usual pattern, specifically in vv. 22–27. In this way a mutuality in the covenant relationship is signified. The command that they should 'return to their tents' has an echo in the law code at 16:7, with an implication that the law is effective for Israel not only when gathered at the place of worship but in all its life (see 'Comment' there).

31. The solemn ratification continues with a resumption of the concern that the people's obedience should continue into the future, permanently; a concern that is closely linked in ch. 4 (as here) to the themes of the encounter at Horeb and the teaching of the commandments (4:9, 40). Obedience to the covenant is focused on the laws that Moses would teach, here called 'the commandment(s), laws and statutes' (31). The first of these three (strictly a singular) is here added to the pair that is already familiar from 4:1; 5:1 (see on those passages); the trio occurs again at 6:1; 7:11. In 6:1 the singular *miṣwâ*, 'command(ment)', stands in apposition to 'the laws and statutes'. According to this text, therefore, it is a way of referring to the whole teaching of Moses. This indeed is the most common usage of the singular *miṣwâ* in Deuteronomy (the plural 'command(ment)s' is more frequent; on two occasions the singular refers to a specific law, viz. 15:15; 31:5). The common usage of the singular occurs a number of times in the phrase (with variations): 'this (entire) commandment that I command you this day' (see 6:25; 8:1; 11:8, 22; 17:20; 19:9; 27:1; 30:11). The connection with 'today' shows that the term has essentially the same meaning as 'laws and statutes', that is, it refers to Moses' teaching in its entirety, and not strictly to the Decalogue.

The present verse (31; cf. 7:11) differs from the pattern in 6:1 because it inserts 'and' between 'the command' and 'the laws and statutes', suggesting not apposition, but that the 'command' and 'the laws and statutes' refer to different things. SamP has a different reading from MT, both here and at 7:11 (see 'Notes on the text'), conforming the phrase to 6:1, and this may be the best solution. (N. Lohfink [1989] thinks there is a development within Deuteronomy in the meaning of 'laws and statutes', so that it ultimately refers only to Deut. 12 – 26. In my view this involves a reconstruction of the textual history which is not convincing; see my response in McConville & Millar 1994: 126–127.)

32–33. Only in these last two verses does Moses now return to the direct speech to the people with which the chapter opened (5:1), and exhort them to obey the commands that have been given. The logical sequel to v. 31 has been found in 6:1 (Mayes 1979: 174). Verses 32–33 have been thought intrusive because they assume that the law has already been given. However, they may be seen as an anticipatory exhortation that provisionally brings to a close the section dealing directly with the Decalogue. The idea of 'deviating' or turning aside occurs in Deuteronomy in different senses (cf. 2:27; 11:16). Here and in a few other cases it denotes obedience to the Torah (17:11, 20; 28:14; cf. Josh. 1:7; 23:6; 2 Kgs. 22:2). The preponderance of important covenantal texts in this list suggests that the phrase is used to express obedience in a summarizing way, to denote complete obedience. Finally, the topics of life, long life, and the good of the land return in a great accumulation (33) as the consequence of obedience. The rhetorical effect of these two verses suggests that a unit is thus rounded off (cf. the theme of 'life' in 4:1, 26, 40; 5:3). The Decalogue is given, its ongoing role in the community assured by Moses' mediation, and the whole is concluded with a strong exhortation.

Explanation

With ch. 5 Deuteronomy turns to its main account of its central event. The links with the preliminary narrative are crucial, for by now it has been established that Israel receives its charter for life from the God who has brought them from slavery and promises to bring them into a land of freedom. Covenant here receives specific content (though it will be subject to change and development, as the further laws will show). Yet as law it has freedom at its heart, a point well illustrated by the memories of slavery in vv. 6, 15. There is even a kind of 'eschatological' thrust in this portrayal – further realized in laws such as those in Deut. 15 (which makes a contribution to the emancipation of women, as the Sabbath law does here). With this eschatological perspective the covenant of Yahweh with Israel is seen to be related to the theology of creation. (Birch et al. [1999: 116] have made this point well in showing that the story of the conflict with Pharaoh at the exodus is about the restoration of creation order out of the 'chaos' of the kind of rule exercised in Egypt.) When the Decalogue is read in this light, legalistic and pedantic interpretations of it can be avoided.

The Decalogue is firmly set within the life of ancient Israel. Even the small differences from the Exodus version show that in principle it requires reflection and reapplication. Religiously, it belongs to a world in which polytheism and the worship of idols are the norm. Its commands concerning family relationships make social assumptions quite different from those of the modern West, and it has a relationship with the practice of law in Israel, perhaps as a kind of 'basic law' that provides a rationale for statute and process as exemplified in the deuteronomic code. For these reasons it is not a 'pure' or universal ethic.

This does not mean that it is irrelevant to the modern world. On the contrary, its location in a 'real world' fits it to speak to all manner of 'real worlds'. Its 'religious' commands, which initiate the whole, teach that right behaviour cannot be isolated from right thinking about the nature of the universe, and from the character and sovereignty of God. Modern idolatry (at least in the West) is more likely to take the form of a dichotomy between God and the empirical world when it comes to ethical and political decision-making, than to carve images from wood or stone. The exclusion of God includes the 'privatizing' of religion and a practical belief in the autonomy of natural and physical laws. His displacement from science, art and public life, with the associated claim to the autonomy of human reason, may be a modern form of having 'other gods in his Presence', or indeed of 'taking his name in vain'.

The first four Commandments give rise to controversies still. Many Protestants have felt that the use of the icon in other traditions infringes the Second Commandment's ban on images. Yet there has been rapprochement between some Orthodox and evangelical Christians that might not have been expected a generation ago. We have seen that the context of the original prohibition of images was polytheistic, and the theological debates between the OT and Canaan are of a different sort from modern debates about the representation of God. The essence of the ban on images seems to be to avoid the idea that God can be manipulated or in any sense made subject to the processes of history; and this is a bigger issue than the question of icons.

The Sabbath command has a well-established place in Christian practice, with the transference of the idea of the 'Sabbath' to Sunday, the 'first day of the week'. The earliest Christians may have worshipped on both days. Within the Decalogue, the Sabbath represents that whole side of Israel's life that corresponds to what has been called the 'ceremonial' law, that is, the feasts and sacrifices. As Christian theology regards sacrifice as redundant in view of the atonement of Christ (letter to the Hebrews), the Sabbath may be regarded in the same way. 'The Son of Man is Lord even of the Sabbath' (Mark 2:28); and 'Sabbaths', for Paul, are but a shadow of what is to come (Col. 2:16–17). While the Christian Sunday should be regarded as a gift of God's providence to a world in need of rest and the opportunity to worship, its observance is not strictly that of the 'Sabbath'. The principle of acknowledging the primacy of God in human life cannot be satisfied by the Sunday gathering alone. In particular, the relationship between Sabbath and 'Jubilee' is fruitful, especially at the dawn of a millennium. The heart of the Sabbath is to acknowledge a profound relationship between religion and the social order; there can be no Sabbath-keeping that endures any kind of oppression of the poor and weak (cf. Amos 8:5–6). And the eschatological connotations of the Sabbath are closely related to this: the idea of a 'rest' that still remains for the people of God is taken up by Hebrews (Heb. 4:1). In this perspective lies a reconciliation of the twin foundations of the Sabbath command in creation and covenant.

The latter six commands were seen to be rooted in time and place also. However, they deal with topics that have applications to modern societies too. Honouring parents (especially older parents) must take different forms in days when, even compared with a few generations ago, patterns of family life have changed rapidly (because of social mobility, for example, or because both young married partners work outside the home). Yet the concept of a connection between God, the family and the social fabric may still be maintained, though it requires careful nuancing. Institutionalized care for the elderly may be necessary in many cases, and can be the best way for some people to provide for older relatives. But it can also become a poor substitute for filial duty. The prohibitions of murder, adultery and theft had, as we saw, positive correlatives in respecting and promoting the well-being of others. Laws may be seen as minimal requirements, while the spirit behind them counsels much more (Wenham 2000: 79–80). The ruthless ambition that ruins the hopes of others, the sly affair, the unscrupulous deal or dishonesty in accounting, the malicious rumour – all fall under the shadow of the Decalogue's brief commands. The final command stands over them all, showing that their orientation is away from self-gratification and towards the fulfilment of others. The Decalogue, in the context of Deuteronomy's programme for life in the land, has everything that could be developed into the most sublime ethical vision, as we have it above all in Jesus' Sermon on the Mount (Matt. 5 – 7). The Decalogue's specific historical setting and character do not condemn it to irrelevance, but are consistent with the idea of the laws and constitution of Israel as a 'paradigm' (C. J. H. Wright 1990) capable of reapplication in ever new forms in many societies.

The establishment in this chapter of the immediate relationship of each new generation to God in covenant relates to our understanding of how the Decalogue may be used theologically. The Horeb event retains its unique status in Deuteronomy as constitutive of the covenant, yet at the same time it is capable of re-realization. And the point applies not just to the Moab generation, but rather to all. As the relationship between Horeb and Moab gains its fuller development in Deuteronomy (notably in chs. 29 – 31), it becomes clearer how this is so. Moses the mediator dies before Israel enters the land, and his role of mediating the words of God is formally enshrined in the written Torah, kept by the ark of the covenant and read every seven years at the Feast of Tabernacles (31:9–13, 24–26). In this model is a warrant not only for passing on a tradition but also for teaching and interpretation. The apparent conflict in Deut. 5:4–5 arises, therefore, from the need to hold important things together: the direct responsibility of each generation to keep covenant with God, and the need to keep understanding the changing ways in which Torah can guide and regulate the life of his people. That guidance must take the form, if it is true to its source, of a concern to bring the people of God into genuine liberty, by a full commitment to the good of the other and of all; and in doing so to offer the world an example of the nature of the divine will for ordering the whole creation.

DEUTERONOMY 6:1–25

Translation

[1]Now this is the commandment, that is, the laws and statutes that the LORD your God instructed me to teach you to keep in the land you are crossing over to occupy. [2]They are given so that all your life you and your children, and their children, may fear the LORD your God, and keep all his statutes and commands with which I am charging you, and thus have long life. [3]Hear, then, Israel, and be careful to keep them, so that you may enjoy well-being and grow in number, as the LORD the God of your forefathers promised you, in a land flowing with milk and honey.

[4]Hear, Israel! The LORD our God, the LORD is one. [5]You must love the LORD your God with all your heart, all your being, all your strength. [6]And these instructions I am giving you today you must know by heart, [7]and school your children in them. You shall speak of them whether you are sitting at home or out on a journey, when you go to bed and when you get up. [8]Tie them on your hands as a sign, and as frontlets on your forehead; [9]write them on your doorposts and on your gates.

[10]When the LORD your God brings you into the land he swore to your forefathers Abraham, Isaac and Jacob that he would give you, a land of fine, large cities that you did not build, [11]houses full of all kinds of wealth that you did not supply, cisterns hollowed out that you did not cut, and vineyards and olive-groves that you did not plant, and when you eat your fill, [12]then be careful not to forget the LORD, who brought you out of slavery in the land of Egypt. [13]It is the LORD your God whom you must revere and worship, and by whose name you must swear. [14]You must not go off to other gods, gods of the nations around you. [15]For the LORD your God who is among you is a jealous God, and the anger of the LORD your God would so rage against you that he would sweep you off the face of the land. [16]Do not put the LORD your God to the test as you did at Massah. [17]Be very sure to keep the commands of the LORD your God, and his precepts and statutes, which he has commanded you. [18]Do whatever is just and good in the LORD's sight; so it will go well with you, and you will come and possess the good land, fulfilling the LORD's sworn promise to your forefathers; [19]and you will drive out your enemies before you – as the LORD also promised.

[20]When in days to come your son asks: 'What is the meaning of the precepts, statutes and laws the LORD our God commanded you?' [21]you are to say to him: 'We were slaves of Pharaoh in Egypt, until the LORD brought us out of Egypt with a strong hand; [22]the LORD performed signs and great and terrible deeds, and brought plagues on Egypt, and on Pharaoh and his household, before our eyes. [23]He brought us out of there, in order to bring us to this land and give it to us, fulfilling his sworn promise to our forefathers. [24]The LORD commanded us to keep all these laws and fear the LORD our God, so that we might have well-being all the days of our lives, just as today. [25]And we shall be held righteous, if we are careful to keep all these commands before the LORD our God, according to his command.'

Notes on the text

1. See note on 5:31. MT is preferred here to the forms with 'and' in LXX, Syr and QL.

3. 'in a land flowing . . . ' Hebr. lacks 'in'; LXX consequently takes 'land' as the object of 'promised to give' (hence 'as the LORD . . . promised to give you a land'). But this strains the conjunction *ka'ᵃšer* (which is usually 'as' = 'according as'). The solutions are either to supply *bᵉ*, 'in', or to take the last phrase as an accusative of place (Weinfeld 1991; cf. GKC 118g).

4. 'Hear, Israel! The LORD our God, the LORD is one.' For this translation see Moberly 1990; the response by Veijola [1992]; and Moberly's further note in 1999: 125. And see 'Comment' below.

8. *ṭōṭāpōt*, 'frontlet', is found only here, at 11:18 and Exod. 13:16. The derivation of the word is obscure. It is translated with *tᵉpillîn* ('phylacteries') in the Targums.

24. *ṭôḇ* may be a verb here (cf. on 5:33), in this case an inf. construct (so Weinfeld 1991: 336).

'just as today': the form is *kᵉhayyôm*, not the more usual *kayyôm* with assimilated def. art. The distinct forms are noted in GKC 35n., but both forms are combined with *hazzeh* in Deuteronomy, and mean the same thing.

Form and structure

Together with ch. 5, ch. 6 forms a unified argument (see 'Form and structure' on ch. 5, and N. Lohfink 1963: 290–291). Conceptually, the two chapters are linked by the idea of extending the laws given on Horeb into the regular lives of the people into future generations.

Verses 1–3 were at one time seen as one form of introduction to the law code, couched partly in the plural. They are now more often taken closely with 5:27–33 and as the culmination of the discourse immediately following the Decalogue (Weinfeld 1991: 327). This view has been supported by stylistic analysis (N. Lohfink 1963: 66–68). Lohfink shows that there is no 'join' between chs. 5 and 6; rather, 'one must speak of a single, conscious formation of the whole text' (1963: 151; my translation; cf. Christensen 1991: 133–135). Key verbs in 5:27–31 and 6:1–3 (hear, do, fear, keep, teach, do) are organized palinstrophically (that is, in an extended chiasmus), with 5:32–33 as the centre of the pattern, highlighting the Mosaic role in teaching the word of Yahweh, and the relationship between Israel's obedience and its long duration in the land. This pattern also shows that the structure of the discourse overrides variations between singular and plural address, (1, pl.; 2–3, sg.). Further, the same progression of thought ('the LORD commanded . . . I command', 1–2) is present here as in the Decalogue discourse (5:22–27; cf. Braulik 1986a: 54).

Even so, the passage has wider connections. Its 'Hear ... Israel' (3) recalls the same phrase in 5:1. Its foreshadowing of future life in the land ('keep all his statutes ... and thus have long life', v. 2) moves the thought of 5:3 forward ('all of us who are alive here today', i.e. the Horeb generation) in a way that is consistent with the basic structure of the argument in these two chapters. The 'Hear ... Israel' also makes a transition to the next phase of the larger section 5:1 – 6:25, namely 6:4–25, because of the repetition of that phrase in 6:4. The shift to singular address in vv. 2–3 continues in v. 4.

Deut. 6:4 is sometimes seen as the paranetic introduction to the law code, the original introduction being at 4:45 (Mayes 1979: 176; cf. above on 4:44–45). Deut. 6:4 is new in the sense that it marks the beginning of the words that Moses has hitherto been introducing. However, the substance of the verses that follow continues from the Decalogue address, having at its heart the primary command to be loyal to Yahweh alone. Its extension from this into obedience to all commands of Yahweh reflects the logic of the Decalogue discourse. N. Lohfink (1963: 158) notes parallels between 6:12, 14, 15 and 5:6, 7, 9 respectively; and even finds that the *Hauptgebot* (i.e. the fundamental law commanding worship of Yahweh alone) and the laws conceived as a totality are interchangeable.

The heart of the exhortation (4–19) pictures life in the land stretching into the future, and its relation to covenant faithfulness. Within this passage, vv. 4–9 are a fundamental command to keep faith with Yahweh in this and future generations; vv. 10–15 develop this with an exhortation not to 'forget' Yahweh, after experiencing his bounty (cf. 8:11–19), and vv. 16–19 reflect the shift from the basic demand for loyalty to the obligation to keep the commands in general, in an echo of 5:32–33. The last section, vv. 20–25, returns to the theme of teaching/learning, which has been developed since 5:1 (Yahweh tells Moses what he must teach the people; they then teach subsequent generations, 5:1, 31; 6:1; cf. 4:5). The teaching of children is resumed specifically from 6:7 (cf. 6:2; 4:9). The words 'in days to come' (20) also contrast with 'today' in 5:3; and the conditions for continued 'life' in the land (24) make a similar connection, this time by way of an echo of 6:2.

At two points in this section there are links with Exod. 13, namely at v. 8 (Exod. 13:9, 16) and vv. 20–21 (Exod. 13:14). The context is the teaching of children and the significance of ongoing practices in terms of the exodus from Egypt. Deuteronomy sets this instruction in the context of commandment-keeping, rather than of the dedication of the firstborn (as in Exodus).

Comment

6:1–3

The opening expression, 'This is the commandment' (1), is singular, with the following 'laws and statutes' in apposition (cf. on 5:31 and 'Notes on the text' both there and above). The phrase as a whole refers to the body of Mosaic teaching that is shortly to be given, and that is to be taught and to have validity for the life of the people in the land. As Yahweh commanded Moses to teach the laws, so now he commands the people to keep them in perpetuity. The transition from plural to singular address in v. 2 has the effect of picturing the people as a whole. The words 'all your life' (2) therefore convey primarily the life of the whole people, continuing over generations. If the lifelong faithfulness on the part of individuals also is implied, this is secondary here. Verse 3 brings together a pair of similar-sounding key words in the paranesis, 'hear' and 'keep' (*šāmaʿ* and *šāmar*), suggesting careful, sustained obedience. The long life in the land and the many descendants who will result again refer to the whole nation in all its generations, and hark back to the promise to Abraham of land and offspring (Gen. 12:1–3; see on 1:8). For the 'land flowing with milk and honey' compare Exod. 3:17, there also closely associated with the patriarchal promise. Promise and command are tightly interwoven here.

Indeed, the ethical dynamic of Deuteronomy is illustrated in these verses. The possession of the land is a given; Israel is going over to possess it (in the 'deep structure' of this statement they are going over because Yahweh is taking them, according to the patriarchal oath). That being so, Moses teaches the people to keep the commands (1) *so that* they may fear Yahweh and keep his commands, *so that* they may have long life in the land (2), with a similar extension in v. 3. This progression is not strictly logical, yet it is central to the thought of Deuteronomy.

6:4–9

4. The famous 'Shema' ('Hear, Israel! The LORD our God, the LORD is one') is an elusive construction in Hebrew, because it consists of a small number of words whose interrelationships are not explicit. The confession of faith in Hebrew is *yhwh ᵉlōhênû yhwh ʾeḥād*, lit. 'the LORD our God the LORD one'. It is possible to render each of the two phrases here either with or without the verb 'is', or indeed to provide the verb between the two clauses. There are therefore the following four possible translations. 1. 'The LORD is our God, the LORD alone' (or, 'Our God is the LORD, the LORD alone', Miller 1990: 98). 2. 'The LORD our God, the LORD is one.' 3. 'The LORD is our God, the LORD is one.' 4. 'The LORD our God is one LORD' (see NIV and mg.). LXX reads *kyrios ho theos hēmōn kyrios heis estin*, which underlies NT (Mark 12:29). This can be translated by the traditional English AV (4. above), or by 2. above (as adopted by more recent translations: NIV, NRSV; cf. Craigie 1976a: 168 n. 8). In terms of Hebrew syntax, however, option 4. seems least likely because it involves qualifying a proper name with an attributive adjective. The oddness of this is clearer if we read it as 'Yahweh our God is one Yahweh'. This is obscured in Greek because *kyrios* is a common noun.

Between the other renderings the chief difference concerns whether to translate *'eḥad* as an adjective, 'one', or an 'adverb', 'alone'. Both of these make good sense. Deuteronomy plainly requires the worship of Yahweh *alone*. This is part of the force of the Decalogue, and it is developed both in the present chapter (13–15) and in ch. 7. Israel's covenant with Yahweh entails having no other gods. It is debatable whether Deuteronomy is 'monotheistic' in a theoretical sense. Yet the confession may rightly be seen as implying monotheism, in common with other developments of the First Commandment of the Decalogue both in Deuteronomy and in the prophets (Deut. 32:39; Zech 14:9; Is. 43:11; 44:6, 8; 45:5–6, 18, 21–22; 46:9; cf. Mark 12:32). The important primary point, however, is that the covenant makes the relationship between Yahweh and Israel exclusive. The immediate consequence of the declaration of oneness is the command: 'Love the LORD your God' (5). This is the language of covenant loyalty (Moran 1963a). Set against the history of Israel in its land it prohibits the pragmatic worship of several gods at once, or any kind of syncretism. But it is not a simple numerical point; it declares that Yahweh alone is worthy of covenant love (cf. Moberly 1999: 132).

However, the phrasing of the confession seems to imply more than this. It differs from the First Commandment (Deut. 5:7) in that the emphasis falls heavily on the word 'one', in its final climactic position – so much so that it has even been suggested (though it has not been widely followed) that the word *'eḥad* may be another name for Yahweh; 'Yahweh is "ONE"' (C. H. Gordon 1970). The effect of this is to suggest that 'oneness' is in some sense part of Yahweh's nature. The nuance shifts therefore from 'uniqueness' to 'unity', or integrity. Yahweh is one and indivisible. This may have been intended to prohibit the worship of Yahweh in a variety of manifestations, like Baal (1 Sam. 7:4; S. R. Driver 1895: 90), or even at a variety of places (von Rad 1966: 63), though this last is too much influenced by the belief that Deuteronomy centralizes worship in Jerusalem. The integrity of Yahweh is better understood, however, according to the development of the present chapter, that is, in terms of his power to deliver Israel, his entitlement to their obedience and his capacity to bless them in the land he will give. Zech. 14:9, which is best translated, 'Yahweh will be one, and his name shall be one' (cf. NRSV, against NIV), projects the same message on to an eschatological canvas, involving the recognition of all the nations.

5. The command to love the LORD 'with all your heart, all your being, all your strength' is one of the characteristic ideas of Deuteronomy (cf. 4:29; 10:12; 11:1, 13, 22; 13:4; 19:9; 26:16; 30:2, 6, 10, 16, 20; cf. Josh. 22:5; 23:11, 14). Love of Yahweh as covenant loyalty is fleshed out in Deuteronomy in a specific way, namely as gratitude to him for his special love towards and deliverance of them (6:10–11, 21–23; 10:12, 15). The gratitude is to be expressed in obedience to his commands (6:6–9; 10:12–13; 11:1), based in deep and wholehearted commitment. The phrase 'all your heart' might possibly be rendered 'all your mind'. The association of the words *lēb*, *lēbāb*, 'heart', with the intellect is clear from Jer. 5:21; Hos. 7:11. The translation 'heart' is suitable, since 'heart' in Deuteronomy is typical for penetrating to the seat of the will (as in English 'heartfelt'). 'Being' here translates *nepeš*, often taken as 'soul', but indicating a person's life or vitality. The force of the phrase is to require a devotion that is single-minded and complete. The present passage (like 2 Kgs. 23:25) introduces 'strength' to the phrase (contrast 4:29), adding the idea of a person's full capacities, perhaps including natural abilities and even resources.

6–9. These verses expand the idea of wholehearted obedience. The commandments, that is the whole teaching of Moses, are to be 'upon your heart', reiterating the need for inward obedience (6). They are likewise to be passed on to the next generation, not simply by enforcing them as a law code but by making them the fabric of life and conversation (7). Finally, symbols of them are to be always before them (8–9). The terms in v. 8, 'sign', 'frontlets', are used first in Exod. 13:16 of the dedication of the firstborn, and in that case must be understood metaphorically. The reference here is to words. In principle, words too might be 'bound' and 'written' metaphorically about the person, as certain sayings in Proverbs testify (e.g. Prov. 3:3, specifically of love and faithfulness, but also of the parents' instruction, 3:1–2; cf. Prov. 6:21; 7:3). Such passages generally echo Deuteronomy's insistence on internalization of outward requirement (cf. also Deut. 10:16; 30:6). A metaphorical reading of v. 8, therefore, would be true to the spirit of the book. Yet a literal interpretation of v. 8 is made possible by v. 9, which would be hard to take in a metaphorical sense (cf. S. R. Driver 1895: 92–93). And Judaism took the command literally, as we know from the discovery around the Dead Sea of phylacteries containing biblical texts. It is impossible to decide this question satisfactorily. There is no conflict in Deuteronomy's understanding, however, between outward sign and inward condition; its concern is that there should be harmony between the two. Here, the law of God is one with piety and lifestyle.

6:10–15

10–12. The loyalty command is now developed in a specific way. This paragraph recalls Yahweh's oath to the patriarchs, deliverance from slavery in Egypt, gift of land and requirement of faithfulness, by way of explanation of the confession of faith in v. 4. Verse 10, like v. 3, has an echo of 1:8, with its allusion to the three patriarchs who received the promise at first. The idea of land as gift and blessing is then developed in concrete terms (10b–11; cf. 8:7–10). The good things named do not have to be acquired, according to the usual duty of a king. The reference to 'cities that you did not build' (10) recalls the duty of kings in Mesopotamia to build cities as part of incorporating new territory into their kingdom (Ahlström 1982: 27ff.). Territory and cities are also in their gift, by royal grant (cf. N. Lohfink 1981: 95). The idea that Yahweh himself has met the royal obligation in this respect is filled out by the city lists in Joshua.

The land has been acquired by Yahweh. It is a work already accomplished, containing all that is needed for life, and in that sense comparable to Eden. But plenty brings with it the temptation to forget the giver; and therefore the command to remain loyal to Yahweh is reinforced (12). The decision to obey or disobey is not straightforward, but complicated by moral weakness. This explains Deuteronomy's whole paranetic approach, and especially the typical exhortation to 'be careful' (lit. 'guard yourselves'), to remember that all this blessing is due to Yahweh, who brought them out of Egypt (several times referred to as the 'house of slaves' in Deuteronomy, cf. 5:6; 7:8; 13:5[6], 10[11]).

13–15. The command 'not to forget' proceeds naturally into a requirement to be faithful to Yahweh (13). The sentence structure stresses the absolute requirement to worship him and not others: 'Yahweh you shall fear ... him you shall serve ... in his name you shall swear.' The three terms used here amount to a representation of religious devotion. 'Fear' (here translated 'revere') is the most general word for the worship of Yahweh, both in Deuteronomy (cf. 4:10; 5:29; 6:2 and frequently) and elsewhere (cf. Job 1:1). Service is both worship and obedience; and to 'swear in the name of' identifies the God whom a person worships (Jer. 12:6). Verse 14 follows this with a prohibition of worshipping other gods, recalling 5:7 (notice that the name of Baal is not mentioned here or elsewhere in Deuteronomy), and v. 15 returns to the language of 5:9, also in the context of false worship. It is idolatry, above all, that will draw down the wrath of Yahweh on his people.

The line of thought introduced here is developed more fully in 8:7–20, where the emphasis shifts slightly from the danger of defection to other gods to the danger of complacency.

6:16–19

16. Verse 16 recalls the connection between the place-name Massah and the verb to 'test' (*nissâ*, twice here). Testing involves a question about the capacity of the person tested. The recollection of Massah (Exod. 17:7; cf. Deut. 9:22) fits well in the present context because Israel's 'testing' of the LORD there involved questioning whether he could take them safely through the wilderness and into the promised land. There too Israel was tempted to think Egypt a better option than the prospects ahead (Exod. 17:3), a great act of unbelief, reminiscent of the people's refusal to go up into the land from Kadesh-Barnea (Deut. 1). The central point of this paragraph, therefore, is that Yahweh is capable of keeping his promise that Israel will enter the land.

17–19. The people's obedience to his commands (17–18a) is, as elsewhere, a correlative of Yahweh's fulfilment of the promise. It is not necessary to suppose that commandment-keeping here is a prerequisite of land possession in a legalistic sense (*pace* N. Lohfink [1981: 98], who attributes vv. 17–19 to DtrN, along with 11:8, 22–25; cf. 'Explanation', below). The reappearance of command-keeping in these verses, following the basic loyalty command in vv. 10–15, is also a function of the typical movement within chs. 5 – 6.

6:20–25

20. The child's question is similar to that in Exod. 13:14, but it is asked here about the meaning of the commandments (rather than about the dedication of the firstborn). The question-and-answer format in these verses is important, because it embodies the nature of Deuteronomy as instruction in the commandments for all time (note 'in days to come', lit. 'tomorrow', as opposed to the ubiquitous 'today'). It fits, by the same token, with the motif of teaching the next generation (4:40; 6:2, 7). It is easy to see how a passage such as this might readily become 'liturgical'. There is no evidence that it originally constituted a 'creed', however, detached from its present context, as it fits naturally into the paranesis of Deuteronomy. The question and answer appropriately round off the present section, which has been dominated by the idea of making the once-for-all commandments at Horeb available and valid for all time.

21–22. The substance of the answer follows familiar lines, with the powerful deliverance from Egypt at its heart (cf. 4:20, 34). Verse 22 somewhat abbreviates 4:34, though it adds *rāʿîm*, literally 'evil', here 'terrible', to compensate.

24–25. These verses extend the thought, establishing a connection between the past (exodus), and the future (possession of land). The need for commandment-keeping is brought into this context, and these two final verses form in themselves a reflection on the relationship between command and blessing. The word order of the Hebrew is essentially retained in the translation above, showing its ABBA pattern. It opens and closes with exhortations to obey, and in the middle there is a correspondence between 'have well-being' (lit. 'good') and 'we shall be held righteous' (lit. 'it will be righteousness for us'). This creates a close connection between several elements: commandment-keeping, the righteousness thus established for the Israelites, and the blessings of the land. Righteousness (*ṣᵉḏāqâ*) is fundamentally a quality of God, which becomes an ethical imperative for Israel (33:21). As such, it is at once rectitude, acquittal and the condition brought about as a result. The relationship between the right act and the consequence as 'righteousness' is illustrated by 24:13. Righteousness in this case, then, indicates a standing in God's sight (cf. also Gen. 15:6; Ps. 106:31; and see on Deut. 9:4–6). Again, however, the structure observed above shows how inextricably linked righteousness and blessing are, as opposed to the logical causalities of legalism (see also McConville 1984: 14–15).

Explanation

Deut. 6, with ch. 5, puts into effect the relationship between the Decalogue on Horeb and the deuteronomic teaching that is to characterize the life of Israel in its entire future (a relationship first articulated at 4:13–14). The fundamental deuteronomic call to loyal obedience in 6:4 stands at the head of the instruction that is then unfolded as far as ch. 26.

The dominant thought in the chapter is the oneness of God, which we have explained above as implying both singularity and integrity. This oneness as uniqueness is the justification of the call upon Israel's wholehearted devotion. And the oneness as integrity has its consequence in the goodness of the commandments they are obliged to keep. This connection between the character of God and the gift of his commands implies a unity in the created order, embracing the material, political and ethical. There is, as we saw on vv. 24–25, a profound balance between 'righteousness' and 'good' (as elaborated by Schmid 1968a). At this point the centrality of a *creation* theology in Deuteronomy – better known for its covenantal theology – is most evident. (The book of Exodus has this in common with Deuteronomy; see Fretheim 1991 for elaboration.) Yahweh as lord of creation is always implied in the connection between commandment-keeping and well-being. In this chapter, the creational power of Yahweh is also to the fore in the pictures of a plentiful land that is his to give (10–12), and indeed in his axiomatic right to give a land to one nation at the expense of another (18–19).

This unity of God, with its continuity between the material, political and ethical, has seemed to some theologians to carry within it the danger of totalitarianism. Brueggemann (1979) aligned creation theology with the oppressive power structures of Canaan, which he saw as having invaded Israel in the form of the Davidic-Solomonic official theology, a view that can be traced to von Rad's (1966: 131–143) exclusion of creation theology from Israel's earliest formulations of its faith. (Brueggemann later modified his position on this; 1997: 159–164.) Gunton (1993: 22–24) has shown, in the context of Greek philosophy, how the attempt to understand the world as a unity, in a challenge to the plurality of traditional gods, gave rise to the danger of seeing 'god' simply as 'an unchanging principle of order'. In politics, a 'unitary deity, whether theist or deist, is commonly seen to be at the root of totalitarian or repressive forms of social order' (1993: 25). The modern insistence on the rights of the 'many', therefore, has perceived a need to throw off the idea of the One (1993: 26–27, citing Nietzsche). In the interpretation of Deuteronomy, furthermore, there are precedents for its exploitation in order to oppress (Deist 1994). The fear of totalitarianism, indeed, is one of the motives leading to the demand for pluralism (Brett 1978).

In biblical theology, the oneness of God is conceived in such a way as to avoid the entailment of oppression. In the OT story, this is because it impinges on the human partner by means of an invitation into relationship. Israel is invited into an open future with Yahweh in which its assent is and continues to be required (cf. Gunton 1993: ch. 6). The currency of the 'order' in Yahweh's world is justice ($s^e\underline{d}\bar{a}q\hat{a}$, $sedeq$ occur at 1:16; 16:18, 20; 25:15; 33:19, mainly in the judicial realm). When this is made the counterpart of 'good' (6:24–25), the order that is pictured comes at the end of a story of deliverance from bondage in the house of Pharaoh (20–23), whose oppressive regime negated the divine order (cf. Fretheim 1991: *passim*). The order in Yahweh's world, as opposed to the fixed political-religious order of Egypt, represented by the rigid control of Pharaoh and the principle of *maat*, was one in which people were exhorted to righteousness in freedom – the reverse of all Pharaoh-like regimes.

In this way, the divine order embraces human freedom (and thus, incidentally, creation may be reclaimed as the horizon of OT theology, as is done by Knierim 1995). This has consequences for God. The prophetic picture of God grieving over the sin of Israel implies a kind of powerlessness (cf. Seifert's [1996] treatment of metaphor in Hosea, which she sees as a well-chosen vehicle to express this). In the NT, the divine readiness for relationship derives especially from the conception of the one God as trinity. The inclusion of Jesus within the deity as 'Son of God' expresses the power of God in a way that is as far removed as possible from totalitarian coercion (cf. Bauckham 1999: 36–40; N. T. Wright 1991: ch. 6).

The relationship into which Israel is called with God is that of love. The idea of human love of God must be understood in relation to its object. There is a danger of importing inappropriate connotations into it because the idea of love occurs (quite properly) in a variety of contexts, such as family, friendship and romance. The essential aspect of this love is loyalty, as the appearance of love language in political treaties shows. However, there is an emotive side to the love between God and humans too. This reaches its highest expression in the OT in Hosea, in which God is depicted in an inner agony over contrary impulses to judge and to save (Hos. 11:8), and in which the 'steadfastness' of covenant love (*ḥeseḏ*) takes on the nuances of 'compassion'. This loyalty is expressed in heartfelt adherence to Yahweh, the measure of it being an attachment to his commandments (hence the sequel to v. 5 in vv. 6–9). For this reason it can be said that love of God has a cash value in love of neighbour (Moberly 1999: 138–140), since the commands of God aim at a society in which each promotes the good of the other.

These are the issues that underlie the deuteronomic ethic. Echoes of later theological debates about law and grace are not really heard here. This means that the question whether the gift of land (salvation) precedes the command to obey, or the command precedes the promise, does not go to the heart of this discourse. (The case in point is the attribution of 6:7–19 to DtrN.) The context of these and similar verses is the function of command-keeping in living in the freedom of Yahweh's world. The impossibility of reducing the ethics of Deuteronomy to a law–grace formula is best illustrated in 6:1–2, where the result of command-keeping, along with possession of the land and long life, is fear of Yahweh! Obedience to Yahweh needs no justification outside itself. The logic of Deuteronomy knows too the power of learning and habit, just as it knows of the profound unity of inward and outward reality in the life of the spirit (6:8–9).

DEUTERONOMY 7:1–26

Translation

[1]When the LORD your God brings you to the land you are going over to occupy, and drives out many nations in your path – the Hittites, Girgashites, Amorites, Canaanites, Perizzites, Hivites and Jebusites, seven nations stronger and more numerous than you – [2]and the LORD your God gives them over to you so that you defeat them, you must utterly destroy them; you must make no covenant with them, or show them any mercy. [3]Do not intermarry with them, either by giving your daughters to their sons or by taking their daughters for your sons, [4]for that would turn your children away from following me to worship other gods; then the LORD's anger would rage against you and quickly destroy you. [5]Instead, you must treat them like this: break down their altars, smash their sacred pillars, cut down their Asherah poles and burn their idols. [6]For you are a people holy to the LORD your God; the LORD your God chose you to be a people particularly for him, out of all the nations on earth.

[7]It was not because you were a more numerous nation than others that the LORD took delight in you and chose you, for you were the smallest of all the nations. [8]It

was only because he loved you, and in order to keep the promise he made by oath to your forefathers, that he brought you out by his great strength, setting you free from slavery, from Pharaoh, the king of Egypt. [9]Know then that the LORD your God is indeed God, the trustworthy God who in faithful love keeps covenant with those who love him and keep his commands, as far as a thousand generations. [10]But those who reject him he will requite with destruction; he will not delay in requiting those who reject him. [11]So keep the commandment, the laws and the statutes, with which I am charging you this day.

[12]Because you obey these laws, keeping them carefully, the LORD your God will in faithful love keep covenant with you, as he promised on oath to your forefathers. [13]He will love and bless you, and make you grow in number; he will bless your offspring and your crops – your grain, wine and oil, the young of your herds and the lambs of your flocks, in the land he promised your forefathers on oath that he would give you. [14]You will be blessed more than any other nation; there will be neither sterility nor barrenness among you or among your livestock. [15]The LORD will take away from you all diseases; and the terrible ailments that you suffered in Egypt he will no longer bring upon you, but will afflict those who hate you with them. [16]You will devour all the nations that the LORD your God is giving over to you, not sparing them, and you shall not worship their gods, for they would be a snare to you.

[17]If you say to yourselves: 'These nations are more numerous than we; how can we drive them out?' [18]you must not be afraid of them: be sure to remember what the LORD your God did to Pharaoh and all Egypt: [19]the great trials of strength that you yourselves witnessed, the signs and wonderful deeds, the strong hand and arm stretched out by which the LORD your God delivered you; so the LORD your God will do to all the nations of which you are afraid. [20]The LORD your God will put panic among them, so that even those who are left, or who try to hide from you, will perish. [21]You must not be in dread of them, for the LORD your God is among you; he is a great and terrible God. [22]The LORD your God will drive out these nations before you little by little; you will not be able to make an end of them quickly, otherwise the wild beasts might become too many for you. [23]The LORD your God will give them over to you; he will throw them into complete confusion, until they are destroyed. [24]He will give their kings into your hands, so that you blot out their names from under heaven; not a man will be able to resist you, until you have destroyed them all. [25]Burn the idols of their gods; do not desire for yourselves the gold and silver with which they are overlaid, or take it; it might become a snare to you, since it is abhorrent to the LORD you God. [26]Bring no abhorrent thing into your house, or else you shall become subject to destruction, just like it; treat it as something loathsome and abhor it, for it is subject to destruction.

Notes on the text

3. Lit. 'you [sg.] shall not give your daughter [sg.] to *his* son, and *his* daughter you shall not take for your son'. The unexpected singular ('his') seems intended to balance the second-person singular address adopted here. It may envisage an actual arrangement between two fathers.

4. The singular 'your [i.e. thy] son' continues in this verse. It is followed by a plural verb in MT, lit. 'and *they* would worship other gods'. SamP, LXX and Vg have a singular verb here, presumably adjusting to a stricter grammar. MT is acceptable, however, since the singular 'thy son' must be understood distributively.

'following me'; Moses' speech on behalf of God occasionally portrays his words as if in direct speech (cf. 11:14–15; 17:3; 28:20; 29:4–5; cf. Jer. 8:22 – 9:3[2] for what seems to be a fusion of the prophet's words with God's).

9. Note the names for God here: lit., 'Yahweh your *'elōhîm* is *'elōhîm*, [cf. 4:35] the faithful *'ēl*' (see 'Comment').

'who in faithful love keeps covenant': lit. 'will keep covenant and steadfast love (*ḥesed*)', cf. v. 12; the phrase is a hendiadys, where the two nouns help to explain each other.

10. 'Those who reject him': lit. 'hate him', cf. 5:9. The phrase is plural only in its first occurrence here, and is immediately followed by a singular ('with destruction', lit., 'to destroy him').

11. 'the commandment, the laws and the statutes': on this as an appositional phrase, see note on 5:31.

13. 'land' is here *hā'aḏāmâ*, not *hā'āreṣ*, as in v. 1. The choice of this word is motivated by the subject-matter, and specifically the 'crops' (lit. 'fruit of the earth', 14).

14. 'neither sterility nor barrenness': lit. 'no sterile one, either male or female' (*'āqār wa'aqārâ*).

15. 'all diseases': *kol-maḏwê*; contrast Deut. 28:60, which has singular *maḏweh*; the plural is clearly correct here because of following *hārā'îm*.

17. 'to yourselves': lit. 'in your heart'.

'Us ... we': lit. 'me ... I'.

20. 'The LORD your God will put panic among them': 'panic' is *haṣṣir'â*, frequently taken as 'hornet', here and in Exod. 23:28; Josh. 24:12. The meaning 'hornet' is suggested by the ancient translations, including LXX, and similar metaphors for invading armies are found in Deut. 1:44; Is. 7:18–19. In Exod. 23:27–28 there is a parallel with *'êmâ*, 'terror', and for this reason 'panic' is adopted here. See also 'Comment'.

22. '*these* nations', *hā'ēl* is written defectively for *hā'ēlleh*, as 4:42.

24. 'until you have destroyed them all': an inf. construct with *ḥireq*, anomalously, in the first syllable of *hišmiḏ'ekā*; see note on 3:3.

Form and structure

Deut. 7 has important similarities with several Exodus texts, notably Exod. 23:20–33. The passages have in common Yahweh's promise to drive out the existing nations of Canaan, the call to Israel to avoid worshipping their gods and to destroy vestiges of their religion, and promises of fertility and freedom from sickness. There is a broad correspondence even in the structure of the two, each beginning and ending with the themes of defeat of the nations, intertwined with rejection of their worship. There is no evidence, *pace* Mayes (1979: 181), that these two themes were originally developed independently, or that this chapter can be divided into separate layers according to each. The intrinsic connection between the destruction of the other nations and worship appears from a number of OT texts concerning war, including the narrative of conquest under Joshua (e.g. Josh. 4 – 6), and the Philistine wars (1 Sam. 4), in both of which the ark of the covenant plays a major role. It is demonstrated also by the close relationship of theme and structure between Deut. 7 and 12, Deuteronomy's great worship chapter; see, on the latter, 'Form and structure'.

There are also specific and even verbal similarities between the present passage and the Exodus one. 1. The unusual term *ṣirᵉ'â*, 'panic' (Exod. 23:28; Deut. 7:20; see 'Notes on the text'). 2. The qualification that the expulsion of the enemies will not happen all at once, because of the danger of wild animals gaining a foothold (Exod. 23:29–30; cf. Deut. 7:22). 3. The nations as a 'snare' (*môqēš / tiwwāqēš*) to Israel (Exod. 23:33; Deut. 7:25). Deut. 7 has developed the Exodus text in certain ways, for example by expanding the list of blessings, in keeping with the book's strong emphasis on that subject (Exod. 23:25–26; cf. Deut. 7:13–14).

Our text also incorporates the theme of election from Exod. 19:5–6 (Deut. 7:6), and the reflection on Yahweh's faithful love 'as far as a thousand generations', together with his judgment on those who hate him, from Exod. 20:5–6 (Deut. 7:9–10).

Deut. 7 has thus rearranged previously existing material as part of its distinctive theological discourse. In Exodus the theme of election is raised before the giving of the Decalogue and the law code, but the treatment of the other nations comes after these (20:22 – 23:19); Deuteronomy, in contrast, brings together these two topics (election and other nations) and places them before the law code (chs. 12 – 26). Deuteronomy's organization in relation to these topics rests on its perception of a correlation between the two. (It may also owe something to Deuteronomy's greater concern with the topic of land.) Its incorporation of Exod. 20:5–6, furthermore, allows the punishment of 'those who hate him' to relate potentially (though not necessarily) to the other nations (see 'Comment'). And it reflects a methodology that seeks to work through the theological implications of the covenant as far as possible, a feature that is attested also in its promotion of the narrative of the golden calf (Deut. 9 – 10; cf. Exod. 32).

There are frequent changes of singular and plural address in this chapter, as follows: vv. 1–4, sg. (except 'against you', 4); v. 5, pl.; v. 6, sg.; vv. 7–8, pl. (up to 'he brought you out'); vv. 8 (from 'and he redeemed you') to 11, sg.; v. 12, mixed; vv. 13–26, sg. (except 'you shall burn', v. 25). As elsewhere, this is not a guide to literary analysis (see Introduction), but simply a feature of the style.

The chapter is a literary unit. Some see 7:1–11 as a continuation of ch. 6, while 7:12 opens a section that runs to 8:20 (see Christensen 1991: 164). This is partly because of the verbal echo: 'because you obey (7:12) … because you do not obey' (8:20), featuring the same relatively unusual word for 'because' [*ʿēqeḇ*]). But, as Weinfeld (1991: 372) rightly notes, such a division fails to recognize the unity of the chapter, which is both literary and conceptual. N. Lohfink (1963: 182) also argued that the unity of the chapter cannot be the result of a slow, haphazard process, but shows evidence of a conscious shaping of material. He found in particular a carefully constructed concentric pattern in 7:6–14, at whose centre stand vv. 11–12, with their double command to keep the commandments, and which begins and ends with the theme of Israel's distinctiveness from the other nations. This pattern was overlaid in the final structuring of the text, however. The structure may be represented in the following ways (N. Lohfink 1963: 186–187):

1–6	Command		1–6	Paranesis
7–15	Blessing	OR	7–15	Blessing
16	Command		16–26	Paranesis
17–24	War paranesis			
25–26	Command			

Lohfink stresses the close connection between oath, command and blessing at vv. 11–12 (see below). His structure, however, seems to mix formal and theological categories, and to divert from the relationship between the themes of holiness/election and of blessing.

The following, slightly different structure brings these relationships out more clearly (and additionally finds a parallel in the form of ch. 12; see on that chapter; cf. also McConville 1984: 60; O'Connell 1992b):

1–6	Destroy false worship
7–11	Israel as holy people
12–16	Blessing
17–26	Destroy false worship

Comment

7:1–6

1–2. In this opening exhortation, vv. 1–2a are subordinate clauses, expressing again one of the basic assumptions of deuteronomic thinking, that God is giving his people land. The first direct command (2b) is a consequence of this, a call to carry out the *ḥerem*, or ban of destruction (see 2:34, and 'Comment'). The importance of *ḥerem* as a theme of the chapter is clear from its recurrence at v. 26. This signals a shift from the themes of Deut. 5 – 6. The emphasis moves from the exodus and the words of Yahweh to the conquest and occupation. While the First Commandment (not to worship other gods) undergirded Deut. 5 – 6, its implications are now extended to confront the issue of worshippers of other gods in the land Israel is to occupy. The *ḥerem* has lain dormant as a theme since chs. 2 – 3, though implicit in chs. 4 – 6, but now it comes to its fruition. The present passage has a close parallel in Exod. 34:11–16, which serves as a prelude to the renewal of the covenant after the great golden-calf apostasy. Both passages require removing the nations (though Exodus is less strict, demanding only that they be 'driven out'), extirpating their religion, and refraining from assimilation to them by marriage.

In this call to the *ḥerem* we meet the first enumeration in Deuteronomy of all the peoples of the promised land, already familiar from Exodus (cf. Exod. 3:8, 17; 13:5; 23:23; 34:11). Deuteronomy's first demography of the land had named only Canaanites and Amorites, using the terms in a general way to describe the whole population (see on 1:7). The more differentiated listing here reflects the diversity of population in pre-Israelite Palestine. A similar list occurs in Deut. 20:17, as well as in Josh. 3:12; 9:1; 11:3; 12:8; 24:11; Judg. 3:5; 1 Kgs. 9:20. Of these texts, the full sevenfold enumeration occurs only at Josh. 3:10; 24:11, besides this one. The majority of texts have only six, omitting the Girgashites. A longer list is found at Gen. 15:19–21.

The composition of the lists reflects a combination of historical and rhetorical factors. There is a tendency for the Canaanites, Amorites and Hittites to come in the first three positions, being perhaps the most important constituents (cf. also Ezek 16:3, 45). In one pattern, typical of Exodus, Canaanites take prime position (but Exod. 34:11 has 'Amorites'); in another (as here, Deut. 20:17; Josh. 9:1; 12:8), the Hittites have the honour. One explanation offered for this is that 'Canaan' and 'Hatti' represented the whole land at various times (Weinfeld 1991: 362–363); the earliest six-name lists had Canaan first, the latest had Hatti (Ishida 1979). However, this does not quite meet the point, as the lists are differentiating between peoples, rather than reaching for generalizing terms. It is sufficient to observe that the greater come first.

The Hittites embrace the influx of peoples from Anatolia after the fall of the great Hittite empire that had vied with Egypt for control of Palestine in the mid-second millennium BC. Canaanites and Amorites have already been located on the coastal plain and in the hill country respectively (see on 1:7). The lesser groups, the Hivites, Jebusites and Perizzites, occupied specific areas. Hivites are associated in the OT with Shechem (Gen. 34:2), Gibeon (Josh. 9:7; 11:19) and Mt Hermon (Josh. 11:3). They have been traced to an original home in Anatolia. Jebusites famously preceded the Israelites in Jerusalem (Josh. 15:63; 2 Sam. 5:6), and may also have been Anatolian (note 'Hittites' at David's court in Jerusalem, 1 Sam. 26:6; 2 Sam. 11:6). Perizzites cannot be linked with any place of origin, but often appear in combination with 'Canaanites' (Gen. 13:7; 34:30; Judg. 1:4–5). Finally, Girgashites, like the Hittites, Hivites and Jebusites, are also thought to have come from Anatolia (Karkisa; Weinfeld 1991: 363).

The variation in number (sixes and sevens!) is due simply to the fact that the biblical authors are not aiming to be encyclopaedic, but follow rhetorical as well as historical criteria. The lists in general serve the purpose of describing the population in its full extent and variety. In Exod. 3:8, 17, the lists serve the theme of the plenty of the land, and so depict it as capable of sustaining all these peoples. In other Exodus texts, and here in Deut. 7:1, the accent shifts to the theme of Yahweh's war against the nations. The present text has counted seven nations in keeping with the idea of seven as a number of fullness, and fitting for a command to rid the land thoroughly of its existing population. But this device is not sustained in all the lists that promise the expulsion of the nations, not even within Deuteronomy (20:17). (LXX mistakenly thought the sevenfold enumeration in this text prescriptive, and often supplies 'Girgashites' in texts where it is omitted in MT.)

2–4. The command to destroy the seven nations completely is followed by further commands prohibiting intermingling in any way (2b–4). This is strictly illogical. It is intended, however, to explain the *ḥerem* requirement. The heart of this is in v. 4b, where the nations are seen as a temptation to worship gods other than Yahweh, the most fundamental breach of the covenant (cf. 1 Sam. 12:20; 2 Kgs. 18:6 for the same phrase in formulaic expressions of faithfulness to Yahweh). Intermarriage was a potent factor in the mixing of cultures and religions in Israel's world. The singular address in the present prohibition, as well as the singulars 'daughter ... son ... daughter ... son' (3; see above, 'Notes on the text'), evokes the marriage agreement between respective fathers (see further 'Comment' on Deut. 22:13–19 for the social assumptions here). The consequence is a powerful social bonding. Marriage within Israel serves to strengthen the fabric of the covenant people (see above on 5:16); marriage outside it serves to weaken that fabric, because it compromises the allegiance of the people to Yahweh. Solomon and Ahab furnish the outstanding examples of this in the OT (1 Kgs. 11:3; 16:30–33). The idea of a holy people is therefore hedged around in these verses, with an insistence on the need to keep separate from adherents of false religion. And if the command preserves an unexpected compromise between rigour and practicality, this corresponds to the course of the history that would follow Israel's entry to the land.

5. The procedures against Canaanite religion reveal something of its trappings. The plural 'altars' corresponds to the many places where the peoples worshipped their gods. Stone pillars (*maṣṣēḇôṯ*) were frequent features of cult places in Canaan and Israel. The symbolism of the pillar is often thought to be phallic, and thus combining with the female imagery of the Asherah pole to produce a powerful fertility synthesis. However, religious symbolism need not be constant or uniform, and a number of OT texts show that they were in certain contexts acceptable within Israel's worship. Jacob's *maṣṣēbâ* at Bethel is a memorial of God's theophany there (Gen. 35:14). Moses himself set up twelve of them at Sinai, as a symbol of the twelve tribes' commitment to the covenant (Exod. 24:4), and Joshua's 'great stone' at Shechem (Josh. 24:26) had a similar function. The significance of stone pillars depends therefore on the context in which they are found. This is the reason for their inclusion in Deuteronomy's provisions here, and their actual destruction as part of the measures taken by Judah's later reforming kings, Hezekiah and Josiah (2 Kgs. 18:4; 23:14).

The 'asherim' are unequivocally Canaanite in the OT texts where they occur. The term 'Asherah' (the singular form) is used in the OT to refer both to the goddess of that name (1 Kgs. 18:19), the consort of El, according to the Ugaritic texts, though later, it seems, of Baal (see Cross 1973: 13–46, esp. 32), and to a wooden object associated with her worship (Judg. 6:26). The setting up of wooden objects in worship is very ancient, and was not necessarily originally attached to that goddess, though they are so in the OT (see 'Comment' on 16:21). That wooden objects are in view here is implied by the verb 'cut down' (and cf. the burning of the object in Judg. 6:26). For this reason none survive, and their exact form is not known. They may have been poles, carved in such a way as to represent the goddess Asherah, or stylized trees, such as date palms (Olyan 1988: 1–3, and further bibliography there; Keel 1997: 140–143 for illustrations of tree symbolism in temple iconography). (They have sometimes been mistakenly thought to be living trees, perhaps because of the translation 'plant' in Deut. 16:21. This is better taken as 'set up', however; see on that verse.)

It is clear that there was Yahweh worship in Israel, in the time of the monarchy, that included the use of *maṣṣēbôt*. Two of these were found in the temple to Yahweh at Arad, in the holy of holies. Asherim may also have been used in some Yahweh worship. Olyan argues for this, for example, because of silence on the subject in Amos and Hosea, and by arguing that texts that do condemn it were influenced by the Deuteronomist (e.g. Mic. 5:13; Olyan 1988: 16–17). Such texts make it possible that asherim were used in Yahweh worship, as opposed to Baal worship, but do not prove it. The epigraphic evidence from Kuntillet 'Ajrud, a site in the northern Sinai, probably shows only that an asherah symbol featured in a cult of Yahweh in that area (Emerton 1982). The view that the goddess Asherah was known as consort of Yahweh, in succession to Canaanite El, has insufficient support from this much debated text (*pace* Olyan 1988: 23–37).

7:6-11

6. The underlying reason for the uncompromising line taken on other peoples and their worship is that Israel is 'holy' to Yahweh (6). The holiness of Israel in Deuteronomy is always explained in terms of Yahweh's having chosen them as his own people 'out of all the nations on earth' (cf. 14:2; 26:19; 28:9). This last phrase echoes v. 1 (there the word is *gôyîm*, here it is *'ammîm*; the two are synonymous in this context). Deuteronomy thus recalls Exod. 19:5–6, which it follows in its general sense (a people set apart from all other nations to be 'holy'), and especially in the term *s^egullâ*, 'a people particularly for him'. The noun, which refers elsewhere to a king's private fortune (1 Chr. 29:3; Eccles. 2:8), expresses the special affection of Yahweh for the people. Its equivalent in Akkadian and Ugaritic describes the *king* as the special possession of the god (Greenberg 1951; Weinfeld 1972: 226 n. 2). The term also occurs in treaty contexts, in which the the vassal is described as the *s^egullâ* of the overlord (Weinfeld 1991: 368, on a thirteenth-century BC Hittite treaty with a Ugaritic vassal). It has a double appropriateness in Deuteronomy, therefore. Its application to Israel is part of Deuteronomy's understanding of the people as such enjoying a direct relationship with Yahweh, without the needed mediation of a king; and it expresses the people's vassal relationship to him. The same emphasis probably also explains why Deuteronomy omits, here and in similar passages, the phrase 'kingdom of priests' (Exod. 19:6). The idea of 'priesthood', as a metaphor of dedication to God, apparently did not suit Deuteronomy's idea of the whole people as an integrated entity before God, in which the priest is not set up as the ultimate model of holiness. The special language of this verse therefore coheres well with the model of Israel that is elaborated in Deut. 16:18 – 18:22 (see on that section).

Israel's holiness thus derives from its chosen status. It does not follow, however, that it is divorced from considerations of covenant conditionality, and thus made absolute or inherent. This is sometimes held, on the grounds that the present verse omits the conditional clause in Exod. 19:5 (Weinfeld 1991: 367). Such an interpretation fails to reckon with the careful theologizing of 'covenant' in vv. 9–11 (see on those verses). A contrast is also often observed between holiness in Deuteronomy and the concept as it is found in the 'priestly' parts of the Pentateuch (Weinfeld 1991: 61; Braulik 1986a: 63). It is true that in the latter it is a condition that can be maintained in greater and lesser degrees, depending on the person's 'purity', in both moral and ritual senses. Deuteronomy has no portrayal of the geography of holiness as in the tabernacle of Exodus, nor does it have extensive regulations governing either the personnel of the cult (the priests) or its actions (sacrifices); (for the 'priestly' view of holiness see Jenson 1992). A 'cultic' view of holiness does find a place in Deut. 14:3–21, which echoes Lev. 11, and embraces the language of 'cleanness' and 'uncleanness' in relation to permissible and impermissible foods. And Deut. 23:1–14 reviews criteria of admissibility to the *qāhāl* (cultic assembly), which include physical conditions. Deuteronomy's theology of holiness, therefore, does not aim to exclude other OT expressions of it. However, it places Israel's status as holy people in the context of its exhortation to them to keep faith with the covenant in their whole life.

The language of choice, or election, is used in Deuteronomy in a way that coheres with its dominant thrust. As already noted on 4:37, it contrasts specifically with the idea of the election of the Israelite king, and of his capital on Mt Zion (1 Sam. 10:24; 2 Sam. 6:21; Pss. 78:70; 132:13; cf. also. 89:3[4], where the noun *beḥîr*, 'chosen one', is used of David). Deuteronomy, in contrast, highlights the direct extension to the whole people of Yahweh's love for and choice of the forefathers (4:37; 10:15). In this theology of election it is close to Is. 40 – 66, which is often said to 'democratize' the Davidic covenant (Brueggemann 1968; cf. Is. 41:8; 55:3; 65:9). Here too the whole people (Israel, or Jacob) is the object of choice, and a connection with the patriarchs is made.

OT scholarship typically sees the deuteronomic concept, along with that of Is. 40 – 66, as an exilic reaction against the idea of the election of David and Zion (Mayes 1979: 60–63; Braulik 1986a: 63–64). However, the election of the people as such was certainly known to the prophet Amos in the eighth century (Amos 3:2; the verb is *yāḏaʿ*, not *bāḥar*, which links the thought, incidentally, with the patriarchal election tradition; cf. Gen. 18:19). So the theory that the election of the people as such was simply a consequence of the demise of the Davidic dynasty is not without difficulties. I have argued in the Introduction that Deuteronomy's programme as an alternative to the political models of the ANE aims to resist the adoption of such a model in Israel. This implies that the election of David departs from the deuteronomic ideal, the converse of the more common view. (For my view of the relationship between Deuteronomy and the 'deuteronomistic' historical books, in which election comes to be applied to David [1 Kgs. 8:16; 11:34], see McConville 1998.) In Deuteronomy's application of the term 'choose' to the sanctuary (12:5, etc.), the king (17:15) and the priest (18:5), we may discern a further opposition to election's being subsumed by the Jerusalem royal-sanctuary establishment (see 'Comment' on those texts).

7–8. To Yahweh's choice is now added the idea of his love (as it was in 4:37), expressed by two terms, *ḥāšaq* ('took delight in', 7) and *'aha̱ḇâ* (8). Love is known in ANE treaty language to denote the mutual loyalty of the treaty partners (Moran 1963a). And this is an important dimension of it, where love takes flesh (on God's side) as a determination to keep his promise to Abraham, and (on Israel's side) as a requirement to be faithful to God to the exclusion of others. This connotation of love as exclusive loyalty no doubt lies behind the metaphor of marriage used in Hosea to express the covenant relationship. Yet neither in Hosea nor in Deuteronomy can love be evacuated of its emotive aspect. Hos. 11:1–4, 8–9 powerfully conveys Yahweh's deep attachment to his people, so strong that it will not let him execute his rightful anger on account of sin. In the present context that emotional bond finds voice in the first term used, translated 'took delight in', which is used in Deut. 21:11 of sexual attraction (cf. Gen. 34:8), and in Ps. 91:14 of the worshipper's close relationship with God.

The idea of Israel as 'the smallest of all the nations' contrasts with the promise to Abraham that it would be exceedingly numerous (Gen. 15:5), which is reflected in Deut. 1:10; 10:22. The perspective here, however, is that of the people's beginnings in Egypt, whereas the promise to Abraham anticipates generations of growth, and is considered to have been fulfilled in principle by the people that stands at Moab. The smallness of Israel accords well with their sense of the far greater strength of the peoples of Canaan when they first approached the land (Num. 13:26–33; Deut. 1:28). It is in any case an important perspective on Israel as such, which might take on special significance in any number of particular historical situations (such as the Babylonian exile, which many scholars see as the time of the origin of this idea; it is an exaggeration to claim that 7:7 'stands in contradiction to' 1:10; 10:22, as Weinfeld [1991: 369] does).

Yahweh's love for Israel is demonstrated by the deliverance from Egypt, a frequent theme in Deut. 1 – 6 (cf. 6:21–22). Here a new term ($p\bar{a}\underline{d}\hat{a}$) appears, translated 'setting you free' (8). In other texts in Deuteronomy, the 'redemption' of Israel from slavery is made the basis of commands to treat the slave and the foreign resident well (15:15; 24:17–18). Its dominant sense in the book, therefore, is the legal freeing of a slave, and conferring the rights and privileges of independent status (see also 9:26; 13:5[6]; 21:8).

In the sacrificial sphere this term means 'redeem', that is, ransom by means of a gift in substitution, as of firstborn children by the sacrifice of a suitable animal (Exod. 13:13). This practice is used in Exod. 13:14–16 to explain the Passover, where the firstborn of Egypt were killed as a prelude to the freeing of Israel, and it becomes a memorial of that deliverance. The narrative of the Passover may, therefore, be hinted at here, though in Deuteronomy it is never marked out from the 'signs and wonders' of the exodus in general. (6:22 is a case in point, where the death of Pharaoh's firstborn is suggested by the phrase 'and his house'; 'Passover' is mentioned by name only in 16:1–8, the law governing its observance.)

9–10. These verses strongly recall 5:9–10, with some expansions. The theme is Yahweh's faithfulness to his covenant. The term $b^e r\hat{i}t$, 'covenant', is introduced here, alongside $\d{h}esed$, 'faithful love', where $\d{h}esed$ stood alone in 5:9–10. This has the effect of allowing 'covenant' and 'faithful love' to define each other. Yahweh is characterized (more literally than above) as 'Yahweh your God ($^e l\bar{o}h\hat{i}m$), (the) trustworthy God ($h\bar{a}'\bar{e}l$), who keeps covenant and faithful love'. Of the two words here translated 'God' the former belongs to the expression 'Yahweh your God', common in Deuteronomy. The latter term (*'ēl* prefixed by the definite article, 'the') must be taken as generic, that is, a general term for God (or god); that is, not the name El, well known in forms such as El Shaddai. The effect is to say that Yahweh alone among gods is trustworthy, and thus the note of polemic against other gods may just be heard once more. Trustworthiness and faithful love are close in meaning, and go to the heart of the OT's portrayal of Yahweh. His devotion to his chosen people cannot be compromised by anything in himself. And this now gives content to covenant, in a way that is consistent with the fulfilment of the ancient oath to Abraham that is recalled in the theology of election.

It is not the whole picture here, however, that is surprising in its continuation. For the beneficiaries of this undying love are not Israel as such, but 'those who love him and keep his commands'; and in contrast, those who have reason to fear his resolution are 'those who reject him'. The requirement to 'love' him echoes his love by which he chose them (8), as well as the great, all-embracing command already met (cf. 6:5). And it provides its own comment on the commandment-keeping that goes with it; this belongs within a relationship of reciprocal devotion. The judgment on those who reject him is sometimes set out as a fragment of poetry, as from a liturgy (see NIV), because of its structure:

A   requite
B   those who hate him
C   destroy
C'   not delay
B'   those who hate him
A'   requite

Its emphasis falls on the idea of requital, that is, a full repayment in kind (the verb is *šillēm*, related to *šālôm*, and having the connotation of completeness). The meaning is matched by the chiastic form. The full picture of covenant here, therefore, is of faithful love returned by faithful people. The passage departs from the formula found in the Decalogue (Exod. 20:5; Deut. 5:9, cf. Exod. 34:6-7; Num. 14:18), where punishment is extended to future generations (see on 5:9). This change is not in the interests of 'individualism' as such (*pace* Weinfeld 1991: 371), but simply asserts the moral basis of the covenant, against a false doctrine of election. The last verse in the section, v. 11, again puts commandment-keeping in this context.

In these verses 'holiness' and 'chosenness' are put in a quite new light, so that the theology of holiness that emerges from the chapter as a whole is complex. Indeed there is a pointer here to the prophetic controversy with an ideology of holiness and chosenness that presumes upon such status (see 'Explanation' for further comment). This is because the moral issue lies between God and human beings as such. The distinction between Israelites and Canaanites, though prominent initially, has receded here, and the way lies open to those reinterpretations of election that occupied the prophets. Ultimately, the issue is not about being Israelite, but about being righteous before God (cf. Amos 5:24; Is. 51:4–6; Prov. 11:5).

7:12–16

12. The discourse now puts a different slant on the nature of the reciprocal commitment entailed in the covenant. The structure of v. 12 mirrors that of vv. 9–11; there, the exhortation to obey God's commands is plainly a consequence of the covenant of faithful love, which is presented as established. Here, in strict grammar, the law-keeping is a condition of God's keeping his covenant of faithful love. This has been seen as an intrusion of a 'legalistic' point of view into the text, as if to correct the preceding verses (Perlitt 1969: 61). There is an inconsistency, however, only if one has an over-exclusive model of law and grace, in which either one or the other must have absolute priority (thus against Mayes 1979: 186). The discourse of Deuteronomy does not favour such a model. Rather, its repetitions and rhetorical balances express the many-sidedness of the great themes it treats. The sharp opening, 'Because (*'ēqeḇ*) you obey', protects against presumption on God's promise. The absoluteness of the oath to the patriarchs should not give rise to any separation between enjoyment of covenant status and obedience to its standards. The following blessings, vv. 13–16, are thus predicated on a relationship in which Israel is remaining true. The question whether Israel *can* lose its privileged status can be answered only with a 'yes'. And in fact there is an echo of both v. 10 and v. 12 in 8:20. There, a destruction of Israel is hypothesized, like that of the nations Yahweh once drove out in their favour (7:10); and this is 'because' (*'ēqeḇ*) they did not obey Yahweh. The whole discourse of Deut. 7 – 8, therefore, both asserts the truth of Yahweh's election of Israel and problematizes it; that is, it shows that a wrong concept of election will have disastrous results.

13–16. The blessings catalogued in vv. 13–16 assume a covenant-keeping Israel. In the terms of that assumption there is an echo of 'those who hate him' (10) in 'those who hate you' (15), that is, the nations that are Israel's (and Yahweh's) enemies. But this equation also is predicated on Israel's faithfulness to the covenant.

The blessings themselves explicate 'land'. Here 'love' shows what it will mean in practice (13), issuing in blessing, always the result of covenant faithfulness (cf. 11:26–29; 28:1–14). This means first an expansion of numbers, in fulfilment of the promise to the patriarchs (Gen. 15:5; Deut. 1:10). Such an expansion was a necessary practical condition of filling, and thus holding, the promised land (the size of nations is an issue in the chapter, vv. 1, 7). The blessing operates not only on the grand scale, however; it comes down to the level of families, hence 'your offspring'. This is not sentimental. The welfare of families depended on children to work the land and provide for their elders in later life; children were greatly desired, and in numbers (Ps. 127:3–5). Blessing as increase applies also to the land itself ($'^a d\bar{a}m\hat{a}$, twice here), and to flocks and herds. Land is not abstract, but the means of life. All these fruitfulnesses, even children, interrelate and amount to life itself.

The underlying point is, once again, that Yahweh alone is the true God. The issue for Israelites in the land of Canaan was precisely this: who is the God who has power to 'give' in this place? And the answer in practice for many Israelites was Baal, and the other gods known by the Canaanites. Hosea, in the eighth century BC, had to reassert that it was Yahweh, not Baal, who was the true giver of 'the grain, wine and oil' (the same trio as here, standing for fertility in general; Hos. 2:7–9[9–11]).

The connection between practical blessing and the theme of election appears strongly in vv. 14–16. The people of Yahweh will not merely enjoy the blessings necessary to life, but will do so in a qualitatively different way from other nations. The picture of a people free from childlessness and disease is idealized, as is the concept of the total destruction of the nations (see on vv. 2b–4). The latter theme is now returned to (16), to emphasize the indissoluble connection between faithfulness to Yahweh and the possibility of life itself. It has, if anything, a new ferocity ('not sparing them'). And it expresses the rationale of radical separation in the term 'snare' (repeated in v. 25). In the act of giving everything to Israel, Yahweh knows the fatally powerful attractions of the gods of the other peoples.

7:17-26

17–21. The final section of the chapter returns to the exhortation to oppose the peoples of the land radically, and makes it a matter of Israel's belief in Yahweh. The logic that says the weaker must yield to the stronger (17) has already been challenged by the contrary logic of Yahweh's decision to choose Israel (6–7). That reasoning is now developed into a rationale for the wars of Yahweh's people. In these, the essential elements are, first, that Yahweh himself is in the midst of them, the 'divine warrior', and consequently that the people should not fear (cf. Deut. 20:3–4). The command not to fear is prominent here (18a, 21), and linked to the recollection of what Yahweh has already done in bringing the people out of Egypt with a show of his strength (18b–19; cf. 4:34; 6:22). The thought and language are strongly reminiscent of 1:26–31 (note 1:29), where fear cost Israel its first opportunity to possess the land. The present exhortation shows that fear to oppose the nations is not merely an initial threat but a permanent possibility; and that narrative portrayed unmistakably how much they stood to lose. Significantly, the premiss of the present speech is that, even as they stand in Moab, and with the example of Egypt as well as of the defeat of the Transjordanian kings behind them (2:26 – 3:7), they continue to fear the nations (19b). The folly of such fear, and thus of the failure to trust in God, is brought out with ironic force in v. 21, which shows that the reason not to fear enemies is that it is Yahweh himself who is 'terrible', or to be feared. Yahweh indeed sends a disabling 'panic' among the opposing nations (20; cf. Exod. 23:28; Josh. 24:12). The translation 'panic' (rather than 'hornet', see 'Notes on the text') is supported by v. 23. The need for trust in Yahweh, and for belief that he is the one to be feared, is illustrated by a story such as that of Gideon. This would continue to be the key to possessing the land in reality (see Judg. 7:9–11). The same story provides an example of the panic that causes an enemy's defeat (Judg. 7:17–24).

22–24. Verse 22 comes as a surprise in a context in which the defeat of the Canaanites is portrayed as quick and complete, providing a rationale for the actual continuance of the non-Israelite population after the people's entry. A number of points may be made. First, the concept of a complete annihilation of the nations is always a kind of ideal, symbolizing the need for radical loyalty to Yahweh on the part of Israel (see on 7:2–3). Secondly, this tension between total conquest and actual cohabitation with the nations runs through the whole narrative of occupation in both Joshua and Judges. (The older tendency to see Joshua and Judges simply as representing opposite viewpoints on this is no longer tenable; Joshua itself knows that the conquest was not swift and complete, and juxtaposes sweeping statements like 11:21–23 with realistic concessions, as in 15:63; 16:10; 17:12–13; see Polzin 1980. For the view that Joshua is informed by centuries-long experience of cohabitation with non-Yahwist populations, see Mitchell 1993.) Thirdly, Judges offers two rationales for the persistence of non-Israelite populations (Judg. 2:20–23; 3:1–4). The rationale in our present text differs from these, but is consistent with the immediate context, which assumes that Israel will need actively to fill the land, and presumably time in which to do so (Deut. 7:13). It is best to think of v. 22 not as intrusive, but as representing the realism that characterizes not only Deuteronomy but the historical books that follow. The same juxtaposition of ideal and real is found in Exod. 23:27–30.

Nevertheless, the promise of complete dominance of the other nations climaxes in v. 24. While the defeat of Kings Sihon and Og is much celebrated in Deuteronomy as a kind of paradigm of Israel's victories (Deut. 1:4, etc.), and Pharaoh is called king of Egypt (7:8), this is the only place in the book where the kings of other nations are referred to as a generality, though it is a marked feature of the book of Joshua (e.g. Josh. 12). The designation portrays the conflict between Yahweh and the nations as a power struggle, in which Yahweh alone is truly king. The picture of Yahweh's universal sway is the premiss of his power on Israel's behalf (cf. 3:24; 4:32–34).

25–26. The chapter returns finally (25–26) to the theme of the dangers of false worship, which has been the rationale for the opposition to the nations from the start. These verses extend the basic command of v. 5 to cover the misappropriation of the materials in the idols that, being under the 'ban', are destined for destruction. The temptation to compromise in this respect by 'desiring' the silver and gold (the word 'desire', or 'covet', is as in the Tenth Commandment, 5:21, expressing a strong craving) is illustrated in the story of Achan (Josh. 6:18–19; 7). Whether v. 26 anticipates recycling the materials as objects of worship or simply as spoils of war is unclear. But the language used of the materials shows that they are regarded as abhorrent. The key words are *tôʿēḇâ*, 'abhorrent thing, abomination' (25–26), and *šiqqēṣ*, 'treat as loathesome, detest' (26). These are technical ways of characterizing that which is under the ban, and which therefore cannot be allowed to have an existence in contact with Yahweh or his people. Abhorrence is expressed in our text by both noun and verb (*tôʿēḇâ*, *tʿb*); similarly, the verb 'treat as loathesome' has its counterpart in the noun *šiqqûṣîm*, 'loathesome thing' (not used here, but cf. Hos. 9:10). The materials of the idols are objectively 'abhorrent' in Yahweh's eyes, and therefore to be actively 'abhorred', or radically rejected, by Israel. The command is reinforced by the use of both verbs together in v. 26, each with its double form of infinitive absolute and imperative ('abhorring you shall abhor, loathing you shall loathe'). Failure to maintain integrity in this respect would mean that the people themselves would become subject to the ban.

Explanation

The present chapter is the main exposition in Deuteronomy of the book's most controversial themes, the election of Israel and the consequent radical rejection of other nations. Three topics may be identified for consideration.

First, is any reconciliation possible between the idea of God's selecting one people for a relationship with himself and the idea of God as having a universal interest in humanity? On the face of it, the contradiction between the two appears complete. It is hard for the Christian reader to assimilate the OT texts that show a ruthless attitude towards enemies, whether in Deuteronomy, Joshua, the Psalms or elsewhere. And it is harder still when such texts become the pretext for warlike and oppressive behaviour, even in modern times (see the discussion on God as one in Deut. 6). Such readings of the OT texts represent an absolutizing of holiness, one of the great theological dangers. One understandable Christian response to this problem has been to set the gospel in opposition to the 'nationalistic' religion of the OT. Christ commanded his followers to love their enemies; this must imply a judgment on the hatred of enemies found in so many OT texts.

Yet this rejectionist hermeneutic does not tell the whole story. One more positive view of Israel's election sees it as lying on the way out of polytheism in the direction of a theology of creation. Only when Yahweh is king of heaven and earth can he *choose* (Rendtorff 1981: esp. 78–80; cf. 10:12–15, where the election of Israel is grounded in creation). In addition, election statements are closely connected with Yahweh's commands (7:9–11; 10:12–13; 14:1ff.; Rendtorff 1981: 85; and see further below). Rose (1975: 97–98) also brings election into connection with Yahweh's commands, although he sees this as a process in which, in the uncertain times of the seventh century, deuteronomistic redactions hedge election theology about with conditions. Either way, election has been theologized in terms of ethical responsibility.

The relationship between election and universality has been pursued in a rather different way. Against the view that Israel's account of God's dealing with it is merely anachronistic and even offensive is the belief that the particular is a necessary precondition of the universal. God shows his interest in the whole world by showing it in the case of one people. On this view, God's history with Israel becomes a 'paradigm' for his dealing with any or every nation. O'Donovan (1996: 23) has expressed it in this way, noticing also how the self-understanding of Jesus mediates between God as ruler of Israel and as ruler of the world, and how the early church took up the same way of thinking: 'For in the church's understanding Israel's political categories were the paradigm for all others. Jesus belonged to Israel; and Israel was, for him as for his followers, the theatre of God's self-disclosure as the ruler of the nations.'

The possibility that the rule of Yahweh as expressed in Israel will become relevant to the world at large arises through the medium of Torah. The priority of Torah over election is expressed in Deuteronomy when Torah is made the focus of the nations' perspective on Israel (4:6–8), and when the main expositions of the place of Torah in Israel's life (chs. 4 – 6) precede the main exposition of its election (ch. 7). Israel, the chosen people, is subject to Torah, with the principles of righteousness and justice that it enshrines. And Torah, standing for the divine authority that lies behind all political authority, is therefore the principle of all government (O'Donovan 1996: 65–66). Furthermore, Israel's story with God, as it is continued in the 'Deuteronomistic History' (Joshua–Kings) is the story of its success and failure in respect of these things, and its own subjection to judgment on the basis of them (1996: 69).

Two further things follow from this idea of Israel as paradigm. The first is that the idea of the divine rule never becomes an abstraction. The rule of God is always realized in particularities, that is, in the context of particular national traditions. O'Donovan goes further than this and says that Israel's story implies the validity of a plurality of national traditions, as opposed to universal, imperial government, which the OT strongly rejects (1996: 71).

Secondly, Israel's experience of judgment followed by salvation becomes the basis of hope for other nations. The whole story of Israel becomes paradigmatic, including its failure to keep covenant, but also in turn the judgment on the nations that, in their own rejection of divine rule, were in their time the instruments of Yahweh's wrath on Israel (Is. 10:5–10; Jer. 50 – 51; cf. O'Donovan 1996: 69), followed by Israel's restoration to land, independence – and to Torah (Deut. 30:1–10).

The problem of the election of Israel can therefore be turned to positive account, as the story of God's saving intentions for all humanity. This too is the thrust of the whole OT story. Indeed, the Bible as a whole may be said to wrestle with this issue of the universal and the particular. On the broadest canvas, the covenantal story (of Israel) comes in after the introduction of chaos into the world created 'good' (Gen. 1 – 3), and leads into universalizing perspectives, both in the OT (e.g. Is. 40 – 66) and in the NT.

The specific problem of the sentence of destruction on the nations of Canaan has been treated above (see 'Explanation' of Deut. 2). Its theological function is to express the rejection of forms of rule that were not subject to the divine rule. These can be seen as a kind of 'chaos', and the divine war against the idolatrous nations therefore as an act of salvation, in the sense of establishing the possibility of the divine rule in the world, which alone could offer it hope.

The radical rejection of other nations as a thoroughgoing cultural confrontation has also been explored by C. J. H. Wright (1990), who helpfully adopted the idea of Israel as paradigm in relation to its laws. On the ban on intermarriage as a rejection of idolatry, see also Knoppers (1994), who traces the theme in Exod. 34:11–16; Josh. 23:2–16; Judg. 3:6–7; 1 Kgs. 11:1–2.

DEUTERONOMY 8:1–20

Translation

[1]Be careful to keep the whole law with which I am charging you this day, in order to have life and to grow in number, and to come into possession of the land the LORD promised on oath to your forefathers. [2]Remember the whole journey that the LORD your God led you on these forty years in the wilderness, in order to humble and test you, to know what was in your hearts and whether you would keep his commands or not. [3]And he did humble you, making you hungry and then feeding you with manna, which neither you nor your forefathers had known before, to teach you that human beings do not live by food alone, but they live by

everything that comes from the mouth of the LORD. [4]The clothes on your back did not wear out these forty years, nor did your feet swell. [5]Understand then in your hearts that the LORD your God disciplines you, just as a man does his son. [6]Keep the commands of the LORD your God, following in his ways, and revering him.

[7]When the LORD your God brings you into a delightful land, a land of streams, springs and underground waters that gush forth in valley and hill, [8]a land of wheat and barley, of vine, fig and pomegranate, a land of olive oil and honey, [9]a land where you will eat food in plenty, and lack nothing, a land whose stones are iron and from whose mountains you will mine copper, [10]and when you eat and are satisfied, and bless the LORD your God for the delightful land he has given you, [11]then be careful not to forget the LORD your God, by failing to keep his commands, laws and statutes with which I am charging you this day.

[12]For you might be tempted – when you eat and are satisfied, and are living in fine houses that you have built, [13]when your herds and flocks increase, and you are rich in silver and gold, indeed when you have everything in great quantity – [14]to become proud, forgetting the LORD your God, who brought you out of slavery in the land of Egypt, [15]who led you in that vast and terrible wilderness, with its poisonous snakes and its scorpions and its waterless wastes, who produced water from the flinty rock [16]and fed you manna in the wilderness, a food your forefathers had not known, all to humble you and to test you, yet to do you good in the end; [17]you might be tempted to say to yourselves: 'Our own strength and energy got us all this wealth.' [18]Then remember that it was the LORD your God who gave you strength to be successful, in order to confirm his covenant promised on oath to your forefathers, as he has done this day.

[19]But if you do forget the LORD your God and go to worship and bow down to other gods, I stand to witness against you today that you will certainly perish. [20]Just like the nations that the LORD is destroying before you, you too will be destroyed, because you would not obey the LORD your God.

Notes on the text

7. *kî* is here taken as 'when', introducing a conditional sentence, not as 'for', explaining what has preceded. For analogies see 6:10; 18:9: *kî attā bā'*..., 'when you come...' The main statement then follows in v. 11. Formally, it is not always easy to discern when a 'when/if' clause finishes in a conditional sentence, and when the main clause begins, since both types of clause are often introduced with *waw*-consecutive. Exegetical decisions, therefore, depend on what makes best sense in the context. See also 18:6–8, and 'Comment' there.

12. On the syntax of the passage beginning *pen*, 'lest', see below, 'Form and structure'.

16. 'in the end'; the term is *bᵉaḥᵃrîtᵉḵā*, lit. 'at *your* end', referring not merely to the end of the journey to the land, but also to the idea of a final

condition or destiny. This 'end' is more than a point on a timescale, rather a goal reached. The expression is reminiscent of the prophetic 'in the latter days', with its eschatological overtones (cf. Is. 2:2).

Form and structure

A simple logic informs the whole chapter. The journey in the wilderness has been an assay, to know whether the people can and will remain faithful, and to teach them that they have cause to do so (by the provision of manna); similarly, the possession of the land will tempt them to be unfaithful; then they must stand firm, remembering the lessons of the desert.

The structure reflects this strong sense of purpose. It is an argumentative chapter. Its aim is to persuade Israel to remember Yahweh and keep his laws (1, 19–20). The first sub-section, vv. 2–6, contains several infinitives (concentrated in vv. 2–4), expressing purpose. It ends at v. 6, which recalls the theme of v. 1 (keeping the commandments). There are also repetitions of vocabulary between v. 2 and vv. 5–6 ('go in the way', 'heart', 'keep the commandment' [*miṣwâ*]; N. Lohfink 1963: 190).

There follow two sections (vv. 7–11, 12–18) that are syntactically extended, in order to motivate by spelling out the grounds for obedience. Verses 7–11 form a long conditional sentence (see 'Notes on the text'). The opening *kî* is best translated 'when', on analogy with 6:10, rather than 'for' (as NIV; N. Lohfink 1963: 192; Weinfeld 1991: 391). This means that the passage should not be seen as a self-contained statement, grounding the preceding vv. 1–6, and ending with the rather static assertion in v. 10 that they would eat their fill and 'bless' the LORD (NIV). Rather, vv. 7–11 constitute a single conditional sentence, whose apodosis (the 'then' clause) falls in v. 11. (The sentence is similar to 6:10–19.) This has the effect that, while it makes a sharp contrast with the time of hardship in the desert (2–4), it belongs integrally with vv. 12–18, expressing the strong moral danger associated with possession of the land.

Verses 12–18 also achieve a taut argument by means of a series of clauses subordinated to the double climax in vv. 17–18: 'you might be tempted to say ... Then remember...' The translation adopted has tried to express this by means of a single sentence spanning vv. 12–17. Verse 12 actually opens with the word *pen*, 'lest', and is followed by a series of verbs with *waw*-consecutive (lit. 'and', but capable of a variety of subordinating nuances). The translation expresses this with 'you might be tempted', which is adopted to try to express the force of the sentence; it is repeated in v. 17, where the *waw*-consecutive should be read as resuming the force of the 'lest' in v. 12.

The structure of the chapter may be illustrated thus (following N. Lohfink 1963: 189):

1	Paranetic scheme
2–6	Argument (*Beweisführung*)
7–18	Command sequence (*kleine Gebotsumrahmung*)
19–20	Conditional curse

Lohfink (1963: 195) also finds a chiastic structure superimposed on this, centring on v. 11, which highlights the chapter's theme of dependence. It is: A 1; B 2–4; C 7b–9; D 11; C' 12–13; B' 14b–16; A' 19–20. This is preferable to Fishbane's analysis of vv. 1–18: A 1, B 2–3, C 6, D 7a, E 7b–9, D' 10b, C' 11, B' 15–16, A' 16. According to this, vv. 7b–9 (E, the anticipated bounty in the land) form the centre of the passage (Fishbane 1985: 328–329). It is imperfect, because it does not account for the culmination of the argument in vv. 17–18, 19–20, nor does it identify the nub of the chapter's argument.

We have already noticed a close formal connection between chs. 7 and 8 (see on ch. 7, 'Form and structure'), with the unusual term *'ēqeb* (7:12) finding an echo in 8:20, which suggests a closure at the latter verse. The chapters also share echoes of the Decalogue (here vv. 14, 19), the idea of the oath to the patriarchs as 'covenant' (*bᵉrît*; 7:12; 8:18), the only blessing-and-curse texts in Deut. 5 – 8 (7:12–26, 8:19–20), and concentric forms (N. Lohfink 1963: 197). For these reasons Deut. 7 and 8 can be seen as belonging closely together within the larger structure of chs. 5 – 11. See also O'Connell (1992b: 265), who regards chs. 7 and 8 as complementary; ch. 7 urges Israel on to activity and courage, while ch. 8 wants them to understand their dependence on Yahweh.

The present chapter finds important echoes in three other passages, Deut. 32:10–18, Hos. 13:4–8, and Deut. 17:14–20. The first restates in poetic form the thought in Deut. 8: the sustaining in the wilderness (32:10–12), rich provision in the land (32:13–14), 'Jacob's' satiation leading to 'forgetting' Yahweh (32:15–18), and a connection with idolatry (32:16–17). The passage is followed by a declaration of intent to punish (32:19–27).

The thought in Hos. 13:4–8 is similar, with surprisingly close echoes of Deut. 8, extending even to vocabulary, mainly in Hos. 13:4–6: 'from Egypt' (Deut. 8:14; Hos. 13:4), 'satisfied' (*śāba'*, Deut. 8:12; Hos. 13:6), 'hearts lifted up' (Deut. 8:14; Hos. 13:6), 'forgetting' (Deut. 8:11, 14, 19; Hos. 13:6). Other elements are also present, for example 'feeding', though the terms used differ (Deut. 8:3; Hos. 13:6). And there are terms in common, though the contexts in which they are used differ: 'eating' (Deut. 8:12; Hos. 13:8), 'did not know' (Deut. 8:16; Hos. 13:4).

In places Hosea resembles Deut. 32 more closely than Deut. 8. For example, Hos. 13:4 is like Deut. 32:12, 17 (they knew no other God); and Hos. 13:7–8 echoes the language of punishment in Deut. 32:24.

Hosea and Deut. 32 also have in common that they look back on Israel's rebellion as an accomplished fact, Hosea attaching his critique to a further taunt about kings (Hos. 13:9–11), which has some echoes of Deutero-nomy's warning in Deut. 17:14–20. Deut. 8 has also been linked with Deut. 17:14–20 in the sense that both warn against the dangers of complacency arising from wealth; the former passage has even been linked with Solomon (as has the latter), and has been seen as a generalizing of the implied criticism of Solomon in 1 Kings.

There is a complex picture of interrelationships here, therefore, which is more easily described than accounted for, in terms of linguistic compar-isons alone. The four passages all express the moral dangers of plenty, concomitantly with idolatry, in a way that may be called 'deuteronomic'. On general grounds I have taken the view that Deuteronomy itself (rather than Hosea) is the source of this thought. Within Deuteronomy, it seems that Deut. 32:10–18 reflects on Deut. 8 and 17:14–20 (see on that chapter). Hos. 13:4–8 may then draw on all the Deuteronomy texts.

Comment

8:1–6

1. The chapter opens with a typical requirement to keep the command-ments (*hammiṣwâ*, the law as a whole; see on 5:31; 6:1). The perspective moves from the immediate present of Moses' address ('today') to an anticipated long future in the land. The phrase 'so that you may live' (here translated 'in order to have life') applies to the people in their totality and throughout their generations, as is clear from the accompanying 'grow in number' ('multiply'). The logic of the verse, therefore, is not that Israel must obey here and now in Moab and thus qualify to enter the land in the immediate future. Rather, it is in line with the rhetoric of chs. 5 – 6, which established a connection between the laws as given on Horeb and the ongoing teaching and interpreting of them in the people's future settled existence. This verse is sometimes seen as making a contrast with the thought in the rest of the chapter, as it is held to place obedience logically before possession, and therefore to be 'legalistic' (N. Lohfink 1981: 98). However, Deuteronomy's rhetoric variously displays both sides of a complex thought: on the one hand, Yahweh gives, therefore Israel must obey (as in 7:11); and on the other, Israel must obey in order to continue to possess (7:12, and here; see also on 7:12). The appeal to the promise to the patriarchs in this verse finally keeps this balance.

In this context, the verse specifically introduces the theme of the chapter: the need for the people to remain faithful to the covenant during their whole existence in the land. Craigie (1976a: 184–185) has rightly pointed out that the theme of dependence on Yahweh is reinforced by a sustained comparison between life in the desert and in the land. In this way ch. 8

forms part of Deuteronomy's validation of the commands once given at Horeb for Israel's future in the land, and in all new situations.

2. The call to 'remember' strikes a vital chord in deuteronomic paranesis, being embedded in the concept of a deliverance from slavery which then becomes the ground of covenant faithfulness (cf. 5:6, 15; 7:18). Its importance here is signalled by its repetition in v. 18, and by the corresponding and repeated warning not to 'forget' (11, 14, 19). Israel's memory is directed to the journey in the desert, characterized as a time of Yahweh's care (cf. 1:31). The term 'led you' is literally 'caused you to go' (a hiphil, or causative, form), which encapsulates Yahweh's responsibility and enabling in all of the people's progress. The phrase 'these forty years' is resumed from 2:7, and is a further echo of the theme of chs. 1 – 3, in which the punishment of the forty-year delay to enter the land in the desert became a testimony to Yahweh's care.

3. The time in the desert is now additionally seen as a test of Israel. This is a neat reversal of the 'testing' of Yahweh by the people at Massah (6:16). Its focus on whether Israel would obey the commandments is also a shift from the test of faith that was entailed in the initial command to take the land (1:8). The testing in the desert is related to the provision of manna, as it was also in the parallel passage in Exod. 16. There, it was given not only in answer to physical need, but as a test of the people's willingness to believe and follow God's commands (his *tôrâ*, 4), concretized in the Sabbath command (22–30). Deuteronomy enhances this connection by making the test relate to the habit and life of faith, ignoring the particular application to Sabbath-keeping. The test is 'to humble ... you ... to know what was in your hearts and whether you would keep his commands or not ... to teach you [make you understand]...' (2–3). While Deuteronomy has in common with Exodus a concern with obedience to Yahweh's commands, it looks for a faithfulness that goes deeper than obedience in particular instances, or mere acquiescence in written requirements (cf. 10:16; see also Fishbane 1985: 326–328). (Deuteronomy will go on to show, in 9:1 – 10:11, that Israel failed the test of the desert. However, this is not the right point in the argument at which to bring this out, or to reflect on the consequences of it.)

The faithfulness required by Yahweh is expressed in trust. In this respect the present text is exactly like Exodus. But here the point is made as a general principle. This is the purpose of the well-known v. 3b. Jesus' adoption of the passage brings out a contrast between material and spiritual 'food', in the context of his fasting in the wilderness (Matt. 4:4), and this has widely influenced understanding of the verse in question (see Perlitt 1981: 403–404). Jesus' refusal of miraculous food in that context is a strange inversion of the divine provision of it here. The thought in this place is not directly a contrast between material and spiritual, but an assertion that people do not secure their well-being in their own strength. The final phrase, 'by everything that comes from the mouth of the LORD', may imply utterances as commands which, by their wisdom, are a source of life, or as acts of providence, that is, whatever is created by God's word (S. R. Driver 1895: 107; NRSV mg.). The former meaning is certainly at home in Deuteronomy, with its close connection between obedience and life. Yet the latter is strongly suggested here, because the temptation to self-sufficiency is a central theme of the chapter, which will be developed in vv. 12–18. The case of manna as a warning against self-sufficiency is stressed especially in vv. 15–18, which echo v. 3b.

It is striking that the lesson on dependence concerns not Israel alone but humanity (*hā'āḏām*). This universal dimension has been met before in Deuteronomy in connection with Yahweh's universal rule (4:32–40). There it was associated with the election of Israel, which it in a sense recast (see on 7:7–11). Here Israel's experience is explicitly made a paradigm of human experience in general, and there is an echo of the Genesis creation narratives' assertion of the divine interest in all humanity (Gen. 1 – 3).

4. The point about dependence on Yahweh is carried on in v. 4, with the miraculous arresting of normal wear and tear, a point confined in the Pentateuch to Deuteronomy (cf. 29:5[4]; Neh. 9:21), and perhaps to be taken rhetorically rather than literally (S. R. Driver 1895: 108).

5–6. These verses complete the picture of a continuing, responsive relationship between Yahweh and people. The father–son metaphor has been used previously to express Yahweh's care (1:31); here it is turned to discipline, to show that that is tempered by love. Discipline has appeared before in Deuteronomy, as a function of God's 'voice' (4:36; this is therefore a second echo of 4:32–40 in these verses; see above on *'āḏām*, v. 3); here it involves the loving provision of the manna, and the other miraculous signs of care. Finally, the physical journey in the desert is echoed by a metaphorical walking in his ways that means an obedient lifestyle (6, employing the same terms, *hālaḵ, dereḵ*, as v. 2).

8:7–11

7–9. While the land is ubiquitous in Deuteronomy, this passage contains its most vivid portrayal, picturing its natural richness with an accumulation of its features. All is in contrast with the desert. In place of the hand-to-mouth sustenance provided by the manna, the means of livelihood will be present regularly and in abundance. It will be well watered rather than arid, fertile rather than rocky, rich above and beyond basic need, with its variety of vegetables and fruit, oil and honey, replete even with minerals, suggesting the possibility of industry, trade and wealth. The theme of land becomes here an ideal, or dream, of plenty; a well-known theme in the ancient world, where life was often felt to be precarious. Egypt, by its natural configuration, furnished the outstanding example of the contrast between life and death, with its ribbon of fertility along the Nile flanked on both sides by extensive desert zones. The Egyptian story of Sinuhe has its own lyric on the abundant land (see Lichtheim 1975: 226–227). Pharaoh's dreams of plenty and dearth, interpreted by Joseph (Gen. 41), constitute only one example of the theme in Egypt (see *ANET* 31 for a traditional motif of seven lean years). The *Wisdom of Merikare* contrasts Egypt as a place of plenty and order with the chaos and deprivation of the lands of the 'Asiatics' beyond (Lichtheim 1975: 103–104). We have noticed already that it was the king's responsibility to provide the benefits of land, and that in Deuteronomy Yahweh takes that role (see on 6:10–12).

10–11. The extravagant picture of the land is subordinated, as explained above ('Form and structure'), to the exhortation not to forget him. The sequence of thought from v. 10 to v. 11 suggests initial recognition of Yahweh's hand in the rich provision, followed by 'forgetting' (11). The same danger has been heralded before (4:9, 23; 6:12), but here the ingratitude is most tellingly exposed by means of the portrayal of the unstinting gift; and the psychology (or the spiritual lineaments) of forgetfulness is explored trenchantly in the following verses (12–18). It is important to note first, though, that forgetting Yahweh is inseparable from failing to keep his commandments. This connection has been forged already in Deut. 4, which brings together the need for obedience to Yahweh's commands and the prohibition of worshipping other gods. Commentators have sometimes maintained that the present passage originally spoke of a forgetting of Yahweh that was not tied to his commands, thinking that the latter idea came from a secondary, more legalistic hand (Mayes 1979: 192–193). It is difficult to pull these ideas apart with confidence, however; the whole tenor of chs. 7 – 8, with its special development of the concept of election, has expressed loyalty to Yahweh both in personal terms and in relation to his laws (7:9).

8:12–18

The tendency to forget the giver in the very enjoyment of his gift is now developed. The motive to gratitude and praise is dulled by the experience of plenty. This forgetfulness, like its corresponding memory, is a capacity of heart and will, rather than of mind.

In the portrayal of pride that follows, the idea of fullness (*śāba'*, v. 12), resumed from v. 10, is now elaborated into a picture of settled enjoyment of wealth that keeps on growing; note the emphasis on abundance in v. 13 ('increase ... great quantity' translate the same verb, *rābâ*, occurring twice), echoing a theme of v. 9. There is a sense of passing time here: time for houses to have been built, and for herds and flocks to become numerous (contrast 6:11, in which the houses are those left behind by the previous occupants, and the time reference is more immediate). The response, in contrast to the praise in v. 10, is now pride (lit. '[lest] your heart be lifted up', 14a), and forgetting God, who had brought them out of Egypt. Particular stress is laid on the saving acts of God on their behalf – deliverance from Egypt, and miraculous provision of both water and manna in the desert (14b–16). This familiar theme is now made to bring out the irony of Israel's pride and ingratitude. The climax of the point is reached in v. 17, in which Israel imagines that its own power has made it rich.

The connection of thought in vv. 14b–17 resembles that of vv. 2–3, with its testing in order to teach a dependent spirit; that passage then added the thought of vv. 7–10, where blessing led to praise. But here the picture is reversed, for the hard time in the wilderness has been forgotten, and the plenty has led not to praise but to the pride of self-sufficiency. The climax of the exhortation is reached with the plea that they should 'remember' Yahweh instead of forgetting him, and that it was he who gave the land and the strength to enjoy its wealth, in fulfilment of his promise to the patriarchs (18). The picture of rebellion is not inevitable, if the people keep Yahweh before them.

19–20. The chapter concludes with a curse formula, in keeping with the covenantal structure of thought. The tone of persuasion gives way to a different kind of motivation, the warning that rebellion will have consequences in severe punishment. The topic of forgetfulness is continued, but shifted slightly to focus on worshipping other gods, rather than on mere self-sufficiency. The apostasy would also imply disobedience to God's commands. Self-sufficiency, apostasy and disobedience are finally brought together here, as jointly characterizing rejection of Yahweh's covenant.

Moses once called 'heaven and earth' to witness against Israel that they would perish if they committed apostasy (4:26). In a similar formula he now stands as witness himself (*hā'idōtî*). The term can mean simply 'I warn you', but the translation here is equally possible, and is suggested by the covenantal pronouncement. He thus takes the role of witness to the covenantal arrangement in which he has been mediator. The punishment of Israel is simply 'to perish' (cf. 7:4). The verb is expressed in the emphatic form (19), and repeated in v. 20. The due penalty for covenant unfaithfulness, therefore, is a complete end to the people. This does not correspond exactly to the fate that finally befell Judah (2 Kgs. 24 – 25), since it went into exile in 587 BC and later returned (as is actually anticipated in Deut. 30:1–10; cf. Knoppers 1994). It is closer to that of the northern kingdom, which sank without trace in 722 BC (2 Kgs. 17). Complete destruction, however, remains the due penalty for covenant disobedience. The point is made with some irony, for Israel would then be subject to the wrath that had been destined for others, whom God had not chosen to bless.

With this return to the topic of Israel in relation to other nations there is a reminder that the themes of chs. 7 and 8 have been closely connected.

The terms of v. 20 recall those of 7:12 (see on that passage). And the picture of blessing spurned in apostasy (8:12–20) is a mirror image of the blessing bestowed for faithfulness in 7:12–16, in which the wrath of Yahweh falls on the other nations. The point is reiterated that chosenness cannot be taken for granted.

Explanation

The chapter makes important connections with other OT passages (see 'Form and structure'), and the comparison helps to bring out the main themes. Deut. 8 is perhaps the greatest statement of human dependence on God for everything. Verse 3 is a key: it is not (directly) a contrast between the material and the spiritual (as might be supposed from Jesus' words in Matt. 4:4), but between self-dependence and dependence on God. The line of thought in the chapter brilliantly portrays the moral dangers of plenty, and therefore the dilemma of Deuteronomy; in the covenant, God promises rich blessing as part of the relationship he establishes with Israel, yet the blessing itself carries enormous temptation. The danger of wealth to true spirituality also becomes an important NT theme (Luke 18:18–25). While Jesus put a particular spin on Deut. 8:3, there is nevertheless no important difference between that verse and his interpretation of it. Both the Israelites (in accepting the manna) and Jesus (in refusing miraculous food) expressed trusting dependence on God, pointed to him as the true author of all well-being, and resisted the temptation to depend on strength that was independent of him. Deuteronomy's affirmation of the good things of God's creation has no truck with any 'prosperity theology'; this chapter, indeed, is as strong a repudiation of such an interpretation as may be found anywhere in the Bible.

As for the connection between self-sufficiency, apostasy and disobedience, these may seem quite separate in a day when the first of them usually implies a practical atheism. But they are not so distinct in a religious society. For Israel, self-sufficiency would be conceivable within a religious framework, in which gods might be seen as a sanction of success. The fertility cults of Canaan could well have been so interpreted. The closeness of disobedience and apostasy is clear from the First Commandment (Deut. 5:7). When the commands of Yahweh are put in a covenantal context, there is no pure ethic, but rather faithfulness to the giver of Israel's good, expressed in practical terms in both worship and adherence to his laws (this is more fully explained in the 'Explanation' to ch. 5).

The dangers of wealth foreseen in Deut. 8 are sometimes thought to have emanated from a time when Israel was indeed prosperous, such as the reign of Solomon. A very similar theme is struck in Deut. 17:14–20, where the qualifications set upon kingship are strongly reminiscent of Solomon's actual excesses. He too serves as an example of how the enjoyment of

God's blessing can lead into sin. We have already noticed (on Deut. 7) the similarities between Deut. 7:1–4 and 1 Kgs. 11:1–4. But the latter passage is immediately preceded by 1 Kgs. 10:26–29, which reflects on the king's enormous wealth. In Deut. 8, the dangers of wealth are applied to the people as a whole.

The chapter concludes with a covenantal curse formula. Complete destruction for disobedience (v. 19) further qualifies election (cf. on Deut. 7): election is not an unqualified promise; rather, the elect are still subject to covenant requirements. The point is extremely important in relation to the widely held idea in OT studies that God's covenant with Israel was originally a covenant of promise, and that such a covenant was intrinsically superior to covenants that had a conditional element (note von Rad's 'declension from grace into law', 1966: 91). Even so, covenant may ultimately be governed by grace. The adoption of a covenantal form in Deuteronomy does not entail any determinism about the implementation of covenantal curses; the formula of 8:19–20 must be seen in the light of the 'dénouement' (30:1–10; cf. 4:29–31). Here too Deuteronomy finds an echo in Hosea (Hos. 11:8–9).

DEUTERONOMY 9:1 – 10:11

Translation

[1]Hear, Israel: this day you are about to go over the Jordan to dispossess nations that are greater and stronger than you, taking possession of great cities fortified to the sky. [2]They are a mighty people, great in stature, Anakim, of whom you know, and of whom you have heard it said: 'Who can resist the Anakim?' [3]But you shall know this day that it is the LORD your God who is crossing ahead of you; like a devouring fire he will destroy them, and he will bring them to their knees before you; you will indeed drive them out and destroy them quickly, just as the LORD promised you. [4]When the LORD your God has driven them out before you, do not think: 'It is because of our innocence that the LORD has brought us here to possess this land, and because of the guilt of these nations that the LORD is driving them out before you.' [5]It is not because of your innocence or uprightness of heart that you are going over to occupy their land; though indeed the LORD your God is dispossessing these nations before you because of their wickedness, and also in order to fulfil the promise he made on oath to your forefathers, Abraham, Isaac and Jacob. [6]So you must know that it is not because of your innocence that the LORD your God is giving you this good land to possess; indeed, you are an obstinate people. [7]Remember, do not forget, how you angered the LORD your God in the wilderness; from the day that you left the land of Egypt until you came to this place, you have been rebelling against the LORD.

[8]Even at Horeb you angered the LORD so much that in his wrath he was ready to destroy you. [9]When I went up the mountain to get the stone tablets, the tablets of

the covenant the LORD made with you, I remained on the mountain forty days and forty nights, neither eating food nor drinking water. [10]Then the LORD gave me the two stone tablets, written with God's own finger, bearing all the words the LORD spoke to you on the mountain from the heart of the fire on the day of the assembly.

[11]It was at the end of forty days and forty nights that the LORD gave me the two stone tablets, the tablets of the covenant, [12]and the LORD said to me: 'Rise and go down quickly from here, for your people, which you brought out of Egypt, have become corrupt; they have lost no time in leaving the way I commanded them to go: they have made themselves an idol.' [13]The LORD also said to me: 'I have seen this people, and they are obstinate. [14]Let me alone and I will destroy them and blot out their name from the earth, and instead I will make of you a nation stronger and more numerous than they.' [15]So I turned and came down the mountain, while it was ablaze with fire, carrying the two tablets of the covenant in my hands. [16]Then I saw how you had indeed sinned against the LORD your God; you had made for yourselves a molten calf-image; you had lost no time in departing from the way that the LORD your God had commanded you. [17]So I took hold of the two tablets and flung them from my hands, smashing them before your eyes.

[18]Then I lay prostrate before the LORD in prayer as I had done before, without eating food or drinking water, for forty days and forty nights, because of all the sins you had committed, and because you had done evil in the LORD's eyes, provoking him to anger, [19]for I was greatly afraid of the furious wrath the LORD had conceived against you, that it might destroy you. But the LORD heard my prayer that time also. [20]The LORD in his fury was also about to destroy Aaron; but I prayed for Aaron too at that time. [21]As for the sinful thing you had made, the calf, I took it and burned it with fire, then crushed it and ground it thoroughly till it was as fine as dust, and I flung the dust of it into the wadi that runs down the mountain.

[22]Likewise at Taberah, at Massah and at Kibroth-Hattaavah you continually provoked the LORD to anger. [23]Even when the LORD sent you forth from Kadesh-Barnea, and said: 'Go up into the land I have given you, and occupy it', you defied the LORD your God, and would not trust or obey him. [24]You have been rebellious against the LORD since the day he first knew you.

[25]So I lay before the LORD those forty days and forty nights, for the LORD intended to destroy you. [26]I prayed to the LORD, and said, 'O LORD God, do not destroy your people, your inheritance, whom in your great strength you set free, bringing them out of Egypt by your mighty hand. [27]Remember your servants, Abraham, Isaac and Jacob; overlook the hard-heartedness of this people, their wickedness and their sin. [28]For the people of the land from which you delivered us might say: "It was because the LORD could not take them into the land he promised them, and because he hated them, that he led them out to their death in the wilderness." [29]They are your people, your inheritance, whom you delivered by your great strength and with outstretched arm.'

[10:1]At that time the LORD said to me: 'Carve out two stone tablets like the first ones, then come up on the mountain, to me, and make an ark of wood. [2]I will write on the tablets the words that were on the first tablets, the ones you broke, and you shall place them in the ark.' ³So after I had made an ark of acacia wood, and cut two stone tablets like the first ones, I went up the mountain carrying the two tablets in my hands. ⁴And the LORD wrote on the tablets the same writing as before, the Ten Commandments that he had spoken to you on the mountain from the heart of the fire, on the day when you were assembled there; and the LORD gave them to me. ⁵I turned, came down the mountain and put the tablets in the ark I had made; and there they remain, as the LORD commanded me.

⁶(The Israelites travelled from Beeroth-bene-Jaakan to Moserah. There Aaron died and was buried, and Eleazar his son served as priest in his place. ⁷From there they travelled to Gudgodah, and from Gudgodah to Jotbathah, a land of flowing streams. ⁸At that time, the LORD set apart the tribe of Levi to carry the ark of the covenant of the LORD, to stand before the LORD to minister to him, and to bless in his name, as still happens today. ⁹It is for this reason that Levi did not receive a part of the land as their inheritance, as their fellow tribes did; the LORD is their inheritance, as the LORD your God promised them.)

¹⁰As for me, I remained on the mountain forty days and forty nights, just as the first time; this time too the LORD heard my prayer, and the LORD refrained from destroying you. ¹¹The LORD said to me: 'Rise and go on the journey ahead of the people, so that they enter and take possession of the land I promised on oath to their forefathers to give them.'

Notes on the text

9:1. 'dispossess ... taking possession of': these together translate the verb *yāraš*, which occurs only once in the sentence.

3. Three times the emphatic subject pronoun *hû*', 'he', referring to Yahweh, introduces clauses with imperfect verbs. This departure from the usual sequence of *waw*-consecutive with pf. for future acts stresses that it is Yahweh who will act, rather than the action itself. See 'Comment'.

4. 'before you': it is possible to read 'before me', following Ehrlich (1909: ad loc.), who suggested that the second-person singular ending was a misplaced conjunction *kî*, 'for', which originally introduced the next clause. The issue of interpretation that arises may be solved either in this way, or in the more rhetorical way proposed by N. Lohfink (see 'Comment').

9. 'forty days and forty nights': the numeral *'arbā'îm* is followed in each case by the noun in the singular, as is usual for multiples of ten. This is the typical form in the section; cf. 9:11; 9:18; 10:10. In 9:25 each noun is qualified by the definite article, indicating that it is the same period as mentioned before (in that case, v. 18).

12. *hôṣêtâ* (*yṣ*', hiph.), 'you brought out', typically in Deuteronomy; Exodus uses this verb and *'lh* hiph. variously (cf. the parallel passage, Exod. 32:7, for the latter); Deuteronomy uses this verb only once in this sense, at 20:1.

14. 'and I will destroy . . . [I will] blot out . . . I will make . . .': these verbs are all impf. following simple *waw*, a construction that expresses purpose. Therefore one might translate 'that I may destroy', etc. The force seems to be closer to cohortative, however, which can be translated with an emphatic future. This seems to be required in the last instance.

16. *wᵉhinnēh*: often 'behold', but always better rendered otherwise. Here 'I saw *how* you had sinned' is intended to signify that the phrase means more than simply 'I saw *that*', but expresses the immediacy of Moses' shocked reaction. The verb sequence is without *waw*-consecutive, and is therefore translated staccato, again expressing the immediacy of Moses' reaction.

21. The destruction of the calf is introduced with a phrase that indicates a change of subject-matter: 'As for the sinful thing . . . I took . . .' This is not the form used for narrative sequence, and the syntax therefore agrees with the fact that the events narrated in vv. 15–21 are not strictly sequential. A reconstruction of the chronology puts the burning of the calf before the intercession, not after (see 'Comment').

22. 'Likewise at Taberah': 'likewise' translates *waw*, 'and'.

'. . . you *continually* provoked': this represents pf. of *hāyâ* followed by ptc.; the translation is influenced by the tendency of the chapter to represent Israel as habitually rebellious (see 'Comment').

24. 'since the day *he* [Yahweh] first knew you' follows SamP; MT has 'I' (Moses). The case for the former is strong (cf. Hos. 13:5), since the idea of Moses' first knowing the people is not so significant.

25. 'those forty days and forty nights': see on v. 9.

'intended': the verb *'āmar* more commonly means 'say', but can also mean 'think' or, as here, 'intend'.

27. Lit. 'Do not turn towards the hard-heartedness'; *tēpen* is the shortened form of 2 m. sg. impf. of *pānâ*.

28. Lit. 'the land might say'; the verb is plural, however, and the phrase is clearly shorthand for 'the people of the land'. SamP supplies the word *ʿam*, 'people', and LXX follows suit; these are probably rationalizing additions, however.

10:6. The new topic is signalled by the syntax, with the subject, 'and the Israelites', placed first in the sentence, breaking the sequence of *waw*-consecutives. The reversion to the former topic is marked in the same way in v. 10.

9. Levi is here pictured as one of the twelve brothers, and therefore has a singular verb in Hebrew. The point is really made about the tribe, however, hence the plural used in the translation.

10. The sentence begins with *wᵉ'ānōḵî*, lit. 'and I', i.e. 'as for me', and continues with the perfect tense. As in v. 6, the change of topic is marked by placing the subject first.

Form and structure

Relation to other texts in Deuteronomy and the Pentateuch

Deut. 9:1 – 10:11 is based partly on the narrative of the golden calf in Exod. (24:12–18) 32 – 34, which catalogues the apostasy, amounting to a breach of the covenant just made on Mt Sinai (= Horeb; Exod. 32:1–10); Moses' intercessions for the people (Exod. 32:11–14, 31–32; 33:12–16; 34:9); the annulling of the covenant (Exod. 32:15–20); punishments for the apostasy (Exod. 32:25–29, 35); an assurance of God's continuing presence (Exod. 33); and the renewal of the covenant (Exod. 34). Of these elements, Deuteronomy retains the apostasy, Moses' intercession (reduced to one) and the covenant renewal, omitting the punishments and the issue about God's presence (see below for reasons for this). It also reorders events to some extent. Whereas in Exodus Moses' first intercession takes place during the first period on the mountain, immediately after God tells him that Israel has sinned (Exod. 32:11–14), in Deuteronomy he does not pray then, but only after he has seen the apostasy for himself (Deut. 9:16–18). The outcomes of the intercessions differ somewhat also: Exodus has one categorical change of heart on God's part (Exod. 32:14), and one qualified response, in which he announces a limited punishment (32:33–34), before the covenant renewal (34:10–35); Deuteronomy simply says twice that God heard Moses' prayer (Deut. 9:19b; 10:10). Furthermore, Deuteronomy is less clear on the number of periods Moses spends on the mountain. In Exodus it is apparently three times (Exod. [24:18] 32:15, 30–31; 34:2), with the first and third each lasting forty days (24:18; 34:28); Deuteronomy's account requires only two (see below). The forty-day period, however, together with the element of fasting (Exod. 34:28), becomes an important motif in Deuteronomy's account.

Deut. 9:1 – 10:11 not only recalls Exod. 32 – 34, but also echoes Deut. 1 and Num. 13 – 14, and the reports there of Israel's failure to take the land in the first instance through lack of faith (Deut. 9:1–2, 22–24). The themes of apostasy and covenant renewal, therefore, are spliced more firmly into that of occupation of land than in Exodus.

Deuteronomy also varies from Exodus in its 'running order' of events following the covenant at Sinai/Horeb: while Exodus incorporates its law code into the covenant narrative (Exod. 21 – 23), Deuteronomy postpones that to chs. 12 – 26; Exodus follows the covenant narrative with instructions about the tabernacle (Exod. 25 – 31), while Deuteronomy, lacking those, includes before its golden-calf narrative the reflections on regular teaching of the law (ch. 6) and on election and sin (chs. 7 – 8).

Because of the differences between Exodus and Deuteronomy in their general chronological scheme, earlier commentators sometimes tried to relocate the passage in Deuteronomy; after 5:31, for example, in order to allow the apostasy to follow directly on the conclusion of the covenant, as in Exodus. Such efforts are misguided, however. Rather, the memory of the events recorded here is shaped according to Deuteronomy's own developing argument. Unlike Exodus, Deuteronomy uses the apostasy to illustrate a general tendency in Israel's religious life, specifically in connection with the justification for the occupation of the land of Canaan by a people of this sort in preference to other nations. The narrative of the apostasy, therefore, is built into the movement towards the land, which we have seen to be a major element in Deuteronomy's portrayal, and which I have called the 'journey' theme. This explains, incidentally, why it omits: 1. the punishments recorded in Exodus, since they bore upon that incident in particular, and 2. the issue about God's continuing presence, since that is transformed here into that of Israel's suitability as covenant partners in the land.

In the developing argument in Deut. 1 – 11, the passage 9:1 – 10:11 continues to reflect on Israel as Yahweh's chosen people, and on their title to the land (9:26–29). (Cf. N. Lohfink 1963: 205, on the alternation of the themes of life in the land [chs. 6; 8] and conquest of the land [ch. 7; 9:1 – 10:11].) Chs. 7 and 8 are particularly echoed. The theme of dispossession of existing inhabitants is signalled by repetition of yāraš, '(dis)possess', in 9:1–6. (In this connection Braulik [1997b: 64–65] has noticed that the use of yāraš in 9:1–6 displays a reflection on the relation between law and grace that repudiates both a legalistic [nomistic] understanding of covenant faithfulness and a secularized 'success' ideology. It does so by means of a sevenfold repetition of the verb, in alternating qal [simple] and hiphil [causative] forms.) The theme of memory (9:7; cf. 8:2, 11, 14), connected with Yahweh's deliverance from Egypt, recalls Israel's failure to give due recognition to Yahweh (8:11–19). Correspondingly, the theme of self-reliance (9:4–5) also recalls that in 8:12–17. And underlying this passage, as also chs. 7 – 8, is the explanation of Israel's title to the land in terms of the ancient promise to the patriarchs (9:27; cf. 7:8; 8:18); here, indeed, it is the motivation used by Moses in his intercession.

A number of commentators, influenced by Noth's thesis that passages with plural address are deuteronomistic, have found that the 'Horeb' sections of the present passage are later additions to the basic paranesis of Deuteronomy (Mayes 1979: 195; Minette de Tillesse 1962; Aurelius 1988: 10; Braulik 1986a: 75–77). N. Lohfink (1963: 200–218) inverts this order: the Horeb passages are prior. However, in my view law and paranesis are again inseparable. Talstra's linguistic analysis of Deut. 9 – 10, though he broadly follows Mayes in his tradition-critical observations, concludes that the 'Horeb' texts do belong in the basic paranetic layer of these chapters (Talstra 1995: 207; cf. 205, 209).

The structure of Deuteronomy 9:1 – 10:11

It is difficult to work out a systematic chronology of the events reported, because Moses' periods spent on the mountain are not catalogued in that way. For example, at 9:18 Moses is abruptly back on the mountain, though we have just read that he has come down (15). And in 10:1 he is commanded to come up, even though at the end of ch. 9 he was still there. The narrative requires at least two periods on top of the mountain: the first in 9:9–14; the second in 9:18–21, 25–29, and possibly a third, in 10:1–3. The reference in this place, however, might be to the second period. This is to be preferred because of 'At that time' (10:1a), and in spite of the renewed command to come up (10:1b), which may be taken as resumptive. In either case 10:10 refers to the second time on the mountain, because of the reference to the intercession. Deuteronomy has retained Exodus's pattern of two forty-day periods, but has incorporated the intercession within the second period, along with the instruction to renew the covenant.

The chronology, however, is somewhat overshadowed by the pattern of references to 'forty days and forty nights'. Lohfink has argued that the five mentions of 'forty days' structure the narrative into: 9:9–11, covenant made; 9:12–17, covenant broken; 9:18–21, amends made for covenant breach; 9:25 – 10:5, covenant renewed; 10:10–11, Moses continues to lead the people (rather than becoming the head of a new nation, 9:14; N. Lohfink 1963: 215–216; followed by Weinfeld 1991: 427). This is not quite satisfactory because it leaves parts of the section out of account, and because the second reference to 'forty days' does not quite introduce his second section, but belongs within the first. A more comprehensive analysis is needed, therefore.

An important element is the fact that the parts of the section are precisely framed by passages that remind one of Israel's 'journey' towards the land. Commentators tend to regard 9:22–24 and 10:6–9 as intrusions. However, together with 9:1–3, 8, and 10:10–11, they form a series of progression markers, which show that the issue in Deuteronomy's telling of the golden-calf incident is Israel's fitness to enter the land. The whole section is framed by a reminiscence of Israel's first failure to enter the land, in 9:1–7, and in 10:11, which gives permission at last for the final approach. Deut. 9:1–7 is followed immediately by a passage that records the making of the covenant on Horeb, its breach, the first report of Moses' intercession, and further examples of Israel's covenant unfaithfulness (9:8–24). And the final division records Moses' intercession (9:25–29), the renewed instruction to make tablets of the covenant (10:1–5), the setting apart of Levi for ark-bearing duties on the way to the land (10:6–9), and the resumption of the journey as God's response to Moses' intercession (10:10–11). These divisions are not hard and fast. The structure offered is closest to Talstra's, which is based on a distinction between 'The negative itinerary of a rebellious people' and 'God's reaction in the positive itinerary' (Talstra 1995: 200). The structure of 9:1 – 10:11 may therefore be briefly expressed as follows:

9:1–7   Israel will possess, but not by its power or
                   righteousness
9:8–24   Israel's rebellions at Horeb and elsewhere
9:25 – 10:11   Covenant renewed and journey resumed

Comment

9:1–7

1–2. The command 'Hear, Israel', or the 'Shema', is elsewhere closely associated with exhortations to keep the commands (4:1; 5:1; 6:4). Here it is followed immediately by a declaration that the land is about to be possessed. The themes of journey and command are very close here, therefore, and in fact Horeb will loom large in the verses that follow. Possession of the land, in an important sense, *is* command.

The verb *yāraš*, 'possess, dispossess', occurs numerous times in Deuteronomy in combination with 'go over' (*'ābar*) or 'go' (*bô'*), but here with both verbs. This, together with the concentration of occurrences of the verb in the section (vv. 1, 3, 4 [twice], 5 [twice], 6, 23; 10:11), indicates a resumption of the idea of an imminent march into the land. Such a concentration is matched only in chs. 1 – 4 and 11. The opening statement (1) is echoed in 10:11, following the command to Moses to continue on his way, so that the people might 'go' and 'possess' the land, bringing closure to the whole section. The echoes in vv. 1–2 are of ch. 1 in particular, where the people feared to go into the land because of the giant Anakim (1:28). The promise there that Yahweh would go ahead of the people and fight for them (1:30) is now repeated (9:3), and indeed the phrase 'as the LORD promised you' (9:3) may echo that earlier occasion. The qualification of 'Anakim' with 'of whom you know' (9:2) may also contain such an echo. The recollection of the former occasion is clearly deliberate, and has two effects. 1. It reaffirms that there will be a further opportunity to take the land, in spite of failure then. 2. It hints that failure is a possible consequence, even though all is in place for success. It is this quality of the argument that brings narrative and command so close together; the purpose of this narrative is that Israel should obey.

3. The first word of v. 3, 'But you shall know', makes a little contrastive echo of 'whom you know' in v. 2. The effect is to stress Yahweh's irresistible power as he goes ahead of his people, and perhaps suggests a transformation from the experience of fear to that of trust, inspired by a vision of what Yahweh was about to do. The phrase 'like a devouring fire' (3) is repeated from 4:24, where it was part of a warning to Israel against idolatry; here, in contrast, it stresses how Yahweh's enemies cannot stand before him. The syntax emphasizes that it is Yahweh who will accomplish the victory over the peoples of the land (see 'Notes on the text'), implying that Israel's weakness before the nations is not a hindrance. In the second half of the verse, however, the subject changes to Israel ('you'), affirming that, as a result of Yahweh's initiatives, Israel will in fact dispossess and destroy their enemies. An important connection between Yahweh's action and Israel's is thus established. That they will do it 'quickly' (3) is a way of pronouncing its certainty and completeness (as 7:4; cf. also 4:24, and note on 7:22). In this chapter the same adverb appears in vv. 12, 16, of the speed of the people's apostasy in the golden-calf episode. A contrast is thus made between what Israel can do in faith, and what it has done in the past in rebellion.

4–6. The issue here is strictly between Israel and Yahweh, with the wickedness of the other nations incidental to the point. The point is that Israel has no right of itself to inherit the land. These verses are therefore like 8:17, which warned Israel against thinking it had acquired the land by its own strength. Here, however, the category is legal. The mistake Israel makes lies in thinking it is receiving the land from Yahweh because of its own rectitude, and, correspondingly, because of the unrighteousness of the other nations already in the land (4). Yahweh then counters by accepting the latter proposition, but rejecting the former. This interpretation requires reading v. 4b as a continuation of Israel's speech in v. 4a, even though it ends 'before you', rather than 'before us'. There are strong reasons to do so, whether one adopts a text-critical solution (see 'Notes on the text'), or Lohfink's stylistic-critical one, namely that the speech gradually reverts to Yahweh (or better, to Moses) in preparation for his response in v. 5.

The advantages of reading v. 4 as entirely in the mouth of Israel are: 1. as an answer to the criticism that v. 4b comes too soon, unhelpfully anticipating v. 5b (S. R. Driver 1895: 111), and 2. that it allows v. 5 to form a satisfying reply to v. 4, point by point (N. Lohfink 1963: 200–204). Israel's proposition, then, is an interpretation of Yahweh's decision to allow them to possess the land while at the same deciding against the other nations. According to it, Israel itself is receiving the land because of its own 'innocence', while the other nations are losing it because of their guilt. Accordingly, ṣeḏāqâ, 'righteousness', and rišʻâ, 'wickedness', are here to be understood in legal terms, as they are again in 25:1 (cf. also Ezek. 18, *passim*). (Reimer [1997: 751], however, opposes this reading, though he accepts in principle that ṣaddîq can mean 'innocent' [1997: 749].) Yahweh's response is that while the other nations are indeed guilty, Israel should not think that by the same token it is innocent. On the contrary, it is not for legal reasons that Yahweh's decision has been made, but only because of his ancient oath to Abraham, Isaac and Jacob (5). The assertion that Israel has no claim to innocence is made into a thesis in v. 6 ('you are an obstinate people', lit. 'hard, stiff of neck'; cf. Exod. 32:9; 33:3, 5; 34:9). The image implies a refusal to turn the head in order to listen (Weinfeld 1991: 407).

7. The opening section finishes with an exhortation to 'remember' and 'not forget', recalling the main rhetorical theme of ch. 8. The people is now characterized as habitually contrary, in the context of its journey from Egypt to the plains of Moab, the last phrase, 'you have been rebelling against [Yahweh]', adopting a continuous tense to make the point strongly. This prepares for the argument in the rest of the chapter. The passage probably also underlies the argument of Paul in Rom. 10:3–4, and his idea of righteousness that comes from faith (cf. Braulik 1986a: 74–75; but see also the 'Explanation', below, for a qualification).

9:8–24

8. The thrust of the narrative that now follows is in line with that of vv. 1–7 (against Braulik [1986a: 75–77], who sees the core of 9:8 – 10:11 as a 'juristic-legal' text in tension with the 'gospel' of 9:1–7; see also 'Form and structure'). The continuity between v. 7 and v. 8 is signalled by the syntactical link between the two, with the word $\hat{u}b^e\hbar\bar{o}r\bar{e}b$, 'and at Horeb', in an emphatic opening position. Verse 8 is also linked to v. 7 by its repetition of the verb 'you angered' (*qṣp*, hiph.), which recurs in vv. 19 (qal) and 22 (hiph.), giving it a framing function in vv. 8–24, and summarizing the critique of Israel in this section. The other verb in v. 8, 'destroy' (*šmd*, hiph.), is characteristically used of Yahweh's destruction of the other nations (2:12, 21–23), but also expresses his turning of that intent upon Israel in the case of covenant unfaithfulness (cf. 6:15; 7:4). The theological summation in this verse is deuteronomic; neither of the main verbs here occurs in the Exodus account.

9–11. The record of Moses' ascent of Horeb is told in the first person (unlike Exodus), and is engaged abruptly (9). The memory of the formative Horeb event forms the backcloth to the whole narrative. The phrase 'on the day of the assembly (*qāhāl*)' (10; cf. 10:4) employs the regular term in Deuteronomy for Israel as a cultic assembly (cf. 23:2–4), but refers in this case to the gathering of the people at Mt Horeb. The allusion to the stone tablets (regularly 'tablets of the *covenant* [*b^e rît*]' in Deuteronomy; contrast 'tablets of the *testimony* [*'ēdût*]' in Exodus, e.g. 31:18) recalls primarily Deut. 4:13, though the phrase 'written with God's own finger' (10) follows Exod. 31:18. The 'words the LORD spoke to you on the mountain' are the Ten Commandments (4:13). (As we saw in Deut. 5, Deuteronomy is clearer on this identification than Exodus is, and the difference in terminology is part of their distinctive elaborations of the Horeb event.) For 'from the heart of the fire' see on 4:12; 5:22–27. The first forty-day fast (9, 11) corresponds to that recorded in Exod. 24:18; cf. 32:1.

12–14. These verses contain the report of the great apostasy, the making of an image at the very moment when the covenant was being concluded.

The phrase 'have become corrupt' (12) has been met already as a way of speaking about a basic perversion of true worship (see on 4:15–19). The passage follows Exod. 32:7–10 fairly closely. Each contains a command to Moses to go down from the mountain because of the people's hastily committed idolatry; the implied disassociation in '*your* people that *you* brought out of Egypt'; the charge that they are 'obstinate' ('stiff-necked'), and Yahweh's resolve to destroy them and make a nation of Moses instead. Deut. 9:12–14 lacks some of the details of Exodus (that the idol is specifically a calf, and that the exodus from Egypt is attributed to the gods it represents; Exod. 32:8). Conversely, certain details are added: Moses is to go down *quickly*, echoing the speed of the people's idolatry (12ab), and the people offered to Moses will be 'stronger and more numerous' than Israel (not just 'a great nation', as Exod. 32:10), ironically echoing 'seven nations stronger and more numerous than you' (7:1), and indeed the reference to the Anakim in the present passage (9:2).

15–16. The narrative of Moses' descent continues to show divergences from the Exodus account, chiefly abbreviating. 1. There is no record of an intercession before Moses' descent to the scene of the crime; and that recorded in v. 18 apparently occurred in his second period on the mountain (cf. Exod. 32:11–14, and see 'Form and structure'). 2. The characterization of the tablets is more general (15b; cf. Exod. 32:15–16). 3. The vivid depiction of the noise of the feasting (Exod. 32:17–19a) is omitted. Conversely, Deuteronomy adds a reminder that the mountain was 'ablaze with fire' (15), frighteningly juxtaposing the holiness of God with the terrible sin. And now the image is said to be a 'calf' (16). Calf and bull images were common in the ANE, a symbol of creative power and fertility, and a form in which the Canaanite gods El and Baal were both imaged. The expression 'molten calf-image' is probably contemptuous, implying that this thing was merely metal. While ANE religions did not crudely identify image and god, the OT is fiercely opposed to any representation of the divine, as is clear from the first two commandments. (See on 5:7–10, and also 4:15–19, for the OT's critique of image worship.)

17–18. The smashing of the tablets, promoted to a position prior to the intercession (17), creates a different kind of dramatic effect from the account in Exodus. There, Yahweh's repentance of his intent to destroy the people is already in place before the covenant is symbolically annulled in the breaking of the tablets (Exod. 32:14). Here, in contrast, the covenant lies in pieces before any such relenting. The arrangement of the material is so concerned with this logical order of events that it suddenly places Moses back on the mountain (the significance of 'before the LORD', 18) without explicitly narrating a new ascent (see on 'Form and structure'). The crucial significance of the intercession for the maintenance of the covenant is thus enhanced. This first report of it focuses on Moses' sacrificial bearing in it rather than on its content (which is kept until vv. 26–29), and this is developed more fully than in Exodus.

19–21. Moses' fear for the people (*yāgōrtî*, 'feared greatly, dreaded') is also brought out expressly (19a). The personal quality of the relationship between Moses and Yahweh functions in the latter's change of heart: 'the LORD heard my prayer that time also' (19; cf. the less personal 'the LORD relented and did not bring on his people the disaster he had threatened', Exod. 32:14). And the habitual nature of Moses' prayer is emphasized in 'that time also' (19b), which may have in mind occasions subsequent to this, as S. R. Driver pointed out (1895: 115; cf. Num. 11:2; 14:13–20; 21:7–9). Moses then includes a special intercession for Aaron (20), whose guilt in the affair, though acknowledged, is thus treated much less severely than in Exodus, which has no place for this brotherly touch.

The destruction of the calf must presumably be taken to have happened after Moses' descent of the mountain, and therefore, strictly, before the prayers reported in vv. 18–20. The account, as we have observed, is not strictly sequential, and this indeed is indicated by the syntax of v. 21 (see 'Notes on the text'). The burning, grinding and disposal of the calf in a wadi echoes the report in Exod. 32:20, as well as conventional ANE language for the liquidation of an enemy (such as the defeat of the god Mot by the goddess Anat; Weinfeld 1991: 411–421). As such, it may not be necessary to imagine each of these procedures literally. The account serves as a model for the cultic measures of the reforming kings (1 Kgs. 15:13; 2 Kgs. 11:18; 18:4; 23:4–15). The present passage omits the grim finale in Exodus, 'and made the Israelites drink it', presumably a trial of guilt intended to identify transgressors for punishment (Weinfeld 1991: 413), in line with a tendency here to play down the special punishment of the people for the sin of the calf, and to stress the success of Moses' prayer and God's graciousness.

22–24. This short section continues the argument that Israel has been habitually rebellious. Syntactically it corresponds to v. 8, adding to Horeb a number of places along the wilderness journey (for the places named cf. Num. 11:1–3, 4–34; Exod. 17:1–7; Deut. 6:16). These places were scenes of complaint against God, tantamount to a rejection of his whole purpose to liberate them for himself. The listing of such places evokes the opening words of Deuteronomy (1:1b–2), which set the journey itself as the stage for the action and the thought of the book. An explicit memory of the rebellion that aborted the first attempt to occupy the land follows in v. 23, echoing also 9:1–2 with its allusion to the Anakim. These links with the journey theme well suit the tendency of Deuteronomy's version of the golden-calf narrative to make it typical of Israel's character rather than a singularly important event. It fits, too, with the form of the intercession, which also became typical. The point is rounded off in v. 24, which makes Israel's rebelliousness formally coterminous with its existence as Yahweh's people (see 'Notes on the text', and cf. v. 7).

25. The reference here is to the second period on the mountain, first mentioned in v. 18, as is indicated: 1. by the definite article in the phrase 'those [the] forty days and forty nights' (see 'Notes on the text'), and 2. by the explanatory 'for the LORD intended to destroy you'. The content of Moses' prayer is now conveyed. It corresponds in outline with Exod. 32:11–13. S. R. Driver's objection (1895: 116) that it cannot be the same intercession as recorded there, since that one occurred before the breaking of the stone tablets, is ungrounded, as it underestimates the extent to which Deuteronomy is prepared to rearrange chronology in order to weave its argument. For the same reason, the fact that the prayer now recorded does not agree with Exod. 34:9 need not disturb us, though that prayer occurs in connection with the making of new stone tablets (Exod. 34:1–4), as this one does. Exodus too is pursuing an argument, in its case concerning the continuing presence of Yahweh with Israel. For such reasons the details of the two accounts do not readily match.

26–27. The prayer contains two pleas for Israel. First, Moses appeals to Yahweh's oath to the patriarchs, already partially fulfilled in the deliverance from Egypt. Verse 26 adopts the language of election ('your people, your inheritance'; cf. 4:20; 1 Sam. 10:1), closely associated, as always in Deuteronomy, with the mighty acts of Yahweh in the exodus (cf. 3:24; 7:8 for the terms used). Election is then traced back to the patriarchs, and the argument from this is made to prevail over the fact of Israel's persistent rebelliousness, which has been the theme of the chapter. Verse 27, in fact, returns to the terms of vv. 4–6, which established that Israel was not receiving the land because of its innocence. 'Hard-heartedness' is lit. 'hardness' ($q^e\check{s}\hat{i}$), echoing the 'obstinate', or 'stiff-necked' ($q^e\check{s}\bar{e}h$-'$\bar{o}re\bar{p}$) of v. 6. 'Wickedness', or 'guilt', is the virtually the same term as applied to the other nations (5; there $ri\check{s}\hat{a}$, here $re\check{s}a$'), and now expressly to Israel for the first time, thus finally extinguishing any possible delusion that Israel was in any sense better than the other nations (Aurelius 1988: 27).

28–29. The second ground of Moses' appeal concerns the reputation of Yahweh in the eyes of the nations (28). This is developed beyond Exod. 32:12, in which, in the case of God's punishment of Israel, the Egyptians are imagined to conclude that Yahweh meant evil towards his people, and more in line with Num. 14:16, where such a case leads to the calling into question of the power of Yahweh itself. The thought is natural in the ancient world, in which the fortunes of peoples are bound up completely with the power of their gods, and it recurs in other places in the OT (e.g. Ezek. 20:8–9 and *passim*). In this passage, the Egyptians are not named, which allows the prayer to have a general reference. The prayer also retains the possibility that they have suffered 'because he hated them', an inversion of the truth that Yahweh has chosen them because he loved them (7:8), and thus a special challenge to Yahweh's own word. If the two branches of this argument based on Yahweh's reputation do not add up logically, this is due to its force as a rhetorical proposition, intended to move him by any means possible. Both rest on aspects of Yahweh's intention to make Israel his own people that have been developed at length in the book to this point. The final verse (29) closes the prayer with a summary statement of deliverance and election together, in familiar terms (for the final phrase, cf. 4:34).

10:1–5

1. The momentum now begins to swing in a positive direction. After the failure of the first attempt to seal the covenant with its validating sign of the stone tablets, the making of new tablets points in the direction of fresh opportunity (cf. Talstra [1995: 198–200], who traces a 'positive itinerary' in 9:25 – 10:11, in contrast with a 'negative itinerary' in 9:1–24). 'At that time' provides a link with the intercession in 9:25–29, and suggests that this conversation between Yahweh and Moses is conceived as taking place at the same time as that prayer (see 'Form and structure'). It is impossible to reconstruct an exact chronology of Moses' second ascent, his intercession, the cutting of the tablets and the making of the ark. (For the same reason it is again unfruitful to try to reconcile the account with that of Exodus, where the ark is made by Bezalel after Moses' return from the mountain, Exod. 37:1–9.) The material is arranged here in order to lead from the nexus of rebellion and covenant breach into one of covenant renewal and the possibility of continuance. The new tablets are in every way like the first, and contain the same words (namely the Ten Commandments, v. 4; cf. on v. 10).

2–5. The construction of the ark serves the new forward-looking purpose (3, cf. v. 1b). It was not mentioned in relation to the first tablets, but is now introduced as part of the arrangements for maintaining the covenant in perpetuity. Its function is to contain the tablets of the covenant (2b, 5), in conformity with the practice whereby treaties were deposited in religious shrines (cf. 1 Sam. 10:25, note 'before the LORD'); indeed, it was customary for kings to keep copies of treaties in the 'footstools' of their gods (that is, where the god is depicted sitting on a throne).

Deuteronomy's treatment of ark and tablets, however, has been widely thought to presuppose a quite different theological concept from the ark in Exod. 25 – 31, especially 25:22, where its location in the Holy of Holies of the tabernacle is part of the portrayal of God's presence there, and his promise to 'meet' Israel in the regular worship. It is often characterized as the throne, or even the footstool, of Yahweh in that place (Haran). According to the well-known view of von Rad and Weinfeld, based partly on v. 5, the ark in Deuteronomy is merely a box for the tablets. It is thus evacuated of the more 'religious' significance that it has in a number of OT texts, in which it signifies God's presence, as in the 'holy war' (Num. 10:33–36; cf. von Rad 1966: 103–124; Weinfeld 1972: 63 n. 3, 208–209).

The difference between Exodus and Deuteronomy on the subject of the ark, however, has to be understood in the respective contexts of the two books. Exodus makes its transition from Sinai to the regular worship in the tabernacle in its own way, with a focus on the nature of God's presence. (Exod. 34:29–35 makes an important bridge between the unique event on Sinai and the regular worship.) Its golden-calf narrative (Exod. 32 – 34) is subordinate to the theme of presence, and Moses' intercessions there are bound into the theme (esp. Exod. 33:13–16). Deuteronomy, in contrast, subordinates its golden-calf narrative to its own distinctive theological argument concerning Israel's fitness to be God's covenant partner in the land. In that context the treatment of the ark and tablets has a minor role within a demonstration of the people's habitual unfaithfulness and Yahweh's decision to be gracious nevertheless.

To claim, therefore, that Deuteronomy and Exod. 25 – 31 have different theologies of the ark is to fall into the fallacy of assuming that every reference to a phenomenon conveys the writer's whole concept of it. Deuteronomy and Exodus agree that the ark contained the tablets of the covenant (cf. Exod. 25:16, where they are referred to as the 'testimony', hā'ēḏût, cf. Exod. 31:18). Since, as we have seen (on ch. 4), there is no fundamental difference on 'presence' matters between P and D, it is clear that this is not a text with an agenda about presence. The different theological purposes of Deuteronomy and Exodus in their respective arguments about the golden calf should not be extrapolated into different overarching theological concepts.

5. When Moses turns and comes down the mountain for the second time, his action makes an exact contrast with his first turning to descend (9:15). On that occasion he came down to find the image of the calf and smashed the tablets (9:16–17); now he comes with the new tablets, and houses them in the ark. The closure achieved in the words 'there they remain, as the LORD commanded me' shows that a foundation has been laid on which the covenant might now be firmly established.

10:6–9

6–7. Verses 6–9 are widely regarded as an intrusion into the main narrative, hence the parentheses usually adopted in translations (Vermeylen 1985b: 202). Craigie (1976a: 200 and n. 6), for example, thinks vv. 6–7 may be an extract from a separate travel record, noting the similarity especially with Num. 33:30–33, though rightly supposing that there is no direct dependence of either text on the other. The itinerary, when compared with that in Num. 33, is at best partial and representative. Perhaps this fragment is chosen because it mentions the place where Aaron is said to have died (which differs, incidentally, from Num. 33:37–38). Either Deuteronomy has found a different tradition about the death of Aaron, or it is less concerned with the precise location than with illustrating the arangements for the worship in the context of the continuing journey to the land. In any case, the inclusion of these verses is not untidy editing. Indeed, again following Craigie (ibid.), the allusion to Aaron's death, not at Horeb following the sin with the calf, but later in the journey, may show that Moses' prayer (9:20) was heard, just as 10:1–5 is an answer to the main part of the prayer, for Israel's survival.

8–9. More generally, verses 6–9 are among the journey markers that we have repeatedly seen to have been firmly wedded to the developing argument of Deut. 1 – 11. Yet the passage is specifically appropriate to the context. The mention of Aaron suggested a contrast between the arrangements for worship instituted by Yahweh and the false worship of the golden calf. More importantly, the reference to the ark (10:1–5) now occasions a comment on ark and priesthood alongside the tablets, with echoes of the sanctification of the priesthood of the line of Aaron, as well as the role of the Levites in ark-bearing (6b, 8; cf. Num. 3). The terms used for Levi's duties are applied elsewhere to priests (Num. 6:22–27; cf. 8:23–26). Deuteronomy does not systematically distinguish separate roles and privileges for 'priests' and 'Levites' (see further on 18:1–5), even though there are hints of such distinctions within 10:6–9. On occasion, however, it appears to express itself more exactly. (Cf. 21:5, where the 'priests, the sons of Levi' are said to have been chosen to 'bless' and to 'serve' in Yahweh's name. In Joshua [chs. 3; 6], furthermore, the priests are found bearing the ark, perhaps because the occasion is especially solemn.) The relaxed approach to such details in Deuteronomy accords with its present purpose: to consider the basis on which Israel as a whole might sustain a covenant with Yahweh.

The ark is referred to here as 'the ark of the covenant of the LORD'. While a simpler form of the name, 'ark of Yahweh/the LORD', is also attested (Josh. 3:13; 4:5; 1 Sam. 5 – 6, *passim*; 2 Sam. 6, *passim*), the present form is not new with Deuteronomy (cf. Num. 10:33; 14:44; and other 'old' texts, Judg. 20:27; 1 Sam. 4:3–5; 2 Sam. 15:24a). It is hard to determine, on the basis of these texts, which form is 'older', and in any case it cannot be shown to be a product of deuteronomic ideology (with Weinfeld 1991: 421). (This is true even though the word *beˆrît* appears, because of awkward Hebrew syntax, to have been introduced for clarification into certain already existing texts: Josh. 3:14, 17 [Weinfeld, ibid.]. The term also appears alongside the strongly 'cultic' concept of Yahweh enthroned on the cherubim in 1 Sam. 4:4.) As a name for the ark, however, the form used here suits well Deuteronomy's concept of the covenant (*beˆrît*) as the Ten Commandments (4; cf. 4:13), its designation of the stone tablets as 'the tablets of the covenant' (9:9), and the present argument in particular, which concerns covenant renewal. (See on 9:9, for the use of *'ēdût*, 'testimony', instead of *bᵉrît*, 'covenant', in Exodus.)

The tribe of Levi's vocation to serve Yahweh in the official worship entails a disqualification from having its own tribal territory, this being the practical significance of the statement that 'the LORD is their inheritance' (9). The priests' entitlements in return for their duties are elaborated in 18:1–8, which assumes that they live throughout the tribal territories of Israel, are entitled to serve at the main place of worship, and have their living both from such service and from certain private lands that they may hold. The same principle of perquisites from the cult in lieu of tribal territory is maintained in Num. 18, esp. vv. 20, 24 (where it is reiterated separately for both 'priests' and 'Levites'), and in Josh. 13:14; 18:7; cf. 14:3b. In Num. 35:1–5 there are instructions for Levites to receive towns and 'pasture lands' in 'the inheritance the Israelites will possess'. And this requirement is met in Joshua, where cities are allocated to the Levitical tribe (Josh. 21). The story of the priest Abiathar, in the time of David and Solomon, sees him banished by Solomon to his private estates (1 Kgs. 2:26). The present allusion, like vv. 6–7, presupposes that such arrangements are already known, most clearly in the phrase 'as the LORD your God promised them' (9b). Scholars doubt whether this can be an allusion to Num. 18:20, on the grounds that that text refers to the priests ('Aaron') alone, not to the whole tribe (S. R. Driver 1895: 123–124; Weinfeld 1991: 422–423). The reference could of course be to a promise unrecorded in the Pentateuch. Yet it is in accordance both with Deuteronomy's pattern of assimilation of available material, not least in the present passage, and also with its habit of thinking of the Levitical tribe as a whole, that it should allude to Num. 18:20, together with v. 24 of the same chapter, in this way.

10:10–11

10. Moses now reverts to his own role in the narrative, signalling the change of subject syntactically, beginning with the emphatic pronoun 'I' rather than using the normal narrative sequence, just as he had signalled a change in v. 6 (see 'Notes on the text'). This suggests, incidentally, that vv. 6–9 are not a simple intrusion but are fully built into the discourse. He refers to the second period on the mountain, when he prayed for Israel (9:18–20, 25–29) and received the new tablets (10:1–5), with an allusion to the first period ('just as the first time'; cf. 9:9). The phrase 'this time too' is identical with the last words of 9:19b, which, as we saw, referred to other later intercessions of Moses. The echo of that passage shows that the narrative of the Horeb events is reaching its closure.

11. Verse 11 is highly significant, because it gives the signal for renewed movement towards the land. This is the all-important outcome of the recollection of Israel's repeated failures to be faithful keepers of the covenant, the topic of 9:1 – 10:11. The covenant is intact, in spite of their rebellions, and because of the oath to the patriarchs. The command to Moses, 'Rise and go on the journey', corresponds to Exod. 32:34; 33:1. But its closest echoes are within Deuteronomy. In 2:24, Yahweh says to the people, 'Rise, go on your journey', by way of his command to enter the land and conquer the Transjordanian kings (cf. 2:13). By the same token, the command contrasts with 9:12, where Moses is told to 'Rise and go down quickly from here', which leads to the discovery of the apostasy. The issue in all these passages is whether the people has Yahweh's blessing to continue the journey into the land, and the present text is the final word on the matter: Moses may now at last go ahead of them to the verge of the occupation itself.

The command, addressed as it is to Moses, states only that *they* (the people) may go in. It thus obliquely calls to mind the exclusion of Moses himself from entering the land (3:23–29) and anticipates his death on Mt Nebo (ch. 34). Moses' role has been indispensable, not least in his intercessions, but it will have its terminus before the last stage of the journey.

Explanation

Deut. 9:1 – 10:11 continues the argument, which has been building since ch. 7, about the basis on which Israel might properly occupy the land of Canaan. It has been established in chs. 7 – 8 that Israel's election neither originated nor continues in its own intrinsic qualities. It was not greater than other nations (7:7), and has no right to say that it took the land by its own strength (8:17). There was, moreover, the beginning of a reconception of the basis of Yahweh's covenant loyalty (7:9–10). Finally, despite Israel's election it could fall under the ultimate covenantal curse of the loss of the land (8:19–20).

The present passage follows 7:7 and 8:17 by arguing that Israel is not only no greater than other nations; it is no more righteous either. The passage aims above all to give the lie to the idea that Israel might in any sense have some merit that other nations do not have, as the basis for its status as the elect of Yahweh. The nub of this argument is in 9:4–6, where quasi-legal terms are used to show that the people is 'guilty', just like the other nations, and the point is put beyond all doubt in 9:27.

It follows, then, that its election is entirely by the grace of God, or by his 'love' (7:8; cf. 10:15). This thesis is pursued by two means. First, it is framed by the metaphor of the 'journey'. The opening verses, 9:1–3, reach back to chs. 1 – 3, in which the qualification of Israel to proceed into its inheritance was established on the basis of faith in Yahweh. There, too, land possession by its own strength was ruled out (1:41–45); land could be given only by God (1:30; cf. 9:3). The present pericope finishes too, like a final green light, with a renewed command to proceed on the way into the land (10:11). All the reflection on Israel's persistent 'guilt' falls between these two boundaries. The covenant is broken because of Israel's sin, but renewed by God's grace, and so the people may enter the land.

The second means of showing that Israel's election is only by the grace of God is the account of the apostasy in the incident of the golden calf. The telling of this is in important respects different from that of Exod. 32 – 34, such that simply to try to harmonize the two is misguided. While Exodus presents the episode as a catastrophic beginning of the covenantal relationship, comparable in respects to the flood following creation, Deuteronomy sees it more as an illustration of a general truth about Israel, namely that it has nothing intrinsic to make it a suitable covenant partner. In this sense it belongs inextricably within Deuteronomy's own theological discourse. The special characteristics of the narrative here (catalogued above, 'Form and structure') help to pursue the theme of Israel's covenant suitability. An example is the fact that no particular punishments are recorded here, since the issue at stake concerns the general viability of Israel as a whole, and perpetually, as covenant partner.

Broadly, the narrative pursues a contrast between (on the one hand) the failure of Israel to keep covenant, leading to the breaking of the first tablets, and (on the other) the continuance of the covenant nevertheless, symbolized in the making of new ones. This balance is summed up neatly in a contrast between 9:15–17 and 10:5, each beginning '(so) I turned', but leading in the one instance to Moses' discovery of the apostasy and to his breaking the first tablets, and in the second to the housing of the new tablets in the ark. This covenant renewal, based in principle on the grace of God because of Israel's inability, is very close to the prophetic new-covenant idea (Jer. 31:31–34).

The resulting argument is a theological and ethical analysis that, in important respects, comes close to the Pauline doctrine of justification by faith, or righteousness that comes from faith (cf. Braulik [1986a: 75], who rightly sees 'gospel' in this proclamation). Common to both is the tracing of the basis of election, not to intrinsic merit, but to the antecedent promise to the patriarchs (7:8; 9:27; cf. Rom. 11:28; Gal. 3:15–29). The Horeb scenario helps to express this point, by showing that Israel's status with God is not based on its capacity to keep the covenant (here against Braulik [ibid.], who sees 9:9 – 10:11 as being in tension with 9:1–7). In this sense the outcome of the golden-calf narrative is indeed like that of Exod. 32 – 34 (see Moberly 1983: 88–93, on Exod. 34:9).

The similarities with Paul must be carefully understood. Modern NT scholarship has realized that Paul's doctrine of justification by faith was part of his redefinition of the true covenant *community* (N. T. Wright 1991). This puts him very much in line with Deuteronomy, where the 'unrighteousness' of Israel is part of the election theology that embraces the exodus deliverance, the Horeb covenant and the gift of land, and that opens up the possibility of redefinition of the covenant community in 7:8. This means that the NT's extension of the OT in this respect is *not* to be understood as a change from corporate to individual models of salvation. The nature of the covenant community awaits still further development in Deuteronomy (see on ch. 12). But it is left to the NT to draw the Gentiles into a covenant community finally redefined in Christ.

DEUTERONOMY 10:12 – 11:32

Translation

[12]So now, Israel, what does the LORD your God demand of you? Only that you revere the LORD your God, continue in all his ways, love him, and worship the LORD your God with all your heart and being, [13]keeping the commands of the LORD, and his laws, with which I am charging you this day so that you may prosper. [14]Truly, to the LORD belong heaven, the highest heavens, and the earth with everything in it; [15]yet it was in your forefathers that the LORD delighted; he loved them, and chose their descendants after them, that is yourselves, out of all the nations, as is still the case today. [16]So you must circumcise your hearts, and do not again be stubborn. [17]For the LORD your God is God of gods and lord of lords; he is the great God, mighty and terrible; he acts impartially and accepts no bribe; [18]he ensures justice for the orphan and widow, and is loving to the outsider, giving him food and clothing. [19]So you must love the outsider; for you yourselves were outsiders in the land of Egypt. [20]Revere the LORD your God; worship him, hold to him, and swear in his name. [21]He is your praise, your God who has done these great and terrible things that you yourselves have seen. [22]Your forefathers were only seventy strong when they went to Egypt; but now the LORD your God has made you as numerous as the stars of the sky.

[11:1]Love the LORD your God and keep that with which he has charged you – his laws, statutes and commands – always. [2]Today you shall understand the discipline of the LORD – not your children, since they have not known or seen it – his greatness, his strong hand and mighty arm, [3]the signs and deeds that he did among you in Egypt, to Pharaoh king of Egypt and his whole land, [4]what he did to the Egyptian army, with its horses and chariots, causing the water of the Reed Sea to overwhelm them when they were pursuing you, and destroying them once for all; [5]and what he did for you in the wilderness, bringing you to this place, [6]and what he did to Dathan and Abiram, the sons of Eliab of the tribe of Reuben, how the earth opened up and swallowed them, in the midst of Israel, together with their households, their tents and every living thing that stood with them. [7]It is you who have seen with your own eyes this whole great work of the LORD that he did.

[8]Keep all the commands, therefore, with which I am charging you this day, so that you have the strength to enter and take possession of the land you are crossing to occupy, [9]and so that you may remain long in the land the LORD promised on

oath to your forefathers that he would give to them and to their descendants, a land flowing with milk and honey. [10]For the land you are entering to occupy is not like the land of Egypt from which you came, where you had to plant your seed and then irrigate it by foot as in a vegetable garden; [11]rather, the land you are crossing to occupy is a land of mountains and valleys watered by rain from heaven, [12]a land the LORD your God cares for, his eyes constantly upon it, from the beginning of the year to its end.

[13]'If you steadily obey my commands with which I am charging you today, and love and worship the LORD your God with all your heart and being, [14]then I will give you rain on your land in its due time, both autumn and spring, so that you may gather your grain, your wine and your oil; [15]and I will give grass on your fields for your cattle, and you yourselves will eat your fill.'

[16]Be careful lest your hearts be enticed away and you bow down and worship other gods, [17]for then the anger of the LORD would be kindled against you, and he would shut up the heavens, so that there might be no rain, and the earth might not yield its fruit, and you would quickly perish off the good land that the LORD is giving you.

[18]Rather, write these words of mine on your heart and being; tie them as a reminder on your hands, and as frontlets on your forehead. [19]Teach them to your children; speak about them whether you are sitting at home or out on a journey, when you go to bed and when you get up; [20]write them on your doorposts and on your gates. [21]Do this, so that you and your descendants may remain long in the land the LORD promised on oath to give to your forefathers as long as the sun stands over the earth.

[22]If you are careful to keep and practise all these commands with which I am charging you, if you love the LORD your God, follow all his ways and adhere to him, [23]then the LORD will drive out all these nations before you, and you will dispossess nations greater and stronger than yourselves. [24]Every place on which you tread will be yours; your borders will stretch from the wilderness to Lebanon, from the River Euphrates to the Mediterranean. [25]No-one will be able to oppose you. The LORD your God will send fear and terror of you across the whole land as you invade it, just as he promised you.

[26]Now pay attention; I am giving you a choice today between a blessing and a curse: [27]the blessing if you obey the commands of the LORD your God with which I am charging you this day, [28]and the curse if you do not obey the commands of the LORD your God, but leave the way that I am today commanding you, and go after other gods whom you have not known. [29]When the LORD your God brings you into the land you are crossing to occupy, you shall set the blessing on Mt Gerizim and the curse on Mt Ebal. [30](As you know, these mountains are beyond the Jordan, towards the west, in the land of the Canaanites of the Arabah, near Gilgal, by the oaks of Moreh.) [31]When you have crossed the Jordan and entered the land the LORD your God is giving you to possess, and have settled down to live in it, [32]then be careful to keep all the statutes and laws I am laying upon you this day.

Notes on the text

10:12. *l^eyir'â*, 'to fear'; the noun *yir'â* is regularly used in place of the inf. construct of *yr'* in constructions with the preposition *l^e*.

15. QL has *'al kēn*, 'therefore', instead of MT *raq*, 'only, even so'. MT suits better, since God's special love for Israel is intrinsically surprising in view of his universal lordship.

17. *wa'^adōnê*, 'lord of': the form is plural (sg. in SamP, cf. Syr); the plural of this noun is common in the expression, *'^adōnāy*, 'O Lord', and with other suffixed endings (e.g. Exod. 21:4). It occurs in other plural forms also, however; e.g. Gen. 42:30, 33 (construct, as here); Is. 19:4.

20. The narrative sequence is broken by putting the grammatical object 'the LORD your God' first, to stress that it is he who is to be feared, not others. The pattern is repeated in the next two clauses.

QL has *tiqrab* for MT *tidbāq*. The difference arises from a scribal error confusing *d* and *r* (a frequent error), and also transposing the consonants. MT is preferable because the verb appears elsewhere in Deuteronomy in paranetic texts (11:22; 13:5, 18; 30:20), while *qrb* does not.

22. *b^ešib'îm nepeš*, lit. '*as* seventy persons'; the preposition is so-called *beth essentiae* (GKC 119i).

11:2. The syntax is difficult, for two reasons. 1. The term 'your children' is preceded by *'et*, though it is not obviously the object of a preceding verb. This is to be explained on the assumption that some verbal idea is implicit in what has gone before, such as 'I do not mean...' (see GKC 117l). 2. Even so, the sentence lacks something. In the phrase translated here as an interjection ('not your children, since they have not known or seen it'), 'it' is supplied, as the verb lacks an expressed object. It may anticipate 'the discipline' as object, though it seems strictly to be the object of 'you' (in 'you shall understand'). Braulik (1986a: 87) favours a rearranging of the text, incorporating v. 7 within v. 2, with this result: 'Today you shall understand that the LORD has disciplined you. For it is not your children, who did not know or experience the discipline of the LORD your God, but you yourselves who have seen with your own eyes the mighty works that the LORD did...' This allows 'the discipline' to be the object of 'children who have not known', without confusion. However, the untidiness may be put down to rhetorical style (with Craigie 1976a: 208).

6. SamP adds 'and all the men of Korah', probably supplied from Num. 16:32.

8. 'commands' is actually the sg. *hammiṣwâ*, standing for the commandments as a whole; see on 5:31; 6:1.

9. 'to them and to their descendants': SamP has simply 'to their descendants'. Cf. v. 21.

10. 'you came [out]' is plural in an otherwise singular passage; in this case the change may be due to dittography of the final *m* with the following word, *miššām* (as QL, and with Weinfeld 1991: 433).

11. 'watered by rain from heaven': lit. 'it drinks water according to the rain from heaven'.

12. 'the beginning of the year to the end of year' (lit.): the first case of *šānâ*, 'year', has the definite article, the second not. The imbalance is odd, and corrected by SamP and other versions, which supply the article in the second case. It may be best to omit it in both cases.

14 – 15. MT shifts from 'I' meaning Moses to 'I' meaning Yahweh. SamP and LXX substitute 'he', rationalizing. Yet we have noticed such shifts before; cf. 9:4b, and 'Notes on the text' there.

18. The phrase *dᵉbāray 'ēlleh*, 'these words of mine', lacks a perhaps expected definite article on *'ēlleh*. However, when the noun is determined by a possessive suffix the article is usually omitted from demonstratives (GKC 1126y).

22. *kî 'im*, often 'rather'; but here it is the protasis of the sentence that continues in v. 23.

24. 'from the wilderness to Lebanon': MT has 'from the wilderness and Lebanon', as Josh. 1:4, which, however, continues 'to the Great Sea'. The present verse, in contrast, appears to need '*to* Lebanon' for reasons of both balance and sense. The simplest amendment is to suppose that *wᵉ'ad* has fallen out before 'Lebanon'. Josh. 1:4, however, may have read the Deuteronomy text and made sense of it in a slightly different way.

30. 'towards the west': lit. 'on the road of the setting of the sun', that is, the central east–west road leading from Jericho through the Judean hills into the heart of the land (Seebass 1982: 27).

'As you know': lit. a rhetorical question, 'Are they not?'

The geographical description here is odd. The sentence reads (lit.) 'across the Jordan, on the road of the setting of the sun, in the land of the Canaanite dwelling in the Arabah, over against Gilgal, by the oaks of Moreh'. The first two elements point west in a general sense. The next two indicate the area where Israel would cross the Jordan at their first entry to the land. This is a long way from Shechem. The 'oaks of Moreh', however, are associated with Shechem in Gen. 12:6. Even so, the plural form here (oaks) has echoes of the 'oaks of Mamre', in the deep south, near Hebron. The specific location is thus couched in terms that are also imprecise, reminiscent of the imprecision in the opening verse of the book (1:1).

MT has *'ēlônê*, 'oaks', pl., as in Gen. 13:18; 14:13; 18:1, all with 'Mamre' (Hebron). Gen. 12:6, however, has 'oak [sg.] of Moreh', located near Shechem. Deut. 11:30 alludes to the latter, though influenced by the other usage. SamP amends to 'oak', and adds for clarification 'over against Shechem'. This reflects the Samaritans' belief that Shechem was the 'chosen place' of worship (in the terms of Deut. 12:5), and also a sense that the geographical details here need a little sharpening. The singular is followed by LXX, as in all the above cases; LXX may be an interpretation of the plural form, rather than evidence of an actual singular in Hebrew. The verse has led to the suggestion that the crucial covenantal ceremony was relocated by Judahite authors to a southern position (Rose 1994: 522; cf. Eissfeldt 1970).

31. This verse is taken as the protasis of vv. 31–32 (with NRSV against RSV; obscured by NIV).

Form and structure

General

Deut. 10:12 – 11:31 is a unified speech not unlike 4:1–40 (see Weinfeld 1991: 453–454, for similarities). It is, however, quite different in structure. While it has a particular function as a kind of summation of themes up to this point, it also expressly prepares for life in the land, and provides a transition from the exposition of the main deuteronomic themes to the law corpus.

The whole speech is *forward-looking*, though it draws extensively on themes and motifs in 1:1 – 10:11. There is a mixture of the familiar and the new angle (e.g. on Egypt and the Reed Sea). Surprisingly, Horeb is not directly mentioned, giving way in the thematics of the speech to the anticipation of land. There are, however, echoes of Horeb: 1. in the restatements of the principal law (10:12, 20; 11:16–17); 2. in the 'commandment(s)' (11:8); and 3. in the implied contrast with Mts Ebal and Gerizim. The absence of Horeb comes from the rhetorical purpose of this section. The problem that arose there is in the past. Yahweh has heard Moses' intercession; now the people are to go to the land, keeping the commands, and 'circumcising their heart' (cf. 10:16). Even so, Israel remains at a place of present decision (10:12; 11:1–2, 8, 13, [18], 22, 26–32).

The following aspects belong to the speech's forward-looking character.

First, it covers the whole range of Israel's life, from the election of the patriarchs to the occupation of the land. There is a conscious historical perspective in 10:15, which, unlike 7:6ff., distinguishes between God's love for the forefathers and his election of Israel. The historical perspective sweeps from the promise to the patriarchs, through the exodus from Egypt, to Israel's present position on the border of the land, where they are now as 'numerous as the stars in the sky' (10:22; cf. 1:10). The climax of this is in 11:22–32, with a new description of the land, and the solemn ceremony in it, which is now mentioned for the first time.

Secondly, it foregrounds the land (11:8–12, 13–17). Egypt is dealt with in a unique way, tracing the stages of Israel's involvement with it, like a journey. 1. They *went to* Egypt few, but now are numerous (this growth in numbers is only here and at 26:5 in Deuteronomy; cf. Exod. 1:5). 2. They came *out of* Egypt (the Reed Sea tradition appears only here in Deuteronomy). 3. The land is described as '*not like* the land of Egypt' (11:10), an expression occurring only here (cf. 7:15, on diseases); the good land is otherwise compared with the wilderness.

Thirdly, there is a prophetic colour in this look forward ('what does the LORD your God demand of you?', 10:12; cf. Mic. 6:6–8; 'circumcise your hearts', 10:16; cf. Jer. 4:4, suggested there too by the patriarchal allusion in Jer. 4:2).

Fourthly, the principle of the law is anticipated in 10:18–19; cf. 14:28–29; 15:15; 16:20; this also recalls 1:16–17. The memory of Dathan and Abiram echoes the theme in the laws of 'purging the land' of wickedness (see 'Comment' on 11:6).

Fifthly, in the phrase 'not your children' (11:2) there is a curious echo of 1:39, where the phrase 'your children' referred to the Moab generation. This new contrast moves the lens on to the next generation(s), though it still calls the present generation to obedience.

Structure

Commentators divide the speech differently, especially after 10:12–22. The analysis adopted here is closest to Mayes (1979) and, to an extent, G. Seitz (1971) (contrast Christensen 1991).

10:12–22   This passage is bracketed by 'and now' (12a, 22b). It is also unified by the call to love and serve God, thus developing 6:5, and this implying also love of the weak (cf. 1:16–17).
11:1–7   The speech returns to the principal theme: the call to love God on the grounds of his deliverance from Egypt.
11:8–17   This section focuses on the theme of land, with concomitant themes of command, blessing, conditional blessing and curse, and warnings against other gods (cf. 7:12ff., 17–26; 8:19–20). Within this section, vv. 8–12 and vv. 13–17 have a parallel development.
11:18–21   These verses take up the teaching of the commands; cf. 6:6–9. Verse 21 appears to bring closure to the themes of the speech, but does so only relatively.
11:22–25   Yahweh's gift of the land here echoes 1:7.
11:26–32   The speech closes with the announcement of the ceremony of curse and blessing to be carried out at Mts Ebal and Gerizim, a ceremony that will be more fully developed in ch. 27. The passage also leads directly into the detailed commands of chs. 12 – 26. And it has undertones of 1:1–5, in the phrases 'commands' and 'beyond the Jordan'; and it resumes the 'journey' theme, now having in view the journey from Mt Horeb to Mts Ebal and Gerizim.

Comment

10:12–22

12–13. The opening words, 'So now Israel', as in 4:1, mark a turning from historical reminiscence to command. In both cases the historical reminiscence has focused on the grace of God in Israel's life despite the difficulty experienced by the latter in keeping the covenant. The wording of the exhortation that then begins (12a) varies from 4:1, being not directly command but rather a rhetorical question similar to Mic. 6:8. The question is immediately answered (12b), in this too like Mic. 6:8. Though the exact terms of the two answers differ, they have much in common. Micah teaches the need for justice and righteousness, and indeed that these should be 'loved'; he puts this, furthermore, in the context of relationship with Yahweh ('walk humbly with your God'). This requirement of a heartfelt love of what is right, based in loyalty to Yahweh, is the stuff of Deuteronomy too. The terms used in our text are familiarly deuteronomic, recalling especially the speech following the Horeb encounter in Deut. 5: 'to revere (fear)' (cf. 5:29; 6:13); 'to continue [walk] in all his ways' (cf. 5:33); 'to love [God] … with all your heart and being [soul]' (cf. 6:5; 4:29); 'to worship [serve]' (cf. 6:13); 'keeping the commands' (cf. 6:17); 'so that you may prosper [for your good]' (cf. 6:24). This clustering has the marks of a recollection and summation. The elements in v. 12b are grouped closely, whereas they were more widely spread in ch. 6. To an extent they occur in the same order as in the passages noted in chs. 5 – 6 (cf. N. Lohfink 1963: 227), though this correspondence is not perfect. The connection between loving God, obedience to his commands and enjoying prosperity cannot be strictly rationalized, here any more than elsewhere in the book. These are all parts of a unified picture.

14–16. Verses 14–15 bring together two theological statements that seem at first glance to be at odds, namely Yahweh's universal rule, and his election of one nation, Israel. The translation adopted here ('Truly') is an attempt to capture both the strong affirmation in v. 14 and the fact that it prepares for a continuation that is in some sense unexpected or at odds with that affirmation. The universality of Yahweh's rule is articulated also in 4:32–40 (note the repeated 'there is no other', 4:35, 39; cf. also Neh. 9:6). It is the basis in Deuteronomy of the whole story of Israel's deliverance from Egypt and the gift to it of its land at the expense of others. It thus leads inevitably to the question of election. That theme was treated first in 7:6–11, many of whose terms (esp. vv. 6–8) occur again here, with some variations (there the patriarchs received an oath, while Yahweh chose 'you'; here he chose the patriarchs together with their 'seed', i.e. the present Moab generation).

We have seen already that Deuteronomy acknowledges the inherent difficulty in the idea of the election of one nation by the universal God (see

'Comment' on 7:6–11). The same acknowledgment may be found here in the syntax of vv. 14–15. The first word in v. 14 is often translated 'behold' or 'see', but this is overly literal. The effect of *hēn* in conjunction with the following *raq* ('yet', 15) is a concession: 'although ... yet', as adopted by NRSV (contrast RSV). There is an issue in this concession that is not fully developed here (how Yahweh's universal rule might yet be expressed; see 'Explanation'). This passage, like ch. 7, is content to develop the connection between Yahweh's universality and Israel's elect status by means of an exhortation to be faithful. In ch. 7 this takes the form of a call to obedience (7:11–12). Here Moses resorts to the more 'prophetic' device of spiritualizing a ritual requirement. Circumcision, as a mark of Israel's elect, holy status, is associated with the covenant with the patriarchs (Gen. 17:9–14). The specific links between that covenant and the present text are unmistakable (there Yahweh makes a covenant with Abraham and his 'seed', or descendants, and gives circumcision as a mark of it). Deut. 10:15–16 echoes these elements. Circumcision, however, is now of 'the heart'. In this way Deuteronomy insists that the election of Abraham, Isaac and Jacob, now extended to their 'descendants' in the Moab generation, must have an inner reality. (There is a similar development in Jer. 4:1–4, which, in v. 2a, echoes the promise to Abraham [Gen. 12:3b], as well as spiritualizing circumcision in v. 4.) That inner reality is explained in terms of the character of the people, which has just been exposed in the preceding account of the golden-calf incident and other instances of rebellion (9:1 – 10:11) by means of the expression 'do not again be stubborn' (cf. 9:6).

17–19. The parallelism of 'God of gods and lord of lords' (17) is also found in Ps. 136:2–3 in a hymn of praise, and is therefore a kind of formulaic expression. The first epithet, taken in a strict sense, asserts Yahweh's superiority over other gods, but in practice does not need a pantheon to make sense of it. It means simply that he is absolutely supreme. The phrase 'lord of lords', like its close neighbour 'king of kings', is used in the ANE of human kings, affirming their superiority over all other human kings. (This usage is actually found in Ezek. 26:7 and Ezra 7:12 of Nebuchadrezzar and Artaxerxes respectively.) Some similar texts prefer 'lord of kings' to mean the same thing (Dan. 2:47, Aram.; and Tg to the present text). The sequence 'great ... mighty and terrible' is also applied to God in the prayer in Neh. 9:32 (and cf. Deut. 7:21). 'Great king' is well known in the ANE (at Ugarit and in Akkadian) as a formula for the king (cf. 2 Kgs. 18:28; Ezra 5:11; Dan. 2:10), and its application to Yahweh is found in Ps. 48:3, as well as here. The word 'mighty' alone (*gibbōr*), referring primarily to warriors, is used several times of Yahweh in the OT (e.g. Ps. 24:8; Is. 42:13) casting him as a man of war (cf. Exod. 15:3). The effect of the expressions in this verse is to say that neither any other God nor any human king can match the authority of Yahweh. In this sense v. 17 echoes and continues v. 14, with its claim to Yahweh's universal power.

The royal attributions continue with the characteristics postulated in vv. 17b–18. The picture is of a king exercising just and merciful rule. The trio 'orphan, widow and outsider' is regular in Deuteronomy. It is not by definition the same as 'poor' (see 'Comment' on 14:28–29), yet in this case it certainly stands for vulnerability, perhaps because these groups would have had no rights of their own in a lawcourt. Responsibility to protect the weak was part of the ideal of kingship in the ANE, most famously illustrated by the prologue to the law code of King Hammurabi in the early second millennium BC (*ANET* 163–180), and found also at Ugarit. Such responsibility, delegated by the god, appears in a number of OT psalms, where it is laid upon the Davidic king (Pss. 72; 146:7–10). In our text, however, it is exercised directly by Yahweh himself. This is consistent with Deuteronomy's reduction of the role of the human king (see on 17:14–20). The enforcement of Yahweh's impartiality is, in Deuteronomy, the responsibility of the lawcourts (1:16–17; 16:19; cf. Exod. 23:3, 6–8). The command to 'love the outsider', however (19), extends the 'royal' responsibility to Israel as such. At the same time it becomes another example of deuteronomic penetration beyond the external act to the heart or attitude (cf. Lev. 19:18, where 'love' also reaches beyond the law, though there the horizon is other Israelites). The appeal in this text is grounded in gratitude to Yahweh, because he had mercy on Israel while they were 'outsiders' in Egypt. The same point is made in the law concerning slave release (Deut. 15:15).

20–22. The first part of the great speech in 10:12 – 11:31 (i.e. 10:12–22) now ends with renewed exhortations to fear and worship Yahweh, again using familiar language. Verse 20 is almost identical to 6:13, adding only 'hold to him', strengthening the plea not to be seduced to other gods (the same verb occurs in 11:22; 13:5; 30:20). In the fashion of deuteronomic rhetoric, the appeal is immediately given grounding (21), here in terms of the great acts done in Egypt and the wilderness (cf. 4:34; 26:8). The phrase 'He is your praise' appears also in 26:19, which shows that it refers to the fame or glory of Israel because of what Yahweh has done for them (cf. 4:6 for a related idea; also Ps. 22:25[26]). The train of thought concludes (22) with an allusion to the promise to the patriarchs that the people would become numerous (Gen. 22:17; Deut. 1:10; 26:5). This echoes v. 15 and the election theme. The contrast is made with the small numbers of the family of Jacob that originally went to Egypt to avoid famine (Gen. 46:27; Exod. 1:5). In this way a sense is given of a promise fulfilled, and of the position of Israel on the threshold of a new stage in its life. The resumption of the phrase 'and now' (22) from v. 12 creates a fine balance between the need for obedience expressed there and the promise reaffirmed here.

11:1–7

1–2. The command to love God, fleshed out in obedience (1), is repeated from 10:12, and leads into a rehearsal of the basis for this in Yahweh's acts of salvation. The combination (2) of memory, or 'knowledge', and discipline in the wilderness is picked up from 8:2–5. Here 'you shall understand' is a command (lit. 'you shall know', *wîḏaʿtem*). (For the difficult syntax of v. 2 see 'Notes on the text'.) The distinction between the present (Moab) generation and their 'children' makes an interesting contrast with 5:3, where the present generation is distinguished from their 'fathers'. Deuteronomy's focus on the experiences of the Moab generation cannot be taken pedantically, since its concept that *this* generation saw the signs at the exodus sets aside the distinction between the exodus and Moab generations that Deuteronomy elsewhere acknowledges (1:34–40). Elsewhere, too, the covenant at Moab is extended to the participants' descendants, in line with Deuteronomy's sense of the solidarity of Israel in all its generations (29:14–15[13–14]; cf. Lenchak 1993: 104). In the present text, as in 5:3, therefore, the effect is rhetorical, and aims to focus on the immediacy of the experience and the urgent responsibility to remember and obey.

3–7. This passage is a kind of hymn, using repetition to build up a picture of Yahweh's acts in saving Israel from Egypt. The phrase 'what he did' (*ʾăšer ʿāśâ*) occurs in each of these verses. (In vv. 3 and 7 *ʾăšer* follows 'deeds/work', and is therefore translated 'that'.) This argument from history has a precedent in 8:2–6 (see 'Comment' there). Formally, there is some correspondence with the 'historical prologue' element of the treaty (G. Seitz 1971: 81ff.). The narrative of Yahweh's saving acts is entirely typical of Deuteronomy's grounding of the call to obedience (as in vv. 8–17) in the need for gratitude. Two elements, however, appear only here in Deuteronomy's recollections of the acts of salvation, namely the crossing of the Reed Sea, and the punishment of Dathan and Abiram (cf. 6:21–25; 26:5–9).

4. The absence otherwise of an explicit allusion to the crossing of the Sea is remarkable in a work that makes so much of the saving acts, and because the deliverance at the Sea is so prominent in other parts of the OT literature (see Childs 1967). It may perhaps be explained in terms of Deuteronomy's somewhat generalizing tendency, which, as we have seen, may also explain its substitution of 'Horeb' for 'Sinai' (see on 1:2; 4:10). The terms used for the destruction of Pharaoh's army ('causing the water … to overwhelm them') are unique in the OT's accounts of the event. Deuteronomy thus displays both its knowledge of the tradition and its freedom in conveying it.

6. The same is true of the record of Dathan and Abiram's rebellion. The full account of this event is found in Num. 16, which records the rebellion of Dathan and Abiram against Moses' leadership (16:12–14) alongside the more specifically priestly challenge to Moses and Aaron of Korah (a non-Aaronite Levite; Num. 16:3, 8–11). Deuteronomy draws freely on the account in Numbers, being basically similar to Num. 16:32, but also adopting the term 'tents' ('households') from Num. 16:26–27. It uses its own word for 'opened up', and adds the phrase 'every living thing that stood with them'. The omission of Korah from the passage is often explained in literary-critical terms (the Korah passages in Num. 16 being from the source P; so Weinfeld 1991: 444). It could equally follow Deuteronomy's habit of passing over the priest–Levite distinction, thus picking out Dathan and Abiram as representing rebellion in general. The inclusion of this event in the list makes it primarily a saving act, that is, from an enemy within. This fits with the idea in Deuteronomy of the danger of sin to the community as a whole (cf. 13:5; 19:13; 21:9).

7. The list of saving acts, though unique, sums the whole activity of Yahweh for Israel. This is expressed in v. 7, which embraces it all in the unifying expression 'this whole great work' (with RSV, 'all the great work'; S. R. Driver [1895], against NRSV; Weinfeld [1991: 432], 'every great deed'; and cf. Judg. 2:7, 10, where NRSV also translates 'all the great work').

11:8–17

8–9. The next main paragraph, vv. 8–17, continues the thought of vv. 1–7 by taking the narrative of Yahweh's saving activity on into the possession of the land itself. As in that passage, there is a balance between command and promise. Following the commands in vv. 1–2 and the rehearsal of Yahweh's acts (3–7), we now meet a reiteration of the basic command (8–9; cf. v. 1), as a preparation for entering the land that Israel is in fact about to occupy (9, 10–12). This expression of the command is very similar to 6:1–2. In both these places the commandments are summed up in the single word *hammiṣwâ*, and each also has the prospect of land inheritance. The full range of Israel's life, from the promise to the ancestors to an unlimited future, is represented in vv. 8–9. (Even though there is no actual reference to future generations, in contrast to the parallel 6:2, this is implied in the idea of long life in the land.) The idea of strength to enter the land is new here (8), but expresses the need for both physical and moral courage to obey the command/promise, in a challenge that would be repeated to Joshua at the moment of impending entry (Josh. 1:9).

10–12. The promise of the land prompts another vivid description of it, such as we have met before in Deuteronomy (cf. 6:10–11; 8:7–10), and as are found in covenant forms at the end of historical prologues (Baltzer 1971: 22, 29–30, 46). The contrast with Egypt (cf. 7:15) adds a new twist with an allusion to the need the irrigate there, using the available water to its greatest possible extent; in the promised land, in contrast, the watering will be done by the rain from heaven, conceived as the direct gift and responsibility of Yahweh himself (cf. 28:12). The land literally 'drinks' the heavenly water supply, suggesting both ease and plenty. The relationship between Yahweh and his land is at its most intimate here, as he 'cares for' it, watching it the year round to ensure that the watering is adequate to keep it fruitful (12). The 'caring' is literally 'seeking', with a suggestion of devotion. The idea is mirrored by Israel's 'seeking' the place that Yahweh will choose for them to worship him (12:5).

13–17. The thought of vv. 8–12 is largely repeated in vv. 13–15, with some further specification. The command to obey resumes the idea of loving God wholeheartedly (cf. 10:12; 11:1), a keynote of this whole section. And the promise of rain now spells out the rains of autumn and spring, the so-called former and latter rains (cf. Jer. 5:24). The logic of loyalty to Yahweh reaches its conclusion (16–17) when it excludes the worship of other gods. Love of Yahweh to the exclusion of other deities was also linked with Yahweh's provision and blessing in 7:1–6, 13–14. And the connection of thought finds an echo in Hos. 2:8–9[10–11]. The warning is also reminiscent of Deut. 8, where the possibility of the people's 'forgetting' Yahweh had potentially disastrous consequences; in both places the prospect of final loss of the land, and thus of life itself, is held out (17; cf. 8:19–20). This warning marks a significant resting-point in the development of the theme that began at 10:12.

11:18–21

These verses strongly resemble 6:6–9, the elements coming in a slightly different order (11:18b = 6:8; 11:19 = 6:7; the promise of long life also pulls in 6:2–3). For comment see on that place. The argument here deliberately resumes that fundamental exhortation to Israel, in line with the tendency in 10:12 – 11:32 to re-present important themes. According to one view, the repetition of the passage at this point signals the closing of the main part of the argument following the Horeb narrative, which had begun with the 'Hear, Israel!' at 6:4 (Weinfeld 1991: 453–454).

11:22–25

This short passage re-expresses the basic promise of conquest. As usual, a balance is kept between command and promise, but the emphasis is on the latter. Verse 22 once again exhorts to wholehearted obedience (cf. 10:12). Then the passage returns to two aspects of the basic promise. First, Israel will drive out nations greater and stronger than itself (23; cf. 7:1, 17; cf. 1:28). And secondly, there is a description of the limits of the land (24). Comparable descriptions come at 1:7 and 34:1–2, thus at the beginning and end of the book. Another is found in Josh. 1:4, in a passage (1:3–5) closely resembling this one. The occurrence of such a description at this point, therefore, is an important structuring mark, signalling the end of the first major section (chs. 1 – 11). This is the simplest of the three boundary descriptions (closer to Josh. 1:4 than to the deuteronomic ones), but specifying north–south and east–west axes (the Sinai wilderness to Lebanon in the north; the Euphrates [east] to the Mediterranean), rather than naming parts of the land (cf. also Gen. 15:18–19; and see 'Notes on the text'). Verse 25 draws together the two aspects of the promise, v. 25b recalling 7:24a. The allusion to the past promise (25c) is another small indication that an argument is being rounded off.

11:26–32

26. The identification of 11:26–32 as a small section in itself arises from several factors. The first is its strong new beginning (lit. 'See!'; cf. 4:5; 30:15 [N. Lohfink 1962: 42 n. 44]; 1:8, 21; 2:24, 31 [N. Lohfink 1960]). Usually the expression introduces a declaration that Yahweh has given the land (as an accomplished fact), but, in the first two cases cited here, it is followed by a command to obey, or choose. The present instance is the only one followed by a participle, rather than the perfect, suggesting the imminence and urgency both of the occupation of the land and of the choice now to be made (N. Lohfink 1963: 232–233).

The second distinguishing element in these verses is their thematic focus, also fixed in v. 26. What Yahweh now 'gives' is, strikingly, 'the blessing and the curse' (not 'the land', as might be expected following the verb *nātan*, 'give'). 'The blessing' and 'the curse' are technical terms here, from the language of treaty and covenant, and in Yahweh's imposition of them he is asserting his role as the primary and authoritative participant in the covenantal relationship that is being instituted. The verb *nātan* ('give') might in this instance be more naturally translated 'set'; the play on ideas is unmistakable, however. To the question, 'What does Yahweh give?' the expected answer in deuteronomic terms is 'The land'; so here that presumed answer is anticipated with the correction, 'Yahweh gives the *possibility* of land.' The gift of land is in one sense an accomplished fact; in another, its possession is bound to be a matter of Israel's choice and agreement. The terms of holding it are covenantal, and covenants are marked by the twin possibilities, and motivations, of blessing and curse. This covenantal rationale is at the root of the dialectic between divine gift and human responsibility everywhere in the book.

The third factor marking out 11:26–32 is its formal correspondence with everything that follows in chs. 12 – 28 (as noticed by N. Lohfink 1963: 234). Blessing and curse (11:27–28) correspond to 27:11 – 28:68; the prescription regarding a ceremony on Mts Ebal and Gerizim to mark the covenant is repeated in 27:1–8; and the final summarizing command to keep the commands of Yahweh (11:31–32) is the theme of the entire law code that is about to begin (chs. 12 – 26). This structural role marks the passage as particularly important.

27–28. The blessing and curse depend on Israel's response to the fundamental requirement of all Deuteronomy's preaching, namely to adhere to Yahweh rather than to other gods, and to do so by keeping his commands. As usual in Deut. 1 – 11, these two elements (loyalty and obedience) are essentially one (cf. on 4:9–14, 15–19; also on 8:19). The content of blessing and curse is not spelt out here. This has been clear from the preaching so far, however. The blessing comprises a long life of peace and prosperity in the land that is Israel's by reason of inheritance; the curse entails loss of the land, and consequently of life.

29–30. The announcement of the covenantal ceremony to be enacted on Mts Ebal and Gerizim is a significant landmark in the book so far. Nothing in the legal and narrative materials that we know to lie behind Deuteronomy prepares for this requirement. Furthermore, the reticence of Deuteronomy about naming the regular place of worship in chs. 12 – 26, though it plays a major part there, makes the careful instructions about location in this case all the more striking. Even so, the geographical details in v. 30 have caused puzzlement, because they do not locate the mountains precisely, and even seem contradictory (see 'Notes on the text'). That is, the directions for Shechem in the north seem to be short-circuited by southern place-names (Arabah, Gilgal), though 'Moreh' makes a specific link with Shechem. Some have tried to explain the problem in terms of religious developments and the re-use of old traditions (e.g. an old Shechem ritual was relocated to the area of Gilgal and Jericho after the exile, the names of Gerizim and Ebal being allowed to stand symbolically for blessing and curse; Seebass 1982). However, the peculiarities of the text need no special explanation. Generally speaking, they indicate that, from the perspective of Moab, Shechem is on the other side, in the land of the Canaanites. And the north–south dimension brings the ceremony at Shechem into theological connection with the crossing of the Jordan at Gilgal.

The mountains' position in the heart of the promised land, overlooking the ancient city of Shechem, carries historical symbolism. The patriarchs knew Shechem (Gen. 12:6); indeed, the sons of Jacob had a victory over a Canaanite population there (Gen. 34). That story, though in some ways unedifying, told of a refusal to make a covenant with the people of the land (despite a pretence of being willing to do so, 34:8–24), because of the Shechemite prince Hamor's rape of Jacob's daughter Dinah. It has a number of 'deuteronomic' overtones, therefore (cf. esp. Deut. 7:2–3). The story of Abimelech, the son of Gideon who was made king over Israel at Shechem (Judg. 9:1–6), has echoes of *false* covenant-making in the name of the temple there (Baal-berith, 9:4, i.e. 'Baal of the covenant'; cf. 9:46, which varies to El-berith, using the name of the chief god of the Canaanite pantheon). The importance of Shechem, therefore, may be to emphasize the deuteronomic insistence that only a covenant with Yahweh will be true and valid for Israel.

The ceremony is obviously important to the writer, since the requirement is recorded twice, the two instances of it bracketing the law code, thus binding it into the covenantal framework of the book. The significance of the ceremony is further emphasized by the account of its execution in Josh. 8:30–35.

The role of Mts Ebal and Gerizim at this juncture may be brought into correspondence with that of Mt Horeb in the events unfolded so far. The relationship may be seen as one of progression. Just as Horeb played a major part in the development of Yahweh's covenant with Israel, so now will these twin mountains in the heart of the land. Shechem, as we have seen, is a suitable symbol of covenant faithfulness to Yahweh. As such, it may be seen as a worthy next stage on Israel's 'journey', a journey both in the plain sense and in the sense of its life of faith. This perspective on the presence of Ebal and Gerizim in this chapter, moreover, may explain why Horeb has receded into the background, following 9:1 – 10:11, in which it was prominent.

For the syntax of vv. 31–32, see 'Notes on the text'. This final sentence in Deut. 1 – 11 leads directly into the law code. The basic deuteronomic logic is contained here: Yahweh is giving Israel the land; correspondingly, Israel must obey his commands. The balance between gift and command is, as always, carefully held, here by a double use of the participle 'giving' (*nōtēn*; translated in the second instance, above, by 'laying upon', since the sense in that case is not so much donation as imposition). The terms of this sentence are taken up in 12:1 (see below), so that a bridge is formed between the long prelude to the law code and the code itself.

Explanation

The theme of this long and varied speech is set by the opening question (10:12a), with its prophetic overtones (cf. Mic. 6:6–8). The answer to the rhetorical question is given in terms that express the deuteronomic demand for obedience at its most fundamental level (12b), terms that are then repeated, wholly or partly, at other points (11:1, 13, 18). It is nothing less than a discourse on loving God. As such it becomes one of the profoundest expressions of deuteronomic theology, because it develops this love commandment fully in the context of covenant faithfulness. Here love and command are not at odds; neither can transcend the other. Deuteronomy contains its own response to those who think its theology primitive or legalistic, and it is this: loving God means loving him as he is, that is, as he has made himself known; he has made himself known to Israel in covenant at Horeb, in which he has given his commandments.

The commandments are not detachable from the question of who he is, which is why the preaching in Deuteronomy can run seamlessly from the exhortation to obey the commandments to the warning not to run after other gods (11:13, 16); 11:16–17, in fact, is a first major climax of this speech.

It is the close connection between ethical imperatives and the person of Yahweh that distinguishes his requirements from those of law as such. The need for justice and righteousness was by no means confined to Israel in the ancient world. It was the duty of kings to organize society justly; at the top of the Hammurabi stele, over the mass of laws inscribed on the main part of it, a god (Shamash or Marduk) is represented as handing the laws to the king. There, however, the relationship of the god to the laws themselves is somewhat detached. In Deuteronomy it is intimate. Here Yahweh not only initiates the standards inscribed in the law, but embodies them, and is even their executor (10:17–18), thus incidentally taking the role of 'king'.

The election of Israel is once again brought again into connection with the universality of Yahweh (10:14–15), as in Deut. 7. Both these passages prepare for the question how Yahweh's universal rule might be expressed in the light of the election of Israel; in the former it was clear that the command to act righteously undermined any notion of election that could be taken for granted, or transmitted on merely national grounds; here the answer is in terms of the inward realizing of the marks of election (circumcision, 10:16). This, too, is a prophetic note (cf. Jer. 4:4). It is also taken up by Paul in Rom. 2:25–29, to show that true love of God does not depend on the physical mark of belonging to the Jewish people, but on 'circumcision of the heart, by the Spirit' (2:29). This is what makes a true 'Jew'. Paul's revolutionary extension of the covenant privileges to Gentiles, on the basis of faith, is therefore fully prepared for in Deuteronomy and the prophets.

In close connection with circumcision of the heart is the idea of God's grace, for the need for this still hangs over the present speech, following from the narrative of the golden calf in 9:1 – 10:11. In this speech it is chiefly stressed by means of the themes of creation and election. (It will be further developed at a later point, in Deut. 30:6, which takes up the metaphor of circumcision of the heart, but there makes Yahweh the subject of the action, in the manner of the theology of the new covenant; cf. Jer. 31:33; 32:39, and see 'Comment' on Deut. 30:6.)

Blessing is a major theme in the speech, with a description of the fruitfulness of the land, and the promise of rain (11:10–17). Peace and security in a land truly Israel's own belong to the picture (11:24–25). A note of warning must always be sounded when such language is used, for direct translations into modern politics are deeply misguided. Deuteronomy's promises of peace, prosperity and secure boundaries belong to the time of ancient Israel. History and theology have come a long way since then. The traditional Christian 'spiritualizations' of crossing the Jordan and entering the promised land (as in the hymn 'Guide me, O thou great Jehovah' and in some negro spirituals), though they adopt typology in an oversimplified way, have the virtue of avoiding such dangerous identifications. Theology has to find ways of adopting the dynamics of giving God his due in the real world of human relationships that do not fall into such traps. The laws that follow in Deut. 12 – 26 cannot be applied literally and directly; they do affirm, however, that the people of God, wherever and whenever they are, have a responsibility to promote all practical ways of doing what is right in the world, as well as in their private lives.

Finally, the call to love God and the pictures of promised blessings are drawn together in the first programmatic statement of the alternative possible outcomes of the covenant commitment, the blessing and the curse (11:26–32). Only then are the hearers ready to hear the laws themselves, whose role and function in the covenant have been the subject of so much of the discourse so far.

DEUTERONOMY 12:1–32

Translation

¹These are the laws and statutes you shall be careful to keep in the land the LORD the God of your forefathers has given you to possess, for as long as you live on the earth. ²You must completely destroy all the places where the peoples you are driving out have worshipped their gods, on the high mountains and hills and under every green tree. ³You shall break down their altars and smash their sacred pillars, burn their Asherah poles and cut down the images of their gods, and so destroy their names from that place. ⁴You shall not worship the LORD your God in that way.

⁵But you are to seek the place the LORD your God will choose, out of all your tribes, to put his name there as its dwelling-place; and you shall go there. ⁶You must take your burnt offerings and sacrifices there, your tithes and contributions, your vow offerings and freewill offerings, and your firstborn of herd and flock. ⁷You shall eat there before the LORD your God; and you shall rejoice in everything to which you put your hand, together with your households, because the LORD your God has blessed you.

⁸You are not to do as we are doing here today, each what seems right to him. ⁹For you have not yet come into the rest and inheritance the LORD your God is giving you. ¹⁰But when you have crossed the Jordan and are living in the land the LORD your God is giving you as an inheritance, and live in security, having rest from your enemies around, ¹¹then you shall bring everything I am commanding you to the place the LORD your God chooses, to make a dwelling for his name there: your burnt offerings and sacrifices, your tithes and contributions, and the choicest gifts that you have vowed to the LORD. ¹²You will rejoice before the LORD

your God, together with your sons and daughters, your servants and maidservants, and the Levites who live in your cities because they have no territorial share of their own in your inheritance.

[13]Be sure not to make your burnt offerings at any place you see, [14]for it is at the place the LORD chooses in one of your tribes that you must make your burnt offerings, and do all that with which I am charging you.

[15]However, you may slaughter and eat meat whenever you like, as much as the LORD your God has blessed you with, in any of your cities; the ritually unclean and clean alike may eat it as they would eat gazelle or deer. [16]But you must not eat the blood; pour it out on the ground like water.

[17]You may not eat in your cities the tithe of your grain, wine or oil, or your firstborn of herd or flock, or any vow you have made, or freewill offering or contribution. [18]These you must eat before the LORD your God in the place the LORD your God will choose, together with your sons and daughters, your servants and maidservants, and the Levites who live in your cities; you will rejoice before the LORD your God in everything you do. [19]Be sure you do not neglect the Levite as long as you live in your land.

[20]When the LORD your God enlarges your territory, as he has promised he will, and you think, 'I want to eat meat', because you are hungry for meat, then you may eat meat whenever you like. [21]If the place the LORD your God will choose, to put his name there, is at a distance from you, you may slaughter from your herds and flocks that the LORD has given you, in the way I have commanded you, and eat meat in your cities whenever you like. [22]Indeed, you may eat it as one eats gazelle or deer, the ritually unclean and clean together. [23]But be sure not to eat the blood; for the blood is the life, and you must not eat the life together with the meat. [24]Do not eat it; pour it out on the ground like water. [25]Do not eat it, and thus you will have well-being, together with your descendants, for you will be doing what is right in the eyes of the LORD. [26]Only take the holy things and the vows that you vow and go to the place the LORD will choose, [27]and offer there your burnt offerings, both the flesh and blood, on the altar of the LORD your God; the blood of your sacrifices too must be poured out on the altar of the LORD your God, but the flesh you may eat. [28]Be careful to obey all these commands with which I am charging you, in order that you and your descendants may have well-being for ever, because you do what is good and right in the eyes of the LORD your God.

[29]When the LORD your God has cut off before you the nations you are going across to dispossess, and you have driven them out and live in their land, [30]be careful not to be ensnared by them, after they have been destroyed before you, and you seek their gods, thinking, 'How do these peoples worship their gods? I too want to do as they do'; [31]you must not do so to the LORD your God. For every abhorrent thing that the LORD hates they do for their gods; they even burn their sons and daughters in sacrifice to their gods. [32]Every command that I am giving you you must be careful to do; neither add to it, nor take away from it.

Notes on the text

3. The suffix on *mizbᵉḥōtām*, 'their altars', is odd, being the form normally attached to a singular noun; 7:5 has the expected form, *mizbᵉḥōtêhem*, as has SamP here.

5. *yibḥar*, 'will choose': SamP substitutes *bāḥar*, 'has chosen', here and regularly, in accordance with its view that the place was indeed Mt Gerizim. The imperfect suits an openness on the matter of choice, while the perfect makes it an accomplished fact.

lᵉšiknô, 'for its/his dwelling': the form presupposes a noun, *šeken*, not otherwise attested (cf. Craigie 1976a: 217 n. 9; Keller 1996: 15), and this is accepted in the translation here. Because of the *hapax legomenon*, interpreters often emend to *lᵉšakkᵉnô* (*škn* pi., 'to make dwell'), in conformity with v. 11. (Laberge [1985: 211–212] notes that the form in MT *suggests* a piel, but the Masoretes stopped short of pointing it either as such or as qal.) There is, in any case, ambiguity concerning whether the suffix refers to 'it', that is, 'the name', or to 'him', that is, Yahweh. MT's punctuation, with *athnah* at the word *šām*, 'there', provides 'to place (*lāśûm*) his name there; *his* dwelling you shall seek' (see Keller 1996: 16–17). However, the verb *tidᵉrᵉšû*, 'you shall seek', is required to complete the command begun at the beginning of the verse: '(to) the place he will choose'. This syntax, together with the analogy of v. 11, suggests '*its* dwelling', i.e. a reference to the name.

LXX reads *epiklēthēnai*, 'to call (over)', here and regularly, avoiding the force of *šākan*, 'dwelling', in line with its concern to stress the transcendence of Yahweh.

11. LXX adds 'today' after 'everything I am commanding you', here and elsewhere (cf. 14, 28). LXX probably conforms these texts to the pattern elsewhere in Deuteronomy.

14. 'in one of your tribes': though the word 'one' (*'aḥad*) can in other contexts do duty for the distributive (thus 'in any of your tribes'; cf. 15:7; 16:5, and Fenton 1989: 24–25, following Welch 1924: 48), when contrasted with 'any place you see' (13) the meaning is on balance 'one' (NRSV; cf. Keller 1996: 29–30). Similarly, since v. 5 has been clear on the point, v. 14 should be read in its light.

15. The phrase 'whenever you like' can be used to refer to place rather than time, i.e. 'wherever you wish' (cf. 2 Sam. 3:21; 1 Kgs. 11:37, and Fenton 1989: 28–31). The decision between 'whenever' and 'wherever' in the present context is a balanced one. The spatial permission would correspond nicely with the restriction of sacrifices to the chosen place. The scales are tipped towards a temporal permission, however, because the spatial point is covered by 'in any of your cities' (15, cf. 21).

18. 'your sons … daughters … servants … maidservants': these are singular in Hebrew.

20. 'whenever you like': cf. on v. 15.

22. 'as one eats gazelle or deer': the construction is niphal followed by the direct object, marked by *'eṭ*; this is strictly illogical, as 'the gazelle and deer' should be the subject of the passive verb; the niphal effectively gives an impersonal construction in this case, however: 'as one eats'.

27. 'the blood of your sacrifices too': there is no word for 'too', but the word order suggests it by putting subject before verb in the clause.

28. 'Be careful to obey': SamP and LXX have 'to do', after which *dᵉḇārîm* might be translated 'things', rather than 'words'. This makes the verse a command to carry out the sacrifices according to the laws just given. MT's 'obey these commands' is preferable because of general analogy in Deuteronomy.

28. There is some textual support for 'today' after 'with which I am charging you'; cf. on v. 11.

Form and structure

Chapter 12 in the context of Deuteronomy

With ch. 12 the long central section of Deuteronomy opens (chs. 12 – 26), known generally as the deuteronomic law code. This is not quite accurate, because the laws are cast within the form of Moses' second speech, and they are attended by exhortation and motivation in the style familiar from chs. 1 – 11. Even so, there is a definite shift at this point into specific regulations. The commands that occupy chs. 12 – 26 are unmistakably the 'laws and statutes' for which the preaching has prepared the hearers at length in chs. 1 – 11 (4:1, etc.). Because of the change in content, the section now beginning has been compared, as far as its form and literary setting are concerned, with the specific stipulations found in treaties. The instructions here are not quite like those of treaty stipulations, however, since they are indeed more like law, and it is right, therefore, to see a certain assimilation of treaty and law code forms in Deuteronomy.

Although there is a new departure here, there is also strong continuity. Deut. 12:1 is closely linked with 11:31–32, repeating the references to the gift of the land, and to the laws and statutes. Indeed, there is a chiasmus involving these terms, together with the plural pronoun 'you', thus (with G. Seitz 1971: 40):

A 'You'
B Formula of gift of land (*'ereṣ*)
C Keep (*šāmar*) the laws and statutes
C¹ Keep (*šāmar*) the laws and statutes
B¹ Formula of gift of land (*'ereṣ*)
A¹ 'You'

In this way the strong connection between motivation (on the basis of Yahweh's gift) and obedience is reiterated at the outset of the main body of laws.

Notwithstanding the point just made, 12:1 opens with a kind of superscription, 'These are the laws and statutes', which recalls certain other announcements of laws, namely 1:1; 4:44, 45; 6:1; 29:1[28:69]; 33:1 (G. Seitz 1971: 23). These are not all strictly announcements of laws yet to be promulgated, and they are not a guide to the structure of the book in themselves (5:1, for example, is a more important beginning than 6:1). Even so, they all mark transitions in some sense, and in this case a strong one.

Relationship with other law codes (Exod. 20 – 23; 34; Lev. 17)

We have noticed several times that Deuteronomy re-presents in distinctive form material that lies behind it. Specifically, we saw that following its version of the Decalogue it did not proceed directly to the law code, as in the case of Exodus (Exod. 20:22 – 23:33, the Book of the Covenant [BC]), but interposed a long section of exhortation, including the golden-calf narrative, which Exodus had left till later. The law code that follows here has many points of contact with BC, not least that it begins with a law about the place of worship (Exod. 20:22–26). (Exod. 34:11–28, a shorter text parallel to Exod. 20 – 23, does likewise; see N. Lohfink 1991f: 175 for the view that Deuteronomy has drawn on both of these earlier texts.) Deut. 12 is often contrasted with Exod. 20:24–25 on the matter of how many altars are permitted. It is also contrasted with Lev. 17, which requires that sacrificial worship during the wilderness wanderings be made at the tabernacle only. Deuteronomy's law of the place of worship is thought stricter than that of Exodus, but less so than that of Leviticus. (See 'Comment' for elaboration of these points; and Introduction.)

Structure of Deuteronomy 12

In keeping with the primacy of the subject of ch. 12 in the law code (namely worship), the treatment of it is careful and complex. The sub-sections of the chapter are as follows:

A.	12:1	Superscription
1.	12:2–4	Destroy Canaanite religious sites
2.	12:5–14 (8–12)	Worship Yahweh at his chosen place
3.	12:15–28 (20–28)	Permission to slaughter non-sacrificially
4.	12:29–32 [13:1]	No adoption of Canaanite worship

This pattern may be elaborated in greater detail (see McConville 1984: 67 for an attempt; it is slightly modified here). The progression of thought is then: 1. Israel is not to tolerate Canaanite worship in its midst, and is to destroy the places where it is carried on (2–4). 2. In contrast, after they have entered the land and peace has been achieved, they are to worship only Yahweh according to his choice of a worship place (5–14). 3. Since there is to be no proliferation of worship places, the issue of slaughtering animals for food in the localities of Israel is raised, and is settled by the permission to slaughter non-sacrificially (15–19). This is articulated carefully, so as to avoid any improper manipulation of blood (20–28). 4. Finally, the argument returns to a warning not to copy the religious practices of Canaan (29–32[13:1]). The progression of thought closely follows that of Deut. 7, as already noticed:

1. 7:1–6   Destroy Canaanite worship
2. 7:7–11   Israel as holy people
3. 7:12–16 Blessing
4. 7:17–26 Destroy Canaanite worship

The first and fourth elements obviously correspond. The second elements agree in marking out Israel from other nations, in ch. 12 specifically in the realm of worship. And the third elements correspond in regard to the blessings of the land: 7:12–16 makes the fundamental point, while 12:15–28 reflects on how they might be enjoyed in the context of the worship regulations. (The correspondence is not exact, since 'blessing' is evident also in the basic regulations about sacrificing, 12:7. Yet in broad outline it is striking.)

Critical scholarship has explained the composition of Deut. 12 as the result of a complex literary and religious-historical growth, based on the repetitious style and other factors.

First, the several expressions of the command to worship Yahweh at a place of his choosing have led to the belief that several versions of the command have been brought together in the chapter. The versions are as follows: vv. 2–7, 8–12, 13–19, 20–27/28 (G. Seitz 1971: 187, 206–212); alternatively, vv. 2–3, 4–7, 8–12, 13–19, 20–28, 29–31 (N. Lohfink 1996: 130). The earliest version is almost always thought to be vv. 13–19, because it is in the singular (G. Seitz 1971: 208; cf. Mayes 1979: 222; Levinson 1997: 24).

Secondly, not only does the call to centralize in general occur variously, but the place formula itself is expressed in different forms – broadly speaking, a long form and a short form – both in ch. 12 and elsewhere in the law code (G. Seitz 1971: 212–214). In addition, the different forms use different terms for 'to place (the name)', namely *šākan* and *śûm* (see 'Notes on the text'). The occurrence of these two verbs is sometimes taken to suggest different traditions. De Vaux (1967) noted that while *šākan* was more frequent in Deuteronomy, *śûm* was preferred in DtrH (Joshua–Kings), and that the former was earlier.

These differences have generally been thought to betray signs of development in relation to religious events in ancient Israel, with Josiah's reform at their centre. Besides the matter of different forms in itself, the first occurrence of the formula (12:5) is thought to specify a single place of worship exclusively, while the older forms were not explicit on this point.

Thirdly, the parts of the chapter are held to make different theological points (e.g. vv. 2–4, 29–31 aim at Canaanite worship, while the central parts concern internal worship arrangements; Reuter 1993: 110). 'Canaanite' religion is often taken to be a cipher for something else, either worship at sanctuaries other than Jerusalem, or indeed Babylonian religion (Reuter 1993: 111, on vv. 5–7, 20, 28). The latter case presupposes a progression from a pre-exilic to an exilic setting, with the result that the issue of relating to Babylonian religion presents itself, and this is then thought to be in mind in the anti-'Canaanite' passages (so also Keller [1996: 38–42], for whom vv. 2–7 are late exilic or early post-exilic).

The view taken here proposes, in contrast, a unified view of the chapter. Responses to the arguments outlined can be made only briefly.

Against the first argument two points may be made. 1. The supposed earliest form of the altar law (13–19) scarcely amounts in itself to a coherent requirement. It refers only to burnt offerings, but then makes a provision for non-sacrificial slaughter which relates to *zebah* sacrifices (the sort that comes to the altar only in part). This law, if it were self-standing, would raise the question whether all *zᵉbāhîm* were now abolished, without being explicit enough to resolve it. The command in vv. 13–14 is better taken as resumptive, and v. 15, with its limiting *raq*, as an adjustment in the light of the whole argument that has gone before. (N. Lohfink [1996: 136–137] also thinks vv. 13–19 cannot be an original centralizing law, for similar reasons, though he thinks it is in essence the oldest part of Deut. 12.) 2. There is no counterpart anywhere else in the law code to the compilation of several pre-existing laws on the same topic.

Secondly, the different forms of the place formula are not a sure guide to a tradition history of the formula. Certain cases of the short formula are best understood as presupposing more elaborate forms (e.g. Deut. 31:11; Josh. 9:27; G. Seitz 1971: 214), and therefore there can be no presumption that short forms in general constitute a distinct type of the formula (see also N. Lohfink 1991f, and his reply [1995b] to Reuter's challenge [1993]; also Halpern 1981a: 23). As for *šākan* and *śûm*, the idea that these represent diverse traditions is less convincing when it is agreed that the shorter forms of the place formula presuppose the longer. Further, there appear to be no special theological issues at stake in Deuteronomy's use of these terms in relation to the divine presence, even if problems were subsequently felt by LXX and the Masoretes (see 'Notes on the text'; also

'Comment'). On the question whether the chapter contains various messages about a single sanctuary, see 'Comment'.

Thirdly, the idea that Deut. 12 contains within it fundamentally different theological issues overlooks the theological coherence of the argument (as set out above). There are, furthermore, strong stylistic features of the passage that are best explained on the assumption of its unity. The use of repetition, obviously, is an important part of its teaching style. But it is more than repetition. Rather, there is a progressive dialogue between the two poles of the argument, namely: 1. that the people must sacrifice at the place of worship chosen by Yahweh, and 2. they are free to slaughter and eat meat at any place. The repetitions, with a tendency to expansion, constitute progressive mutual qualifications.

Deuteronomy 12 and Josiah's reform

Lying behind the whole discussion is the question whether or in what way the laws here relate to the reforms of Kings Hezekiah and Josiah in the seventh century BC. The issue affects all the laws in the code, especially those concerning the cult, but also the judicial legislation. (See on 16:18 – 18:22, and Introduction.) Studies of the laws have often found the marks of the reform upon them, conceived generally as centralizing the whole administration of Judah in Jerusalem. The postulate of different forms of the altar law could be reconciled with the concept that pre-Deuteronomic laws, which did not have a background in centralization, were gradually revised in favour of the new, centralized system. The hypothetical older versions of the altar law were a case in point, culminating, however, in 12:2–7, which was held to be the product of the reform and to be exclusive. (Welch [1924: 57–59], who denied that Deuteronomy was largely a product of the reform, conceded that this passage was so. A classic example of the approach, for all the laws, is Horst 1930.) The question whether the formula in 12:5 is exclusive is taken up in the 'Comment' (below).

The principal reasons why the present commentary does not accept that the law can be a programme for Josiah's (or Hezekiah's) reform are based on an interpretation of the book as a whole (as explained in the Introduction). Essentially, they consist in the belief that Deuteronomy's radical view of the nature of religion, while not by definition anti-cultic, cannot align itself with measures that enhance the interests of a particular sanctuary, a priestly class or a royal administration conceived along lines that owe more to ANE ways of thinking than to Deuteronomy's concept of the covenant with the people of Israel. This runs counter to the common idea that Deuteronomy's altar law supports the Jerusalem institutions. It means too that Deuteronomy is in line with Jeremiah's critique of the practice of worship in the temple (Jer. 7:1–15; note v. 12), and not, as de Vaux (1967: 220) thought, that Jeremiah opposed Deuteronomy on the matter.

Finally, it is a fallacy to argue that Deuteronomy must have centralization in Jerusalem in mind on the grounds that the law is obviously taken to refer to Jerusalem in the books of Kings (2 Sam. 7; 1 Kgs. 8:29; 2 Kgs. 21:4; 23:27). From the perspective of Josiah's time, the law must naturally be understood in relation to Jerusalem; but the OT knows that it could in principle have applied to other places too (Josh. 9:27; Jer. 7:12).

Comment

12:1–7

1. The law code begins with an announcement that the laws are about to be declared, similar to other such announcements (5:1; 6:1). The form found here, however, where 'laws and statutes' stands alone, is found only at 5:1; 11:32, 12:1 and 26:28, that is, at the beginnings and endings of the long preamble to the laws (chs. 5 – 11) and of the laws themselves (chs. 12 – 26). The phrase marks out these sections as the body of laws and commands to which it refers (i.e. chs. 5 – 26; here with Braulik [1970] rather than with N. Lohfink [1989], who limits the intended scope of the phrase to chs. 12 – 26; see discussion in McConville & Millar 1994: 126–127). The giving of the laws, therefore, fundamentally continues the Decalogue, applying those basic commands into the life of Israel. This is in line with the argument in chs. 5 – 6, that the authority of the Decalogue would continue to be expressed through the properly constituted authorities in Israel.

The keeping of the laws and statutes is linked closely with the formula of the gift of the land. The intimate relationship between keeping the covenant commands and the enjoyment of land is articulated in brief compass, just as in the immediately preceding verses. In a sense, too, these are laws *for* the land ('the laws ... you shall be careful to keep *in the land*'), since many of them make sense only in a settled situation, in cities and tribal territories. It would be wrong, though, to say that chs. 12 – 26 are in principle for the land only, while chs. 5 – 11 are for all time (N. Lohfink's position; see 'Form and structure'). Rather, the close relationship between Decalogue and subsequent laws inaugurates a hermeneutical process, according to which its provisions may be adapted to new situations, the authority to do so being invested in the appropriated institutions, represented in Deuteronomy by Moses.

The words 'land' (*'ereṣ*) and 'earth' (*'ᵃdāmâ*) occur together in v. 1. The translation here makes a choice concerning the latter which implies that they are not synonymous in the verse. The matter is not so clear, since both terms are used elsewhere in the book to mean both 'land' (territory) and 'earth'. In 11:8–9, both terms clearly refer to the land (cf. 4:38, 40). In 26:1–2, in contrast, the two terms mean respectively 'land' (territory) and 'fruitful ground'. In 4:17–18 *'ereṣ* is the whole earth, while *'ªdāmâ* is ground as such. The phrase 'as long as you live on the earth' occurs also in 4:10, where *'ªdāmâ* means the whole earth; in other places, this and similar phrases refer to life in the land itself (4:40; 30:20; 32:47). However, a mere repetition of the idea of land as territory would be a tautology here; it is best therefore to understand the phrase by analogy with 4:10.

It is noteworthy that the formula of the gift of the land occurs here with the verb *nātan*, 'give', in the perfect, instead of the otherwise regular participle *nōtēn* ('is giving'; 28:52 is another exception to the rule). This may help to signal the new phase in the book's argument; it is time to consider the laws.

2–4. The first specific command in the law code (2–3) concerns the destruction of Canaanite places of worship, root and branch. The term 'places' is notable (2). Deuteronomy avoids the term 'high place' (*bāmâ*), typical in the historical books (Joshua–Kings). The term 'place' can sometimes simply be translated 'sanctuary' (e.g. Gen. 12:6; see REB), but needs the context to determine this. Deuteronomy's usage is in keeping with its general avoidance of specific terms for cultic things, including 'temple', or 'sanctuary' for Yahweh's chosen place.

In the present discourse, 'places' corresponds to the chosen 'place' in v. 5. Their plurality contrasts with the singular there, and there is at least a rhetorical correspondence between their many places and their many gods. Plurality of places is probably not an issue in itself here. In Deuteronomy's critique of Canaanite religion the concern is simply that Israel should avoid the worship of other gods. There is a certain scathing note, however, about the indiscriminateness of the Canaanites' worship, 'on the high mountains and hills, and under *every* green tree'. There was indeed a tendency for places of worship to be found on hills and in groves (cf. 'oak of Tabor', 1 Sam. 10:3; also 'Gibeah', or 'Gibeat-Elohim', a sanctuary town literally meaning 'hill', or 'hill of God', 1 Sam. 10:5, 10). The point is echoed also in Hosea (4:13; cf. Weinfeld 1972: 366–370). This indiscriminateness has perhaps something in common with the absurdity of fashioning a 'god' out of a piece of wood (Is. 44:9–20). It also contrasts with the stress on Yahweh's choice in respect of his place of worship (5).

The specific command to destroy the Canaanite worship places (3a) is similar to 7:5, with a slightly different distribution of the verbs (see 'Comment' there).

Verse 3b rounds off the command to destroy, repeating the verb used in v. 2 (*'bd*, pi.). The effect of destroying the accoutrements of worship at a place is to destroy the 'name' of the god worshipped there. Place and name are strongly associated in this verse. The identification of a place with God, or a god, is well known from OT narratives (cf. Jacob's naming of

Bethel, 'house of God', Gen. 28:19; and of Peniel, 'face of God', Gen. 32:30). Other place names in the OT were probably based on gods' names (e.g. Beth-Shemesh, 'house of Shamash', the sun-god; Jericho, cf. *yārēaḥ*, 'moon', hence the moon god). The religious associations of a place of worship went deep; the logic of this command is, then, that the only sure way to protect Israel from sliding into the worship of the gods of the land was to eradicate the physical remains of it, with their long and powerful memories. ('Place' at the end of v. 2 occurs in the singular, despite 'places' in v. 2, and must be taken distributively.)

The laconic prohibition in v. 4 sets the positive instructions about worshipping Yahweh in opposition to the picture of Canaanite worship just sketched. Literally it is 'you shall not do so to the LORD your God'; that is, you shall not worship in the way they do. This is echoed in v. 31, and therefore it is a leading idea in the whole chapter that Israel should be qualitatively different from the nations (see also on v. 31, for comment on the temptation to be like them).

5. The phrasing of this first formulation of the law of worship follows directly from the command that has preceded: 'you shall ... destroy their names from that place [3] ... But [to] the place [Yahweh] ... will choose ... to put his name'. The correspondence is clear (extending even to the singular number in both cases), and so the topic of the new command is quickly established. The term 'place' is tantalizingly unspecific, seeming deliberately to avoid available words for 'temple' or 'sanctuary' (such as *hêkāl*, 'temple'; *bayit*, 'house'; *miqdaš*, 'shrine'). This is in keeping with Deuteronomy's tendency not to use the technical language of holiness that we find in Exodus–Leviticus. But, more importantly, it belongs to the particular rhetorical force of the book, which exploits the potential of the word *māqôm* to refer to both 'land' and 'sanctuary', and thus to establish a correspondence between the two (see further below, still on v. 5).

The present verse begins, continuing the sharp contrast with Canaan, 'But (to) the place', though English translations find it hard to convey this with any elegance. The phrase 'to the place' is complemented by 'you shall seek'. The verb *dāraš* can usually be translated 'seek' or 'enquire' (though recall 11:12, where it means 'cared for'). When followed grammatically by the preposition *'el*, as here, it has rather the sense of turning to, or choosing, often with God (Job 5:8; Is. 8:19b), or false religious inter- mediaries (Deut. 18:11; Is. 8:19a; 19:3) in view (cf. also Is. 11:10). 'Seek', therefore, is not the ideal translation here; certainly not if it implies merely trying to identify something, as in a guessing game. The meaning is that the Israelites should decide to resort to Yahweh's place of worship, as a deliberate choice of him and rejection of the other nations' gods. The command therefore forms an ideal sequel to the warnings in vv. 2–4.

Prior to this choice of Israel's, however, which is essentially a response, is that of Yahweh. The most characteristic feature of the command is that the place is the one that Yahweh will *choose*. This is a key idea in

Deuteronomy. Israel itself is the people chosen by Yahweh (7:6). Yahweh will also choose both king (17:15) and priest (or 'Levi', 18:5). Yahweh's choice is therefore set over against any claim on Israel's part to assert its own rights in fundamental matters concerning its life. Yahweh's choosing is akin to his 'giving' of land, blessing and life. Together the two ideas express his primacy in Israel's affairs.

Yahweh's prerogative in choosing the place is more important than any identification of it. Even so, the phrase 'out of all your tribes' suggests at least that a single place is in mind. While other occurrences of the formula, such as v. 14, might be taken as 'in any of your tribes' (see on that verse), and thus imply several sanctuaries in various parts of the land, it is difficult to understand this phrase in the same way. (See above, 'Form and structure'.) The point has been one of the strongest suits in the argument that Deuteronomy's altar law is concerned to centralize the worship of Yahweh in one place after a long period of multiple sanctuaries. When compared with Exod. 20:24-25, the difference in this respect is immediately noticeable. There Yahweh says, 'in every place where I cause my name to be remembered I will come to you and bless you', which evidently allows for a plurality of sanctuaries. (SamP's variant 'in the place' is presumably a change in favour of its Shechem interpretation, and proves that MT's plain reference is to a plurality.) The question then is whether the present law intends to teach that there should be only one sanctuary, in the sense of the theory of centralization, or whether it has some other force. Any interpretation must deal with the fact that the place is not identified by name. Those who see this as a centralization law have argued that everyone would have known that Jerusalem was meant, and that the silence on the name is merely consistent with the Mosaic fiction. However, other views are possible. Serious cases have been made for the law's having originally applied to other places (such as Shechem, Bethel, Shiloh), and this from medieval Jewish commentators, such as Rashi, to modern critical scholars; and perhaps the law even referred to several sanctuaries in succession. (Exod. 20:24-25, incidentally, could also be taken this way.) In my view, the silence concerning the name of the place is intended to resist the making of the wrong kind of claims about any particular temple institution. The point will be returned to below 'Explanation'.

The law is in line with that of Exod. 20:24-25 in this important respect, that the chosen place is where Yahweh's *name* will be known. In the terms of Exodus, he will 'cause it to be remembered'. Here, he will choose the place in order to put his name there. The immediate force of this is to make a contrast with the commands in vv. 2-3. As the Israelites are to destroy both the other gods' 'places' (2) and their 'names' (3), so they are to seek Yahweh's 'place' and he will put his 'name' there. The essential point of the altar law, therefore, is faithfulness to Yahweh. The true place of worship is one that is known to belong wholly and unequivocally to Yahweh. The point is strengthened by occurrences of an Akkadian phrase that closely parallels the Hebrew (Akk. *šuma[m] šakānu[m]*, cf. Hebr. *šākan šēm*), and means literally 'to place the name'. The usage of this phrase that comes closest to the present text occurs in two Amarna letters (EA 287.60–63; 288.5–7), in which a Canaanite king of Jerusalem, Abdi-Heba, acknowledges Pharaoh's lordship there (de Vaux 1967; Schreiner 1963: 163). (The parallel, however, cannot determine the meaning of our text, without exegetical support; cf. Keller 1996: 110–115; also Wenham 1971a.)

The idea of putting Yahweh's name at the place is filled out by the expression 'as its dwelling-place' (*l^{e}šiknô*). This is similar to v. 14: 'to make his name dwell there' (*l^{e}šakkēn*). The text in v. 5 is unusual, but it should be retained rather than emending in favour of the latter (see 'Notes on the text'). Even so, a comparison with v. 11 makes it likely that the present phrase means 'its dwelling-place' as opposed to 'his', i.e. Yahweh's (against MT's punctuation).

This raises the question what is meant by Yahweh's name 'dwelling' in the place. The idea of the name arises in connection with the temple in DtrH (2 Sam. 7:13; 1 Kgs. 8:29, 43–44, 48; 11:36; 2 Kgs. 21:4). Many scholars think that this 'name theology' asserts that Yahweh himself does not dwell in the sanctuary, but only in heaven, the 'name' being a kind of hypostasis representing him. Deuteronomy and related literature would therefore react against an unduly immanentist theology, stressing God's actual presence in an almost tangible sense, as is alleged to be found in older and priestly texts, especially associated with the attribute of God's 'glory', and the enthronement and war metaphors associated with the ark of the covenant (von Rad: 1953: 38–39; Weinfeld 1991: 192–196). The argument draws heavily on 1 Kgs. 8:27–30. That passage is misunderstood, however, no account being taken of 1 Kgs. 8:1–12, which has a strong sense of Yahweh's actual presence. The repeated 'before the LORD' in the present and related passages in Deuteronomy itself (12:7; 14:26) also makes the theory impossible (I. Wilson 1995: 164–165, 191–97). Nor does the use of either of the verbs, 'put' (*sûm*) or 'make dwell' (*šakkēn*), alter the point. (*šakkēn* would tend to support a more 'immanentist' concept of the divine presence; cf. Exod. 25:8; 29:45; etc. It might then be a late exilic assertion that Yahweh would once more dwell in Zion; Keller 1996: 170. But this rather assumes what it wants to prove.) The verb *šākan* certainly became a springboard for later Jewish theological reflection on the nature of the divine presence, leading to the concept of the *Shekinah*, which was a kind of representative of God at the sanctuary. But the present text is not directly concerned with conceiving the nature of God's Presence, and it is wrongly used in pursuit of such arguments. (For fuller discussion, see McConville & Millar 1994: 110–123. Keller [1996: 147–152] has a modified form of the traditional view in which he argues that the 'name' theology affirms Yahweh's immanent presence strongly, and is compatible with a natural reading of 'before the LORD'.) It is not clear either that the expression 'for its dwelling' implies a reference to the ark and tabernacle (Craigie 1976a: 217). Deuteronomy has very little to say about either of these, and its use of the term *šākan* can hardly have the force to make such a point. The point is simply that Israel must worship at the place where Yahweh himself has chosen to be present.

As Israel 'came' to the land (*bô'*, qal, 1:20, 31; 4:1 and *passim*), so they must now 'come' to the chosen place. There is therefore a correspondence between the journey from Egypt through the wilderness to the land and the coming of Israelites regularly to the place of worship. In one text the correspondence is strengthened by the use of *māqôm* (1:31) to designate the place where Moses and Israel now stand (Moab), on the verge of the land. There is therefore an important rhetorical dimension to the use of the word *māqôm* to mean 'sanctuary' in the present passage. As Yahweh brings Israel to the 'place' (= land), Israel should bring its offerings to the 'place' (= sanctuary). At its simplest, the worship of Israel responds to the salvation of Yahweh in the exodus and gift of the land. (In Deut. 1 – 11, Israel's 'coming' occurs by Yahweh's power; now it is a command.) More profoundly, there is a suggestion that in a sense it re-enacts that journey of salvation, in which, too, they were in the presence of Yahweh. (See also N. Lohfink 1995c: 219–260, esp. 232–244.)

6. When Israelites come, they are to 'bring' their offerings to Yahweh. The word is another form of the verb for 'come' (*bô'*, now in the causative hiphil conjugation; cf. 11). The verbal correspondence between *bô'* (hiphil) here and *bô'* (qal) in 1:20, etc. (as the immediately preceding paragraph) once again helps to make the point that Israel's worship is a response to the gift of Yahweh. This correspondence is parallel to that between the two possible meanings of *māqôm* that we have just noted.

The list of sacrifices and offerings simply stands for the full range of these. 'Burnt offerings' and 'sacrifices' represent respectively whole offerings, where the whole animal is consumed on the altar (cf. Lev. 1:3–13), and blood-sacrifices, where the blood and fat are consumed and the flesh is eaten by priests and other participants. The regulations and different occasions for the latter are enumerated in Lev. 7:11–18. (See also 12:27, below, where the distinction is made clearly.) The pairing often stands for the whole range of sacrifices, since they are the principal types. Vow and freewill offerings are subsets of the latter (Lev. 7:16). Tithes and firstborn offerings, or firstlings, have their own regulations in due course (14:22–29; 15:19–23). The 'contribution', lit. 'what is lifted up in the hand', was an additional offering accompanying a sacrifice, or part of the sacrifice itself, given to the priest (Lev. 7:14, 32, 34; Num. 18:8). The pairing 'tithes and offerings' is found in Mal. 3:8 to denote the whole range of offerings for the work of the temple.

It is not the purpose of Deuteronomy here to give full instructions for sacrifices; other texts have that function (esp. Lev. 1 – 7). The omission of certain sacrifices from the list (notably the 'sin offering' and 'reparation' offering; cf. Lev. 4 – 5) is not surprising, therefore, since Deuteronomy does not aim to be a comprehensive guide to ritual worship. The point of the list is to say that all Israel's worship must be conducted in the proper way, at the chosen place. And the overriding point is to say that its response to God should be wholehearted.

7. Israel's worship is now depicted as happening at the chosen place 'before the LORD'. The plain meaning is that he is actually present, just as he has been present with Israel during their journeyings to the land (1:31). There is no engagement here with the issue of how he is present. His presence is part and parcel of his having chosen the place as the location where he should be worshipped and known. However, there is a distinct echo of the first decisive encounter between Yahweh and Israel at Horeb (4:10). The 'chosen place', therefore, in some sense corresponds to Horeb. In Israel's 'journey', the 'chosen place' is among that sequence of places where Yahweh encounters Israel. As the 'today' of Moses' exhortation is made a model for Israel's response to Yahweh in all future times, so the encounter at Horeb is given an entry into all future time through Israel's worship at the chosen place – wherever and whenever that might be.

The picture of worship as community feasting and rejoicing is one of the hallmarks of Deuteronomy's depiction of Israel before God. The connection between worship and feasting is not in itself surprising (cf. Exod. 24:11 for a classic example), and, as we have noted, animal sacrifice did not always mean the complete destruction of an animal, for some of it was often kept for consumption by the offerers. However, this regular portrayal of the official worship as a tremendous social event is a peculiarity of Deuteronomy (cf. 12:12; 14:26). The significance of 'with your households' is that Israel is pictured as a community together in its worship of Yahweh. This will be seen to have important ramifications in terms of caring for the poor in certain of the laws (e.g. 14:22–29). And the rejoicing of Israel is a response to the promised blessings, now realized, in that everything the people do is successful. The feasting is in itself a participation in the blessings given. Israel at worship, in obedience, togetherness, prosperity and joyful feasting, is a cameo picture of the covenant people in active and harmonious relationship with God.

12:8–12

8–9. The command 'not to do as we are doing here today' makes a contrast with the behaviour required in vv. 5–7, just as v. 4 contrasts it with the worship practices of the Canaanites. The characterization of the Moab generation as undisciplined is unexpected. The contrast between this 'today' in a description of the people's actual behaviour and the 'today' that we have met frequently in the exhortation is striking. The idea that the people were ill-disciplined in matters of religion is odd, too, if one has in mind the rules and narratives concerning the tabernacle (Num. 1 – 10). However, there are plenty of Pentateuchal reminders of Israel's tendency to rebel against Yahweh (e.g. Num. 25), and Moses has dwelt long on their habitual unfaithfulness in a passage just before this (9:1 – 10:11).

The importance of the analysis, however, is its correspondence to the structure of the history to follow Deuteronomy (Joshua–Kings). In the passage before us, a period of unruliness is to be followed by the achievement of peace in the land, at which time the chosen place may be established as the worship centre for Israel (9). And in the historical books, too, there is disorder before the building of the Jerusalem temple, during which time the lack of discipline was tolerated (1 Kgs. 3:1–2); the expression 'each [doing] what seems right to him' (8) also echoes texts in Judges deploring the degenerate behaviour of Israelites (Judg. 17:6; 21:25). Furthermore, there is a concept that the peace achieved by David at last fulfilled the conditions that could lead to the building of the temple (2 Sam. 7:1; the term used there, 'the LORD had given him *rest* [*hēnîaḥ*] from his enemies' is taken up from 12:10, and also corresponds to the noun 'rest' [*mᵉnûḥâ*], v. 9).

It is this structural correspondence that gives the key to understanding the statement here. This is not to say that the potential meaning of it is exhausted by the story that is actually told in Joshua–Kings, since Deuteronomy tirelessly makes clear that the entry into the inheritance is a matter of Israel's faithfulness, not an unalterable divine historical plan. The same point precisely underlies Deut. 1, with its narrative of deferred enjoyment of the land.

10–11. The historical structure of vv. 8–9 is then resumed in v. 10 as a prelude to the repeated command to bring sacrifices. In this verse the familiar noun *naḥᵃlâ*, 'inheritance', is echoed by the verbal form *manḥîl*, 'causes to inherit', just as the noun 'rest' (9) is followed by its corresponding verb (as we have just noted). God's gift as a dynamic act is thus emphasized. So too is the idea of 'rest from enemies' as a key element in the gift and blessing of the land (cf. 3:20; Josh. 1:13, 15; 2 Sam. 7:1), filled out with a further phrase, 'live in security' (*beṭaḥ*), a term belonging to the 'faith' vocabulary of the OT and conveying trust, that is, the trust that does not have to fear. The idea returns at 25:19, virtually at the end of the law code, while the present passage stands close to the beginning. (The 'rest' of Israel in these texts makes an interesting contrast with that of Yahweh in Ps. 132:8; the difference is in line with Deuteronomy's tendency to avoid the type of holiness concept found in the Davidic/Zion election texts.)

The command to bring offerings to the chosen place (11) is repeated from v. 6. The 'place formula' now occurs in a short form, abbreviated from v. 5, though still containing the important idea of 'making his name dwell there' (see on v. 5, and also 'Form and structure'). The list of offerings is once again representative. The phrase 'the choicest gifts that you have vowed to the Lord' has an interesting echo of Yahweh's 'choice' of the worship place. The idea that Israel's worship is a response to Yahweh's gift is therefore once again hinted at (cf. on v. 6).

12. The command to rejoice 'before the Lord' repeats that in v. 7, but the general term 'households' there is expanded to specify not only the offerer's family, but also servants and Levites. The inclusiveness recalls the Sabbath commandment (also a religious celebration involving 'rest'), especially in its deuteronomic form (5:14). The Levites, too, are in a dependent position, having no territory of their own (see on 10:8–9), but living scattered throughout the territories of the other tribes. (For further comment on this, see on 18:6–8.) They must therefore be included in the celebration.

The command here assumes that the principal hearer is a householder in Israel. That is, in this case at least, the implication of the singular address. (It is not, however, a general explanation of it in Deuteronomy; its more usual function is to express the unity of Israel in principle as a moral agent and covenant partner with Yahweh; for the range of meanings of the singular address in Deuteronomy see McConville 2002b.)

12:13–19

13–14. These verses are best regarded as finishing the basic sequence of exhortations begun in vv. 2–7, where the warning not to imitate the Canaanites is followed by instructions regarding correct worship. Here the command not to worship 'at any place you see' (13) recalls the Canaanite indiscipline in this respect (2b).

The command to worship only at the chosen place appears yet again in a slightly different form (14). Whereas v. 5 had a place chosen 'out of all your tribes', v. 14 has 'in any of your tribes' (see 'Notes on the text'). This has led many to think that vv. 13–14 are the relic of an older and less strict law than v. 5 (see 'Form and structure'). But in my view vv. 5 and 14 should be read each in the light of the other. Verse 14, coming after v. 5, suggests that the important thing about the chosen sanctuary is not that there is only one, fixed and unchangeable for ever; rather, it is that it should be chosen by Yahweh. Neither v. 5 nor v. 14 would be adequate to legislate either for the singleness or for the plurality of the place of worship. This is supported by the fact that the term 'out of all your tribes' (5) never recurs in the book; the abbreviating forms, which occur frequently, focus on the fact that Yahweh has chosen the place for his name.

15. Following the law restricting worship to Yahweh's chosen place, a practical consequence is now considered, namely that the people would be unable to partake of sacrificial meals at a sanctuary close at hand. The turn in the argument is marked by the conjunction 'only' (*raq*). The assumption in the present law is that, hitherto, meat (i.e. of 'clean' animals, fit for human consumption; cf. 14:3–21) might be consumed only if slaughtered as part of a sacrificial ritual (cf. Lev. 17:2–9). The permission then given is radically new, therefore, allowing meat to be eaten without first being offered in sacrifice (so-called 'profane slaughter'). Since this eating is outside the normal sacrificial sphere, all may partake, at any time (see 'Notes on the text' for 'whenever you like'), including those who may be temporarily excluded from ritual participation due to some 'uncleanness' (15b; cf. Lev. 13 – 15 for examples of this, with rituals for resolving the problem).

The gazelle and the deer are 'clean' game animals (Deut. 14:5), that is, they may be eaten subject to the restriction regarding the disposal of blood (Lev. 17:13), and do not fall under sacrificial regulations. The profane slaughter of animals suitable for sacrifice is thus put on a par with animals that may be killed in hunting. The phrase 'as much as the LORD your God has blessed you with' shows that the concern of the permission is to ensure that the people may enjoy the gift of the land fully; whether participating in sacrificial meals at the sanctuary, or eating in their towns, they are enjoying the blessings of Yahweh.

16. The reservation (another turn in the argument, and so another 'only') that the one who slaughters the animal must drain off the blood respects a concept that lies deeper than sacrifice, namely that the blood represents the life of the animal and must not be consumed (Lev. 17:8–9; cf. Gen. 9:4–6). (An example of the application of this principle is furnished by the account of Saul's celebration of victory in 1 Sam. 14:31–35, which is best taken as an example of a profane slaughter in terms of the present text; see further McConville 1984: 43–52. Cf. also 2 Sam. 23:16. The same concept also underlies the decision of the Council of Jerusalem that Gentile Christians should be free from the ritual regulations of the Torah, except that they should abstain from eating blood; Acts 15:20.)

17–19. In the rhythmic and somewhat circular style of Deuteronomy, vv. 17–19 essentially repeat vv. 11–12. They have a definite rhetorical function, however, as is clear from the opening words of v. 17, namely to insist strongly that the permission just given has strict limits and does not relax the basic command concerning sacrificial worship. There is again a certain tendency to expand in the repeated material (as v. 12 expanded on v. 7), the substance of the tithe and firstlings being specified in v. 17 as the tithe of vegetable produce. The 'grain, wine and oil' correspond, incidentally, to the products that sum up the blessings of the land (7:13). The provision for the Levite (18) is as in v. 12, with a phrase ('in everything you do'), as well as the command to rejoice, reintroduced from v. 7. Finally, the instruction to care for the Levite is reiterated.

12:20–28

20. This passage further articulates the permission to slaughter freely, just given in vv. 15–19, with some expansions. Verse 20 introduces a new element to the reasoning behind the permission to slaughter freely. It is not in itself the primary reason, which remains implicit in vv. 15–19, namely that the land is big enough in itself to prompt such a concession (see v. 21). Rather, it develops that provision, allowing for expansion of the land. The thought is therefore analogous to 19:8–10 (note the identical introductions in 12:20; 19:8), where provision is made for three *further* cities of refuge to be added to the three first set aside (19:1–7), in the case of further expansion of the territory. Both 12:20 and 19:8 consider this prospect in relation to a promise made, which is specified as the promise to the patriarchs in 19:8. The expansion of the land, therefore, may be seen as the ultimate possession of the whole land. A tension may be perceived here between what is apparently the dominant idea in Deuteronomy, that the land is to be conquered all at once, and an idea of progressive occupation. If so, this is analogous to the pattern found in Joshua, where, for example, Josh. 13:1 is surprising after 11:23. (Joshua sets aside just six cities of refuge in Josh. 20, in accordance with Deut. 4:41–43; 19:1–7, but implying that even then the work of conquest remains to be done.)

21–25. Verses 20b–25 reiterate the substance of vv. 15–16 with a strong tendency to expansion. The basic reason for the need for free slaughter is spelt out in v. 21. The permission is reiterated at greater length (22). So too is the restriction regarding blood disposal (23–25), with an added motivation in terms of a promise of long life in the land.

26–27. The thought finally returns to the other pole of the argument in the present chapter, namely the need to offer sacrifices only at the chosen place. The turn in the argument is now for the third time signalled by the conjunction 'only' (*raq*). A new term is deployed in v. 26, 'the holy things', a designation for everything that must come to the altar. (In 26:13 the same term occurs in the singular, referring to the tithe, and specifically to the special application of it in the third year to the needs of the poor; cf. 14:28–29. The confession there recognizes that in its normal use it is designated for the altar.) The tendency in these verses is to reinforce the need for rectitude in basic sacrificial practice. Verse 27 spells out the distinction already referred to in our discussion between burnt or whole offerings and those that are only partially consumed on the altar (see on v. 6).

28. The long section on the sacrifices is rounded off with a final exhortation, which recalls v. 1. In its projection of a long life in the land for an Israel that obeys Yahweh and acts justly, it suitably summarizes the picture in the chapter, where Israel has been depicted enjoying the fruits of the land, and at the same time worshipping Yahweh and rejoicing in his presence. There is a balance between the 'doing' involved in the worship regulations here, and the hearing and obeying that form the substance of the paranesis. To keep the commands is to be constituted as Yahweh's people, behaving in an appropriate way. (There is no need, therefore, to accept SamP's 'to do', instead of MT's 'to obey'; see 'Notes on the text'.) And to be so constituted is also to have life. The close connection between right behaviour and enjoying the blessings of being Yahweh's people is also expressed syntactically: '[you will have] well-being, *because* you do what is good and right'. The 'because' hides a condition, yet 'if' would be too strong; the point is to express a correlation within a synthetic picture composed of doing good and right and experiencing the blessing of being Yahweh's people (cf. 6:24-25).

12:29-32[13:1]

29-30. The final part of the chapter returns to its opening theme (2-4), the danger of adopting the religion of the nations. The paradox of their destruction before the advance of Israel, yet their continuing potential influence, has been noticed before (7:2-4), and is openly acknowledged here (30). Above all, the holy people of Yahweh must not be like the other nations. The programme for Israel's worship in ch. 12 was, right at the beginning (12:4), set over against the practices of Canaan; the same contrast now returns, put in the mouths of Israelites, as if to express the likely strong temptation to be like the nations, in spite of their origins in deliverance from them (cf. Deut. 17:14; 1 Sam. 8:5; and esp. 2 Kgs. 17:7-12). The power of the temptation is indicated in the term 'be ensnared' (cf. 7:25, though there the 'snare' was in the actual silver and gold of the idols). There is an important verbal parallel, too, between 'seek their gods' and the command to 'seek the place the LORD ... will choose' (5, etc.), which casts the foreign religion as a falsification of that of Yahweh, bidding to occupy its place in the minds of his people.

31. This leads to a repetition of the categorical prohibition of imitation (31a; cf. 12:4). Finally, the Canaanite practices are 'abhorrent' to the LORD, meaning that they are absolutely to be rejected because of his holiness, and subject to destruction (this echoes 7:25-26; see on that text for fuller comment). The sacrifice of children is then cited as the worst such abhorrent thing, yet also symbolic of the depravity of the whole gamut of them (cf. also 18:9-10, where it is prominent in a context about divination). There is strong evidence from archaeology that child sacrifice occurred in Phoenician religion (see Heider 1985: 196-203), though the evidence is less clear in other areas. The OT records such acts (2 Kgs. 3:27; 16:3; 23:10; Jer. 7:31; 19:5; 32:35. It is clear from the present text, as well as from the first two Jeremiah ones just mentioned, that actual sacrifice is meant, because the verb 'burn' is used. In 2 Kgs. 3:27 the child is made a 'burnt offering'. It is sometimes argued that, in the other texts mentioned, where the verb 'make pass through' is used (cf. also Lev. 18:21; 20:2–5), something less appalling is in view. However, 'handing over to Molek' is also now understood to imply child sacrifice; Heider 1985: 258–273; Day 1989: 31, 67–68).

In Deuteronomy the command not to imitate the Canaanites is strongly associated both with the command to destroy them and with the 'abhorrent' things they do, particularly child sacrifice (cf. the sequence 7:2–4; 12:4, 30–31; 18:9–10; 20:17–18; and N. Lohfink 1995c: 255–260).

32[13:1]. The exhortation to Israel to be holy in the realm of religion and worship has come to a powerful climax, and the whole reaches its conclusion with a word about both the paramountcy and the sufficiency of the words of Yahweh, echoing 4:2.

Explanation

Worshipping God alone

The regulations for Israel's worship are, first, an expression of the First Commandment, which requires the exclusive worship of Yahweh (5:6–7). That commandment has so far been elaborated in the exhortations following the confession at 6:4, and also in the exposition of Israel's holiness in ch. 7. Indeed, the whole paranesis of Deut. 5 – 11 can be understood as a reflection on it, rooted as it is in Yahweh's deliverance of the people from Egypt. The regulations in ch. 12, standing at the beginning of the law-code section of the book, now express the status of Israel as holy to the one God Yahweh in its life of worship. Here as in ch. 7 the holiness of the people is the basic theological substance. That holiness, as we know from ch. 7, belongs to the people as a whole, not because of their intrinsic merits, which have explicitly been ruled out (9:1 – 10:11), but because of Yahweh's 'choice', and his consequent deliverance of them from Egypt. The same concepts underlie the picture here, and this is why the commands concerning worship are preceded by a renewed instruction to destroy the paraphernalia of worship of the gods followed by the peoples of the land (12:2–4).

The positive portrayal of Israel before God requires a corresponding negation of the ways of the other nations, effectively a restatement of the *herem*, that area of life that cannot exist in God's presence (though the term is not used here; cf. 2:34). This is expressed not only by vv. 2–3, but also by the repeated command not to imitate the nations (4, 31), and by the contrasts between their 'places' and Yahweh's 'place', their names and Yahweh's name (2–5). As Nelson (1997: 53) puts it, Israel and other nations are 'on opposite sides of an impenetrable social barrier'.

C. J. H. Wright (1996: 8–17) has developed the idea of Deuteronomy as a social and religious critique of the culture of Canaan, finding in it 'missiological significance'.

The name of God and his being

The name of Yahweh must now be considered from a positive point of view. If it is not a mere device in an argument about the divine presence, as I have argued, why is it so important? The answer cannot be separated from Yahweh's acts of self-disclosure to Israel. The revelation of his name to Moses (Exod. 3:14; 6:3) is located precisely in the context of the great, paradigmatic act of deliverance that is narrated in that book, and that becomes crucial to the entire deuteronomic paranesis. Indeed, the enigmatic quality of the disclosure in Exod. 3:14 ('I am/become who I am/become'), receives content from the narrative that follows (a point that is well developed by C. Seitz 1999a). The name of Yahweh, therefore, is about who he truly is.

The relationship between the name of God and his saving actions means that there is something open and ongoing about it. His name can be fully known only in the context of the unfolding biblical story. Thus, the God who delivered Israel from Egypt becomes known in time as the God who saves his people from the bondage in Babylon that their own sin had brought upon them (Is. 40 – 55). And for the Christian reader, God is known in the end in his self-disclosure in Christ, which is both a new thing and a continuation of the disclosures in the OT. Bauckham (1998) has shown convincingly how the NT draws him, both as pre-existent and risen Christ and as the crucified Jesus, into that which is predicated of God in Jewish monotheism – even though Judaism carefully excluded angels and intermediaries from divine status. (Bauckham thus opposes a route to the divinity of Jesus that travels via a belief that divinity was in fact predicated of such beings, as in M. Barker 1992.)

There is not yet explicit 'messianism' here. A messianic reading, however, will find contact points in the promise of the divine presence into an indefinite future, and the access of a people, holy and undifferentiated, to that presence. The promise of the 'name' in particular is evocative for Christology, as we see from Jas. 2:7, which echoes the language of the 'place formula' in its LXX form: the name in question is Christ, and the 'place' is the people of God.

The worship of Israel

The elements in the picture of Israel at worship are not accidental, but parts of a carefully conceived composition. In it, Israel has come to the land, brought there by Yahweh in fulfilment of his promise. In response, they present themselves in worship, at a 'place' chosen by him, and which in a sense corresponds to the land itself. The people, in its wholeness, gathered in worship at the place chosen by Yahweh, is the people as it most truly is.

First, its worship is response: as Yahweh has given them a land, so now they bring produce of the land itself to his place in offering (6).

Secondly, the worship has a strong social and ethical dimension. The unity of the people in worship knows no hierarchy or divisions. This depiction of the sacrificial activity is not concerned with the role of the priests; no king leads or represents the people (contrast 1 Kgs. 8:62–66); neither does even a Moses or a Samuel. The 'place' is not a royal-sacral complex in which the people's right of approach is relativized or mediated. The space in Deut. 12 belongs to Yahweh and to Israel. The people itself, in its households, gathers before Yahweh. This integrity of the people is no light or sentimental thing, but makes demands. It involves the inclusion of slaves, or servants, in the big picture of the people of God, as well as the Levites, who have no substance of their own. (The picture is filled out in 14:29, to include widows, orphans and resident aliens.) Those who, in terms of the social structure of Israel, have no power, and particularly no land, of their own, are, even so, fully part of the 'landed', holy people of God. When Israel is truly itself, in worship, it can brook no division or self-interest within it. Israel as it truly should be will have 'no poor among you' (cf. 15:4; and N. Lohfink 1990a; 1995f).

In this realization of Israel's wholeness, the people is to *rejoice* before Yahweh. The worship is festal. The 'sacrifices' are the occasion of feasting (only v. 27 reminds the reader of the rights of the altar). In worship the promised blessings of the land are fulfilled (cf. 7:13–14). Blessing, there-fore, is not simply quantifiable as the produce granted by the covenant partner, Yahweh, but is known in the act of the people's being truly itself. It has a dynamic quality, being enacted in the religious and social life of the people, and thus further realized (as a number of the laws will illustrate, e.g. 15:12–18). This rejoicing of the people of God is no accidental extra, but is essential to the picture, and even has an eschatological quality.

Thirdly, this worship life of Israel with Yahweh has an open future. This is implied in the idea of covenant itself. But it is now expressed in the idea of the chosen place of worship. The 'place' is an echo of the encounter between Israel and Yahweh at Horeb; as the people gathered there 'before Yahweh' (4:10), so do they now at the 'place'. This seems to me to be the most important thing about the place in Deut. 12 – 26. The 'oneness' of it may have theological significance, as a kind of ideal correlate of Yahweh's choice (although it has been rightly pointed out that there is no logical necessity in this; N. Lohfink 1987: 223). More important, however, is the fact that it is not named.

An open history

At one level, the view of many commentators that this is merely consistent with the setting of Deuteronomy before the entry to the land, and therefore before the events that followed could be known, is satisfying enough. But, at another level, the namelessness of the place has about it an irreducible openness. The recognition in the historical books that Jerusalem corresponds to the chosen place (1 Kgs. 8:29) should not be confused with an irreversible claim on Jerusalem's behalf by Deuteronomy. This idea, that history could end in a specific place with its institutional trappings, runs counter to the thrust of Deuteronomy itself, which is perfectly echoed in Jeremiah's critique, with its direct reference to our present chapter (Jer. 7:11–15; note v. 12). Rather, the 'place the LORD will choose' brings for ever into Israel's life the principle that the covenant must always be renewed in a life of decision that finds itself constantly at Horeb, being called into covenant in an open history consisting of many times and (perhaps) many places. There is power in this concept for the prophetic critique of all institutionalism that has lost sight of its foundational purpose.

In portraying the worship thus, Deuteronomy does not abolish 'institution' as such, or become anti-institutional for its own sake. There is 'cult' still in Deuteronomy, despite the widely canvassed concept of desacralization. The sacrificial language and requirements of ch. 12 are incomprehensible apart from a shared background in knowledge of such a world, and it is implicit (and occasionally explicit; 12:27) that such requirements must be met. In what follows, there is both cult and law, as there must be in all human society. Yet none may claim to be the end of history. Or, rather, that too is a matter of God's 'choice' in the open future that he presents to Israel.

DEUTERONOMY 13:1–18[2–19]

Translation

[1][2]If there should arise among you a prophet, or one who gives dream oracles (and he foretells a miraculous sign or a portentous event, [2][3]and the sign or portent he has foretold comes about), and he says, 'Let us follow other gods (whom you have not known); let us worship them,' [3][4]you must not listen to what that prophet or dreamer says; for the LORD your God is testing you, to know whether you love the LORD your God with all your heart and being. [4][5]It is the LORD your God whom you must follow and revere, and his commands you must keep; him you must obey and worship, and to him you must cling. [5][6]And that prophet or dreamer must die for speaking lies concerning the LORD your God, who brought you out of Egypt, setting you free from slavery; and for trying to force you from the way the

LORD your God commanded you to go. So you shall root out the evil from among you.

[6][7]If your brother (your mother's son), your son or your daughter, your wife with whom you sleep, or your closest friend entices you secretly by saying, 'Let us go and worship other gods' – gods whom neither you nor your forefathers have known, [7][8]gods of the peoples around you, whether close by or at a distance, from one end of the earth to the other – [8][9]you must not give in or listen to that person. Show neither pity nor mercy, and do not give him asylum; [9][10]you must kill him! Your hand must be the first to strike when he is put to death, the whole people following after you. [10][11]Stone him to death for trying to drive you away from the LORD your God, who brought you out of slavery in Egypt. [11][12]And let all Israel hear this and be afraid, so that this wickedness is never done among you again.

[12][13]If you hear a rumour about one of your cities that the LORD your God has given you to live in, [13][14]that some rabble among you has begun to lead the inhabitants of their city astray, saying 'Let us go and worship other gods', gods whom you have not known, [14][15]and if, when you have made an exhaustive investigation, you find that the report is true and established, and that this abhorrent thing has in fact happened among you, [15][16]you must put the inhabitants of that city to the sword, subjecting it to utter destruction, with everything that is in it, including the cattle. [16][17]All its goods you are to collect together into its public square, and burn the city together with its goods as a whole offering to the LORD your God. Let it be a deserted mound for ever; it must never be rebuilt. [17][18]Do not keep back anything from that sacrificed city for yourself, so that the LORD may turn from his anger to show you compassion, and in that compassion make you great in number, as he promised on oath to your forefathers, [18][19]provided you obey the LORD your God and keep all his commands with which I am charging you today, and do what is right in the sight of the LORD your God.

Notes on the text

1–2[2–3]. The syntax is awkward. The phrase 'and he says' is strictly 'saying', and is best taken to follow v. 1a (after 'dream oracles'). Verses 1b–2a should then be taken as a parenthesis. The order of events, therefore, is that the exhortation to worship other gods is followed and supported by a sign, rather than that the sign is given first, to impress, followed by the instigation of apostasy.

2[3]. 'whom you have not known': the phrase is odd in the mouth of the false prophet, and better regarded as the comment of the narrator. This is easier in the parallel vv. 6[7], 13[14], where the phrase comes at the end. LXX and 11QTemple (the Temple Scroll from Qumran) transpose the phrase to the end of the line here also. The MT should be kept, and the narrator's comment considered to have intruded untidily into the quotation of the prophet's words (cf. 9:4, and 'Notes on the text'). This is supported by the singular address in 'you have not known', which is frequent in the discourse of Deuteronomy (and the present passage), and perhaps less likely to be used by the prophet (*pace* Dion 1991: 151).

5[6]. 'he must die': *yûmāt* is 3 m. sg. hoph. impf. ('he must be caused to die'). The translation 'speaking lies' derives *sārâ* from the root *srr* rather than *sûr* ('depart', thence 'rebel'). Other OT texts where the noun should certainly or probably be translated thus are Deut. 19:16; Jer. 28:16; 29:32; Is. 59:13. There are also Akkadian equivalents: *šībūt sarrātim*; *dabābu sarrātim* (see Dion 1991: 153). For the exodus as the basis of the loyalty requirement, cf. 10[11].

6[7]. 'your brother': SamP and LXX add 'your father's son or' before 'your mother's son'. MT is to be preferred, as the versions seem to want to make the text explicitly monogamous. MT probably represents an older situation in which polygamy was evisaged (Dion 1991: 153). The qualification is then in line with the tendency in the verse to specify intimacy.

9[10]. 'you must kill him!': this follows MT, against LXX's 'You must report him'. LXX assumes *haggēd taggîdennû* (*ngd*, hiph., 'tell') instead of *hārōg tahargennû* (*hrg*, 'kill'). The Hebrew words could be confused by a scribe, and the difficulty in deciding between the two phrases lies in the fact that each idea (reporting and killing) is present in the context. LXX is widely preferred by translations and commentators (see Dion 1991: 154), and has indirect support from Jer. 20:10. Levinson's (1995) text-critical study, however, has probably reinstated MT, and has also shown that it is closest to the analogy of VTE.

16[17]. 'whole offering' is to be preferred to the adverbial rendering of LXX, 'completely', as in Is. 2:18; cf. Lev. 6:16; Deut. 33:10 (see Dion 1991: 155–156, for an Akkadian analogy).

Form and structure

Deut. 13:1–18[2–19] lays in place an important element in the elaboration of Israel's covenantal commitment to Yahweh. The portrayal in ch. 12 of the people at worship before him was built on the concept of the elect people, which presupposed exclusive loyalty. The need for such loyalty is now the theme of ch. 13. The close connection between the two sections of the Mosaic discourse is illustrated by the topic of the temptation to follow the gods of other nations (12:30), which is the central topic of ch. 13.

The prohibition of worshipping other gods is well established in the OT (Exod. 34:14; 22:20[19]). The framework of the demand for loyalty here, however, is specifically covenantal. The royal political systems of the ANE imposed covenantal obligations not only on subject peoples but also on officials, and on citizens in general. The people's covenantal obligation to the king required incentive and the possibility of enforcement, and therefore the obligation both to reject and to reveal any conspiracy to break it. Close parallels to Deut. 13, both in form and in concept, exist in Hittite and neo-Assyrian treaties, and in Hittite instructions to royal officials (Weinfeld 1972: 92–94). Typical of the treaties is the command to expose any plot against the king. The seventh-century Vassal Treaties of Esarhaddon (VTE), in common with Deut. 13, specify prophets and close family as potential fomenters of rebellion (VTE 108–22; Weinfeld 1972: 97–99; Levinson 1995: 55), and the Sefire treaty envisages whole cities defecting (Weinfeld 1972: 99). These are exactly the categories specified in Deut. 13. (The question whether Deuteronomy is directly dependent on VTE must be addressed in the 'Comment' below, which must take into account the relationship of the curses in Deut. 28 to the same Assyrian source. See also on that passage.)

The covenantal background of Deut. 13 accounts for many features of the chapter: the danger to the covenant from conspiracy to defect, the need for denunciation, and the 'love' – or loyalty – command. These features belong to a way of thinking that is widely attested in the ANE, from the Hittite to the neo-Assyrian periods. The affinities with VTE in particular, however, have led to the common view that Deut. 13 is King Josiah's response in his covenant document (Deuteronomy) to the covenant imposed on Judah since the time of Hezekiah by the Assyrian king (Frankena 1965; Weinfeld 1972: 100).

The argument of the chapter adopts an 'if . . . then' form, found widely in ANE laws, including laws commanding covenant loyalty such as VTE. It is composed of three sections so formed: vv. 1–5[2–6]; 6–11[7–12]; 12–18[13–19]. The sections follow a similar pattern: the instigator is quoted as urging rebellion with the words, 'Let us go after (and worship) other gods', always qualified as 'gods you have not known'; the people are warned not to yield to this, and to make the conspiracy known; and the death penalty is prescribed.

Comment

13:1–5[2–6]

1–2[2–3]. The first group who might incite to sedition are those who claim a religious authority and special access to knowledge (1[2]). The term 'prophet' (*nābî'*) is the commonest in the OT for those who give words from God. In itself it does not guarantee that the person speaks truly in God's name. In Deut. 18:15–22 Moses promises that God will raise up a prophet like himself in the future, and he is distinguished from others who, though 'prophets', do not speak Yahweh's words; indeed, as in the present text, these might speak 'in the name of other gods'. The need to tell true prophets from false ones is felt as a problem in the OT, because there were evidently many who bore the name and status of prophet in society, but who had no word from Yahweh (cf. Jer. 28).

Alongside the prophet is mentioned 'a giver of dream oracles' (or simply 'a dreamer of dreams'). The dream is a well-known means of receiving a revelation from God, both in Israel and the ANE. (Joseph furnishes an example from the OT; Gen. 37.) In Egypt, Mesopotamia and Canaan, dreams were given by gods, and sometimes actively sought in times of crisis. Kings in particular received dreams, giving assurance of the god's assistance, or direction for a course of action. And other officials had dreams on the king's behalf. (A case of the latter is the Canaanite king Keret, known from the Ugaritic texts, who is given a dream by El, which shows him how his royal dynasty may be secured by succession; *ANET* 142–149.)

In the OT God gives a number of dreams, and in one text this even seems normal for his prophets (Num. 12:6). God's appearance to Solomon in a dream is an important confirmation of his kingship (1 Kgs. 3:1–15; the text has been compared to a dream given to the Pharaoh Thutmosis IV [*ANET* 449], and see Herrmann 2000).

There is, therefore, no hint of disapproval in either of the terms used here in themselves. Neither occurs in 18:10–11, 14 in the list of those intermediaries who are abhorrent to Yahweh (in contrast to his true prophet, 18:15–19). The point here is not to warn against certain types of official as such, but only in so far as they aim to seduce Israel to the worship of other gods. VTE also warns against prophetic figures (*rāgimu*, *maḫḫû*, and *šā'ilu*) leading people astray (116–117; Weinfeld 1972: 98. The last-named term may refer to a figure who sought dream oracles).

The words of the agitators, 'Come, let us go after other gods', correspond closely to the political sedition in the Hittite instructions to officials: 'Come, let us join another (king)', and in VTE (318–335). The parallel illustrates the special nature of the Yahweh covenant, in which Israel has a direct covenant, not with a king, but with Yahweh himself. The religious loyalty demanded of Israel has a political correlate, of course, since defection to other gods could and often did imply subjugation to a political power associated with them.

The gods the agitators invite Israelites to follow are described as 'gods you have not known', a characteristic formula in the chapter (also in vv. 6[7], 13[14]), and elsewhere in Deuteronomy (11:28; 28:64; 29:26[25]). The latter set of passages shows that the idea is important in the covenantal structure of the book (in the threats of curse, and in an explanation why the curse finally fell on Israel). The phrase carries with it the assumption that Yahweh is the God whom Israel has known. While he is never referred to in precisely these terms ('Yahweh, whom you have known'), this is the content of the whole narrative of the exodus and the basis of the election theology. And Yahweh, indeed, has 'known' Israel (9:24). The unknownness of the gods, then, is not just a factual observation. Rather, the phrase expresses the full force of the rejection of Yahweh involved in Israel's choice of other gods. It also conveys something of the folly and uncertainty of making such a choice (28:64–68). And there is an interesting contrast with the Anakim, 'whom you know' (9:2), and who were defeated before Israel by Yahweh. The contrast has something ominous about it, therefore: there is no promise that this fearsome and *un*known people will be subdued in the same way.

The form 'that you have not known' has been met already in connection with the manna in the desert (8:2–3, 16), and, there as here, the 'not knowing' is applied to the patriarchs as well as to the present generation (note v. 6[7]). In both cases, too, the unknown thing is said to 'test' Israel (3[4]). The common denominator, therefore, is the 'knownness', the trustworthiness, of Yahweh, which should be sufficient to enable Israel to follow him in the desert, and also to resist the temptations of great promises from new quarters. (See 'Notes on the text' for the phrase as the narrator's, not the prophet's.)

The prophet or dreamer may support his incitement to rebel with a 'sign' or 'portent'. This might be any unnatural event, which would give the impression that the prophet had special insight or control. The terms are familiar from the narrative, where Yahweh has delivered Israel from Egypt to the accompaniment of these (4:34). Here too, therefore, there is a special challenge to the covenant with Yahweh; signs and portents are the province of Yahweh in Israel's life, belonging especially to their history with him on which the covenant is based. (On the relationship between the sign and the incitement see 'Notes on the text'.)

3[4]. The issue at stake in the confrontation with the false prophet is whether Israelites will 'love' Yahweh. As we have seen, this concept is at home in the ANE tradition of treaty and covenant, in which it amounts to loyalty. The formula 'love the LORD your God with all your heart and being' (3[4]) is specifically deuteronomic (6:5; 10:12). In the context it is not directly paranetic, but expresses the terms of the test: will the people's loyalty stand up to powerful religious temptation?

4[5]. The sign of such loyalty is spelt out in v. 4[5]. The emphasis in the verse is thrown consistently on to the person of Yahweh by means of the word-order, which places him first in all the clauses in the verse. The first requirement is to 'follow' him, contradicting the agitator's suggestion of 'following' others, as does the term 'worship' (or 'serve'). The string of expressions quickly characterizes in familiar terms the kind of life required by the deuteronomic covenant (cf. 10:20; 30:20). It consists not only of obedience to commands, but of unswerving devotion, and thus demonstrates a fundamental choice for Yahweh. Such a passage is entirely to be expected in the present argument (a demand for loyalty), and it need not be regarded as a secondary expansion, as some do, partly on the grounds of the second-person plural address in vv. 3b–4[4b–5] in an otherwise singular context (see Weinfeld 1972: 97 n. 4 for examples of change of number in extrabiblical treaties). The incitement to worship other gods runs counter to the legal freeing ('redemption') of Israel from slavery in Egypt (5[6]; see on 7:8).

5[6]. The death penalty is the expected outcome for the conspiracy. In terms of the political analogy, it amounts to treason, which was subject to the death penalty. By extension, this applies to a fundamental breach of the covenant with Yahweh, enshrined in the First Commandment (5:6–7), which is echoed here in the words 'who brought you out of Egypt'. It has been argued that, wherever the death penalty is then applied in Deuteronomy, it has a specific connection with covenant breach (Phillips 1970: 1–2). This overstates the case; the death penalty should be seen in the context of ANE law more generally. Even so, there is a specific and logical connection with covenant breach.

The term 'speaking lies' is often translated as 'urging rebellion', deriving the noun from a different verb (see 'Notes on the text'). Both options make sense in a covenantal context (for ANE analogies see 'Notes on the text'). The choice made here is influenced by the powerful idea of 'falsehood' as a characterization of covenant disloyalty, especially in Jeremiah (see Jer. 28:16; 29:32, where the present phrase occurs).

The formula 'root out the evil from among you' is unique to the law code of Deuteronomy (cf. 17:7, 12; 19:13, 19; 21:9, 21; 22:21–22; 24:7; 26:13–14), though echoed in Judg. 20:13. Apart from 19:19, all cases carry the death penalty, and even there it could do so. It is impossible to say whether it existed as a formula separately from the contexts it now has in Deuteronomy. Its implication of the solidarity of Israel and its connection with the death penalty suggest a home in covenantal thinking, and it is not surprising to find its first appearance in Deuteronomy in its present context. The threat to the solidarity of Israel in the present case has as its background the concept of a united covenant people, as depicted in ch. 12. One of the main themes of Deuteronomy is precisely such a united people, directly in relationship with Yahweh, and forming a deep bond together, for which the term 'brothers' is frequently adopted, and most characteristically expressed in worship (see on ch. 12). This being so, rebellion (even of a few) strikes at the heart of the true nature of Israel. The logical remedy is excommunication, here enacted by the death penalty, but aiming to enable the life of Israel to continue.

13:6–11[7–12]

6–7[7–8]. Verse 6 envisages that an Israelite might be pressed by a person very close to him to give up the covenant with Yahweh in favour of other gods. The qualifications here stress intimacy. Birth by the same mother ('your mother's son'), connotes special closeness; cf. Joseph and Benjamin, sons of Rachel. The phrase '(your wife) with whom you sleep' concentrates the mind on the most intimate aspect of that relationship. This dilemma is the logical correlate of the command to 'root out evil', where the imperative of loyalty affects the covenant partner most deeply. The enticement is expressed in the same terms as before, with only a further qualification of the 'gods', namely that they might be gods worshipped anywhere, near or far (7[8]). The main development in the argument is that the person who is approached in this way should show no mercy. This is for obvious reasons, since the guilty party is personally dear, and the consequences for him will thus affect the person himself. In a political context this has the hallmarks of totalitarianism, a system of informing on neighbours and therefore of deep mistrust. The logic is similar when transferred into the realm of religious covenant. Any justification can only be in terms of the nature of God and of the society that is thus protected (see 'Explanation').

8–9[9–10]. The person approached in this way is, of course, to resist the attempted seduction. But his responsibility extends further, to the need to take measures against the guilty party. The penalty for enticing to covenant breach is death, and it is to be carried out without fail. I have adopted here the translation 'you must kill him!' with MT and against LXX and many commentators (see 'Notes on the text'). The change reflected in LXX may be attributable merely to a scribal error, or to a deliberate wish, evident also in other textual witnesses (Syr, Tgs; see Levinson 1995: 43–47), to avoid the implication that the culprit is to be put to death on the initiative of one person alone, bypassing the law requiring two witnesses (17:6–7). The reading 'kill him!' gains some further support from VTE, however, where a discovered plot against the king's life is to be dealt with by the discoverer acting alone if he can (VTE 130–46; Levinson 1995: 58). The force of Deut. 13:9[10] is like VTE in demanding the speedy execution of the plotter.

Does the text then require the discoverer of the rebel to act alone? The difficulty felt by the versions may not be so acute as it appears to be. The interpretation of the text must take into account the regular use of the second-person singular in Deuteronomy to address the people collectively. The number varies in ch. 13, but the collective singular appears in the first paragraph at vv. 1–3a[2–4a], 5b[6b]. The singular is regular in vv. 6–11[7–12], and must be taken as a collective at least in vv. 7[8], 10[11], where the reference to an individual would not make sense. In the nature of the case in question, however, it sometimes refers to the individual who has discovered the plot. The addressee moves back and forth, therefore, between this individual and the collective. The difficulty comes at v. 9a[10a], where the individual reference is suggested by what follows in v. 9b[10b], and this supports the idea of perfunctory execution by the discoverer. However, v. 9b[10b] also shows that the execution is in fact the corporate responsibility of the people. After the categorical command to kill the traitor, it is specified that the discoverer should cast the first stone, as is required of the witnesses in 17:6–7, followed by all the people. It follows that the singular address in v. 9a[10a] should not be taken to refer exclusively to the discoverer; rather, it establishes that capital punishment is due for enticing others to break the covenant, and the context shows that it is the responsibility of the covenant people to carry it out. There is no need, therefore, to see a contradiction between 13:9[10] and 17:6–7. The former passage draws out the basic implication of covenant loyalty in the case of the defector to other gods; the latter puts such a case in the context of legal practice.

The best example in the OT of a case such as this is, ironically, Jeremiah, who is watched by his 'close friends' (not the same term as here) for an opportunity to 'denounce him' (the phrase is the same as Deut. 13:9a[10a], LXX; see 'Notes on the text'). The charge of breaking the covenant with Yahweh would have been the basis of a plot to kill Jeremiah (cf. Jer. 11:19; 37:13).

11[12]. The second case of enticement to sedition closes with a theological point analogous to that which rounded off the first (5b[6b]). The capital punishment is not only the proper penalty for the crime, but also has the effect of ensuring that Israelites should not let themselves be tempted in this way in the future. The loyalty of the whole people, undivided, to the covenant is again the principle underlying the point.

12–18[13–19]. The final scene of enticement to covenant breach involves a whole city. The language of vv. 12–13[13–14] is charged with indignation that a city from among those given by Yahweh should defect. The term 'some rabble' ($b^eliyya'al$) has a connotation of meanness (cf. 15:9), and is used regularly for people who foment mischief (cf. 1 Sam. 10:27; 1 Kgs. 21:10). The scenario of a whole city going over to the enemy is perfectly intelligible in a world in which borders were less fixed than in the modern day, and is envisaged also in the Sefire treaty (see Weinfeld 1972: 99). Such a case is tantamount to the city's putting itself outside the covenant, and on a par with the Canaanite cities of the land before Israel. The fate prescribed for them, therefore, derives from the *ḥerem*, or 'ban of utter destruction' (15[16]; cf. 2:34; 3:6; 7:2). Like Jericho, it is to be destroyed entirely, a kind of sacrifice to Yahweh, with not even its cattle allowed to be taken as booty (Josh. 6:21). The term 'whole offering' (16[17]) is a sacrificial term known in Israel and beyond (Lev. 6:15–16; 1 Sam. 7:9). It is based on a word meaning 'whole' (*kālîl*), and is in that sense like the 'burnt offering', but broader in that it need not refer to an animal sacrifice. In the Sefire treaty, as here, the city is given first to the sword.

The city of Gibeah becomes such an offering in the war between Israel and Benjamin (Judg. 19 – 20). The crime committed in Gibeah is instigated by a 'rabble' (19:22, the same term as in Deut. 13:13[14]). It is then regarded as an offence that calls in question the status of Israel, which is depicted in its unity, and with reference to the exodus (19:30); the offence has to be punished in the name of Israel (20:10). In the war that follows, Gibeah is first put to the sword, then burned, apparently as a 'whole offering' (*kālîl*; 20:37–40; cf. 20:48).

The severe fate meted out to the rebellious city, like the executions prescribed for individual offenders, has as its aim the continuance of the covenant life of the people of Yahweh (17b–18[18b–19]). The promise of great numbers is fundamental to the patriarchal promise, and character-istic of the idea that Israel is on the verge of a future in which the promises have yet to reach full fruition. The promise, typically, is balanced with a concluding exhortation to keep the commands of the covenant.

Explanation

The chapter is commonly interpreted as part of King Josiah's covenant with the people of Judah in the context of his reform (Dion 1991: 206; Weinfeld 1972: 100). As always, there are problems with this location of the text. The assumptions in it are consistent with the thoroughgoing concept in Deuteronomy that the people as such are the supreme responsible agent under Yahweh's sovereignty. The absence of the king in the text, then, is no mere device born of the artificial Mosaic setting. If Josiah was a ruthless king who wanted to protect his covenant with the people at all costs, it is more likely that he would have done so in less ambiguous terms, like other despots. Deuteronomy's vision of Israel is deeply at odds with the idea of royal tyranny. The law, rather, aims to protect the covenant between Yahweh and people.

Is it none the less a repressive, totalitarian measure? The provision for all members of the community to become a sort of 'secret police', watching their own families, has very unpleasant resonances. The answer to this charge can be met only on the basis of a wider view of the book. It rests on Deuteronomy's view that the people of Yahweh is a free people, a people of liberated strangers (*gērîm*), who have been brought into fellowship with Yahweh, whose nature is to liberate. The 'oneness' of Yahweh, far from producing totalitarianism, issues in freedom, inclusive-ness and justice, in accordance with the picture we have seen in ch. 12. Ch. 13 should be read together with ch. 12, and thus be seen as the measure that protects Israel characterized as it was there. As Braulik (1986a: 103) put it: 'Apostasy "in your midst" destroys that which makes Israel Israel.'

The death penalty belongs to the fact that Israel's constitution had a real presence in a political-religious world; it was itself a political-religious entity. In the NT, the church is not constituted in this way. It remains a covenantal community, however, called into the service of God, in a world (then as now) in which many gods made their own claims. The NT, too, protects its covenant by placing allegiance to God above all other claims, even valid ones. Jesus made it plain that the service of God preceded family ties (Mark 3:31–35; Matt. 10:37–39). And Paul required what amounted to excommunication in order to ensure the integrity of the church (1 Cor. 5:11–13).

DEUTERONOMY 14:1–29

Translation

[1]You are children of the LORD your God; you must not lacerate yourselves or shave the hair on your foreheads in mourning for the dead. [2]For you are a people holy to the LORD your God, and the LORD chose you to be a people particularly for him out of all the nations on earth.

[3]Do not eat anything abhorrent. [4]These are the animals that you may eat: the ox, the sheep, the goat, [5]the deer, the gazelle, the roe-deer, the wild goat, the ibex, the antelope and the rock-goat, [6]any animal in the animal world whose hoofs are divided to make a split hoof, and which chews the cud. That you may eat. [7]However, among animals that chew the cud or have split hoofs you may not eat the camel, the hare and the rock-badger, for these chew the cud but do not have split hoofs; they are ritually unclean for you. [8]Neither may you eat the pig, because, though it has split hoofs, it does not chew the cud; it is unclean for you. You must not eat their flesh, or touch their carcasses.

[9]You may eat the following from among creatures that live in the water: any that have fins and scales you may eat, [10]but any that do not have fins or scales you may not eat; it is ritually unclean for you. [11]You may eat any ritually clean bird. [12]But these are the birds you may not eat: the eagle, the vulture, the osprey, [13]the buzzard or any kind of kite, [14]any kind of raven, [15]the eagle-owl, the short-eared owl, the long-eared owl and any kind of hawk; [16]the tawny owl, the screech owl, the little owl, [17]the desert owl, the Egyptian vulture, the cormorant, [18]the stork, any kind of heron, the hoopoe and the bat. [19]All winged insects are ritually unclean for you; they are not to be eaten. [20]You may eat any ritually clean insect.

[21]You may not eat any creature that has died naturally; you may give it to a resident alien who lives in your cities for him to eat; or you may sell it to a foreigner; for you are a people holy to the LORD your God.

You may not boil a kid in its mother's milk.

[22]You must be careful to set aside a tithe of all the yield of the seed that comes forth in the field year by year. [23]Then you shall eat it before the LORD your God at the place he will choose as a dwelling for his name: that is, the tithe of your grain, wine and oil, together with the firstborn of your herd and flock, so that you may learn to revere the LORD your God all your life. [24]If the journey is too long for you to carry your produce, because the place the LORD your God chooses as a dwelling for his name is at a distance from you – because the LORD your God will bless you – [25]then you may sell it for money, keep the money in your hand, and go to the place the LORD your God chooses, [26]buy with the money whatever you desire, whether

beef or lamb, together with wine and strong drink – anything you wish; eat it there before the Lord your God, and rejoice, together with your household. [27]And you must not neglect the Levite who lives in your cities, because he has no territorial share of his own among you.

[28]After three years, bring out the whole tithe of your crops for that year and store it up in your cities. [29]Then let the Levite come, because he has no territorial share of his own among you, and also the resident alien, and the orphan and the widow, who are in your cities, and let them eat their fill so that the Lord your God may bless you in all your labour.

Notes on the text

6. 'any animal in the animal world': this is taken as appositional to the preceding string of animals, as it appears to be a summarizing description of that group. The final verb phrase is then resumptive. 'That' is the feminine object pronoun referring strictly to 'any animal' (*bᵉhēmâ*), but having a general reference to vv. 4–6 as a whole.

8. 'it does not chew the cud': MT has only the noun 'cud', lacking the verb (*yiggōr*), which should be restored with SamP, LXX; cf. Lev. 11:7.

12. *zeh* is masculine despite the feminine gender of *ṣippôr* in v. 11; in this introductory form it is gender neutral.

20. 'clean insects': this requires the translation of *'ôp̄* as 'insects', though it more usually refers to birds or flying creatures generally. However, as Milgrom points out, the term *ṣippôr* is used for 'birds' at v. 11 (where Lev. 11:13 uses *'ôp̄*), and this makes it likely that the shift to *'ôp̄* in Deut. 14:20 takes its cue from *šereṣ hā'ôp̄* (19), and refers in this case to insects (Milgrom 1991: 498–499).

21. '*a* resident alien', '*a* foreigner': the nouns have the definite article, but this is a case where the article specifies a class, and the sense requires translation with the indefinite.

'and he shall eat it' (here translated 'for him to eat'): the *weqatal* form typically indicates a future tense in a sequence of actions. In this case there is a stronger relationship with the preceding clause, suggesting either purpose or result. The translation here is meant to adopt the latter, but note NRSV's 'for them to eat' (purpose).

'you may sell': inf. abs., following the syntactical function of the imperfect 'you may sell'.

22. 'that comes forth': the form is a participle, meaning lit. 'that goes out/forth'; the participle *hayyōṣē'* is masculine in form, therefore agreeing strictly with 'seed' (*zar'ekā*, m.) rather than 'crops' (*tᵉbû'at*, f.; with Morrow 1995: 78). *yāṣā'*, 'go out', can be followed by an object noun, denoting the place from which something goes out (Morrow, ibid., citing Gen. 44:4; Exod. 9:29, 33).

24. 'too long for you to carry': lit. '(too long) so that (*kî*) you are unable to carry'. The conjunction *kî* here means 'with the result that' (GKC 166b). Verse 24 consists of a number of *kî* clauses, introduced by an initial conditional *kî*, to which the following three are subordinate. The *weqatal* form that opens v. 25 announces the apodosis of the sentence, that is, the 'then' clause, indeed, a series of 'then' clauses extending through v. 26. The translation adopted is similar to NRSV; NIV is slightly different. The force of the sentence is that the LORD's blessing of the people with increased territory may result in the distance to the chosen place being too great for them to carry the tithe produce there, and therefore special rules apply.

27. 'And you must not neglect the Levite': the verb is missing from LXX, and the syntax in MT is unusual. Without 'you must not neglect', v. 27 would follow naturally from v. 26: 'together with your household, and the Levite who lives in your cities...' Andersen (1974: 93) defends the clause as 'adjunctive', but LXX may represent the better text.

Form and structure

Deut. 14 consists of what seem at first glance to be quite different kinds of laws: first, laws regulating acceptable and unacceptable kinds of food (1–21), followed by a development of the laws on tithes and first-lings (22–29). They are linked, superficially, by the topic of 'eating', and more importantly by their relationship with the concept of Israel's holiness.

The food laws belong to the 'purity' regulations that are at home in the 'holiness sphere', a world of thought best represented in the OT by the book of Leviticus (see 'Explanation'). The counterpart to these instructions in that book is found in Lev. 11. It is difficult to determine the nature of the relationship between the texts on ordinary literary grounds. In general, Deut. 14 is shorter, although it does more than Lev. 11 to specify the animals that may be eaten (Deut. 14:4; cf. Lev. 11:3, 9, which restrict themselves to basic criteria). Yet Lev. 11 is more complete and coherent as an account of purity/impurity in relation to what may be eaten, and this may argue for its priority. For example, the general permission in Deut. 14:20 seems to presuppose some body of assumed knowledge, such as Lev. 11:21–22, which specifies exceptions to the rule about winged insects (so Milgrom 1991: 698–699). Deuteronomy's expansions, in contrast (14:4), do not enhance the regulations themselves, since the main clean animals need hardly be specified, but are perhaps in keeping with the positive focus of the chapter on what may be eaten. (See further Milgrom 1991: 698–704, for further arguments for the priority of Lev. 11; cf. also Firmage 1990; S. R. Driver 1895: 163–164.)

Both chapters have an evident connection with Gen. 1 in their division of the creatures into those that inhabit the three spheres of earth, water and sky, and there may be a deliberate echo of the classification there. The restriction on what may be eaten qualifies the general permission to eat all creatures given in Gen. 9:3 (where the term *remeś* has the sense of 'all living creatures'; see Wenham's [1987: 192–193] discussion of 9:3), and this restriction may be understood in the context of the covenantal obligations laid upon Israel and variously elaborated in Leviticus and Deuteronomy, as opposed to the freedom granted in the pre-Mosaic world.

The connection between the dietary laws and the 'holiness-chosenness' theme is announced in 14:1–2. These verses could follow very suitably on from 12:31, continuing the holiness idea in terms of distinction from the Canaanites. The dietary laws, therefore, have been incorporated into the rationale of Deuteronomy's law code, which began by developing the basic implications of the First and Second Commandments (in chs. 12 – 13), and continue by enunciating the holiness of Israel in terms of its ritual and worship practices. Both Braulik (1993: 321 n.) and Kaufman (1978– 9: 122–129) relate 14:1–21 specifically to the Third Commandment (5:11), Braulik entitling it, 'Yahweh's holy people in its ritual difference from the peoples of other gods'.

The structure of vv. 1–21 is as follows:

1–2	Israel as holy people, and initial prohibitions
3	Prohibition of eating any abominable thing
4–20	Elaboration of the basic prohibition
21	Final prohibitions, with holiness rationale
22–29	The law of tithe

There are signs of careful patterning of this material. 1. The set of specific permissions and prohibitions is framed by the categorical prohibitions in vv. 3, 21a. These in turn are explained by a statement that Israel is a people holy to Yahweh (1–2, 21b). 2. The nature of the patterning of these parts is illustrated by the presentation of the singular–plural phenomenon in them. The alternation between singular and plural second-person address is not congruent with the division of the material, but rather overlaps the 'joins'. The distribution is as follows: 1, pl.; 2–3, sg.; 4–20, pl.; 21, sg. (22–29, sg.). This suggests a deliberate variation in the number as part of the patterning. A certain semantic motivation for the change is visible in vv. 1–2: 'you [pl.] are children ... you [sg.] are *a* people holy ...'

In vv. 4–20, the alternation between permission and prohibition is a function of the basic distinction between Israel and Canaan, or the 'mimesis' of 12:4, 31. There are slightly different patterns in vv. 4–10 and vv. 11–20. 1. In vv. 4–10, initial commands are followed by positive and negative ramifications, and motivating (final) exhortations (e.g. 3, 4–6, 7–8; 9a, 9b, 10a, 10b; Morrow 1995: 67). 2. In vv. 11–20, the positive command frames the passage (11, 20); the negative commands come between (12–19).

In vv. 22–29 the holiness rationale does not appear on the surface. The laws must be understood in this context, however, by reference to ch. 12, where the image of the people at worship in joyful unity 'before the LORD' was seen to be a portrayal of it precisely as holy people. The law governing the tithes and firstlings (14:22–27) stands in close relationship with 12:17–19, which it develops, in a manner parallel to the development already seen within 12:(15–16), 20–28. These verses relate to tithes *and* firstlings, together a substantial part of the offerings (even though a further law relating to firstlings will appear at 15:19–23). There is also a link between the present law (14:22–27) and 12:15–28 in the concept of further extension of the land, and provision for offerings in that case. (See 'Explanation'.)

If the dietary laws are connected in Braulik's scheme with the Third Commandment, he relates the tithe law to the Fourth. This is because he sees a pattern in 14:22 – 16:17, incorporating the specific laws of sacrifice and feasts at the chosen place (14:22–29; 15:19–23; 16:1–17). Throughout the laws in this section there is an interest in periodicity: the ordinary tithe is set aside yearly (14:22); the tithe is handled differently on a three-year cycle (14:28–29); release from debt and slavery is required in the seventh year (15:1, 12). (These seven-year cycles are different, the former being a fixed cycle, while the latter refers to the various enslavement periods of individuals, which could expire in any year.) The firstlings sacrifice returns to an annual pattern (15:20). Finally, the laws of the feasts themselves reflect the sabbatical structure (16:8; Braulik 1993: 325–326). The tithe law also manifests the Sabbath commandment's concern for the weak (5:14).

However, there are links between the dietary laws and the tithe law. The tithe law is bound into the holiness theology in its immediate context by means of the motif of eating, which it shares with the dietary laws. The concept of the tithe as a feast is peculiar to Deuteronomy. The Pentateuch's other laws of tithe are Num. 18:21–25 and Lev. 27:30–33. In the former, it is seen as a perquisite of the Levite. In the latter, too, tithes are assumed to be the property of the sanctuary and its personnel, and to be capable of being redeemed by the donor for money (in effect, substituting money for produce). Tithes in Leviticus also include animals, whereas Deuteronomy speaks of vegetable tithes only. There are, of course, points of contact between Deuteronomy and the other two texts. Deuteronomy and Numbers have in common the need to provide for the Levite; and Deuteronomy and Leviticus share the possibility of a money transaction. Clearly, however, there are quite different perspectives on these things in the several laws. Some of these may be explained by the theological arguments within which they are cast in the respective books. (Historical-critical interpretation has tended to suppose that the laws are simply different and that they must have operated at different times and/or places; S. R. Driver 1895: 169–171. For an attempt to explain the differences in a way that assumes a continuity in the institution of tithe, while allowing for contextual motivation in Deuteronomy, see McConville 1984: 68–87.)

In Deut. 14 as a whole, the 'holy people' logic is fused into the cultic life of Israel (as in ch. 12), here by means of the eating theme. Holiness is elaborated in terms of what may and may not be eaten, and how. From different angles, a basic distinction is carried through between what is acceptable for the holy people and what is not: this is represented in the discourse by a series of contrasts between 'thou shalt' and 'thou shalt not'.

This is not to say that holiness in the OT is completely explained by this theological function of the dietary laws in Deuteronomy. The 'holiness spectrum' in Israel (that is, the organization of life into the categories of holy, clean, unclean, abominable) has been explored penetratingly by Wenham (1979a: 18–29) and Jenson (1992: 56–88), mainly in relation to Leviticus. Drawing on anthropological studies, notably of Mary Douglas (1966), they have shown that these concepts are fundamental means of structuring human experience, often into binary opposites (such as life and death, God and chaos), and also other more nuanced relationships (Jenson 1992: 62–65). From this point of view, the language and actions of the holiness sphere become symbolic of important dimensions of life. Furthermore, such an understanding does not apply to Israel alone, but to many societies, including Israel's own neighbours. The attention given by Deuteronomy to the dietary laws, therefore, must be seen in terms of the book's specific interests. It turns to the opposites embedded in the permissions and prohibitions to help to portray Israel's whole life as belonging distinctively to Yahweh.

Comment

14:1–2

1. The idea of Yahweh as Israel's 'father' has appeared already at 1:31 (see there for related texts) and 8:5, in the latter passage as part of the elaboration of the theology of holiness and election in chs. 7 – 8. Sonship is in parallel here with holiness and chosenness in vv. 1–2, the latter verse being virtually identical with the important expression of election theology in 7:6 (see there for comment). The force of the verse is that Israelites are children of Yahweh, not of any other god (since the idea of sonship of a god is not in itself unusual in the ancient world). The addition of 'sonship' at this point, however, strengthens Deuteronomy's view of election, which puts the whole people in an immediate covenantal relationship with

Yahweh (whereas in other contexts it is the king who is regarded as God's 'son'; Ps. 2:7).

2. Verses 1–2 show, therefore, that the chapter is to be seen as a continuation of Deuteronomy's election theology. The initial prohibitions, of self-inflicted laceration and shaving the temples in mourning for the dead (2), are also prohibited in Lev. 19:27–28, with a motivation similar to the one here (that Israel should be holy like Yahweh). In some OT texts these mourning activities are mentioned as if they were rather neutral (Is. 22:12; Jer. 16:6). Self-laceration, however, clearly played a part in the worship of other gods (Hos. 7:14; 1 Kgs. 18:28; cf. Jer. 47:5). In the Ugaritic literature, the god El gashes himself in mourning for dead Baal (*ANET* 139; and see Craigie 1976a: 229–230). This ritual act, therefore, was part of mourning rites in general among the peoples around Israel, but it may also have played a part in the festivities attending the myth of the dying and rising god (Baal in Canaan, or Tammuz in Babylon; cf. Ezek. 8:14). The strong theme of Israel's distinctiveness continues here, therefore, following from 12:4, 31.

14:3–21

3. The section opens (3) with a general prohibition of eating anything 'abhorrent' to Yahweh, the term used in Deuteronomy for any thing or any practice that is totally unacceptable to him (7:25). The characterization of 'unclean' food in this way brings it into the realm of practices prohibited because associated with false religion.

4–20. The dietary laws themselves follow a tight pattern (see 'Form and structure'), governed by the dual command, 'you may eat . . . you shall not eat'. The passage has many similarities with Lev. 11:2–23, both following the order: land animals, fish, birds, winged insects. The two are not identical, however. Lev. 11 is more repetitive in style (for example, regarding the camel, hare and rock-badger, vv. 4–6; and the expansions on the uncleanness of certain fish, vv. 10–11). Deut. 14:4 specifies animals that may be eaten, while Lev. 11:3 states only the criteria of cleanness. Lev. 11:21–22 specifies winged insects that may be eaten, while Deut. 14:19–20 makes general restrictions. The exclusion of all winged insects in v. 19 is qualified by the permission to eat all 'clean' insects (20; for the translation 'insects' here see 'Notes on the text'). It is possible that the verse has in mind the regulation in Lev. 11:21–22 (Milgrom 1991: 499).

With the exception of Lev. 11:21, the animals that are named are virtually identical, although there are slight differences in the order between Lev. 11:4–6 and Deut. 14:7; and Lev. 11:17–18 and Deut. 16 – 17. Lev. 11 also adds a number of further creatures in vv. 29–30, in a section that is not paralleled in Deuteronomy, and that largely concerns rules for dealing with uncleanness.

Deut. 14 has an important terminological difference from Lev. 11 in its avoidance of the term *šeqeṣ*, which in the latter place is used of a number of the creatures that may not be eaten (11:10–13, 20, 23). Lev. 11 actually has both terms, where *ṭāmē'* is used of the quadrupeds that may not be eaten, while *šeqeṣ* is confined to creatures of the water and air. One explanation of this is that *ṭāmē'* in Lev. 11 connotes impurity even to the touch, while *šeqeṣ* means impurity only from eating (so Milgrom [1991: 656–659], who relates the explanation to the origins of both fish and birds in water, according to Gen. 1). Deut. 14 applies *ṭāmē'* to all the cases, presumably because it is not interested in developing the laws of uncleanness as such, but is making a simple distinction in line with its subordination of the material to its theology of holiness.

Of the creatures, a number cannot be certainly identified. The following have a high degree of certainty: ox, sheep, goat, deer, gazelle, roe-deer (4–5); camel, hare, rock-badger (hyrax) and pig (7–8); raven (or crow), hawk, stork, hoopoe, bat (12–18). The others have some degree of uncertainty. Houston (1993: 29) leaves them untranslated, claiming that to translate would give 'a totally spurious impression of certitude'. To his list might be added, however, the eagle (12), though it is sometimes also given as 'vulture' (*HALAT* 3:691). Other renderings involve a degree of guesswork, and also assume that the text contains groupings, hence the continuations in vv. 5b, 12–17. The identifications of S. R. Driver (1895: 159–163) continue to be influential.

The principles underlying the original classifications into clean and unclean categories are unclear, as they must be, to an extent, in view of the uncertainty about identifications. A number of observations may be made. 1. Some of the unclean creatures were apparently used in the worship of other gods (Is. 65:4; 66:3, 17; Ezek. 8:9–10). 2. Several of the prohibited species are scavengers or meat-eaters. This may make them unacceptable either for hygienic reasons (Albright 1968: 154–155), or because they consumed blood (G. R. Driver 1955: 5ff.) and/or fed on carrion, which would cause those who ate them to infringe cultic prohibitions of these things. 3. There is some correspondence between (on the one hand) permitted animals and (on the other) animals used in sacrifice and other well-known animals in Israel's environment that were useful for food (such as the gazelle and deer).

As we have seen ('Form and structure'), these observations do not yield a full explanation for the system developed here. Considered from an anthropological point of view, it may have developed for a variety of reasons, including some or all of the above. The system as such cannot be understood as a rejection of Canaanite practices, since other ANE peoples both ate and sacrificed the same domestic animals as Israel, and there was a widespread avoidance of the pig, again in both sacrifice and in ordinary consumption. (The texts cited above, however, may show that it was used in some aberrant practices.) There is some advantage in Douglas's view that 'cleanness' means a wholeness or perceived suitability in terms of the element that the creatures inhabit, and according to specific criteria. This may be supported by the patterning of both Lev. 11 and Deut. 14 after the threefold division of earth, sky and water in Gen. 1. Yet it is not certain whether the criteria offered (cud-chewing and cloven hooves in the case of the animals) logically precede the identifications, or whether inclusions and exclusions are established first in practice (Houston 1993: 65, 116–117). The concept of distinctions between clean and unclean creatures is probably very old and widespread (as are institutions such as temples, priesthood and sacrifice). Fundamental explanations of systems such as this, therefore, have to reckon with criteria that have developed out of common usage and religious prescription, the two being related.

The more important question for interpretation is how Deuteronomy fits the system into its development of the theology of Israel's holiness. It is clear that there is such a conscious application of the permissions and taboos (which may have had a separate existence, and on which Lev. 11 may also have drawn in pursuit of its own theological interests). The introduction in v. 3 plainly fits with its pattern of demands and prohibitions in consequence of the premiss of Israel's holiness, as well as with the theme of eating food in the present chapter. And the catalogue in vv. 4–20 is a suitable development of the categorical command in v. 3. The principle of a distinction between Israel and Canaan is maintained both in v. 3, with the term 'abhorrent' (cf. 7:25–26), and in v. 21 (in contrast to Lev. 17:15, which subjects 'resident aliens' to the prohibition of what dies by itself), in line with the tendency established in 12:4, 31. The deuteronomic incorporation of the dietary laws, therefore, must be seen as part of its thesis concerning the holiness of Israel in contrast to its neighbours. (Its simple distinction between 'clean' and 'unclean', in contrast to the more complex picture in Leviticus, is part of this.) Such a contrast cannot be drawn in detail from the specific classification of prohibitions, however. Rather, this very important part of Israel's life is drawn into the picture, being developed, of a people whose whole existence expresses its holiness to Yahweh.

21. Deuteronomy is categorical in its prohibition of the flesh of creatures that have died naturally, and is thus different from Lev. 17:15–16, in which the eating of such meat makes a person ritually unclean (whether native or resident alien), but which provides for restoration to the normal 'clean' state. In Leviticus, only the priest is barred from eating such meat (Lev. 22:8). The difference may be explained by Deuteronomy's concept of Israel as such as holy, because of Yahweh's choice, and according to which it generally avoids expressing the special rights and duties of the priesthood. Leviticus, in contrast, is occupied with the adminstration of holiness, and therefore with dealing with situations that arise. The exclusion of the resident alien and foreigner from the rule for Israel is consistent with Deuteronomy's theme of the special status of

Israel, as in other cases (cf. 15:3; 23:20 – of the 'foreigner' only); and the contrast with Leviticus may suggest a certain ideal vision on the part of Deuteronomy.

The prohibition of boiling the kid in its mother's milk (also at Exod. 23:19b; 34:26b) presumably has in mind some fertility practice in the cult of another god. Evidence for it has been thought to exist in a Ugaritic text (*CTA* 23.14 [= *UT* 52.14]), but it is not certain that the text is relevant (see Keel 1980; Knauf 1988). The rejection of the practice, whether in Israel or elsewhere, may derive from a sense that the cooking of the kid in the milk, which was intended to give it life, infringed a natural boundary, and was an unacceptable mixing of the spheres of life and death (see also Carmichael 1974: 151–153).

14:22–29

22. The basic command is contained in v. 22, and must be understood as a setting aside of produce as a gift to God (see 'Notes on the text' for the syntax). The practice of tithing produce was widespread in the ANE, and the gifts came to sanctuaries for the maintenance of the priesthood and worship there, often in the context of the royal cult. The tithe laws in Num. 18:21–25 and Lev. 27:30–33 show more clearly the connection between the tithe and maintenance of the religious system. In the first case it is the perquisite, or prescribed income, of the Levite; in the second, it is seen in terms of money equivalency, which again shows its character as a kind of taxation. The deuteronomic law, typically, regards the tithe in a quite different aspect, since it has no brief to legislate for the rights of a particular sanctuary. Its own concern is expressed in the two extensions of the basic requirement that follow.

23. The first extension of the basic requirement portrays the tithe as a feast involving all Israel at the place of worship chosen by Yahweh. It thus directly develops the picture first painted in ch. 12, where the people was to bring all its offerings to the chosen place. The allusion to the place is here brief and formulaic, taking for granted the fuller formulations in ch. 12, especially 12:5. The content of the tithe corresponds to the chief vegetable elements used in Deuteronomy to characterize the blessing of Yahweh (7:13), here filled out by reference to firstlings of herd and flock in order to represent meat produce. The first extension of the law has the aim that Israel may 'learn to revere Yahweh', an expression used elsewhere in Deuteronomy to motivate obedience to the laws in general (4:10; 17:19). Here the celebration of the tithe itself becomes a means by which Israel may learn to 'fear' the LORD.

22–27. This second extension of the basic command is analogous to the permission to slaughter freely in 12:15–27. It envisages the difficulty arising from distance from the sanctuary in the event of the expansion of the land in due course (cf. 12:20; and see 'Notes on the text'). In that case a provision could be made for non-sacrificial slaughter, but in this case the close connection between tithe and sanctuary is maintained by means of the device of pecuniary transactions, first in the locality, then at the sanctuary (26). This device does not relax the cultic requirement, since its effect is to enable the worshipper and his household to participate in the feast at the chosen place. (The 'profane slaughter' in 12:15–27 had the same effect, since it ensured that true sacrifices would be feasts for all Israel there too.)

The envisaged celebration is a further example of the united Israel rejoicing before the LORD, as a symbolic representation of its nature as the chosen people, complementing the portrayal in ch. 12. The echoes of that passage are strong, comprising not only the location at the chosen place, but the feasting, the idea of the consumer's freedom of choice and satisfaction ('whatever you desire' [26] is a phrase similar to that found in 12:15, 20, 21), and the inclusion of households and the Levite in the feast (see on 12:7, 12; and 'Notes on the text'). The law of the tithe requires both extensions of the basic command for its completeness; it is only in the second extension that some of the most typically deuteronomic elements occur (as Brin [1994: 35] allows in his study of 'double' laws, though he thinks it more likely that the second extension came later), enabling the formulation of the law to fulfil its theological purpose (see 'Explanation').

28–29. The final provision for the tithe is remarkable because it finds no point of contact with other tithe laws in the OT and because it provides for the use of the tithe without its coming to the sanctuary. Every third year, instead, the produce earmarked as tithe is stored in the localities as part of a welfare system. (The third-year tithe seems to be known to Amos, who makes an ironic reference to 'tithes every three *days*' in his criticism of the people's religious activism.) In fact, the link with the sanctuary is not entirely broken, because the proper disposal of the third-year tithe must be properly declared in a confession there (26:12–14), where its nature as a 'holy thing' is carefully preserved (13). The tithe thus becomes, formally and institutionally, a way of securing means for those who have no property of their own in Israel. That this is the right way to construe the grouping of Levite, widow, orphan and resident alien – rather than by the blanket designation as 'the poor' – has been shown by N. Lohfink (1995f: 11–14; 1990a). Levites are not by definition poor; neither are widows, orphans or resident aliens. Deuteronomy, moreover, does not use any word for 'poor' in its laws relating to these classes. The aim of the law is to provide an alternative means of access to Israel's wealth, in the absence of their control of land. They may not have had access, by their own right, to the court system either (N. Lohfink 1995f: 14–15; and cf. 10:18).

This law, therefore, is not, properly speaking, a 'welfare' provision; it rather ensures that these groups within society can participate fully in Israel's enjoyment of Yahweh's blessing, which is their entitlement as members of the holy people. (For this reason the present law has no direct bearing on the law of the fallow year [Exod. 23:10–11], *pace* Kaufman [1984: 282], who thinks it shows that law had ceased to provide sufficiently for the poor; see also 'Comment' on Deut. 15:1–18, and 24:17–22.)

Explanation

Deut. 14 brings together two passages that contribute in quite different ways to its theology of holiness. Some have found them so different as to be incompatible, the one borrowing a form that articulates holiness in terms of ritual requirements (3–21), the other articulating a holiness that must be expressed in the nation's life, worship, ethics, and the promotion of social mechanisms that protect every individual. (Mayes [1994] fitted the former to the category 'ascribed holiness' and the latter, in contrast, to that of 'achieved holiness'.)

The food laws, however, are adopted not wholesale, but purposefully. While the laws in Deuteronomy and Leviticus have in common their concern for Israel's holiness, this is developed differently in each book. By comparison with Lev. 11, the laws in Deut. 14:3–21 do not constitute a rigorous regulation of dietary rectitude, and they seem to be free to presuppose the more detailed provision of such a set of laws (e.g. at v. 20; and cf. the assumption of the clean–unclean distinction at 12:15, 22). Verses 1–2 establish a connection between these laws and the main expression of Israel's holiness in Deut. 7, and they are in fact conformed to the idea of the holiness of all Israel, and its separateness from non-Israelite people (see on 14:21). Interestingly, they reveal Deuteronomy's attitude to cultic things. There is no question of abolishing such requirements; that was left to Jesus (Mark 7:15). Rather, an existing institution or convention is given new force within the context of the wider argument. (In the same way circumcision as such is scarcely undermined by the appeal in 10:16.)

If the dietary laws insist in their own way on the wholeness of Israel in its obligations to Yahweh, it is important that they are followed by the tithe law. In it, holiness is conceived as the people united in joyful worship 'before the LORD', as in Deut. 12 (cf. 'Explanation' of that chapter). The tithe was evidently important in Deuteronomy's programme, featuring in chs. 12, 14 and 26, and thus, in a sense, framing the law code. The code is actually selective in its portrayal of sacrifices and offerings in Israel. Those that are developed, from the list in 12:6, are only the blood sacrifices, the tithes and the firstlings, to which are added the three annual feasts (16:1–17). The choice is presumably motivated by Deuteronomy's concern to portray Israel rejoicing and experiencing blessing in the worship. This is crucial to its picture of a brotherhood before Yahweh.

The special provision in vv. 28–29 is remarkable – one of the best expressions of Deuteronomy's aim to create a society in which no-one would be permanently disadvantaged, or consigned to a second-class status. Deuteronomy is otherwise realistic about the likely persistence of poverty (15:11), as even Jesus was (Mark 14:7). Yet the ideal is a constant project for Christian people. And it is not just 'charity', but the conferring of worth, dignity and belonging. Israel as paradigm for just societies is nowhere more powerful than here. The inclusion of the 'resident alien' is surprising, in the context of a rationale that derives from Israel's holiness. His two appearances in the chapter make an interesting contrast; he is excluded from the dietary requirements, yet included in the provision for those without property (cf. van Houten 1991: 82). It is one of the points at which Deuteronomy's strict focus on Israel as the chosen people shows a propensity to give way to a more inclusive logic.

DEUTERONOMY 15:1–22

Translation

[1]Every seventh year you shall make a release. [2]This is the law regulating the release: every creditor shall release what he has lent to his neighbour. He shall not press his neighbour, his brother Israelite, for the LORD's release has been proclaimed. [3]You may press a foreigner; but you must release any claim that you have on your brother.

[4]However, there shall be no poor among you, because the LORD will certainly bless you in the land the LORD your God is giving you to possess as an inheritance, [5]if only you strictly obey the LORD your God by being careful to keep all this commandment with which I am charging you this day. [6]When the LORD your God blesses you as he has promised, you will lend to many nations and borrow from none; you will rule over many nations, and they will not rule over you.

[7]If one of your brothers should become poor among you, in any of your cities in your land the LORD your God is giving you, do not harden your heart or be tight-fisted against your impoverished brother. [8]Rather, open your hand generously to him and liberally lend him enough to cover whatever he needs. [9]Be sure not to entertain the mean thought that the seventh year, the year of release, is near, and look with ill-will on your impoverished brother, giving him nothing; then he would cry to the LORD against you, and it would be counted as sin in you. [10]Rather, give generously, and do not be grudging as you give to him, for because of this the LORD your God will bless you in all your work, and everything that you put your hand to. [11]For there will always be poor in the midst of the land; that is why I am commanding you to open your hand generously to your brother, to your needy and poor in your land.

[12]If a Hebrew brother (or sister) sells himself to you and serves you for six years, in the seventh year you shall let him go from you a free person. [13]And when you let

him go a free person, you shall not let him go empty-handed. [14]Rather, you shall provide for him liberally from your flocks, your threshing-floor and your wine press; give him of that with which the LORD your God has blessed you. [15]Remember that you were a slave in the land of Egypt until the LORD your God delivered you; it is for this reason that I give you this command today. [16](However, if a bondservant says: 'I do not wish to go from you', because he loves you and your household and feels well off there, [17]then take an awl and thrust it through his earlobe into the door, and he will be your slave for life. You must treat a female servant in exactly the same way.) [18]Let it not seem hard to you when letting him go from you a free person, for he has served you for six years, and has been worth twice as much as a hired servant to you. And the LORD your God will bless you in all you do.

[19]Every male firstborn born in your herd or flock you must dedicate to the LORD your God; you shall do no work with the firstborn ox, or shear a firstborn sheep. [20]Before the LORD your God you shall eat them, year by year, at the place the LORD will choose, together with your household. [21]But if an animal has a blemish, if it is lame or blind, or has any serious defect, you must not sacrifice it to the LORD your God, [22]but eat it in your cities, the ritually unclean and clean alike, as you would eat gazelle or deer. [23]But you must not eat its blood; pour it out on the ground like water.

Notes on the text

2. What is released? The syntax of v. 2a has been read in several different ways. 1. The whole phrase *kol baʿal maššēh yāḏô* is the subject of the verb 'release'. It then means (awkwardly) 'every owner of a loan that he has made', both *baʿal* and *maššēh* being construct forms (North 1954). 2. With the same syntax *maššēh* may be 'pledge' (a security taken on the loan). The sense then is not 'remit a loan' but 'release [i.e. give back] a pledge' (so C. J. H. Wright 1990: 170–171). 3. The noun *baʿal*, 'owner', 'master', may stand in itself for 'creditor', *maššēh yāḏô* being the object (Horst 1930: 59–60). In this case the object may yet be either 'the one who has taken a loan by his own hand' (where *maššēh* is a hiph. ptc. as verbal noun; Horst, ibid.), or 'that which he has lent by his own hand', i.e. 'his personal loan' (where *maššēh* is a noun meaning 'loan'; Morrow 1995: 91–92).

'his neighbour ... his brother Israelite': the former term is absent from LXX, and some Hebrew MSS lack the word 'and' between them. The latter term has sometimes been regarded as a gloss, to emphasize the theology of brotherhood in the chapter (Mayes 1979: 248). Yet, in the absence of the former from LXX, the text-critical arguments are not conclusive.

3. *tašmēṭ* is the only example of *šmṭ*, hiph., in the OT. It is not clear whether the hiphil has the same force as the qal (as in v. 2), in which case *tašmēṭ yāḏô* would mean 'your hand shall release' (where *tašmēṭ* is 3 f. sg.

and *yāḏô* the subject); or a causative force, in which case *tašmēṭ* must be 2 m. sg., and the phrase would mean 'you shall cause your hand to release'. In either case, what is released remains to be decided. That is, is it the debtor, 'your brother' (*'eṭ 'āḥîḵā*, where *'eṭ* is taken as the sign of the definite object)? Or is it the loan, in which case the whole phrase *'ᵃšer yihyeh lᵉḵā 'eṭ 'āḥîḵā* must be taken as the object, meaning either: 1. 'that which belongs to you which you have placed with your brother' (where *'eṭ* is the preposition 'with'), or 2. 'the claim that you have on your brother' (Morrow 1995: 92), where *'eṭ* is one of the handful of cases in which it means 'in respect of' (cf. e.g. Num. 3:46; Judg. 20:44; and GKC 117m). This last is preferred here. It might also mean, in practice, a return of any pledge held against the kinsman.

4–5. The 'if' clause in v. 5 could depend on either of the two clauses in v. 4. The alternative to the translation here would be: 'There will be no poor among you (for the LORD will bless you...), if only you will strictly obey...' The close link between v. 5 and v. 4b is preferable, however: 1. because of the causal relationship generally in Deuteronomy between blessing and obedience (note the close similarity between this clause and 11:13–14; and 2. because of a structural similarity between the two clauses (Morrow 1995: 94).

6. 'When the LORD...': the first phrase, beginning with *kî*, is taken as a temporal clause, rather than as explanatory of the previous clause ('because'), by analogy with 12:20; 14:24.

8. 'open ... generously'; 'liberally lend': the two phrases are formed with infinitive absolutes, emphasizing the force of the main verb.

12. 'Hebrew': the term *'ibrî*, with its feminine *'ibriyyâ*, occurs only here in Deuteronomy, in this following Exod. 21:2. In its origins it may have referred to a social class, perhaps even to those who had to sell themselves into slavery (if the supposed parallel with the term *ḥabiru* is correct), rather than to Israelites as a nation, and that is probably its sense in Exod. 21:2. The parallel with 'your brother' in the present verse does not prove that the term now refers to Israelites as such (*contra* Mayes 1979: 250–251). Its function here, assuming it knows the Exodus law, is deliberately to widen its scope to include women on their own terms.

14. For the form *yiqbeḵā*, 'your winepress', lacking *dagesh forte* in *b*, see GKC 93k.

'give him of that with which the LORD your God has blessed you': *'ᵃšer* is taken as the relative pronoun 'that which' and as the second object of 'bless' (GKC 177ff). It is often taken otherwise, as the equivalent of *ka'ᵃšer*, a form supported by SamP and LXX, thus: 'as the LORD your God has blessed you'.

18. 'seem hard to you': MT's 'in your eye' (*bᵉ'ênekā*) should be emended to 'in your eyes' (*bᵉ'ênêḵā*) with SamP.

'twice as much': this restores the traditional understanding of the term *mišneh*, with Lindenberger 1991, and against some recent translations as 'the equivalent of' (Craigie 1976a: 235; Braulik 1986a: 115; NRSV), based on a supposed parallel term from Alalakh.

Form and structure

Deut. 15 is dominated by the idea of 'release', both of debts and of debt slaves, and includes with the laws concerning this a law governing the firstlings sacrifice (19–23). The concept of 'release' is not confined to the Bible in the ancient world. It was a common practice for kings, soon after their accession, to issue decrees of 'justice' (*mīšarum*), proclaiming 'freedom' (Akk. *andurārum*; examples in *CAD* A II.115b–117b), by annulling debts and freeing debt slaves. Hammurabi's law code apparently tried to bring some system into this practice by requiring the release of debt slaves after three years' service (CH 117).

The biblical laws of release also aim to bring regularity into the practice of slave release. In the Jubilee, people who had had to give up property because they were economically hard pressed were allowed to return to it (the term $d^e r \hat{o} r$, 'freedom' [Lev. 25:10], is the equivalent of Akk. *andurārum*). Both Exodus (21:2–6) and Deuteronomy have their own laws concerning 'release', which also have the Mesopotamian practice as background. Here too it is not kings who make releases, at their own initiative and without compulsion, but Israel itself (addressed in the singular in Deut. 15:12–18; cf. Exod. 21:2), and according to a compulsory, regular pattern.

The relationship between the various laws is not wholly clear. Deuteronomy probably reads Exod. 21:2–6, yet is no mere extension of it (see 'Comment'). The biggest difficulty in connecting the three laws lies in the fact that while Lev. 25:39–46 puts slave release in the context of the Jubilee, but says nothing about a seventh-year release of either debts or slaves, Exodus and Deuteronomy provide only for seventh-year releases and say nothing about the Jubilee. These difficulties are usually resolved by supposing that the laws simply emanate from different times in Israel's history. There are analogies, however, for the different kinds of laws represented here in second-millennium Mesopotamia. And the laws can be regarded as facing different kinds or degrees of indebtedness. In particular, only Lev. 25:39–47 envisages the restoration of forfeited patrimonial land (see further Chirichigno 1993: 302–343).

The laws of release are obviously closely related to the law of the tithe, which began to provide a structure in Israel for maintaining a balance and equity in society, and especially for giving access to the wealth of the land to those who had no property rights of their own. The laws of release now address the same issue from another angle.

As we saw when discussing the tithe law (ch. 14, 'Form and structure'), the laws of ch. 15 may be related to the Fourth Commandment (the

Sabbath, 5:12–15; Braulik 1993: 321–322). The first specific reason in this case is the prevalence of the number seven (15;1, 9, 12). The concern for the weak also echoes 5:14, and the grounding of the command to release the slave is the memory of Israel's own slavery in Egypt (15:15; cf. 5:15). The idea of the oneness of Israel is also highlighted by the sevenfold ocurrence of the term *'aḥ*, 'brother', in this chapter (Braulik 1991b: 38).

The juxtaposition of vv. 1–18 and 19–23 is part of a pattern of distribution in Deut. 12 – 18. Both the tithe law (14:22–29) and the firstlings law (15:9–23) take their cue from 12:6, and indeed the resumption of the topic of the tithe includes again a mention of firstlings (14:23). There seems, therefore, to be a conscious pattern of recurrence, a certain spreading of the laws that relate expressly to worship at the chosen place, interspersed with other laws, which are nevertheless connected in some way. One effect is to put worship at the centre of all of Israel's life. Merendino (1969: 123), for example, saw a pattern in chs. 15 – 16 that related the laws of release directly to Yahweh, and drew them into the cycle of laws of worship.

Another effect, in this context, is to complete a progression in 14:22 – 15:23 that leads from a picture of the household at worship (14:22–27), through images of deprivation and restoration, and back to an image of the household at worship (Braulik 1993: 326). There are also rhetorical connections between the two sections (see 'Comment' on 15:19). And finally, the memory of the exodus underlies both the laws of release (15:6, 15) and the law of firstlings, which is closely connected with the exodus in Exod. 12 – 13. Deut. 15:18, in fact, makes a link between the two laws with an echo of Exod. 13:15 in its vocabulary.

Comment

15:1–6

1. The law in vv. 1–11 is commonly known as the law of debt release, although this is slightly misleading, as it bears more broadly on the relation between lending and the year of release. Its closest relative among the Pentateuchal laws is Exod. 23:10–11, which says nothing of remission of debts, but provides only for the land to lie fallow one year in seven. The term used there for the 'release' of the land is the same (in a verbal form) as the one used here for the release of debts. In 15:1 itself, there is no mention of debt (hence the translation given). However, in Exod. 23:10–11 there is a connection between the fallow year and care for the poor. And the idea of a seventh-year release in itself is the important factor common to the passages.

2–3. Deuteronomy develops the law of the fallow year into procedures relating to debt in that year. If it was unclear in Exod. 23:10–11 whether the fallow year occurred on a universal cycle (Phillips 1970: 75), this is now explicit in Deut. 15 (hence the mean-minded calculation in v. 9; and cf. 31:10–11).

The question is raised what is actually meant by the release. In both v. 2 and v. 3 there are options that allow the object of the 'release' to be either the debtor or the loan. (The syntactical possibilities are discussed in the 'Notes on the text'. The third option noticed there, 'the pledge' [cf. REB] does not fit easily with v. 3.) So which interpretation leads to the most satisfactory interpretation of the passage?

Even the precise import of the term 'release' can be derived only from an interpretation of the passage as a whole. The view taken here is that the creditor gives up a certain right in respect of the loan. The idea of his 'pressing' the debtor obviously involves insistence on payment. The pressure could arise from the practice of securities, or 'pledges', taken on the loan at the outset (24:6, 17). This might extend to a portion of land or of the produce of it for the duration of the loan (C. J. H. Wright 1990: 171–172). In the latter case, a clear connection emerges between the fallow year and debt release, since the debtor, if deprived of the produce of a part of his land, would be in even worse difficulty during the fallow year, since there would be no new seeding that year, and therefore the yield would be only what grew of itself (against Phillips 1970: 77–78).

The same point bears on the question whether the release is a cancellation or a deferral. Again, it is hard to decide this from the vocabulary alone. If, however, the debt release is involved with the fallow year, a deferral is more likely. And a system of loans is more likely to operate if the creditor is not expected to give up all entitlement to be repaid in the seventh year. The system of loans laid down in Deuteronomy evidently has the benefit of the debtor in view, and the motive to lend is the well-being of the needy (7–9). The same point is clear from the prohibition of taking interest on loans from fellow Israelites (23:19–20[20–21]). Even so, the self-interest of the creditor is not ignored, as may be inferred from the general permissibility of taking pledges. And, both in relation to the seventh year and to interest-taking, the creditor is given more freedom in relation to the foreigner. (The foreigner, who may be a trader and only temporarily resident, would in any case not be subject to the rules governing debt release; cf. C. J. H. Wright 1996: 188.)

The special relationship among Israelites is articulated in v. 2, where the ordinary term for a neighbour or friend is further qualified by the term 'brother', which then recurs a further six times in the chapter (see 'Notes on the text').

4–5. Verse 4 marks a sharp contrast with vv. 1–3, because it holds out the deuteronomic ideal that there shall be no poor. The statement 'there shall be no poor' is best taken as a command, whose force comes from the clauses in vv. 4b–5 (see 'Notes on the text' for the syntax). The gift of Yahweh's blessing carries with it an imperative to ensure that no-one fails to benefit from it. The transition from vv. 1–3 to vv. 4–5 is a move from the real to the ideal, the two passages linked by the intention to prevent poverty among the weak. The contrast between real and ideal is even sharper when v. 11 is drawn into the picture: 'For there will always be poor in the midst of the land.' The command in v. 4, however, becomes no less urgent because of the recognition that, in the world of contrary interests and mixed motives, the ideal state will not be attained. The ideal is nevertheless strongly held out, the picture of absence of poverty being closely related to the familiar command to keep the whole commandment (5). (This is one of the few cases within the code where the term *miṣwâ* occurs in the singular, referring to the whole deuteronomic law; cf. 17:20; 19:9.)

6. This ideal is reinforced in this verse by a picture drawn from the world of international commerce, in which Israel is depicted as a creditor nation, independent of external control (cf. 28:12). It is directly related to the memory of the exodus, the deliverance from enslavement to a foreign nation and the poverty that went with it, which are also recalled in v. 15. And it belongs within the theme in Deuteronomy that expresses the blessing of a covenantally faithful Israel in terms of its exaltation over other nations (26:16–19; 28:1, 13). The 'blessing' promised in v. 6 is probably best aligned with the promises of expansion of territory that we have seen already in laws concerning worship (12:20; 14:24), and the translation 'when the LORD...' is based on these analogies (see 'Notes on the text').

15:7–11

This paragraph extends the thought in vv. 1–2. The logic is that the likelihood of a creditor's recouping the full value of the loan is lessened by the nearness of the year of release. Some commentators regard the creditor's anxiety (9) as evidence that the loan would be cancelled altogether, since mere deferral would not be so serious (e.g. Braulik 1986a: 111). Cancellation would not involve the loss of the whole loan, only what remained outstanding. The proportion of this would be greater the less the time that remained to the 'release' (C. J. H. Wright 1996: 188). However, even if the 'release' implies only deferral (as argued above), the true cost of the loan will still have been reckoned in relation to the number of years before it was due. If the security on the loan was the produce from a piece of 'pledged' land, then the loss of that produce in the year of release, and possibly in the next as well, would be a considerable deterrent to lend (C. J. H. Wright 1990: 172–173).

7–8. The command in this case is a strong exhortation, since refusal to lend was presumably not legally actionable, the hortatory language being especially strong in v. 8 with its doubled verbs (the urgency is conveyed in the translation by adverbs; see also 'Notes on the text').

9–10. There is also a concentration of forms of the verb 'give' in vv. 9–10. This has a clear echo of Deuteronomy's predominant use of this verb to refer to Yahweh's gift of the land to Israel. The exhortation thus hints strongly at a reciprocal obligation on the part of those Israelites who have benefited most from Yahweh's blessing, and it squarely faces the fact that lending as envisaged in the law may well be to the cost of the lender. Indeed, the typical deuteronomic dynamic of Yahweh's blessing leading to Israel's willing response leading to Yahweh's further blessing is immediately invoked in v. 10.

10–11. The appeal to generosity in vv. 10–11 resumes the language of v. 8. It finally extends the scope, as far as the borrower is concerned, from 'your brother' to 'your needy and poor in your land' (11). If this seems to contradict v. 4 ('there shall be no poor'), the exhortation aims, even so, at the ideal. There is no contradiction in effect between these two passages: the holding out of the ideal in the midst of a more realistic set of proposals belongs to what Goldingay (1987: 153–166) has called Deuteronomy's 'pastoral strategy'.

15:12–18

12. If a person's debt problems became extreme, the consequence might well be that the debtor himself and/or members of his family had to enter the service of the creditor (Lev. 25:39 [cf. 2 Kgs. 4:1–2]; Neh. 5:4–5 [cf. Is. 50:1]). Slavery, or, better, slave release, is the subject of two separate Pentateuchal laws besides this one (Exod. 21:2–6; Lev. 25:39–46), all three having distinct features. The subject of all three is debt slaves, as opposed to 'chattel slaves', that is, those who had the status of slave permanently. There is a clear distinction between these two types in Mesopotamian law, the debt slave having greater rights than the chattel slave. The OT also knows both types (Chirichigno 1993: 145–185), the law in Leviticus (25:44–46) making a sharp distinction between the two, allowing only foreigners to be enslaved permanently. Deuteronomy (15:17) allows debt slaves to become permanent slaves by their own choice. A similar situation is dealt with by Exodus (21:5–6), although in that place there are cases in which a female slave may not go free (when she is given as a wife to the slave, or when she has been sold as a slave wife; vv. 4, 7–10).

Deut. 15:12–18 shares with the Exodus law the release (or manumission) in the seventh year (12), and the impoverished person's option to remain permanently in service (16). The Levitical law is different from both, in that it says nothing about a seventh-year release, but only about the great release in the fiftieth year, the 'Jubilee', which related to both slaves and to ancestral land. One further text is relevant, namely Jer. 34:13–14, which evidently recalls the present law, and also the theological connection between it and the exodus from Egypt (cf. Deut. 15:15).

In Deuteronomy, as in Exodus, the freedom of the impoverished person is a restoration to full independence in the community (the significance of the term *ḥopšî*, 'free', v. 12; Exod. 21:2; cf. 21:26). In both laws too, the manumission is due in the seventh year, dated from the beginning of the service. This seventh year, therefore, is different from that in 15:1, which was on a universal cycle. There is, of course, a connection of thought between the two 'seventh years', since both bear on the restoration of the unfortunate to a viable place in society (see 'Form and structure'). Only Deuteronomy makes a connection between the two kinds of release in this way.

Indeed, Deuteronomy develops the basic law quite independently, such that, for three reasons, it cannot be seen as a simple development of the Exodus law (N. Lohfink 1996; against Japhet 1986: 68–69).

First, the subject of the action is the impoverished person. In Exodus the master buys a slave; here the impoverished person 'sells himself' (or perhaps 'is sold') into service. (The verb, a niphal form, can be translated either as a passive or as a reflexive. The reflexive translation lays more emphasis on the initiative of the impoverished person, but a clear decision on the point cannot be made.)

However, the difference from Exod. 21:2 ('When you buy a slave...') is striking, because the impoverished person is not called 'slave' (*'ebed*). His service is admittedly described by the corresponding verb (*'ābad*), yet that has a broader usage, and the variation from Exodus is significant. In fact, the stereotypical master–slave vocabulary is entirely avoided before v. 17; the protagonists appear only as 'I – you – he/she' (Lasserre 1995: 487). The designation 'slave' is used only after the impoverished person's choice of permanent service (17). (The term used there for the woman is *'āmâ*, analogous to *'ebed*, but it too may be taken to refer to the woman in the chosen status of permanent bondage.)

With the avoidance of the term 'slave' at this stage goes the designation of the impoverished person as 'brother', establishing the equal standing of all Israelites in principle in the covenant community. The phrase 'a Hebrew brother (or sister)' (12) is literally 'your brother, whether a Hebrew or a Hebress'. The term 'Hebrew/Hebress' has been thought to refer to a landless class within Israel, echoing an older sociological meaning (C. J. H. Wright 1984; and see 'Notes on the text'). However, it is likelier that the term itself is picked up from Exod. 21:2 (where the word may indeed retain a sociological nuance) and used here as part of the concern to establish the equality of men and women in terms of the law of release (Chirichigno 1993: 278). The term 'Hebrew/Hebress' is here in apposition to 'brother', and should in this case be equated with 'Israelite' (Lasserre 1995: 483 n.). There seems also to be no reason to suppose that those who have entered service are only the dependants of the impoverished person (here against Chirichigno [1993: 281], who deduces the point from the analogy with CH 117; as he agrees, however, vv. 16–17 could not well apply to the debtor's wife).

Secondly, as already noticed, the law puts the woman on a par with the man in the matter of debt and slavery. Since women could be property-owners (2 Kgs. 8:3), they could also fall into debt. The importance of this aspect of the law is reinforced by the return to it in v. 17b.

13–14. Thirdly, the law requires the master to provide generously for the impoverished person on releasing him or her (13–14), whereas Exodus merely regulated the release. This element, in fact, is the heart of the deuteronomic law. It is expressed in terms that stress the dignity of the person being released. 'Provide' (14) is based on a word meaning 'garland' or 'necklace', a rare term that expresses honour and even extravagance. There is perhaps a memory of the jewelry that was part of the rich provision of the Israelites by the Egyptians when they released them at last from slavery to go into the bounty of their own land (Exod. 12:35–36; cf. Chirichigno 1993: 290). The provision in this case is to consist of the produce of the land, referred to in terms reminiscent of deuteronomic descriptions of Yahweh's blessing (13; cf. 7:13).

There are two motivations to obey. First, the phrase 'give him of that with which the LORD your God has blessed you' places no limit on the amount, but says clearly that the person being released has a fundamental interest in the good of the land; as an Israelite he too has a rightful share in this blessing. The provisioning, incidentally, does not prove that the person being released is landless; the assumption is rather that he or she has somewhere to return to.

15. The second motivation to the owner, a wealthy person, is that he must remember that the nation's very origins were in slavery, until the people was released by Yahweh. (The singular address in this verse is nicely ambiguous; it could be the communal singular address to the nation, or a direct address to the individual owner; it may not be necessary to decide between the two.) The release of people who have had to enter the service of others, therefore – and indeed generosity towards them – is an appropriate response both to him and to them.

16. The rule governing the impoverished person's option to remain in permanent slavery differs from that in Exod. 21:5–6 in ways that arise from the new emphases in the present law. The decision to remain is not motivated here by the desire to remain with a family that cannot accompany the man to freedom (as in the case where the wife and family have come by the gift of the owner; Exod. 21:4). Deuteronomy does not raise the question of wife and family, but because of the spirit of it, and the heightened concern for women generally, it is fair to suppose that it does not intend to make the restriction made in Exodus. Here the envisaged reason for staying is simply that he is well off where he is (16c). There may well have been reasons for someone in service to fear the responsibility of independence. But the little phrase has a sting for the owner too, implying that conditions in service should not be hard to bear.

17. Deuteronomy shares with Exodus the ceremony of ear-piercing, which happens here simply at 'the door'. Deuteronomy does not employ the phrase in Exod. 21:6 usually translated 'before God', indicating in practice a judicial setting (cf. Exod. 22:7–13; not, therefore 'before the household gods'; Phillips 1970: 74–75). The deuteronomic usage need not be seen as a 'desacralizing' move (i.e. by removing the ceremony from the sanctuary court to the home in the context of cult centralization; Braulik 1986a: 115; cf. Mayes 1979: 252). The reason for the omission is the deuteronomic address to the whole people as such, omitting any special reference to judicial procedures (cf. on 13:9; also Chirichigno 1993: 299). The act may well have required witnesses to give it legal standing, and, indeed, it is unclear whether 'the door' is at the owner's house or at the sanctuary. In any case, Deuteronomy passes over the circumstances of the procedure, focusing instead on its meaning for the master and the slave.

18. Deuteronomy thus distinguishes, in its own way, between the person who enters the temporary service of another Israelite and the permanent slave. Its law stands in a certain contrast with that of Lev. 25:39–46, which makes no mention of a release of slaves after six years' service, but only at the Jubilee (i.e. in the 'fiftieth' year in a cycle of 'sabbatical' fallow years; Lev. 25:8–12). The Jubilee law seeks to preserve the citizenship of the impoverished Israelite, not by the right of release after six years, but by insisting explicitly that he is not properly a 'slave' (*'ebed*, the term used by Exodus), but a hired labourer (*śākîr*; Lev. 25:39–40). Deut. 15 has an echo of this in v. 18, in which the six-year service of the impoverished person is put in relation to that of a hired labourer (see 'Notes on the text' for the translation of the phrase), and he becomes a 'slave' (or 'bondman') only by his choice and after the ceremony of ear-piercing. The structure of the law remains different from that of Lev. 25, yet they share a concept of service that is not 'slavery', based in the status of Israelites as 'brothers' (Lev. 25:47). It is exaggerated to say that Deuteronomy polemizes against Lev. 25:39–46 by reapplying the possibility of perpetual slavery from foreigners to Israelites (Japhet 1986: 87–88). (See also 'Form and structure'.)

The final exhortation to the owner has another echo of the Exodus: Pharaoh several times 'hardened his heart' against releasing Israel, but it must not 'seem hard' to the owner to release the slave (18). While the Exodus narrative shares with the deuteronomic law the verb *šālaḥ*, 'send away', the usual verb for 'hardening' in Exodus is *ḥāzaq* (Exod. 7:13, 22; 8:15; 9:35; cf. 7:14, 16; etc.), not *qāšâ* as here. However, one text, Exod. 13:15, makes a link between the 'hardening' (in this instance *qāšâ*), the 'sending away', and the Israelite sacrifice of firstlings. Not only is this echoed in Deut. 15:18, but it is also suggestive as a cue for the next law in our section, on the sacrifice of firstlings (19–23).

15:19–23

The firstlings law follows the same structure as the other laws of sacrifice and offering hitherto, namely a basic command to make the offering and then to eat it at the chosen place, and finally an instruction governing some special cases (cf. 12:6, 7, 15–27; 14:22–27; Morrow 1995: 126).

As with other deuteronomic laws, this law can be understood only in its context, and is closely connected with the laws of release in 15:1–18. The command to 'do no work with the firstborn ox' recalls not only the Sabbath law (5:14), but also the vocabulary of service/slavery in 15:12–18. (The connection with slavery is also established by reference to Lev. 25:39, where the same expression [*lōʾ taʿăbōd bᵉ*] is used to prohibit the making of true slaves; McConville 1984: 95–96.) Firstlings are seen as representing the blessing of flock and herd, and therefore their status as gifts to the altar is passed over. The extension of the celebration of the feast to all Israel is a bold assertion that all Israel is holy (as in the case of the tithe, where the essential issue is the same).

There are also parallels between the firstlings law and the laws of release. For example, there is a similarity between the terms for 'press', or 'exact' (15:3) and 'shear' (15:19), and these form a catchword link between the passages (McConville 1984: 96). The common thought is that Israelites should not be tempted to keep or grasp for themselves something they might regard as their own, but rather to be ready to give it, in the first instance, to the hard-pressed fellow Israelite, and in the second to God (Morrow 1995: 127, though see also p. 122). Structurally, too, the law follows suitably on the laws of release, picturing all Israelites as free people participating in the feasting and rejoicing that express their character as Yahweh's holy people.

19. The requirement to offer firstlings is expressed in several Pentateuchal laws (cf. Exod. 13:2, 11–16; 22:30[29]; Num. 18:15–18). The principle underlying it is that every firstborn creature, including the human (Exod. 13:2), belongs in a special way to Yahweh. Human firstborn were 'redeemed' by the substitution of an animal sacrifice, as were domesticated animals that were not suitable for sacrifice (Exod. 13:13). Exod. 22:30[29] specifies that the requirement refers to male offspring only, and must be fulfilled on the eighth day after birth.

The 'consecrating' of the firstborn meant in practice that it must be either sacrificed or redeemed, as it belonged, in cultic terms, to God's holy sphere. The sacrifice, however, is understood in Num. 18:15–18 as one of those that were not entirely consumed on the altar, but of which the flesh could be eaten, in this case by the priests. The confinement of the flesh to the priests meant that it still belonged within God's holy sphere. (The suggestion that the consecration of the firstlings must originally have meant that their sacrifice was a burnt offering is therefore unnecessary; Brin 1994: 185–187.)

Finally, the law in Lev. 27:26–27, which says that firstlings shall not be consecrated (same term as Exod. 13:2; Deut. 15:19), is in the context of property freely given (and therefore consecrated) to Yahweh. It means that one cannot give as a freewill offering that which must be given anyway; it cannot be 'consecrated' because it is already 'holy'. It is therefore not in conflict with the laws in Exodus and Deuteronomy which require the firstlings to be 'consecrated', in the sense of affirming that they are in fact holy to Yahweh (so also Morrow 1995: 123, rightly opposing Weinfeld [1972: 215] on the point).

The basic command in the present law (19a) requires the consecration of the firstborn male of flock and herd, essentially as do the laws in Exodus. Everything else, however, is new and different. The command not to work with the firstling (19b) may assume that the law of Exod. 22:30[29] is not in force or is abrogated, perhaps because, according to Deuteronomy's perspective, in the expanded territory there could not in practice be frequent trips to the chosen place for every consecration sacrifice (Morrow 1995: 127).

20. In fact, the firstlings sacrifice is now to occur only yearly in the context of a great feast there. The eating of the meat of the sacrifice is not confined here to the priests; rather, the people themselves are allowed to participate.

21–23. Deuteronomy is alone, too, in prescribing for the consumption of blemished firstlings. The banning of defective animals from the altar is not unique in itself (cf. 17:1; Lev. 22:22–25). But, outside the present text, exclusions from the general requirement apply only to firstlings of animals that are ritually unclean (Lev. 27:27; Num. 15:16). The permission to consume defective firstlings 'in your cities', finally, provides a parallel with the other cases in which holy things, freed from the altar, can be eaten by 'the ritually unclean and clean alike', subject only to the requirement to dispose of the blood correctly (see on 12:15–16).

Explanation

It is clear from a reading of the prophets that the oppression of the rich by the poor was a problem in Israel just as much as in other parts of the ancient world (Amos 2:6; Mic. 2:8–9; 3:1–4; Is. 5:8; Prov. 22:22). The laws of debt release and slave release aim to eradicate such inequities. Their theological basis is the 'brotherhood' of Israelites in a community that owes its existence to its deliverance by Yahweh from slavery in Egypt. The status of the person temporarily enslaved is maintained by the extension of the term 'brother' to him or her, and by the provision that he or she should return in due course to independence. The principles in the laws cut across all calculation for advantage (cf. Lev. 25:35–38; Cholewinski 1976: 242–243). The affirmation of the full membership of the disadvantaged in the community is a function of the holiness of Israel.

The essence of the laws does not lie in their degree of humanitarianism; that in itself would be hard to establish (cf. CH 117, which releases the debt slave after only three years). The biblical laws do not create an ideal society in some absolute sense. Rather, they are orientated to certain widespread contemporary social/economic structures and bring to bear on them the thinking of the covenant. Even the release of slaves and debts need not be motivated by humanitarian concern, but rather by force of economic necessity; this was true of the proclamations of 'justice' and 'freedom' by the Mesopotamian kings, as it no doubt was also of Zedekiah (Jer. 34). It could indeed be true of certain modern aid packages. Deut. 15 goes far beyond this, setting a precedent, in its theology of the 'brother-hood' of members of the covenant community, for breaking down all barriers and for recognizing that mere humanity brings with it entitle-ments to enjoyment of God's creation in freedom and dignity. The principle of voluntary self-restraint in the matter of gathering personal wealth, with a view of the support of others' independence, is radical, and a sharp challenge to most modern economic thinking.

The 'release' idea, especially the Jubilee, is taken up in both the prophets and the NT. In Is. 58:6 the LORD declares the true 'fast' to be the freeing of the oppressed, using the term found in Deut. 15:12 (*sālaḥ ḥopšî*). But here the idea is extended to all who suffer economic oppression. In Is. 61:1, the 'servant of the LORD' declares that he is sent to 'proclaim liberty' (*dᵉrôr*) to the captives, in a picture of a restored Zion that is known for its righteousness in all the earth, and has eschatological features (61:1–11). Jesus combines these passages in his description of his own ministry in Luke 4:18–19, a passage that sets the tone for Luke's portrayal of Jesus' life in terms of Jubilee and 'release', the 'year of the LORD's favour' (Luke 4:18) recalling the Jubilee itself. Modern interpretation of Luke avoids the extremes of seeing Jesus' words as either a call for an actual Jubilee or a complete spiritualization of it (Seccombe 1983: 44–69). Rather, God's deliverance in its deepest sense is manifested in his healings; healing the blind is a sign of the light that illumines spiritual darkness. Jesus shows a love of justice in the real and everyday, and at the same time proclaims a kingdom with a strong eschatological aspect, a 'freedom' that amounts to a universal restoration of all things.

DEUTERONOMY 16:1–17

Translation

[1]Observe the month of Abib, and keep the Passover to the LORD your God. For it was in the month of Abib that the LORD your God brought you out of Egypt by

night. ²Sacrifice as a Passover offering to the LORD your God sheep and cattle at the place the LORD chooses as a dwelling for his name. ³Do not eat anything leavened with it. For seven days you are to eat unleavened bread with it, 'bread of affliction', because you left Egypt in great haste, so that you remember, as long as you live, the day when you left Egypt. ⁴No yeast must be seen anywhere in your land for seven days; and of the meat that you slaughter on the evening of the first day, nothing is to be left over till the morning.

⁵You must not sacrifice the Passover offering in any of the towns that the LORD your God is giving you. ⁶Rather, sacrifice the Passover offering at the place the LORD your God chooses as a dwelling for his name; do it in the evening, at sunset, the time of your departure from Egypt. ⁷Cook it and eat it at the place the LORD your God chooses; and, in the morning, go back to your tents. ⁸For six days you are to eat unleavened bread; on the seventh there shall be a solemn assembly to the LORD your God; you shall do no work.

⁹Count off seven weeks; begin to count the seven weeks from the time when you first put the sickle to the standing grain. ¹⁰Then keep the feast of Weeks to the LORD your God, offering an appropriate freewill offering which you shall give according to the measure with which the LORD your God has blessed you. ¹¹And rejoice before the LORD your God – you and your son and your daughter, your male and female slave, the Levite who lives in your cities, the resident alien, the orphan and the widow who live among you – at the place the LORD your God chooses to make a dwelling for his name. ¹²Remember that you were slaves in Egypt, and be careful to keep these laws.

¹³Keep the feast of Booths for seven days after you have brought in the produce from your threshing-floors and winepresses. ¹⁴And rejoice in your feast, together with your son and your daughter, your male and female slave, the Levite, and the resident alien, the orphan and the widow who live in your cities. ¹⁵For seven days you are to keep the feast to the LORD your God at the place the LORD chooses. When the LORD your God blesses you in all your produce and all your work, you will surely be joyful.

¹⁶Three times a year all your males are to appear in the presence of the LORD your God at the place he will choose: at the feast of Unleavened Bread, the feast of Weeks and the feast of Booths; and they must not appear before the LORD empty-handed, ¹⁷but each with a gift corresponding to the blessing the LORD your God has given him.

Notes on the text

2. 'as a Passover offering': this translation takes 'sheep and cattle' to be the object of 'sacrifice' and *pesaḥ* as a complement (with Morrow 1995: 129). *pesaḥ* could equally be taken as the direct object, with 'sheep and cattle' as a second object ('sacrifice the Passover, sheep and cattle'). *pesaḥ* is translated here 'Passover offering', not 'the feast of Passover' as in v. 1, for contextual reasons.

5. 'in any of your towns': this is an occasion when 'one' has to be translated 'any'; cf. 'Notes on the text' on 12:14.

6. 'the time of your departure from Egypt': the term translated 'time' (*mô'ēd*) has the sense of 'appointed time', 'agreed time'. In Exod. 13:10; 23:15 it refers to the date of the Passover, hence NIV's rendering of the present passage as 'on the anniversary of your departure'. The immediate context makes possible a reference to the time of the day, however, taking 'the time' in apposition to the preceding phrase. The evening time is also part of the prescribed timing of the Passover (Exod. 12:8; Lev. 23:5).

10. 'the feast of Weeks': strictly '*a* feast of Weeks', since *šābû'ōt* is undetermined; however, the reference is to an established event, and therefore the definite article is justified in translation.

'an appropriate freewill offering': the word *missat* is a *hapax legomenon*, apparently meaning 'sufficiency'. There is no need to emend the text. The 'appropriateness' of the offering is linked by the second half of the line ('which you shall give ... ') to the abundance of the harvest (10b).

15. 'When the LORD your God blesses you ... ': for this understanding of *kî* + impf. + *weqatal* cf. 13:12–14[13–15].

16. 'appear in the presence of the LORD': this takes the verb 'see' (twice in the verse) as niphal, with MT. The phrase following, then, '*et p*ᵉ*nê yhwh*, is an 'adverbial accusative', hence 'in the presence of the LORD'. Many believe it is preferable to follow K and read the verb as qal, the following phrase being a simple accusative, hence 'to see the face of the LORD' (Morrow 1995: 160). The strongest support for this is Gen. 33:10, where the phrase 'like seeing the face of God' is very similar to the phrase here, and must be read as a qal + direct object. The possible theological motivation for pointing the consonantal text as niphal is obvious, especially in view of such texts as Deut. 4:12. However, the niphal reading is ancient, underlying LXX, and it is not certain that MT is wrong. Cf. also Exod. 23:15; 34:20; Ps. 42:2[3].

17. The line has no verb of its own, but runs on from 'they must not appear' in v. 16.

'with a gift corresponding to the blessing': the phrase consists of two parts, each beginning with *k*ᵉ, 'like', therefore lit. 'as his gift so the blessing'.

Form and structure

Deut. 16:1–17 contains Deuteronomy's laws governing the three main feasts of Israel: namely Passover-Unleavened Bread, early harvest (or Weeks, or Pentecost) and late harvest (or Ingathering, or Booths). The command to keep three annual feasts appears in three other places: Exod. 23:14–18; 34:18–26; Lev. 23; cf. Num. 28–29. In addition, the narrative of the institution of Passover-Unleavened Bread (Hebr. *maṣṣôt*) is found in

Exod. 12 – 13. A number of important elements are well established across these texts: the attendance of all adult Israelite males at the three feasts; the close relationship between Passover and Unleavened Bread; the timing of Passover-Unleavened Bread in the month of Abib, or the 'first month' (Lev. 23:5); the seven-day duration of Unleavened Bread; the association of Unleavened Bread with the exodus from Egypt; the command not to appear before the LORD 'empty-handed'; and the command to consume the meat of the Passover sacrifice entirely, leaving none till the morning. There are links, too, with the theme of Sabbath, for example in Exod. 23:10–13; 34:21, but most pronounced in Lev. 23, which casts the laws on feasts in a calendar that includes the weekly Sabbath (23:3) and the Day of Atonement (23:26–32), and specifies a number of 'holy convocations' (e.g. 23:7, 27–28), which are like Sabbaths in that no work is to be done on them.

Deut. 16:1–17 has all of these elements in some form, though it lacks the detailed specifications of Lev. 23. The connection with the 'Sabbath' appears explicitly in v. 8, and implicitly in the fact that the term 'seven(th)' occurs seven times in 16:1–17 (cf. Braulik 1997b: 63–79). It also shares with Exod. 12:11 the rationale for the Passover celebration that Israel came out of Egypt 'in haste'.

In addition to these elements shared with the wider tradition, however, the present passage also has features that are characteristically deuteronomic: the themes of rejoicing before Yahweh and the inclusion of slaves and the other vulnerable classes (11, 14); the memory of Israel's own slavery in Egypt (12); and the explicit location of the feasts at the 'chosen place' (6, 11, 15, 16), which makes a surprising contrast with the provisions elsewhere that Passover should be kept in the homes of Israel (Exod. 12:46; see 'Comment').

The differences between Deut. 16:1–17 and the other related texts are often explained in terms of the development of Israel's religious history. Deuteronomy is thought to have been the first to combine Passover and Unleavened Bread, which many think were originally distinct festivals, partly because Passover is not named in Exod. 23:14–18.

However, it is impossible to trace separate origins of the two celebrations. It has been proposed that Unleavened Bread was originally a Canaanite agricultural festival. But there is no evidence that it was ever anything other than a feast commemorating the exodus from Egypt, since it is regarded in this way in the text generally held to be the earliest (Exod. 23:15; so, rightly, Mayes 1979: 255). Nor is it convincing to argue that Deuteronomy combines the two in the context of Josiah's centralization of worship (against Mayes [1979: 256], though in fact he thinks the combination was a restoration of an older unity of the two).

There are signs that Passover-Unleavened Bread was already known as a combined celebration in Exodus, because of 34:25, which evidently glosses 23:18, and specifies the 'feast' in that place, too, as the Passover (here against Levinson [1997: 69–70] and others, who take Exod. 34:25c to be post-deuteronomic). The likeliest explanation of the form of the laws in Deuteronomy, therefore, is not that it is attempting to make decisive changes in the worship of Israel, but that it brings distinctive emphases to bear on a well-established body of law concerning the feasts. The boldest of these is the assimilation of Passover to the concept that all sacrificial worship happens at the chosen place.

In these laws, Deuteronomy interacts somewhat freely with the body of material that is available to it, here as elsewhere. (For this reason, Levinson [1997: 53–97] finds in them a clear example of Deuteronomy's radical transformation of previous practice. Levinson shows clearly that Deuteronomy systematically redeploys terms and phrases from older laws in order to create something quite new. In my response to his thesis [McConville 2000c], I differ with him on the occasion and orientation of the book's stance.)

The form of the laws conforms to patterns we have observed in other laws. Indeed, they bring to a culmination the cycle of laws on worship that began in ch. 12, and particularly the group of laws in 14:22 – 16:17, which share an interest in the structure of Israel's time (see again 'Form and structure' on ch. 14). The annual feasts connect with the 'year by year' of 14:22; 15:20, as well as focusing on the weekly sabbatical rhythm. The purpose of the formulation of the laws here, however, has supremely to do with the characterization of Israel as the holy people liberated to worship Yahweh, as we shall see. (The special features of the laws, including the location of the feasts at the 'chosen place', are commented on further below; see also McConville 1984: 112; 2000c.)

Comment

16:1–8

1. The opening, 'Observe the month of Abib', reminds readers of the Fourth Commandment ('Observe the Sabbath day', 5:12), and also the law about the feast of Unleavened Bread in Exod. 23:15; 34:18. (The month Abib [March–April], the first month in the ancient Hebrew calendar [cf. Exod. 12:2], is called after the 'new ripe corn' of that season. It was later called by the Babylonian name Nisan; Neh. 2:1; Est. 3:7.) The opening phrase, which seems imprecise and even odd, is best understood as presupposing the fuller command in Exod. 23:15: 'You shall observe the feast of Unleavened Bread at the appointed time in the month of Abib.' And, indeed, behind both texts lies an assumption of knowledge of the timing of events; the calendar for the month is most fully spelt out in Lev. 23:4–8 (cf. Exod. 12:1–6).

Here, what is said in the Exodus texts of Unleavened Bread is applied directly to Passover. This is the first strong indication that Deuteronomy will speak of Passover-Unleavened Bread as a single entity, whereas the texts ascribed to P (Exod. 12:1–20; Lev. 23:5–6) distinguish clearly between the one day (or night) of Passover, the fourteenth of Abib, and the seven days following (fifteenth to twenty-first), on which no leaven is to be eaten. (There too, however, the Passover itself is to be eaten without leavened bread; Exod. 12:8.) But we are familiar by now with Deuteronomy's readiness to subordinate the detail to its dominant argument. (It is misleading, incidentally, to translate 'month' as 'New Moon' here, as is sometimes done [Levinson 1997: 68 n. 51], though the word can mean this; cf. Ps. 81:3[4].) The phrase 'by night' is not in Exod. 23:15; 34:18, but comes from the narrative of the institution of the Passover (Exod. 12:6, 12; cf. 12:30–31).

2. The Passover is to be 'sacrificed', following the terminology of Exod. 12:27; 35:25, though other texts have the more neutral 'slaughter' (Exod. 12:6, 21). The sacrifice is to be made from the flock and the herd and held at the 'chosen place' (2; on this formula, see on 12:5). Strictly, the Passover sacrifice is of a lamb (Exod. 12:3, 21, thus in both P and JE). Deuteronomy uses less prescriptive terms, allowing larger cattle to be used either for the Passover sacrifice itself or for the feast more generally. The change is motivated by the regular pairing in Deuteronomy of flock and herd as symbols of Yahweh's blessing in the context of sacrificial worship (17:13; 12:17, 21; 14:23), and its (consequent) relative lack of concern for exactitude in those matters. The terms used may also be suggested by a consideration of other sacrifices that would accompany the Passover proper (cf. the sacrifices in Num. 28:19; 2 Chr. 30:15, 24!).

The location of the combined feast at the 'chosen place' is consistent with Deuteronomy's concept, which locates all of Israel's worship 'before the LORD' and at his instigation. It is often held that Deuteronomy overrides the family character of Passover in the interests of its alleged centralizing ideology. It is true that the institution of Passover has a family setting, derived from the logic of its origin in Israelite homes in Egypt (Exod. 12:1 – 13:10), and indeed it is conceived as being celebrated in homes on all future occasions (Exod. 12:21–24). However, all texts concerning its celebration assume that it belongs to the whole community of Israel as such (Exod. 12:6, 47), and many texts envisage sacrifices at the sanctuary in connection with it (Lev. 23:4–8; Num. 28:16–25; cf. 2 Kgs. 23:21–23; Ezra 6:19–22; 2 Chr. 30; 35; Luke 2:41; and the Jewish tractate *Pesachim* 5:5–7).

The aspect of the family and the home, still visible in the private nature of the Gospels' Last Supper, is somewhat overshadowed in Deuteronomy by its stress on the setting at the sanctuary (but see on v. 7, and, for fuller argument on the point, McConville 1984: 107–110). It is not clear how the command to commemorate the first Passover by daubing blood on the lintels of the home 'as a perpetual ordinance' (Exod. 12:23–24) was put into practice in Israel. There is no reference to it in any of the laws or narratives other than the foundational narrative in Exod. 12 – 13.

3–4. Verses 3–4a elaborate the seven-day abstention from anything leavened, fundamental to the feast of Unleavened Bread, together with the rationale for it in Israel's hasty departure from Egypt (already in Exod. 23:15). Here too, however, the fusion of Passover and Unleavened Bread is clear. The command not to eat anything leavened 'with it', that is, with the Passover (3a; cf. Exod. 12:8b), is run together with the prohibition of leavened bread in the seven days following as well (3b–4a). The link between the eating of unleavened bread and the haste of the departure is found in direct connection with both the Passover meal (Exod. 12:11) and the eating of unleavened bread (Exod. 12:39). The term used here is from the former context, but is now subordinated to the seven-day prohibition. Finally, a Passover element returns in v. 4b (cf. Exod. 12:10; 23:18; 34:25).

The arena within which leaven is banned is the whole territory of Israel (4; cf. Exod. 13:7). This suggests that the true arena of the feast is the whole land. In practical terms this means that those who are not at the sanctuary (women and children, in view of v. 16a) are also considered to be participating in the feast and are bound by its rules. The prohibition of eating anything leavened applies explicitly to homes throughout the land in other texts (Exod. 12:15, 19–20). It also applies to the participants in the central feast when they return to their 'tents' (7) on the day after the Passover proper (see below). In this way, the concept of the pilgrimage feast (*ḥag̱*) is transformed, since it is not celebrated wholly at the sanctuary.

5–6. Verses 5–8 expand the command to eat the Passover at the chosen place. Verse 5 makes the usual deuteronomic contrast between the cities and the chosen place (cf. 12:15; 14:28), and between what must be done at the latter and what must be done in the localities (cf. 7–8). The location of Passover at the chosen place allows it to become part of the expression of Israel's true character through communal worship before Yahweh. (On the relation of this command to Exod. 12:7, 22, 46, which locate the sacrifice and the meal in houses throughout the land, see 'Explanation' for comment.) The place datum is matched by a time datum: 'in the evening, at sunset, the time of your departure from Egypt'. The last phrase is sometimes taken as a reference to the day of the month (NIV). On balance it probably refers to the time of the day, in keeping with v. 1; the evening is the set time for the Passover meal (Exod. 12:8; Lev. 23:5; and see 'Notes on the text').

7. The 'cooking' of the Passover sacrifice is often contrasted with the 'roasting' prescribed in Exod. 12:9, which also prohibits 'boiling', the same term actually used here. The translation 'cook', however, is due to the capacity of the verb to refer generally to food preparation (McConville 1984: 117–118). Levinson (1997: 73) opposes this. His criticism of the

view taken here, however, pays no attention to the respective contexts of
Exod. 12:9 and the present text.

The people are now commanded to return to their 'tents'. The word
'tents', applied to the people's homes, is infrequent in Deuteronomy, and
elsewhere refers to their temporary dwellings in the desert (1:27; 5:30;
11:6). Otherwise, even in the present context (5), Deuteronomy speaks of
the people's 'gates', or cities, and their 'houses' (6:11; 7:26; 21:12; etc.).
The command here is an echo of 5:30, in which they are also told to return
to their tents, immediately after the appearance of Yahweh on Mt Horeb
and the giving of the Ten Commandments. We have noticed before a
certain correspondence between Mt Horeb and the chosen place (cf. on
Deut. 12). Here the counterpoint in Deut. 5 between the place of worship
(Horeb) and the Israelites' desert dwellings finds a correspondence in
relation to the regular worship in the land, now between the chosen place
and the people's homes in the land. In each case the implication is that,
though the people retreat from the place of direct encounter with Yahweh,
they remain in touch with it, symbolically gathered around it in spite of
physical distance (cf. Braulik 1986a: 118).

It is difficult to decide whether the reference to 'tents' implies temporary
dwellings that the people brought for the duration of the feast, or their
actual homes (though I formerly took it as the first of these; McConville
1984: 109–110). The symbolism of v. 7b is effective in either case (cf.
Morrow 1995: 144–145). The extension of the feast into the whole land,
implied in v. 4a, is the main point of this command.

8. The 'sabbatical' overtones of the law of Passover-Unleavened Bread
come out strongly in v. 8, where the 'six days' have been said to be in
contradiction with the seven in v. 3 (Mayes 1979: 254). However, the
seven-day picture is consistent throughout the passage, the six-plus-one
pattern in v. 8 being made to correspond to the structure of the week, in
which six days of work are followed by a Sabbath of rest. The question
remains how the seven days of Deut. 16:1–8 relate to the eight required by
the more detailed laws (Lev. 23:4–8). In fact, vv. 7b–8 may hint at a
known eight-day structure, the six-plus-one in v. 8 following on 'the next
morning' in v. 7b. In that case, the preference for a seven-day concept can
be explained only in terms of the motivation of the author to cast the law
within a sabbatical structure (see also 'Form and structure'). Verse 8
corresponds to v. 1, whose terms echoed the Sabbath command, and thus
the law is framed by the concept of Sabbath.

The last day of the celebration is called a 'solemn assembly', as in Exod.
12:16 (where the first of the seven days is also characterized in this way; cf.
the 'holy convocation' in Lev. 23:8; the term 'solemn assembly' occurs in
Lev. 23:36 and Num. 29:35 in connection with the feast of Booths). The
meaning is that no work must be done on that day. In the latter texts, the
solemn assembly is located in the tabernacle, since it is to be marked by
sacrifices. Other texts, too, show that a 'solemn assembly' was held at a

central place of worship (Joel 1:14; 2:15–17; 2 Kgs. 10:20–21). The present text makes the location of the assembly ambiguous, following the instruction to 'go back to your tents' in v. 7. The ambiguity belongs to Deuteronomy's deliberate merging of Passover and Unleavened Bread, and its confusion of the boundaries between the celebrations at the chosen place and throughout the land.

16:9–12

The feast of Weeks is known in the earliest code as the feast of Harvest (Exod. 23:16a), but it is most commonly named as here (Exod. 34:22; Num. 28:26). In all the codes (except Deuteronomy itself) it is expressly associated with the 'firstfruits' of the barley harvest, somewhat generally in Exod. 23:16a; 34:22a; Num. 28:26, but spelt out in detail in Lev. 23:9–21. The last-named passage specifies an offering of a sheaf of the first mature grain (Lev. 23:10–11), then seven weeks to allow for its full ripening and harvesting, which is followed by the celebration of harvest itself in the early summer (Lev. 23:15–21).

Deuteronomy specifies more than the codes in Exodus, stipulating the seven-week lapse between the harvesting of the first ripe grain and the celebration of the completed harvest; thus presupposing a system of reckoning like that in Leviticus. Instead of cataloguing in detail the offerings due at the feast (as Leviticus does), Deuteronomy requires a 'freewill offering' in proportion to the amount harvested, and thus articulates once more its theology of grateful response to Yahweh's blessing (10; and see 'Notes on the text'). The feast is depicted, like the other great religious occasions in Deuteronomy, as a joyful celebration by the whole people without distinction at the chosen place (11; cf. 12:7, 12; 14:26–27). Only here is the feast expressly made a memorial of the deliverance from Egypt (12).

16:13–15

The feast of Booths is called the feast of Ingathering in the earlier codes (Exod. 23:16b; 34:22b). It marks the gathering in of all the produce that ripens during the summer months, such as grapes, dates and olives, and is thus in an agricultural sense 'the end of the year' (Exod. 23:16b). The precise timing is spelt out in Lev. 23:33–36, as beginning on the 'fifteenth day of the seventh month', soon after the Day of Atonement (26–32).

Deuteronomy is again more succinct. Its terminology ('Booths') corresponds to Lev. 23, as does the seven-day duration of the feast (not yet in the older codes), at the holy place, during which the people lived in 'booths' or tents (Lev. 23:42). Here, too, Deuteronomy presupposes a timetable, but focuses on its typical concerns: rejoicing; the whole people; the response to Yahweh's blessing in joyful celebration together at the chosen place. The feast of Booths was apparently in itself joyful above all other events, and elsewhere, too, associated with the deliverance from Egypt (Lev. 23:40, 43; Ps. 81:5[6]). It is referred to a number of times in the OT simply as 'the feast', suggesting it was felt to be the most important of the three annual pilgrimage festivals (e.g. 1 Kgs. 12:32; 2 Kgs. 8:2, 65; Ps. 81:3[4]). In Deut. 31:9–13 it is this feast that is singled out for the solemn seven-yearly reading of the book of the law.

16:16–17

This summarizing passage mainly restates the well-known requirement of three annual pilgrimages at which offerings were expected (Exod. 23:14–15; 34:20, 23), with the deuteronomic tailpiece requiring proportionality between blessing and gift. (See 'Notes on the text' for comment on 'appear in the presence of Yahweh'.) The need to appear 'not ... empty-handed' echoes in this context Deut. 15:13, recalling that the released slave has both the right and the obligation to participate in this feast.

It is surprising that the law now specifies that only males shall go to the chosen place, in view of vv. 11, 14, as well as 12:12, 18 and similar texts, and indeed 15:12, 17, which had established the equal right of the Israelite woman to share in the economic and religious life of Israel (see on those texts). It is also surprising to find the first of the feasts called simply 'the feast of Unleavened Bread', in view of the careful re-presentation of it as of a piece with Passover in vv. 1–8. It is probably best to think of the terms here as a citation of earlier law, even though the practice has been reconceived by the developments hitherto in the present chapter, in which, chiefly, Passover and Unleavened Bread have been presented as a single entity. The marriage of these, and the citation here, assert that Passover is one of the pilgrimage feasts of Israel, and also reinforce the fact that Unleavened Bread is essentially a celebration of the deliverance from Egypt.

Explanation

Deuteronomy's laws on the feasts of Israel exemplify both its respect for existing legislation and a certain readiness to interpret and apply it in new ways. The fusion of Passover and Unleavened Bread is not entirely new in Deuteronomy. However, it has carefully woven together elements of existing laws and traditions on the separate institutions into a seamless whole. The result is to conceive the double feast as occurring both at the chosen place, the scene of all Israel's worship involving sacrifice in

Deuteronomy, and throughout the land (Exod. 12:46). This is quite a different conception from other Passover laws, which think of the celebration as taking place in homes throughout the land, while maintaining its all-Israel character (Exod. 12:47), and even requiring sacrifices at the sanctuary in connection with it (Lev. 23:8; Num. 28:16–25). Deuteronomy has achieved the needed balance between the family character of Passover and its status as a feast of Israel by means of its fusion with Unleavened Bread. The all-Israel nature of the feast is here asserted in typical Deuteronomic fashion by locating it at the chosen place, while the decentralized aspect of it is mediated by the eating of unleavened bread throughout the territory (4), and by the rather elusive dismissal 'to your tents' on the day after the Passover feast (7).

The concept of Israel assembled together before Yahweh at the chosen place as the highest expression of its status as his holy people is thus maintained, even though Passover itself had the strongest possible association with the home in its origins and in other requirements concerning its celebration. Here more than anywhere else, Deuteronomy has had to interact carefully and creatively with law and tradition in order to maintain its vision. Its answer is to create a fusion between the act at the sanctuary on the first day and the act throughout the land on the following six. This whole nexus is, then, only in retrospect (16), designated *ḥag*, or 'pilgrimage feast', giving a new twist to that concept. (For the view that the present law makes Passover as such a *ḥag*, see Levinson 1997: 93–94, and my response in McConville 2000c.)

The distinctiveness of Deuteronomy's presentation of Passover is ultimately governed by the pre-eminent place it gives to the divine act in the exodus from Egypt as the decisive event in Israel's existence. The concept of Israel rejoicing together 'before Yahweh' is the supreme expression of its chosenness as Yahweh's people, and the culmination of the deliverance from Egypt. This is the theological motive for bringing together Passover and chosen place. The same dominant force of the exodus idea is visible in the other feasts; while the connection is made elsewhere regarding the feast of Booths, it is new in Deuteronomy in relation to the feast of Weeks. The structure of the laws to this point in the book (chs. 12 – 16) also helps make the point that all Israel, without qualification, participates in the celebrations of its holy status.

The connection between Passover and God's deliverance of his people is maintained in the NT. The events of Holy Week, the crucifixion and resurrection of Jesus, occur against the background of the feast of Passover (John 13:1). His Last Supper is itself a Passover meal, with the bread and wine of the feast reinterpreted as his body and blood, symbolizing the deliverance that would be brought about by his own sacrifice, as the Paschal lamb. The connection is made, for example, in John 19:36 (cf. Exod. 12:46). John's Gospel significantly calls the old feast the 'Passover of the Jews' (John 11:55), suggesting that the 'Passover' for Christians is now something quite different. The imagery of Passover-Unleavened Bread is adopted by Paul in 1 Cor. 5:7–8, where the unleavened bread is recast as 'sincerity and truth', and the holy people of God 'celebrate[s] the feast' in the light of Christ's sacrifice (note the idea of the people assembled in the presence of Christ through God's spirit in v. 5).

DEUTERONOMY 16:18 – 18:22

Translation

[18]Appoint judges and officers [officials] in all the cities the LORD your God is about to give you, according to your tribes; and let them judge the people justly. [19]Do not pervert justice, or show favouritism or accept a bribe; for a bribe makes the wise blind, and subverts the cause of the innocent. [20]You must rigorously pursue justice, so that you may have life, and possess the land the LORD is about to give you.
[21]Do not set up an Asherah pole, made of any kind of wood, beside the altar of the LORD your God which you shall make for yourselves. [22]And do not erect a sacred pillar; for the LORD your God hates these things.
[17:1]You must not sacrifice to the LORD your God an ox or a sheep that has a blemish, or anything wrong with it at all; for that would be abhorrent to the LORD your God. [2]If there should be found among you, in any of the cities the LORD your God is about to give you, any man or woman who does evil in the eyes of the LORD your God, and breaks his covenant [3]by going and worshipping other gods – the sun or the moon or the stars in the sky – which I forbade you to do, [4]when you hear the report of this, you are to make careful enquiries. If the report is true, and this abhorrent thing has been done in Israel, [5]you are to lead out to the city gates the man or woman who has done this vile thing, and stone him or her to death. [6]The death sentence may be passed on the evidence of two or three witnesses; no-one may be put to death on the evidence of a single witness. [7]The witnesses themselves must strike the first blow in carrying out the sentence; then the rest of the people shall follow. So you shall purge the evil from among you.
[8]If a matter arises for judgment, and it proves too difficult for you to decide, that is, whether it is one kind of homicide or another, or one kind of plea or another, or one kind of assault or another, matters of dispute in your city courts; and you go up to the place the LORD your God will choose, [9]and come before the Levitical priests, and the judge who is in office at the time; and you enquire of them, and they declare to you the decision in the case, [10]you must follow carefully the ruling that they give from the place the LORD will choose, and be sure to put into effect all that they instruct you to do. [11]Act exactly in accordance with the law as they explain it to you, and the decision they give you; do not depart from it in any way. [12]Should anyone be presumptuous enough not to listen to the priest who serves the LORD your God there, or the judge, he must die; so you shall root out evil from Israel. [13]And let all the people hear about this with fear, so that they do not act presumptuously again.

¹⁴When you have come into the land the LORD your God is giving you, and you have occupied it and settled in it, and you say, 'Let us appoint a king over us, like all the nations around us', ¹⁵then you may indeed set over you a king whom the LORD your God chooses. You may appoint a king from among your fellow Israelites, not a foreigner, who is not your brother. ¹⁶However, he must not gather many horses for himself, or take the people back to Egypt in order to gather horses; for the LORD your God has told you that you must not go back on that road again. ¹⁷Nor may he accumulate wives, for then he would be led astray; and he must not amass silver and gold. ¹⁸Rather, when he is enthroned in his kingdom, he must write for himself in a book a copy of this law that is kept by the Levitical priests. ¹⁹He shall have it beside him, and read from it all his life, in order to learn to revere the LORD his God by keeping all the requirements of this body of law, and putting these statutes into effect. ²⁰This is so that he might not lord it over his fellow Israelites, or turn away from these commands in any way; rather, by keeping them, he will ensure that he and his descendants will reign long in Israel.

^{18:1}The Levitical priests, the whole tribe of Levi, are not to have a territorial share or inheritance with Israel. The offerings by fire to the LORD are their inheritance; these they shall eat. ²They are not to have a territorial inheritance among their fellow Israelites; the LORD is their inheritance, just as he promised them. ³This shall be the priests' due from the people: when anyone sacrifices an ox or a sheep, they must give the priest the shoulder, the jaws and the stomach. ⁴You shall also give him the first of your grain, wine and oil, and the first fleece when you shear your sheep. ⁵For the LORD your God has chosen him from all your tribes, together with his descendants for ever, to stand and minister in the LORD's name. ⁶When, then, a Levite comes from one of your cities in any part of Israel, where he is resident, and comes at his own wish to the place the LORD will choose, ⁷and ministers in the name of the LORD his God like all his fellow Levites who stand and serve the LORD there, ⁸he shall have his due share to eat, besides what he may receive by trade with family property.

⁹When you have come to the land the LORD your God is giving you, you must not learn to follow the abhorrent practices of those nations. ¹⁰Let no-one be found among you who makes his son or daughter pass through fire, or who practises divination or soothsaying, or who looks for omens or practises sorcery, ¹¹or anyone who casts spells or enquires of a ghost or a familiar spirit, or who seeks oracles from the dead. ¹²For anyone who does these things is abhorrent to the LORD, and it is because of such abhorrent things that the LORD your God is dispossessing them in favour of you. ¹³You are to be undivided in your allegiance to the LORD your God. ¹⁴These nations that you are dispossessing listen to soothsayers and diviners; but the LORD your God has not given to you to do this.

¹⁵Instead, the LORD your God will raise up from among your brothers a prophet like me; you must listen to him. ¹⁶This is in answer to your request of the LORD your God at Horeb on the day you were assembled there, when you asked to hear the voice of the LORD your God no longer, and to see that great fire no longer, lest you die. ¹⁷The LORD said to me, 'What they have said is good. ¹⁸I will raise up for them a prophet like you among their brothers, and put my words in his mouth, and

he will convey to them whatever I command him. [19]And anyone who does not listen to my words, spoken by the prophet in my name, I will personally call to account. [20]But if a prophet presumes to utter a word in my name when I have not commanded him to do so, or speaks in the name of other gods, he shall die.' [21]And in case you are uncertain how to know when an utterance is not from the LORD, [22]when a prophet speaks in the name of the LORD and what he says is not fulfilled and does not come about, then it is not a word that the LORD has spoken. The prophet has uttered it presumptuously; you need have no fear of him.

Notes on the text

16:21. *lō' titta' 'ªšērâ*, 'set up an Asherah pole': the verb is most often 'plant'. But see below, 'Comment'.

17:5. The second occurrence of 'the man or the woman' is absent from LXX, Vg. It may have been repeated by error in MT.

8. 'whether it is one kind of homicide or another', lit. 'between blood and blood': for the interpretation see Levinson 1997: 128.

18. Hebr. *'et mišnēh-hattôrâ hazzō't*, 'the (a) copy of this law', is mistranslated in LXX as *to deuteronomion touto*, 'this second law' (see Introduction).

19. 'his God'; a few MSS and some forms of the Greek OT have 'thy God'. This is likely to reflect harmonization to the more dominant expression in Deuteronomy.

18:1. MT has 'they shall eat the LORD's offerings by fire *and his inheritance*' (*wᵉnahªlātô*). S. R. Driver (1895: 214) takes 'his' to refer to Yahweh, rather than to Israel, which seems required because of the 'and'. The 'inheritance' then refers to 'other sacred dues' not covered by the fire offerings. However, it is unlikely that these should be referred to as Yahweh's 'inheritance', since the idea is not paralleled in this sense (contrast Deut. 4:20, where Yahweh's 'inheritance' is the people of Israel). LXX translates 'their [the priests'] inheritance', presupposing a text that has no 'and', and the Hebr. *nahªlātām*). This is the basis of my translation, which also produces a good balance in the line ('they shall have no [land] inheritance ... the offerings are their inheritance').

15. Lit. 'from your midst, from among your brothers'. LXX and SamP have 'from the midst of your brothers', as v. 18, and cf. 17:15. MT should perhaps be retained as *lectio difficilior* (the more difficult reading).

Form and structure

The next section of Deuteronomy may be regarded as a separate unit because of its subject-matter. This is the case even though there is no very definite structural marker at 16:18. The next familiar introductory formula comes at 17:14, which is in the middle of the section I have marked off, with a further one at 18:9. Here, the discourse runs on from the regulations on the feasts, with a direct instruction that has no introduction of its own. It is linked, by way of the vocabulary of 'gift', to the preceding section (see 'Comment').

Nevertheless, there now comes a sequence of laws and commands that are united by a concern with the political and religious organization of Israel. An opening paragraph (16:18–20) lays down a general principle, and provides for the establishment of a judicial system. This is followed by two laws about sacrifice (16:21 – 17:1; see 'Comment' on their placement here). The judicial theme is developed in 17:2–13, with procedures surrounding testimony and referral to a higher legal authority, involving both judges and priests. Provision is then made for the appointment of a king (17:14–20), and for the livelihood of priests (18:1–8). And the section is rounded off with instructions about the place of the prophet in the religious and political spectrum (18:9–22). The laws about the king and the prophet are headed by introductory formulas recalling the gift of the land (17:14; 18:9).

The laws in question may be described as a constitution for Israel (cf. Halpern 1981b: 226–233; Rütersword̈en 1987: 89–90). While there is some justice in this, it must be said that there is no evidence of these laws' separate existence before or apart from their incorporation into Deuteronomy, as is clear from the fact that they are not marked off structurally as a separate unit. The introductions in 17:14 and 18:9 show that the section has been adapted to the larger context of the book as a whole. Yet the separate existence of the laws, and even their pre-deuteronomic grouping as a body of laws governing aspects of the constitution of Israel, cannot be ruled out. While the collection of laws in this section can hardly be seen as a complete constitution, for reasons that we shall note, it was extraordinary and radical in the ancient world, and has also had a powerful effect on the modern one.

Deut. 16:18 – 17:13 concerns the appointment of officials for the process of law in Israel. Other Pentateuchal passages presuppose the existence of judicial procedures but do not specify them (Exod. 21:1–3, 6–8; Lev. 19:15). The passage recalls Deut. 1:9–18, in which Moses prescribed a judicial organization in order to relieve his own heavy burden of leadership. The prominence of that passage in Deuteronomy shows the importance of the present theme in the book. And it seems that the provision for a judicial system in the land is seen as a continuation of the arrangement first conceived in relation to Moses.

There are important similarities between the two passages. The principle of impartial justice is paramount. The people themselves are to choose the officials. The judicial system is organized according to tribes. There is a second level of authority, in the former case Moses himself, in the present case a high court sitting at the place of worship. In both cases, while the institutions and processes are entirely human, it is recognized that judgment is ultimately God's, this being reflected in our law in the presence at the place of worship of 'the levitical priests' alongside the judge (17:9; cf. 1:17).

There also important differences between the two passages. The former prescribed a division of the people into units as small as ten, which seemed to have military overtones, or which were suitable, perhaps, to a people on the march. The key terms are 'leader' ($r\bar{o}$'$\check{s}$) and 'commander' ($\acute{s}ar$), though the terms 'judge' and 'official' also feature (1:15–16). The present passage, in contrast, envisages a division according to both tribes and cities (16:18). The terms 'leader' and 'commander' are absent, and the focus is now on 'judges' and 'officials'. The differences between the two passages can be accounted for in terms of their settings in the book. The context of the former is the narrative of the journey into the land, with its echoes of the Israelites' resistance to the hardships of the wilderness, and its anticipation of initial encounters with the peoples of the region. The present text envisages settled existence in cities throughout the land, and is the first law in Deuteronomy (and the only one in the Pentateuch) providing explicitly for a judiciary in the localities.

The provisions here differ from those of Exodus, in which legal processes are said to occur simply 'before the $^{e}l\bar{o}h\hat{\imath}m$, that is, either 'before God', or 'before the judges' (Exod. 21:6; 22:6–14[7–15, EVV]). In Deuteronomy, too, the functions of court and sanctuary overlap at the highest level, but Deuteronomy makes a typical provision for regular life in the locations throughout the land (cf. 12:15–25). A similarity between the requirements here and the reform of King Jehoshaphat (2 Chr. 19) has often been noted (Crüsemann 1996: 83–98); Jehoshaphat appointed judges up and down the land and established a high court in Jerusalem presided over by 'Levites, priests and the heads of families of Israel' (2 Chr. 19:8). He may thus be reinstating an old arrangement (although this is not expressly said).

It is common to argue, in contrast, that these laws governing the judiciary arise out of Josiah's reform, as part of its perceived secularizing tendency (Weinfeld 1972: 233–236; Gertz 1994: 28–97). It is certain, however, that a civil judiciary existed in the cities before Josiah's time (as Weinfeld [1972: 235–236] agrees; cf. Deut. 22:13–19; 25:5–10; Ruth 4; Hos. 7:7; 13:10; Is. 1:26; 3:2; Mic. 7:3; and Reviv 1989: 61–66). And the few references outside Deuteronomy to a judicial role of priests are not inconsistent with the deuteronomic picture (Is. 28:7; Ezek. 44:24; and see S. R. Driver 1895: 207). It is not clear from Deuteronomy, therefore, that the introduction of judges can be traced to an independent Josianic layer. It is rather part of Deuteronomy's general concept; in respect of legal process, it provides for the appointment of a secular judiciary in the cities, while preserving the rights of the priests at the central sanctuary, along with 'the judge' (17:8–13). The new thing in the deuteronomic law is simply the need to provide for a judiciary throughout the land. On the relation of judges to priests and elders see 'Comment' (and on 21:1–9).

The second main paragraph of the section (17:2–7) also recalls Deut. 13, because it shares with it the topic of enquiry about and punishment for idolatry. Ch. 13, however, focuses first on the discernment of false prophecy, and then on the penalty of death, whether for false prophets, or for any who lead astray to idolatry, or indeed for whole cities that have gone over to the worship of other gods. The focus in the present text, however, is on the judicial process, and especially on the responsibility of witnesses. In this way, the sin of idolatry is used as the prime example of what constitutes a crime in Israel. As that topic stands at the beginning of the specific laws of the law code (in ch. 13), so it also has a prominent position in this special section on the judicial process.

17:14–20

The law on the king is one of the most remarkable and important in Deuteronomy. It comes in the sequence of laws about officials in Israel, only after the regulations about the judicial functions of priests and judges (16:18 – 17:13). Its late appearance in the sequence corresponds to the role that is given to the king in Israel's constitution. A king in the ancient world was typically the chief executive in all departments of the life of the nation; here, the appointment of a king is not an absolute requirement, but subject to the demand of the people (17:14). It is the limitations placed on the king (17:16–20) that make the laws on the administration of Israel so radical. The deuteronomic picture of the king contrasts, in fact, not only with kingship as it was exercised in the ANE, but also with the reality of it in ancient Israel. The kings of Israel and Judah assumed rights that are not provided for here.

The fact that the king law does not easily fit with the Israelite practice of kingship has led to quite diverse assessments of its origin. It is dated variously from a time before the rise of the monarchy, to Solomon's time or soon after, to Josiah's reform or similar antecedent reforms, or to the exile. Almost the only point of agreement is that 17:18–19, with its picture of a king studying and keeping Torah, is not part of the original law (Mayes 1979: 273; Zobel 1992: 110).

The case for a setting in Josiah's time rests on the belief that the law is part of the programme for the reform. Weinfeld (1972: 168) thinks that Josiah's scribes produced an ideal constitution in 16:18 – 18:22, with Moses as the implicit ideal king, and Josiah as the actual one, a king who 'reveals a clear anti-Solomonic attitude'. In his view, Deuteronomy supports what he calls 'Royal intervention in matters of religion' (1972: 163). The problem with this is that King Josiah, in his reform (2 Kgs. 22 – 23), acts in a way that is incompatible with the deuteronomic law; that is, he assumes total charge of the affairs of the state, including religion, while Deuteronomy's constitution clearly restricts the king's powers. Further, it is not Moses who is the supreme human authority in Deuteronomy's constitution, but the people.

For this reason, others have argued that no actual king would have tolerated such limitations on his power (Perlitt 1994), and that the law represents idealistic exilic thinking about a constitution after the experiment of the monarchy has failed. However, if the law cannot be Josianic, the alternative to an exilic dating is a much earlier one than Josiah. For Alt (1959), the king law was an important factor in his argument that the home and thought-world of Deuteronomy was close to that of Hosea. Some find its ultimate origins in the law of the tribal league, and think it may have been promulgated in the time of Solomon or soon after (Cross 1973: 221 n., 223; cf. Noth 1966: 28–41). The echoes here of Solomon's wealth, vast stables and harem are unmistakable (17:16b–17; cf. 1 Kgs. 4:26–28; 10:14–29; 11:1–8). But the law is more than a mere reaction against one king; it is part of the whole picture that is built up in these chapters, and that belongs to the earliest pictures in the OT of the struggle to establish the Israelite state.

18:1–8

In the laws to date on the administration of Israel, there have been a number of allusions to the high priest, and to the Levitical priests in general, in their judicial capacity (17:9, 12), and as guardians of the Torah-constitution (17:18). The present law fills out the picture that those laws begin to paint, by giving the rationale for the priestly role at the sanctuary, and by showing how individual priests relate to that role. Even here, however, the picture is not full or systematic, for the text assumes, and cross-refers to, information that may be known from elsewhere. The phrase 'as he promised them' (2) recalls Num. 18:20, which enunciates, as if for the first time, the principle found here, in the context of an enumeration of perquisites of priests and Levites (in the more differentiated parlance of P). There seems to be no good reason to think that our text does not have Num. 18:20 in mind (*pace* S. R. Driver 1895: 214–225, who thought the reference was to an unknown text, and Mayes 1979: 276–277, who saw Deut. 18:2 as a late addition).

The argument is essentially as follows. *Verses 1–2*: Levites do not have land, because their 'inheritance' is Yahweh; *vv. 3–4*: an illustration of this in the concrete terms of their perquisites from the sacrifices; *v. 5*: a link with the motif of Yahweh's 'choosing', previously applied to the sanctuary and the king, giving the priest a place in the administrative scheme; *vv. 6–8*: a further illustration of the priest's enjoyment of his perquisites, as it relates to his tenure of property in the land. This explanation may be supported by an observation on the structure of the passage. Verse 1 introduces two terms, *ḥēleq* and *naḥᵃlâ*, which, when applied to other tribes, refer to tribal territory. Each of these is then picked up again in the following verses, in the reverse order: *naḥᵃlâ* in vv. 3–4, understood as the priest's sacrificial dues; *ḥēleq* in vv. 6–8, referring to Levitical cities and personal property. The priest's right to a share of the sacrifices and to specially set-aside estates within the tribes is effectively a tax system supporting the administration's bureaucracy (McBride 1993: 75).

The law is often seen in the context of Josiah's reform. The connection rests on the proposed collocation of Deut. 18:6–8 with 2 Kgs. 23:8–9, which reports that King Josiah, in abolishing the 'high places' of Judah, brought the 'priests' who had presided there to Jerusalem, and made some provision for them, but did not allow them to officiate in the temple. The present law is then interpreted as an attempt to secure the livelihood of those priests, an attempt that failed because Josiah did not admit them to the altar (Wellhausen 1885: 146–147; cf. Ahlström 1982: 51 n. 39). On this view, Deuteronomy's concern is based on a natural sympathy for the Levites, which it shows elsewhere (12:12; 14:28–29). It suffers from two main handicaps: 1. that Deuteronomy refers principally to 'Levites', especially in vv. 6–8 (i.e. not 'priests of high places'), and nowhere suggests that this group has in any sense misbehaved; 2. that it fails to understand the reason for the law's placement here, as part of Deuteronomy's thinking about the constitution. It is unnecessary to suppose that the present law is a failed attempt to mitigate effects of Josiah's reform (so, rightly, Mayes 1979: 278–279).

18:9–22

The present section rounds off not only the series of laws on the legal institutions (16:18 – 18:22), but also the extensive first division of the laws (chs. 12 – 18). On this larger canvas it returns to an important theme of ch. 12, namely the need to be distinct from the other nations in life and worship. The passage opens with the formula of the gift of the land (cf. 12:1); and there are specific echoes of that chapter in the themes of dispossessing the peoples, and the prohibition of their abominable practices. The provision for the prophet, therefore, is in the context of the strong deuteronomic theme of the distinctive relationship between Yahweh and Israel.

As the final section in 16:18 – 18:22, it completes the laws about Israel's institutions. Following the laws concerning judge, priest and king, we now have the law of the prophet, or, better, about the true way of hearing the voice of Yahweh. The climactic final position of this section stresses the primacy in Israel's affairs of the divine word. A commentary on Deut. 5:23–27 in vv. 15–19 extends the role of Moses to future prophets.

Comment

16:18–20

18. The section beginning lacks a clear introductory formula, like that of 17:14, with a 'when' (*kî-*) clause and a reference to Israel's coming into the land. It may be compensated for by the clause that follows the word 'cities' (lit. 'gates'), as it regularly does, namely 'the LORD your God is about to give you' (cf. 16:5). The instruction is thus conformed to the deuteronomic framework. Indeed, the repetition of the land-gift formula in v. 20 marks this passage off as a well-rounded expression of the deuteronomic theology.

The verb 'give' also features in the opening command, though it is translated above as 'appoint'. This is another instance, therefore, in which the verb 'give' echoes its use in the formulaic phrase in vv. 18, 20. The appointment of judges is thus seen as a response to the divine gift of land, just as the offerings were (as in 16:17).

The verb 'give', as regularly in the formula of land-gift, is a participle, conveying a present action, hence the translation 'about to give'. A simple reconstruction of the chronology, therefore, is that when the people come into the land they are to make judges in their towns. The deuteronomic chronology is not simple, however, for the time clause here is balanced by the clause at the end of v. 20: 'so that you may ... possess the land the LORD is about to give you'. That keeps the possession firmly in the future. Here as elsewhere, there is a tension between the occupation of the land as a decisive event in history and as a permanently future possibility, which has its obverse in the possibility of loss.

The people of Israel is addressed as a whole unit in the singular (that is, not to the judges themselves, though the continuation in v. 19 shifts the focus in that direction; this point is not always recognized [e.g. Zobel 1992: 189; and see further McConville 2002b]). In the 'constitution' of Israel the people as such bear the overarching responsibility, appointing judges, officials and also the king (17:14), though it is God alone who appoints priest and prophet. The judges and officials presumably had separate duties, the latter acting, perhaps, as recorders or sergeants-at-arms. The judges themselves will have been appointed from among the city's elders, perhaps on the basis of special knowledge of the laws (S. R. Driver 1895: 200). The elders of a city had a role in the administration of its affairs and, as is well known, would congregate at the city gate. The book of Ruth (4:2) portrays a specially gathered group of them as witnessing a case in tribal law or custom. Elders and judges, and indeed priests, are named together in Deut. 21:2, 5. In that place the main action is undertaken by the elders, who appear to exercise a representative role on behalf of the city, while the presence of the judges and priests ensures that legal requirements are observed (cf. Weinfeld 1972: 234). Judges appear alone in a judicial role 25:1–2. There is no reason to think that the appointment of judges in Deuteronomy replaces an older system in which elders as such had a judicial role (*contra* Phillips 1970: 22).

The phrase 'according to your tribes' (18) has seemed to some commentators to be in tension with the distribution of judges by city, and therefore an addition to the original law (Gertz 1994: 34). The settlement in cities, however, is not at odds with the tribal organization of Israel. The record of settlement in Joshua lists the occupied cities according to tribe, and there is a tendency for territorial name and patriarchal eponym to be fused in genealogical lists such as 1 Chr. 1 – 9 (Reviv 1989: 51). It is likely that, in early Israel, cities and villages were occupied by smaller and larger kinship groups. As city culture developed, it may well have cut across early tribal organization, and, with the establishment of a royal capital, in due course it certainly did so. Here, however, as the judicial organization is established, the rights of the patriarchal leadership of old Israel are recognized. This is important in the concept of Israel that is outlined in these chapters, for they amount to a strong anti-centralist tendency. (See further below on the law of the king, 17:14–20.)

19–20. The opening statement of fundamental principle in legal process is now filled out with appeals to integrity in operating it. Deuteronomy knows that the existence of statute and due process, though necessary, is no guarantee of right practice. Two important terms are used in close combination in v. 18, namely *mišpāṭ* and *ṣedeq*. This combination is known also in the prophetic books, for example Amos 5:24 (where we find the related form *ṣᵉdāqâ* for *ṣedeq*). The pair of terms expresses both the basis and practice of law. While the word *mišpāṭ* refers to the individual case, a just decision, *ṣedeq* is the more abstract quality that underpins such decisions, namely justice. An appeal for the love of justice thus brackets this opening paragraph of the laws governing legal practice. The paragraph closes (20) with the repetition of 'justice' (*ṣedeq*, lit. 'justice, justice you shall seek'), a technique for emphasis.

In this appeal, the 'thou' address, which in v. 18 (as generally) is directed at the people as a whole, shifts to addressing those who would be engaged in the regular practice of law. The specific prohibitions relate to favouring one of the parties, perhaps because they are poor (Exod. 23:3), and to taking bribes, which would favour the rich. These warnings are known already in Exodus, including even some of the motive clauses also found here (Exod. 23:3, 6–8, esp. 23:8). Deuteronomy's 'the wise' broadens the picture from the Exodus text's 'officials' (Exod. 23:8), and may be influenced by the requirement of wisdom for the appointed officials in Deut. 1:13, 15. It also makes the phrase into a more general maxim, a point about human behaviour rather than mere procedure. On the last phrase of v. 19, NRSV is probably right, with 'subverts the cause of those who are in the right'. NIV's 'twists the words of the righteous' is also possible, since the word *dābār* may be taken as either 'word' or 'cause'. The two translations give slightly different angles on miscarriage of justice, but that is the essential point. Verse 19 is echoed closely in 1 Sam. 8:3, where Samuel's sons, acting as judges, 'accepted bribes and perverted justice'. This is the first of numerous links between our passage and the narrative in 1 Sam. 8 – 12 concerning the constitution of Israel.

16:21 – 17:1

Judicial passages (16:18–20; 17:2–13) are interspersed with cultic ones (15:19–23; 16:1–17; 16:21 – 17:1) in this part of Deuteronomy, and this is therefore a feature of deuteronomic organization of its laws that cuts across thematic blocks. Inserted into the sequence on legal practice, therefore, there now appear three prohibitions from the sphere of the cult, each introduced by the strong particle *lō'*, also found in the Decalogue. The first two prohibitions bear directly on the claim of Yahweh to Israel's exclusive loyalty, recalling the First Commandment, and this theme is continued in the following passage concerning judicial procedure (17:2– 8). The third (17:1) is strongly reminiscent of 15:21, that is, the law requiring animals brought for the firstling sacrifice to be perfect. It may be deliberately repeated from that place to make a point about the quality of devotion demanded of Israel (though it does not follow that 17:1 rounds off a section that began at 15:19 [Rütersworden 1987: 27–28]; the organization of the discourse is more fluid than that). The placement of the three laws here, in the context of laws about Israel's body politic, may function to affirm that the fundamental law for Israel is adherence to Yahweh. (In the reference to the Asherah pole and the idea of 'abhorrence' to God, 17:1, there are echoes of the first and basic warning against conformity to the worship of Canaan in Deut. 7:25–26; cf. 12:31; 13:15.) Specifically, they make a suitable introduction to 17:2–8, where the pre-eminent 'crime' is the worship of other gods. The alternation of cultic and judicial laws here, then, is not a merely formal feature, but has a specific rationale in the context.

21. The words *'ašērâ* ('Asherah pole') and *maṣṣēbâ* ('sacred pillar') appear in the singular only here in Deuteronomy; otherwise they refer to Canaanite cult objects marked for destruction by the Israelites when they occupy the land (7:5; 12:3; see on those places). Deuteronomy uses the word *'ašērâ*, not to refer to the goddess Asherah, but to designate a wooden object used in worship; for this reason it is often translated 'Asherah/sacred pole' (NIV, NRSV), though the shape of the object is unknown. It is better to regard it as an object that is 'set up', rather than as a tree that is 'planted' (NIV mg.), taking the verb *nāṭaʿ* in a sense that is found also in Eccles. 12:11; Dan. 11:45 (cf. Rütersworden 1987: 24). The practice of setting up wooden objects in worship contexts is cited from

Hittite (Rütersworden 1987: 123–124 nn. 134–136) and Assyrian (Spieckermann 1982: 216 n. 122) sources. It is not exclusively Canaanite, therefore, and apparently goes back to the second millennium (Rütersworden 1987: 27). It follows that this prohibition is not simply a controversy with Canaanite practices (contrary to Merendino [1969: 156], who thinks this is so because of *tôʿēḇâ*, 'abhorrent', in 17:1; but this term does not always imply anti-Canaanite polemic; cf. 25:13–16; Rütersworden 1987: 120 n. 99). It follows, too, that there is no necessary relationship between the sacred pole and the goddess (as implied by NIV mg.). Nor need it be supposed that Deuteronomy knows of a belief that Asherah was the consort of Yahweh (see Handy 1994: 73–74; Day 1986a).

22. The setting up of 'sacred pillars' as objects in worship was an ancient practice, familiar to the patriarch Jacob (Gen. 28:18, 22; 35:14). It could also be done simply as a memorial (Gen. 31:45, 51; 2 Sam. 18:18). In Deuteronomy and DtrH the combination of Asherah poles and sacred pillars is a byword for idolatry (1 Kgs. 14:23; 2 Kgs. 17:10; 18:4; 23:14). The placing of a sacred pole beside the altar of God was a particular offence against the true worship of Yahweh; the act is attributed in Kings to Manasseh, who appears there as the most flagrant apostate (2 Kgs. 21:7; cf. 23:6). Yahweh's 'hatred' of these symbols of the worship of other gods is echoed in the prophets' critique of false worship (Is. 1:14; Amos 5:21).

17:1. The command to offer perfect animals for sacrifice was met first in the law of firstlings (15:21), but is now stated as a general principle. This principle is spelt out in Lev. 22:17–25, and is applied in that book's laws on sacrifices (e.g. Lev. 1:3, 10; 3:1). Disobedience to the principle is castigated by the prophet Malachi (Mal. 1:6–8). It runs deeper than mere opposition to Canaanite practice (in any case, it is not clear, even from Lev. 22:25, whether Canaanites also had such a requirement). Right practice in worship had an important ingredient of 'wholeness', which applied to priests as well as to the animals they offered (Lev. 21:16–23). The point of the command, therefore, is not simply 'giving one's best' to God (though that may be Malachi's point); the concept is strictly cultic, namely that wholeness is appropriate to the holy sphere (see Wenham 1979a: 23–25). Infringement of this principle is 'abhorrent' to God (see on 7:25–26), a concept that normally denotes apostasy in Deuteronomy.

17:2–7

2–4. This passage brings the primary sin in Deuteronomy's concept, idolatry, into the sphere of the judicial process. It is linked to the preceding cultic prohibitions by the theme of apostasy, and specifically by means of the term *tô'ēbâ* (4; cf. v. 1). The worship of sun, moon and stars as a violation of the covenant of Yahweh (2–3) recalls Deut. 4:19; cf. 4:13 (and see 'Comment' there on the relationship between idolatry and the keeping of covenant and Torah; see also Josh. 23:16 for the same connection). Such worship was widespread in the ANE. The need to expose and eradicate apostasy was the theme of Deut. 13, where it is called *to'ēbā* (13:15[14, EVV]), and is punishable by death. This was to be enforced in the cases of false prophets, individuals and whole cities. The process of enquiry and sentence applied there to the last of these, in an action that was a function of the religious-political assembly (13:15–16[14–15, EVV]). Here, in contrast, the same process is elaborated for individuals; that is, the action prescribed is strictly judicial. The crime of apostasy is therefore brought explicitly into the judicial process.

The responsibility of the individual is emphasized by the repeated phrase 'man or woman' (2, cf. v. 5 [twice, but see 'Notes on the text']). It has been suggested that the explicit inclusion of women might reflect the special involvement of some of them in certain forbidden cults (cf. Jer. 7:18; 44:17, and Braulik 1992a: 125). However, Deuteronomy elsewhere insists on the rights and duties of individuals (including both women and servants) more expressly than do parallel texts (see on 5:14b; 15:12, 17), and its even-handedness here is in line with that tendency. The laws of Deuteronomy protect the individual, but are also based on his and her personal responsibility before the law.

5. The condemned person is executed at the city gates, that is, probably, at the place of judgment. In Leviticus and Numbers, execution took place 'outside the camp' (Lev. 24:14; Num. 15:35; P texts), i.e. in an unconsecrated place, since sin is conceived there as offence against holiness (Lev. 20:3). Some have contrasted this concept with that of Deuteronomy, drawing attention to the pedagogical purpose of punishment in the latter (Deut. 17:13; 21:21; Braulik 1992a: 125–126). However, in normal life in the cities of Israel the concept 'outside the camp' could scarcely apply. The theology behind the punishment is to 'purge the evil from among you' (7), linking this passage to 13:6[5, EVV], where it is also used of apostasy. The justification for execution in the case of capital crime is the idea of the integrity of Israel in covenant with Yahweh.

6–7. Responsibility for the whole process in view here – the hearing of the report, the enquiry, and the execution of the offender – rests with the whole community (the 'you' form is singular throughout). In this respect Deuteronomy is like Leviticus (Lev. 24:14). However, the special responsibility of the witnesses is specified. The need for more than one witness is stated categorically in a law in 19:15, to minimize the possibility of false witness because of personal prejudice. There was a strong deterrent penalty for false witness (19:16–21). The addition of a third witness, allowed in our text as in 19:15, is a further precaution, perhaps for cases when the accuser is counted as one of the witnesses.

17:8–13

This section returns to the regulations for judicial decisions in the cities begun in 16:18–20 (the term 'gates', meaning cities, is taken up again from there; 17:8). It concerns the function of the court at the place of worship in relation to the local courts; as the tribal leaders in the wilderness were to bring hard cases to Moses (1:17), so now such cases, first heard locally, would come to the high court consisting of judge and priests. The activity of judging civil and criminal cases is thus a case of Deuteronomy's synthesis of the civil and religious spheres. Deuteronomy's forward look is maintained with the phrase 'at the time' (9). Five questions arise here. 1. In what circumstances should cases be taken to the high court? 2. What kind of procedure was undertaken there? 3. Who is responsible for such referral? 4. What is the main focus of the regulation? 5. Why is the punishment for disobedience to the court's ruling so severe?

8–9. 1. The need for local judges to consult a more competent authority may be illustrated by the fine judgment required in a number of biblical laws, as in the Book of the Covenant (Exod. 20:22 – 23:19). For example, was a homicide murder or manslaughter (Exod. 21:12–14)? How serious was an assault, or a theft (Exod. 21:18–21)? When does negligence become culpable (Exod. 21:28–29)? How great was the threat to the victim in the case of theft (Exod. 22:2–3[1–2])? Under what category of law should a case be heard ('one kind of plea or another')? To these difficulties might be added the problem of discerning the most accurate testimony; false witness is specified elsewhere as a matter for the high court (Deut. 19:16–21).

2. The word translated 'too difficult' has in some contexts the connotation of 'wonderful', or belonging to the divine realm. For this reason some scholars think that the difficulty of the case is such that it requires an oracle of God to settle it (Horst 1930: 133 n. 324); this is why the case is referred to the court at the place of worship, so that the priests there can consult God for guidance. However, this cannot be demonstrated from the term itself, which can simply mean 'impossible' (2 Sam. 13:2; Rüterswörden 1987: 45). The kind of enquiry envisaged is thoroughly judicial. The series of legal possibilities noted above suggests a specifically legal kind of deliberation that would require the expertise of those who were highly trained in law.

3. The collective address in the singular shifts once again to focus on the actual representatives of Israel who would bear the responsibility. The law assumes that the local court would decide to refer a case to the high court, and representatives of the local jurisdiction would presumably present the case there.

10–11. 4. The central point of the present regulation concerns the carrying out of the decision of the high court. The law, like a number of others, is in the form of a rather long 'if … then…' sentence. Many translations (incl. NIV, NRSV) assume that the command (the 'then') comes in v. 8 ('if a case is too difficult ... then go to the place ... '). However, the point at which the apodosis (the 'then' clause) begins cannot be determined from the syntax itself, but must be judged from the context. The best sense seems to be that referral to the high court is taken as read; the competence of the sanctuary in legal matters did not need to be proven or instituted. The command begins at v. 10. We are left to infer, therefore, that the court consisted of Levitical priests and at least one judge (9). There is no need to suppose that priests and judge had different spheres of responsibility (the priests in ceremonial law, the judge in civil; such distinctions are not finally convincing in thinking about Israelite law). Rather, the high court brings together the sacral and civil powers. The exact relationship between the two is not spelt out. The authority of the final decision, however, seems to repose in the 'priest' (12; presumably the senior priest, or high priest), whose pronouncement of the court's decision lends it its indisputable authority. (This is preferable to supposing a conflict between the singular in v. 12 and the plural, 'priests', in v. 9.)

The point of the regulation seems to be that, when the high court was consulted, its decision must be implemented. The high court is not strictly a court of appeal; there is no second trial here, nor does the responsibility for the trial pass irrevocably to the high court, for the local representatives are charged with implementing the decision. The heart of the command, therefore, comes in vv. 10–11, with its insistence that the high court's decision be followed in every point. The terms used for the decision are typically deuteronomic: the judges' decision is a 'word', which they 'teach' (10); it is an instruction (*tôrâ*) taught, and a judgment pronounced (11). The *tôrâ* in this instance could be the larger body of law contained in Deuteronomy (McBride 1993: 74), or merely the instruction relating to the case in point. In favour of the former interpretation is the fact that it is 'taught', or explained, by the judges; the judgment itself is then represented by *mišpāṭ*, in the same verse. Even if the latter translation is preferred, however, the authority of the decision rests in the fact that it is based on the Torah, the instruction given to Israel through Moses.

12–13. 5. The sanction for failure to carry out the decision of the high court is death. This extreme penalty is designed to assert the rights of the high court as an instrument of theocratic rule in Israel. Dissent from its decision is 'presumption' (*zāḏôn*), that is, a deliberate defiance of God. The root idea is pride, and when directed against God it deserves the severest punishment (cf. Jer. 50:31–32; the term occurs again in Deut. 18:22, where it refers to a prophet's false claim to have spoken in God's name). The severe sanction would also have a practical purpose. Dissent from the arbitrator's judgment might be highly likely in a case that was difficult in the first place, and where there was much at stake for the contesting parties. We cannot tell whether all sides in the case were represented in the deputation to the high court. It was paramount, therefore, that the local jurisdiction had the authority to carry out the decision that was handed down.

17:14–20

14–15. The law opens with the formula of land-gift, a significant reaffirmation of Yahweh's right to give land, in a law that will deal with the Israelite king. (Rüterswörden [1987: 57–58] and Zobel [1992: 113] oppose N. Lohfink [1981] and García López [1985], who argue that the introductory formula must be deuteronomistic. Zobel thinks García López's argument is too narrowly linguistic.) The sequence of Yahweh's gift and Israel's occupation is common in Deuteronomy (5:31; 9:6; 11:31; 12:1; 15:4; 16:20). Here it is supplemented with 'settling' (cf. 2:21–22; 11:31; 12:29), to give the effect of a time-span from first arrival to an indeterminate future point. The series of 'when' clauses continues to 'and [when, or if] you say'. It therefore permits, but does not require, such a request.

The phrase 'like all the nations around us' is otherwise found only in 1 Sam. 8:5, 20. The story in 1 Sam. 8 echoes our passage, recording the moment in Israel's history when the people did what is envisaged here. In that place their request is regarded as sinful (7). It does not follow, however, that a request in the terms found here was necessarily wrong. In 1 Sam. 8:7, Yahweh points to a whole history of sin against him as the context of the request; and the addition in 1 Sam. 8:20 is significant: '…and go out before us and fight our battles', a right that is not granted to the king in the deuteronomic law (cf. Boecker 1969: 91–92).

The essential criteria for Israel's appointment are that the king should be the one chosen by Yahweh, and that he should be a 'brother' Israelite. The 'choosing' formula ('… that/whom the LORD your God will choose'), with its look to the future, strongly resembles that which more commonly applies to the place of worship (12:5; etc.). While the theme of Yahweh's choice is important generally, and is used of the people (7:6) and of the priest (18:5), this familiar formula is used only of the place of worship and the king. At one level, this is because, from Deuteronomy's perspective, Yahweh's choice of king and place of worship still lie in the future. But the pairing is interesting also because the choice of king and of place of worship is important in the theology of Zion, especially in certain psalms, as exemplified by Ps. 2:6–7. In that context, the king is David and the place is Jerusalem, or Zion; and furthermore, David is Yahweh's 'son', and Zion his dwelling-place, which he will defend from his enemies. Together, king and holy place are celebrated as symbols of God's love of Israel.

Deuteronomy, however, speaks with a different voice. Indeed, the terms of the 'Zion theology' are conspicuous by their absence. In particular, the king is not called Yahweh's son (Ps. 2:7; 89:26[27]; 2 Sam. 7:14). Rather, he is a 'brother' in Israel. Here as elsewhere, brotherhood distinguishes the Israelite from the 'foreigner' (cf. 14:21; 15:3). But in this case it also affirms that in principle the king is not exalted over his fellow Israelites; they are not at his disposal. This view of the king corresponds with the primacy given in these chapters to the judicial process, which is controlled by the people themselves, who appoint the judges, and by Yahweh, whose authority is represented by the priest (17:9, 12). (On the question why Deuteronomy differs from certain psalms in this way, see 'Explanation'.)

16–17. Specifically, the king is now constrained in three ways: he must not engage in trade with Egypt in order to build up large royal stables; he must not have a vast harem, and he must not become wealthy. Each of these relates to established prerogatives of kings, in the military, economic and political spheres, in all of which the king was supreme. By conventional standards, therefore, these were the marks of success. And by them no Israelite king was more successful than Solomon.

However, the prohibitions here are echoed in the prophets. The multiplication of horses and wealth is condemned in Is. 2:7–9, and of horses again in Mic. 5:10[9]. Both these prophetic passages have more extensive similarities with the present section of Deuteronomy: Is. 2:6 echoes the proscription of foreign magical practices in Deut. 18:9–14, and Isaiah's criticism here culminates in an accusation of idolatry (8; cf. Deut. 16:21 – 17:1). Mic. 5:10–15[9–14] includes divination and Asherim in its accusation. Some see this threefold prohibition as being the core of the law and as having originated in prophetic circles (Mayes 1979: 270), and think for this reason that the core of Deuteronomy's requirement has prophetic origins (Mayes, ibid.). It is also possible, however, that the prophets echo the deuteronomic law; indeed, they may know a sequence of laws similar to those contained in Deut. 16:18 – 18:22, although this cannot be demonstrated.

The warning against returning to Egypt has sometimes been read, in conjunction with Deut. 28:68, as evidence of a trade in Israelite slaves in return for horses (Mayes 1979: 272), or as a resort to Egypt for help in desperate times (Reimer 1990: 226). The present passage, however, is better understood simply as a moral reversal of the exodus from Egypt, upon which the whole concept of Deuteronomy (Yahweh's gift of land to his chosen people) is predicated. This is explicit in v. 16c, which recalls the idea of Israel's first refusal to enter the land as an 'Anti-Exodus' (see on 2:1). It is echoed, too, in the prophets' denunciations of seeking alliance or refuge in Egypt (Is. 30:1–7; 31:1–3; Jer. 24).

Wealth and wives played an integral role in developing a king's power base. A king would acquire wealth by taxation, which presupposed in turn a centralized administration that threatened the old patriarchal structure of Israel. This is what Samuel spells out in 1 Sam. 8:11–18, namely an economy centred on the royal house. Foreign trade, too, would be conducted with and on behalf of the king, as the visit of the Queen of

Sheba to Solomon illustrates (1 Kgs. 10). Marriages could also consolidate foreign alliances, as they did for Solomon and Ahab, with implications for increased wealth and national security (cf. 1 Kgs. 3:1; 9:16–17a). This brought with it, however, the danger or necessity of adopting the worship of other gods (1 Kgs. 11:1–8; 18:4). The political importance of wives, or concubines, is also shown in the story of the revolt of David's son Absalom, who made the possession of the king's concubines a powerful tool in his rival bid for the kingship (2 Sam. 16:20–23). These prohibitions, therefore, fit perfectly with the picture of a king who is simply a brother Israelite.

18–19. The king is now required to make for himself a copy of 'this law' (*tôrâ*; see 'Notes on the text'). The reference is to the book that Moses is later said to have written, the 'book of the *tôrâ*' (28:61) which, when completed, was put into the care of the Levites (31:9). It is only here in the law code (chs. 12 – 26) that the term *tôrâ* refers to that completed book. This is significant for our understanding of this part of Deuteronomy. The regulations for the officials function in part, as we have seen, to show that Israel is to be distinct from the other nations at the precise point of kingship. If the law of the land is not to be framed by the king as a typical ANE royal administration, then what is the basis of the constitution to be? The answer is the Torah.

The significance of the Torah as a topic in Deuteronomy could not be more strongly portrayed than by this reference in the book to the book itself. The point has been well elaborated by Sonnet, who shows how this text anticipates the transformation of Moses' speeches into a book. By making the king the book's arch-reader, 'Moses' speech projects its own reception – via the representativity of an exceptional reader' (Sonnet 1997: 79). (The book, incidentally, cannot simply be equated with Deuteronomy, since Deuteronomy contains material expressly not in the category of Moses' speech; Sonnet 1997: xi. But see also his qualification of this on pp. 260–261.)

The view advocated here differs from those that regard vv. 18–19 as a Deuteronomistic addition to the original law, however, on the grounds that they presuppose Moses' finished book, and because v. 20 follows smoothly from v. 17 (Mayes 1979: 273; Rütersworden 1987: 89–90). Such a view conceives the Torah requirement placed upon the king in terms of exilic and post-exilic Judaism, in which Torah-reading characterized the pious Jew. The king is thus seen as a kind of ideal Israelite, a pious individual (Braulik 1992a: 129). It is true that the king is to have a close relationship with God (hence 'his God', a link, albeit muted, with the Davidic king's special relationship with God). In my view, however, the king's subordination to the law belongs within a programme for the state of Israel, in which the Torah is the supreme authority (McBride 1993).

20. The final verse stresses that the purpose of the law is that the king should not lord it over his fellow Israelites. The warning against departing from the whole law 'to the right or to the left' is paralleled in 5:32; Josh. 1:7. The reference to the commandment (*miṣwâ*) presupposes the law on the Torah in vv. 18–19, and refers to the whole deuteronomic law (cf. 15:5; 19:9). In the immediate context, the idea of turning away from the commandment 'to right or left' echoes the turning away from the 'word' (sc. of the *tôrâ*) to right or left in 17:11, where *tôrâ* refers to the instruction, or judgment, given by the high court. There is an extension here to a broader sense of Torah, but the echo implies a role of the king in administering the whole system of justice. Such a role is not spelt out in detail. That is, it remains unclear whether a king, if appointed, would assume a responsibility for judicial matters in the high court (McBride 1993: 74). The tendency of the laws in this section would suggest that that is not envisaged. The consequence of his obedience to the administrative role assigned to him, however, is a continuing dynasty, in an echo of the conditional promises to the Davidic kings (1 Kgs. 2:2–4), but evidently with less power.

18:1–8

1–2. The translation 'Levitical priests' is common in EVV for the phrase that is literally 'the priests the Levites', which is found several times in Deuteronomy (17:9, 18; 24:8; 27:9) as well as in other texts (Josh. 3:8; 8:33; Jer. 33:18). It is syntactically awkward, and therefore its meaning is unclear. Taken together with the phrase that follows it here in apposition ('the whole tribe of Levi'), it reflects an assumption in Deuteronomy that priests must belong to the tribe of Levi (cf. 'the priests the sons of Levi', 21:5; 31:9), and conversely that Levi is the priestly tribe. This last point has sometimes been put in such a way as to set Deuteronomy at odds with the laws on priests and Levites in Exodus and Numbers, where the priests are sons of Aaron, that is, one branch of the tribe of Levi. The term 'Levites', in contrast, refers to other members of that tribe, who take a subordinate role to the Aaronide priests (Num. 3:5–10).

Many have argued, therefore, that Deuteronomy simply does not know of the distinction that is maintained in P (Emerton 1962). Other translators, in contrast, have tried to harmonize Deuteronomy with Exodus and Numbers by supposing that 'the whole tribe of Levi' is not in apposition, but means rather '*and*, or *indeed*, the whole tribe of Levi' (NIV; G. E. Wright 1954). This is supported by an argument that Deuteronomy elsewhere distinguishes between priests and Levites (27:9–14; 31:9, 25; cf. Abba 1977a: 261). However, it is not certain that the two terms in those places refer to different groups. And in 18:1 it is more natural to take the phrase 'the whole tribe of Levi' as a true apposition, and to explain the relation of Deuteronomy to Exodus and Numbers differently.

Deuteronomy is concerned here to show only that the priestly tribe has no land inheritance, and therefore must live off the proceeds of its official responsibilities. Its usage is more akin to that of Joshua than of Exodus–Numbers, where a use of 'Levites' to designate the whole tribe (Josh. 14:4) co-exists with a more precise usage that distinguishes priests from non-priests (Josh. 21:4; McConville 1984: 140). The former usage occurs, as it does here, where the point is that the priestly tribe must forgo a land inheritance because of its official responsibilities.

The Levites' forfeiture of a territorial inheritance because of their priestly role is recorded in a number of OT texts (Num. 26:62; Josh. 13:14; 14:4–5; 21). It is expressed positively in the statement that 'the LORD is their inheritance' (2; cf. 10:9; Josh. 18:7). The idea of the Levites' abandonment of a natural right is echoed in the oracle in Deut. 33:8–11, where it is put in terms of primary family relationships (33:9a). They subordinate these to their fundamental loyalty to Yahweh, a picture that is supported by the record in Exod. 32:25–29. The oracle conforms to the concept of a tribal identity that is bound in a special relationship with Yahweh, and implies non-possession of a natural right. Levites are still 'brothers' of their fellow Israelites, a status that is not compromised by the playing down of family ties in 33:9a. (The abandonment of natural ties as a mark of devotion to God is recalled in Jesus' memorable declaration that 'whoever does the will of my Father in heaven is my mother and brother and sister'; Matt. 12:50. Here the Levitical principle is extended to all who would be disciples.)

This term, 'inheritance', is normally reserved for a land allocation to the other tribes (e.g. Josh. 13:7). The idea that Yahweh himself is Levi's 'inheritance' is, therefore, directly linked to its land forfeiture. The actual content of Yahweh as inheritance is twofold. 1. It is an entitlement to proceeds from the sacrificial worship at the sanctuary. Num. 18:9–24 specifies these in detail, making distinctions between the rights of priests and 'Levites'. Our text is closer to the general expression of the point in Josh. 13:14, where 'offerings by fire' are designated as the 'inheritance' of Levi, that is, the whole tribe. 2. It is an entitlement to cities to live in throughout the various tribal territories, together with surrounding pasture land (e.g. Josh. 21:3, where these are called their 'inheritance'). The last provision is paralleled in Egypt, where priests were excluded from territorial possession, as in Israel, and where they were permitted to own temple lands (Ahlström 1982: 50–51).

The provision makes clear that Levites were not to be offered mere crumbs, but could actually build up personal wealth; though this seems to have been somewhat at the discretion of the host tribes, as is implied by the appeals to Israelites elsewhere in Deuteronomy not to neglect the Levite (12:19). This kind of personal or family wealth is illustrated by the case of Abiathar, banished to his city Anathoth, and to his 'fields' (1 Kgs. 2:26; cf. Jeremiah, the priest from Anathoth [Jer. 1:1], who sold a field

[Jer. 32:6–15], and Amos 7:17, which implies that the priest Amaziah had land).

3–5. In the specification of the dues for the priests the terminology now varies from 'Levitical priests' to 'priests' (3). The motive for the change may lie in the expression *zeh yihyeh mišpaṭ hakkōhᵃnîm* ('this is the right [or due] of the priests'), which echoes *zeh yihyeh mišpaṭ hammelek* ('this is the right of the king') in 1 Sam. 8:11 (see above on 17:14–20). These may both be fixed expressions. Here too, however, the priestly tribe as a whole is meant, as is clear from v. 5, where the priest is said to be chosen 'out of all your tribes'. The priests' right or due is their customary entitlement, as attested in the narrative of Eli's sons (1 Sam. 2:12–15, though the implication there is of a 'due' exceeded or disregarded). The phrase establishes a further connection, therefore, between this part of Deuteronomy and the picture of Israel's development in the early chapters of Samuel.

The enumeration of the dues is different in important respects from the regulations in Num. 18:9–24 and Lev. 7:28–34, and is perhaps a summary statement based on a particular practice. The 'first[fruits]' of grain, wine and oil (4) has echoes in Num. 18:12, but, while Deuteronomy specifies a gift from the first fleece (4), Numbers has olive oil (12), together with the wave offerings and firstlings (11, 14–16; see on Deut. 15:19–23). It is Lev. 7:28–32 that specifies which parts of the sacrificed animal should fall to the priests, and these differ from Deuteronomy. It is not possible to reconcile the various data; there may have been fluidity in the customs. Deuteronomy is perhaps not attempting to legislate for the first time on this, or to do so exhaustively; it knows of other legislation, and here chiefly wishes to make a point about the place of gifts in the context of provision for the bureaucracy.

The priestly tribe has been chosen by Yahweh (cf. 21:5; 1 Sam. 2:27–29). This completes the quartet of entities so described: the people, the sanctuary, the king and the priest. This does not quite add up to a portrayal of the body politic (since it omits the judge and the prophet). But it echoes the ANE association of king, priest and sanctuary that dominated most societies. Deuteronomy submits the whole organization of Israel to the criterion of Yahweh's choice, giving priority to his choice of the people.

The terms 'stand and minister' are used regularly for priestly service (Deut. 17:12; Exod. 28:43; though the former is also used more generally, as in 1 Kgs. 17:1); and the phrase 'and his descendants' echoes the provision that Aaron's sons should be priests in perpetuity (Exod. 28:4, 43b). The phraseology again suggests that Deuteronomy is aware of other legislation, which we know from Exodus and Leviticus, but that it applies what may be true of priests specifically to the priestly tribe at large.

6–8. The final paragraph of this section rounds it off with a picture of the Levite enjoying the rights that have been spelt out in the previous verses. The person in question ('the Levite') is none other than the 'Levitical priest' (1) or the 'priest' (3). The terminological variation in the section is not so great as appears in translation. The term 'Levite' is virtually the same as the word 'Levi' (1). It means in effect 'member of the tribe of Levi', and that is what is chiefly in view here: the rights and solidarity of the individual Levite, or priest, in the priestly tribe. Verses 1–2 established that Levites were fully 'brothers' in Israel, while putting that status in relation to their special relationship with Yahweh; now the focus is on their 'brotherhood' within the priestly tribe (7).

The meaning of vv. 6–8 can be understood by a consideration of its syntax. It consists of a string of clauses beginning with 'if'. In such cases, the point at which the 'if' clauses give way to a 'then' clause must be judged from the context. (This is because the second and subsequent 'if' clauses are introduced simply by 'and', which may also introduce a 'then' clause). In vv. 6–8 the question is whether to read: 'if a Levite comes ... then he may minister' (Craigie 1986a: 257–259; Steuernagel 1923: 68; RSV; NIV); 'they shall also have equal shares ...'; or 'if a Levite comes, and ministers, he (they) shall also have equal shares' (NEB; S. R. Driver 1895: 217; Mayes 1979: 278; Braulik 1992a: 132–133). The former is closely associated with the questionable interpretation of this passage as a claim on behalf of the displaced 'priests of the high places' (2 Kgs. 23:8–9) to enjoy parity of status with the Jerusalem priests. This, however, is not the issue here, since, as we have argued, the status of the Levite is not in doubt (cf. von Rad 1953: 122); rather, the issue is the right of all Levites/priests to enjoy certain benefits because of their priestly functions.

The final verse (8) brings together the Levite's proceeds from the altar (*ḥēleq*) with his property rights, the two aspects of the provision for him adumbrated in v. 1. The term *naḥᵃlâ* does not appear here, however. Rather, we have the obscure term *mimkārāyw 'al hā'āḇôṯ*, often translated 'from the sale of his patrimony'. It may refer, not necessarily to selling off the family silver, but to such income as might be achieved from personal, family property.

The situation envisaged in these verses is not a permanent relocation of a country priest to the central sanctuary, though that is often inferred from the mistaken connection with 2 Kgs. 23:8–9. It may envisage only a temporary tour of duty at the sanctuary by a Levite who comes from one of the cities set aside for him in any part of the land (Josh. 21; cf. Haran 1978: 119–120).

18:9–14

These verses are framed by the idea of Yahweh's gift of the land (9, 14). The land-gift formula is not placed randomly here, but applies to a particular case the general teaching that the gift has been made on condition that the land should be occupied worthily. Israel in the land is generally to avoid the 'abhorrent things' done by the nations (see 'Comment' on 12:31), and in the present case this relates to the realm of communication from God. Verse 14 has the most succinct statement in Deuteronomy of the conditionality of the gift: 'The LORD your God has not given to you to do this', or 'he has not *thus* given you'. The point is often missed in translations, which, properly enough, understand 'give' as 'permit' or 'allow'. God's gift of land has a particular outcome in view, namely a people in loyal relationship with him (see further on v. 13).

9. The phrase 'Those nations' assumes that they have previously been identified. The immediate allusion is to 17:14, the introduction to the law of the king. This confirms a continuity of thought between the laws on institutions as framed here: in that case a practice of the nations was permitted; in this case another is prohibited. The expression 'you must not learn' is the obverse of the positive commands elsewhere to 'learn' the commands of Yahweh in order to obey him (4:1; 5:1). The issue is ethical. And here, as elsewhere, the whole ethic of Deuteronomy is put in relational terms: the right way is a commitment of the whole self to Yahweh; the wrong way is the opposite commitment, to the ways of the nations and their gods. The 'learning' of obedience to Yahweh is expressly put in terms of conflict with other nations in Judg. 2:3; 3:2. The verse strongly resembles 12:29, and, with v. 10, the connection between imitation of the nations and the sacrifice of children in 12:29–31.

10–11. The need to hear a word from the deity was universally felt in the ancient world, and a whole array of esoteric arts and practices grew up around it, together with various kinds of experts in them. The magicians of Pharaoh (Exod. 7:11), the wise men of Nebuchadnezzar (Dan. 2:2) and even the Magi of Matthew's Gospel (Matt. 2:1) echo that world of thought. Ezekiel, too, has a mocking picture of the king of Babylon consulting his means of divination as he conducts his campaign of conquest: 'he shakes the arrows, he consults the teraphim, he inspects the liver' (Ezek. 21:21[26]); respectively, a kind of drawing of lots, a taking of oracles, and the practice known as extispicy, or haruspicy (examining entrails). Kings, in particular, resorted to such means in order to make important decisions, as in times of war. The banning of these superstitious practices, therefore, is consistent with Deuteronomy's rejection of the whole religio-political apparatus of the ancient world.

The list of forbidden activities covers a range of such practices. The common theme is the attempt to gain knowledge or guidance, or to exercise power over the deity or other people by magic and secret procedures. The sacrifice of children is named here in this context. (See also on 12:30–31 for this practice as symbolic of the abhorrent things of Canaanite religion. The specific context may be the cult of the god Molek, the god of the dead; see Day 1989: 67–68.) The king of Moab, losing ground in battle against Israel, made a burnt offering of his son and heir, to try to persuade the deity by the act of self-sacrifice itself, or to discern how to turn the tide of events (2 Kgs. 3:26–27).

Divination is a general term for the use of esoteric means to determine the likely course of events. It is sometimes used in a neutral sense of prophets in Israel. In Mic. 3:11 it occurs in company with other activities that are legitimate in themselves, but abused by their practitioners (cf. Is. 3:2–3). The OT records a number of cases of seeking answers from Yahweh that are not adversely judged (e.g. the taking of Urim and Thummim; Lev. 8:8; Deut. 33:8; cf. Judg. 6:36–40). The force of the term here, therefore, derives from its association with means of knowledge used by other nations, the hopeless divination directed to false gods. It may also, in that case, be an umbrella term for what follows.

Soothsaying is a kind of divination practised by the Philistines (Is. 2:6) and the apostate King Manasseh of Judah (2 Kgs. 21:6). It is disparaged in several prophetic texts (Mic. 5:12[11]; Jer. 27:9; Is. 57:3), and is condemned in Lev. 19:26, but its precise nature is not known. The taking of omens is also listed among the crimes of Manasseh (2 Kgs. 21:6; cf. 17:17), and forbidden in Lev. 19:26. Joseph in Egypt, however, used his cup for the purpose, perhaps by 'watching the play of light' on the liquid (S. R. Driver 1895: 224).

With sorcery and the casting of spells, we move from seeking guidance to the attempt to exercise control by supernatural means. Mic. 5:12[11] implies that 'sorceries' involved using something, no doubt considered potent, in the hand. In Exod. 22:17, the practitioner (in that case female) is to be put to death. The casting of spells is based on a word meaning 'bind', which presumably relates to the intended effect on another person (cf. Ps. 58:5[6]).

The last secret art named is necromancy, that is, the attempt to communicate with the dead in order to predict or determine events, famously resorted to by Saul in the cave of the medium at En-Dor (1 Sam. 28). Saul has the woman call up the ghost ('ôḇ) of Samuel there (8). 'Ghost' and 'familiar spirit' (yidd^e'ōnî) are often named together. The former can refer to the spirit of any dead person. The latter term is often mentioned together with it, and may be indistinguishable from it. However, because of a semantic connection with the verb 'to know' it is sometimes conjectured that it means 'familiar spirit', that is, a particular spirit that attends the one who consults it. Alternatively, the knowledge hinted at in the name might be that which it is thought to impart.

The present passage seems to be explicitly recalled in 2 Kgs. 17:17 and 21:6, as part of the case against 1. the northern kingdom of Israel and 2. King Manasseh of Judah, the paradigmatic apostate according to Kings.

12–14. These verses are a kind of reprise of the preceding. The new element is in v. 13. The command here is literally 'You shall be complete [or perfect with] the LORD your God'. The word is used frequently in sacrificial texts to refer to the unblemished animals that are required for sacrifice (Lev. 1:3; 3:1). But it is found too in the prophets to express the more abstract notion of truth (Amos 5:10). And it often appears, as here, in expressions that are ethical and relational (Ps. 18:23[24], 'I am perfect with the LORD'). The emphasis is on integrity in relationship, and this expresses well the whole ethical tenor of Deuteronomy. The verse is by no means out of place in the present connection, as some have thought (G. Seitz 1971: 31). It shows, rather, that the prohibitions in these verses have their meaning in the context of a choice between devotion to Yahweh and allegiance to other gods.

18:15–19

15. The declaration that Yahweh will raise up a prophet like Moses now comes in direct contrast to the vivid picture of the practices of the other nations. The contrast is achieved by a repetition of the word 'listen' (15; cf. v. 14), which thus makes a connection between vv. 9–14 and 15–19. The promise is made starkly, with the word 'prophet' placed in the strong initial position (lit. 'A prophet from your midst, from your brothers, like me, will the LORD raise up'). The emphasis is on the prophet. It is by this means that Yahweh will speak, not by others. The immediate qualification of the prophet, as of the king, is that he shall be an Israelite (and therefore free from the taint of foreign religion). Only then is he likened to Moses.

16–17. The way in which he is like Moses is the subject of vv. 16–17. As for Yahweh's 'raising up' of the prophet, this contrasts with the 'choosing' of the priest and king (17:15; 18:5). The difference may lie in the type of function. In the case of king and priest, Yahweh affirms his right to choose in relation to official public ceremonies performed by the people. In the case of the prophet, in contrast, it seems that there is no corresponding ceremony of institution; rather, the prophet will be appointed by Yahweh as need arises; the question of the recognition of the true prophet (20–22) then follows from this.

Verses 16–17 are a commentary on 5:23–27, and explain what is meant by the 'prophet like Moses'. The (lit.) 'day of the assembly' refers to the encounter with Yahweh at Mt Horeb when the covenant was first made (ch. 5). Deut. 5:23–27 tells how the people fear they will die because of the sight and sound of God, and therefore demand that Moses act as mediator between them. The present verse reverses the order of sight and sound from 5:24, somewhat diminishing the force of the vision in the process, perhaps to focus more directly on the idea of the word. Verse 17 shows clearly the connection of thought between the two passages, with its direct quote from 5:28c. There, the LORD approved the people's request that Moses should mediate his word to them; here the same sequence of thought results in the provision for that function of Moses to continue

(18). This is the sense in which the prophet, or prophets, of the future would be like Moses.

18–19. It can hardly be the case that this difference between the two passages is evidence of a later hand in the present passage (Mayes 1979: 282). Rather, the provision for Moses' role to continue is consistent with the orientation of the book towards the future life in the land, with all its changing scenes. The 'raising up' of the prophet need not mean a single act, or a single individual, therefore. It rather envisages a succession of prophets, as and when the LORD deems it right. His freedom in this regard *could* result in an Elijah passing on his mantle to an Elisha (2 Kgs. 2:1–14). But the role of the prophet is neither essentially dynastic nor a permanent office in the deuteronomic view. In Samuel's time it could be said, 'The word of the LORD was rare in those days' (1 Sam. 3:1). But when prophets spoke, they did so because the LORD had 'put his words in their mouth', as with Moses (18; cf. Jer. 1:9).

The sense unit is complete with v. 19, which returns to the key idea of 'listening to' God's word. Failure to obey God's instituted means for Israel must result in punishment. While, in the case of the legal verdict of priest and judge, this could take the form of judicial punishment (17:12), in the case of the prophet it might be only spiritually discerned and prosecuted.

20–22. If failure to obey the voice of the prophet might be discerned spiritually only by the LORD, so too might the voice of the prophet himself by the people. The vulnerability of the hearers to betrayal by a plausible false prophet makes his lying words a specially heinous crime. To speak words *not* put in his mouth by Yahweh is called 'presumption', that strong term used in 17:12 for disobedience to the central court. Here, however, the sin is on the part of the one who would represent God, not the hearer, and again can be only spiritually discerned.

The provision here, then, is for cases where someone has claimed to give a prophetic word of judgment. This is different from the cases in Deut. 13 and 17:2–7, which address the problem of enticement to worship other gods, and from Jer. 28, where a false oracle of salvation is in view. Here the danger is not that the people should fail to hear Yahweh's voice, or that they should go over to other gods, but that they might needlessly *fear* (22). The remedy for uncertainty is similar to that offered by the book of Jeremiah for a false prophecy of salvation, namely that the word would be tested by whether it came about (cf. Jer. 28:9). The problem with such a test is that the proof may come too late! (It may not do so, however, as Hananiah's sudden death [Jer. 28:12–17] demonstrated – a striking, and non-judicial, fulfilment of v. 20, albeit in the converse case: 'that prophet shall die'.) It makes best sense, however, as a test that might be applied to a prophet's record over time (Craigie 1976a: 263). Even this would need supplementary criteria, however, in the case of Jeremiah, whose words of judgment did not come about for some forty years! That book adds to this criterion the proof that lay in a prophet's character (Jer. 29:22–23).

It is surprising, perhaps, that the possibility of false prophecy is envisaged only from this one point of view. It is unnecessary, however, to suppose that the passage is consequently later than Jeremiah, when the onus might be thought to be on the prophet of salvation to prove his credentials.

Explanation

This section of the book plays a key role in establishing its theology and orientation. Its significance can be understood only in relation to the deuteronomic view of Moses and the Torah.

In 4:13–14 and 5:23–27 the role of Moses is established as the one who mediates the Torah to Israel. Deuteronomy, as we saw, distinguishes between the Decalogue and the subsequent laws, the latter being conveyed to Israel by means of the 'teaching' activity of Moses. That role, however, can obviously be maintained only while Moses is alive. And we have been prepared for the death of Moses from the first chapter of the book (1:37–38), the narrative of the event itself being the subject of the final chapter. The death of Moses may even be seen as a kind of hermeneutical key to the whole book (cf. Olson 1994). There is, then, this tension between the absolutely crucial role of Moses in the mediation of the Torah and the fact that he cannot accompany Israel into the land, where the Torah must be put into effect.

It follows that the role of Moses has a paradigmatic function in Deuteronomy, and one of the book's real purposes is to show how that function may be performed in the actual life of the people. This was already signalled in 1:9–18, in which the topic of Moses' inability to do all the work of judging the people, even in his own lifetime, was broached. And in the present section the succession of Moses is addressed explicitly in the law concerning the prophet (18:15–20).

The succession of Moses is broader than the prophet alone, however, and consists in all the arrangements put in place for the effecting of Torah in the covenant community. This is what is provided for in the present chapters. There are several elements in the synthesis.

First, the essential element is the supremacy of Torah itself as that which embodies the qualities of justice and righteousness (16:18–20; cf. 4:8 for Torah itself as 'righteous'). This supremacy is symbolized by the provision that the king should keep and study his own copy of 'this Torah' (17:18). The point is that the source of authority in Israel, in contrast to other nations, is not the king himself but the divine word. (The king, indeed, as we saw, is not even a necessary part of these institutions.) It is Torah that mediates the qualities of justice and righteousness (16:18–20), which emanate ultimately from the character of God himself (cf. 10:17–19).

Secondly, the responsibility for implementing the Torah lies, in principle, with the people as such. This is entailed in the address in 16:18 to Israel as a corporate entity. The sovereignty of the people in its administration of the Torah is invested in practice in the assembly. The classic gathering of the assembly was at Horeb ('the day of the assembly', 9:10), but the assembly is reconstituted at each of the annual feasts, and at every seventh Feast of Tabernacles there is a special reaffirmation of the Torah as the final authority in the people's life (31:10–13). In this way it is embedded in the life of the people for all generations (13); Moses is dead; long live the Torah!

The day-to-day responsibility for the rule of Torah falls, however, to the judges in the cities of Israel, who are appointees of the assembly (16:18), and to a high court at the main sanctuary, consisting of a judge (or judges) and priests (17:8–13). In this combination the responsibility of the people is joined with the prerogative of God, for the priest is chosen by him, and represents his sovereignty in the people's life.

It is because of this careful conceptualization of the organization of the people that these chapters have had terms like 'polity' and 'constitution' applied to them. The supremacy of the Torah is worked through systematically. In these chapters several offices are reviewed in succession: judge, priest, king, prophet. The genius of Deuteronomy lies in the mutuality of these. These provisions of Deuteronomy bear a resemblance to what in later times came to be known as the 'separation of powers', and, indeed, early modern democratic theory found support here (see Halpern 1981b: xx–xxviii, 226–233; N. Lohfink 1993b). The concern not to concentrate power in one office stands out most clearly in the place given to the king. His role is the antithesis of that of the ANE monarch, who was supreme in all affairs of state. This king is emphatically subject to the real authority, the Torah, which is administered by the assembly, and watched over by the prophet.

Thirdly, the prophet's role is distinctive. While the judges are appointed by the assembly, the prophet is raised up by God. It is the prophet who has the special responsibility of calling the people to faithfulness to all its obligations. (On the significance of the prophet as the key figure in the covenant community, see O'Donovan 1996: 77–78. O'Donovan reads Deuteronomy differently from the thesis offered here, and sees the prophet as the distinctive biblical means of ensuring the obedience of government, *rather than* the distribution of political functions; 1996: 65.)

These arrangements, therefore, are quite radical in the world of the OT. The inspiration for them lies in the larger concept of Deuteronomy. On the canvas of the Pentateuchal narrative, Deuteronomy follows the narrative of the world's descent from created order into chaos, both natural and political (in Genesis and Exodus). In that context it aims to provide for a re-realization of the orderliness and blessings of creation. And it does so in a way that takes account of sin in the political sphere, by aiming to preclude by legislation the possibility of depotism and oppression. The checks and balances in its potentially kingless system stand in direct opposition to the monarchical power politics of Egypt, and of its smaller clones in Canaan.

This comprehensive concept of religious and political life calls for two further observations.

First, it must be brought into connection with the OT's other prominent view of king and polity, namely the Zion theology (see above on 17:15). In this, the king appears to unite powers that Deuteronomy puts asunder. Ps. 72 exemplifies the ideology that makes the king responsible under God for justice and righteousness in Israel. Some treatments of Deuteronomy find no tension here, thinking that 17:14–20 may be reconciled with the pictures of just kingship offered in Hezekiah and Josiah, and indeed that DtrH (in its first edition) culminates in a celebration of Josiah's reform as an implementation of deuteronomic ideals. It is better to admit, however, that the two visions are different (see McConville 1998), and to follow the OT's own way of explaining matters, by thinking of the Zion theology as an outcome of Israel's checkered history with Yahweh. The books of Kings finally portray an institution that failed to bring justice and right-eousness, let alone peace, to Israel. So too the Psalms, which know of the fact of exile, express bewilderment at the fortunes of the Davidic promise (Ps. 89), and yet go on to reaffirm that *Yahweh* is king, in spite of the loss of the Davidic dynasty (Books 4 and 5; see McCann 1993).

The ideal of human kingship, introduced by the story of human failure and the gracious accommodation of God to it (in 1 Sam. 8 – 12; 2 Sam. 7), remains, however, for messianic appropriation.

Secondly, the view advocated here proposes a kind of regulation of the whole life of Israel. What is elsewhere in the power of kings is here in the power of the people. This means that what is at stake is not explicable in the 'desacralizing' terms used by Weinfeld. The issue is not more or less advanced views of religion: Deuteronomy is concerned, not to reduce the cultic-religious life of Israel as such, but rather to subject all to the regulation of Torah.

DEUTERONOMY 19:1–21

Translation

[1]When the LORD your God has rooted out the nations whose land he is giving you, and when you have settled down and are living in their cities and houses, [2]set apart three cities within your land which the LORD your God is giving you to possess. [3]Work out distances, and divide the land the LORD your God is giving you as an inheritance into three areas; and these cities shall be places in which homicides may seek asylum. [4]These are the circumstances in which a homicide may take refuge

there and live: when he strikes another unintentionally, and had not previously been at enmity with him; ⁵when, for example, he goes into a wood with another to fell trees, and as he swings the axe to cut down a tree the head of the axe flies off the handle and hits the other, killing him, then he may take refuge in one of these cities and live. ⁶For if the distance to the city were great, the 'avenger of blood' might overtake the homicide in hot anger and kill him, though he did not deserve to die, since he had not previously been at enmity with the dead man. ⁷That is why I am instructing you to set apart three cities.

⁸And if the LORD your God further enlarges your territory, as he promised on oath to your forefathers, and gives you the whole land which he promised to give to them, ⁹because you have been careful to keep all these commands with which I am charging you this day, that is, to love the LORD your God and follow in his ways as long as you live, then you are to add three more cities to these three. ¹⁰In this way no innocent blood will be spilt in the land the LORD your God is giving you as an inheritance, nor will blood-guilt be upon you.

¹¹If, however, a man who has been at enmity with another lies in wait for him and attacks and kills him, and then seeks asylum in one of these cities, ¹²the elders of his city shall send and extradite him from there and hand him over to the 'avenger of blood', and he shall die. ¹³You shall not have pity on him, for thus you will purge the guilt for the death of the innocent person from Israel, and your well-being will continue.

¹⁴You must not move your neighbour's landmark, set up by those who come first into the inheritance you are about to receive, in the land the LORD your God is giving you to possess.

¹⁵The testimony of a single witness against anyone shall not stand, regarding any crime or sin that he may have done; a case may be established only on the testimony of two or three witnesses. ¹⁶If a malicious witness accuses another falsely, ¹⁷the two who are at odds must appear before the LORD, that is, in the presence of the priests and the judges who are in office at the time, ¹⁸and if the judges, having made careful enquiries, find that the witness is false, and has falsely accused his brother, ¹⁹then you shall inflict upon him whatever punishment he had intended to bring upon his brother. So you will root out evil from among you. ²⁰Then others, when they hear this, will be afraid, and no-one will do this sort of evil among you again. ²¹You shall not have pity: life must be given for life, eye for eye, tooth for tooth, hand for hand, foot for foot.

Notes on the text

3. 'Work out distances'. The phrase is sometimes translated 'Build roads to them' (NIV, RSV; cf. S. R. Driver 1895: 231). In the latter case the noun *derek* is taken simply as 'road' and the verb *tākîn* (*kûn*, hiph., 'prepare', 'establish') as the physical building of it. In the translation adopted here the action is rather a 'fixing of the way', in the sense of determining distance (cf. *HALAT* 2:443b).

'and these cities shall be places in which homicides may seek asylum': the phrase 'and these cities' is not expressed in Hebrew, but rather the impersonal 'and *it shall be* for the homicide to flee to'.

4. 'These are the circumstances': lit. 'This is the word', meaning possibly, 'This is the law (for)'. However, the context suggests the translation chosen here.

'and live': for the syntax cf. 5:24 and 'Notes on the text' there.

5. 'swings the axe': lit. 'is driven (*ndḥ*, ni.) upon the axe'.

6. 'in hot anger': lit. 'for his heart is hot' (*ḥmm*, 3 m. sg. impf. qal).

9. 'in his ways': cf. LXX 'in *all* his ways', and 10:12; 11:22; 30:16.

10. Strictly, 'innocent blood' (NIV), rather than 'the blood of an innocent person' (NRSV), though the latter is correct at v. 13. MT has *dām*, 'blood', in the absolute (though a few MSS conform it to the construct, as in v. 13), with *nāqî*, 'innocent', following as an adjective.

13. 'purge the guilt for the death of the innocent person': lit. 'the blood of the innocent person'; contrast v. 10. In this case 'blood' is in the construct, and 'innocent', having the definite article, is to be read as a noun.

16. 'accuses another falsely': the verb *'ānâ*, 'answer', is used in the sense of giving testimony; cf. 31:21. The question here is whether the following noun, *sārâ*, 'falseness, rebelliousness', refers to what the accused is said to have done, or to the falseness of the witness himself. The former is adopted by NRSV ('to accuse someone of wrongdoing') and NIV ('to accuse a man of a crime'); cf. Craigie 1976a: 269; S. R. Driver 1895: 235. Against it are: 1. the fact that it seems to define the nature of the accused's wrongdoing (as apostasy), when the issue is the truthfulness of the witness; and 2. the analogy of 19:18, *'ānâ šeqer b^e*, where the same construction is used to refer to the false witness itself; see *HALAT* 3:806b.

19. 'you shall inflict upon him': lit. 'you shall do to him'. LXX, *kai poiēsetai*, 'it shall be done to him', suggests a different Hebrew reading from MT (perhaps *w^ena'ᵃśeh*). The plural form in MT, in a mainly singular context, may be a further reason for emendation.

19–20. LXX, Syr, Tg have plurals in vv. 19–20, where MT has singular. MT regularly uses singular in such contexts.

Form and structure

Chs. 19 – 25 form a distinct sub-section of the book, comprising laws on various subjects, in a style that is generally less hortatory than in chs. 12 – 18. There are some traces of themes and rationale in the organization of these laws, as we shall notice. In the schemes of Kaufman (1978–9) and Braulik (1993) they cover the second half of the Decalogue, that is, the Sixth to the Tenth Commandments. Thus 19:1–13, on the unintentional homicide, is the first of a series on aspects of homicide, or, in Braulik's phrase, on preserving life (see on ch. 5, 'Form and structure', and Braulik

1991b: 62–63; 1993: 321–322). The law on unintentional homicide is balanced by the provision for the unsolved murder (21:1–9). Between them fall the laws on warfare (ch. 20), which in their own way bear upon the justifiable and unjustifiable taking of life.

Deut. 19 falls into three parts: a law on cities of refuge (1–13); a law on the landmark (14), and a law concerning witness (15–21). The chapter is about judicial process as much as about homicide. In this sense it has a connection with the laws on such procedures in 16:18 – 17:13; specifically, the law of witness in 19:15–21 closely echoes 17:6–7. This focus on process makes the chapter a suitable transition into the next phase of laws in chs. 19 – 25. The law on the landmark seems intrusive in 19:14, but its position among laws concerning homicide may be intended to stress the life-and-death significance of boundaries in an agricultural society.

Comment

19:1–13

1–3. A significant new beginning in the argument of Deuteronomy is signalled by the terms of 19:1, which, with its use of the verb *kārat*, hiph., echoes 12:29, the only other place in which this form of the verb occurs in Deuteronomy (Gertz 1994: 118–119). The perspective, therefore, puts the wars of conquest behind, and envisages Israel in possession of the enemies' goods (cf. 6:10–11). Deut. 12:29 came at the end of the major chapter on arrangements for worship in the land after occupation, and at the beginning of specific laws on the subject; this one stands at the head of a wide range of laws to be applied in the land. The theme of cities of refuge itself appears at important junctures in the narrative of conquest (Num. 35; Deut. 4:41–43; Josh. 20).

The OT's primary law of refuge is in Exod. 21:12–14. The basic assumption, shared by all the OT's laws on the subject, is that no-one should be condemned unjustly as a murderer. Unlike laws in the ANE, no distinction of penalty or procedure is made in this respect between slaves and free people.

Cities of refuge as such are not specified in Exod. 21, but only the precise place of refuge, namely an altar at a sanctuary (14; cf. 1 Kgs. 1:49–53; 2:28–34). However, the phrase 'I will appoint for you a place' (13, NRSV) may be taken to mean a specific city, since it implies that not any place (and perhaps not any sanctuary) would do. Provision for cities of refuge is then taken up in the passages in Numbers, Deuteronomy and Joshua. The establishment of cities of refuge does not necessarily supersede the notion of an altar as the symbol of divine protection of the innocent fugitive, but it extends sanctuary in practice into the jurisdiction of a city's authorities (see on vv. 11–13). The city itself is clearly conceived as the locus of sanctuary in Num. 35:25–28, and that concept is apparently shared by Deuteronomy. The spread of texts on cities of refuge across a range of sources (Num. 35 is assigned to P) speaks against the theory that Deuteronomy has abolished an older 'sacral' concept of sanctuary in a doctrinaire way. It is possible that Hos. 6:8–9 alludes ironically to the refuge cities of (Ramoth-)Gilead and Shechem (Phillips 1970: 101–102; cf. Milgrom 1981: 299–310).

Num. 35:9–28 provides for six cities of refuge, drawn from the Levitical cities both in Transjordan and in the area west of the Jordan, to be appointed by Israel when they enter the land. Deut. 4:41–43 sets out the basic conditions for resort to cities of refuge, and names the three allocated for the region of Transjordan, in the context of the narrative of its conquest. The present passage (19:8–10) resumes the theme, providing not only for three cities in the area west of the Jordan (in line with Num. 35:13–15), but for a further three in the event of complete occupation of the territory promised by God. The picture is completed with Josh. 20, which incorporates elements of both Num. 35 and Deut. 4 and 19, and names three cities in the area west of the Jordan in addition to the three specified for Transjordan in Deut. 4:43. Josh. 20 is therefore like Deut. 4:41–43 in specifying cities of refuge in the context of the narrative of conquest.

3. The distribution of the cities, as appears from the identifications in Deut. 4:41–43 and Josh. 20:7–9, is regional, and aims to ensure that a fugitive should find one within a reasonable distance. The present text is alone in specifying that distances should be worked out in the context of a tripartite division of the land (3). (The translation adopted here is preferred to the frequent 'Build roads to them' [NIV; cf. S. R. Driver 1895: 231], and best represents the concern for proximity; cf. NRSV; Craigie 1976a: 265–266; see also 'Notes on the text'.)

4–7, 11–13. Verses 4–7 give an example of a hypothetical accidental homicide. Two conditions determine it: 1. the killing is a purely accidental event, and 2. the perpetrator and victim have not previously been at loggerheads with each other. The converse is covered in vv. 11–13. The distinction between accidental and intentional killing elaborates that made in Exod. 21:13–14, though without adding to it substantively. The law, indeed, does not cover all possible cases (such as the accidental killing of someone who has been a known enemy, or a deliberate action which is not intended to kill but which nevertheless has that result). Such possibilities are reviewed more fully in Num. 35:16–25, where a distinction between pure accident and unpremeditated harm is known. (The latter concept also occurs in Hammurabi's Code; CH 206–208.) The present law, however, simply confirms the principle that innocent blood should not be spilt as a result of a false conviction.

The law does, however, presuppose a legal process, though again this is more fully documented in Num. 35. The protagonists in the case are the 'avenger of blood' (6), the elders of the killer's city (12) and (presumably) the elders of the city of refuge. The issue is not one of vengeance in the sense of a blood feud, but one of responsibility to ensure expiation of blood-guilt. This is why the elders of the killer's city play a role (12), as they do also in the case of the unsolved murder in 21:1–9. (Elders may be taken to have a representative function, in contrast to the strictly legal function of judges, who are not mentioned here.) The role of the 'avenger of blood' should probably be seen in this light also.

The term 'avenger of blood' is the traditional translation of a phrase that is literally 'redeemer of blood' (*gō'ēl haddām*). It is not immediately obvious whether the 'redemption' relates to the deceased person, the *gō'ēl* thus being analogous to the 'kinsman redeemer' known from the story of Ruth and Boaz (Ruth 3:20), and implying some kind of personal restitution; or whether it relates directly to 'blood', and therefore refers to a duty to protect innocent blood. (The term 'protector of blood' has been proposed as an alternative translation, based on the latter interpretation; Phillips 1970: 103–106.) In either case, he is the main agent responsible for ensuring that blood-guilt incurred by the killer is expiated, probably under the authority of the killer's city's elders. (The story in 2 Sam. 14:4– 11 does not determine whether the 'avenger of blood' represents the victim's family or the killer's city, though it depicts the family as in the forefront of demands to hand over the killer.) The possibility that the 'avenger of blood', in his eagerness, might catch his quarry and execute him before he reached sanctuary (6), accentuates the purpose of the cities of refuge, namely to ensure a fair trial. The law of refuge aims to facilitate this, not to override it.

8–10. The possibility of enlarged territory, in fulfilment of the promise to the patriarchs (8), envisages the full possession of the promised territory, as in 12:20 (see 'Comment' there). That full possession is made conditional on obedience to the covenant in typical deuteronomic terms (9; cf. 10:12; 11:22; 30:16; and see 'Notes on the text'). The three further cities provided for here are not appointed in Josh. 20, or anywhere else in the OT narrative. This may be consistent with the implication in much of that narrative that Israel never fully kept the conditions of the covenant and therefore never fully possessed the land. (This explanation of the concept of full possession of the land is preferable to that which finds in it evidence of expansion of the territory of Judah under Josiah; so Brin 1994: 36–37.)

The basic aim of the law on refuge is expressed in v. 10, namely to protect innocent life, and at the same time to prevent blood-guilt falling on Israel. This could happen not only through murder, but by the wrongful execution of an innocent person. The concepts underlying the law are complex. It aims, of course, to secure justice for the innocent individual by protecting him from wrongful retribution. But it also aims to protect Israel from the effect of sin on the whole land and its people. This concern falls more exactly into the category of ritual impurity than into that of judicial measures against sin. That is, the wrongful killing of a falsely accused person would be like the sin of murder in that it would bring impurity on the land. The city of refuge, therefore, not only protects the refugee, but also quarantines him because of the effect that his own death at the hands of the avenger of blood would have on the land. This dimension emerges more clearly in the law in Num. 35:32, in which the refugee is prohibited from returning to his home before the death of the high priest. This may have the practical effect of allowing the hot blood of revenge to cool. It may also meet the possibility that the refugee is in fact guilty and that his return would therefore make the land impure. Indeeed, in Numbers the refugee is like the murderer in that no 'ransom' can be accepted for him (cf. Num. 35:31), suggesting that the permission to flee to a place of refuge is at the same time a kind of banishment. This aspect, however, is mute in Deuteronomy, which thus emphasizes the humanitarian dimension of the law. (For treatments of atonement in relation to both sin and ritual impurity, see D. P. Wright 1992; 1991.)

19:14

The prominent place here of the law forbidding the moving of a landmark is matched by the curse on anyone who does such a thing (Deut. 27:17), and by severe sayings of the prophets and wisdom writers (Hos. 5:10; Prov. 23:10–11; Job 24:2–4). The offence no doubt covers the sly stealing of areas of arable or pasture land, in terrain where there were no hedges or roads to mark boundaries clearly. The difficulty of dealing with such a crime in law may explain why the offence is subjected to a curse in Deut. 27. But the prophetic and wisdom sayings cited suggest that the law goes further, to include the deliberate taking over of the land of the poor by the powerful. This could occur as land seizure in payment of debt, as presumably envisaged in Is. 5:8, or simply by reason of greater strength (Mic. 2:2), the moving of the boundary marker being a removal of the evidence of ownership (see Craigie 1976a: 332). The story of Ahab and Naboth illustrates the motive and the crime (1 Kgs. 21). That story also sheds light on the law's reference to 'inheritance', the legal right of the owner lying in the ancient gift of the whole land as an 'inheritance' to Israel, so important in Deuteronomy, and in the concept of distributed inheritances embodied in Josh. 13 – 21.

The prominent position of this law shows how closely the need to respect the life and means of others is bound up in Deuteronomy with the prohibition of murder itself.

19:15–21

15. The law requiring more than one witness for an outright conviction appears also at Num. 35:30, as well as at Deut. 17:6. In the former case it occurs in close association with the law on cities of refuge, as it does here. The connection between the two lies in the need for due process in the trial of the one accused of murder. The concern in Deut. 17:6 is similar, in the context of an accusation of idolatry.

16. The present law develops what was implicit there, namely the possibility of false witness, and how this should be prosecuted. The 'malicious witness' is described both as a 'violent witness', a phrase that gives notice of the vicious motive, and also as one who testifies 'falsely' (see 'Notes on the text'). Whether he actually was so could not be known until it was proved; the phrase therefore anticipates that the process about to be described will demonstrate the witness's wicked intentions.

17–21. The case anticipates a witness coming forward alone, in spite of the provision just recorded. Of course, a legitimate witness may hope or expect that others would report too. In the event in question none does. The enquiry that follows still takes the accusation seriously. It is not said whether such an enquiry might, after all, decide against the person accused; presumably, in view of the categorical v. 15, this could occur only if the thorough enquiry made by the judges discovered further witnesses. The thrust of the law, however, is to provide sanctions against witnesses who used the lawcourts to try to take revenge on a personal enemy, or otherwise to gain an advantage at someone else's expense.

The dispute must be brought to the main sanctuary (as indicated by 'before the LORD', v. 17), as with all difficult cases (17:8). The judiciary in this case consists of 'the priests and the judges who are in office at the time'. (Cf. 17:9, where the judge is singular; the plural in this case may mean that local judges are drawn into the enquiry.) The punishment is a case of the so-called 'law of talion' (cf. Exod. 21:23–25; Lev. 24:17–20). The justice is 'poetic', the malicious person's intention being turned precisely against himself. The law of talion, however, also has a strong element of limitation. Just as importantly, it treats all people as exactly on a par, as do all the laws of Deuteronomy, in contrast to ANE law codes (note esp. Lev. 24:22a).

Interestingly, as the law condemning false appropriation of land is illustrated by the story of Naboth, so is potency of false witness, in that case procured by the ruthless king (1 Kgs. 21:10; note the *two* false witnesses).

Explanation

The laws in this chapter are unified by the concept of preserving human life. This is not a bare requirement, but falls within a clear moral framework. The abhorrence of murder (5:17) is the premiss on which the chapter is based, even though neither here nor elsewhere in the book is there a law devoted to the ordinary prosecution of murder. The justice of the death penalty for one guilty of murder is expressed in 19:11–13, and in the law of talion, v. 21 ('life . . . for life').

The laws here can be clearly understood as elaboration of the fundamental requirements of the Decalogue. This is because they deal with matters that arise around the edges of murder, especially the possibility of wrongful conviction, and even the consequential crime of perjury, where the misfortunes of others are turned to another's advantage. Such instances, like the case of murder itself, are also abhorrent, for they too involve the spilling of innocent blood. Not only the murderer but the community as a whole, in its judicial capacity, might become guilty of the ultimate violence, the spilling of innocent human blood being the archetypal crime, which pollutes the earth and causes a breach between God and human beings (cf. Gen. 4:10; 9:5–6, where the sanctity of human blood is linked with the creation of humanity in God's image).

For these reasons, the justice that pursues the guilty must equally zealously protect the innocent. The cases of the boundary marker and the false witness show a deep insight into the inventiveness of human wickedness. Law aims to be practical and enforceable, but it is framed in knowledge of the human heart. And the provisions here have a certain prophetic edge, because they reveal the possibilities of corruption. It is for these reasons that the biblical law codes themselves sometimes shade over into exhortation to the heart, where actions are engendered (Lev. 19:18b).

The law of talion (21) has acquired a bad reputation as a kind of byword for vengefulness, in opposition to a spirit of forgiveness. The principle is sometimes reconciled with Christ's command to forgive enemies by pointing out that the former has its context in the lawcourt, while the latter is appropriate to personal relationships. This is only partly true. A lawcourt, in any society, is obliged to impose penalties laid down, and is not entitled to 'forgive'; it might properly show leniency, however, where there are signs of remorse. Indeed, in certain instances a victim might decide not to press charges, in a spirit of forgiveness. Sometimes whole societies find that they have no hope of a future apart from a strong movement of forgiveness (as the peoples of South Africa and Northern Ireland, among others, have found).

Yet lawcourts are bound to uphold the standards that undergird a society's laws. It is those standards to which the law of talion makes a firm contribution, by asserting the irreducible sanctity of human life. There is no other currency into which human life may be translated. The prince or tycoon must take the consequences of his destruction of the pauper. This is the absolute difference between biblical and other ancient laws. It can remain a bulwark in a modern society in which human life is, in many ways, regarded as a disposable or tradable commodity.

DEUTERONOMY 20:1–20

Translation

[1]When you go to war against your enemies, and see horses and chariots and an army greater than yours, do not be afraid of them, for the LORD your God, who brought you out of Egypt, is with you. [2]When you are about to engage in battle, the priest shall come forward and speak to the army. [3]He shall say to them: 'Hear, Israel! You are about to engage in battle with your enemies this day. Do not be faint-hearted or fearful; do not flee in panic, or be terrified by them. [4]For it is the LORD your God who marches with you, to fight for you against your enemies, and give you victory.'

[5]Then the officials are to say to the army: 'Has anyone built a new house and not yet settled in it? Let him return home, in case he should die in battle and another settle in it. [6]Has anyone planted a vineyard and not yet harvested its first crop? Let him return home, in case he should die in battle and another harvest it. [7]And has anyone become engaged to marry a woman, but has not yet married her? Let him return home, in case he should die in battle and another man marry her.' [8]The officials shall go on to say to the army: 'Is anyone fearful or faint-hearted? Let him go home, lest he cause his brothers to lose heart like himself.' [9]When the officials have finished addressing the army, they shall appoint commanders over it.

[10]When you approach a city to make war against it, you must offer it terms of peace. [11]If they accept the terms and open their gates to you, then all the people in it shall serve you as forced labour. [12]But if they do not make peace, but engage you in war, then begin siege warfare against them. [13]And when the LORD your God gives them over to you, you shall put all the men to the sword. [14]But you may take as plunder all the women and children, and the cattle and all the goods of the city, all its spoil. You may consume the spoil of your enemies, which the LORD your God has given you.

[15]That is how you are to deal with all cities that are at a great distance from you, that is, cities that do not belong to these nations here. [16]As for the cities that belong to these nations that the LORD your God is giving over to you as an inheritance, you must leave nothing alive. [17]Rather, you are to devote them to destruction: the Hittites, Amorites, Canaanites, Perizzites, Hivites and Jebusites, as the LORD your God commanded you. [18]This is so that they may not teach you to do all the abhorrent things they have done for their gods, and you sin against the LORD your God.

[19]When you are laying siege to a city, and you undertake a long-drawn-out war against it in order to take it, do not destroy its trees by taking an axe to them, for you can eat from them. Do not cut them down, therefore. Are trees of the field people, that they should be besieged by you? [20]However, you may cut down any tree that you know is not fruit-bearing and use it to build siege-works against a city that is at war with you, until it falls.

Notes on the text

1–2. 'Army' is strictly 'people'. The word is sometimes used in this military sense, and the context shows that this is the sense here. The distinction between 'army' and 'people' is not as we might expect today, however (see 'Comment').

2. $k^eq^orobkem$: prep. k^e with inf. construct of verb $qārab$, 'draw near'. For the form see GKC 61d. The clause is temporal ('when'), giving the sense of contemporaneous action.

5. 'officials': this is preferable to 'officers' (NIV), which gives the impression that these are the military leaders themselves, whereas v. 9 makes clear that they are not.

$yēlēk$ $w^eyāšōb$: lit. 'let him go and return' (also v. 6). These are two jussives, as is clear from the sense; but note also that the jussive of the 'hollow' verb ($šûb$) differs in form from the imperfect.

8. $yimmas$: 3 m. sg. ni. of $māsas$, 'to melt'. The niphal sits oddly with the following sign of the accusative, $'et$, and for this reason the hiph. $yāmēs$ is adopted by SamP (followed by LXX, Syr, Vg), meaning 'cause to melt'. There is an analogy with MT's construction in 12:22, however (see note there), which may suggest that MT is correct.

9. 'they shall appoint commanders': thus with NIV, against NRSV, 'the commanders shall take charge'. There is no analogy for such a use of $pāqad$. NRSV is perhaps influenced by the supposition that the officials in question are subordinate and unlikely to have the authority to appoint commanders. Alternatively, 'they' is impersonal, and the meaning is simply, 'the commanders shall be appointed' (S. R. Driver 1895: 238).

13. 'And when the LORD your God gives them' ($ûn^etānāh$ $yhwh$): or possibly 'And the LORD your God will give them'.

14. 'consume': often translated 'enjoy' or 'use', but is strictly 'eat'.

19. 'Are trees of the field people?' The interpretation as a question takes its cue from LXX. The Hebrew should be repointed $he'ādām$, i.e. with the interrogative particle rather than the definite article.

Form and structure

The laws on warfare in Deuteronomy are the only ones in the OT. Deut. 20 contains the main ones (see also 21:10–14; 23:9–14; 24:5). These are positioned here because of the connection of thought between war and homicide, the subject of ch. 19, both under the influence of the Sixth Commandment prohibiting murder. The thought that connects these laws with Deut. 19 in particular is the question of legitimacy and illegitimacy in the taking of human life. The answer to this question comes in vv. 11–13, with a further proviso in vv. 16–18. The treatment of the theme affirms that Israel's war is properly Yahweh's war (1), then draws in regulations on the preparations for war (2–4), the muster of troops (5–8), the appointment of leaders (9), the conduct of the war (10–15), the special principles that govern war within the promised land (16–18), and restrictions on the use of trees in siege-works (19–20).

These divisions are marked syntactically with a sequence of conditional sentences. The first main section is vv. 1–9, beginning with a 'when' (*kî* with impf.) clause, on which a number of further clauses depend. This section is also framed by the idea of 'fear' (1, 8–9). A second section is signalled by another similar opening at v. 10, and the final section in the same way at v. 19. The clauses concerning the 'holy war' (15–18) are introduced differently. The phrase 'That is how you are to deal with' (lit. 'Thus you shall do') in other places introduces additional laws (cf. 22:3, and Brin 1994: 37–38). In this case it appears to resume the requirements of vv. 10–14, with their permission to spare the lives of women and children when reducing a defiant city, in order to lead into the restriction laid down in vv. 16–18, beginning with the conjunction 'only' (*raq*), which withholds such permission for cities close at hand.

This syntactical structure shows that the main topic is 'ordinary' warfare, defined as war against 'cities that are at a great distance from you' (15), the war in the land being introduced only in a parenthesis. The context addressed is a settled one (5–7), not that of the tribes massed on the plains of Moab. No special occasion of war is specified. Rather, these are general principles and regulations, such as other nations also had (similar at points to these; see 'Comment' on vv. 5–7). The subject, moreover, is the conduct of war, not the justification of it, whether in general or in particular.

Comment

20:1–9

1–2. The law is concerned with war fought by Israel, after settlement in the land, against external enemies. In the ancient world, 'going out to war' was a seasonal thing, a regular activity of kings to expand their kingdom for the glory of their gods. An echo of this is found in 2 Sam. 11:1: 'at the turn of the year [i.e. spring] when kings go out [to war]'. (The words 'to war' are missing in MT, but present in many manuscripts and probably original; see *BHS*.) The case of David's war against the Ammonites in that chapter is a good example of the sort of war envisaged here. According to 2 Sam. 7:1, David had fully occupied the promised land by military victories; the war against Ammon was undertaken after this in response to a studied insult and preparations for an attack on Israel (2 Sam. 10:1–6). The war of conquest, therefore, would not end all wars. Israel, as a political entity within the world of its day, was bound to be involved in political and military strategy.

The address (in the singular) is to the people as a whole. This in itself sets Israel apart from other nations, where the king was responsible for war, and is in line with Deuteronomy's concept of a people that bears authority in itself, through properly appointed officials, under the kingship of Yahweh. The 'army', indeed, consists of the whole people gathered for the purpose, not the standing armies of the days of the kings (the term at the end of v. 2 is simply 'the people', hā'ām). The picture rather resembles that found in Judges, in which the tribes supply fighting men as need arises.

3–4. Common to both the original war of conquest and later wars would be the idea that the whole people constitute the fighting force, and that the war is undertaken by Yahweh. For this reason the issue on the eve of the conquest is pictured: though enemies might seem invincible, the war was Yahweh's, who had overcome the might of Egypt to deliver his people (cf. 1:28–31; 8:14). This being so, they should not fear any foe. The issue was played out in 1:26–46. 'Victory' (4) is strictly 'deliverance' or 'salvation'. Thus, though Israel is depicted as 'going out' to war against distant enemies, the issue is still conceived as a threat to them from forces hostile to Yahweh. The conflict has a spiritual dimension. The key point in the laws about war is faith in Yahweh.

The part played by the priest symbolizes the fact that the war belongs to Yahweh, just as war in general was religious in the ANE. In Joshua (3:1–4), priests play a prominent role in the military march on the land, carrying the ark of the covenant ahead of the people. Deuteronomy says nothing about the ark of the covenant here (and little elsewhere; cf. 10:8). Its interest in the priest in this instance is as the one who places the forthcoming war under the authority of Yahweh. His opening words, 'Hear, Israel!' (3), are reminiscent of the Mosaic basic call to obedience and faith in Yahweh (6:4; cf. 4:1; 5:1). They declare that the war is to begin, and call the people to fight under Yahweh. It may be, too, that the priest has a kind of judicial role here, extended from his judicial role in legal affairs (cf. 17:9; 21:5), to represent the judgment of Yahweh among the nations (Braulik 1992a: 144).

20:5–9

5–7. The 'officials' have both judicial and military responsibilities (cf. 1:15; 16:18; and see 'Comment' on the former passage). In this case they have oversight of the muster, that is, the gathering of the troops. Their formal declaration of exemptions is part of that responsibility.

The first three exemptions (5–7) are echoed in the curse in 28:30. The underlying thought in both cases seems to be that people have an inalienable right to enjoy the basic elements of the blessings promised in the land. The parallel with Deut. 28:30 is a clue to an understanding of these exemptions. The type of curse there is known as a 'futility curse', that is, one in which an action intended to produce a certain result is frustrated. The futility curses probably express an underlying fear that something begun but not finished might have ongoing destructive influence in life (de Bruin 1999: 29, 32, following Schmid 1976: 405–406). Exemptions from war are known throughout the ANE, as the Ugaritic text *CTA* 14.2:96–103 shows. The idea is also found in the ancient Sumerian poem *Gilgamesh and the Land of the Living* (*ANET* 48 line 50; so de Bruin 1999: 21; Craigie 1976a: 273). It may be present, too, in Ps. 68:6[7]: '[Yahweh] sends the "bachelor" home.' In our text it is combined with the form of the futility curse. It expands the curses in 28:30 so as to draw out possible consequences. The corresponding opposite thought may be found in Jer. 29:5–6.

Theologically, the exemptions are linked here with the concept of 'rest' in the land (12:9), which means freedom to enjoy its benefits without pressure from enemies (Carmichael 1974: 118–128). The one who has built a house should be able to live in it; the term used means, in certain contexts, 'dedicate' (e.g. 1 Kgs. 8:63), and the noun, *ḥᵃnukkâ*, is best known in connection with the rededication of the temple after its desecration by Antiochus IV Epiphanes and the Jewish feast that commemorates it. The meaning here, however, is probably simply 'first use or enjoyment', in line with the other instances in the context (Reif 1972). The person who has established a vineyard, the work of several years before the first harvest (five years, according to Lev. 19:23–25), should enjoy the long-awaited fruit of that harvest. He then, literally, 'profanes' it, that is, puts it to its first use for food, following the dedication of the first crop to Yahweh. (The provision may be contrasted with the law in CH 60–63, in which a five-year period of labour is required of the tenant-farmer by the owner, so that the *owner* may not be deprived of the fruit of his land.) The man who has married should be able to begin married life with his bride. The related law in 24:5 specifies a year as the mimimum period of this exemption. The idea of consummation, and therefore of having children, is included in the marrying.

In the cases of house and vineyard, there are, no doubt, additional entailments of establishing legal ownership, and, in the case of marriage, of ensuring perpetuation of a man's name through offspring. Implied in all these are the right of individuals to have their share in the 'inheritance' of Israel, the land given by Yahweh. Property played an important part in legal status too, the prohibitions in the Decalogue (or at least the second half of it) being largely comprehensible in terms of the rights of individuals not to have their basic rights infringed.

The final exemption, marked off by its separate introduction, is surprising, and belongs closely with the concept of war as Yahweh's, with its implication that Israel should not fear (cf. v. 3). The criterion is put into practice in Gideon's war with Midian (Judg. 7:2–3), where the huge reduction that resulted is turned to the purpose of demonstrating that the victory actually is Yahweh's. The permission not to participate in the war, in a context in which the army consists in principle of the whole people, is remarkable. This voluntarism is memorialized in the famous Song of Deborah, which celebrates the victory of Deborah and Barak over the Canaanite alliance under Jabin of Hazor (Judg. 5; note 'the people offer themselves willingly', 5:2; and conversely the failure of certain sections of the people to participate, 5:17, 23). While the people is formally 'called up' by the tribal officials, the principle on which they fight is that of willing participation, seen as a function of their obedience to and trust in Yahweh.

When the officials have established the forces who will fight, the commanders for the battle are appointed (see 'Notes on the text').

20:10–14

10. The procedures outlined in these verses are quite different from the kind of warfare commanded in 7:1–2, and apply to ordinary warfare conducted by the people after settlement in the land (see above on v. 1). The offer of peace concerns the kind of relationship that will exist between conqueror and conquered after the war, in accordance with the universal practice of treaty-making in the ANE. (The Hebr. *šālôm* is more than 'peace' here, being closer to 'peace treaty'. It is similar, therefore, to Akk. *salīmum*; Craigie 1976a: 276 n.)

11. A defeated city could be laid under tribute or, as here, subjected to forced labour. The case of the Gibeonites illustrates the dictation of terms to a city that surrenders (Josh. 9). These people persuaded Joshua that they were not native to the land but had come from a distant place, and so Joshua made a 'peace treaty' (*šālôm*) with them (Josh. 9:15; cf. 11:19; 2 Kgs. 18:31). They thus escaped the 'devotion to destruction', and were spared to become servants of the Israelites. (The case is peculiar, because Gibeon was actually a city in the land, yet it exemplifies the treatment of a city outside it. However, Joshua actually subjected numerous Canaanite cities to forced labour; see 'Explanation'.)

12–13. The recalcitrant city is punished by the slaughter of all its men. This is not the 'devotion to destruction' that befalls the cities of the land itself, but rather an emasculation to ensure no further threat. The victory is portrayed in terms similar to the victory in the promised land: Yahweh gives the enemy into the hand of Israel (cf. 3:2–3; 7:24) and they are allowed to take plunder, including, in this case, the women and children. (A further law governing the capture of a woman in war is found at 21:10–14.)

14. The Israelites may 'consume' (the translation takes account of the literal 'eat', while trying to convey the sense of 'enjoy') the benefits that fall to them as a result (cf. 6:10–11). (The motif of eating is a key signifier of blessing, e.g. in chs. 8 and 14.)

20:15–18

15. The explanatory v. 15 functions as an introduction to the next short section, which brings a distinction not yet signalled (see 'Notes on the text'). Special regulations arising from distance have occurred before in Deuteronomy (12:20–27; 14:24); here the distinction between 'far and near' has a new meaning, signifying the difference between places within the promised land and places beyond.

16–17. The general rules for warfare do not apply to the special situation of the imminent conquest of the promised land, which Yahweh claims as his own in order to give to the Israelites. There the *ḥerem* applies, that is, the 'complete destruction' of an enemy as a kind of sacrifice to God (see on 2:34; 7:2–3). The book of Joshua narrates the implementation of this 'destruction', especially in the cases of Jericho and Ai (Josh. 6 – 8). The rule of the *ḥerem* is that 'you must leave nothing alive' (16; cf. Josh. 11:14), that is, destroy 'everything that breathes'. This is variously interpreted as people and animals (Josh. 6:21, Jericho) and as people only, the livestock being available as booty (Josh. 8:2, Ai). At both Jericho and Ai the booty was included in the 'devotion to destruction', which in this respect, too, distinguishes the *ḥerem* from ordinary war.

ḥerem was a phenomenon widely known in the ancient world, but it appears originally to have been used selectively as a special religious act, perhaps in fulfilment of a vow. There is an echo of this in Num. 21:2–3 (where the place where the city had stood is named Hormah, after the *ḥerem* applied to it). The same is probably true of the *ḥerem* pronounced by the Moabite King Mesha on the Israelite city of Nebo. Deuteronomy, however, presents the entire conquest of the land as falling under the terms of the *ḥerem*, the booty falling to Israel (6:10–11). Many commentators think that the present regulations are a deuteronomic addition to the general law on warfare, representing a systematizing of the older concept of *ḥerem* (Mayes 1979: 294; Levinson 1997: 40; Brin 1994: 39).

The nations enumerated correspond to those named in 7:1, with the omission of the Girgashites; the list occurs in two forms, either with or without this people (see 'Comment' there).

18. The rationale for the destruction of the peoples of the land, that they might lead Israel to worship false gods, is similar to the one in 7:4 (cf. 12:30; Judg. 2:1–3).

20:19–20

19–20. The final two verses return to the main theme of the chapter – ordinary war beyond the limits of the land – the idea of siege making a link with v. 12. The preservation order on trees is supported by the rhetorical question in v. 19b (see 'Notes on the text'); trees do not make war, and therefore should not be destroyed. This scarcely means that trees have a higher value than human beings; only that they have a place in the natural order, yet are without the moral responsibility that humans have. The exemption of non-fruit-bearing varieties (20) introduces a further criterion for the protection of trees, namely their usefulness for food. Food is one of the essential blessings of the promised land. Here there is an extension to produce outside the land also, belonging to other peoples. The intention is presumably that, even in waging a war against a population, Israel must not permanently damage its ecosystem. A particular war may be justified for some reason, but the possibility of life for a people must not be removed for ever. The food-producing potential of the trees is in relation to the indigenous people; the besieging Israelites may, however, use them for their own needs on the occasion in question. Deuteronomy comes close here to a theology of creation, alongside its highly developed theology of covenant.

Explanation

The deuteronomic law of war is part of the biblical story of Israel. The command concerning the *herem* for the peoples of the promised land relates to the phase of the story told in Numbers–Joshua, that is, the conquest of Canaan. The main part of the law in Deut. 20, however, is connected with the subsequent history, told in the books of Samuel–Kings, when Israel undertook wars against such nations as Ammon (2 Sam. 10 – 11), Syria (1 Kgs. 20), and Moab (2 Kgs. 3). The present law and these narratives are about securing Israel's 'rest' in their land. The correspondence between the law and the narrative is not exact. The Israelites who conquered Canaan, for example, put numerous cities in the promised land itself to forced labour, having failed to drive them out (e.g. Josh. 16:10; 17:13; Judg. 1:28–35). Solomon apparently subjected Israelites to it (1 Kgs. 5:27), though perhaps temporarily (see 9:21–22). Conversely, the Amalekites, not a people of the land, are to be 'devoted to destruction' by Saul, who fails to do it and is censured for it (1 Sam. 15; note vv. 3, 8–11). All this is irregular, in the logic of the biblical narrative, and a function of Israel's failure fully to obey the covenant and to enter into its blessings.

Modern Christian readers ask what purpose such a law can have for them. More disturbingly, how can the God who is love, and who commands love of enemies, command the annihilation of men, women and children in a 'holy war'? Early in a new millennium we may well ponder a thousand years of 'holy wars', all having disastrous, and lengthy, consequences. In answer to the question why the Bible contains a law about war, the following three points may be made.

1. War is simply an inevitable part of life, like law and punishment, and therefore Israel, as a nation among nations, must prepare for war and

know how to conduct it. All nations had laws and customs governing war. If Israel is to fight wars, however, it is to do so at the instigation of Yahweh and under his leadership.

2. Is the deuteronomic law merely of historical interest, therefore, or can it speak in any way to modern warfare? It is essential to realize that it cannot be used to condone any kind of 'holy war'. The identification of God's purposes with the interests of any nation cannot be carried over from the OT to the NT age, since in Christian theology 'Israel' is now identified with Christ and his universal church, which has no earthly armies. The Crusaders were tragically wrong just on this. But the temptation to confuse 'just war' and 'holy war' is still very much alive, even in the secular West, and should be opposed at every turn.

However, the laws concerning 'ordinary' warfare in Deut. 20 can have a bearing on matters of conduct of war. Most accept that wars are sometimes necessary. Pacifism – the dominant position of the church in the first three Christian centuries (Hays [1996: 341] prefers the term 'nonviolence') – is far from so these days (but see the defence in Yoder 1994; Kreider 1988). It remains very hard to decide whether any particular war constitutes a 'just war'. And in fact Deuteronomy's law does not directly address the matter, since it assumes that Yahweh will lead the nation into wars, and even that Israel's interests are by definition identical with his. Even so, if a war may ever be justified, on the ground rules explicated by St Augustine, then Deuteronomy's requirement of restraint in the case of a people that surrenders (10–11), of limitation in the effects of warfare (19–20), and of humane treatment in the case of captives (21:10–14) have a bearing, and indeed have entered into modern thinking about warfare.

3. But the most important perspective on the laws of warfare is the part they play, along with the narratives of conquest, in symbolizing God's war on evil. Christians may wish to 'spiritualize' this, and to hold that the earthly wars of Israel correspond to wars in heaven between the forces of good and evil. It is true, of course, that there is 'spiritual warfare'. But spiritualization of the struggle between good and evil is not the whole truth, for it may simply transpose the problem of war from one sphere (earth) to another (heaven). Apocalyptic literature, like the book of Daniel, knows of a correspondence between earthly wars and heavenly ones; this is the significance of the conflict between the 'princes' of Persia and Greece, who are opposed by the 'prince' Michael, who leads God's heavenly armies (Dan. 10:20 – 11:1). Evil and conflict take earthly forms, and cannot, in the end, be separated from the war in heaven.

DEUTERONOMY 21:1–23

Translation

¹If the body of one who has died violently is found lying in the open country, in the land the LORD your God is giving you to possess, and it is not known who killed him, ²your elders and judges must come and measure the distances to the cities that are near the body. ³When it has been established which city is nearest the body, the elders of that city shall take a heifer which has not yet been worked, or put under a yoke, ⁴bring it to a wadi that has a perpetual flow and that has not yet been ploughed or sown, and break its neck, there in the wadi.

⁵Then the priests, the sons of Levi, shall come forward, for the LORD your God has chosen them to serve him and to pronounce blessing in the name of the LORD, for by their word shall all disputes and cases of assault be settled. ⁶And all the elders of that city, being nearest to the dead man, shall wash their hands over the heifer whose neck has been broken in the wadi, ⁷and declare, 'Our hands did not spill this blood, nor did we witness the crime. ⁸Make atonement for your people whom you set free, O LORD, and do not let the guilt for innocent blood remain on your people.' And the blood-guilt will be forgiven them. ⁹So you will purge yourselves of the guilt for innocent blood, when you do what is right in the LORD's sight.

¹⁰If, when you go out to war against your enemies, the LORD gives you victory and you make captives of them, ¹¹and you see a beautiful woman among the captives and desire her, and you take her as your wife ¹²and bring her into your house: have her shave her head, trim her nails ¹³and put off the clothes in which she was captured. She shall live in your house, mourning her mother and father for a full month. After that you may go to her as her husband, and she shall be your wife. ¹⁴If, after all, she does not please you, let her go free. You must not sell her for money, or trade her, since you have had your way with her.

¹⁵If a man, having two wives, prefers one to the other, and, while both have given him sons, the eldest son belongs to the wife he does not love, ¹⁶on the day when he divides his inheritance among his sons, he may not give the eldest son's share to the son of the wife he loves in place of the son of the unloved wife, who is actually the firstborn. ¹⁷Rather, he must acknowledge the son of the unloved wife as his firstborn, and give him a double share of all that belongs to him. For he is the first issue of his manhood, and the right of the firstborn belongs to him.

¹⁸If a man has an unteachable and rebellious son, who refuses to obey father or mother, and, though they discipline him, he does not listen to them, ¹⁹the father and mother must bring him to the elders of the city at the city gate, ²⁰and say to them: 'This son of ours is unteachable and rebellious; he will not obey us; he is a drunken profligate.' ²¹Then all the men of the city shall stone him to death. Thus you will purge yourselves of the evil; and all Israel shall hear of it and be in awe.

²²When a man has been convicted of a capital offence, and he has been put to death and hung on a tree, ²³his corpse must not be allowed to remain on the tree overnight; be sure to bury it on the same day, for a hanged man is accursed by God; do not defile the land the LORD your God is giving you as an inheritance.

Notes on the text

1. 'and it is not known who killed him': a verbal circumstantial clause; see GKC 156d, f, g.

2. SamP adds 'and your officials', probably a late addition.

3. Lit. '(and it shall be) the city that is nearest the body, the elders of that city . . . ': the syntax of the first clause is loose, but it pictures a stage in the proceedings before the action required of the elders. This is missed by translations that simply begin, 'The elders of the city that is nearest . . . ' (NRSV, NIV). With the translation adopted here cf. EÜ.

6. 'nearest': though the adjective is plural, strictly qualifying 'elders', many translations translate it as if feminine singular agreeing with 'city', thus 'the elders of the city nearest the body . . . ' The present translation offers an interpretation of the text as it is (cf. EÜ).

7. 'declare': the combination *'āmar*, 'say', and *'ānâ*, 'respond, testify', occurs several times in the laws with this sense of solemn declaration. It is not far from the sense of 'testify' (cf. *'ānâ* in 19:16, 18).

'spill': the consonantal MT text suggests a feminine singular, as if following the singular 'our hand', though MT in fact has 'our hands'. The ancient versions regularize this, making the whole phrase either singular (Syr) or plural (LXX, SamP, QL, Tg). MT is pointed to read plural, despite the consonantal form.

8. 'whom you set free': LXX adds 'out of the land of Egypt', conforming to other texts where the verb occurs, and where Egypt is specified in some way, though not precisely as here (7:8; 9:26; 13:6; 15:15; 24:18).

9. 'the guilt for innocent blood': LXX adds 'and it will be well with you', by analogy with 19:13.

10. 'your enemies': singular in some versions, and followed by singular in MT ('the LORD gives *him* into your hand'). There is some mobility between singular and plural in this term, because of its collective meaning; cf. 20:1 and *BHS*.

14. 'trade her': the verb is used only here and at Deut. 24:7 in the OT. It is often translated 'treat as a slave'. In both places, however, the implication of such treatment seems to be bound up with the idea of the right to sell.

18. 'though they discipline him, he does not listen to them': this might be taken as a circumstantial clause (cf. on 21:1), because it expresses repeated action, and is parallel in content to the preceding clause.

21. 'the evil': some LXX MSS have 'the evil one' (also at 13:6), which is a possible reading of the Hebrew.

23. 'accursed by God': the phrase has sometimes been read 'an affront to God', which makes a smooth transition to the following idea of defilement of the land. LXX and Gal. 3:13 support the reading adopted here.

Form and structure

The laws in Deut. 21, like those in chs. 19 – 20, continue to show a connection with the Sixth Commandment, the prohibition of murder. More precisely, they deal with restrictions and procedures surrounding the legitimate taking of life – in the justice system and in war – and thus the prevention of shedding innocent blood. The law concerning the unsolved murder (21:1–9) has a correspondence with the law of the accidental homicide (19:1–13), each ending with the aim that Israel should not incur guilt for the shedding of blood (19:13; 21:9). Both laws also begin with a form of the land-gift formula (19:1; 21:1), focusing on the underlying purpose of the laws that Israel should not desecrate the land they are possessing, a point that recurs in 21:23b. And each demonstrates the responsibility of all Israel to ensure that the proper measures are taken (cf. Braulik 1991b: 70–72).

Further links operate between the laws in the chapter and in chs. 19 – 20. The war theme (ch. 20) is continued in 21:10–14. It is possible that this section originally belonged closely with the material in ch. 20, but that it has been repositioned in order to make a transition into the family laws, concerning inheritance and the rebellious son, in 21:15–21. The law of the captive wife is best understood in a polygamous context, and therefore has this in common with the following law of inheritance, dealing with a man's sons by two different wives (Braulik 1991b: 71). This law in turn forms a link between the captive wife who is rejected (21:14) and the 'unloving' son (21:18–21; Kaufman 1978–9: 136). Kaufman (1978–9: 135) also observes a progression from greater to lesser, from laws concerning Israel's institutions (19:1 – 21:9), through family, to criminals (21:22–23) and finally animals (22:1–4).

The association of these laws with the Sixth Commandment does not mean that every law must be strictly accounted for in this way; other organizational criteria are called into play, as we have noticed. However, the laws here that do not involve the taking of a life (21:10–17) reflect the corresponding positive requirement that human beings should be respected and their life and dignity made possible.

Comment

21:1–9

The laws in the present chapter are all 'casuistic', that is, they consist of conditions, signalled by opening *kî-* ('if') clauses, which are followed mainly by series of *waw*-consecutives with the perfect tense. The first division is vv. 1–9, dealing with the unsolved murder.

Here the condition is contained in v. 1, which ends with a circumstantial clause ('and it is not known who killed him'); all the succeeding clauses belong to the apodosis (the instructions). The series of *waw*-consecutives is broken at v. 6, where the subject, 'all the elders of that city', is placed in the emphatic first position with the verb following in the imperfect tense, the direct speech in vv. 7–8, and the closing exhortation (9). These breaks in the pattern highlight respectively the importance of the main participants, what they say, and the reason for the action.

1. The law focuses, therefore, on the responsibility of Israel to make atonement for the blood that has been shed. Both these elements, Israel's responsibility and shed blood, are highlighted in the land-gift formula, the former because of the direct address to Israel. The formula also uses the term *'ᵃdāmâ* for 'land', which has connotations of 'earth' or 'ground', and in this instance is reminiscent of the 'earth' that was polluted by Abel's blood (Gen. 4:10–11). As we noted on 19:8–10, the spilling of blood has the consequence not only of making the murderer liable to judicial penalty, but also of making the land itself ritually impure. We consider below how the ceremony relates to the guilt arising from the murder and to cleansing the land of the impurity that results from it.

The phrase 'if *x* is found' occurs several times in this group of laws (also 22:22; 24:7; cf. 17:2). It implies discovery by the community, but perhaps also exposure to the sight of God, and therefore an offensive thing that must be removed from sight (cf. on v. 23; and Carmichael 1974: 45–46, citing Daube 1969).

There is no provision here for an enquiry or for the pursuit of the murderer. The case concerns the discovery of the body of someone who has died violently. The term *ḥālāl*, 'pierced', accompanied as here by the participle *nōpēl*, 'fallen', is also used of those who have died in battle (1 Sam. 31:1; Ezek. 32:20). The law does not address the question whether the homicide came into the categories considered in 19:4–7, 11–13. The phrase 'and it is not known who killed him' may imply, however, that enquiry has been made and has failed to discover the perpetrator. The verb 'killed', *hikkāhû* (*nkh*, hiph.), is the same as the one found in 19:4, used of the homicide who is entitled to resort to the city of refuge; it is therefore neutral on the question of intent. For the purposes of right procedure, however, the assumption is made that there is guilt for the shedding of innocent blood, and that it must be dealt with appropriately.

2–3a. The responsibility for the necessary propitiatory ritual that lies on Israel falls representatively on the officials of the city nearest to the body, as the proper authorities to carry it out on behalf of all. (A legal responsibility of cities for an area around them was also known in Babylon and elsewhere in the ANE; Driver & Miles 1952: 110–111.) This does not mean that the city is held responsible for the crime, or is suspected of it; nor is it liable for compensation to the family of the victim; contrast CH 23–24; HL 6). Rather, unatoned blood-guilt affects the whole community, and the officials of this city act to make amends on its behalf. (Cf. the blood-guilt that remained on Saul's house for his murders at Gibeon, resulting in famine on the whole land; 2 Sam. 21:1–14; Gertz 1994: 171.)

The ceremony involves three categories of officials, namely judges, elders and 'the priests, the sons of Levi' (5). In v. 2 the elders and judges presumably represent the cities in the vicinity of the crime, since the single city that must undertake the atonement ritual has not yet been determined. Each city will have had elders by virtue of seniority and standing, and judges, by the provision of Deut. 16:18. The role of elders, in a matter concerning the relations of the city with the community outside, was representative (cf. 19:12; Judg. 8:14, 16), while that of the judges was, of course, judicial. Their duty here was presumably to preside over the measuring to ensure that no dispute arose on the point of distance. After the nearest city has been determined, the elders of that city take centre stage; the elders in v. 3 are therefore a more restricted group than those in v. 2 (cf. Gertz 1994: 162–163). The judges, having done their work, apparently recede from the scene.

3b–4. The ritual itself, the killing of a heifer that has not yet been used for work, in a wadi-bed that has not been cultivated, is without exact parallel in the OT. It is scarcely a sacrifice, since there is no altar, and the breaking of the neck is expressly not a sacrificial method (cf. Exod. 13:13). An atonement ceremony in which an unworked heifer is burned outside the camp is recorded in Num. 19:1–10, but the occasion is unspecified and the action different from this one.

There is a possible connection with the scapegoat, in which a goat is sent to 'Azazel', that is, a deserted place, loaded with the sins of Israel, on the Day of Atonement (Lev. 16:1–22). The wadi-bed would resemble a desert, being rocky and unsuitable for cultivation. The symbolism of the perpetually flowing stream (not typical of wadies, which normally dry up in summer) is different from the demonic Azazel image, yet could serve the same function of carrying the sins away from the populated area.

A different explanation is that the action replicates the execution of the criminal that has not proved possible (Janowski 1982: 165–166; cf. Gertz 1994: 167 n., for the interpretations that have been offered). The last of these would meet the need of a compensating death as propitiation for the capital offence (Phillips 1970: 94; Num. 35:31–33). Yet there was apparently no such need in the case of the accidental homicide (Deut. 19:1–13), so this cannot have been an absolute necessity. Indeed, the law in Numbers that demands the death of the murderer also says that atonement cannot be effected except by his death. This is an important limitation, preventing the execution of some other innocent person instead of the guilty one (cf. 24:16).

5. The role of 'the priests, the sons of Levi' is the hardest to discern in the ceremony. As Wellhausen (1889: 359) noted, 'they come late, have nothing to do, but simply cannot be left out' (i.e. in the view of some redactor). Their formulaic designation refers to both religious and legal functions. In terms of the latter, they form part of the 'high court' constituted at the main sanctuary for difficult legal cases (17:8–13). A rationale for their presence here could be that it symbolizes the effectiveness of the ritual performed by the elders of the nearest city for all Israel.

6–9. The ritual is explained in connection with the prayer of the elders (8); it is best understood as a visual representation of the removal of sin and its effects from the land (cf., somewhat differently, Carmichael 1996: 132–134). If there is also an element of propitiation, it follows that there is a certain limitation in the concept of compensatory death, since no person other than the actual murderer may be executed (Phillips 1970: 34; cf. Deut. 24:16). The present law shares this, too, with the case of the accidental homicide.

The elders wash their hands, probably as a sign of innocence (Ps. 26:6; Matt. 27:24). This is reinforced by the prayer and the final comment (8–9), which shows that the aim of the whole process has been to protect the community from the guilt of shedding innocent blood, and the consequences of it.

21:10–14

10–13. In the law concerning the woman taken in war (10–14), the first 'if' (*kî-*) clause is followed by a number of *waw*-consecutive clauses with perfect tense that continue to spell out the conditions (thus differently from the preceding law). The series of conditions could terminate either at the end of v. 11 ('and you take her as your wife') or after the first clause of v. 12 ('and you take her into your house'). The latter has been preferred here (with NRSV), because the series of actions up to that point coheres as a set of conditions; that is, this is what might be supposed to happen in the case of a woman seized in war. The instructions then begin in the middle of v. 12, with 'have her shave her head', and consist of five further *waw*-consecutive clauses (to 'for a full month'). The law culminates in a new sequence of clauses, beginning with a conjunction with imperfect ('after that you may go to her'), with instructions following, again initially in the form *waw*-consecutive + pf., and incorporating instructions for the circumstance that she is displeasing to him in some way.

One practical purpose of the law may be to enable a marriage to take place in circumstances that make the usual familial contract impossible (Pressler 1993: 11–12). However, the syntactical structure shows that the main concern of the law is that the captive should be treated with dignity, by being allowed to mourn, and then by being given the full rights and status of a wife. The assumption of the law is polygamous, like the following (15–17).

14. The eventuality in v. 14a, that the man is not pleased with her and wishes to divorce her, is not confined to a case such as this, but could arise

following any marriage (cf. 24:1). The man's action may amount to a
formal divorce, although there is no mention here of the bill of divorce
described in 24:1. The verb is the same in each case (*šillaḥ*); here, however,
the emphasis is on the woman's freedom. She must not be traded with, as
if she were a slave. (The only other occurrence in the OT of the verb used
here for 'trade' is in 24:7, where it means making a slave of a person by
selling him or her; cf. Brin 1994: 28 n.) Rather, her case is like that of the
slave whom her master marries but then divorces (Exod. 21:8–11). The
fact of her marriage to a free Israelite means that she must be treated as a
free Israelite herself. The final clause, 'because you have had your way
with her', uses a verb that typically means 'rape' or 'humiliate'. In this case
it may mean specifically that the sexual relationship that came with
enforced marriage to the free man has conferred social equality on her
(Braulik 1992a: 155).

21:15–17

The syntax of the law of the firstborn's inheritance is couched in
oppositions, arising from the two possible courses of action open to the
testator. The first instruction is a strong negative, 'he may not give the
eldest son's share to the son of the wife he loves' (16b), followed by an
equally strong command, 'Rather (*kî*), he must acknowledge the son of the
unloved wife as his firstborn' (17), the law finishing with the grounds for
the command (again introduced with *kî*, 'for', 'because') 'for he is the first
issue of his manhood, and the right of the firstborn belongs to him' (17).

The law rests on the custom, widespread in the ANE, that the first son
receives a double share of the inheritance, meaning that he receives twice
as much as the share of any other son (see MAL B 1). It does not mean
'two thirds', therefore, a misconception that has sometimes arisen because
in fact only two sons are in question here, and on the basis of Zech 13:8,
where again only two groups are in view (cf. Brin 1994: 240–242;
Westbrook 1991: 18–20). The divided property might in practice remain
undivided, the portions being administered together (cf. Deut. 25:5–10;
and see Westbrook 1991: 118–141).

The case addressed is strongly reminiscent of the story of Jacob, who
favoured the son of his second but beloved wife Rachel (namely Joseph),
and whose firstborn, Reuben, lost the right of the firstborn because of his
misdemeanour with Jacob's concubine Bilhah (Gen. 49:3–4). Joseph
received the 'double share' when his two sons, Ephraim and Manasseh,
each inherited tribal territory in the promised land (Gen. 48:5; Josh. 14:4a;
cf. 17:14–17). Jacob's action runs counter to the law of Deuteronomy; it
may be that the law recalls his action and refuses to allow it to become the
norm (cf. Carmichael 1974: 139–140). The primary concern of the law
may be to protect the interests of the mother of the firstborn.

21:18–21

18–20. The law of the rebellious son is formed rather like the law of the unsolved murder (1–9), that is, an opening conditional (*kî-*) clause, followed by two circumstantial clauses ('who refuses to obey' and 'though they discipline him, he does not listen to them'), followed by a series of *waw*-consecutive clauses expressing the instructions, interrupted by direct speech (20), the whole culminating in a motive clause (again *waw*-consecutive + pf.): 'thus you will purge the evil', and a final subject + impf.: 'and all Israel shall hear of it and be in awe'.

The case of the rebellious son goes beyond matters of family alone, for, as we have seen (on the Fifth Commandment, 5:16), the family unit is an essential part of the larger political and religious fabric. Respect for parents was therefore a basic element in a right attitude to the whole society and indeed to God. A law in Exod. 21:15 demands the death penalty for 'striking' father or mother; the word 'strike' can mean 'kill', but need not, and a special law requiring death for parricide would probably be superfluous. Lev. 20:9, which prescribes death for 'cursing' parents (cf. Deut. 27:16), shows that lesser crimes against parents were regarded as meriting the supreme penalty.

The judicial action of father against son was a feature of ANE law. In Babylon, a son could not be disinherited by the father's wish alone, but a just cause had to be proved in court (CH 168–169). These laws allow for a 'second chance', as if to ensure that the son was punished only for persistent faults. The same concern is present in the biblical law in the clause 'though they discipline him, he does not listen to them' (18), which, by its tenses, indicates repeated action (see 'Notes on the text'). The disciplining will probably have included corporal punishment (Prov. 23:13–14), which could even have been publicly known (cf. Deut. 22:18). The offences are not specified, except by the words 'he is a drunken profligate' (20), which is probably not the whole cause of the parents' action, but 'an example of what might be said on such an occasion' (S. R. Driver 1895: 247–248).

21. The law is harsh compared with Babylon, where the severest punishment is amputation of the hand for striking the father (CH 195). The harshness corresponds to the fact that rejection of parental authority is tantamout to breach of the covenant in Israel. The parents' motive, moreover, in taking this unlikely action against their own son, might be understood in terms of their devotion to the covenant, or, more probably, in order to safeguard the integrity of their own name, family and even property from dangers to them arising from possible crimes committed by the son (cf. on 22:21). The law may be placed along with laws on homicide, instead of with laws concerning authority as such (16:18 – 18:22) because rebelliousness of this sort might lead to the worst crimes. Even so, there is no evidence of such measures actually having been taken in the OT.

21:22–23

22. This series of laws beginning with *kî* finishes with the law of the hanged man. In this case MT has *wᵉkî*, '*and* if', instead of simple *kî*, suggesting that the compiler of this group of laws indicates in this way that it is coming to a close. (The ancient versions, however, appear to read simple *kî*.) The conditions are expressed in v. 22; that is, the execution and the hanging are part of the given set of circumstances that are legislated about. The issue concerns what to do with the body, and this is addressed with a prohibition, a strong command, an explanatory clause and a final prohibition.

23. The 'hanging' is not the form of execution, which is normally stoning, but some form of impalement of the body, in a custom that was widespread in the ancient world (cf. Gen. 40:19; Est. 2:23; CH 21). The intention was a public shaming of the criminal (cf. Josh. 10:26–27), apparently designed to show that he was under the curse of God (see 'Notes on the text'). The display is restricted to one day so that the presence of one so cursed might not 'defile' the land. The image of the land defiled by a dead body brings the chapter full circle to the opening image of the land defiled by the body of the murder victim.

Crucifixion, common in the Hellenistic period, continued the ancient practice of public exposure, though it was at the same time the means of execution. The removal of Jesus' body from the cross before nightfall observes the present law (Matt. 27:57–58; cf. Acts 5:30). The idea of the exposed body as cursed by God is taken up by Paul as part of his demonstration of Christ's atoning death for sinful people (Gal. 3:13; 2 Cor. 5:21).

Explanation

A number of related concerns inform the laws in this chapter. Paramount is the idea of the land as the arena of life, prepared by Yahweh for the Israelites. The victim of the unsolved murder and the body of the executed criminal frame the chapter – strong images of the offence of death, especially violent death, to Yahweh's intention to give life by means of the land (cf. Carmichael 1996: 133). The 'defilement' of the land consists in this perversion of its status as life-sustaining, and the offence to Yahweh that comes with it. At this point Deuteronomy is not far from the ideas underlying prohibitions in Leviticus and Numbers. Homicide, along with idolatry and forbidden sexual relationships, made the land 'unclean', so unclean that they could result in the land 'vomiting out' the offenders (Lev. 18:24–30; 20:2–5; Num. 35:33–34; and see Wenham 2000: 136).

Along with this basic postulate goes the need to protect the inheritance of individual Israelites and their families within the land. This is at the heart of the law of the rebellious son, which poses a threat to his family's foothold in its inheritance.

Similarly, the absolute necessity to protect and uphold human life and dignity is represented here in the law concerning the captured woman, and in the limitation on retribution that prevents any but the criminal himself being executed for murder.

In these ways the laws promote the concept of Yahweh's gift of the land to Israel, for life and well-being, along with the need to uphold justice and human dignity. The offence of sin to Yahweh is not forgotten. The powerful image of the man executed for murder and exposed to public humiliation is double-edged. The offensive presence of violent death itself is cut short, because it perverts the purpose of the land in God's eyes; yet it is not prohibited, but rather permitted within the set limits, in order to express the repugnance to Yahweh of the violation of human life. The death of the criminal both calls to mind the violence (of whatever sort) for which he has been condemned, and the justice of the retribution. In the same way, the death of Christ exhibits the suffering of the innocent at the violent hands of the guilty, and expresses God's judgment on the guilty (2 Cor. 5:21).

DEUTERONOMY 22:1–30[22:1 – 23:1]

Translation

¹Do not look on as your neighbour's ox or sheep goes astray, ignoring it, but take it back to your neighbour. ²If your neighbour is not close by, and you do not know who he is, keep the animal with you until your neighbour comes looking for it; then give it back to him. ³Do the same with his donkey, or his clothing, or anything that your neighbour loses and you find; you must not ignore it. ⁴Do not look on as your neighbour's donkey or ox lies in the road, ignoring them; help him lift it up.

⁵A woman shall not wear an item suitable for a man, or a man dress like a woman, for anyone who does these things is abhorrent to the LORD your God.

⁶If, while on the road, you find a bird's nest, in a tree or in the open country, and there are fledglings or eggs in it, and the mother is sitting on the young or on the eggs, do not take the mother together with the young. ⁷Let the mother bird go, and take the young for yourself; in this way it will go well with you, and you will have long life.

⁸If you build a new house, make a parapet on the roof, so that no blood-guilt might come upon your household because someone falls from it.

⁹Do not sow two kinds of seed in your vineyard, or the whole crop will be forfeit to the sanctuary, both the produce of the seeds, and the fruit of the vine itself. ¹⁰Do not plough with an ox and a donkey together. ¹¹Do not wear clothes made of wool and linen woven together.

¹²Make tassels on the four corners of your garment with which you cover yourself.

¹³If a man marries a woman and, when he comes together with her, dislikes her, ¹⁴and falsely tries to blacken her name publicly, claiming, 'I married this woman, and when I had intercourse with her, I did not find the evidence of her virginity', ¹⁵then the young woman's father and mother must produce the evidence of her virginity to the elders of the city in the gate. ¹⁶The young woman's father shall say to the elders: 'I gave my daughter to this man in marriage, and he rejected her. ¹⁷He falsely accused her, saying he did not find the evidence of her virginity; but here is the evidence of my daughter's virginity.' And they shall spread the garment before the city's elders. ¹⁸Then the city's elders shall take the man and punish him. ¹⁹They shall fine him a hundred pieces of silver, and give them to the young woman's father, because he tried to blacken the name of an Israelite virgin. And she shall be his wife; he may never divorce her.

²⁰But if the accusation should be true, and no evidence of the girl's virginity could be produced, ²¹the young woman must be taken to the door of her father's house and the men of her city shall stone her to death, because she has done a heinous thing, prostituting herself in her father's house. Thus you shall purge evil from your midst.

²²If a man is found sleeping with another man's wife, the two shall die; you shall purge evil from Israel. ²³If a young woman is engaged to be married, and a man comes upon her in the city and has intercourse with her, ²⁴you shall bring both of them out to the city gate and stone them to death: the woman because she did not cry out, though she was in the city, and the man because he forced his neighbour's wife; you must purge evil from your midst. ²⁵But if the man comes upon the engaged woman in the open country, and overcomes her and has intercourse with her, then only the man, who lay with her, shall die. ²⁶But you shall do nothing to the woman; she has done nothing deserving death, for her case is like that of a man who is attacked and killed by another. ²⁷For the engaged woman was taken in the open country, and though she cried out, there was no-one to help her.

²⁸If a man comes upon a young woman, a virgin who is not yet engaged, and forces her to have intercourse, and they are found, ²⁹the man who forced her must give fifty pieces of silver to the young woman's father, and she shall be his wife, because he has had his will with her. He may never divorce her.

³⁰[23:1]No-one may marry his father's wife, for then he would bring shame on his father.

Notes on the text

1. SamP adds, after 'sheep', 'or any beast of his'. SamP is slightly fuller and rationalizing in this and the following few verses. In this case the addition may be motivated by the different animals named in v. 4.

2. 'comes looking for it': SamP adds 'from you,' which slightly alters the tone to 'asks/demands it of you'.

4. MT lacks the object particle *'eṭ* before 'his ox'; SamP supplies it.

9. 'the whole crop': cf. Exod. 22:29; the term *m^elē'â* is the feminine adjective 'full' here functioning as a noun.

'will be forfeit': the textual tradition hesitates between verb forms that have the crop as subject (as MT, Syr [hith.], and translation here) and a form that makes the farmer the subject: 'lest thou make forfeit' (*taqdîš*, SamP; cf. Deut. 15:19).

12. 'your garment with which you cover yourself': the verb (*ksh*, pi., + prep. *b^e*) seems to be capable of a reflexive sense, as also in Gen. 38:14. The ancient versions show some tendency towards a definite reflexive (hith.): Syr, Tg, Vg in this case; SamP, Syr, Tg at Gen. 38:14.

14. 'evidence of virginity': this phrase translates the single noun *b^etûlîm*, which in its few other occurrences in the OT means 'virginity' itself (Lev. 21:13; Judg. 11:37–38; Ezek. 23:3, 8). In this case it must refer to the evidence of it after the first act of intercourse.

15. 'young woman': the word *na^'arâ* unusually lacks the final *h* (the *mater lectionis*), here and frequently in vv. 15–29; other MSS, together with SamP and QL, have it.

29. 'had your will with her': alternatively, 'raped, violated'; in 21:14b, however, the point is not the violence of the act but the conferral of status of wife by virtue of it. There is some analogy with that text here.

Form and structure

Kaufman treats 22:1–8 as part of the group of laws related to the taking of life (thus 19:1 – 22:8; Kaufman 1978–9: 134–137; cf. Mayes 1979: 306). It is better, however, to see 22:1–12 as a unit, having elements that relate to that theme, but also elements that prepare for the next theme of sexual misconduct (22:13–29; Braulik 1991b: 72–73). Verses 1–12 are also formally united by being principally apodictic (direct commands), rather than casuistic, like the laws surrounding them. Braulik (1995a: 150) also thinks 22:1–12 derives from Lev. 19:19, and that this text served as a starting-point for the argument here.

A connection with homicide, understood as a positive concern for the life of the other, may be perceived in vv. 1–4, 6–8; the prohibition of transvestism, however (5), along with the laws on mixing materials (9–11), and possibly the instruction in v. 12, relate more readily to the series on adultery that follows (Braulik 1991b: 73–74). The unit formed is characterized by catchword links (e.g. 'ox', 'sheep', 'donkey', vv. 1, 3, 4), 'house' (2, 8) and 'garment' (3, 5). Verses 8–9 are linked by 'house/vineyard' (also associated in 20:5–7; Carmichael 1974: 156–157); vv. 9 and 10–11 by the theme of mixing; and vv. 11 and 12 by the motif of clothing (Braulik 1992a: 163). In addition, vv. 9–12 probably have sexual connotations, and therefore lead into the laws on adultery (Carmichael 1974: 166).

The next section, 22:13–29, consists of laws on the theme of adultery, and therefore corresponds to the Seventh Commandment (5:18). The theme continues to v. 30 (though v. 30 itself falls outside the basic structure of vv. 13–29), and in Braulik's view to 23:15 (see below on v. 30). Most of the laws here have no counterpart in BC (except vv. 28–29; cf. Exod. 22:16–17). Laws on adultery are found in ANE lawcodes, e.g. LE 17–18, 25–31; CH 127–132; MAL A 12–16. These laws deal with different levels of seriousness of the offence, the need for adequate proof, and the setting of punishments. In some cases they are virtually a function of property laws (especially in LE), and distinctions are made between illicit sex with free women and with slaves (LE 31). The deuteronomic laws differ in having no place for private judgment in matters of adultery; sexual crimes are crimes against society (Boecker 1980: 113), and premarital sex is punishable by death. More importantly, only in the deuteronomic law does the interest fall not only on the offended husband but also on the woman's situation, and only here do the judges have an obligation to protect her honour (Locher 1986: 3).

Locher (1986: 107–110) has argued that 22:13–21 may be the 'protocol', or legal document, of an actual legal decision, citing Sumerian parallels for this as a way of producing law (cf. Rofé 1987: 131). This could explain the 'narrative' elements in the law, the speech, and the fact that the introduction knows the outcome (14). On the 'double law' in vv. 23–27, Locher cites cuneiform parallels, and argues that it can therefore be regarded as a unified composition.

Deut. 22:13–29 has a clearly worked out structure. 1. Verses 13–22, concerning married women, are balanced by vv. 23–29, which deal with unmarried young women. 2. Each of these sub-sections is similarly structured, with a pair of 'alternative' cases (13–19, 20–21, and 23–24, 25–27), followed by a third, related, case. 3. The punishments are chiastically arranged (A, damages, 19; B, woman executed, 21; C, man and woman executed, 22; Cʲ, 24; Bʲ, 25; Aʲ, 29). 4. Each individual law is composed of the same elements: definition of status, circumstances surrounding the offence, evidence required, punishment, a comment (see Wenham & McConville 1980 for fuller explanation). The structuring devices used may explain why the most general law (22) comes in the middle rather than at the head of the section.

Otto (1994: 190–191) explains the structure slightly differently, showing a concentric pattern within the 'alternative' laws of vv. 23–24, 25–27, and seeing v. 22a as the general rule introducing what follows. For this he finds an ANE parallel in MAL A 12–16 (cf. Otto 1995a: 257–261; against Stulman [1992], who thought vv. 25–27 were a later addition). Otto has not observed the wider structure in vv. 13–29, however. The laws in 22:13–19 have wider links within chs. 19 – 22; the 'disobedient daughter' (23:20–21) corresponds to the disobedient son in 21:18–21, both in subject-matter and in composition (Carmichael 1974: 168).

Comment

22:1–12

1. The obligation to help the other is also found in Exod. 23:4–5, where it is expressly the person's enemy whom he is required to help (meaning another Israelite, with whom he is at odds, perhaps even in some legal matter). The series of laws in Exodus (23:1–9) aims to protect the weak from exploitation. The present law makes the obligation to assist the other person general, that is, to the 'brother' Israelite. The language of brotherhood is motivational, since these requirements may not be enforceable (Braulik 1992a: 160). It is based on the deuteronomic insistence that all Israelites have their substance as fellow members of the covenant community of Yahweh (cf. 15:1–18). The word 'ignore' (1, 3, 4) literally means 'hide oneself', implying pretending not to see. There is a sharp contrast between the 'seeing' ('look on') and 'hiding oneself' (vv. 1, 4), which shows the main point of these laws; seeing trouble constitutes an unavoidable obligation to help.

2–3. In the law of the stray animal, vv. 2–3 are extensions of v. 1. The laws pass over a multitude of possibilities; the line between keeping an animal safe until its owner is found and keeping it for one's own benefit might be a fine one. In Babylon, the unauthorized 'safe keeping' of an animal, or other property, could mean the death penalty (CH 7). Indeed, the terms of the owner's request to have his animal back (2b), once he has appeared, might well be a demand implying suspicion of wrongful possession (note the 'plus' in SamP; see 'Notes on the text'). It may not be accidental that v. 3 has echoes of the Tenth Commandment (5:21).

It is not specified how far away is meant by 'not close by' (2; the Temple Scroll set it at three days from the temple in the case of the law of profane slaughter [12:21; 11QTemple 52:14]; Brin 1994: 37–40). The further condition, 'and you do not know who he is', is presumably alternative, not additional. In these unclarities some leeway is left to the finder's judgment, and the appeal of the law is that in these negotiable situations he should genuinely act in the interests of his fellow Israelite.

5. In the law against transvestism, the woman must not wear 'an item suitable for a man'. The term is general, and therefore not strictly clothing. Indeed, it can have military connotations, which fit here with the word used for 'man' (*geber*, often man as warrior). The man must not wear female dress. The concern is either to discourage homosexuality, or to prohibit transvestite practices found in Canaanite and Mesopotamian worship (Braulik 1992a: 161–162). The latter is suggested by the word 'abhorrent' (cf. 12:31).

6–7. The protection of the mother bird has an analogy with the fruit trees, spared in siege warfare (20:19–20). The common idea is preserving the means of life. There may also be a respect for the mother bird as life-giver, echoing the law forbidding boiling a kid in its mother's milk (14:21; Carmichael 1974: 151–153; cf. 12:25; Braulik 1992a: 162). The promise of long life recalls other passages (including 4:40; 5:16). The law is best not linked with the Fifth Commandment, however (on the grounds of 5:16), since it corresponds better with the theme of preservation of life and the means of life. The expression 'the mother together with the young' has echoes in Gen. 32:11[12] and Hos. 10:14, contexts where it implies destruction (Carmichael 1974: 153).

8. The concept of negligent manslaughter here is found also in Exod. 21:28–32 (the goring ox), and in Babylon in CH 229–230. Negligence is also punishable in Exod. 21:33–34. Flat roofs in ancient Israel were places were people relaxed, and this is a simple safety measure. It is another case of concern not merely not to kill, but actively to care for the lives of others at one's own cost. The 'falling' – to death – has an echo of 21:1, which shares the specifically deuteronomic concern, found here, not to 'shed innocent blood', polluting the land.

9–11. The three illicit mixtures in these verses have a counterpart in Lev. 19:19, with small differences (in that place the animals may not interbreed, the mixed crop is in the field, not the vineyard, and the mixed materials of the garment are not specified). The original reason behind these commands may be an ancient taboo against unnatural or abnormal combinations (Driver & Miles 1952: 320). A form of this occurs in Deuteronomy also in 14:3–20 (clean and unclean food), with its concern for distinct created categories. The offence in v. 9 results in forfeiture to the sanctuary, the probable meaning of the Hebrew word 'sanctify' in this place. Both the seed sown between the vine rows and the grapes themselves are forfeit (see 'Notes on the text').

The shifts in the deuteronomic laws compared with Exodus and Leviticus, however, also seem to have sexual connotations (vineyard, Song 8:11–12; ploughing, Sirach 25:8; cf. Carmichael 1974: 159), a point reinforced by their proximity to the following laws on adultery (Braulik 1991b: 77). The particular mixture of wool and linen may have been worn by prostitutes (Carmichael 1974: 164–165). The word for the mixture (11) is not Hebrew, and is thought to be Egyptian.

12. The wearing of tassels on the corner of the garment is also commanded in Num. 15:37–41, where it is made a reminder to keep the law. That thought is not expressed here (Deuteronomy has other visible tokens of this; 6:8–9). The more mundane point in this case is apparently to weight down the garment so that it should not display the person's 'nakedness'. The garment is literally 'your covering with which you cover yourself', the idea of covering being emphasized by the repetition (see 'Notes on the text'). The garment as a 'cover' appears also at Exod. 22:26–27, and the concern for modesty at Exod. 20:24–26. In this place, too, then, there is a sexual connotation.

22:13–30

13–14. The laws begin with the special case of an accusation by a newly married man that his wife was not a virgin when she married him (see 'Notes on the text'). The expectation of virginity on the part of a bride was universal in Israel and Mesopotamia. (Locher cites a number of Babylonian laws that illustrate the point; 1986: 195–196, 202, 232–237.) Remarriage was not excluded, however, as is clear from Deut. 24:1–4 (Lev. 21:13–15 sets a higher standard for the priest than for others). And in Babylonian marriage documents, the demand for virginity is set aside in the cases in question (Locher 1986: 234–235). The issue, therefore (in both areas), does not seem to be virginity as such, but rather the honour of the woman. That is, the point is not a simple guarantee that she will become the mother of the man's own children rather than of someone else's. It concerns her character more generally.

The man's accusation is signalled as mischievous by the phrase 'falsely tries to blacken her'. Even the phrase 'dislikes her' suggests an unjustifiable rejection (as in 24:3), supported by no explanation in the text (contrast 24:1; there is reproach in the father's use of it in v. 16). The accusation itself, as an attempt to end an unwanted marriage, suggests that divorce was not easy. The substance of it, in plain terms, is that after the first act of intercourse there was no blood on the covering of the wedding couch as evidence that the bride had been *virgo intacta*.

15–17. This triggers a defence of the woman, already carefully prepared. The preservation of the sheet was presumably a matter of wedding ritual, the initial placing of it, its presentation and entrustment to the parents all being part of the festivities, certifying that the parents had fulfilled their part of the bargain; their daughter was indeed marriageable. (Braulik [1992a: 165] reports that such rituals are still known in certain Arab societies. Wenham [1972] argues in contrast that the blood-stained sheet is evidence of menstruation prior to marriage, showing that the woman is not pregnant; he is followed by Mayes [1979: 310]; but see the response of Pressler [1993: 26–27].) The parents are responsible for the defence, and the court consists of the elders of the city (17), because the integrity of marriage, and any offence against it, are matters of concern to the whole society.

Pressler (1993: 22–24) has argued, alternatively, that the formal accusation is brought to the courts by the parents, the husband's charges having been made informally in the community. This does not seem to account adequately for v. 21, however, which deals with the eventuality that the man's charge is proven. (Pressler [1993: 30] regards vv. 20–21 as secondary.)

18–19. The false accuser is subjected to corporal punishment, no doubt as an act of public demonstration that the woman was innocent. It might be thought that the law of talion should apply in this case, as it is laid

down in 19:15–21 that the false witness be liable to the punishment that
would befall the victim of his slander, in this case death (21; Levinson
1997: 109). It is not clear why this is not so. (Pressler [1993: 24] finds the
answer to this in her view that the formal accusation has been brought not
by the husband but by the parents, so that the issue in court is that of their
family honour, not the honour of the bride herself.) However, the talion
requirement is also relaxed in the case of false accusation of adultery in a
number of Babylonian laws; Deuteronomy is thus in line with other laws
on this, even in respect of the tension with 19:18–19 (cf. Locher 1986:
378).

Alternatively, attempts have been made to find some form of talion
principle in the law. Merrill (1994: 30) finds it in the prevention of his ever
divorcing her. The prevention of divorce neatly mirrors the accuser's
intention to end the marriage at once, and at the same time reverses the
position of the woman, who, instead of being rejected, receives greater
than usual protection. The case addressed in 21:15–17 illustrates the sort
of situation that might subsequently arise.

The fine of 100 shekels, paid to the father, is twice the amount of
the marriage price specified in v. 29, previously paid by the husband to the
father, and which the husband must have wanted to retrieve as part of his
plan (Pressler 1993: 28). There is an aspect of talion in the double
restitution. This element in the punishment reveals, incidentally, that
marriage was conceived in some sense as a purchase, widespread in the
ANE (cf. Exod. 22:16–17; Gen. 34:12; 1 Sam. 18:25). Yet the concept of
'purchase' in relation to a wife needs qualification: it was not a transaction
like others, but a mark of the value placed on a wife (Boecker 1980: 102).
(There might, equally, be a dowry [Gen. 24:53], as in the ANE; that is, a
gift from the father to the daughter, which gave the woman some
independence, and might be worth more than the marriage price; CH
163–164; Boecker 1980: 102.)

20–21. In the obverse of the first case, the eventuality that the woman's
innocence cannot be proved is considered. This law serves to show the
seriousness of the charge brought against the woman. It is characterized as
a 'heinous thing', or 'folly', a strong term in Hebrew (note the parallel
'iniquity' in Is. 32:6). The behaviour often takes a sexual form (e.g. 2 Sam.
13:12–13), and is almost always, as here, followed by 'in Israel' (cf. Gen.
34:7; Josh. 7:15; Jer. 29:23), showing that such behaviour was reprehensible in Israel, and must be visibly rejected by it (the stories in Gen. 34 and
Judg. 19 – 20 are virtually enactments of this point). The term 'prostitution' is equally strong, and is used frequently as a figure for Israel's
idolatry, the ultimate treachery (Lev. 20:4–6; Hos. 4:12–15; Ezek. 16:15–
29). The offence, therefore, as covenant breach, is punishable by death.

The guilt of the young woman falls by implication on her family, as
the place of execution is the door of the family's house. The repetition
of 'father's house' stresses the point. The association of the woman's sin

with the father's house is complex: the family shares in the woman's guilt, since the parents have wittingly or unwittingly given her in marriage although she was not marriageable; it suffers the shame of her condemnation; and it participates (willingly or not) in the reprobation of the sinful offspring, as it did in the case of the rebellious son (21:18–21). The principle contained in the Fifth Commandment (5:16) operates, namely that duty to Israel as a whole begins with duty to the parents, and they in turn bear the responsibility for teaching the child the right way to live in the covenant (cf. 4:40; 6:7). The execution at the hands of the men of the city shows that the sin was an offence against all Israel, and this is reinforced by the formulaic last phrase (cf. 21:21b). Only in Israel was sexual intercourse before marriage punishable in this way. (See Rofé [1987], who thinks this was not a real law, but the work of a moralist; with response by Pressler [1993: 31].)

22. The basic case of adultery involves a man and a woman who is married to someone else (cf. Lev. 20:10). It assumes that the relationship is consensual, as the verb ('sleeping with') implies no force. The adulterous act must be discovered, and thus witnessed. This means that mere accusation is inadequate, and there is no provision here for the sort of 'ordeal' found in Num. 5:11–31 and CH 132, designed to discover the truth by a kind of divine guidance. Both parties are subject to the death penalty, as is also the case in some ANE codes (CH 129; MAL A 15). In the latter, however, there is a possibility of reprieve in the gift of the husband, either total, or in the form of commuted, but still equal, penalties. This is not permitted in the OT, because the offence is not private, but ultimately against God, and therefore irreducible. The deuteronomic law, therefore, is not innovative in the sense of making the woman equally liable with the man in the case of adultery, as some have argued (Phillips 1970: 110–112; Pressler rightly opposes: 1993: 33–34). But it is more strict.

23–24. The focus switches to the woman not yet married but 'engaged' or betrothed. This is a stronger commitment than in modern times, implying that a contract has been made, and the marriage price paid, though the woman still lives in her father's house (Boecker 1980: 113). She is therefore called a virgin betrothed ($b^e\underline{t}\hat{u}l\hat{a}\ m^e{}'\bar{o}r\bar{a}\acute{s}\hat{a}$), designating this status. The offence in view is consensual, because the terms imply no force (the man [lit.] 'finds' her and 'sleeps with' her), and because of the circumstance that no-one heard her cry out. These things being so, the case is like that in v. 22.

25–27. The case now has its obverse; it is like the previous one in so far as the virgin betrothed has intercourse with a man who encounters her, but different in that it happens 'in the open country'. The encounter is here assumed to be a case of rape, and this is reflected in the terms: he 'overcomes her and has intercourse with her'. She is presumed innocent, because her cries (if she did cry out) could not have been heard. Only the man is executed. It is a point of simple justice (also found in CH 130; cf.

LE 26). And the assertion in v. 27 reads like an acquittal; not a mere 'not proven', but a legal declaration of the woman's innocence, necessary to preserve her standing. In this 'benefit of doubt', the need to 'purge the evil' is not applied in some mechanical way, as if to leave no loopholes; the overriding concern is to avoid the shedding of innocent blood, in this case that of the defenceless victim. (The piece of comparative law in v. 26 shows how the legislator was concerned to classify cases and rightly view the protagonists, both during and after an enquiry.)

These related cases are a good example of the pairing of 'alternative' laws. They do not cover every conceivable possibility, such as a woman raped in the city but prevented from crying out by force or threat, or of consensual illicit intercourse 'in the open country'. The two laws almost certainly operate together to establish parameters within which wise counsel might prevail (Eichler 1987: 72).

28–29. The law has a counterpart in Exod. 22:16–17, which may illustrate the importance of the case. (The fact that in Exodus she is seduced, not raped, apparently makes no legal difference; Pressler 1993: 36–41.) The laws come full circle in terms of the woman's status. This young woman is not yet engaged, and therefore the offence against her may be made good by marriage to the man who has raped her. The logic is strictly in keeping with the legal and social code. The young woman, having been violated, and this being known, becomes less eligible for marriage, with all the consequences of insecurity, including the financial loss to the parents. The law therefore makes the offender liable to compensate for these things, even depriving him of the right to divorce the woman in the case of her marrying him. (There is a certain analogy with the law of the captured woman in 21:14; see 'Notes on the text'.)

The fifty shekels is presumably the prevailing marriage price (doubled in v. 19 for the false accuser). It need not mean that the woman, or her father, is obliged to accept the marriage (cf. Exod. 22:17). Deuteronomy goes further than Exodus, first in excluding the possibility of a formal marriage followed quickly by divorce, and second by fixing the bride-price (Carmichael 1974: 169).

30[23:1]. This isolated law on a prohibited affinity in marriage is different in theme from the other marriage laws in the chapter, and undeveloped, in contrast to Lev. 18:6–18; 20:19–21. It is probably regarded as the basic or typical law. Specifically, it prohibits the son's taking as wife a woman who had previously been his father's (cf. 2 Sam. 16:21–22). The assumption is polygamous; the son's own mother is not in question. The father was accorded special respect in the matter of his sexual privilege, and the potential offence against this is indicated in the phrase 'bring shame on', lit. 'uncover the nakedness'. Sexual relations with a man's wife 'uncovers the nakedness' of the man, that is, exposes him to shame in his most intimate life; the offence is the more intense if committed by his sons. The revulsion against this in Israel is expressed in the story of Noah (Gen. 9:20–23).

The verse may fit better with Deut. 23 than with the present chapter (it is 23:1 in Hebrew). It could link the two chapters by means of the theme of purity, first in the area of sex, then in that of the community of worship (Braulik 1991b: 86).

Explanation

The juxtaposition in this chapter of laws linked with homicide and laws concerning adultery suggests a connection between the two. Both forbidden love and an unwanted marriage can quickly bring forth murder. The point should be turned around, however, for these laws aim to ensure that people are able to enjoy all the benefits of belonging within the covenant community. The commands to help one's neighbour recall the appeal to the inner motive found at 15:9. Law in the strict sense might be evaded, but Israelites should not evade their obligations to others; they cannot 'hide' from their need, and merely pursue their own interests (1–4). In the realm of sexual relations, they must not exploit the weak, but ensure that women, especially, be allowed to keep their standing in the community. The laws are informed, as always, by a fine sense of justice; for example, in their profound balance between offence and punishment. Their very incompleteness leaves room for the exercise of that justice by those responsible.

Deuteronomy has in common with ANE law that marriage is comprised within patriarchal, family custom; it is contracted between fathers, and money is exchanged. Furthermore, there are similarities at the level of particular cases, where ANE law can share the basic sense of justice that is found in the OT. The deuteronomic laws on marriage and adultery differ at a deeper level from ANE law, namely in treating marriage ultimately as a function of Israelite society, not of private jurisdiction and property. This means, moreover, that breaches of the exclusive marriage relationship are breaches of the covenant with Yahweh. The motivations in vv. 21, 22, 24 make this point.

This last point raises a major matter of interpretation. Interpretations of the laws concerning adultery reveal the huge differences between ancient and modern society in a particularly sensitive area. Modern readings of the laws experience the patriarchal character of biblical society as a problem. Pressler's exegetically careful interpretation lays much stress on her view that the laws' basic purpose is to protect the male family members, and that this produced an imbalance in the rights afforded to men and women respectively. Her reading of Deuteronomy thus contrasts explicitly with the well-established tendency to regard Deuteronomy as 'humanitarian' when compared with other law codes, biblical and non-biblical.

Furthermore, her thesis illustrates one of the dilemmas in feminist readings of the OT: whether to regard its patriarchal orientation as an insurmountable barrier to their usefulness in a modern age, or to attempt to reread the texts eliminating the patriarchal bias (as much the bias in the modern reader as in the ancient society). This is intrinsically difficult, because it involves judgments about the intentionality of the text, a notoriously elusive concept. Pressler (1993: 42–43) is confident that the laws are not governed by a concern for women; hence, 'The laws prohibiting adultery recognize the rights of the father to the exclusive disposal of his daughter's sexuality and especially the rights of the husband to exclusive possession of his wife's sexuality. The wife has no such reciprocal claim.' However, she concludes: 'The laws also protect the wife from false accusations, and provide for the socially vulnerable girl (22:28–29). It is not possible to distinguish completely in these cases the extent to which the laws protect the girl, and the extent to which they protect the father.' This admission illustrates the hermeneutical problem. It also shows that the quite correct awareness of the cultural distance between societies can result in an unduly hostile approach to the biblical text.

In the interpretation offered above, I have followed the more usual line, that the laws in Deuteronomy have a strong humanitarian concern. This, however, is situated in a society that is certainly patriarchal, in the sense that it is structured patrilineally. Our interpretation, therefore, here as in principle everywhere in the Bible, involves a genuine dialogue with a text that makes social assumptions that are not the same as our own. This is not a warrant to disqualify what we read, but rather, first, to understand what it essentially communicates, and secondly, to question our own assumptions, as well as those of the text.

In my view, these laws exhibit the immense protection and dignity extended to all members of the covenant community, male and female. Adulterous women are subject to legal process in the same way that men are, not dependent on the decision of the offended husband. No distinction is made between free people and slaves. Such distinctions in the ANE codes can result in penalties for certain sexual offences that are more 'lenient' than in Israel. But this does not mean they were more enlightened or tolerant; rather, that some people were valued less highly than others. Furthermore, it is only the Bible that understands these offences as having a religious dimension as sins against God and against his ordering of the world, which goes deeper than the special arrangements of a particular society. The OT stands against the modern idea of private sin, which 'doesn't hurt anyone else', at this point.

DEUTERONOMY 23:1–25[2–26]

Translation

[1][2]No man whose testicles are crushed or whose penis is cut off may come into the assembly of the LORD. [2][3]No-one born of an illicit relationship may come into the assembly of the LORD; as far as the tenth generation, none of his descendants may come into the assembly of the LORD. [3][4]No Ammonite or Moabite may come into the assembly of the LORD; as far as the tenth generation, none of their descendants may come into the assembly of the LORD, for ever. [4][5]This is because they did not meet you with food and drink on your journey out of Egypt, and because they hired Balaam, son of Beor, from Pethor in Aram-naharaim, to curse you. [5][6]The LORD your God refused to listen to Balaam, and the LORD your God turned the curse upon you into blessing, because the LORD your God loves you. [6][7]You are not to promote their peace or welfare ever, as long as you live.

[7][8]Do not regard Edomites as abhorrent, for they are your brothers. Do not regard Egyptians as abhorrent, for you lived as sojourners in their land. [8][9]The third generation of their descendants may come into the assembly of the LORD.

[9][10]When you go out and camp against your enemies, keep yourselves free of all impurity. [10][11]If one of your number is ritually unclean because of an emission of semen at night, he is to go outside the camp, and not come back into it; [11][12]in the evening he must wash with water, and when the sun sets he may return to the camp. [12][13]You shall have a designated place outside the camp, to which you may go to relieve yourself. [13][14]And you shall have a stick as part of your equipment, and when you squat to relieve yourself you shall dig a hole with it, and afterwards cover over the excrement. [14][15]For the LORD your God walks in the midst of your camp to deliver you, and give your enemies over to you; so your camp must be holy, so that he might not see any shameful thing, and cease to go with you.

[15][16]You shall not hand back to his master any slave who has sought refuge from him with you. [16][17]Let him stay with you, in any place he chooses in any of your cities, as it suits him; do not oppress him. [17][18]Let no Israelite, man or woman, be a cult prostitute. [18][19]Do not bring the earnings of a prostitute, or the pay of a male prostitute, into the house of the LORD your God in fulfilment of any vow; for both of them are abhorrent to the LORD your God.

[19][20]You must not exact interest on any loan made to a fellow Israelite, whether of money or food, or anything that is normally lent at interest. [20][21]You may exact it of a foreigner, but not of a fellow Israelite, so that the LORD your God may bless you in all that you put your hand to in the land you are entering to possess.

[21][22]When you make a vow to the LORD your God, you must not be late in paying it, for the LORD will not fail to seek it from you, and you would be guilty of sin. [22][23]If you refrain from vowing, you shall be guilty of no sin. [23][24]Be sure to fulfil in act what you have promised to the LORD your God that you will do, and fulfil the vow you have freely made with your own lips.

[24][25]When you go into your neighbour's vineyard, you may eat your fill of grapes, just as you desire; but you may not fill a container with them. [25][26]When

you go into your neighbour's cornfield, you may pluck ears of corn by hand; but you may not take a scythe to your neighbour's corn.

Notes on the text

2[3]. 'as far as the tenth generation, none of his descendants may come into the assembly of the LORD': the words 'his descendants' are not present in Hebrew, but the idea is indicated by the word *lô*, 'for him', the '*l*ᵉ of reference' (S. R. Driver 1895: 260); the sense is roughly 'the tenth generation of his'. The same construction recurs in vv. 4, 9. (This particular phrase is missing from LXX.)

3[4]. 'as far as the tenth generation': see previous note. The phrase sits oddly with the following 'for ever'. The two may perhaps be reconciled by supposing that the latter means 'indeed, for ever', as an explanation of the effective meaning of the preceding. Alternatively, if LXX represents the best text in v. 2[3], then perhaps this phrase has come into MT secondarily in both verses (Mayes 1979: 316).

4[5]. 'did not meet ... hired': the former verb is plural, the latter singular. The singular refers perhaps to Balak, king of Moab, in particular.

10[11]. 'because of an emission of semen': this is not expressly said, but presumably intended by the euphemistic '(because of) something that happens' (*miqqᵉrēh*, see next note); the implication of involuntariness may be part of the preservation of decency.

The word *miqqᵉrēh* is explained in two different ways: 1. as the noun *miqreh*, 'something that happens', having *dagesh forte* in the letter *q*, in order to make the following *shewa* more audible (GKC 20h); or 2. prep. *min* followed by noun *qāreh* (construct *qᵉreh*, same meaning as *miqreh*; HALAT 3:1062; also S. R. Driver 1895: 263). The latter is syntactically more straightforward.

12[13]. 'a designated place': the term is *yād*, normally 'hand', but capable of bearing a range of meanings (e.g. 'memorial', 1 Sam. 15:12); in this case it means either 'place' (LXX has *topos*) or a sign pointing to a place.

12[13]. 'to relieve yourself': Hebr. simply repeats 'outside', another euphemism for the sake of decorum. So also v. 13[14].

13[14]. 'as part of your equipment': this follows the MT *hapax legomenon* '*ᵃzēnekā*, presumed to mean something like 'quiver', based on an Aramaic expression; LXX has read '*ᵉzōrekā*, 'your girdle'.

17[18]. 'cult prostitute': two forms appear, masculine and feminine (*qādēš*, *qᵉdēšâ*), related to the word for 'holy' (*qādôš*); cf. 1 Kgs. 14:24; 15:12; Hos. 4:14.

18[19]. 'prostitute', 'male prostitute': the terms are different from those in the preceding verse; they are, respectively, the ordinary word for a female prostitute, and the word 'dog', a term of contempt (cf. Phil. 3:2).

19[20]. *yiššāk*: 3 m. sg. impf. qal *nāšak*, 'pay interest'. The construction is impersonal: 'one pays interest'. The hiphil of the verb appears three times in this and the following verse, in the corresponding sense of 'lend at interest', 'make [someone] pay interest'. In the first instance, in the present verse, it is followed by the noun *nešek*, 'interest', in a kind of double accusative (cf. 'vow a vow' in v. 21[22]).

Form and structure

The first part of ch. 23 can be taken together with ch. 22 and the commandment prohibiting adultery, because the theme of sexual integrity makes a natural link into that of the integrity of the people of Israel, certain of the individual laws having an explicit sexual theme (22:30 – 23:2[23:1–3]; 23:17–18[18–19]). Other laws within this section are placed there by association; 23:9–11[10–12] has a different angle on the sexual theme in relation to the assembly, now constituted as military camp. Verses 12–14[13–15] continue the focus on the camp, without the sexual theme. The law on the refugee (23:15–16[16–17]) may also be suggested by the topic of war (as a foreign refugee might well defect in such a situation; Kaufman 1978–9: 138). Equally, it forms a transitional step into the next collection of laws, beginning at 23:19, which can be gathered under the heading of stealing, or the Eighth Commandment (Kaufman 1978–9: 137–141; Braulik 1991b: 79–101. Braulik takes the influence of the Seventh Commandment only to 23:14[15]).

The passage 23:1–8[2–9] addresses nations in the reverse order to that in which they were met in the exodus–conquest narrative, giving the sequence: Canaanites, Ammonites-Moabites, Edomites, Egyptians (Braulik 1992a: 169). It also reverses the order in Deut. 2 (Edom, Moab, Ammon), and makes the same distinction between the Edomites, who are brothers, and the others, who are not. Deut. 23 therefore knows that chapter as well as Num. 22 – 24.

Comment

23:1–14[2–15]

1–8[2–9]. This first section governs admission to the 'assembly of Yahweh'. This phrase occurs in Deuteronomy only in the present chapter. Elsewhere the 'assembly' is the whole people of Israel gathered at Horeb ([4:10]; 5:22; 9:10; 10:4; 18:16) or in one case in Moab (31:30). The present chapter looks forward to the assembly at worship in the land. Entitlement to participate was in principle open to all Israelites, a point that Deuteronomy is at pains to stress (e.g. 12:12; 16:11), even if it is unlikely that the whole community could ever in practice do so (and 16:16 seems to recognize that it would in fact be men, and perhaps heads of families, who would do so).

However, the question of admission to the assembly is raised at this point, since Israelites would rub shoulders with non-Israelites during the nation's life in Canaan. (The incompleteness of the *ḥerem*, or 'sentence of destruction', is recognized by both Deuteronomy and the book of Joshua; see on 7:2–3.) The fact of a mixed population, together with a doctrine of the election of Israel, led to the reflections on qualification for membership of the assembly found here. It is not surprising that Deuteronomy should be careful about these things, since the assembly appears to have military connotations as well as worship ones, and these rules are immediately followed by others on ritual cleanness in the military camp (9–14[10–15]; in that case its roots are in enmity with some of the very peoples named here. Nevertheless, the assembly is not entirely closed to them. The inclusions and exclusions may relate to the Abrahamic formula by which nations are blessed or cursed according to their attitude to Abraham's descendants (Gen. 12:3).

1–2[2–3]. The first excluded group refers to people who have been ritually mutilated in the context of the worship of other gods (1[2]; cf. 14:1). The second prohibition bears upon the *mamzēr*, 'bastard'. This can refer to the offspring of an incestuous or forbidden marriage (cf. 22:30), to a marriage between an Israelite and a foreigner (cf. 7:3), or to the offspring of ritual prostitution (2[3]; cf. 17–18[18–19]), and thus, in religious terms, of a foreign god. The word is used only twice in the OT, so it is hard to be sure which of these is likeliest. (The other occurrence of it is at Zech 9:6, where it is applied metaphorically to 'a mongrel people' [NRSV].) (The translation offered here keeps all options open.) I prefer the last, however, which means taking the parallel with the cultic regulation in v. 1[2] to be decisive rather than the juxtaposition with the following command concerning the Moabite and Ammonite. This allows a gradual progression from Canaanite worshippers through prohibited foreigners to foreigners who may in time join the assembly of Yahweh. It also acknowledges the fact that though Moab and Ammon are products of incestuous relationships (see next), and this might suggest a link with the present verse, this fact about them is not decisive in their exclusion from the assembly (see on vv. 3–6[4–7]).

In this case, both types in vv. 1–2[2–3] would occur among the Canaanite population, and the command is in line with the radical deuteronomic rejection of Canaanite worship. The *mamzēr* undergoes the severest exclusion from the assembly, 'as far as the tenth generation', that is, effectively, in perpetuity. (Perhaps the first group is not expressly included in this because the possibility of procreation does not exist in their case, assuming that the mutilation precedes and pre-empts marriage.) The 'eunuch' of Is. 56:3–5 is probably in a different category, because his mutilation is probably not a mark of a particular religious commitment (see 'Explanation').

3–6[4–7]. An associative link between the preceding verses and these verses may be provided by the fact that Moab and Ammon were the product of illicit unions between Lot and his daughters (Gen. 19:30–38). This probably explains why Ammon is lumped together with Moab in this allusion to the hiring of Balaam against Israel (4–5[5–6]; cf. Num. 22 – 24), although Ammon does not feature in that narrative, and there is no record of its strong resistance to Israel's progress to the land elsewhere. The present passage shares the view of Numbers that Moab actively resisted Israel's progress. (This is passed over in Deut. 2:9, which is interested only in the fact that Israel has no right to the territory of Moab, which has also been apportioned by Yahweh. The implication that Moab actually helped Israel, 2:29, may simply be the rhetoric of war.)

The rejection of Moab and Ammon is explained, however, not by the associative link based on illicit offspring, but by their refusal to help Israel on its journey. This is an offence against nature and the hospitality ethic that was and is strong in the East. It goes deeper, however, implying a resistance to Yahweh's purpose to bring his people to their land. Yahweh's defeat of the magic of Balaam is based on his covenantal commitment to Israel ('the LORD your God loves you', 5[6]; see on 7:8), which in turn rules out any such commitment between Israel and Moab and Ammon (6[7]; cf. 7:2). The ban on Moabites and Ammonites entering the assembly of the LORD is permanent ('as far as the tenth generation'). The terms of v. 6[7] imply a turning back upon itself of the curse on Israel that Moab sought. Nevertheless, the exclusions of Moab and Ammon prove not to be absolute (see 'Explanation').

7–8[8–9]. In contrast to Moab and Ammon, Edom's 'kinship' with Israel is a ground for treating them differently (7[8]; cf. 2:4). The degree of kinship is closer in Edom's case than Moab's and Ammon's, their ancestor Esau having been the brother of Jacob. (This close affinity can become a reason for special punishment, when Edom behaves in a hostile way to Israel; Obad.; Amos 1.) Edom is not to be treated as 'abhorrent', the term used by Deuteronomy to describe anything seriously offensive to Yahweh in the cultic realm (cf. 7:25–26; 12:31; the form is verbal here, nominal there).

Egypt is treated in the same way. In this case an ethical reason is given, namely that they showed hospitality to Israel. The period in view is the immediate aftermath of the settlement in the time of Joseph, rather than the enslavement that came later (Gen. 46 – 50; cf. van Houten 1991: 101). The present text takes the longer and generous view, therefore. Egypt's hospitality is in sharp contrast to the portrayals of the prohibited nations, and in conformity to the demand made of Israel itself that it show kindness to the sojourner (14:29; cf. 10:19 for the same logic). Edomites and Egyptians have a real prospect of entering the assembly of Yahweh, after only three generations. The time lapse presumably allows for demonstrable assimilation. But the permission shows that belonging to Israel depends ultimately on faith, not on bloodline (Braulik 1992a: 171; against van Houten on this, 1991: 101).

9–14[10–15]. A general instruction, requiring ritual purity in the military camp, is followed by two examples. There is a connection with the basic rules for warfare in ch. 20, both in the subject-matter and in the opening words, 'When you go out...' The rules that follow apply, therefore, to warfare generally (as in the bulk of ch. 20), not only within the promised land (cf., however, 1 Sam. 4:1, where Israel 'goes out' against the Philistines, within the land). The concept is that Yahweh 'walks in the midst of your camp' (14[15]), reminiscent both of the progress of Israel through the wilderness, and also of its wars against the Philistines and other enemies in the land, in which the divine presence was symbolized by the ark of the covenant (1 Sam. 4:3–4). The camp itself is holy, therefore, much as it was in the wilderness period, and presumably beyond the strict confines of the promised land. (The military-cultic assembly, gathered round the ark, is depicted in Num. 10.)

The rules are concerned with cultic improprieties (like the laws in Num. 5:1–4). The term in v. 9[10] is rather general, lit. 'evil thing'; and in v. 14[15] the more specific *'erwâ*, 'shame', or 'nakedness' (cf. Exod. 20:26 for this term, where there is a similar ritual concern). The first example probably refers, by analogy with Lev. 15:16, to the emission of semen. Since this happens in the military camp, it cannot take place during intercourse, and the expression used may therefore imply that it occurs involuntarily (see 'Notes on the text'). It is also possible that the vague phrase is meant to cover other kinds of uncleanness arising from bodily discharge (Craigie 1976a: 299). In Lev. 15:16–18 the context is not military, and it can therefore apply to an emission during intercourse.

The second example (12–13[13–14]) continues the topic of uncleanness by bodily discharge. Even though the object of the uncleanness is kept outside the camp, it is still covered by earth, implying a degree of holiness even in the camp's vicinity. (On the meaning of *yād*, 'designated place', see 'Notes on the text'.)

The concern in these rules arises from a concept of holiness as applying tangibly to persons, places and things that have close contact with Yahweh. This is more typical of the 'priestly' parts of the Pentateuch than of Deuteronomy (especially the regulations for the tabernacle, priests and sacrifices). However, Deuteronomy here shares the idea that there is a propriety in worship that is not strictly ethical, but has to do with the right ordering of all of life.

15–16[16–17]. There is a catchword link, in the verb *hiṣṣîl*, between vv. 14[15] and 15[16], respectively 'deliver' and 'sought refuge' (Braulik 1992a: 172–173). The refugee is described as a 'slave' or 'servant'. The term is *'ebed,* which can imply quite a high status in ANE societies, but nevertheless total subordination to a master. The word is avoided in the deuteronomic law of slave release up to the point at which the debt slave voluntarily accepts permanent slave status (15:17). For this reason the refugee is more likely to be a foreigner than an Israelite (with Braulik 1992a: 173; Craigie 1976a: 300; against Weinfeld 1972: 273 n.; Patrick 1985: 133).

Also in favour of this is the permission for the refugee to reside 'in any of your cities' (15[16]), implying freedom of residence anywhere in the land. (The phrase, incidentally, is reminiscent of Yahweh's choosing of a place of worship 'in one/any of your tribes'; 12:14.) Furthermore, international treaties regularly require the return of runaways (see e.g. *ANET* 200), and all the ANE law codes deal with the issue, as a problem of social order as well as of property (CH 16ff.; CE 49ff.; CL 12–13; Boecker 1980: 86–87).

Deuteronomy's law is unique in the ANE, and consistent with the book's structural resistance to political tyranny, perhaps with an implication that it should not make treaties with other nations (Craigie 1976a: 301; though 7:2 is strictly about treaties with the peoples of the land of Canaan). The 'oppression' of the refugee that is forbidden here is like the oppression of weak Israelites by the rich and powerful (all its uses, except one, Is. 49:26, relate to oppression of Israelites by Israelites; van Houten 1991: 52; e.g. Exod. 22:20; Lev. 19:33; Jer. 22:3; Ezek. 18:7). This implies that the refugee is to be allowed not only to reside in the land, but to have freedom in it. His status is somewhat like that of the Israelite who has served his six years in restitution for unpaid debt, and who is able to return to an independent life.

17–18[18–19]. Cult prostitutes, male and female, were a feature of the the religion practised by the peoples of Canaan (cf. Gen. 38:21–22). The words used in v. 17[18] are closely related to the word 'holy'. Sexual intercourse with them may have been seen as a fertility ritual, the sexual act corresponding to the deities' sexual fertility, designed to secure plenty in the agricultural sphere. The opposition to the practice here is in keeping with Deuteronomy's rejection of all forms of Canaanite worship, and especially the association of sexuality with the deity, Deuteronomy's one God having no sexual characteristics. Presumably the male and female prostitutes mentioned in v. 18[19], using other terms (see 'Notes on the text'), are the same persons. The law implies that money earned by them was used for the maintenance of the temple and its personnel (Mic. 1:7 illustrates this in a metaphorical allusion). Verse 18[19] shows that recourse to a cult prostitute might be made in fulfilment of a vow, and therefore that the activity formed part of popular religion.

'Both of them' (i.e. male and female cult prostitutes) are 'abhorrent' to Yahweh, the deuteronomic term for what is cultically reprehensible (7[8]; 7:25–26; 12:31). The historical and prophetic books show that Israel adopted the practice, however, and it took reforming kings to remove them from the places of worship in the land (1 Kgs. 14:24; 15:12; Hos. 4:14).

19–20[20–21]. The OT's laws against interest-taking are unique in the ANE. Of the several Pentateuchal laws, Deuteronomy's is the most comprehensive, forbidding interest-taking on anything whatever (cf. Exod. 22:25; Lev. 25:36–37). In other nations, interest might be levied not only on money, but on a wide range of goods that might be lent, at rates of between 20% and 50%. Deuteronomy also differs from the other Pentateuchal laws in not specifically focusing on the poor, but apparently applying the rule to Israelites generally. Even so, the underlying point of the prohibition is presumably to make help accessible to the poor without its then becoming a new burden (Matthews 1994: 126).

The spirit of this law is close to the laws in 15:1–18, in which the normal canons of commercial activity are undermined by Deuteronomy's insistence that people live for the interests of the other, even at personal cost, in the matter of the material necessities of life. The ban on interest-taking is the other side of the appeal not to withhold a loan from the needy person, even when it is unlikely that the capital will be recovered (15:9). The promise of blessing reminds the people that it is Yahweh who gives wealth, and therefore they need not make selfish calculations about acquiring it.

The separate rule for foreigners applies here as in the case of recovering loans (15:3). The difference is not 'racial', but a matter of different regulation for international trade, in which Israelites no doubt paid interest as well as received it. The possibility of strictly commercial loans between Israelites does not seem to be addressed, and is therefore perhaps not excluded (Brin 1994: 86).

21–23[22–24]. The vow was a promise made to God, which normally entailed making a sacrifice (cf. Lev. 7:16–17; Ps. 22:25[26]). Alternatively, it could mean dedicating goods or even persons (1 Sam. 1:11), although Lev. 27 allows any of these to be commuted into money. Vows, by their nature, did not have to be made, a point brought out strongly in vv. 22–23[23–24]. Once made, however, they were binding. The practicalities of this are worked out in Num. 30:2–17. The present law affirms both the voluntariness and the obligation (cf. Eccles. 5:4–5[3–4]), and puts the obligation to Yahweh in terms of personal truthfulness and integrity. Failure to keep a vow puts someone in a position of sin. Indeed, the thought of debt may not be far away, which would make an associative link with vv. 19–20[20–21].

24–25[25–26]. These two provisions, unique to Deuteronomy, are consistent with its concept of the obligation of each Israelite to all brothers and sisters within the covenant community. As in the prohibition on interest-taking, economic life is made subject to social need. The freedom to eat the neighbour's produce is a strong depiction of the teaching that the fruitfulness of the land is Yahweh's gift to the whole people. The restrictions on this freedom prevent the exploitation of a neighbour, whose interests are carefully protected not only here but elsewhere (e.g. 27:17).

Explanation

This is one of the few chapters of Deuteronomy in which specifically ritual regulations are dealt with (cf. 14:1–21). While much of the book addresses Israel as a known entity, the first section of ch. 23 asks who may belong to Israel, or, strictly, to the assembly of Yahweh. The answer given is surprising in view of the rigorous opposition to the nations other than Israel, and their gods. Membership of the assembly, it turns out, is not restricted to those descended from Israel, but is, with qualifications, open to others. The potential inclusion of Egyptians and Edomites is very significant. It establishes that the 'assembly' of the covenant people is ultimately a spiritual community. By the same token, the first category of those who are excluded may well be Israelites who have adopted foreign religious practices (14:1–2[2–3]). It is possible that the admission of foreigners, with its criterion of the attitude to Israel of the people in question, takes into account the promise to Abraham, 'I will bless those who bless you, and whoever curses you I will curse' (Gen. 12:3).

The particular exclusions and restrictions in Deut. 23 arise from conditions that prevailed at a certain time. The cultic exclusions relate to contemporary religious practices. The memories of Egypt and Edom are favourable, while Moab and Ammon are regarded as hostile. Moab and Ammon are generally so regarded in the OT (cf. Amos 1:13 – 2:3; 2 Kgs. 24:2; Neh. 13:3). The record concerning Edom is more mixed (note 2 Kgs. 3, where Edom joins with Israel and Judah against Moab), but is on balance more often hostile (Amos 1:11–12; Obad.).

The resonances of Deut. 23 in the OT also vary. There is at least one restrictive application of 23:1–8[2–9], and a number of texts that tend to loosen it. Neh. 13:3, alluding directly to the passage, narrates how the community of returned exiles excluded all foreigners, thus actually going against the intention of the law of Deuteronomy. Lam. 1:10 is sometimes thought to confirm the restrictions of Deut. 23, when it laments that foreign nations entered the temple, 'those you had forbidden to enter your assembly'. As this refers to invading armies, however, it does not correspond well with the law.

The predominant tendency of the OT in relation to Deut. 23, however, is to qualify even further the idea of restriction by birth, and the exclusions prove not to be absolute. Most strikingly, Ruth the Moabitess becomes the ancestress of King David, Israel's greatest king, and the primary organizer of its worship life (Ruth 4:13–22). Amos deals with all peoples equally on ethical grounds; Yahweh's favour does not depend on descent, therefore, but (conversely) is in principle available to all. In Edom's case its 'brotherhood' with Israel only brings the greater condemnation for its enmity (Amos 1:11). Is. 56:3, proclaiming God's salvation to the post-exilic community, abolishes all restrictions on foreigners and eunuchs becoming members of his people. Many commentators find here a direct relaxation of the restrictions imposed by Deut. 23. This is probably correct, even though the correspondence between the 'bastard' (23:2[3]) and the 'eunuch' (Is. 56:3–5) is not exact, and therefore the allusion is general and indirect (see 'Comment'). Finally, even the Ammonites gain a measure of reinstatement in the book of Judith (14:10), when the Ammonite Achior is converted to Judaism.

Clearly, the question of legitimate membership of the people of Israel was ever alive and controversial. We have seen that even when Deuteronomy deals with election it does not restrict this absolutely to ethnic Israel (see on 7:9–10). Even so, Deuteronomy envisages the extension of Yahweh's salvation in terms of people of other nations joining the assembly of Yahweh. It does not yet have a 'missionary' thrust. The book of Isaiah extends the vision of Yahweh's aim to save the nations, but there, too, their inclusion is conceived as a coming to Zion (Is. 2:2–4; 60 – 62). It is only in the NT that the idea of election is reconceived so as to make all distinctions between ethnic Israel and the Gentiles irrelevant. This is at the heart of the argument in Romans (esp. Rom. 1 – 4, 9 – 11).

From the laws in Deut. 23:15–25[16–26] it emerges that the constitution of Israel as a society of liberated people, equally entitled to the benefits of Yahweh's gift of land, means that its law is essentially non-commercial, unlike other ANE laws (Brin 1994: 85). The refugee is not to be handed back (perhaps for reward, as suggested by other law codes), oppressed or exploited, but allowed to join in the economic welfare of the people. The ban on interest-taking shows that economic life is in itself one of the means of expressing the co-operative and mutual character of the society, as does the permission to take casual benefit from the produce of others. This is a radical social-economic theory, and one of the lesser-known points of contrast between Deuteronomy and the ancient world. In its laws about use of wealth, Deuteronomy provides the basis for the prophetic critiques of greed and oppression in Israel. The sting in those critiques derives not from a general theory of justice or wealth redistribution, but from the vision of a society wholly distinct from others in its moral basis, in which the use of wealth is in and of itself a function of the calling of Israel to be a brotherhood. As much in this respect as in its rigorous monotheism, Deuteronomy presents a challenge to the modern church and world, for no modern theory of society or economics is quite like this.

DEUTERONOMY 24:1–22

Translation

[1]If a man marries a woman, and she does not please him, because he finds some reason to take offence at her, and he writes her a certificate of divorce, gives it to her and sends her away, [2]and if, after leaving him, she marries another man, [3]and the second man also rejects her, writes her a certificate of divorce, gives it to her and sends her away, or if the second man who has married her dies, [4]her first husband, who divorced her, may not take her back as his wife, after she has been declared defiled; for that would be abhorrent before the LORD, and you must not defile the land the LORD your God is giving you as an inheritance.

[5]When a man has married a new wife, he shall not go with the army to war, or have any other responsibility laid on him; he shall be free for his household for one year, to make glad the woman he has married.

[6]No-one may take a pair of millstones, or even the upper millstone, as security for a loan; for that would be like taking a life itself as security.

[7]If a man is found kidnapping one of his brothers, of the people of Israel, and trying to barter or sell him, the kidnapper must die; so you shall root out evil from your midst.

[8]In cases of serious skin disease, be sure to heed and follow whatever instructions the Levitical priests give you; what I have commanded them, you shall be careful to do. [9]Remember what the LORD your God did to Miriam on the journey from Egypt.

[10]If you lend anything whatever to your neighbour, do not go into his house to take a security for the loan. [11]Wait outside, and the man to whom you have made the loan will bring the pledge out to you. [12]And if he is a poor man, do not sleep in his pledged garment. [13]Be sure to return it to him before sunset, so that he may sleep in his own cloak; he will bless you, and you will be in the right before the LORD your God.

[14]Do not oppress the wage-earner, one who is poor or needy, whether a fellow Israelite or a stranger in your land, in one of your cities. [15]Give him his wages on the day they are due, before sunset; for he is poor, and he sets his heart on them; otherwise he will cry to the LORD against you, and you will be in the wrong.

[16]Fathers must not be put to death on account of their sons, or sons on account of their fathers; each one shall die for his own sin. [17]Do not pervert justice in the case of the stranger or the orphan; and do not take a widow's garment as security for a loan. [18]Remember that you were slaves in Egypt, and the LORD your God set you free from there; that is why I command you to keep this law.

[19]When you reap the harvest in your field and accidentally leave behind a sheaf in the field, do not go back to get it; let it be for stranger, the orphan and the widow, and the LORD your God will bless you in all your work. [20]When you beat your olive trees, do not go over them again; leave the residue for the stranger, the orphan and the widow. [21]When you gather the grapes from your vineyard, do not glean afterwards; leave the rest for the stranger, the orphan and the widow. [22]And

remember that you were slaves in Egypt; this is why I am commanding you to keep this law.

Notes on the text

4. *ḥuṭṭammā'â*: the verb form, a hothpael or huthpael, is unusual, and is broadly equivalent either to hophal or to hithpael. The possible meanings, therefore, are: 1. 'after she has been declared unclean' (as hophal; Warren 1998: 43 and n.; and close in meaning to piel as in Lev. 13, *passim*), and 2. 'after she has made herself unclean' (as hithpael). Walton's (1991) translation, 'after she has been made to declare herself unclean', includes both reflexive and declarative force. The declarative meaning is preferred here in keeping with the interpretation of the law as a whole that is adopted (see 'Comment').

5. 'to make glad': this accepts MT's piel form of the verb, with its causative (or factitive) meaning, and *'eṭ* as sign of the direct object; against Syr, TgJon, Vg, which are based on the qal, and mean 'rejoice with' (where *'eṭ* is taken as 'with').

10. *taššeh*, *maššā'ṭ*: the verb 'to lend' exists in two forms, *nāšâ* and *nāšā'*. The former appears here in MT, while the related noun, *maššā'*, is more closely related to the latter, and contains the letter *'ālep̄*. SamP has the verbal form with *'ālep̄*, here and in v. 11. The hiphil verb is indistinguishable in meaning from the qal, which is used in v. 11.

11. *nōšeh*: see on v. 10.

13. *śalmâ*, 'cloak', a by-form of *śimlâ*.

'in the right': lit. 'right(eousness) will be to you'; cf. v. 15. The phrases in both verses are taken in the sense of legal guilt and innocence; cf. on 9:4–6.

14. 'do not oppress the wage-earner': this translation accepts MT *śākîr* against QL *śākār*, which reads 'do not deprive the poor or needy person of his wages' (adopted by Braulik 1991b: 79–89). As the noun *śākār* occurs in the following verse, it is likelier that MT's distinction between them is right.

15. 'in the wrong': lit. 'it will be sin in you'.

20. *tĕp̄ā'ēr*: *p'r* I, pi., meaning to re-inspect for fruit after the first beating; only here in the OT.

Form and structure

The broad themes of the integrity of the people and justice for all its members continue here. There is a family orientation in vv. 1–6, where a law setting limits to the practice of divorce and remarriage (1–4) is followed by three others (5–7) that aim to secure the well-being of the family. Many of the laws protect the individual, under the rubric of Deuteronomy's doctrine of the 'brotherhood' of all Israelites and their entitlement to full participation in the inheritance of the land. There is a heavy concentration of parenetic 'motivations' in the chapter, notably from v. 8 on. That verse brings into focus the responsibility of the lawcourt, and the duty of Israelites to obey its decisions (cf. 25:1–3).

The classification of the laws according to Decalogue order makes 24:8 – 25:3 (Braulik 1992a: 179–180), or 24:8 – 25:4 (Kaufman 1978–9: 141) correspond to the Ninth Commandment, prohibiting false witness in court (5:20). The prohibition of false witness is thereby loosely interpreted as 'fairness to one's fellow as regards both his substance and dignity' (Kaufman 1978–9). For Kaufman, the 'fellow' extends all the way to the domestic animal (25:4), which comes at the end in a descending order of socio-economic priority. The motivation clauses show, however, that Deuteronomy aims at a kind of truth and justice that ultimately lie beyond the power of any legal jurisdiction.

Deut. 24:10–18 can also be identified as formally separate, a 'social torah', closely connected with Ezek. 18:5–20, with which it shares the topics of pledge-taking (24:10–13; Ezek. 18:7, 12, 16), oppression of the poor and needy (24:14–15; Ezek. 18:18), the separate responsibility of each generation for their own standing before God (24:16; Ezek. 18:1–20, throughout), and the declaration that one is 'righteous' or not (24:13; Ezek. 18:20). Braulik thinks Deuteronomy is based on Ezekiel at this point, and, behind the latter, on a temple entrance liturgy that formally pronounced worshippers righteous as they entered (cf. Ps. 24; Braulik 1992a: 181; cf. Braulik 1991b: 104–105). Against this, Deut. 24:16 is a precept of the lawcourt, with echoes in Mesopotamian law, while Ezek. 18 theologically develops the idea of generational independence in relation to the exilic sense that the disaster of exile had been brought upon them by the sins of the fathers (Ezek. 18:2). Deuteronomy's sequence is consistent with the book's positive encouragement to develop a kind of society that reflects its covenantal basis, from the heart.

Deut. 24 shares with 15:1–18 a particular concern for the poor (24:10–15). The laws concerning the poor arise only in cases related to debt. It is such cases that call forth Deuteronomy's appeal to the Israelite's compassion, based on the doctrine of covenantal brotherhood, according to which there should be no poor, that is, as a permanent class (15:4). The interest in the vulnerable classes (24:17–22) is related to the topic of the poor, though strictly distinct (see on 14:28–29).

Comment

24:1–4

This is the only law concerning divorce in the OT. It presupposes the practice of divorce, in which the husband has extensive rights, the giving of a certificate, and the dismissal from the home. The syntax of vv. 1–4 is almost universally taken as a protasis, consisting of several 'if' clauses (vv. 1–3), and one apodosis (a 'then' clause, v. 4) as in the translation here. This goes back to LXX, and is adopted in most modern translations and commentaries. The alternative, found in AV and now advocated by Warren, is to find a first apodosis in v. 1, implying that the law enacts the permission to divorce (Warren 1998: 42–45). Syntactically, this is possible (cf. 19:16–19 for a complex apodosis; 18:6–8 for a complex protasis).

In favour of the majority interpretation, however, is the very specific focus of the law, in which the need for proper procedure as a prelude to the prohibited case is crucial. A general law of divorce can hardly be embedded here. And, indeed, the practice of divorce is presumed also in 22:19, 29. (The NT discussions, which play a part in Warren's argument, cannot decide the grammar of 24:1, because they assume the speakers' interpretations, which are influenced by contemporary thinking.)

It does not follow, however, that the dissatisfied husband was obliged to give his wife a certificate of divorce. In a comparable case (CH 141) the husband can either grant a divorce or keep the offending wife in the status of a slave. The present law, therefore, postulates an instance in which the husband has in fact given her a divorce.

1. The occasion of the husband's desire to divorce is not specified. The term used, 'some reason to take offence' (*'erwat dābār*), occurs also at 23:14[15], where it refers to anything 'shameful' or 'indecent' that must be hidden from Yahweh in the context of his holy presence in the camp of Israel. The regular meaning of the word *'erwâ* is 'nakedness', which ought properly to be hidden (Exod. 20:26), and which, when exposed, brings shame (Is. 47:3; Ezek. 16; 23). The woman's offence cannot be adultery, as there are other, severer, laws against that (Deut. 22:22; against Otto 1992). It is, therefore, some unspecified form of unacceptable behaviour. The law does not criticize the husband for his action, which presumably means that his action is deemed to be justified. Indeed, the point of the phrase 'some reason to take offence' may be that the offence establishes that he is exempt from any requirement to restore money received from her family at the time of the marriage.

2–3. The second divorce is passed over quickly. No value judgment is implied about the second husband's behaviour. However, the term used here is the same used of the man who makes an unjustified accusation in 22:13. It is an open question, therefore, whether the second husband's action is justified. The essential point of this sequence, however, is to establish the legal position of the woman as a prelude to the decision to be articulated in v. 4.

4. The regulation that is now made is a restriction on the first husband, who may not remarry the woman. The reason is that 'she has been declared defiled'. The word 'defiled' is regularly used for cultic uncleanness, that which is unacceptable in the holiness sphere. And the sexual realm is one of those in which defilement might occur (Pressler 1993: 50–51). In this case the defilement may be understood in one of two ways, depending on how the verb is read (see 'Notes on the text'). Either it means that she has been declared to be 'defiled' (or 'unclean'), perhaps (in part) by the giving of the certificate in a publicly witnessed act (Warren 1998: 43), or it means that she has made herself 'defiled', presumably by her remarriage.

Does this 'defilement' arise from whatever caused the divorce in the first place, or from the fact of the second marriage following the first? Divorce and remarriage are not likely to be the problem in themselves, for there is nothing elsewhere in the laws to suggest this. The possibility of return to the first husband, however, introduces a new element. One suggestion is that a return in this way would be in practice a form of legalized adultery (Craigie 1976a: 305) or 'wife-swapping' (Patrick 1985: 135). Yaron's (1966) view is related, namely that the law protects the second marriage. This faces the difficulty that the prohibition of return to the first husband endures even beyond the death of the second husband (Pressler 1993: 52–53).

However, the general theory that the restoration of the first husband would make the second marriage 'adulterous after the fact' (Pressler 1993: 61) is quite strong. The 'defilement' in that case would be, in practice, the adulterous relationship that the second marriage now constituted. This, perhaps, does not fully explain why the defilement is predicated of the woman only, or why the defilement seems to be an already established fact, rather than arising by virtue of the restored first marriage. Pressler's interpretation is rather too influenced by her view that the responsibility to avoid polluting the land (in this case by adultery) is an entirely male affair, and that the woman is essentially a victim of male interests.

More convincing is the profit motive. The law aims to protect the woman from exploitation by a husband who may have a false motive in terms of personal gain, if in fact the second divorce had resulted in divorce money being paid (so Westbrook 1986; Wenham & Heth 1997: 225–227, contrast 106–111). A husband motivated in a cynical way may even reduce her to the status of a slave (cf. CH 141). This interpretation also fits with Braulik's (1992a: 177) thesis that the present law falls within the section of the laws that derives from the Eighth Commandment (against stealing).

What precisely constitutes the defilement of the woman, then? As the second marriage is not regarded as adulterous, the 'defilement' cannot simply be equated with that which results from adultery (Lev. 18:20). The sense of the verb here (unique in this form) is best understood, in my view, by analogy with the piel forms in Lev. 13, in the sense of 'declare unclean'. The woman has been treated as if unclean by the sequence of events. This originates in the first husband's public rejection of her for some fault. Yet this is not the sum of what is involved in declaring her unclean, for then the second marriage would be irrelevant to the point of the law (so against Otto [1992], who thought the declaration itself prevented restoration). It must also involve the idea of her being driven into the second marriage, and perhaps her poor treatment in that too. The woman is a victim in the case, and the use of the language of uncleanness trades on the terminology from the realm of adultery in order to show that she has been ill-treated. The first husband, in particular, has forfeited his right to marry her because he shamed her, driving her as a result into a second marriage.

The 'defilement' attributed to the woman forms a catchword link into a motivation clause (4b), condemning the sin as 'abhorrent' to Yahweh. The term usually refers to apostasy, but can be extended to the sexual and other ethical spheres (see on 7:25–26).

24:5–7

5. This addition to the exemptions from military service in 20:5–8 is clearly suggested by the preceding law. It is intended to support the married couple, and marriage itself, by protecting against the premature death of the husband. He is free from other official duties as well, which would distract him from his family life (contrast 1 Kgs. 15:22). His freedom is 'for his household', the aim being therefore to make the marriage the basis of a flourishing home. He will at the same time 'make glad' his new wife (see 'Notes on the text'). This is no doubt an image of married bliss, but it has the practical purpose of laying strong foundations to lessen the likelihood that problems will arise in the marriage. (Several laws concerning marriage difficulties in CH address circumstances in which the husband has been absent, or has failed to put domestic arrangements on a secure footing; CH 133–136.) Behind the hope of a happy marriage, there were also economic tensions that might arise on the death of a young man who was childless (see on 25:5–10, where a case of this sort is treated).

6. It was common practice to give and take 'pledges' as securities on loans, both in Israel and in the ANE (see further on 15:1–3). In Israel, as in Babylon, limits were put on the practice, in order to safeguard the debtor's means of subsistence (G. R. Driver & Miles 1952: 214). The embargo on taking a mill as pledge shows how important this was to the ordinary family's livelihood. (The mill consisted of two parts, a lower channelled stone and an upper millstone, both essential to make it work.) The laws concerning securities on loans, or 'pledges' (in this verse and vv. 10–13, 17), have a thematic connection with the law prohibiting interest-taking (23:19–20). (In Exod. 22:25–27 they are grouped together.) The connection lies in the restriction of the imperatives of an economic system out of compassion for the needy (see on 23:19–20). A connecting thread may also be discerned between these and the preceding law, in that they preserve the mainstays of the economy of a household (in this case the means of producing food), thus tending to preserve it from failure due to poverty, resulting in debt slavery (Braulik [1992a: 178], who points to the connection in Jer. 25:10). The motivation clause, 'for that would be like taking a life itself as security', points up the discrepancy between the value of a life and the need to protect one's loan.

7. The word used for 'kidnapping' is literally 'steal', of which this is the most serious instance. The only other occurrence of the word in Deuteronomy is in the Eighth Commandment (5:19). This is also the only case of the death penalty for 'stealing', both here and in the corresponding law in Exod. 21:16 (and CH 14). The present law has deuteronomic characteristics, in that it specifies the victim as an Israelite, and indeed as a 'brother' (lit. 'a person, of his brothers, of the sons of Israel'). The motive for the kidnapping is profit. No Israelite may be sold or bartered, which implies enslavement, possibly into a foreign land (cf. on 21:14, and 'Notes on the text' there). The crime therefore deprives the victim of the benefits of belonging to the covenant community, which explains the severe penalty here. The law is motivated with a call to 'root out evil from your midst', frequent in the laws (see on 13:5[6], where it is also connected closely with 'brotherhood').

24:8-9

8. The topic of this law is the sort of skin disease (not exclusively leprosy) that rendered an Israelite ritually 'unclean', that is, unable to participate in the worship life of the people as long as the condition prevailed. It is the only instance of such a law in Deuteronomy, the extensive regulations occurring rather in Lev. 13 – 14. It echoes the limitations set out in 23:1–8[2–9], and to that extent is concerned with the integrity of the people in a ritual sense. However, the law is almost all 'motivation', the real interest falling on the need for Israelites to obey the decisions of the central court, presided over by the priests and judges (cf. 25:2; 17:8–13). The typically deuteronomic verb 'keep' (šāmar) occurs three times in this dense exhortation, together with the idea of 'doing' as Moses commanded, and a verb (yārâ, hiph., 'teach', 'instruct') that is connected with the noun tôrâ, and used only of the priests' (or Levi's) instruction in Deuteronomy (cf. 17:10–11; 33:10).

9. When the example of Miriam's affliction with leprosy is invoked, with the consequence of her temporary exclusion from the assembly (9; cf. Num. 12), the point seems to be that failure to obey the court (and thus Yahweh) is what excludes, not the skin disease itself. (The translation given here, as NIV, preserves this balance of the exhortation, against NRSV's 'Guard against an outbreak of a leprous skin-disease'.) The dense

deuteronomic language, together with the allusion to the exodus, seem to mark this as a new beginning in the structuring of the laws (see 'Form and structure').

24:10–18

10–13. A further law governing pledge-taking prohibits distraint of goods as security. The prohibition of entering an individual's home guards against violence or arbitrariness on the creditor's part. The command to return a cloak at night ensures that humane regard for a neighbour prevails over economic imperatives (as in 23:19–20, 24–25; and see on v. 6 above). The outcome of respect for this exhortation is that the creditor will be 'in the right before the LORD your God'. NRSV's 'to your credit' is weak; NIV's 'it will be regarded as a righteous act' is better. The effect is to extend the concept of being in the right legally beyond the reach of the court. Yahweh himself is judge, and the person who respects the spirit of the law receives the verdict of innocent. The concept is similar to that in 9:4–6, but now predicated of the individual. The aim is to foster an attitude of deep respect for the principles of the covenant, which protect the interests of all in Israel. The result is a harmonious relationship between the people ('he will bless you'), and the approbation of God (see also above, 'Form and structure').

14–15. Oppression of the poor is the parade example in the OT of social sin, the antithesis of the spirit of the covenant. Other laws against it are found in Lev. 6:2, 4 [5:21, 23]; 19:13b, and it appears across a spread of OT literature, especially the prophets and wisdom literature. The victims of oppression are basically characterized as the 'neighbour', to bring out the treachery of it (Lev. 6:2, 4 [5:21, 23]. Specifically, they are the poor (Amos 4:1; Prov. 14:31; 22:16), and (sometimes) the politically weak (the stranger, widow, orphan; Ezek. 22:7, 29; Zech. 7:10). The relation of oppression to the economics of loan, debt, interest and pledge emerges in Lev. 6:2, 4 [5:21, 23]; Ezek. 22:12.

The language of poverty is confined in Deuteronomy to chs. 15 and 24, perhaps because of the rationale in 15:4 ('there shall be no poor among you'). The present law, however, is expansive compared with the law in Lev. 19:13b, which makes a similar provision for prompt payment of the hired servant. The severe need of the wage-earner is stressed, and a note of exhortation struck. Just as the poor person's pledged garment is to be returned before sunset (24:12–13), so he is to be paid by the same time. His situation on the edge of survival cannot tolerate delay. Once again, economic calculation is to be subordinate to compassion. And the court of appeal is Yahweh himself. If the creditor fails to show compassion, he may avoid the sentence of a court, but he will be 'in the wrong' with Yahweh (contrast v. 13).

The protection of the law extends to the stranger, here explicitly a foreigner, since he is set in contrast to the Israelite 'brother'. This inclusion of the foreigner is a specifically deuteronomic concern (but cf. Lev. 19:33–34).

16. This is a fundamental statement of the legal accountability of the individual. The 'sin' is that which puts anyone 'in the wrong' legally, the term with which v. 14 finishes, making a connection with the present verse. This law is sometimes contrasted with the idea that Yahweh's punishment extends to the third and fourth generation (Exod. 20:5–6; Deut. 5:9–10), but those statements do not have the lawcourt as their setting (see 'Comment' on the latter). The Book of the Covenant knows that the sin of a father will have bad effects on the next generation of his family, but does not actually involve them in his punishment (Exod. 22:23).

The closest affinity with the present verse in the OT is in Ezek. 18, but there the basic legal principle is extended into the broader context of the religious-ethical responsibility of the exile generation for its own standing before God (cf. Jer. 31:29–30). The law establishes a limitation (as does the law of talion), and is set against a tendency in the biblical world to impugn whole families for the offences of a member of them. The context of this tendency is not exclusively legal, but can operate in the realm of curse (2 Sam. 3:29) and vendetta (2 Kgs. 14:6 – which invokes the present law, evidently against what might have been expected), and indeed the *ḥerem* (divine sentence of destruction, Josh. 7). Vicarious punishment is allowed in the law of Hammurabi (CH 230), but can equally be limited in the ANE (MAL A 2; G. R. Driver & Miles 1975: 381).

17–18. Deuteronomy's general law requiring integrity in the administration of justice occurs at 16:18–20. Laws forbidding perversion of justice are also found at Exod. 23:3, 6, either in favour of the poor or at their expense. Other laws protected the stranger from oppression in a general sense (Exod. 22:21–24[20–23]; 23:9), but without implying that he had legal rights. The present law extends the principle of judicial integrity to the stranger (foreign resident). This is the clearest requirement of his inclusion in the public life of Israel, though the general trend is clear in the present chapter (24:14) and elsewhere (14:28–29).

Here as elsewhere, the stranger stands along with the other disadvantaged classes, the orphan and the widow (cf. 27:19). As we have noticed before, these are not strictly the same as the 'poor', but rather those whose independent legal standing may not be recognized. In the present text the inclusion of the orphan and the widow is syntactically awkward, and the principal train of thought runs from the protection of the stranger to the memory of Israel's own slavery in Egypt, and its deliverance from there, couched in the legal parlance of 'redemption' (see on 7:8). The command about the widow is also slightly different, offering a close parallel to vv. 12–13.

24:19–22

The topic of the socially disadvantaged continues with this threefold command, which gives them a stake in the three typical crops of the land, 'the grain, the oil and the wine' (cf. 7:13). Similar laws are found in Lev. 19:9–10; 23:22, where the command is stronger, namely to leave some of the harvest deliberately ungathered; and in Exod. 23:11, there in the context of the sabbatical year. The underlying idea in this law is the same as at 23:24–25[25–26], namely that all members of the covenant society have rights, in principle, to a share in the blessings of the land, which is ultimately Yahweh's gift to the people as a whole. Here again, this principle overrides all other economic and property considerations. The promise of blessing in return for respect for this principle recalls 15:10; 16:15. And, again, obedience is motivated by a memory of slavery in Egypt.

Explanation

The chapter is full of expressions of core principles of Deuteronomy. Together with ch. 15 it contains the greatest concentration of laws demonstrating in practice the nature of Israelite society as the people in covenant with Yahweh. The fundamental concept is that of the land as given to Israel by Yahweh as an 'inheritance', made explicit in v. 4, but underlying all the laws here. It is Deuteronomy's counterpart to the great rationale for the jubilee in Lev. 25:23: 'The land is mine; it shall not be sold in perpetuity.' In each case it is asserted that property can only ever be held provisionally.

The paradigm of the exodus is the obverse of this theory of the land. Israel's status is that of those who have been set free, legally, from their status as slaves in Egypt. Their new situation is the opposite of such status and contradicts it. For this reason the 'inheritance' principle is supported in the present chapter by three allusions to that deliverance. All the commands that tend to protect the independence of families and individuals, especially the poor and the socially vulnerable, are designed to resist and defy the notion of slavery. The structure of society and economics must not be allowed to re-admit slavery, once abolished, by the back door.

Indeed, all economic calculation and self-interest is relativized by the radical idea that land (which should be extrapolated to wealth and substance in general) is a function of Yahweh's intention to sustain his covenant with his people, in their entirety and integrity. The purpose of the land is the blessing of all Israel, conceived as brothers and sisters. The covenant means an irreducible commitment to co-members of the covenant community as a correlate of the commitment of each to Yahweh.

All the parts of this chapter (which therefore follows coherently from the note struck at the end of ch. 23) correspond to this programme. The law restricting divorce aims to protect women, and at the same time marriage and the family. The presence of a specialized law on a single aspect of divorce, rather than a general law of divorce, may be explained in this way; that is, the topic of marriage is not developed independently here; rather, one measure preventing abuse of it finds its place among other provisions for the protection of the family and the individual. (When the text is taken up in other parts of the Bible it is introduced into other kinds of arguments. Jer. 3:1–9 is a metaphorical reflection on this passage, where the 'bride' is idolatrous Israel, and the 'marriage' to the second husband has come to stand for harlotry. Jesus takes it up as part of his setting a higher standard than the law [Matt. 5:31–32; 19:3–9]. The famous 'Matthean exception' belongs to the new high standard that he sets; it does not determine the offence in question in Deut. 24:1.)

The movement in the chapter, from marriage to other measures protecting family life, and thence to commands protecting the poor and disadvantaged, is part of the laws' connected reflection on what it means to be the people of Yahweh. In the middle of them comes the important statement that each person is responsible before Yahweh for his or her own moral actions (16). This prevents unjust procedures against innocent people (in this sense it is like the laws protecting the accidental homicide; 4:41–43; 19:1–13). At the same time it establishes the important principle of individual responsibility, even while the integrity of the family, and ultimately of the whole people, is being established.

At the heart of the chapter, attached almost incidentally to a law concerning ritual cleanness (8–9), is a command to respect the instruction of Yahweh, by means of the Levitical priests. The verse abounds with the deuteronomic language of appeal to the moral responsibility of the people. And the allusion to Egypt in this case carries a warning of Yahweh's judgment. The act of deliverance can lead back to exclusion when he is defied. Beyond the reach of the lawcourt to enforce, therefore, lies the figure of Yahweh, the judge, who pronounces innocent or guilty when the needy person (metaphorically) presents his case (13, 15). The pronouncement of innocence, or of righteousness, recalls the justification of Abraham (Gen. 15:6). It is not accompanied here by the language of 'faith' or 'faithfulness', as it is there, and as taken up by Paul in Rom. 4:3. Nor is it properly soteriological. Yet it is not a 'works' righteousness either, in the terms of the dispute in which Paul later found himself. For it is a righteousness that comes from a right relationship to God and neighbour, based in a commitment to God's own purpose to save a people for himself.

DEUTERONOMY 25:1-19

Translation

¹When two men have a dispute and go to court, and the judges make a decision, vindicating the one who is in the right and condemning the one who is in the wrong, ²then if a sentence of corporal punishment is passed on the guilty man, the judge shall have him lie down and flogged in his presence, the number of lashes in proportion to his guilt. ³He may be given forty lashes, but no more, for if he were to be beaten much more than this, your brother would be humiliated in your sight.

⁴Do not muzzle an ox when it is treading out grain.

⁵When brothers live together, and one dies without leaving a son, his widow shall not be put out of the family to become the wife of a stranger; her brother-in-law shall go in to her, and take her in brother-in-law marriage. ⁶And the first son to whom she gives birth shall bear the name of the brother who died, so that his name may not disappear in Israel. ⁷If the man will not marry his sister-in-law, she should come to the city gate, to the elders, and say, 'My brother-in-law refuses to perpetuate the name of his brother in Israel; he refuses to fulfil the obligation of brother-in-law marriage with me.' ⁸Then the elders of the man's city shall summon the man and reason with him; if he persists and says, 'I will not marry her', ⁹the sister-in-law shall come forward in the presence of the elders, pull off his sandal, spit in his face, and exclaim, 'So may it be done to the man who refuses to build up his brother's house!' ¹⁰And the name of the house shall be known in Israel as 'the house of the one whose sandal was removed'.

¹¹If two men fight, a man and his brother, and the wife of the one, in coming to help to free her husband from the one who is beating him, grabs the other by the genitals, ¹²you must cut off her hand; show no pity.

¹³Do not have two different weights in your bag, one large, the other small. ¹⁴Do not have two different measures in your house, one large, the other small. ¹⁵Your weight and your measure must be full and just, so that you may prolong your days in the land the LORD your God is giving you. ¹⁶For all who act crookedly in this way are abhorrent to the LORD your God.

¹⁷Remember what the Amalekites did to you as you were on your journey out of Egypt, ¹⁸how they attacked you when you were on the march, and cut off those at the rear, when you were weary and exhausted; they had no fear of God. ¹⁹And when the LORD your God gives you peace from all your enemies around, in the land he is giving you to possess as an inheritance, you shall blot out the memory of Amalek from under heaven; do not forget.

Notes on the text

2. The subject of *wᵉhikkāhû* should be taken as impersonal, that is, not 'the judge', since the action is then qualified by 'in his presence'.

'if a sentence of corporal punishment is passed on the guilty man': lit. 'if he is a son of lashes', a typical Hebrew idiom.

3. As in v. 2, the subject of the verb is impersonal, hence the passive voice in the translation.

5. 'go in to her': MT *yāḇō' 'ālêhâ* is unusual; SamP's *yāḇō' 'ēlêhâ*, in contrast, is the usual expression for a man's approaching a woman for intercourse (Gen. 29:23, 30).

'take her in brother-in-law marriage': this is expressed by a single verb, *ybm*, pi., related to the noun *yāḇām*, 'brother-in-law'. The noun appears only here, and the verb only here and in Gen. 38:8.

10. 'the name of the house': this translates *š°mô*, lit. 'his/its name'; the antecedent, however, is apparently the (dead) brother's house (9b).

Form and structure

According to the organization of the laws following the Decalogue order, vv. 1–3 (Braulik 1992a: 186), or vv. 1–4 (Kaufman 1978–9: 141; see 'Form and structure' at Deut. 24) are still under the influence of the Ninth Commandment, while v. 5 leads into a series under the influence of the Tenth. The prohibition of false witness, interpreted as 'fairness to one's fellow as regards both his substance and his dignity', applies even to the convicted criminal (1–3), and to the domestic animal (4). The connection of vv. 1–3 with the lawcourt is plain, and makes a link with 24:8, which, on the same view, introduces this group of laws. The former is the high court, however, whereas this is the local city court. (The difference between 'judges', pl., and 'judge', sg., in vv. 1 and 2 is scarcely significant. The laws assume a number of judges at the local courts [19:18; 21:2]; the singular is most easily understood as one who presides in the case in question.)

The law of levirate marriage (25:5–10), unique in the OT, can be connected with the Tenth Commandment (against 'coveting') in the sense that it requires an attitude of unselfishness and a desire to promote the good of the other. It is followed, because of a topical connection, by the law concerning the woman's attack on her husband's opponent (25:11–12), which shares not only the action of a woman but the topic of offspring for the man. Her attack on the husband's opponent may be at the same time a defence of the husband's virility. The theme of acquisitiveness leading to unfair, indeed dishonest, action is resumed in vv. 13–16. Like the levirate law, it is not accompanied by a penalty enforceable in the lawcourt (unlike vv. 11–12).

The final three verses (vv. 17–19) strictly fall outside the laws proper, being an exhortation in terms of the idea of holy war. Recalling the holy-war theme in the long prelude to the laws (esp. chs. 2 – 3 and 7), it now forms part of the laws' closure, making a transition into ch. 26, which rounds off the laws in a different way.

Comment

25:1–3

1–2. The court setting is not legislated for here (contrast 1:9–18), but, as in other places, merely presupposed (cf. 21:1–9). Also presupposed, and not described, is the process, which leads to the establishment of the truth, an innocent party and a guilty party, and consequently (if appropriate) to the punishment of the guilty party. The terms *ṣaddîq* and *rāšāʿ* are best taken, in this context, to mean 'innocent' and 'guilty' (see on 9:4–6; cf. also 1 Kgs. 8:32, where it is God who vindicates and condemns). Disputes might imply that one party has accused another of a punishable crime, and therefore, by the principle of talion applied in such cases (19:16–21), either party may face punishment, depending on the outcome.

3. Punishment by beating was customary (cf. 22:18; Prov. 10:13), and could be severe (cf. Exod. 21:20–21); even here the limitation to forty lashes suggests that the practice may have run to much more. The purpose of the law, however, is to establish a limit to the punishment, and even to grade it up to that limit, in proportion to the gravity of the offence, calling on the deuteronomic doctrine of brotherhood. It is significant that the explicit intention of the law is not to prevent the death of the offender (though that effect follows), but rather to preserve his dignity. The law, in common with others, notably the laws of debt release and slave release, looks to the restoration of a member of the covenant brotherhood, in this case the offending party, to a dignified place in it. The radical nature of the command lies in the fact that all are treated equally before the law; the possibility of a separate kind of treatment for slaves, in particular, does not arise. (The limitation to forty lashes lies behind the later Jewish practice of administering thirty-nine, allowing a margin of error in case the prescribed limit should be broken; 2 Cor. 11:24.)

25:4

The ox is to be unmuzzled so that it can eat of the corn while it works at threshing it (by trampling it to separate the grain from the husk). This unexpected and isolated provision recalls that domestic animals are also given consideration in the Sabbath commandment, especially in its deuteronomic formulation (5:14). The entitlement of the ox to have what it needs of the farmer's produce for its health is analogous to the rights of the poor and the disadvantaged to consume what they need of another's crops (23:25–26[26–27]; 24:19–22). The wholeness of the covenant society extends even to its livestock. A related provision in Exod. 23:11 extends to wild animals. Paul interprets the command allegorically to refer to the right of the apostle to have his living from the gospel (1 Cor. 9:9).

25:5–10

5–6. A catchword link with the 'brother' of v. 4 leads into the law of the so-called levirate, or brother-in-law, marriage ('levir' being the Latin term for 'brother-in-law'). This is the only law on the subject, but the practice is presupposed in Gen. 38:8 (see 'Notes on the text'), and similar customs are attested in MAL A 30, 31, 33. It stands in a certain tension with Lev. 18:16; 20:21; Num. 27:8–11, but it may be seen as an exception for the specific case in question (so S. R. Driver 1895: 285). Num. 27:8–11 poses a problem too. There the inheritance of a man who has no male heir passes, in order, to daughters, then brothers, then the next nearest kin. The levirate custom is not mentioned. However, the Numbers law would be intelligible in circumstances in which levirate marriage had been refused (as the law of Deuteronomy anticipates), or had otherwise not produced the necessary son. Indeed, the inheritance system proposed there would provide ample motive for the brother-in-law's refusal, as he is a potential beneficiary if his late brother remains without an heir.

The setting is 'when brothers dwell together'. 'Brothers' is here meant in the narrow sense of those who share the same parent (or parents). It is not said whether their father is still alive, or, if not, whether their 'dwelling together' is a typical situation, or an untypical one, perhaps adopted in order in order to avoid dividing up an inheritance (C. J. H. Wright 1990: 54–55). This may have been regarded as something of an ideal situation, rather than one compelled by economic necessity (such as when an inheritance was not large enough to divide). Ps. 133 probably celebrates such a situation. In either case, the different families could have their separate houses (1990: 55).

The levirate law is intended to prevent the widow from remarrying 'outside the family'. The phrase 'outside the family' might in itself mean outside the smallest kinship group, the 'father's house' (*bêt 'āb*), or outside the larger kinship group known as the *mišpāḥâ*, often translated 'clan'. In the context the former seems to be implied. There is probably an economic aspect to this concern to keep the woman within the family, namely to ensure that there is no alienation of property that she may have brought to the marriage, especially land. Similar concerns underlie certain Middle Assyrian laws (cf. MAL A 30, 33). The desire to keep land within the family also explains a number of OT texts, notably Num. 27; 36; Jer. 32. Within the family, however, the widow may have enjoyed a high degree of independence, based upon the property that had been her husband's. The levirate law is not necessarily a measure to deal with the economic need of the widow, and nothing is expressly said here to indicate otherwise. We have observed earlier that widows in Israel were not by definition poor, though they might have been, depending on their former circumstances (see on 14:28–29). The focus is all on preserving the name of the deceased (cf. Pressler 1993: 73).

What social issues were at stake? Or in what way does the law bear upon and regulate existing practice? It is hard to determine this in the absence of direct legal parallels. The events reported in Ruth 4, involving Ruth, the unwilling kinsman and Boaz, do not precisely reflect the same case, as the obligation there is that of the kinsman redeemer (gō'ēl), not of the brother-in-law. In addition, there is a specific issue of redemption of a field, which is not articulated in our law, although the issue of land is implicit. There is a strong analogy between the law and the narrative, however, in terms of a family obligation to the widow and to the name of the deceased husband (3:10), and even in the symbolic removal of the sandal (Loader 1994: 134; cf. T. L. & D. Thompson 1968). The law and the narrative together testify to the powerful sense of obligation within families in Israel. This was both practical, in that it cared for women who were vulnerable following the death of husbands and sons, and principled, because of its costly respect for the deceased. The differences between the law and the narrative show that the customs were complex, and the full range of them is probably not known to us.

7–10. It is possible that the force of the law is to limit the rights of the brother-in-law (who may be the *paterfamilias*) to the particular instance in view, against a convention that gave him the right to take his widowed sister-in-law as wife without further condition. In that case, the brother-in-law marriage is permitted only as a matter of obligation to the deceased brother, as well as to the widow and the brother's posterity. The brother-in-law's refusal to meet the obligation does not result in legal penalties (he is not prevented from inheriting; Patrick 1985: 138). He is merely subject to a ceremony that displays his refusal for all to see. The removal of his sandal by the widow probably signifies a forfeiture of a right or authority (V. P. Hamilton 1992: 567; Frick 1994: 146). In this case, it would declare that the brother-in-law has no conjugal rights with her, since he has declined to take on the only role that would have given him any.

This law, then, is one more that protects the rights of the individual, in this case the widowed woman. (Pressler [1993: 73] agrees, though she sees this as a secondary concern of the law.) She is then free to remain within the 'family', having a social and economic status, and without unwanted conjugal obligations (see Frick 1994: 142–143, 147 for analogous cases from modern anthropological studies). This is the effect of the law, in addition to affirming the right of the deceased husband to have his place in the community respected, even after his death.

The symbolic action of spitting in the face, and the accompanying declaration, demonstrate that shame has come on the brother-in-law and his house. Spitting in the face is a strong symbol that someone deserves to be shunned (Num. 12:14; Job 30:10). In giving an insulting name to the brother-in-law's 'house' there is a certain ironic compensation for the loss of the name entailed by the death of the husband while still childless. The insult is intended to be a just reward for his refusal to do what convention demanded by way of support for his brother and sister-in-law. The insult to the brother, which is evidently intended to be remembered, may even become an oblique memorial to the husband.

25:11–12

The odd circumstance envisaged here has an obvious connection with the preceding, in that the woman's attack on the man who is fighting with her husband is deemed to be an attack on his capacity to have children. The two men are also 'brothers'. The law is not about a sexual attack as such (*pace* Pressler [1994: 109–111], who thinks this is the only case of such a law, arguing that there is nothing similar to protect women; cf. Pressler 1993: 74–77). Rather, it mirrors the preceding case, in which the woman was protected from sexual exploitation.

Discussion of this law has centred on the severity of the punishment, which has been contrasted with the concern to limit the corporal punishment (of a man) in vv. 1–3 (P. E. Wilson 1997: 221). There is no other case of mutilation in the laws, apart from the standard talionic formula (Exod. 21:23–24). Some think this penalty is itself talionic, the woman's hand being the nearest approximation to the male organ she has attacked (Craigie 1976a: 316; Phillips 1970: 94–95). Eslinger (1981) varies the point by suggesting, a little speculatively, that the woman was herself to suffer mutilation of the genitalia, for which 'hand' is a euphemism. On this talionic understanding, the offence is presumably legally actionable only if in fact some harm has occurred. A comparable Assyrian law is predicated on such harm (MAL A 8; G. R. Driver & Miles 1975: 385; Otto 1995a; *ANET* 181).

It has been suggested that the deuteronomic law represents an actual legal decision (Braulik 1992a: 189, and cf. on 22:13–29). Alternatively, it is, in Wilson's words, 'one for the books', that is, a provision in anticipation of the act in question, designed as a deterrent, and informed by the logic of 'shame'. The law would then deter the woman from the act because the punishment would make a permanent display of her crime. The logic of shame would link the law to the limitation placed on corporal punishment (1–3), and the ceremonial humiliation of the recusant brother-in-law (9; P. E. Wilson 1997: 226–229). In favour of this is the fact that the deuteronomic law often specifically aims to deter (19:20; 21:21b).

The command to show no pity belongs to the force of the deterrent (cf. 19:13).

25:13–16

The use of false weights was apparently a widespread abuse in trading in the biblical world. Parallel laws and instructions can be found, for example, in Lev. 19:35–37, and the *Instruction of Amenemope* 16 (*ANET* 423). The prophets condemned the practice (Amos 8:5; Mic. 6:10–12). Larger and smaller weights were false by reference to an accepted standard. The ephah was a measure used for weighing out grain. The traders in Amos 8:5 want to make the ephah small when selling grain, and the shekel large, being a measure of the weight of the silver in which they will be paid.

Crookedness of this sort is just what contributes to the oppression of the poor and vulnerable, as the prophetic texts show. They may, in addition, have difficulty in obtaining justice from a court. The word 'just', used here of the measure itself to mean 'correct' (as in Lev. 19:36), is the word that typically means 'just' in an ethical sense, for example in Deut. 16:20. There is an appeal here for obedience, recognizing that this activity may be hard for the courts to deal with, and it is backed up with a promise of long life in the land (cf. 5:16). There is negative motivation too; unethical behaviour of this sort is condemned as abhorrent to Yahweh with the same word that is used for things that are ritually abhorrent (see on 7:25–26). The word translated 'crookedly' is used of moral evil. It is relatively infrequent, but spread across a range of texts (incl. Lev. 19:35; Prov. 29:27 also parallels it with 'abhorrent', as here).

25:17–19

The Amalekites, a desert people, had been Israel's first enemies on their way out of Egypt, attacking them while they faced the rigours of the desert (Exod. 17:8–15). As a result, Yahweh determined to be their enemy from generation to generation. This resolve underlies the present command.

In subject-matter these verses are different from the laws, though, formally, the command employs the same hortatory devices found there. It is framed by the theme of memory, the infinitive absolute of the verb 'remember' constituting a command in perpetuity (cf. 5:12). Memory, too, is a key category in the ethical language of Deuteronomy (cf. 8:8, 18–19). The command then closes with the idea of blotting out the memory of Amalek. A contextual connection is made with the theme of the laws in 25:5–12, which aim to ensure, in contrast, that the memory of Israelites survives in perpetuity.

The command functions more broadly in relation to the structure of the book, and beyond, however, and its appearance at this point must be explained in this way. Within chs. 12 – 26 it helps to tie the law code into the narrative of the progress from Egypt to promised land. Just as ch. 26 recalls and corresponds to ch. 12, each focusing on Israel's worship at the chosen place at the beginning and end of the law code respectively, so this command corresponds to the sentence against the Canaanite population in ch. 12. The resumption of the idea of 'peace from all your enemies round about' (cf. 12:9–10) establishes this connection.

In the wider literary context, from Exodus to Samuel, Amalek, as Israel's first enemy (Exod. 17), becomes also its last, and stands for hostility to Yahweh's project with Israel. The expression 'peace from all your enemies round about' is crucial once again. In the story of the settlement, that peace is reached with David, as indicated by 2 Sam. 7:1. This sequence shows how important is Saul's war with Amalek (1 Sam. 15), and the significance of his failure to subject them to the sentence of destruction. The undying hostility of Yahweh and Israel to Amalek gains a final OT echo in the book of Esther, where the enemy of the Jews, Haman, is an 'Agagite', that is, an Amalekite (Est. 3:1; cf. 1 Sam. 15:8).

Explanation

The strong commitment to justice in Deuteronomy is evident from the beginning of this chapter, with the limitation of corporal punishment. This measure is significant, not only because of the clear intention to preserve life, but also because of the rationale: even the criminal is 'your brother'. This goes even further than earlier affirmations of brotherhood, which had included the debt slave (15:12–18). Just as the debt slave must be restored to full participation in the life of the people, so must the criminal. This is the force of his protection from degradation. The point is directed not so much at the painful nature of the punishment, but at the fact that he is to be treated by an objectively regulated law under which he has rights as a person, and which is guided by the principle that he remains a full member of the society.

With the levirate law there is a transition to the realm of motivation, an area beyond the reach of the court. The disaffected brother-in-law is not penalized legally for his refusal to meet the traditional demand. He is subjected, however, to a shaming ceremony. This may have had a double function, in part to protect the woman. But it was evidently designed to bring opprobrium on the man. The conventions and laws of Israel reflected here show that the ideals enshrined there could be supported by a strong social will. The man's refusal to perpetuate the name of his brother results, in the poetic justice of Deuteronomy, in his own name being sullied, perhaps for generations.

Though the law cannot be enforced in court, it nevertheless has people's important interests at heart. The action of a brother-in-law who agreed to the widow's request in a case like this would be a costly act of kindness. It is in keeping with the spirit of all the social laws, but extends here even to one who has died, the preservation of a man's 'name' being an inestimable gift. It also has the practical benefit of protecting the social position of the widow. The law recorded here does not, as we have seen, establish the practice of the levirate, but actually limits it in order to protect the woman from exploitation, a concern that it shares with the law governing the double divorce (24:1–4). The law that follows also aims to protect, in this case the wrestler and his offspring. The two laws together show a concern for human life and well-being; the latter does not illustrate a difference made between men and women in respect of their sexual integrity (see 'Comment').

The final law (13–16) nicely illustrates the tendency of all the social laws, namely to look for straight dealing between people, free from all selfishness and dishonesty. It accepts that law is ultimately a matter of grace. This has been clear before, of course; there is no evolution to this point in the laws (cf. 15:9–11). And it is true of biblical law outside Deuteronomy (cf. Lev. 19:18). It conforms, too, to the understanding of the laws expressed in the exhortations that prepare the hearer or reader of Deuteronomy for them. The prefatory appeal of 6:4–9 is inscribed over all the laws, with its central plea: 'love the LORD your God with all your heart, all your being, all your strength.'

Lastly, the warning about Amalek reminds Israel that the laws are about building up a society that can be threatened not only from within but from outside. The reappearance of Amalek here has an ominous quality. There will be those who will seek to destroy the people of Yahweh, and thus frustrate his purpose of demonstrating to the world what a people of God might be like. Deuteronomy's intolerance of peoples who worship other gods can be explained in this way. The people of God must first be built, on principles enshrined in the laws; then it can become 'a light to the nations'.

DEUTERONOMY 26:1–19

Translation

¹When you have come into the land the LORD your God is giving you as an inheritance, and are in possession of it and are living there, ²take some of the first of all the produce that you harvest from your land that the LORD is giving you, put it in a basket, and go to the place the LORD your God chooses to make a dwelling for his name there. ³Go to the priest who is in office at the time, and say to him, 'I declare this day before the LORD your God that I have come into the land the LORD

promised on oath to our forefathers to give to us.' ⁴And the priest will take the basket from you and set it down in front of the altar of the LORD your God.

⁵Then you will make the following confession before the LORD your God: 'My forefather was a wandering Aramean, who went to Egypt and dwelt as a stranger there, with his tiny household. But there they became a large nation, great and powerful. ⁶The Egyptians treated us harshly, afflicted us, and subjected us to cruel slavery. ⁷When we cried to the LORD, the God of our forefathers, he heard us, and saw our suffering, pain and oppression. ⁸And the LORD brought us out of Egypt, with strong hand and arm stretched out, with great terror and with signs and wonderful deeds. ⁹He brought us to this place, and gave us this land, a land flowing with milk and honey. ¹⁰Therefore I have now brought the first of the produce of the land which you have given me, O LORD.' Then you shall set it down before the LORD your God, and worship the LORD your God, ¹¹and rejoice, on account of all the good things the LORD your God has given you and your household – you and the Levite and the stranger in your midst.

¹²When you have finished gathering in the tithe of your produce in the third year, the year of the tithe, and have given it to the Levites, the strangers, the orphans and the widows, so that they may eat their fill in your cities, ¹³then declare before the LORD your God: 'I have removed the holy portion from my house, and given it to the Levites, strangers, orphans and widows, according to all that you commanded me; I have not transgressed any of your commands, or forgotten any of them. ¹⁴I have not eaten any of it while in mourning, or removed it while ritually unclean, or offered any to the dead; I have obeyed the LORD my God; I have done all that you commanded me. ¹⁵Look down from your holy dwelling-place in heaven, and bless your people Israel and the land you have given us, according to your sworn promise to our forefathers, a land flowing with milk and honey.'

¹⁶This day, the LORD your God commands you to carry out these laws and statutes, and to observe them carefully with all your heart and being. ¹⁷You have today confirmed the declaration of the LORD: that he will be your God, that you should walk in his ways, keep his laws, commands and statutes, and obey him. ¹⁸And the LORD has today confirmed your declaration: that you will be a people specially for himself, as he promised you, a people that will obey his commands; ¹⁹and [he has declared] that he will set you high above all nations that he has made, for praise and fame and honour, and that you will be a people holy to the LORD your God, as he promised.

Notes on the text

2. 'that you harvest from your land': the phrase is not in LXX or SamP, and is unusual in the context of the land-gift formula (normally '*the* land').

'in a basket': lit. 'in *the* basket'; the definite article is used when a particular one of a kind is in mind.

3. 'your God' should perhaps be emended to 'my God', with LXX; the

Hebr. suffix (-*kā*) could have arisen by dittography with the following *kî* ('that'); so *BHS*.

5. 'make the following confession': lit. 'answer and say'; the verb *'ānâ*, 'answer', can have the sense of 'confess', 'testify' (cf. 5:20; 19:16, 18).

'dwelt as a stranger' translates the verb *wayyāgor*, otherwise 'sojourned'. The verb is related to *gēr*, 'stranger' (cf. 10:19).

'wandering': on balance, this is preferable to 'dying' or 'starving' as a translation of *'ōbēd*, because the idea of homelessness is further developed in the verse (*pace* Norin 1994; Janzen 1994). Craigie (1991: 321 and n.) has 'an ailing Aramean', and relates this to Jacob's great age when he came to Egypt. The difficulty in deciding between these translations lies in the closeness of the two ideas in the patriarchal history: Jacob 'wandered' (homeless, to Egypt) because he was near to perishing; cf. Ps. 105:12-25, and the echoes there of vocabulary in our passage ('sojourned', 'few in number'; Janzen 1994: 362).

8. 'with great terror': slightly differently from 4:34, where 'terror' is plural.

12. LXX has a significant variation, designating the third-year tithe as a 'second tithe', a concept that became important in Jewish harmonization of the various tithe commands.

17-18. 'confirmed the declaration' (after McCarthy 1981: 183): the two occurrences of *'āmar*, hiph., here are the only two in the OT. N. Lohfink (1969: 530-533) suggested the interpretation 'let someone say', meaning 'agree with what someone says', in this case agreeing to the terms of a covenant. This needs only to be modified by noting that each party's statement contains terms accepted by both. For full explanation, see 'Comment'.

Form and structure

Ch. 26 forms part of the framing structure round the laws. The last specific law ended at 25:16. It was followed by a command to destroy Amalek (25:17-19), which echoed the earlier *ḥerem* commands (7:1-5). This, in turn, is linked with the beginning of ch. 26 by means of the formula of land-gift (25:19; 26:1). And the substance of ch. 26 forms an *inclusio* with ch. 12, by virtue of the instruction to the people to go the place of worship after they have come into the land, bringing offerings (12:5-7; 26:1-2). This is an important and complex literary echo in the structure of the whole book (see 'Comment' for more detail).

A further important echo between chs. 12 and 26 consists in the phrase 'laws and statutes', which occurs as a transitional marker at 5:1; 11:32; 12:1; 12:26 (N. Lohfink 1989: 17-18), therefore bracketing both the first general development of the exhortation to obedience (chs. 5 – 11), and the second detailed one (chs. 12 – 26). All the laws, therefore, are framed by these two chapters (12 and 26), and their important statements about the worship at the chosen place (cf. Otto 1994: 192–194). Ch. 26 not only looks back, however, but also forms a transition to the next important section of the book, the 'blessings and curses', and particularly to ch. 28, which forms the 'blessings and curses' section of the Moab covenant (see 'Comment' on vv. 16–19).

This is a chapter of declarations, the verb *'āmar*, 'say, declare', being a leading motif (3, 5, 13, 17, 18). The first (3, 5–10), on the occasion of the bringing of firstfruits, rehearses the journey of Israel's ancestors into Egypt and slavery, and their deliverance by Yahweh. This basic postulate of the laws has hitherto always been expressed by Yahweh, through Moses; now it becomes Israel's own confession: that Yahweh is Israel's God by virtue of what he has done for her. The second (13–15), linked with the bringing of the tithe of the third year (cf. 14:28–29), affirms that the worshipper has obeyed the commands concerning it. The third (17–18) is Moses' affirmation that both Yahweh and Israel have declared themselves willing partners of the covenant.

The chapter is structured so as to focus on these affirmations. The particular cultic actions both recall the substance of the first major section of the law code and introduce new material. The bringing of 'firstfruits' has not appeared before, though some reference to it might have been expected in connection with the festal calendar (16:1–17). And the procedures named in connection with the third-year tithe are new. Together, however, they appear to be representative of the worshipper's action of bringing offerings. These confessions of faith in the context of worship lead up to the mutual statements of covenant commitment by Yahweh and Israel in vv. 17–18.

Comment

26:1–11

1–2. The familiar introductory formula of Yahweh's gift of land leads into an instruction to bring some of the first ripe grain of the harvest, the 'firstfruits', to Yahweh at the place he will choose for worship. The intention of the instruction is to provide for a regular act of worship, that is, not a single occasion as soon as the people arrive in the land (*pace* Craigie 1976a: 319). This is clear from the phrase 'the priest in office at the time' (3; lit. 'in those days'; cf. 17:9; 19:17).

The bringing of firstfruits of the harvest is mentioned explicitly in other calendars of the major feasts, according to which it occurred in the context of the feast of Weeks (cf. Exod. 23:19; 34:26; Lev. 23:10; Num. 28:26). It is not expressly mentioned in the calendar in Deuteronomy (16:1–17; see 'Form and structure'), and is perhaps deliberately reserved to play this part in the structuring of the book. It is, however, recorded as part of the dues given to the priest in 18:4. The handing of the basket of firstfruits to the priest in this passage presumably corresponds to that requirement. It is still regarded as the worshipper's gift to Yahweh, however, as is clear from v. 10. There is no need to see a conflict between these verses (*pace* Mayes 1979: 332). Gifts of produce to Yahweh are in practice perquisites of the priests in other laws (e.g. Num. 18), and, while this aspect of offerings does not always surface in Deuteronomy, it does so in this instruction about an actual ritual.

3. In the liturgy as recorded, the worshipper makes two declarations, before and after handing over the basket of grain (3, 5–10), which are nevertheless intimately linked. The first (3) sets out the basis on which he comes. It expresses a dynamic that is of the essence of Deuteronomy: Israelites have come into the land (by the power and guidance of Yahweh), and in response they come to the place of worship. This sequence of Yahweh's action and Israel's response, constructed around 'coming' to land and place, was also found in the movement from chs. 1 – 11 into ch. 12 and the following chapters (see on 12:5). Yahweh 'brings' Israel to the land (*bō'*, hiph.; 4:38; 6:10, 23; 8:7; 9:28; 11:29; or 'comes', under his guidance, *bō'*, qal; 4:1; 6:18); in response, Israel 'comes' (*bō'*, qal) to the place of worship (12:5), and 'brings' offerings (*bō'*, hiph., 12:6).

This sequence reappears in 26:1–10:

3   'Go (come) to the priest', at the place of worship (*bō'*, qal)
3   'I have come to the land' (*bō'*, qal)
9   '(Yahweh) brought me to this place (the land)' (*bō'*, hiph.)
10   'I have brought the first of the fruit' (to the place of worship) (*bō'*, hiph.)

This shows that the first declaration (3) is part of a conceptual structure that embraces the one in vv. 5–10 also. The close relationship between 'land' and 'place' of worship is heightened by the use of *māqôm*, 'place', to mean 'land' in v. 9. This echoes the use of the word several times in chs. 1 – 11 to mean the place at which Israel then stood (Moab; 1:31; 9:7; 11:5). The designation of the land (of Canaan) as the 'place' to which Yahweh has brought the people thus marks the progression from Moab into the promised land.

The confession is further remarkable in that it focuses the response required of Israel on to the individual worshipper, who says, '*I* have come...' The ceremony pictured therefore realizes the response expected of all Israelites to the command of Yahweh concerning their life before him in the land. The required confession, that is, of what Israel *shall* say, may be contrasted with what it expressly must *not* say, namely, 'It is because of my innocence that the LORD has brought me here to possess this land' (9:4). This is negated in effect by the development of the confession in vv. 5–10. (Interestingly, that prohibited confession is also couched in the singular, though there the 'I' seems to embrace all Israel.)

4. The altar of Yahweh is mentioned in the law code only in 12:27 (twice), 16:21 and 26:4. The geography of the sanctuary is never pictured in Deuteronomy, as it is in Exod. 25 – 31 (cf. Exod. 27:1–8 for the altar). But the distribution of these allusions conforms with the appearance of major laws concerning the sanctuary in framing positions around the law code, 16:21 occurring after the laws of sacrifices and feasts. The response of the Israelite to Yahweh's blessing is located carefully at the focal point of the worship at the sanctuary.

5–10. The confession itself is often called the 'small credo', after von Rad's (1966: 157–159) theory that it is a self-standing statement of faith, conveying the outline of Israel's most ancient beliefs. It relates in outline the story of Israel's origins, beginning with the journeys of the patriarchs. The 'wandering Aramean' is Jacob, the immediate father of the twelve tribal ancestors, whose long stay in Paddan-Aram among the extended family of Abraham's father Terah (Gen. 28 – 31) is memorialized in the name. This still seems the best view, though some find in the term a meaning close to our 'gypsy', that is, denoting a class that has an unsettled existence (Janzen 1994: 372–373). (On the translation 'wandering', see 'Notes on the text'.)

Jacob was also the patriarch who actually settled in Egypt. The confession continues through the time in Egypt and the expansion in numbers that led to enslavement, to the miraculous deliverance of Israel at the Reed Sea, a story that matches the developed narrative of Exodus–Numbers, as well as other short summaries (Num. 20:14–16; cf. Judg. 11:16; Gen. 15:13–16). It is impossible to isolate an actual ancient credo from these, or to say whether short credal statements preceded the developed narrative or are – as indeed they seem – summaries of the latter. The fact that they are all tailored to their contexts suggests the latter. The topic of the deliverance from Egypt is also a recurring theme in Deuteronomy (cf. 4:34; 5:15; 6:21–25; 7:19; 9:29; 11:2; 26:8). (On the 'signs and wonderful deeds' and Yahweh's 'strong hand and arm stretched out', 8, see on 4:34.)

There are two dominant points in this case. The first is the contrast between homelessness and land. Jacob's 'wandering', as we have noted, is sometimes taken as 'ready to die', and not only the word but also the tradition suggests both these meanings (Ps. 105:12–25, and 'Notes on the text'). Vulnerable and weak ('few in number', cf. 7:7; Gen. 46:8–27), he is accepted as a 'stranger', or 'sojourner', in Egypt, a term that emphasizes homelessness more than the parallel Num. 20:15 (which has *yāšaḇ*, 'dwell'). While there, having no natural right or ownership, his descendants fell victim to oppression, cried to Yahweh and so were liberated into a land of their own. The poles of this arc are 'possessing nothing' and 'possessing plenty'. The second theme of the credo is Yahweh's response to the people's desperate cry (7; cf. Exod. 2:23-25; 3:7, 9), and his favour shown to those who, in oppression, looked for his mercy. The same theme of injustice and slavery that marked the laws deeply (cf. 15:9; 24:16, 18) is here crystallized. Deuteronomy is aligned at this point with other texts that deplore oppression by abuse of power (cf. 1 Sam. 8).

The force of the confession, therefore, is that the worshipper, bringing produce of the land, acknowledges that it is all due to Yahweh's gift of land to Israel in the events that formed the people. The act of worship is essentially agricultural, but, as with the major feasts (16:1-17), it is understood in terms of Yahweh's historical saving acts on the people's behalf. The dominant contrast between homelessness and 'home' explains, in part, why the other great event in the history is missing, namely the encounter with Yahweh at Sinai/Horeb. The absence of that theme is also explained, however, by the fact that the chosen place itself stands in a relation to Horeb as the place where Yahweh now meets Israel, in a typological relationship that we have noted above (see on 12:1-5).

The 'place' (9) is the land of Canaan (see 'Form and structure'), and the plenty that is acknowledged is drawn from the traditional language for the promised land (cf. Exod. 3:17). The offering and confession complete, the worshipper proceeds to join in a festal celebration, probably in connection with the feast of Weeks (10-11; see 'Form and structure'). The instructions for the feast highlight the usual deuteronomic features of feasting (11; cf. 14:29; 16:11, 14); the particular focus on Levites and strangers is consistent with the concern for those who have no intrinsic right to land, and thus answers to the landlessness of Israel's forebears (5).

26:12-15

12. The subject changes from the firstfruits to the tithe, and thus to a later time of year, after the various crops had been harvested, perhaps at the feast of Booths. While the tithe was an annual offering (14:22), the interest in this passage is on the tithe of the third year, which was reserved specially for the disadvantaged (12; cf. 14:28-29). It is worth noting that most of the offerings mentioned in the deuteronomic law are not supplied with a confession like this one; the firstfruits and the tithe of the third year are the only ones. This does not mean that there were no other confessions comparable to these in ancient Israel. We have observed before that the deuteronomic law does not cover every eventuality of life. In the religious life that the law code reflects, the need for the present confession arose because the tithed materials were not being brought to the sanctuary, but rather were being stored up in the cities of Israel (14:28). The confession is therefore a solemn declaration that in a sense substitutes for the act of bringing the goods to the sanctuary. In the logic of ch. 26, with its collection of cultic declarations, the motivation to include this may again lie in the themes of justice and land; landless Israel's occupation of land should issue in care for the landless.

13. The terms of the confession reflect certain cultic or religious concerns. The tithe itself is referred to as 'the holy portion', or strictly 'the holy (thing)'. This word is used only three times in Deuteronomy, though it is frequent in other contexts for the sanctuary, or for the abstract idea of holiness. The occurrences in Deuteronomy are all in chs. 12 and 26: in 12:26 it refers to offerings in general, and in 26:15 it is used in the sense of 'sanctuary' (cf. Exod. 26:33), in this case meaning Yahweh's dwelling-place in heaven. Only in v. 13 is it used of a particular offering. In conformity with this solemn cultic language for the tithe, the word translated 'removed' is the same word used elsewhere to root out evil (13:5; 17:7; 19:19; etc.), and is carefully chosen to express a rigorous separation. This is according to Yahweh's strict command (13b, a reference, no doubt, to 14:28–29), and to regular cultic requirement (14).

14. Three types of cultic transgression are disclaimed here. The affirmation that the worshipper has not removed the tithe 'while in mourning' can be explained by the fact that he would or might have been ritually unclean because of contact with a corpse. It is not necessary, therefore, to suppose that the reference is to the ritual mourning for the dying and rising god, Baal in Canaan, Tammuz in Babylon (cf. Hos. 9:4; Ezek. 8:14; and see on Deut. 14:1–2; thus against Cazelles 1948).

This best explains the second disclaimer, 'I have not ... removed it while ritually unclean', which proceeds to a comprehensive statement that the offerer was in a ritually 'clean' state. The language of cleanness and uncleanness belongs to the 'holiness sphere', that is, the organization of the world according to categories of holiness, regular cleanness and uncleanness or contamination. Just as the offerer could not make offerings in the sanctuary while 'unclean', neither could he handle the third-year tithe in such a condition, even though it never came to the sanctuary. There is a certain parallel with the 'profane slaughter' of 12:15–28, where the blood rite is still to be carried out, even though the slaughter of the animal is not regarded as a sacrifice.

The third disclaimer, 'or offered any to the dead', has been taken to refer to a sacrifice for the dying and rising god, that is, Baal, according to Canaanite myth (Cazelles 1948), or, perhaps more likely, to the god Molek, to whom child sacrifice was made (see on 12:30–31; 18:10–11, and Blenkinsopp 1995: 11). The affirmation thus moves from general cultic propriety to a statement that the worshipper has not been involved in a foreign cult. As child sacrifice to Molek typified the worst excesses of Canaanite religion in 12:30–31, so perhaps does the reference to the cult of the same god here. The worshipper then repeats that he has obeyed Yahweh implicitly (14b), echoing v. 13b.

15. Finally, the affirmation moves into petition. The dwelling of Yahweh in heaven recalls 4:36a (cf. 1 Kgs. 8:27), yet without threatening the idea that he also 'dwells' with his people on earth (see 'Comment' on 4:36). The blessing of the ground is one of the basic promises of Yahweh contained in Deuteronomy (cf. 7:13; 28:4, 11), and the prayer also deploys one of the great Pentateuchal expressions of fruitfulness ('flowing with milk and honey'; cf. Exod. 3:8, 17; Lev. 20:24; Deut. 6:3; 11:9). The worshipper, having declared his faithfulness in responding to all Yahweh's commands, now claims his promises. The image of 'looking down' may suggest sending rain (cf. 28:12; Ps. 85:11[12]).

26:16–19

16. Verse 16 brings the perspective back from the anticipated future ceremonies in the land to Moab (N. Lohfink 1994: 149). The phrase 'this day', in the emphatic initial position in the clause, draws attention to the return to the Mosaic present. There is a return, too, to the deuteronomic main theme, the need to keep the 'laws and statutes', which have now been fully rehearsed. Deut. 26:16 thus echoes 12:1, which marked the beginning of the law code, and announces its closure (see 'Form and structure'). The following verses (17–19) now establish the acceptance of the covenant by both parties.

17–19. The double declaration, by Yahweh and by Israel, as the ratification of the Moab covenant, complements the ratification of the Horeb covenant, recalled in 5:27. Verses 17–18 are mirror images. The double statement ('You have today confirmed the declaration of the LORD ... And the LORD has today confirmed your declaration') expresses rhetorically the two-sided relationship between God and Israel. It thus elaborates the basic covenantal formula, 'I will be your God, and you shall be my people.'

The mutuality of the declaration is striking, so much so that some see the closest formal analogy to be the parity treaty, best exemplified by Hattusili III's treaty with Rameses II (Braulik 1992a: 198). Two near-identical copies of this treaty were found in the Egyptian and Hittite capitals respectively, each setting out the terms of the treaty in the words of the other king. Each first declares his own intention, then his corresponding expectations of the other. Presumably, therefore, each king prepared his own copy, and the two were then exchanged (N. Lohfink 1969: 535–536). A similar practice may be assumed over a lengthy period in ANE politics.

The mutual commitment of Yahweh and Israel follows a similar pattern. The undertaking of each party is spelt out in succession, forming a kind of rhetorical parallelism, with each statement introducing the reciprocal commitment of Yahweh and Israel. Each undertaking has four parts (marked by an infinitive verb in Hebrew), in which the party making the declaration affirms one basic commitment on his part and requires a threefold commitment of the other. This is clear in v. 17. In vv. 18–19 it entails intepreting the first, third and fourth elements as undertakings of Yahweh rather than of Israel, namely 'that you will be a people specially for himself, as he promised you ... that he will set you high above all nations that he has made, for praise and fame and honour, and that you will be a people holy to the LORD your God, as he promised'.

This is not so immediately clear, as the phrases in themselves could be read either way, and the order is not so neat (Israel's own undertaking coming in the second position, not the first). But it is compelled both by the balance of the two declarations and by the repeated 'as he promised you', by which Israel holds Yahweh to promises previously made (e.g. Lohfink 1969: 532–533; cf. McCarthy 1981: 183).

The effect of the Moab covenant is carried forward into the land. It is not accidental that this passage follows directly on one that has put words of acceptance on the lips of the worshipping Israelite in the context of everyday life in the land. The double acceptance in vv. 17–18 constitutes the ratification of the Moab covenant. Covenantal form leads to the expectation of a series of blessings and curses. This will follow in ch. 28, after an interruption (ch. 27) that looks forward to a covenant renewal at Shechem after Israel has come into the land.

The words of ratification of the Moab covenant (16–19) round off the legal section of Deuteronomy on a high note, returning to the theology of Israel's election. They reach back past ch. 12 to the primary exposition of election in 7:6–11. Israel is Yahweh's 'treasured possession' (cf. 7:6). But there is enhancement here, for now they are not merely chosen 'out of all the people on earth', but they are to be set 'high above all nations that he has made, for praise and fame and honour' (cf. 28:1). In 10:21 it was said that 'Yahweh is your praise', meaning that it was he who made Israel worthy of praise among the nations (cf. the thought in 4:6–8). The reversal here has the same effect: Israel will be honoured among the nations. The same threefold expression ('praise and fame and honour') is found also in Jer. 13:11; 33:9 (cf. Zeph. 3:19–20), where it means that Israel should bring honour to Yahweh among the nations.

The trend towards a universal proclamation of salvation is taken further in Isaiah, where, especially in chs. 56 – 66, the triad of terms in this expression appears with some frequency, to denote both the new glory Yahweh will bring to his people when he redeems them after the exile, and the glory they will bring him among the peoples of the earth (60:18–19; 61:11; 62:2–3, 7; 63:7, 12, 14–15; 64:2[1]). The universalistic point emerges less strongly here, the emphasis falling on the honour Yahweh has brought to Israel by making them his own people. It is noteworthy also that, while the terms 'treasured possession' and 'holy nation' recur here, echoing, as in 7:6, the language of Exod. 19:5–6, the phrase 'kingdom of priests' is omitted (see on 7:6 for explanation).

Explanation

The key to understanding ch. 26 is its position in Deuteronomy. Within the structure of the book, with its resemblance to a treaty and law code, it rounds off the long section of laws, signalling this function in the ways that we have noticed above. As the faithful Israelite comes to the chosen place to worship, the command in 12:5–7, 11–13 is pictured in its fulfilment. The nation's obedience is symbolized in that of the individual worshipper. In bringing his offerings and making his confessions (at different times of the year), he is not merely obeying God's commands, but also accepting the terms on which they are given. A note of solemn acquiescence runs through the chapter. Only here in Deuteronomy do we hear the voice of the worshipper at the intimate moment of worship, handing over his offerings to the priest, 'before Yahweh', at the sanctuary. The priest steps out of his habitual anonymity in this book for the purpose. And the worshipper utters what he believes.

The words themselves are intimate, opening with the surprising, 'undeuteronomic' memory of 'my father'. But they quickly open out into the 'we' and 'us' of the people Israel's memory of suffering. The special tension of Deuteronomy is captured sharply in the confession of that pain, born of oppression and homelessness, the cry of anguish that Yahweh heard, and the deliverance into 'a land flowing with milk and honey'. The act of worship at the chosen 'place' symbolizes the secure dwelling of the once enslaved people in 'place', that is, land (9), of their own. The confession is followed by a renewed reminder that deliverance from homeless slavery into 'place' and home brings with it the responsibility to draw the homeless fully into the experience and celebration of rooted belonging (11). This is to echo one of the great themes of the book, an inclusiveness pictured so often in connection with worship (12:12; 14:28–29) and in the implications of the laws (15:12–18; 24:14).

The chapter closes with a renewed general command to keep the commands of Yahweh (16), followed by words of covenant ratification (17–19), in keeping with its thrust up to that point. The declarations recorded here constitute Yahweh's and Israel's mutual acceptance of the Moab covenant, corresponding, therefore, to Israel's words of acceptance of the Sinai/Horeb covenant (Exod. 19:8; 24:3, 7–8; Deut. 5:27). (Apart from the present text, the mutuality of the commitment is clearest in Exod. 24:7–8.) There is no ritual for this covenant ratification; Moses simply says that it has occurred. So it is not clear at what moment it is deemed to have happened. The omission may mean that Yahweh and Israel perpetually re-enter into covenant with each other whenever Israel keeps faith with Yahweh by obeying his commands, conveyed by the teaching of its leaders. A ritual of covenant-keeping follows in 27:1–8, where the scene has changed to Shechem. That shift of focus also says that the covenant must be perpetually renewed.

Finally, the undertaking made by Yahweh to Israel promises it a special place among the nations. This is in line with the perspective of Deuteronomy that Israel is to be a kind of demonstration to the world of what Yahweh has done for his people. The intention of universal salvation in this is at best muted, though we have observed before that election in Deuteronomy is not applied rigidly to the Israel of strict genealogy, but has within it the concept that the chosen people is that which responds to Yahweh in righteousness (see 'Explanation' on ch. 7). The implication of universal salvation is left to other parts of the OT to draw out more fully. The lines from the present passage to Is. 56 – 66 are most noticeable, because of the vocabulary chain 'praise, name and glory', adopted there in a more scattered way. In that place there is an emphasis on newness (e.g. 56:5–6; 62:2–3; 65:15), and a strong sense of Yahweh's praise throughout the world (61:11; 62:7), in language that can be seen as eschatological.

Lines may also be continued into the NT, for example to 1 Pet. 4:16, where the terms of Deut. 26:19 (LXX) are used: 'to *glorify* God because you bear this *name*'. This follows from that letter's adoption of the terms 'a chosen race, a royal priesthood, a holy nation, God's own people' (2:19), which echo the present passage as well as 7:6, and which continue by stating the purpose of this election as the salvation of all nations: 'in order that you may proclaim the mighty acts of him who called you out of darkness into his marvellous light'. We may also notice Paul's admission that he had in himself no 'reason to boast' (*kauchēma*, Rom. 4:2; Deut. 26:19, LXX), and in contrast that he and the Corinthian Christians would be each other's 'boast' on the day of Christ's return (2 Cor. 1:14).

DEUTERONOMY 27:1–26

Translation

[1]Moses and the elders of Israel commanded the people: 'Keep all the commands with which I am charging you this day. [2]And on the day that you cross the Jordan into the land the LORD your God is giving you, set up for yourselves large stones and coat them with plaster. [3]Then write on them all the commands of this law, when you have crossed over to enter the land the LORD your God is giving you, a land flowing with milk and honey, just as the LORD the God of your forefathers promised you. [4]When you have crossed the Jordan, set up these stones that I command you today on Mt Ebal, and coat them with plaster. [5]And build an altar there to the LORD your God, an altar of stones on which you have not used an iron tool. [6]Build the altar of the LORD your God with whole stones, and sacrifice burnt offerings on it to the LORD your God. [7]Sacrifice peace offerings, and consume them there, and rejoice before the LORD your God. [8]And write on the stones all the commands of this law, engraving them clearly.'

⁹Then Moses and the Levitical priests said to all Israel: 'Be silent and listen, Israel. This day you have become a people of the Lord your God. ¹⁰Therefore obey the Lord your God, and carry out his commands and laws with which I am charging you today.' ¹¹And Moses commanded the people that day: ¹²'These tribes shall stand on Mt Gerizim for the blessing of the people, when you have crossed the Jordan: Simeon, Levi, Judah, Issachar, Joseph and Benjamin. ¹³And these shall stand on Mt Ebal for the curse: Reuben, Gad, Asher, Zebulun, Dan, Naphtali. ¹⁴And the Levites shall declare in a loud voice to every man of Israel: ¹⁵"Cursed be the one who makes an image or a molten idol, an abomination to the Lord, the work of a craftsman, and sets it up in secret"; and all the people shall respond, saying, "Amen." ¹⁶"Cursed be anyone who dishonours father or mother"; and all the people shall say, "Amen." ¹⁷"Cursed be anyone who moves his neighbour's landmark"; and all the people shall say, "Amen." ¹⁸"Cursed be anyone who leads a blind person astray as he journeys"; and all the people shall say, "Amen." ¹⁹"Cursed be anyone who perverts justice due to strangers, orphans or widows"; and all the people shall say, "Amen." ²⁰"Cursed be anyone who sleeps with his father's wife, for he has violated his father's bed"; and all the people shall say, "Amen." ²¹"Cursed be anyone who has sexual relations with any animal"; and all the people shall say, "Amen." ²²"Cursed be anyone who sleeps with his sister, whether the daughter of his father or the daughter of his mother"; and all the people shall say, "Amen." ²³"Cursed be anyone who sleeps with his wife's mother"; and all the people shall say, "Amen." ²⁴"Cursed be anyone who kills his neighbour in secret"; and all the people shall say. "Amen." ²⁵"Cursed be anyone who takes a bribe to shed the blood of an innocent person"; and all the people shall say, "Amen." ²⁶"Cursed be anyone who does not uphold the commands of this law by carrying them out"; and all the people shall say, "Amen."' '

Notes on the text

1. 'Keep': the form is an infinitive absolute, used as an imperative also at 16:1 ('plene' form). A few MSS have the 'plene' form here, making this unambiguous in the consonantal text. This reading avoids the difficulty that the consonantal text must otherwise be taken as a singular command in a plural section. Most versions adopt an imperative plural to harmonize. The plural section, however, runs only to v. 2a. It is possible to read the imperative singular, following *hā'ām*, in spite of the following plural.

3. 'to enter': the phrase (*lᵉma'an ᵃšer tābō'*) expressses a strong sense of purpose, which leads some to see the command to write the laws on the stones as a precondition of entering the land (Braulik 1992a: 200, with EÜ mg.). This seems illogical, however, as the people will already have entered the land. The purpose clause should be taken closely with 'when you have crossed over'.

4. Instead of 'Mt Ebal', SamP reads 'Mt Gerizim'. The original text has been altered, either by SamP in favour of the Samaritans' promotion of their sanctuary on Mt Gerizim, or by MT as part of an anti-Samaritan bias. It is hard to decide which. The placing of 'the blessing' on Gerizim (11:29; 27:12) does not decide the issue. Wevers (1995: 417) favours MT. An Old Latin codex, however, has 'Gerizim', and this is unlikely to have been directly influenced by SamP (cf. Braulik 1992a: 200). The textual point is moot, and the translation reads MT. (See also 'Comment'.)

8. 'engraving them clearly': *ba'ēr hêṭēḇ*.

12. *leḇārēḵ 'eṯ hā'ām*, 'for the blessing of the people': the translation avoids the supposition that the tribes themselves utter the blessing. As N. Lohfink (1994: 143 n. 16) says on the phrase, the subject of an action in the infinitive in Hebrew need not be the last-named person (in this case the tribes on Gerizim side).

Form and structure

The anticipated ceremony at Shechem interrupts the flow of Moses' speech. While 28:1 follows neatly from 26:19, both in terms of literary smoothness and in that it introduces the expected blessings and curses of the Moab covenant, ch. 27 reverts to third-person narrative about Moses, now appearing with 'the elders of Israel', and introduces a further covenant ratification, and a set of curses that anticipate and are additional to the blessings and curses in ch. 28. The position of ch. 27 can be explained by considering the structure of the book, however. Just as ch. 26 corresponded to ch. 12 at the beginning and end of the law code, so ch. 27 echoes the passage immediately preceding ch. 12, namely 11:26–32. In fact, the three parts of that short passage are now repeated in reverse order in chs. 26 – 28, as follows (as also Craigie 1976a: 212, slightly differently; cf. N. Lohfink 1963: 233–234):

11:26–28	Blessing and curse pronounced in Moab
11:29–31	Ceremony of blessing and curse on Gerizim and Ebal
11:32	Call to obey commands
26:16–19	Call to obey commands
ch. 27	Ceremony of (blessing and curse) on Gerizim and Ebal
ch. 28	Blessing and curse pronounced in Moab

This structure has the effect of enclosing the laws of chs. 12 – 26 between exhortations to obedience. However, the structuring function of ch. 27 goes further. The speech by Moses and the elders together arcs back to 5:23–27, in which the elders accept and commission Moses' role as spokesman for Yahweh at Horeb. Therefore the elders now declare that Moses has spoken everything that Yahweh has told him on Horeb, and prepare to acknowledge formally their acceptance of Yahweh's words on entry to the land. In this way, a tight connection is made between God's words at Horeb, Moses' speech in Moab and the people's covenant obligations in the land.

While Moses stands with the elders in order to mark the validation of Yahweh's words for all time in Israel, he also stands with the Levitical priests (9). His pronouncement along with the priests (9–10) signifies Israel's formal acceptance of the terms of the covenant. This leads into the ceremony of blessing and cursing (12–13 – of which only curses are recorded, vv. 15–26), in which the Levites play the leading role (14).

Comment

27:1-8

1–2a. Moses and the Levites instruct Israel to keep 'all the commands', or, strictly, 'this whole commandment' (*miṣwâ*, cf. 5:31; 6:1; 17:20; 30:11), meaning the whole body of laws in chs. 12 – 26, which he has just recited 'this day' in Moab. Beginning here, there is a heightened emphasis on the writing of Moses' words, which corresponds to the now rapid movement of the narrative of Deuteronomy towards Moses' death (Sonnet 1997: 95). Moses and the Levites go on to prescribe the ceremony of ratification to be held at Shechem. This is to be done 'on the day' when they enter the land (2). The phrase need not be taken to mean a strict twenty-four hours (cf. P. Barker 1998: 298). In practice, it would take time to reach the area of Shechem; the phrase, in effect, means 'immediately', and is a variant of the regular deuteronomic 'today' of urgent decision, making a specific link with v. 1. The day of Moab and the day of Shechem are brought into unity at the outset. (There is thus no need to think, as many commentators do, that different versions of the command underlie the present text; S. R. Driver 1895: 295–296; Anbar 1985: 307–308.)

2b–4, 8. The ceremony begins with the erection of large stones on which 'the commands of this law' are to be written (3, 8; the 'law' here is *tôrâ*, lit. 'instruction', but referring, like *miṣwâ*, to the whole body of laws in Deuteronomy; cf. 31:24). The stones are overlaid with plaster and written on with a kind of ink, in the Egyptian fashion (Craigie 1976a: 328). The writing of the laws is not only a command but a memorial of Yahweh's gift of the land. The phrase 'a land flowing with milk and honey' (3) occurs also at 6:3; 11:9; 26:9, 15; 31:20 (a distribution that has a certain correspondence with the framing of the law code), and the memorial reaches back to the promise to the patriarchs (cf. 1:21; 19:8).

Ancient and modern interpreters have found it odd that the covenantal memorial should have been erected on Mt Ebal, the mountain of the curse (cf. 13), and have therefore been persuaded that 'Gerizim' was original here (see 'Notes on the text'). The present text can hardly have arisen purely as a matter of anti-Samaritan polemic, however, especially if the setting of the ceremony on the mountain of the curse was likely to be found theologically inappropriate. The symbolism of the location may have the effect of emphasizing that the covenant implies Israel's agreement to accept the curse for failure to keep it. This is in line with the idea of the law as a witness against Israel, in texts that suggest that it will fail to keep the law (31:16–17, 26; P. Barker 1998: 286–289).

5–7. In addition, an altar is to be set up and sacrifices made. There are similarities to other OT ceremonies, especially the covenant ritual in Exod. 24:3–8, where twelve pillars are set up, corresponding to the twelve tribes, sacrifices are offered, and the Book of the Covenant is read and accepted. Memorial pillars are set up, too, in the River Jordan at Gilgal, when the tribes cross into the land (Josh. 4). In neither of these cases are words said to be written on the pillars. However, it was common in the ANE for important agreements to be recorded on stones or stelae, not least in the ratification of treaties (some Hittite treaties; VTE; Sefire; cf. Gen. 31:52–54; Josh. 24:25–27; McCarthy 1981: 195–196, 223). Although Deut. 27:1–8 is widely thought to be a composite piece of writing, vv. 5–7a having been inserted into vv. 1–8 (S. R. Driver 1895: 295; Weinfeld 1972: 165), it is not at all surprising that a covenant ratification should involve both the recording of the treaty with its conditions, and a sacrificial ritual.

Does the location of the ceremony at Shechem mean that it is the 'chosen place', so carefully left unnamed throughout chs. 12 – 26 (but widely thought to refer cryptically to Jerusalem)? The instruction to hold a sacrificial ritual at Shechem has been thought by many scholars to conflict with the deuteronomic altar law (12:5; etc.), because of the belief that the latter requires centralization of worship in Jerusalem. The problem is then solved in various ways: 1. by supposing that vv. 5–7 are a late addition in 'deuteronomic-deuteronomistic style' (Mayes 1979: 340); or 2. by supposing, conversely, that the command is *earlier* than the bulk of Deuteronomy, that is, 'pre-deuteronomic', or even pre-monarchic (Anbar 1985: 309, citing also Cross 1973: 84 n. 15). The rite has also been seen as not requiring a sanctuary setting, because it was not originally sacrificial (Seebass 1982: 25).

This perceived problem is illusory, however, arising only because of the view that Deuteronomy aims to centralize worship once for all in Jerusalem. I have argued, in contrast, that the altar law aims to establish Yahweh's sovereignty in Israel's worship, and that 'the place' is simply wherever he should choose to encounter his people. The ritual foreseen at Shechem is, of course, a unique event, whereas the laws in ch. 12 envisage regular worship. Even so, this is not a crucial distinction between the present ceremony and the regular worship, as may be seen from the strong similarities that 27:6b–7 bears to 12:6–7. The occurrence of Shechem at 11:29 and in ch. 27 makes it impossible to miss the connection between Shechem and the 'chosen place' of chs. 12 – 26. The event at Shechem sets the pattern for Yahweh's choice of 'the place' where Israel should worship him. The silence in chs. 12 – 26 about the name of the place means that the command concerning the place does not reach its definitive conclusion with Shechem, but rather is open to future, different fulfilments. These are all to be seen as re-engagements with the God first met at Horeb.

27:9–10

9. Moses now speaks along with the Levitical priests (see 'Form and structure'). They call the people solemnly to attention, in words that echo the 'Shema' ('Listen!', or 'Hear, Israel!', 6:4) in its simplest form, that is, having no direct object of the verb 'hear' (contrast 4:1; 5:1), and thus in its formal function as a signal to listen. The role of the priest in the muster of the army for battle may be recalled, where again the simple form of the Shema is used (20:2–3). The focus of the address is the declaration that the people have become the covenant people of Yahweh 'This day'. The reference is to the covenant agreement ratified in 26:17–19. It should not be taken to mean that Israel had not already been Yahweh's people before the Moab covenant. Rather, the rhetoric illustrates that it must always enter the covenant afresh. That, indeed, is the essence of the idea enshrined in the Moab covenant itself.

10. It is followed in this case by a further call to hear, now in the sense of obeying Yahweh's laws and commands.

27:11–14

11–13. Moses now speaks alone, distributing the tribes (including Levi) to the two mountains for the formal declamation of the blessing (Gerizim) and the curse (Ebal). (Their actual positions need not involve climbing to the respective summits. In Josh. 8:33, which records the performance of this ceremony, the tribes are said to stand 'facing' the mountains, therefore standing back to back in the valley between; Seebass 1982: 23; Braulik 1992a: 201; and see N. Lohfink 1994: 143 n.) The division partly follows maternal relationship, with order of birth as a secondary ordering principle, and Reuben forming an exception. Alternatively or additionally, the distribution is according to geography, the tribes on Gerizim roughly corresponding to the south, those on Ebal to the north (Mayes 1979: 344; Seebass 1982: 25; the latter finds the six assigned to the curse to correspond to the area still in Assyrian hands following recovery of part of the former northern lands; 2 Kgs. 23:15–20).

Beyond these observations it is hard to find a systematic reason for the distribution. (If Reuben is displaced from his natural priority because of Gen. 49:3–4, how do Simeon and Levi retain their places in view of the same list of blessings; Gen. 49:5–7?) The six tribes assigned to Gerizim and the blessing are descended from children of Leah and Rachel (in birth order): Simeon, Levi, Judah, Issachar (Leah), Joseph and Benjamin (Rachel); while the six on Ebal for the curse include Reuben (Leah, the firstborn, but see Gen. 49:3–4) and Zebulun (Leah's last) and the children of Leah's and Rachel's maids: Gad, Asher (Zilpah; Leah); Dan and Naphtali (Bilhah; Rachel; cf. Gen. 35:22–26; also Gen. 29:31 – 30:24; 35:16–19).

14. The task of uttering the blessing and curse falls to the Levites (Moses will not be there; cf. 1:37–38). There is no need to suppose that the two blocks of tribes actually utter blessings and curses in chorus (see 'Notes on the text', and N. Lohfink 1994: 142–143). The 'Levites' cannot mean the whole tribe of Levi, since the tribe as such is to be gathered as one of the six on (or facing) Mt Gerizim. The term 'Levites' in Deuteronomy denotes members of the tribe of Levi in their priestly capacity. That is, in principle, all of them; and Deuteronomy's main interest in them is that they should be properly provided for as they have no tribal territory (10:9; 14:29). However, while Deuteronomy does not legislate for various functions within the priestly tribe, it knows and assumes that such existed. The 'Levites' here are not clearly distinguished from the 'Levitical priests' (9), since the systematic hierarchizing of the priestly tribe found in Num. 3 finds no expression in Deuteronomy (see also 'Comment' on 18:1).

The Levites' specific role in the ceremony may arise from their responsibility for the written form of the commands of Yahweh, which would in due course be given into their care for keeping with the ark of the covenant (31:9, 25–26; notice there, too, a flexibility in the terms used: 'priests, the sons of Levi'; 'Levites, who carried the ark of the covenant'). In the ceremony, they may be pictured standing by the ark, uttering blessings towards Mt Gerizim and curses towards Mt Ebal. The record of the curses (15–26) has 'all the people' respond to each. This could mean all the people on the Ebal side, or literally all the people; either way, it is, in principle, all the people.

The tribes so gathered constitute the cultic assembly of Israel, this being the clearest picture of it since they were gathered at Horeb (chs. 4 – 5). As it stood at Horeb, so now it stands at a place where the covenant is realized anew. It is this assembly as such that has the authority and responsibility to enter the covenant formally. It is also responsible for enacting and enforcing law in Israel. The law code (chs. 12 – 26) is therefore followed here by a symbolic representation of legal authority in Israel: it is enshrined in the commandments of Yahweh, now written as a permanent memorial; in the anticipated absence of Moses, the people itself is the sole human authority responsible for its administration, and the nature of the law as Yahweh's law is symbolized by the role of the Levites in constituting the people an assembly in his presence.

27:15-26

It is immediately striking that vv. 15-26, in spite of the expectation created in vv. 12-13 of announcements of both blessing and curse, contain only curses. The conventions of covenant-making, together with the symbolism carefully constructed round the two mountains, make it likely that the ceremony was intended to announce blessing as well as curse. Josh. 8:34 seems to confirm this. It is sometimes said that the original list of blessings might have consisted of mirror images of the curses recorded (e.g. Craigie 1976a: 331), but P. Barker (1998: 281) is right to argue that such a list would make little sense. It is improbable, therefore, that ch. 27 represents only a fragment of the original text of the ceremony. This still leaves the question why only curses are recorded, however. I think there are two overlapping answers to this, one to do with the form of the curses recorded, and one literary-theological.

First, the curses differ from those in 28:15-68 in that they correlate with particular offences that an individual might commit. In this they resemble laws and commands, such as are found not only in Deuteronomy but in Exodus and Leviticus, more than treaty sanctions. Several, indeed, correspond to commands in the Decalogue. This formerly led commentators to suppose that curses of this sort are a special type of law. Alt (1989: 114-116) classified them as 'apodictic' law, essentially like the 'thou shalt not' form of the Decalogue. However, this does not explain the 'curse' form of these sayings. It is better to suppose that the curses are closely related to fundamental laws of Israel, but are designed for a particular setting.

The best setting is actually given by the present context, namely the cultic assembly of Israel (which need not always be in a covenantal setting; McCarthy 1981: 198-199 and n.). Their function is to draw within the judicial sphere acts that are punishable – many or all of them by death – but which may easily go undetected. This explains the motif of secrecy that surfaces at vv. 15 and 24, and that may be implied in the other cases by their nature (Bellefontaine 1975). By uttering these formal curses, the cultic assembly meets its responsibility for upholding and carrying out the law, even though it is not able to do so in the case of undetected crime. At the same time, it acknowledges that all sin is against God and that he is the ultimate justicer. The aim of the curses, at this crucial point in the structure of the book, is to 'purge the evil' from Israel (to use terms typical of the deuteronomic law, e.g. 21:21b).

Secondly, to this formal explanation may be added theological and literary ones. Theologically, in the ceremony of curses, Israel accepts the implications for the community of accepting the covenant. In literary terms, while the *Sitz im Leben* of 27:15-26 is somewhat different from that of ch. 28, the two sections have been brought into a literary relationship with each other (esp. by v. 12). This may have had the effect that the set of blessings in 28:1–14 was judged to be sufficient to make the point. Taken over the two chapters (27 – 28), there is a great emphasis on curse (see on ch. 28, 'Form and structure'). The list of curses as presented consists of twelve, a 'dodecalogue', which may assimilate a 'decalogue' of curses by framing it with curses based on fundamental deuteronomic requirements (15, 26; see further on v. 26).

15. The prohibition of images is second only to the command to worship Yahweh alone in the Decalogue (Exod. 20:3–5; Deut. 5:8–10), and it heads the so-called 'ritual Decalogue' in Exod. 34:17. Making images is the chief symbol of turning away from Yahweh in Deut. 4:16, 23, 25. The phrase added here to the basic curse – 'an abomination to the LORD' – borrows deuteronomic language for reprobating anything unacceptable to Yahweh in worship. There is irony reminiscent of the prophets in 'a craftsman ... sets it up' (cf. Is. 44:9–20). The 'secrecy' clause (explained above) aims to prevent the cult of small idols in the home, which might be carried on covertly alongside public official worship.

16. The Fifth Commandment, to honour father and mother, is a cornerstone of Israelite law and society (Exod. 20:12, and see on Deut. 5:16). The curse is directed against failure to honour them, using a strong term for 'despising' or 'humiliating', which appears in only one other place in the laws, in the command not to humiliate the criminal who is flogged (Deut. 25:3). To 'curse' parents was a capital offence according to Exod. 21:17; Lev. 20:9. The verb in the present verse (*qālâ*) is similar to the one used in those places (*qālal*), and a minority of Hebrew texts read the latter. However, MT is in line with the deuteronomic tendency to internalize standards of behaviour, and also with the nature of these curses, namely to regulate what is done in secret.

17–19. These three curses have in common the fundamental imperative of respect and care for the life of the other. On the landmark, the only corresponding prohibitive law is in 19:14 (see 'Form and structure', and 'Comment' there). The occurrence of this curse shows again the central importance of the individual's right to have his share in the inheritance protected, as a matter of life and death. The curse that protects the blind (18) has an echo in Lev. 19:14 (Bellefontaine 1975). It is a special instance of the obligation of care for the vulnerable. The basic deuteronomic requirement of justice is stated in 16:18–20, as the heart of its ethics. The curse (19) puts it at its strongest, demanding it for those who have weak legal standing, according to the command in 24:17 (note also the grouping in Exod. 22:20–23; and cf. Exod. 23:9; Lev. 19:33–34).

20–23. The prohibited sexual affinities receive fuller treatment in Lev. 18:8, 9, 17 ('prohibitives') and Lev. 20:11, 14, 17 ('death laws'). The violation of those conventions is represented first by the case of a man sleeping with his father's wife, which is the primary case in Lev. 18. This need not mean his own mother (cf. Lev. 18:8), though that is expressly prohibited in Lev. 18:7. Such a union is a gross offence to the father. The need for respect for the father in this area is recalled in Gen. 9:20–27, for instance. And this respect would still be expected after the father's death. (The laws on sexual affinities probably aim at situations that arise because of the death of a first husband.)

Two further specific prohibitions in this area are made (22–23). The prohibition of sexual relations applies 'between people who are consanguineous to the first and second degree' (Wenham 1979a: 254). The aim of these laws and conventions is the preservation of the life of the family as the basis of all life in society, the nearest Decalogue command being the fifth (honouring father and mother). The execration of bestiality is also found elsewhere in the laws (cf. Lev. 18:23; Exod. 22:19[18]; Lev. 20:15). Deuteronomy prohibits all sexual intercourse with animals. The word 'all', or 'any', is added here, though it is not in the other laws, as if to make the point that there could be no exceptions. Other peoples allowed intercourse with certain animals, and even practised it in cultic contexts (Bellefontaine 1975).

24–26. Two curses relate directly to the basic law prohibiting murder (Exod. 20:13; Deut. 5:17). The first is against killing (lit. 'striking') another person. The basic prohibitive is in Exod. 21:12. Here as there, the verb 'strike' means in effect 'kill', as also in Deut. 19:4, which the phrase here closely resembles (cf. also 21:1). The occasion is the reverse of that one, however: there the killing was unintentional but known; here it is intentional and hidden. This instance is worthy of the sentence of the lawcourt, but must be consigned to the judgment of God.

The basic law against the use of bribery to pervert the course of justice is in Exod. 23:8. The case of taking a bribe to commit murder, as another case of secret killing, is obviously related to the previous curse. It could arise where the lawcourt cannot make a case against one suspected of murder. It may also be an attempt to beat the 'city of refuge' system in the case of a family's desire for revenge. Like that system, the curse predicates the innocence of the person, and is intended to prevent the shedding of innocent blood (cf. 19:10), which would itself bring guilt on the community.

26. As the opening curse was based on a fundamental deuteronomic principle, in rather expanded form (15), so the last summarizes the deuteronomic command to keep the *tôrâ* entirely, echoing vv. 2–3, 8, and thus uniting the parts of the chapter. Indeed, the curses are framed in this way by twin principles that might be said to sum up the teaching of the book: the worship of Yahweh alone, and faithfulness to his commands, the twin theme developed extensively in Deut. 4.

Explanation

Time and place are of the essence of ch. 27. The difficulties felt by commentators over the erecting of an altar at Shechem, in view of the deuteronomic altar law, misunderstands the nature of that law, which invites Israel constantly into renewed covenant faithfulness as they continue their 'journey' with Yahweh. The altar command in 27:5–7 is entirely 'deuteronomic'. Shechem is a natural place for a primary and historic covenant ceremony because of its important role in Israel's memory as a symbol of covenant faithfulness (see also on 11:26–32).

The purpose of the structure and placing of ch. 27 is to bring about a convergence between the covenant in Moab and that at Shechem (see Millar 1998: 92). This was already prepared for in 11:26–32, which prefaced the law code by anticipating the ceremony now described. At the end of the law code, the mutual statements of covenant ratification lead into the command to hold a ritual ceremony. The 'today' of 26:17–18 is resumed by the 'on the day that' in 27:2. The chronological relationship of the events is important. Moses tells the people while at Moab what they must do in Shechem (1, 9, 11). The structure of Deuteronomy splices the events in Moab and at Shechem into each other. The words of ratification of the Moab covenant in 26:16–19 did not have a corresponding ritual at that point. In the composition of the book, the ritual recorded now bears a relation to that ratification. Moses and the priests say in v. 9, 'This day you have become a people of the LORD your God', referring again to the 'today' of Moab, as in 26:16–19. The 'becoming a people' at Moab is cemented by the ceremony at Shechem.

In fact, the idea of 'becoming a people of Yahweh' is not strictly confined to what happens in either Moab or Shechem. The 'today' of Deuteronomy, as we have seen, is always present. The Moab covenant was itself a new realization of the covenant made at Horeb, in a merging of those two foci (see on 5:1–3). The connection between 27:1 and 5:23–27 is a part of Deuteronomy's securing of this convergence. The super-imposition of the event at Shechem upon the event in Moab is part of the book's theological affirmation that the covenant must always be entered afresh. A covenant-ratification ceremony is expected at this point in the book by virtue of its correspondence to treaty patterns. The placing of it at Shechem is part of the progression of standpoints that is built into the structure of Deuteronomy, especially Horeb–Moab–Shechem, which symbolizes the theology of covenantal re-realization. (The ceremony finishes at 27:26; see on ch. 28 for reasons why the perspective returns there to Moab.) To this spatial factor in the progression of Israel towards its life in covenant with Yahweh corresponds the motif of the writing of Moses' words, which points to the time when he himself will no longer be there as Israel's teacher.

The curse sequence in 27:15–26 expresses the solemnity of the under-taking that Israel makes on entering the covenant. It therefore directly reinforces the formal commitment given in 26:18, and corresponds to solemn covenantal undertakings such as Exod. 19:7; 24:3, 7. Casting the net more widely, there are echoes of the self-curse in imprecations such as

1 Kgs. 19:2, behind which probably lies a sacrificial ritual like the ones alluded to in Gen. 15:9–21; Jer. 34:18. The juxtaposition of imprecation and sacrificial ritual in those texts suggests a real correspondence in Deut. 27 between the sacrifices and the curses.

The format of the sequence is drawn from the sphere of the cultic assembly of Israel, and is based on the need to protect the people from the contamination of undetected and unpunished capital crimes. In this respect it is analogous to the ritual prescribed for the unknown homicide in 21:1–9, and can be regarded as having the same purpose, 'to purge yourselves of the guilt for innocent blood', even though that phrase does not occur at this point (but cf. again v. 25 with 19:10; and see 21:9).

These considerations about the setting and purpose of the curses begin to answer the question why Deut. 27 contains only curses and not blessings also. The curses are part of a ritual in which Israel takes upon itself the full implications of their promise to be Yahweh's people. It explains why a genre that has kinship with law, and bears on the behaviour of individuals within the community, can appear as part of a ritual concerning the whole people. The people is answerable under the covenant for its adherence in its entirety to the covenant. The absence of a blessings section arises from the fact that it is not the place of Israel to utter blessings upon itself. The stance of the two sets of tribes in relation to Mts Ebal and Gerizim is a silent witness to both blessing and curse, but the only voices heard are those of the Levites who utter the words of commitment to – and on behalf of – all the people.

Moreover, the relationship between the curses in 27:15–26 and the curses and blessings in ch. 28 can be explained by the structural relationship of both sections to 26:17–19, which forms a chiasmus:

> 26:17   Yahweh's undertaking
> 26:18–19   Israel's undertaking
> 27:15–26   Israel accepts consequences of its undertaking
> 28:1–68   Yahweh accepts consequences of his undertaking

In Israel's acceptance of its undertaking there is a symbolic affirmation of Yahweh's intention to bless (12), but the words bear especially on its promise 'to be a people holy to the LORD your God' (26:19). Conversely, in ch. 28 Yahweh accepts his own obligation to bless the people (28:1–14), corresponding to the first element in 26:17 ('to be your God'), but also spells out the sanctions that he will apply to secure Israel's obedience (26:17ab).

When the function of ch. 27 is seen in this light, it gives the context for the question whether the chapter embodies a pessimism about Israel's ability to keep the covenant (P. Barker 1998). In my view, it does not in itself imply pessimism on this matter, although in a broad context it fits suitably with passages that do (such as 31:16–17). Barker (1998: 294–300) rightly calls attention to the signs of grace and hope in the chapter; for example, in the significance of the sacrifices for atonement and sacrifice (6–7), and more especially in the location of the ritual at Shechem, where Abraham built his first altar to Yahweh in the land, immediately after receiving the promise that his descendants would inherit it. The memory of the promise to Abraham frames the book (1:6–8; 34:4; P. Barker 1998: 299). It also opens the account of the covenant ceremony held at Shechem under Joshua (Josh. 24:2–4). These point to the promise as the ultimate reality in deuteronomic theology, a theme that will also emerge from our reading of ch. 30.

DEUTERONOMY 28:1 – 29:1[28:69]

Translation

[1]If you truly obey the Lord your God and carefully keep all his commands with which I am charging you this day, the Lord your God will set you high above all the nations of the earth. [2]And all these blessings will come to you and meet you, if you obey the Lord your God. [3]You will be blessed in the city and you will be blessed in the field. [4]Blessed will be the offspring of your womb, and the produce of your land, and the young of your livestock, both cattle and sheep. [5]Blessed will be your basket and your kneading-trough. [6]You will be blessed as you come in and as you go out. [7]The Lord will give your enemies over to you when they attack you; they will be struck down before you; they will march against you by one road, but will flee from you by seven! [8]The Lord will command blessing on you in your barns and in all that you put your hand to; he will bless you in the land the Lord your God is giving you. [9]The Lord will establish you as a people holy to himself, as he promised you on oath, as long as you keep the commands of the Lord your God and live according to his ways. [10]And all the peoples of the earth will see that you are known by the name of the Lord, and they will fear you. [11]The Lord will do you good in abundance; in the offspring of your womb, in the offspring of your cattle and the produce of the earth, in the land the Lord promised on oath to your forefathers to give you. [12]The Lord will open to you his good treasury the heavens, and send rain on your land in its due time to bless all that you put your hand to; you will lend to many nations, but you will not borrow. [13]The Lord will make you the head, not the tail; you will always be in the ascendant, not in decline, as long as you obey the commands of the Lord your God, which today I am charging you to keep carefully. [14]Do not depart from any of the commands with which I am charging you this day, to follow and worship other gods.

[15]If you do not obey the Lord your God, and do not carefully keep all his commands and laws with which I am charging you this day, then all these curses come to you and meet you. [16]You will be cursed in the city and cursed in the field. [17]Cursed will be your basket and your kneading-trough. [18]Cursed will be the offspring of your womb, and the produce of your land and the young of your

livestock, both cattle and sheep. ¹⁹You will be cursed when you go out and cursed when you come in. ²⁰The LORD will send on you curse, confusion and threat in every undertaking that you put your hand to, until you are destroyed and quickly perish because of your evil deeds and because you have forsaken me. ²¹The LORD will send plague to adhere to you, until it obliterates you from the land you are going over to possess. ²²The LORD will afflict you with consumption, with fever and inflammation, with fiery heat and drought, and with blight and mildew; and these will dog you till you perish. ²³The skies above you will be bronze and the earth beneath you iron. ²⁴The LORD will turn the rain of your land into powder, and only dust will descend on you from the skies, till you are destroyed. ²⁵The LORD will hand you over to be struck down by your enemies; you will march against them by one road, but will flee from them by seven! You will be an object of horror to all the kingdoms on earth. ²⁶Your dead bodies will be food for all the birds of the sky and beasts of the land, and there will be no-one to scare them away. ²⁷The LORD will afflict you with boils of Egypt, swellings and skin diseases and itches of which you cannot be healed. ²⁸The LORD will afflict you with madness, blindness and bewilderment. ²⁹You will feel your way at midday just as one who is blind feels his way in the darkness, and you will not succeed in finding it; you will be oppressed and robbed day after day, and there will be no-one to save you.

³⁰You will become engaged to a woman and another will sleep with her; you will build a house but not live in it; you will plant a vineyard, but not harvest its fruit. ³¹Your ox will be slaughtered before your eyes, but you will eat none of it; your donkey will be stolen and you will not get it back; your flock will be given to your enemies, and there will be no-one to save you.

³²Your sons and daughters will be handed over to another nation, and you will see it with your own eyes; indeed, you will wear your eyes out looking for them all day long; but you will be powerless to do anything. ³³The produce of your land, all the fruit of your labour, will be consumed by a people you have not known, and you will know nothing but oppression and abuse all your days. ³⁴And you will be driven mad by the sights that you see. ³⁵The LORD will afflict you with painful swellings on your knees and thighs, of which you cannot be healed; and they will cover you from the soles your feet to the top of your head. ³⁶The LORD will send you, you and your king whom you will set over you, to a nation you have not known, neither you nor your forefathers, and there you will worship other gods, gods of wood and stone. ³⁷And you will be a horror, a byword and an object of derision to all the nations to whom the LORD drives you.

³⁸You will sow large quantities of seed in your field, but obtain only a small yield, for the locust will consume it. ³⁹You will plant and labour at vineyards, but drink no wine or gather the grapes, for the worm will devour the fruit. ⁴⁰You will have olive trees throughout your land, but you will not anoint yourselves with oil, for the olives will drop off. ⁴¹You will have sons and daughters, but they will not remain yours, for they will be taken into exile. ⁴²All your trees and crops will be taken over by the cricket. ⁴³The stranger who lives among you will rise above you higher and higher, while you descend lower and lower. ⁴⁴He will be your creditor, but you will not be his; he will be the head, and you will be the tail.

⁴⁵All these curses will come upon you; they will pursue and overtake you until you are destroyed, because you did not obey the LORD your God, by keeping the commands and laws he laid upon you. ⁴⁶They will be a sign and a wonder among you and your descendants for ever. ⁴⁷Because you did not worship the LORD your God joyfully and wholeheartedly for the abundance of everything, ⁴⁸you will serve your enemies whom the LORD will send against you, hungry, thirsty, naked and lacking everything. He will put an iron yoke on your neck until he has destroyed you.

⁴⁹The LORD will raise up a nation against you from the end of the earth, like a swooping eagle, a nation whose language you do not understand, ⁵⁰a nation whose face is like flint, and which has neither respect for the old nor pity for the young. ⁵¹They will consume the young of your cattle, and your produce, until you are destroyed, for they will leave you no grain, or wine or oil, or your calves or your lambs, until they have ruined you. ⁵²They will lay siege to you in all your cities, until your high fortified walls, in which you have put your trust, come down throughout your land; they will shut you up within your cities in all the land the LORD your God has given you. ⁵³Then you will eat your own offspring, the flesh of your sons and daughters, whom the LORD your God has given you, because of the distress and hardship to which your enemies have reduced you. ⁵⁴The most delicate and coddled man among you will begrudge his brother, or his wife, whom he embraces, or his remaining children, ⁵⁵a share of the flesh of his children that he is eating, because he is left with nothing else, in the distress and hardship to which your enemy has reduced you in all your cities. ⁵⁶The most delicate and coddled woman among you, who would hardly dare set her foot on the ground because she is so coddled and delicate, will begrudge her husband, whom she embraces, or her son or daughter, ⁵⁷the afterbirth that comes out between her legs, and the children she bears, for in her lack of everything she will eat them secretly, because of the great distress and hardship to which your enemies have reduced you in your cities.

⁵⁸If you are not careful to keep all the commands of this law, written in this book, and to revere this glorious and terrible name, 'the LORD your God', ⁵⁹the LORD will afflict you and your descendants beyond measure with terrible and lasting plagues, and with severe and chronic illnesses; ⁶⁰he will subject you again to every disease of Egypt, which you dreaded, and they will cling to you. ⁶¹Even all kinds of diseases that are not written in the book of this law the LORD will bring upon you, till you are destroyed. ⁶²So you will be reduced to a tiny number, though you were as many as the stars in the sky, because you did not obey the LORD your God. ⁶³Just as the LORD delighted over you, to do good to you and to make you great, so he will delight over you by bringing you to ruin, by destroying you, and you will be expelled from the land you are going over to possess.

⁶⁴The LORD will scatter you among all nations, from one end of the earth to the other, and there you will worship other gods whom neither you nor your forefathers have known, gods of wood and stone. ⁶⁵Among those nations you will never have ease, or a resting-place for your foot; there the LORD will give you a trembling heart, failing eyes and despair. ⁶⁶Your life will constantly hang in the balance; you will go in fear both day and night; you will know no security. ⁶⁷In

the morning you will say, 'I wish it were evening'; and in the evening you will say, 'I wish it were morning', because of the terror in your heart, and because of the things you see. ⁶⁸And the LORD will take you back to Egypt in ships, by a way I said to you you should not again see; and you will sell yourselves there to your enemies as male and female slaves; but there will be no-one to buy you. ²⁹:¹[²⁸:⁶⁹]These are the words of the covenant that the LORD commanded Moses to make with the Israelites in the land of Moab, besides the covenant he made with them at Horeb.

Notes on the text

4. 'the young of your livestock' (*ûpᵉrî bᵉhemtekâ*): the phrase is absent from LXX and from the parallel v. 18, and may be due in this verse to homoioteleuton (with *'admātᵉkâ*, as BHS).

20. 'you have forsaken me': unexpectedly in the first person singular. LXX adjusts to 3 m. sg., probably harmonizing to the context. The first person has intruded here under the force of the origin of the speech in Yahweh's own words. Verse 68 is probably a similar case.

22. 'drought', reading *ḥōreb*, rather than MT *ḥereb*, 'sword'.

24. 'and only dust': there is no word for 'only', but it reproduces the emphasis achieved by the Hebrew word-order, which puts 'dust' in the first position; the force is 'only dust', i.e. not the expected rain. It is better to read the line this way (with NRSV) than to take 'and dust' together with 'powder', as it produces a more effective contrast with v. 12.

25. *za'ᵃwâ*: the precise form is found only here and at Ezek. 23:46, while the form *zawᵃ'â* occurs in phrases similar to the one used here at Jer. 15:4; 24:9; 29:18; 34:17; in the latter cases the Q is as in the present verse.

29. 'not succeed in finding it': this assumes that *dᵉrākêkâ*, 'your ways', refers to the road being sought by the blind man. This interpretation fits better if we read the sg. *darkᵉkâ* (with SamP and some MT MSS). The alternative is to find in this clause the more general 'not succeed in any of your ways', since *derek*, 'way', is often used metaphorically with an ethical sense.

48. Note *ḥireq*, anomalously, in first syllable of *hišmîdô*, 'destroyed'; see note on 3:3.

61. 'book of this law' (*sēper hattôrâ hazzō't*): contrast 'this book of the law' (*sēper hattôrâ hazzeh*) in vv. 29:20; 30:10; 31:26; but see also 31:24. The ancient versions show a tendency to conform the present passage to the others. The book referred to is the same.

Form and structure

It is best to suppose that the perspective reverts in 28:1 to Moab and the speech of Moses to Israel, rather than that the blessings and curses in this chapter continue the ceremony at Shechem. This is in spite of the fact that there is no explicit return to the speech of Moses in v. 1, the opening words appear to continue smoothly from the end of ch. 27, and 28:1–14 might be taken to supply the blessings expected since 27:12 (but on this last point see on ch. 27, 'Explanation').

In favour of Moab as the place where these blessings and curses are uttered is the change back to the 'I' style (1; that is, from the speech of the Levites, 27:14), and indeed the resumption in the body of the speech of the focus on 'today' (13–15; cf. N. Lohfink 1994: 145). Further support for this comes from the chiastic relationship between 11:26–32 and chs. 12 – 26, 27 and 28, in which 11:26–27 corresponds formally with ch. 28, and refers to a blessing and curse that Moses sets before the people 'today' in Moab (N. Lohfink 1963: 232–234; but qualified in 1994: 151).

The present form of the text might be supposed to suggest a certain convergence of the perspectives of Moab and Shechem. There may be significance in the distinction between setting the blessing and curse 'before' the people in Moab (11:26) and laying it 'upon' them (11:29), in the sense that they are deemed to become effective only after occupation of the land (Lohfink 1994: 151). In my view (slightly differently, and as explained in ch. 27, 'Explanation'), the blessings and curses are pronounced in Moab, but the fusion of perspectives between Moab and Shechem means that the proposed covenant renewal in Shechem re-realizes the Moab covenant, so much so that the blessings and curses are in a sense transferred to that ceremony. They are, however, in the first instance part of the real covenant concluded in Moab.

The end of the section on blessings and curses is part of the same discussion. Does the opening phrase of 29:1[28:69] ('These are the words of the covenant') conclude the covenant blessings and curses in ch. 28, or does it introduce the new covenantal text in ch. 29? The Masoretic punctuation (reflected in the verse numbering) favours the former view, while the chapter division in EVV leans to the latter (as do N. Lohfink [1962: 32–35], who compares superscriptions in 1:1; 4:44; 28:69; 33:1, and Rofé [1985a: 310]; cf. Millar 1994: 78–79).

The key to the verse lies in comparing 5:2–3, to which it refers. The Horeb covenant was described there, unchronologically, as having been made with the present (Moab) generation. The point of that blurring of temporal horizons was to say that Moses' teaching of the commandments was a new embodiment of the Horeb covenant. That, indeed, is the essence of the Moab covenant. Deut. 29:1[28:69], therefore, expresses that identification. The Moab covenant does not replace the Horeb covenant; it exists alongside (or 'besides') it. This is the only text that expressly describes the relationship between the two covenants, and it shows that the later does not invalidate the earlier. Rather, the two co-exist. This is part of the tendency in Deuteronomy to telescope a succession of covenants into an ever renewed challenge to faithfulness.

Deut. 29:1[28:69] refers back to what has preceded it, as does the same phrase in 29:9[8] (so S. R. Driver 1895: 319). However, ch. 29 also takes its cue from the verse, and therefore Lenchak is right to take it as a transition between the second and third discourses of Moses (1993: 172; see his n. 4 there for further literature on 28:69 as 'subscript' and 'superscript' respectively; and 'Comment' below).

The other major structural issue in ch. 28 is the form of the blessings and curses. It has been widely recognized that, in principle, the existence of blessings as well as curses at the conclusion of a treaty corresponds somewhat to the second-millennium Hittite pattern, in that this has blessings and curses, the curses tending to predominate over the blessings. This differs from the first-millennium Assyrian pattern, which typically has no blessings. The classic exemplar is the Vassal Treaties of Esarhaddon (VTE; see *ANET* 534–541), which contain only the curses that will fall upon those who fail to promote the interests of Esarhaddon's successor Ashurbanipal. The Hittite pattern, in contrast, has both blessings and curses, the curses being slightly longer, and the blessings somewhat formulaic. The curses come first, however, and are shorter than either Deuteronomy's or the Assyrian examples (see e.g. the treaty between Suppiluliumas and Kurtiwaza, *ANET* 205–206; cf. McCarthy 1981: 66–67). Deuteronomy, therefore, is not quite like either of the two known patterns, though its blessings place it, on balance, closer to the Hittite type in form.

Resemblances between parts of the curses in ch. 28 and parts of VTE began to be noticed from the time of the first publication of the latter (Wiseman 1958: 88). These resemblances led a number of scholars to argue that the deuteronomic curses were directly dependent on Assyrian documents (Weinfeld 1972: 121–122). Weinfeld finds the parallel in Deut. 28:26–35 and VTE 419–430. He notices especially the sequence of skin disease followed by blindness in the two texts (Deut. 28:27, 28–29; cf. VTE 419–424), and thinks that, while this sequence can be explained in VTE, by the ranking of the gods Sin and Shamash (who administer these respective punishments), there is no independent explanation of this order in Deuteronomy (Weinfeld 1972: 119–121).

A recent formulation of the theory (Steymans 1995b) goes further than Weinfeld and argues that Deut. 28:20–44 is parallel to VTE 472–493 (= section 56), and that it is an actual translation by scribes at the court of King Josiah of a copy of VTE that was held in Jerusalem. Steymans tries to explain divergences from it as reorderings and expansions, of kinds that were permissible in treaty translation (1995b: 120).

There is space to offer only a brief evaluation of a complicated argument. There are some notable parallels in content and sequence between the texts (e.g. 28:38–40; cf. VTE 490–492: futility curses on food, drink, oil). But the argument for specific dependence is hard to make convincing. Steymans' argument stands or falls by demonstrating specific dependence, in contrast to the alternative, namely that both Deut. 28 and VTE stand within a common tradition. He rules out the latter by showing that Deuteronomy has the same order as VTE at certain points (as in the example just given: food, drink, oil), and that the same elements occur in a different order in other treaties. However, this merely shows that there are no fixed orders. If the parallels between Deuteronomy and VTE were otherwise closer, his argument would carry more weight. But it fails because too often there are important differences between the texts, such as elements in VTE that have no parallel in Deut. 28, or elements in Deut. 28 that lack a parallel in VTE (notably deportation of the people); or because a specific order of elements represents too small a sample to permit significant comparison (e.g. Deut. 28:30: wife, house, vineyard, where he contrasts Deut. 20:5–7; Amos 5:11; Zeph. 1:13; 1995b: 132–133). Furthermore, Deut. 28 can mix items from different parts of VTE (28:26; cf. VTE 425–427, 484; and 28:28–29; cf. VTE 422, 485–486). Finally, Steymans concludes too readily that features of VTE (such as the iron-earth and bronze-sky curse) are its inventions, when it is likelier that they are part of a broad tradition, most of which is still unknown to us (Lambert 1997–8: 398; cf. Dion 1997: 274). In conclusion, at present the theory of the dependence of Deut. 28 on VTE must be considered not proven.

The chapter contains a number of literary forms and sudden changes without logical development. The curses variously affect either individuals or the whole people; the following outline illustrates this (though the domestic and national horizons are sometimes mixed and overlap):

1–2	General introduction to the blessings (national focus)
3–6	A series of short formulaic sayings each beginning with 'blessed' (*bārûḵ*) as a kind of pronouncement (similar to the Beatitudes, Matt. 5:3–11) (domestic focus)
7–14	More discursive blessing sayings (national)
15	Introduction to the curses
16–19	Formulaic curses in a mirror image of vv. 3–6 (domestic)
20–24	Plague, drought (domestic, national)
25–29	Defeat, disease, madness (national, domestic)
30–33a	Futility curses (domestic, national)
33b–37	Enslavement and exile (national)
38–44	Futility curses (domestic), aliens prevail (within the population, domestic)
45–48	General curse (national)
49–57	Reduction and enslavement by an enemy from afar (national)
58–63	A return to 'Egypt', the illnesses of Egypt (national)
64–68	A scattering among the nations, Egypt (national)
29:1[28:69]	'The words of the covenant'

There is a mixing of curses that affect home and family and those that affect the people as a whole, with a tendency to move towards the national focus. The frequency of the phrase 'the LORD will...' is in striking contrast to the curses of the various gods in the Assyrian treaties. The diverse styles and baroque arrangement of the curses do not in themselves entail disunity of composition. Other treaties show the same variety of form (cf. Weinfeld 1972: 128–129, on VTE). One does not need to assume a long process of growth, therefore, but only that the compilers (of VTE as of Deut. 28) have used a variety of forms. The form is consistent with the use of the blessings and curses in an actual covenant ceremony (or ceremonies), rather than just a literary imitation.

Comment

28:1–14

1–2. The condition for obtaining the blessings is stated generally, namely both hearing and doing all the commands that Moses has given at Moab (a reference to chs. 12 – 26). The blessing is initially stated as a lifting of the nation above other nations, recalling 26:19. The same thought is found in 15:5–6, where it is also bound into a command to keep the commandments.

3–6. These 'beatitudes', with their evocation of domestic life, cover the fundamental conditions of life. Verses 3 and 6 correspond to each other, polar opposites conveying comprehensiveness in typical Hebrew style (cf. Ps. 121:8). The intervening blessings relate to fruitfulness of people, ground and animals, as in 7:13, another basic statement in a context that also connected Yahweh's choice of the people and their blessing.

7–10. The focus shifts to the fortunes of Israel as a people. Yahweh's deliverance of them from enemies (7, with its wonderful image of attackers repulsed in disarray) is closely followed by his gift of peace and blessed success in their own land (8; cf. 15:10; 23:20[21] for the expression used). The people's holiness, a correlate of their chosenness (9; cf. 7:6), is not rigidly fixed to genealogy, but conditioned by their keeping faithful to the covenant. The word 'if', here and in v. 13, may be translated 'as long as', or even 'because'; the point is to establish a correlation between blessing and covenant faithfulness, without a strict causal sequence. The conditionals here stand, in any case, under the basic one in v. 1. Israel's blessing and sanctification by Yahweh have the consequence that the nations will know that Israel is 'called [or known] by the name of Yahweh' (10). The phrase, occurring only here in Deuteronomy, identifies the people by the name of their God. (For the concept, cf. Is. 4:1, where destitute women implore a man to allow them to take his name; cf. also Jer. 14:9; 15:16; 25:29; Amos 9:12.) The thought belongs to the deuteronomic theme of

Israel as a witness to the nations by reason of Yahweh's blessing and their keeping his commands (cf. 4:6–8; 26:19).

11–13. There follow further pictures of abundance and of economic ascendancy (cf. 15:6; Mal. 3:10). The context suggests that the ascendancy is that of Israel over other nations (though the echo of v. 13 in vv. 43–44 is addressed to the individual Israelite in relation to the resident alien).

28:15–57

15–19. Following an introductory counterpart to vv. 1–2 in v. 15, the first block of curses (16–19) precisely reverses the blessings in vv. 3–6. There is no apparent distinction of meaning between the different words for 'curse' used in v. 15 (*qᵉlālôt*) and in vv. 16–19 (*'ārûr*; R. P. Gordon 1997b: 492). The formula *'ārûr 'attâ* ('Cursed art thou') occurs only here and in Gen. 3:14; 4:11; Josh. 9:23, though it is in principle formally the same as the pronouncements in Deut. 27:15–26.

20–24. Whereas blessing was held out for everything 'that you put your hand to' (8), now there is the prospect of frustration in every undertaking. The lexicon of words for 'disaster' in v. 20 is headed by one that simply means 'curse' (*mᵉ'ērâ*, related to *'ārûr*), and implies the turning of every good thing to bad (cf. Mal. 2:2). 'Confusion' is what happens to people defeated in war (cf. Deut. 7:23, there of Israel's enemies; 1 Sam. 5:9, 11; 14:20; Is. 22:5), but it can also refer to chaos arising from oppressions within (Amos 3:9). The word for 'threat' occurs only here, but related forms have the sense of threatening confrontation (Mal. 3:11; Is. 30:17). The first-person speech of Yahweh (20) intrudes unexpectedly, but emphasizes that he is the real speaker and agent (see 'Notes on the text').

The picture moves on through plague, other illnesses, drought and disease of crops (21–22), finishing with one of rainless skies and hardened, unproductive earth (24, see 'Notes on the text', and contrast v. 12). The accumulation of horrors rehearses the full gamut of possible disasters, and the consequence each time is the end of the people's life in the land.

25–26. The scene changes from disasters in the domestic sphere to disasters at the hands of enemies. Verse 25a precisely reverses v. 7, while v. 25b echoes prophetic passages that picture the public horror of the people's devastation (see 'Notes on the text'). Israel's terrible fate will make other nations afraid. The exposure of bodies (26) was a humiliation that might be added to the horror of death itself, either in the death penalty (21:22:23) or in defeat in battle (1 Sam. 31:8–10; cf. VTE 425–427, the curse of Ninurta). It is not necessarily a strict sequel to v. 25.

27–29. The sequence of skin disease and blindness is matched in VTE 419–424, the curses of the gods Sin and Shamash (see 'Form and structure'). Disease here is linked to Egypt and the memory of the enslaved past (cf. 7:15; contrast VTE, where the point is exclusion from worship).

The image of blindness is one of helplessness and exposure to exploitation, the reverse of what the laws have aimed to procure for the weak in their life in the land (cf. 27:18; Lev. 19:14). It is, once again, not necessarily a result of the ravages of war (25), but refers to a continuous condition (29c). The ongoing effect of these curses does not contradict v. 21, which promises destruction from the land, since there is no such logical relationship among the curses. The phrase 'there will be no-one to save you' indicates a chaotic situation. The laws had made Yahweh the defender of the weak in the event of oppression by the powerful (15:9b; 24:15b). But now there will be salvation neither by human hand (cf. 22:27) nor by divine (cf. Is. 43:3; Ps. 7:10[11]).

30–33a. These are what are known as 'futility curses', that is, where the proper enjoyment of something is frustrated. Verses 30–31 echo 20:5–7, a permission designed to prevent this kind of non-fulfilment. The order here is slightly different (the wife coming first here, while last there). The images are drawn from domestic life, once again in a chaotic situation in which there is no help (cf. v. 29c; in Deuteronomy the phrase occurs only in these two places and 22:27). With v. 31 cf. 22:1–3. Verses 32–33 change the perspective to the national horizon, but the logic is the same; children should bring benefits to their parents, not to others who capture them, and people should be able to enjoy their own produce (cf. Judg. 6:3–6). Verse 33 extends the enemy oppression into the indefinite future (cf. 29), in contrast to the picture of indefinite peace and security that the covenant aimed to bring (cf. 4:40; 5:33).

33b–35. The sequence in vv. 33b–35 (oppression, 33b; madness, 34; skin disease, 35) inverts that found in vv. 27–29 (Braulik 1992a: 206). There is a shift in focus, however; the oppression is now at the hands of a foreign enemy (33), and the madness (34) is brought on by the horrors of war. The skin disease seems to be purely to complete the balance.

36–37. The theme of oppression by foreigners now extends to captivity in a foreign land (36). The phrase 'you and your king' takes for granted that the thing permitted in 17:14–20 will come about. The allusion to a king in Israel is the second of only two such allusions in Deuteronomy. The tone is deprecatory, and recalls Samuel's scathing opposition to the institution in 1 Sam. 12:25. Their fate in exile, that they will worship other gods, of wood and stone, is presented as a punishment; they will have exchanged the living God for gods that cannot hear them when they call. No determinism is implied (i.e. that gods are inexorably associated with turf; Yahweh is God in heaven and earth, 4:32–38). And the horror of other nations at their suffering contrasts with their intended position as exalted over all the peoples (26:19; 28:1). Verse 37 echoes v. 25, and is more intense; the people's suffering actually becomes proverbial. The words of Huldah (2 Kgs. 22:19) could refer to this verse (because of the term 'horror'; the word is also frequent in Jeremiah, e.g. 2:15; 18:16).

38–44. A further set of futility curses follows, back in a domestic setting

(38–42). There is irony in the contrast between the great labour expended and amount possessed and the poor return, due to factors beyond the person's control (38–39). The humiliation at the hands of the stranger reverses vv. 12–13, though confining the matter to the domestic scene, a reduction in itself.

45–48. This passage forms a first conclusion to the curse section, as is shown by the repetition in v. 45 of the opening words in v. 15. The characterization of the curses as 'a sign and a wonder' (46) is heavily ironic because this expression is used elsewhere in connection with the salvation of Israel (4:34; 7:19; 26:8). Verses 47–48 contain neat contrasts: as they did not serve Yahweh, they will serve their enemies – though the one is freedom, the other slavery; instead of an abundance of everything, they will lack everything. The iron yoke on the neck symbolizes subjugation by Babylon in Jer. 28:14 (cf. vv. 10–13; 27:2–7); the iron cannot be broken in a symbolic repudiation of the sign. The prospect of complete destruction begins to be a refrain: 'until he has destroyed you' (cf. v. 51).

49–52. In spite of the apparent closure in vv. 45–47, there is now a resumption, a kind of sequence that is well known in the treaty curses (McCarthy 1981: 181). From this point to the end of the chapter there is a focus on the ravages of an enemy, resulting in exile. The extended image in vv. 49–57 consists of a negation of the possession of the land, the central tenet of the covenantal promise. Just as Israel stands on the verge of dispossessing inhabitants of Canaan, so another nation will dispossess them. The all-devouring alien nation recalls vv. 32–33, the unknown language somehow intensifying the sense of their cruelty (cf. Jer. 5:15–17). Their devastations undo the essentials of the blessing (51; cf. 7:13; 28:4, 11). And their reduction of high-walled cities that were too much trusted finds a startling echo in the people's first fear to attack such cities at their own approach to the land (52; cf. 1:28).

53–57. The horrors of the siege echo other OT passages that evoke the sudden plunge from prosperity to desperation (e.g. Is. 3:18–4:1; Lam. 2:20). Verse 54 has a hint of remnant language, the verb *yātar* contrasting ironically with v. 11, and echoing Isaiah's pictures of devastation (Is. 1:9; 30:17). There is a black humour in the absurd refinement juxtaposed with the gross images. The crass acts of selfishness in the most intimate relationships convey the brutalizing of people in siege conditions. The images are commonplaces of treaty curses, and need not reflect either the Assyrian depredations or the Babylonian exile in particular (McCarthy 1981: 180; Weinfeld 1972: 127, citing VTE 448–450 [*ANET* 538], and the Treaty of Ashurnirari V.iv.8–11 [*ANET* 533]).

28:58–63

58–61. The references to the 'book' and 'book of this law' in vv. 58, 61 are the first of a number in chs. 28 – 31 (29:19–20, 26; 30:10; 31:26; cf. 31:24), though the motif of the writing of them was signalled at 27:1–8 (see 'Comment' there). As the conclusion of Moses' covenantal address – and of his life – draws near, therefore, the concept of his words at Moab as a written covenantal document comes to the fore. (While the *tôrâ* as such is mentioned a number of times [e.g. 4:8, 44; 17:11; 27:26], there was only one previous allusion to the writing of the laws in a book: in 17:18, where the king is to make a copy of 'this law' for himself. 'The words of the law' are written not only in the book that will be kept with the ark of the covenant [31:9, 24–26], but also on the stones on Mt Ebal [27:2].)

The double reference to the 'book' signals an imminent conclusion to the curses. There is a similar effect in the unusual way of referring to Yahweh's name (58), which looks like a kind of signature. There follow rather generalized curses once more, especially illnesses of Egypt (cf. v. 27), and a clause preventing loopholes (61)!

62–63. The threat of obliteration is nevertheless followed by one that strictly contradicts it, of greatly reduced numbers (62). This shows again the non-logical nature of the accumulation of the curses, though this is, in itself, also severe, and an inversion of the deuteronomic promise of great numbers (62; cf. 1:10–11). Verse 63 is a biting rhetorical twist: Yahweh's joy in blessing turns into joy in bringing destruction. (The phrase in its positive side is echoed in 30:9; Jer. 32:41, both of which look beyond judgment to renewed blessing.)

28:64 – 29:1[28:69]

64. The final paragraph pictures exile. It is a 'scattering among the nations' (64a), a motif found also in 4:27, and adopted in a number of prophetic texts (e.g. Jer. 9:16[15]; 18:17; Ezek. 12:15). The continuation (64b) is different from the prophetic texts; contrast Jer. 9:16[15], where the phrase 'whom neither they nor their forefathers have known' applies not to other gods, as in our text, but to the nations themselves. The similar texts in Ezekiel (11:16; 12:15–16) see the exile as a time of amends. Here, the worshipping of gods of wood and stone is part of the punishment (as in v. 36), and the phrase carries an ironic echo of the idolatry that constituted the sin (cf. 11:28; 13:2; 29:26[25]; 32:17).

65–68. The 'rest' from enemies that came with possession of land (12:9–10) now becomes restlessness in a foreign place (65), and great anguish. There are full circles here. 'Terror' was what the nations in the promised land would feel at the approach of Israel (2:25; 11:25); now it falls in turn on them (67). And the very last of the curses (68) threatens a return to Egypt and the enslavement from which they have just come, as they stand at Moab, facing the promised land.

29:1[28:69]. The phrase 'the words of the covenant' is found only here and in 29:9[8]. The covenant in Moab consists in the renewal of the covenant at Horeb mediated by Moses' preaching of the laws in Deuteronomy. The relationship of the Moab covenant to the Horeb covenant is not one of clean distinction, but rather a new realization. Moses' preaching is, on the one hand, the teaching of the terms of Horeb (5:27; 6:1), but on the other it constitutes the covenant entered into 'today' in Moab (cf. 26:16–19). (On the fusion of the horizons of the covenants see further 'Form and structure'.)

Explanation

Blessing and curse are the rubrics under which all OT history is written: the creation of the first humans is soon followed by sin and a curse (Gen. 3:14–19), but then again by the blessing of Abraham (Gen. 12:2; cf. R. P. Gordon 1997b: 492). The assumption behind this portrayal of reality is the sovereignty of Yahweh in all affairs. The present passage repeatedly insists that Yahweh is the agent ('The LORD [Yahweh] will...'). The singularity of Yahweh contrasts, first, with the polytheism of the treaties. But it also asserts the real effect of the divine decision in human life. Blessing either follows or does not follow, according to his will, not according to that of the people; they may 'put their hand' to all their affairs with full rigour, but the outcome depends on Yahweh (8, 20).

The comprehensiveness of the blessings and especially of the curses aims to show that all of life's possibilities lie within the purview of Yahweh. It is, in a sense, the corollary of his sole sway: 'the LORD our God, the LORD is one' (6:4). The list is not meant to say that all these curses must inevitably come about. They cannot be logically aggregated, and it is mistaken to attempt to assign them variously to different periods. Rather, there is an element of theodicy in them. Where do disasters come from? Some say they come from various gods, displeased for inscrutable reasons. Some will point to blind fate, or the amoral forces of nature. The OT itself knows perplexity about innocent suffering (Ps. 73; Job 24). But all is contained here within a confession of faith, that the universe is ultimately moral.

The blessings and curses are throughout 'deuteronomic'. This does not mean that they do not share themes and even phraseology with the treaty tradition; they clearly do. It means, rather, that there is a unity of concept behind the body of Deuteronomy and the blessings and curses. The chaos depicted in the curses contradicts the kind of conditions that the covenant promised to establish, a number of the curses directly corresponding to certain provisions of the laws (e.g. v. 31; cf. 22:1–3). Motifs of illness, plague, famine, social breakdown, defeat, loss of land, subjection to other nations and their gods, are the obverse of the covenantal promises. Long life in the land, lasting for generations, gives way to imminent death, abducted children and even forced infanticide. It is a promised land and promised freedom from enemies that are now removed by Yahweh's deliberate decision, and turned back to the old Egyptian enslavement (63, 68). Pervading all is the insistence that Yahweh is powerful to bring about both the blessing and the curse (this covenant, unlike the treaties, is not a means of obliging other agencies to help).

The blessings and curses have a rhetorical purpose (apart from their philosophical purpose mentioned a moment ago). While a treaty might be imposed on a lesser state with Machiavellian intentions (sometimes as a device to obtain an excuse for annexation; Parpola 1987: 161), Yahweh's covenant with Israel hoped for the relationship to be established. This is clear not only from texts such as 4:40, but also from the thoroughgoing exhortation in general, and the elaborate law code, which makes actual provision for life in the land. This covenant is no mere pretext.

By the same token, the curses need not be seen as self-validating or irrevocable (in spite of texts such as Num. 22:6; Prov. 26:2): 'The effectiveness of a curse depends on the status of the speaker and the receptivity of the cursed' (R. P. Gordon 1997a: 525). Curses operate, therefore, rather like prophetic oracles of judgment, which intend, not to declare judgment inevitable and fixed, but to turn people from their sins.

In the OT the uncompromising form of the curse is finally juxtaposed with texts of forgiveness. The nature of Yahweh, and of his promises to Israel, is such that the apparent finality of the long maledictory tirade simply prompts the question: can the falling of the curse really be irreversible? The relationship between blessing and obedience has been conditioned all along in Deuteronomy by the recognition that the people were unfaithful before even receiving the gift (chs. 9 – 10). Therefore grace prevails in the structure of the book, and it is no surprise that at this crucial point the freely adapted form of the treaty should be broken, and that the blessing and the curse do not mark the end of the story. Not only here, but elsewhere in the OT, there is renewed blessing beyond the curse (cf. v. 63 with Deut. 30:9; Jer. 32:41; cf. v. 64 with Deut. 30:3; Jer. 30:11).

DEUTERONOMY 29:2–29[1–28]

Translation

²[1]Moses addressed all Israel:

You have seen everything the Lord did before your eyes in Egypt to Pharaoh, all his servants and his whole land: ³[2]the great trials you saw, those mighty signs and wonders. ⁴[3]Yet the Lord has not given you hearts to understand, or eyes to see or ears to hear, until this day. ⁵[4]I led you for forty years in the wilderness; the clothes on your backs did not wear out, or the sandals on your feet. ⁶[5]You ate no bread, and drank neither wine nor strong drink, so that you might know that I am the LORD your God. [7][6]So you came to this place. When Sihon, king of Heshbon, and Og, king of Bashan, marched against us to battle, we defeated them. [8][7]We took their land and gave it as an inheritance to the Reubenites, the Gadites and the half-tribe of the Manassites. [9][8]So observe and obey the words of this covenant, and you will be successful in all you undertake.

[10][9]You stand here today, all of you, before the LORD your God: tribal chiefs, elders, officers, every man in Israel, [11][10]your children, your wives, your strangers in the midst of your camp – from woodcutter to water-carrier – [12][11]so that you may enter solemnly into the covenant of the LORD your God, and its curse, which the LORD your God is making with you this day, [13][12]and so that he may establish you today as a people for himself, and he will be your God, as he promised you, and as he swore to your forefathers, Abraham, Isaac and Jacob. [14][13]And it is not with you alone that I am making this covenant and curse, [15][14]but with those who stand here with us today before the LORD our God and with those who are not here with us today.

[16][15]You know how we lived in Egypt, and how we passed through the territory of the nations where you travelled, [17][16]and you saw their detestable idols and false gods of wood and stone, silver and gold that they have among them; [18][17]let there be neither man nor woman, clan nor tribe, whose heart turns away from the LORD our God today, and who turns to worship the gods of those nations, for then there would be a root from which poison and wormwood would grow. [19][18]Such a person, on hearing the words of this curse, may congratulate himself in his heart: 'I shall be all right, if I act resolutely so that plenty of water may put an end to drought.' [20][19]The LORD would refuse to forgive that person, but rather the LORD's anger and jealousy would rage against him, and all the curses written in this book would stalk him, and the LORD would blot out his name from under heaven. [21][20]The LORD would single him out from all the tribes of Israel to suffer disaster, in accordance with all the curses written in this book of the law.

[22][21]The next generation, your children who come after you, and foreigners who come from distant lands, will see the afflictions of this land, and the diseases the LORD has brought upon it – [23][22]the whole land burned up by sulphur and salt, nothing sown, nothing growing, no vegetation to be seen, a desolation like Sodom and Gomorrah, Admah and Zeboiim, which the LORD overthrew in his raging anger. [24][23]All the nations will say, 'Why did the LORD do this to this land? What was the reason for such furious anger?' [25][24]And they will be told: 'Because the people forsook the covenant of the LORD, the God of their forefathers, which he made with them when he brought them out of Egypt, [26][25]and they went to serve and worship other gods which they had not known and which the LORD had not allotted to them. [27][26]So the LORD's anger raged against that land, and he brought on it every curse written in this book. [28][27]The LORD uprooted them from their land in his anger, rage and great fury, and hurled them into another land, where they are to this day.' [29][28]The hidden things belong to the LORD our God, but the things that have been revealed are for us and for our descendants for ever, that is, to do all that is required by this law.

Notes on the text

5[4]. *śalmōṯêḵem*: SamP, *śimlōṯêḵem* (conforming to 8:4; cf. 24:13).

10[9]. 'tribal chiefs': Hebr. *rā'šêḵem šiḇṯêḵem* is anomalous; Syr and LXX suggest *rā'šê šiḇṯêḵem*, 'the chiefs of your tribes' (cf. 5:23). Other suggestions have included: 1. reading *šōp̄eṯêhem*, 'your judges', in place of *šiḇṯêḵem* (S. R. Driver 1895: 322, citing Josh. 8:33; 23:2; 24:1); and 2. assuming that *šiḇṯêḵem* bears the rare meaning of 'leaders' here (cf. 2 Sam. 7:7; suggested by Barthélemy 1982: 245–246). The first of these is possible, though a scribal error resulting in a more difficult reading is usually considered unlikely. The second is no better, because *šēḇeṭ* always means 'tribe' in Deuteronomy, and indeed in the immediate context (18[17]). Lenchak (1993: 94–95), reviewing these possibilities, also notes the suggestion that MT 'can be understood as a rare variant of the construct relationship', and prefers either this or emendation of *rā'šêḵem* to *rā'šê*. Emendation is the simplest answer in this case.

19[18]. *lema'an sep̄ôṯ hārāwâ 'eṯ haṣṣemē'â*: the phrase is difficult because the syntax may be read in a number of ways. 1. *hārāwâ 'eṯ haṣṣemē'â* may form the object of the verb *sep̄ôṯ*, in which case *'eṯ* is the preposition 'with', and the meaning is, 'so that both the well-watered and the dry might be swept away'. 2. *hārāwâ* may be the subject of the verb, and *haṣṣemē'â* the object, in which case *'eṯ* is the sign of the definite object, thus: 'so that the well-watered may sweep away [put an end to] the dryness [drought]'. Furthermore, the phrase may be either a continuation of the quoted speech of the rebellious person, or the comment of the narrator. If it is the case that the rebellious person continues to speak, it is best to take the clause as in 2. above, giving, 'even though I act resolutely (*kî bišrirûṯ libbî 'ēlēḵ*) so that plenty of water may put an end to drought' (so EÜ; Braulik 1992a: 214).

This positive spin on *bišrirûṯ libbî* is meant to reflect what the speaker might actually say of himself; however, 'in the stubbornness of my heart' is not impossible even on this reading, as the narrator's own point of view might easily be imported into another person's speech. The meaning might be that he is determined to worship the gods of the land in order to bring fertility. Weinfeld (1972: 105–106), on the basis of treaty parallels, thinks the speaker hopes to be safe by keeping his rebellious thoughts to himself. Rofé (1985a: 313) varies the syntax by proposing that *sep̄ôṯ* comes from the (conjectured) root *sp'*, 'feed'. He thinks the speaker hopes his sin will be covered by the faithfulness of everyone else. If the narrator is the speaker, it is best to adopt 1. above, thus, ' "even though I live in the stubbornnesss of my heart"; but this would sweep away both the well-watered and the dry'. For interpretation, see 'Comment'.

22[21]. *haddôr hā'aḥarôn*: 'the next generation', rather than 'a future generation', on analogy with Pss. 48:14[13]; 78:4, 6; 102:19[18] (cf. S. R. Driver 1895: 327).

26[25]. 'which they had known': or possibly 'who had not known them'. Analogy favours the former.

Form and structure

Deut. 29:2[1] – 30:20 forms the next important sub-section of the book. We saw on ch. 28 ('Form and structure') that 29:1[28:69] forms a conclusion to the section of curses and blessings there, and thus to the substance of the Moab covenant. This was because 'the words of this covenant' (29:1[28:69], 9[8]) must refer back to things Moses has already said. Moreover, the horizon, the 'today' of Moab, is the same as that in 26:17–19. In my view, therefore, the Moab covenant is constituted by the preaching of Moses in its entirety in Deuteronomy, and not by chs. 29 – 30 (or 29 – 32), as many commentators argue. These two chapters, rather, explore further the implications of Israel's acceptance of the terms of the covenant, and specifically of the curse. (For an account of the extensive references back to chs. 1 – 28 in chs. 29 – 30, see Lenchak 1993: 114–118.) The key to understanding ch. 29 is the proposition that every curse written in the 'book of the law' is effective for every member of the people; that is what they are entering into 'today'. This is especially the point of vv. 18–21[17–20]. *'ālâ*, 'curse', occurs four times in ch. 29, once more in 30:7, and nowhere else in Deuteronomy (29:12[11], 14[13], 19[18], 21[20]; 30:7).

The logic that begins in ch. 29 runs to 30:20. There is a pattern in the vocabulary of the curse: *haqqᵉlālâ* ('curse', 29:27[26]) is resumed in 30:1, 19; *hā'ālôṭ* ('curses', 30:7), echoes the fourfold occurrence in ch. 29. The 'circumcision of the heart' (30:6) also corresponds to 'heart' in 29:19[18] (twice), where it is rebellious. As well as literary links between chs. 29 and 30, there are also resonances in these chapters of features of chs. 10 – 11, the section that immediately preceded the law code. The idea of circumcision of the heart in 10:16 is not far from the setting forth of blessing and curse in 11:13–17, 26–32, the latter verses (26, 28, 29) showing a concentration of curse vocabulary. The call to 'choose life' (30:19) finds an echo in the offer of long life in the land in 11:9, as does the command to 'love the LORD' (30:20) in 10:12; 11:1. There are, in sum, a number of echoes in chs. 29 – 30 of chs. 10 – 11. The literary and theological frame round chs. 12 – 26, which is closest in 11:26–32 and ch. 27, thus extends both forward and back.

Most elements of the treaty structure can be found in chs. 29 – 30 (historical prologue, 29:2–9[1–8]; statement of commitment, 29:10–15[9–14]; stipulations, 16–20a[15–19a], 28[29]; witnesses and curse/blessing, 30:15–20; principally following Rofé [1985a: 317], who also includes 29:1[28:69] as a 'superscription'). However, it does not appear fully formed, and need not be reconstructed (*pace* Rofé, who postulates certain disruptions in the present text, which have obscured it), because, as I have argued, ch. 29 does not represent a separate covenant, but rather a further sermon with a specific purpose, using covenantal language and thought. By the same token, chs. 29 – 30 are not properly a 'covenant renewal'. (Lenchak [1993: 169] finds a 'dissociation' between the covenants of Horeb and Moab, which confirms 'the possibility of covenant renewal'. In my view, however, the relationship between the covenants is one of convergence rather than dissociation.) The structure of the chapter is as follows:

2–9[1–8]	Historical review
10–15[9–14]	Confirming the covenant
16–21[15–20]	The curse applied to each individual
22–28[21–27]	The curse applied to the whole community
29[28]	A saying about the accessibility of the law

This structure is completed by the parts of ch. 30 as follows:

1–10	Repentance and return
11–14	Accessibility of the law
15–20	Exhortation to 'choose life'

Comment

29:2–9[1–8]

2[1]. This verse initiates a further speech of Moses (the third speech, if we incorporate ch. 27 within the long second; 5:1 – 28:68). Verses 2–9[1–8] are similar to the prologue section of treaties. Typically for deuteronomic discourse, covenant exhortation is preceded by a retrospect upon Yahweh's acts of deliverance in bringing Israel out of Egypt.

2–4[1–3]. Verses 2–3[1–2] use familiar language for the topic, though only here and at 4:34 does this triad of words appear, a stylistic signal of a significant new beginning (cf. ch. 8). Verse 4[3] strikes a note that recalls 8:2–5, which first addressed the issue of Israel's capacity to keep the covenant. There Yahweh tested them to know what was 'in their heart' (*lēbāb*, 8:2), and exhorted them to 'understand [or know] in their hearts' (8:5). Here, he has not yet given them 'hearts (*lēb*) to understand [or know]' (4[3]). Furthermore, though Israel has 'seen' the signs and wonders (3[2]), it has not yet 'eyes to see' (4[3]), that is, to see with true knowledge. The same moral issue is broached as was found in 9:4–6, namely the people's disposition to unfaithfulness to Yahweh. The new note consists in the idea that Yahweh should *give* the people minds (or hearts) to know. (Note how Yahweh's own voice intrudes unexpectedly in v. 6b[5b], strengthening the rhetorical appeal to the hearers; Lenchak 1993: 106; cf. Polzin 1980: 55, 57.) There is, therefore, a similar echo between these two passages as there is between 10:16 and 30:6, where Yahweh declares that he himself will 'circumcise the hearts' of the people (see on 30:6). At this point, however, Israel is still found wanting in its knowledge, that is, the moral understanding that can produce right action.

5–6[4–5]. The allusion to ch. 8 is confirmed by the mention of clothes and shoes that did not wear out, and the 'eating no bread', recalling the miraculous manna (cf. 8:3–4), and by the idea of 'leading' (*hlk*, hiph., in 8:2 and 29:5[4]) for forty years in the wilderness. The idea of proving Israel, so that they may know Yahweh, is the purpose, here as there.

7–8[6–7]. The reference to the victories in Transjordan also takes up the idea of a test of obedience, which had been the issue at the first approach to the land (1:26–33). With Yahweh's help they had eventually been able to conquer (2:26 – 3:7). The present prologue therefore brings us to a point similar to that at which Moses began his first long address (5:1), with the inheritance of land begun (in Transjordan), and the bulk of it lying ahead, still to be taken. Deut. 29:9[8], like 29:1[28:69], refers to the content of the Moab covenant, that is, Moses' preaching in Deuteronomy.

9[8]. The call to obey is a consequence of Yahweh's acts of salvation (cf. the logical connection in 7:6–11, 12ff.); the command succinctly states the real possibility of success, if the people can be faithful. The phrase 'in all you undertake [= do]' echoes and contrasts with 'everything the LORD did' (2[1]), the two forming an envelope round this first paragraph (cf. Lenchak 1993: 174), and expressing forcefully that Israel's obedience is an appropriate response to Yahweh's own acts.

29:10–15[9–14]

Like 26:17–19; 27:9, this passage states Israel's commitment to enter and keep the covenant, the covenant formula standing at the centre (N. Lohfink [1962: 38–39] finds a concentric pattern in these verses as follows: AA': 'before the LORD your/our God', vv. 10[9], 15[14]; BB': 'make covenant', vv. 12[11], 14[13]; C: the covenant formula, v. 13[12].) The phrase 'You stand here' (10[9], only here in the book) emphasizes the formality and purpose of the gathering. So, too, does its syntactical sequel, 'so that you may enter solemnly into the covenant...' (12[11]). The word translated 'enter solemnly' means literally to 'go through' or 'go over' (used mainly in Deuteronomy for 'going over' into the land). It is unique in its sense here of entering into the covenant, and may hint at a ceremony of walking through parts of slaughtered animals in a sacrificial covenantal ritual (cf. Gen. 15:9–10, 17; Jer. 34:18; so Braulik 1992a: 213; McCarthy 1981: 91 and n. 18). This would suit well the character of the present address as a formal acceptance of the implications of covenant participation, namely the full impact of the curses in the event of unfaithfulness.

10–11[9–10]. A further important new thing in the picture of the ceremony, however, is the careful enumeration of the members of Israel (10–11[9–10]; cf. 31:12) ordered 'from greatest to least', that is, from tribal leaders through local leaders (see 16:18), every individual (male), then children and wives, and finally strangers, who may have the lowliest occupations (cf. Josh. 9:27). It is the most inclusive 'participant list' in the OT, enumerating both officials and men, women and children (Lenchak 1993: 101). The liability of each individual under both the terms and the sanctions of the covenant is emphasized in this way. The formal inclusion of the stranger, or 'resident alien', is also established for the first time, although it had already been signalled in all the laws calling for their generous treatment in common with others in socially weak positions (e.g. 14:28–29), as it had been in the inclusion of certain non-Israelites in the 'assembly of Yahweh' in 23:7–8.

13[12]. A form of the covenant formula follows (13[12]), at the rhetorical mid-point of this paragraph. It recalls 26:17–18 (cf. Gen. 17:7; Lev. 26:12; Exod. 6:7), and refers to fulfilment of the oath to Abraham, Isaac and Jacob. The allusion to all three patriarchs has occurred hitherto at significant beginnings (1:8; 6:10, following the Shema), or in passages in which Israel's continuation in the covenant was in doubt (9:5, 27). Its appearance here is echoed by 30:20, the close of the present section. Its function is to reassert the fundamental basis on which the covenant is established, precisely at this point of solemn commitment on Israel's part.

14–15[13–14]. The extension of the validity of the covenant to 'those who are not here with us today' (15[14]) presumably draws in the generations yet to come (cf. 29:11[10], 30:2, 6, 19; Lenchak 1993: 103), in keeping with the concept that covenants are in principle re-realizable in perpetuity, established in 5:2–3 (Lenchak 1993: 104).

29:16–21[15–20]

16–17[15–16]. The next paragraph is the heart of the argument concerning the liability of each individual, and each constituent part, within the whole body of Israel. It echoes Deut. 13, where, too, the crucial measure of covenant faithfulness was the worship of Yahweh alone, and where also the concern was that individuals or groups should not be allowed to go over to other gods and thus lead Israel astray. It also recalls the laws intended to root out sin against the covenant lest the whole people be affected by it (21:9, 21; 22:21). The issue (as in ch. 13) is idolatry. Here, the existence of idolatrous worship in nations around Israel is traced from Egypt itself, and the background to v. 16[15] may be supposed to be the journey, as recorded in Deuteronomy, through or round Edom, Moab and

Ammon and into conflict with the kings of the Amorites (chs. 2 – 3). Hitherto there has been no special mention of their idolatry; that topic has related to the worship of the Canaanite peoples. The terms used here, too, are new (and unique) in Deuteronomy. The term 'false gods' (*gillulîm*) is frequent in Ezekiel (esp. Ezek. 20; the two terms occur together in Ezek. 20:30–31). But now the focus is on the people as they are 'today', in Moab, and the possibility that even now an intention to defect is being harboured somewhere in the camp. The thought fits well with experience (Deut. 9:1 – 10:11).

18–21[17–20]. The danger of the people's harbouring an unfaithful group or individual is now met by an assertion that such a person or persons will not be able to hide from the effect of the curse, for their rebellion will be found out by Yahweh himself. The thought thus echoes the self-curses in 27:15–26. The various possible constructions of v. 19[18] are reviewed above ('Notes on the text'). The translation adopted is in contrast to the most common translation, 'This will bring disaster on the watered land as well as the dry' (NIV; cf. NRSV).

A decision between the two is finely balanced. The immediate context contains two somewhat contrasting ideas: 1. that the wicked individual or group may affect the whole community (18b[17b]); and 2. that Yahweh can single out the wicked individual or group for special punishment (20–21[19–20]). The more common translation is in keeping with the first of these (where 'well-watered' and 'dry' refer to righteous and wicked respectively). The translation adopted here is in keeping with the latter, which seems dominant; namely that Yahweh can single out the wicked, thus protecting the rest. This is why it is better to include the last clause of v. 19[18] within the words of the rebellious person's speech, and take it to reflect his belief that his determined worship of other gods will bring plenty to all. (Rofé's idea [1985a: 313], that the speaker hopes his sin will be covered by others' righteousness, seems improbable. The speaker should be credited with a serious intention, as in Deut. 13.)

In pursuing the guilty it is said that the LORD will not 'forgive' them (20[19]). The word 'forgive' appears only here in Deuteronomy. It occurs a number of times in Kings and Jeremiah, and applies to the whole people in relation to their sins of idolatry. The LORD 'refused to forgive' (same phrase as here) Manasseh (2 Kgs. 24:4) and so brought the punishment of exile on Judah; but he promised forgiveness for his people in the end (Jer. 31:34; cf. 1 Kgs. 8:30, 34, 36, 39 and esp. v. 50).

29:22–29[21–28]

These verses have been seen as intrusive because of the change from the topic of the individual to that of the whole community (Rofé [1985a: 313], who sees v. 29[28] as the real sequel to v. 20[19]). However, the argument now simply reverts to the main line, the responsibility of the whole people to keep the covenant. In addition, the perspective changes to the time of 'the next generation' (see 'Notes on the text'), after the curses have been implemented. The shift in perspective enables a new angle on the disaster to be expressed, namely the horror of those who see it – a conventional topic found in other similar contexts, in the OT and beyond (the closest is 1 Kgs. 9:6–9; cf. Jer. 19:8; 22:8–9; 49:17; 50:13; Ezek. 27:35–36; cf. also the pattern of question and answer about the devastation of a land [Deut. 29:24–28[23–27] in the Assyrian treaty of King Ashurnirari VI with Mati'ilu of Bit-Agusi; Rofé 1985a: 315).

The image is one of a land laid waste with a destruction like that of Sodom and Gomorrah, because of the wrath of Yahweh (Gen. 19). (Note the frequent repetition of the word 'land' ['ereṣ] in vv. 22–28[21–27], as a leading motif [Lenchak 1993: 176]. Admah and Zeboiim are associated with Sodom and Gomorrah in Gen. 10:19; 14:2, 8, and the paradigmatic act of divine wrath against the latter has apparently been transferred to the former in Hos. 11:8.)

The topic of the wrath of Yahweh, in fact, finds its most concentrated expression in the book in these verses, with six nouns for anger deployed. The primary term, 'ap̄, appears five times in this passage out of thirteen in the book (cf. 6:15; 7:4; 11:17; 31:17), typically with the verb ḥrh, 'to burn', and once with the verb 'āšan, 'to smoke' (the verbal form is rare, but has overtones of the theophany at Sinai; Exod. 19:18). The terms qin'â, 'jealousy' (20[19]), ḥ°rî, 'furious anger' (24[23]), and qeṣep̄ (27[26], occur only here in Deuteronomy (though cf. qannā', 'jealous', 4:24; 5:9; 6:15). ḥārôn and ḥēmâ find one other occurence each (13:17[18]; 9:19 respectively). In every instance in which Yahweh's anger is in view, the theme is fundamental breach of the covenant. This explains the heightening of the topic at the point at which Israel solemnly agrees to accept the consequences of entering the covenant.

The reason given to the hypothetical askers (24[23]) for the fate of the people is that they forsook the covenant with Yahweh (25[24]; cf. 31:16: 'they will forsake me and break my covenant'; also 31:20). The covenant he made with them corresponds to the view in 5:2–3, where the Moab generation are effectively the recipients of the Horeb covenant, and also with 29:12[11]. The paradigmatic sin is, as always, idolatry (26[25]). The idea that Yahweh had not 'allotted' the other gods to Israel recalls 4:19, where the idea made a rhetorical contrast with Yahweh's election of Israel for himself (see discussion there). It also reminds the reader of 28:64, where the serving of other gods was part of the punishment of exile. There, too, the gods were gods 'they had not known' (see 'Notes on the text'). The thought is that they have abandoned their relationship with Yahweh, and the life and well-being that came with it, for the futile gods that have brought them only death and deprivation.

27–28[26–27]. Verse 27 looks like a conclusion to the paragraph beginning in v. 22, because of its reference to 'every curse written in this book' (cf. 20–21[19–20]). Moreover, v. 28[27] changes the picture of punishment from wasted land to exile. For these reasons v. 28[27] has been regarded as an addition to vv. 22–27[21–26] (Rofé 1985a: 316). However, v. 28[27] should be seen as the natural conclusion to the whole picture, exile being actually implied by the 'next generation' viewing the devastated land in horror, as if for the first time, in v. 22[21].

29:29[28]

The final reflection is enigmatic. The 'hidden things' may be either 1. everything known to Yahweh but not conveyed to Israel, whether simply the future, or hidden purposes or mysterious ways, in the idiom of the wisdom literature (Braulik 1992a: 216), or 2. hidden sins, in continuity with the theme of vv. 18–21[17–20] (Rofé 1985a: 313). In the former case, the analogy is with wisdom thinking. Job says that wisdom itself is 'hidden' (*str*, ni. ptc., as in the present verse) from all living creatures but God (Job 28:21). The contrast in v. 29[28] between what is hidden and what is revealed then lies between the things that are known only to God, which humans may leave to him, and his laws that he has made known, which they must obey. In the latter case, 'hidden things' as 'hidden sins' occurs in Ps. 19:12[13] (again, *str*, ni. ptc.), in the context, indeed, of a meditation on keeping the *tôrâ*. The meaning of the line in this case is that, while God will take care of sins committed in secret, Israel must be responsible for those that are publicly known.

Both of these possible interpretations, therefore, may appeal to analogy in the OT for support. On balance, it is preferable to take 'hidden things' in the sense of wisdom, because the immediate context does not give a clue to the meaning 'sins' (unless it is contrived by regarding vv. 22–28[21–27] as an interpolation, which is unnecessary). Without such a clue, 'hidden things' is more naturally taken in the wisdom sense. Moreover, the phrase about keeping the law means a general obedience, rather than expressing the specific idea of responsibility to enforce it where they can. The idea in the verse therefore anticipates 30:11–14, with its concept of an available *tôrâ*, that the people are able to keep (Braulik 1992a: 216).

Explanation

The chapter drives home the implications of Israel's agreement to take upon itself the terms of the covenant. It is dominated by the idea of the curse, and the wrath of God that will fall if Israel is unfaithful to the commitment it is willingly taking on. In particular, it stresses that all members of the community are subject to the effects of the curse even if they privately harbour rebellious intentions. In this respect the chapter takes a cue from the self-curses of 27:15–26, which form part of the covenant renewal at Shechem, and where the idea of secret sin was prominent. However, in the logic of Deuteronomy, its immediate antecedent is the blessings and curses pronounced in Moab (ch. 28), which is the scene of this sermon also.

The individual's liability to the force of the curse is a corollary of the elevated place afforded to the individual in the whole ethos of Deuteronomy, enshrined in the paranesis itself, in which the people as such is sovereign, and in the deuteronomic law, which everywhere gives dignity and protection to the individual. It is implied in the moral concept of the inwardness of true religion, symbolized by the metaphor of 'circumcision of the heart' (10:16; 30:6). The acceptance of the curse by the individual, therefore, is a mark of his or her high status in the covenantal arrangement between Yahweh and Israel.

The theme of the anger of God is concentrated in vv. 22–28[21–27] more than anywhere else in the book. Hitherto it has always appeared in close connection with breach of the First Commandment, that is, fundamental breach of the covenant. In 9:19, which also has a cluster of terms for God's anger, Moses prays for Israel after its idolatry with the golden calf. In 13:17[18] the context is the defection of a city in Israel to other gods. In ch. 7 also, the issue is radical separation from Canaanite religion. The theme is present in many parts of the OT, notably the Pentateuch, Psalms and Prophets (e.g. Num. 32:13–14; Is. 10:5; 30:27–33; Jer. 4:26; 21:5; Ezek. 5:15; Ps. 7:6[7]; 21:9[10]). The wrath of God is therefore an important topic in OT theology. In the OT story, it is mostly directed against Israel. This is most apparent when Yahweh acts against his own people in a kind of reversal of the holy war (Jer. 21:5), because of their persistent rebellion against him.

There is, however, a limit and term to his anger. We shall see this in the next chapter (ch. 30). It is also in 1 Kgs. 8, which makes implicit allusions to the present text, while shifting the focus to salvation (see McConville 2000a). In Hos. 11:9, one of the profoundest sayings in the OT, Yahweh declares that he will no longer act in anger against Ephraim (Israel), or come again in wrath – *because* he is 'God and not man'. And in Jeremiah, the so-called Book of Consolation (Jer. 30 – 33) brings wrath sayings into stark juxtaposition with salvation sayings (30:24; 31:1–6). There are pointers in these paradoxes to the cross, where God's wrath and mercy meet, with the triumph, at last, of mercy. The story of his anger, however, with all the emotive quality of the language, is meant to say that the triumph of mercy is no light thing. God's hostility to evil is constant.

DEUTERONOMY 30:1–20

Translation

[1]When all these things have happened to you, both the blessing and the curse that I have set before you, and you lay them to heart among all the nations to which the LORD your God has driven you, [2]and turn back to the LORD your God, you and your children, obeying him with all your heart and being, according to all that I am charging you with this day, [3]then the LORD your God will restore your fortunes, have compassion on you, and turn and gather you from all the peoples among which he scattered you. [4]Even if your banished ones are in the farthest land under heaven, even from there the LORD your God will gather you and bring you back. [5]The LORD your God will bring you back to the land your forefathers once possessed, and you will possess it; and he will make you more prosperous and numerous than your forefathers. [6]The LORD your God will circumcise your hearts, and those of your descendants, so that you love the LORD your God with all your heart and all your being, and thus live. [7]The LORD your God will send all these curses on your enemies, those who hated and persecuted you. [8]But as for you, you will turn and obey the LORD your God, and carry out all his commands with which I am charging you this day. [9]The LORD your God will give you abundance in all that you undertake: in your own offspring, in the young of your livestock and in the produce of your fertile land, for the LORD will turn again to take delight in you, as he did with your forefathers, [10]on the day that you once again obey him by keeping his commands and laws, all that is written in this book of the law, and return to the LORD your God with all your heart and all your being.

[11]For this law with which I am charging you today is not too hard for you; neither is it far off. [12]It is not in heaven, so that one should say, 'Who will go up to heaven for us and get it for us, and proclaim it to us, so that we may keep it?' [13]Nor is it across the sea, so that one should say, 'Who will cross the sea for us, and get it for us, and proclaim it to us, so that we may keep it?' [14]No; the word is very near you, in your mouth and in your heart, so that you can keep it.

[15]See, I have set before you this day, on one hand, life and prosperity; on the other, death and disaster. [16]If you obey the commands of the LORD your God with which I am charging you this day, by loving the LORD your God, living according to his way, and keeping his commands, laws and statutes, you will live and increase, and the LORD your God will bless you in the land you are going over to possess. [17]But if your heart turns away, and you disobey, and are led astray to worship and serve other gods, [18]I declare to you today that you will certainly perish; you will not live long in the land you are crossing the Jordan to enter and possess. [19]I call the heavens and the earth as witnesses against you today, that I have set before you life and death, blessing and curse; therefore choose life, so that you may indeed live, both you and your descendants, [20]loving the LORD your God, obeying him and holding steadily to him, for he will be your life, and length of days, as you live in the land the LORD promised on oath to your forefathers, Abraham, Isaac and Jacob, that he would give them.

Notes on the text

2. The phrase 'you and your children' is placed in Hebrew after 'that I am charging you with this day'; however, as the word 'you' has the form of a grammatical subject ('thou', not 'thee'), it qualifies '(if) you … turn back', rather than following the latter clause. The slight reordering of the sentence (as also NIV, NRSV) is necessary in order to make this clear. The phrase is not in LXX. Its absence would scarcely affect the sense materially, as a future time is predicated in any case; yet it has a certain rhetorical function.

3. *šᵉḇût*: the noun occurs in the OT only in conjunction with parts of the verb *šûḇ*. The same is true of the variant form *šᵉḇît*, 'captivity' (except Num. 21:29; see Ezek. 16:53). MT apparently regards them as interchangeable, and therefore favours the idea 'turn your captivity' (cf. Zeph. 2:7, where the consonantal *šᵉḇût* is 'read' (Q) as *šᵉḇît*, and Job 42:10, where the reverse happens). The ancient versions hesitated between deriving the noun from *šāḇâ* or from *šûḇ* (see W. L. Holladay 1958: 110–112). In modern scholarship, while *šᵉḇît* is connected with the verb *šāḇâ*, 'take captive' (*HALAT* 4:1287), the dominant opinion takes *šᵉḇût* with *šûḇ* (so *HALAT*). The translation 'turn the captivity' is problematical in Job 42:10. Therefore the now common 'restore the fortunes' is best. The phrase also provides one of the few cases of *šûḇ* as a 'qal transitive'; cf. Ps. 85:4[5]; Nahum 2:3, and discussion of these and other possible instances in Holladay 1958: 114–115.

3. 'will … turn and gather': the phrase could mean 'he will again gather'. However, the verb *šûḇ* is so marked in this passage that it is unlikely to bear a weak meaning. W. L. Holladay (1958: 68–69) thinks that in this instance it shows that a previous action on the subject's part is now being reversed (cf. Rofé 1985a: 311, and see also v. 8).

4. *yihyeh niddaḥᵃkâ*, 'your banished ones are': the form of *ndḥ* is a niphal participle with a possessive suffix (*HALAT* 3:636); the phrase is lit. 'your driven one will be'; the translation here follows Craigie 1976a: 361; cf. RSV, 'outcasts'). For a further note on this form see GKC 92b n. 1.

8. 'you will turn and obey', rather than 'you will again obey'; cf. note on v. 3. In this case and the next (9) the decision between 'turn' and 'do again' is balanced. 'Even among the instances where there is assurance that the meaning is "again", there are few that could not *theoretically* carry the meaning "return"' (W. L. Holladay 1958: 67).

9. 'he will turn again to take delight'; the case for translating *šûḇ* simply as 'again' is strongest in this phrase, i.e. 'he will again delight' (S. R. Driver 1895: 330; P. Barker 1995: 172). Yet even here the meaning 'return' (or 'turn again') is likely (Rofé 1985a: 311), that is, because Yahweh had formerly ceased to delight in them (28:63). It is thus a reversal of a previous action as in v. 3 (see also on v. 8).

10. *hakkᵉtûḇâ*, f. sg. following a plural phrase (cf. 29:21[20]). Some ancient versions suppose an original plural. The translation given here ('all that is written') is an alternative solution.

16. 'If you obey the commands of the LORD your God': this phrase is not in MT, and is restored here following LXX, and the parallel in 11:27. In that place the word *'ᵃšer* occurs twice, at the beginning of the phrase that has been omitted here (meaning 'if'), and again immediately following it. The omission probably happened because the eye of a scribe jumped inadvertently from the first *'ᵃšer* to the second (a case of haplography).

Form and structure

I have argued above (on ch. 29, 'Form and structure') that 30:1–20 is part of a unified section of Deuteronomy that runs from 29:2[1] to 30:20. The whole section, in turn, presupposes the blessings and curses that were the subject of ch. 28. The reference to 'these things/words' (1) is in continuity with 29:9[8], and also with 29:1[28:69], which forms a hinge between chs. 28 and 29. So, too, the allusion to 'this book of the law' (30:10) is continuous with 29:20–21[19–20]. The blessings and curses (30:1) are clearly those that also underlie ch. 29, namely the ones spelt out in ch. 28. The blessing re-emerges here, having been out of the limelight throughout ch. 29, but is a reminder that that, too, is one of the possibilities introduced in ch. 28.

There are a number of signs that ch. 30 is a peroration. The return to the metaphor of the 'circumcision of the heart' (6; cf. 10:16) gives a certain thematic closure. References to 'setting the blessing and curse before' Israel frame the chapter (1, 19), and a slight variation of this appears also in v. 15, echoing 11:26. This, too, indicates that all has now been said. The invocation of heaven and earth as witnesses (19) is climactic. And the full form of the promise to the patriarchs, naming all three, occurs in only a few places, and in this case has a ring of finality (cf. on 29:13[12]). These factors show that the chapter is a unity in concept and structure (Lenchak 1993: 177).

The chapter nevertheless falls clearly into three sections: vv. 1–10, 11–14 and 15–20. The first section (1–10) is an extended 'when … then' sequence, organized around the idea of '(re)turning' or 'repenting' (*šûḇ*). The potential meanings of *šûḇ* are carefully exploited in these verses, and applied to a 'returning' on the part of both Israel and Yahweh, and, as regards Israel, to both repentance and return to land. The second section (11–14) is a self-contained explanatory paragraph on the theme of the nearness of the law. And the third (15–20), opening with the structural marker 'See' (cf. 11:26), is a final exhortation to choose life and blessing by keeping the covenant.

The interpretation of the chapter is affected by the understanding of the structure and syntax of vv. 1–10. On this depends our view of the relationship between Yahweh's decision to restore Israel and Israel's willingness to repent and be redeemed.

Structural analyses usually find a fivefold ABCB'A' pattern. An example is that of Vanoni (1981: 74; cf. P. Barker 1995: 166; Braulik 1992a: 219):

A   Protasis (1–2)
B   Apodosis (3–5)
C   Centre (6–8)
B' Apodosis (9)
A' Protasis (10)

The main question here concerns the middle section. Does the important v. 6, with its metaphor of the circumcision of the heart, belong in the 'centre', as in the model above, with the result that God's action of circumcision of the heart is the substance of what is promised? In my view, the accent in the paragraph falls only at v. 8. This is because the series of *waw*-consecutives that resumes at v. 5 continues unbroken to the end of v. 7. The next clear syntactical break comes with *wᵉ'attâ*, 'and you', at the beginning of v. 8.

Therefore, I prefer the following structure (with N. Lohfink [1962: 41], who also has v. 8 alone in the centre, though his analysis is more complicated). Lenchak (1993: 178) has vv. 8b–9 in the centre:

A   Protasis (1–2)
B   Main apodosis (3–7, v. 4 being a
    secondary-level qualification of it)
C   Central exhortation (8)
B' Apodosis (9)
A' Protasis (10)

Both models highlight the careful structuring of the passage to achieve a balance between Israel's obligation to repent and Yahweh's willingness to restore them. This is brought out not only by the use of the verb *šûb* with Israel and Yahweh respectively as subject, but also by the way these contrasting clauses alternate. Each side of the action is filled out, furthermore, with language and ideas that echo major themes of the book: Yahweh's salvation fulfils the promise of blessing to the 'fathers'; Israel's obedience to the Torah must be from the heart.

The main difference between the two models offered here is that v. 6, the promise of the 'circumcision of the heart', occurs respectively in C and B. In P. Barker's view (1995: 169), the effect of placing it in B, that is, in the apodosis (as I have done), 'would be to understand the circumcision of the heart as one of a number of blessings given to Israel by Yahweh as a result of Israel's turning and obedience'; in other words, a legalistic reading. He thinks the inclusion of v. 6 in C indicates 'the priority of

Yahweh's action on Israel's heart to enable Israel's right response' (1995: 170).

However, the theological balance need not follow the syntactical logic so closely. There is a further related question, moreover: namely whether the *kî-* clauses are straightforward 'if' clauses or temporal ones; in the latter case, the strict conditional reading of the text would come further into question. The effect of the structure, in any case, is a formal balance between the idea of the people's obedience to the covenant, and Yahweh's action to restore them. It remains to ask how these two poles are related to each other theologically.

Comment

30:1–10

1–2. Moses' third address now continues by turning attention to a time after 1. the blessings of the land have been enjoyed for an unspecified time, but 2. the ultimate covenantal curses have come about, that is, after Israel has been deprived of its land (28:63–68; 29:22–28[21–27]). 'All these things' are literally 'all these words'. This makes a catchword link with 29:29[28], where the 'words' refer to the commands of the deuteronomic law. Here, however, they refer to the blessings and the curses in chs. 28 – 29. Departing from the pattern of the treaties, whether Hittite, with their blessings and curses, or Assyrian, with their curses only, Deuteronomy now makes possible the thought that the falling of the curses need not spell an absolute end. The treaty pattern is, in a sense, overturned by this development.

The present section, with its singular address, is directed, in principle, to a future generation (cf. Sonnet 1997: 109). In one sense that generation is seen as continuous with the Moab generation that forms the immediate audience of Moses' words. However, the perspective belongs to the message in these latter chapters of Deuteronomy that obedience to the Torah that Moses is bequeathing to the people is continuously renewable.

Verses 1–2 are the protasis of a conditional sentence spanning vv. 1–3. It is not possible on formal grounds alone to decide whether the clauses of this protasis are properly conditional ('if') or rather temporal ('when'). The first clause is introduced with *wᵉhāyâ kî*, which is temporal in 6:10; 11:29; 26:1; 31:21, but conditional in 15:16. Context must decide the meaning. In this case, the opening clause specifies the circumstances that become the basis for the train of thought that follows, and it is therefore best taken as temporal. In our translation, the two following clauses ('and you lay them to heart ... and turn back') are also taken as temporal (with NIV; Craigie 1976a: 361), because their construction with *waw*-consecutive, the 'and' sequence typical of Hebrew narrative, makes this natural. The case for 'if' here, however (adopted by NRSV), cannot be lightly passed over, since it also seems natural that the calling to mind, returning/repenting and obeying should be understood as prerequisites of Yahweh's gracious action. This, however, is a theological judgment, which must be evaluated in relation to a range of texts on the same topic. And analogy by no means compels strict conditionality (cf. Jer. 29:10–13, and below, 'Explanation'). In fact, it is possible to strain the expression of the Hebrew by insisting either that it is conditional or that it excludes conditionality (Braulik 1992a: 216; cf. Aejmelaeus 1986: 197: 'The border line between conditional and temporal is, however, extremely vague'). The whole passage is building up a picture of a balanced set of conditions in which both Israel returns to Yahweh and he delivers them once more.

The verb *šûḇ*, 'repent, return', crucially important in vv. 1–10, occurs twice in vv. 1–2, first in 'lay them to heart' (*šûḇ*, hiph.; cf. 4:39; 1 Kgs. 8:47), then in 'turn back to [Yahweh]' (*šûḇ*, qal; cf. 4:30; 30:10; 1 Kgs. 8:33, 48; also frequently in Isaiah, Hosea, Amos, Jeremiah, 2 Chronicles; W. L. Holladay 1958: 78–79). Together they express the obligation on Israel to change completely. The combination of the verb twice with the noun 'heart', as well as with obedience to Yahweh by means of Moses' instruction, and the extension of this to future generations, recalls the fundamental command in 6:4–9. The 'repenting' is at the same time a 'returning', that is, to an obedience required in the Horeb covenant itself. It is primarily a spiritual act. However, in so far as this returning cannot be reduced to strict precondition, and is both command and promise, it can also prefigure the physical returning to land, which is the theme of v. 3.

3. Yahweh becomes the agent of 'turning' in v. 3. The translation 'restore your fortunes', though the best available (see 'Notes on the text'), hides the fact that the Hebrew (*šûḇ šᵉḇût*) plays on the word '(re)turn'. Outside this text, the phrase is concentrated in Jer. 29 – 33 (29:10; 30:3, 18; 31:23; 32:44; 33:7, 11, 26). In that book, as here, it implies a restoration of exiled Israel (there properly Judah) to its land.

Yahweh himself will 'turn' (as in 'turn and gather', see 'Notes on the text'), and turn everything round for captive Israel. He will not only have compassion on them (cf. Solomon's prayer, 1 Kgs. 8:50), but will actually bring them back to the land he had once given and from which he had lately driven them. (The phrase 'restore your fortunes' is also associated with Yahweh's 'having compassion', *rḥm*, in Jer. 30:18; 33:26. And *šûḇ* and *rḥm* occur together in Mic. 7:19, where W. L. Holladay [1958: 69] translates, 'he shall reverse his anger [see v. 18] and have compassion on us'.) Yahweh's new decision is a radical change of mind. It is motivated purely by his own decision, not by any obligation that might have arisen because of Israel's covenant faithfulness, and that decision is rooted simply in his compassion.

4–5. All the emphasis in these verses (through to v. 7) falls on the actions of Yahweh. The exile envisaged is not specific, but applies in principle to any land, none being beyond the reach or domination of Yahweh. The phrase 'your banished ones' is actually singular, and therefore, while it should probably be taken distributively, it suggests that Yahweh's compassion extends to every single person who has suffered the loss of his or her home (cf. Neh. 1:9; and 'Notes on the text').

The effect of the address to a future generation is that the occupation of the promised land can now be seen as a past event (5), and those who took it are called 'your forefathers', though strictly this refers to the Moab generation, Moses' immediate audience. Once again, the moral solidarity of Israel in all its generations emerges strongly. The future blessing will be like the first in kind: they will enjoy the good of the land, and grow in number – only more so than before.

6. The most dramatic new thing in this promise is that Yahweh himself will 'circumcise [the] hearts' of the people he is restoring (6). This is both like and unlike 10:16, in which Moses exhorted the people to 'circumcise their hearts': unlike, because here it is an act of Yahweh himself, rather than an act of the people. The shift is symptomatic of the perspective of this part of the book. Moses' speech, envisaging the future time, regards the failure of Israel to keep the covenant as an accomplished fact. The text therefore participates in the OT's coming to terms with the problem posed by the broken covenant. That problem could not be solved by a mere turning back of the clock; a new thing had to be done to deal effectively with Israel's sinful disposition. And the answer lay in Yahweh's acting in a completely new way in order to make covenant life with him possible (cf. Jer. 31:31–34; 32:39–40; Ezek. 36:24–27).

The circumcision of the heart is closely connected with the characteristic call of Deuteronomy for love and obedience from the heart, and the term 'heart' occurs frequently in the present passage (three times in the present verse). On such a complete and genuine turning by the people to Yahweh depends their 'life'. The preconditions for life in Deuteronomy had previously been expressed as the keeping of the commands and standards of the covenant (cf. 4:1; 8:1; 16:20). Now it is the consequence of Yahweh's circumcision of the heart, which leads in turn to Israel's love of him. The need for the people to actualize their obedience is not abolished by the concept in this passage, as emerges in part from the structure of vv. 1–10; see 'Form and structure', and 'Explanation').

7. The reversal of fortunes that is explicated in the passage is complete in v. 7, where the covenant curses are now brought to bear on the enemies of Israel. Yahweh's employment of other nations to chastise Israel is only part of the picture of his relationship with them. First, his sovereignty is at stake. Israel does not suffer at their hands because of Yahweh's impotence, but only because of his permission; they will see in due course that he has power over them and their gods. Secondly, their own motivation is itself subject to his judgment. Their 'hatred' and 'persecution' of Israel is culpable, and they will fall under the curse of Yahweh in their turn (cf. Is. 10:5–12; Jer. 25:11–14). The idea that they are subject to the curse is striking, because it suggests that they are implicitly obliged by the moral demands of Yahweh (somewhat as the Oracles against the Nations, esp. in Amos 1 – 2, imply this).

8–10. After the insistence that Yahweh alone can remake Israel's heart, the focus returns abruptly to their own obligations (8). The syntax allows this opening phrase ('But as for you') to be a statement of what will certainly come about in future time. That is, it can be read as narrative, extending the consequences of what Yahweh will do when he has compassion on exiled Israel. It thus makes a bridge into the pictures of a future restored relationship in vv. 9–10. Yet it also expresses what will be expected of Israel at that time. The turning here is clearly a moral change, a conversion back to God, such as the prophets demanded. The content of the changed lives remains what it ever was: obedience to his voice and his commandments, as proclaimed by Moses, 'this day', at Moab. (See 'Notes on the text' on translating *šûḇ* as 'turn' rather than 'again', here and in v. 9.)

Though the logic of the verse refers it to a future obedience by a later generation, its rhetorical force can hardly be missed by the people at Moab. This is clear not only from the opening words, 'But as for you, you will turn' (*wᵉ'attâ tāšûḇ*; cf. the rhetorical force of this in Ps. 85:6[7], where it is addressed to Yahweh by Israel in prayer), but also from 'his commands with which I am charging you this day'. The discourse therefore has a double function, not only revealing that Yahweh's compassion transcends all reciprocal treaty-like obligations, but also continuing to reinforce the present generation's duty to keep the covenant as Moses is spelling it out here and now.

Verse 9 echoes expressions in ch. 28. The threefold blessing – fruit of womb, beast and ground – is a reprise of 28:11, while the new delight of Yahweh, in doing good rather than causing to perish, reverses the curse in 28:63. Blessing finally predominates, therefore, not curse.

Finally, verse 10 restates the duty of covenantal obedience. The verse is syntactically dependent on v. 9, and opens with *kî*, which may be 'if', 'when' or 'because' (or, as here, 'on the day that'). The first of these, 'if', is inappropriate, because it is not strong enough by itself to turn the force of the entire section into a simple conditional sequence (against NIV). Either 'when' (NRSV) or 'because' (EÜ) is suitable, because the point of the verse is to establish a correspondence between blessing and obedience, which is never lost in Deuteronomy, yet here it remains under the strong influence of Yahweh's initiatives in vv. 3–7. (See, however, the discussion in Aejmelaeus 1986.)

30:11–14

The perspective of Moses' speech appears to revert to 'present time', in Moab, an impression supported by the continuation in vv. 15–20, which is clearly addressed to the people who are about to go into the land for the first time. This section (11–14) develops the theme of the 'nearness' of the law (*hammiṣwâ*, that is, the deuteronomic law understood as a whole). The idea as articulated here is new. The closest Deuteronomy has come to this hitherto is 4:7–8, where Yahweh himself was said to be 'near' to Israel, and that nearness was associated with the laws. However, the concept of laws that are 'near', that is, within Israel's capacity to keep, may be considered implicit in Moses' exhortation in general. And the thought has been prepared for in 29:29[28]. This reflection on the 'nearness' of the law is evidently prompted by the preceding passage, which has envisaged a future failure of Israel to keep it.

The law is first declared categorically to be within Israel's reach. It is neither too 'hard' (lit. 'marvellous', but for the meaning here cf. 17:8), nor too distant (11). This metaphor, implying something beyond Israel's capacity, leads into an imaginative expansion of the thought (12–13), embracing the whole creation. The hyperbole recalls 4:32, which set the giving of the law in the context of Yahweh's universal dominion in creation (cf. 4:39). Yahweh, who has all heaven and earth under his sway, has given the law to Israel; no other agent need be invoked in order to compel it. The words may have an additional edge, challenging the ANE idea of epic quests for inaccessible knowledge (as Craigie 1976a: 365 nn. 6, 7). The law is 'in your mouth and in your heart' (14), recalling the basic deuteronomic exhortation in 6:6–7. True love of Yahweh resides in the heart and is fed by the teaching and learning of the mouth (Braulik 1992a: 219–220).

The accessibility of the law runs counter to the theme of Israel's inability to keep it, met in 9:4–6, and the golden-calf narrative more broadly (9–10). And it is, at first sight, curious that a passage such as 30:11–14, addressed to the Moab generation, should come only now, after the blessings and curses (chs. 28 – 29) and a promise of Yahweh's special action to enable a disobedient people (30:1–10). The placing of these verses is essential, however. As we noticed, the time distinction between the future generation, restored from exile, and the present Moab generation, was blurred in 30:8, where the immediate relevance of Moses' sermon to the latter broke through the other perspective. The words in v. 8 ('with which I am charging you today') are now echoed in v. 11, showing that there is a unity of conception between the two parts of the chapter. This means that the affirmation of the accessibility of the commands comes directly under the influence of the promises in 30:3–7, with v. 6 at their heart. The appeal to the Moab generation has its own integrity; but ultimately the realization of an obedient people will depend on Yahweh's new act in compassion.

30:15–20

The dominant theme of these verses is 'life', another extension from 30:6. The noun occurs four times, the verb 'live' twice, and 'lengthen days'/'length of days' in vv. 18 (translated 'live long') and 20. The 'life' theme is in counterpoint with 'death' (15, 18, 19; the 'perishing' of v. 18 makes an ironic contrast with 26:5). 'Life and death' together form an inclusio, or envelope structure (15, 19; Lenchak 1993: 179). There is a strong reminiscence of 11:26–32. Both passages begin with the rhetorical 'See'. This draws attention to what Yahweh has already done and put into effect, whether with 'I have given you the land' (1:8, 21; 2:24, 31), 'I have given you commands' (4:5), or 'I have set before you the blessing and curse ... life and death' (11:26; 30:15).

16–18. Verses 16–18 repeat the twin possibilities of blessing and curse (for the restored beginning of v. 16, see 'Notes on the text'). Keeping Yahweh's commands is contrasted with following other gods, taking up an implication that is ubiquitous in Deuteronomy (cf. 4:9–14, 15–18; 8:11, 19). Command-keeping is qualified by the important phrase 'by loving the LORD your God, living according to his way, and keeping his commands, laws and statutes' (16), which highlights the personal nature of Deuteronomy's ethics. Conversely, the 'heart' is also the seat of rebellion (17).

19. Moses now approaches the final challenge to Israel in his third address, by invoking heaven and earth as witnesses to the covenant that Yahweh is making with his people (19a; cf. Is. 1:2a). This corresponds to a formal element in the treaty convention of the ANE, while refusing the usual polytheism. The 'life' theme in these verses culminates in a strong appeal to 'choose life' (19b). 'This is the high point of Moses' Third Discourse, and perhaps the high point of all Dt' (Lenchak 1993: 113). Israel's 'life' is the goal of the covenant; they have every means at their disposal, by Yahweh's grace, by which to take the opportunity; and all depends on their decision to be faithful to the covenant – not just on one occasion, but continually, as the preaching has tirelessly made clear by its rhetorical use of the term 'today'.

20. The final verse again brings the prospect of 'life' to the fore, for succeeding generations as well as the present one. And such life will fulfil the ancient promise to Abraham, Isaac and Jacob (cf. 1:8), the mention of the three patriarchs announcing a conclusion of the exhortation (see 'Form and structure').

Explanation

The present chapter makes the closest links in Deuteronomy with the exilic preoccupation with the question whether the covenant could continue, and on what basis; cf. Jer. 30 – 33; Ezek. 18:31; cf. 11:19; 36:26 (Merrill 1994: 387). What kind of future is portrayed here? The people is restored to its land, but there is no promise of a restored monarchy, no temple, and not even the deuteronomic altar formula. This deuteronomic vision is distinct both from the books of Kings, which, in considering Judah's post-exilic future, foresee no return to the land at all (1 Kgs. 8:46–53; cf. Wolff 1976: 98); and from Jeremiah, whose restoration has a place, if muted, for both king and temple (Jer. 30:9; 31:12, 14).

Deuteronomy focuses, rather, on a people that has returned to Yahweh by laying to heart all his commands (cf. 1 Sam. 7:3; 1 Kgs. 8:47). The whole structure of Israel as presupposed in the laws is therefore taken for granted here. The first point to be made is that the picture applies to Israel taken as a whole (the singular address in 30:1–10 must be understood of the community as such, as elsewhere in Deuteronomy). (Joyce [1989: 79–87] argues similarly about Ezekiel, in that book's vision of a renewed Israel, though Ezekiel is often held to be the prophet of individualism *par excellence*.)

The concept of this renewed Israel is not simple, however. What can be the meaning of this picture of a historical and political people, occupying its own land, yet characterized by an obedience to God that comes from the heart, which in turn implies a society based on a love of justice and care for the other that we saw to be the foundation of the laws? The answer can only be in terms of the typically deuteronomic tension between legislating for a real historical community and developing a vision for the kingdom of Yahweh. This is not the same as saying that Deuteronomy is 'utopian', a concept that denies any real historical interest or intention. It is simply to say that Deuteronomy is realistic, but also refuses to absolutize any *status quo*. The book's vision of the future, therefore, is anchored in real policies for the present, while allowing the 'kingdom of God' to be always dynamically imminent.

How could such a thing come about without the danger of merely falling back into the old cycle of failure and judgment, with nations mocking the disappointed pretensions rather than admiring the wisdom of Israel and its God? This question, too, exercised the minds of the biblical writers who thought about the exile. They frequently resort to stark contrasts in order to express the idea that Yahweh will now do something quite new in order to overcome the problem. Jeremiah's Book of Consolation (chs. 30 – 33) puts into reverse the story of inevitable judgment that occupies the first half of that book. The salvation promised there comes as a fruition of the purposes of Yahweh, which are shown to have been at the heart of Yahweh's action in the judgment too (Jer. 23:19–20; cf. 30:23–24 – now announcing salvation, Jer. 31). The dramatic new acts of Yahweh are conveyed also by the paradoxical juxtapositions in, for example, Jer. 30:5–7, 8–10 (see also McConville 1993b: 93–97). Ezekiel contrasts Israel's failure with Yahweh's new kind of salvation, with a contrast between a former call to repent that went unheeded (Ezek. 18:31) and a declaration that Yahweh would enable such repentance, in very similar terms (36:26; see Joyce 1989: 57, 126–128). This logical progression is remarkably similar to the deuteronomic one in 10:16; 30:6.

The kind of thinking in such passages culminates in what may be called new-covenant theology, to use the term in Jer. 31:31. The essence of it is the law written on the heart (31:33), again conceived as the heart of Israel as such. Here, and in Jer. 32:39–40; Ezek. 36:26–27, the agency of Yahweh in bringing about the obedience of Israel is prominent. The concept is problematical in itself (how can obedience be compelled by an external agent, in any way that leaves personhood intact?), and the more so in works that devote so much energy and rhetoric to the need for the human party to love and obey in truth. In meeting this challenge of interpretation, writers are prone to pit the call to repent against the grace of Yahweh. (For Deut. 30:1–10 see Wolff 1976: 97–98, who finds different hands at work in vv. 1–2 and 10 and in v. 6; and for Jeremiah, see Unterman 1987: 176–178; W. L. Holladay 1989: 25–35.) Others argue for the necessity of repentance as a precondition of Yahweh's new salvation (Levenson 1975: 208; Craigie 1976a: 363; Schenker 1980: 96, 100–103). Still others emphasize the prior act of Yahweh, enabling repentance (P. Barker 1995: 177–178; Joyce 1989: 128).

Where the call to repent and the assertion of Yahweh's grace are polarized, it is unhelpful. The rhetorical structure of 30:1–10 is often neglected in these debates. As we saw, it effects a balance between Israel's repentance and Yahweh's grace that cannot be reduced. The need for repentance is absolute; so is the decision of Yahweh to act in grace and compassion. The reconciliation of these two imperatives in the Bible always requires travel through a certain moral terrain, from apostasy through reprobation to restoration. This typical journey asserts God's ultimate intention to do good to people in a way that respects and preserves the need for righteous behaviour. The same point emerges from the structure of the flood narrative (cf. Gen. 6:5–7 with 8:20–21) and the apostasy at Sinai (Exod. 32 – 34; note 34:9).

The future of Israel, therefore, is real yet spiritual in nature, and is brought about by the special act of God. These two strands of this great chapter may be brought together with some further reflection on vv. 11–14 in the light of Rom. 10:5–10, which points to a Christological fulfilment of the deuteronomic call to obedience. These verses mean that the perfect obedience to the Torah has been accomplished on Israel's behalf by the Messiah, Jesus, and also that fulfilment of it by faithful people is henceforth achieved by preaching and believing in him. This, according to N. T. Wright (1991: 240–246), is what is meant by 'Christ, the end of the law' (Rom. 10:4). The argument depends on the idea that Israel was bound to fail to keep the Torah so that, in the person of its

Messiah, it might suffer and die on behalf of all (1991: 243). The Pauline argument thus strikes two chords that we have heard in our reading of Deuteronomy: 1. the sense that Israel was incorrigibly unfaithful (9 – 10), and 2. that national election is bound to give way to the vindication of the 'righteous' under the pressure of the deuteronomic demand for love of Yahweh and obedience to him from the heart (see again on 7:9).

But does this reading make void the claim that Israel, as portrayed in the OT, can in any sense be a model for the regulation of modern societies, and indeed for the government of nations? Is there, after all, no political theology here? The answer to this begins with the fact that Israel as a historical people never came to embody the vision set out in these verses. Then we observe that the way Israel is held out as an example to the other nations in Deuteronomy includes not only its having a God who is near, and his excellent laws (4:6–8), but also their dereliction by the same God because of their resistance to him (29:22–28[21–27]). Deuteronomy therefore asks (with other OT literature) how the vision of nationhood under Yahweh's kingship may survive when nationhood itself has been necessarily given up.

Here O'Donovan's (1996: 79–80) concept of the role of the remnant and the faithful individual is helpful. The individualism that is often found in the literature that faces the fact of exile is not individualism in any of its modern senses, but rather focuses on the role of the faithful individuals in conserving the 'memory and hope' (undergirding their society) that can 'reach out towards the prospect of restructuring'. This is the point of the new covenant. Such restructuring can happen, furthermore, in the context of various, or 'plural', national traditions, and indeed cannot occur in a single over-arching governmental structure (O'Donovan 1996: 73).

DEUTERONOMY 31:1–30

Translation

[1]Moses went and spoke these things to all Israel: [2]'I am now 120 years old; I am no longer able to come and go; and the LORD has told me that I shall not cross the Jordan. [3]It is the LORD your God who will cross ahead of you, and he who will destroy these nations as you advance, and you will dispossess them. As for Joshua, he will cross before you, as the LORD has said. [4]And the LORD will do to them what he did to Sihon and Og, the Amorite kings, whom he destroyed, together with their land. [5]The LORD will give them over to you, and you are to do to them as I have charged you. [6]Be strong and have courage; do not give in to fear or panic because of them, for the LORD your God marches with you; he will not fail you or abandon you.'

[7]Moses called Joshua, and in the presence of all Israel said to him: 'Be strong and have courage, for you are to go with this people to the land the LORD promised on

oath to their forefathers that he would give them; you will enable them to inherit it. [8]But it is the LORD who marches before you; he will be with you, and will not fail or forsake you; do not give in to fear or dismay.'

[9]Moses wrote down this law and gave it to the priests, the sons of Levi, who carry the ark of the covenant of the LORD, and to all the elders of Israel. [10]And Moses gave them this instruction: 'Every seven years, in the year of the release of debts, at the Feast of Tabernacles, [11]when all Israelites come to appear before the LORD your God at the place he chooses, you must read this law aloud in the presence of all Israel. [12]Assemble the people – men, women, children and strangers who live with you in your cities – so that they may hear, and learn, and revere the LORD your God, and be careful to obey all the commands of this law. [13]And their children who do not yet know it will hear, and learn to revere the LORD your God as long as you live in the land you are crossing the Jordan to inherit.'

[14]The LORD said to Moses: 'Now the time is approaching when you will die. Call Joshua, and stand, both of you, at the Tent of Meeting, so that I can commission him.' So Moses and Joshua went and stood at the Tent of Meeting. [15]And the LORD appeared at the Tent in a pillar of cloud, and the pillar of cloud stood over the entrance to the Tent. [16]The LORD spoke to Moses: 'No sooner will you have gone to sleep with your forefathers than this people will play the harlot with the foreign gods in their midst, in the land they are entering. Forsaking me, they will break my covenant that I made with them. [17]Then my anger will rage against them, and I shall forsake them, hiding my presence from them. They will become a prey; great evils and distresses will befall them. Then they will say: "Surely it is because our God is not among us that these terrible things have happened to us?" [18]But I will hide my presence from them on that day, because of all the wickedness they have committed in turning away to other gods.

[19]'Now write down this Song for yourselves and teach it to the Israelites; teach them to sing it, so that it may be a witness for me against the Israelites. [20]When I have brought them to the land that I promised on oath to their forefathers, a land flowing with milk and honey, so that they may eat their fill and prosper, they will turn and worship other gods, rejecting me and breaking my covenant. [21]Then, when many catastrophes and distresses befall them, this Song will stand as a witness before them, for it will not pass from the memory of their descendants. And I know indeed the inclination that is already forming in them this day, before I have even brought them into the land I have promised on oath to their fathers.'

[22]So Moses wrote down this Song that day, and taught it to the Israelites.

[23]Then the LORD commissioned Joshua the son of Nun with these words: 'Be strong and have courage, for you will bring the Israelites to the land I have promised them; and I will be with you.'

[24]Now when Moses had finished writing down this law in a book, to the very end, [25]he instructed the Levites who carry the ark of the covenant of the LORD thus: [26]'Take this book of the covenant and lay it beside the ark of the covenant of the LORD your God, and let it remain there as a witness against you. [27]For I know your rebelliousness and hard-heartedness: even while I am still alive among you, this

very day, you have shown rebellion against the LORD; how much more will you do so after my death! [28]Assemble before me all the elders of your tribes, and your officers, so that I can declare these words aloud to them, and let me call heaven and earth to witness against them. [29]For I know that after my death you will become deeply corrupt, abandoning the way in which I charged you to walk. And in days to come evil will befall you because you have done evil in the LORD's sight, provoking him to anger by the things you do.'

[30]So Moses recited this Song in its entirety, in the hearing of the assembly of Israel.

Notes on the text

1. LXX, QL presuppose Hebr. *way^ekal*, 'and he finished', instead of MT *wayyēlek*, 'and he went'. A change from the former to the latter is improbable as a mere scribal error. Mayes (1979: 372–373) argues for the change as deliberate, in order to facilitate the introduction of new material, especially the Song of Moses. But MT makes sense as an introduction to Deut. 31 and should be kept. RSV translates 'So Moses continued to speak', which is possible, but not wholly suitable to the new content that follows.

11. *lērā'ôt*: 'to be seen' or 'to see'? Cf. 16:16, and the preference of many for qal in both these places: see GKC 51l; Morrow 1995: 160. GKC, however, allows that *lērā'ôt* is the correct form of the ni. inf. with preceding prep., eliding *h* (the expected ni. is *l^ehērā'ōt*).

14. MT has lit. 'in (*b^e*) the Tent of Meeting'; LXX modifies this to 'at the doors (of)' (*para tas thyras*), for theological reasons.

19. The verb 'write' is plural in MT, but is followed by 'teach' and 'place [it in their mouths = teach them to sing it]' in the singular. The confusion arises because Yahweh has called both Moses and Joshua to himself at the Tent of Meeting (14), but it is finally Moses alone who writes the Song down in response to this command (22). It is possible to read the consonantal text of v. 19 as plural throughout (*lamm^eduhā*; *śîmuhā*), as assumed by LXX (cf. 32:44). It is best to retain the plural in the initial command, but it is a moot point whether LXX should be followed throughout. Alternatively the first verb ('write') may be taken as singular, with Syr, but in that case *lākem* (lit. 'for yourselves'), must be emended to *l^ekā*, 'for yourself', or to *lāhem*, 'for them', sc. the Israelites.

'for yourselves': this phrase may be taken as a kind of 'middle voice'; it does not mean that the Song is primarily for Moses and Joshua.

21. The verse ends abruptly on 'that I swore/promised on oath'; LXX, Syr, SamP all assume the addition of 'to their fathers'; cf. vv. 7, 20 (and BHS).

23. 'and he commissioned': the subject is Yahweh, not Moses; the change of speaker is not signalled expressly, but is clear from the first-person speech in the last part of the verse (though LXX has altered this to third person in line with its understanding that Moses continues speaking here).

26. 'Take': the verb in MT is an infinitive absolute, which is used elsewhere in Deuteronomy as a command (5:12; 16:1). SamP, LXX and other ancient versions make the plural imperative explicit, in line with the next verb, 'place it'.

29. *qārā'ṯ*: an unusual form of the 3 f. sg. pf. qal, but see GKC 74g, and cf. Is. 7:14.

Form and structure

Deut. 31 – 32 forms a self-contained sub-section, in which the three themes of the transition from Moses' leadership to Joshua's, the deposition of the Book of the Law, and the Song of Witness dominate. There are new and unexpected features. The Tent of Meeting appears here for the first and only time in Deuteronomy. And the Song of Witness itself has not been previously prepared for, and comes in close connection with the topic of the Book of the Law, in a way that is at first sight barely integrated. Scholars have found evidence for a pre-history of the present text in various ways (e.g. Noth [1981: 35], who saw vv. 16–22 as post-Dtr). It is better to see the chapter as a deliberate construction, possibly out of a number of short speeches, the closest parallel to it in Deuteronomy being 1:6–42 (N. Lohfink [1962: 73; 1960: 120–123, esp. 123 nn. 1, 3] calls it a *Redemontage*, a 'montage' of speeches).

The chapter falls into the following divisions:

1–6	Moses tells the people that Joshua will continue the conquest, thus making express links with Deut. 1 – 3
7–8	Moses charges Joshua in the hearing of Israel
9–13	Moses gives the law to the priests and Levites and charges them to assemble the people and read it every seven years (in the year of slave release) at the feast of Tabernacles
14–23	Yahweh commands Moses and Joshua to write the Song of Witness against Israel, and commissions Joshua
24–29	Moses commands the Levites to deposit the Book of the Law, and to assemble the people for the reading of the Song
30	Moses recites the Song to the whole assembly of Israel

Verses 14–23 form a single unit, framed by the topic of Yahweh's charge to Joshua (14, 23). This gives five separate speech events (counting

vv. 1–8 as one), each identified by a different speaker–hearer relationship, in a concentric division, as follows:

A   Moses to the people, on Joshua's succession (1–8)
B   Moses to the Levites on the Book of the Law (9–13)
C   Yahweh to Moses and Joshua on the succession and the Song (14–23)
B' Moses to the Levites on the Book of the Law (24–29)
A' Moses to the people (the Song) (30)

This places the meeting of Yahweh with Moses and Joshua at the Tent of Meeting in the centre section, which also combines the two themes of the succession and the Song, which are respectively the themes of A and A'. The placing of the Book of the Law in the ark flanks the centre.

(N. Lohfink [1962: 74], with a slight variation from the above, finds an alternation of short and long speeches: 1–6; 7–8; 10–13; 14; 16–21; 23. The short speeches have as their theme the installation of Joshua. And the structure places the theophany of v. 14 in the middle of the whole chapter. The four longer speeches are also in a pattern, showing the role of the law in relation first to a bright future, and second to a dark future, the latter foreshadowing the Song. Deut. 31:24–30 together with 32:45–47 [which has no other counterpart before Deut. 29] frames the Song [N. Lohfink 1962: 75–76].)

The unifying factor in this structure is a focus on the means by which the Moab covenant will be realized in future generations of Israel. The succession of Joshua to Moses addresses the need for future leader/ mediators 'like Moses'; the deposit of the Book of the Law corresponds to the writing of the law on the stones on Ebal (27:3, 8), but mediates it permanently into the life of the community by splicing its reading into regularly recurring cultic events; and the Song too is conceived as a permanent witness to future generations of the people's tendency to forget the covenant with Yahweh.

Deut. 31, therefore, belongs closely with ch. 32, the Song itself (indeed, the Song is framed by 31:30 and 32:44–47 – slightly differently from Lohfink, above). It also looks back, of course, since it is the words of the Moab covenant (that is, the preaching of Moses in Deuteronomy) that are contained in the covenant document. This does not require that chs. 31 – 32 be taken as part of a separate unit comprising chs. 29 – 32 (against N. Lohfink 1962, for reasons given above, esp. on 29:1[28:69]). By the same token it is not necessary to read 31:1 as retrospective, adopting the reading of LXX, QL; (N. Lohfink 1960: 77–78; contrast Mayes 1979: 358–359). There is, however, an incongruity in the preparation for the Song in 31:16–22 and the Song itself, which is not wholly pessimistic, but turns from accusation to an announcement of the defeat of Israel's enemies, and then of salvation (32:28–35, 36–43). A parallel may be seen with the emphasis on the curse in chs. 27 – 29 prior to the salvation announced in 30:1–10.

Comment

31:1–8

1–2. It is striking that Moses 'went' to speak to Israel (see 'Notes on the text'), as he has been speaking to them all along. But the opening words are a first signal of the movements in this chapter, which involve changes in the conversation partners and physical movement around the Tent of Meeting (see 'Form and structure'). Verse 1 announces the speech to Israel in vv. 2–6, which connects directly with the narrative of the conquest of Transjordan in chs. 1 – 3. That account first takes up the theme of the death of Moses before entering the promised land; indeed, Yahweh's command that he should not go into it, and (consequently) the succession of Joshua as leader in its occupation (1:37–38; 3:23–28; cf. Josh. 1:2–9). Moses' reference, for the first time, to his great age and the incapacity it brings (2) foreshadows his approaching death (for '120 years', cf. Gen. 6:3; he is also ten years older than Joseph was at his death [Gen. 50:26], an age considered perfect in Egypt).

3–6. The passage focuses on the leadership of Joshua under Yahweh (note how the primacy of Yahweh's leadership is expressed in the chiastic pattern: 3a, Yahweh crosses; 3b, Joshua crosses; 7, Joshua goes; 8, Yahweh marches). Between these two sets of affirmations is placed the memory of the victories over Sihon and Og (4–6), a change to the plural address corresponding to this central passage of the argument, in which there is a further insistence that Yahweh will take charge of the conquest (5). Here the original command to Israel not to fear in the face of the land's inhabitants (1:21, 29) is repeated, with the added words, 'Be strong and have courage', which are actually typical of exhortations to Joshua (31:7, 23; Josh. 1:6–9; but cf. 11:8).

7–8. In vv. 7–8 Moses then 'calls' Joshua (maintaining the sense of action and movement in the series of events), and commissions him in the hearing of all the people, as he was instructed to do in 3:28, a commission that Yahweh will confirm in v. 23.

31:9–13

This section for the first time brings the topics of the ark of the covenant and the Book of the Law together with that of the 'place [the LORD] chooses' (11 – the Levitical priests are already associated with this in 17:9). The following section (14–23) will add to this the tradition of the

Tent of Meeting. The purpose of the present section is to institutionalize the Book of the Law in the worship life of Israel.

9. The focus falls first on the Book of the Law (9). The existence of this book has been presupposed since 17:18 (cf. 28:58, 61), but this is the first explicit statement that Moses wrote it. It is not implied that he writes it only at this point, but, rather, attention is drawn to the writing as part of the series of events that constitutes the establishment of the covenant for all time in Israel, the writing of the terms of covenants being a constituent part of them (Weinfeld 1972: 63–64; Sonnet [1997: 137–138] argues that the beginning of v. 9 should be translated with a pluperfect: 'Moses had written...'). The Book of the Law is additional to the two stone tablets that are kept in the ark of the covenant (10:1–5); it corresponds to the Moab covenant just as they correspond to the Horeb covenant, the juxtaposition of these two emblems symbolizing the close connection between the covenants themselves. There is also a correspondence between God's writing on the tablets and Moses' writing of the Book of the Law (Sonnet 1997: 138). The Levitical priests have charge of the ark, and therefore of the tablets (10:8–9), and now of the Book of the Law (cf. 17:18). The addition of 'and all the elders of Israel' secures the responsibility of the leadership of Israel for implementing the law (cf. 21:2; 27:1).

10–13. There follows a specific provision for perpetuating the law in Israel. Every seventh year, at the feast of Tabernacles (16:16) in the year of the release of debts (15:1), there should be a ceremonial reading of the law. It is a gathering of 'all Israel', an 'assembly', as indicated by the verb 'assemble' (12; *qhl*, hiph., related to the noun *qāhāl*; 23:1). The enumeration of men, women, children and aliens (cf. 29:10–11[9–10]) goes beyond the command in 16:16, and may imply a special obligation on all and sundry to appear in the seventh year.

The purpose of the reading is no different from the general aim of the preaching in Deuteronomy, and the regular teaching that it advocates (6:6–9). Such teaching is not replaced by this major reaffirmation every seven years. The point is to build the law into the worshipping life of the community in perpetuity, so that those who have not previously 'known' (13) may not fail to do so. The institution of the seven-year reading would provide at least two memorable occasions in the formative years of every Israelite. If it was also the occasion of some enactment in relation to the release of debts, this would have a further impressive, demonstrative purpose.

31:14–23

14–15. The meeting of Moses and Joshua with Yahweh at the Tent of Meeting is quite new in Deuteronomy, but it is a high point in the present series of events (see 'Form and structure'). The theme of the transition from Moses' leadership to Joshua's (14, echoing v. 2) is a bell toll for the moment of entry to the land, when this new generation will carry into its proper arena the responsibility for keeping the covenant. The placing of Moses and Joshua at the Tent of Meeting recalls how Moses had formerly met Yahweh there, the pillar of cloud signifying the divine presence (Exod. 33:7-11; Num. 1:1). The Tent of Meeting also symbolized Yahweh's presence with the people when they were on the march, organized in military formation (Exod. 40:34-38; Num. 2:2, 17), and it was the place of theophany to all Israel (Num. 14:10). The appearance of the Tent of Meeting at this point is important for an understanding of Deuteronomy's concept of the presence of Yahweh, as it is brought into connection with the topic of the ark and indeed of the chosen place (cf. vv. 9-11; and see 'Explanation').

The presence of Joshua with Moses was foreshadowed at Exod. 33:11, where he is simply Moses' servant, and at Exod. 24:13, where the servant apparently accompanied his master at the Sinai theophany when all others were excluded. The Pentateuchal narrative, as well as Deuteronomy itself, has prepared us for Joshua's succession (Num. 27:12-23; cf. Deut. 1:38; 3:28). The present event, therefore, is highly climactic in the flow of Deuteronomy (because of both presence and succession ideas); it also points forward to the continuing narrative in Josh. 1:1-9.

16-18. In addressing Moses and Joshua, Yahweh now declares directly that Israel will fail to keep the covenant in the land. This note has been prepared for in 9:4-6 and the golden-calf narrative that followed (9:6 – 10:5), and suggested in 30:1, where it was assumed that the 'curse' would follow the 'blessing'. The immediacy with which the people will turn to foreign gods after Moses' death is reminiscent of the apostasy of the golden calf itself (Exod. 32:1; Deut. 9:12) and of the pattern of rapid relapse in Judges (8:33). The sin of apostasy is characterized (only here in Deuteronomy) as 'playing the harlot', a term that is more frequent in Hosea and Ezekiel (but cf. Judg. 2:17; 8:27, 33). Israel's forsaking of Yahweh is met by his corresponding forsaking of them, a perfect negation of covenant mutuality, and by his 'hiding his face', a concept found in Deuteronomy only here and at 32:20 (being more common in the Psalms, e.g. 10:11). Again it perfectly negates the meeting of Israel 'before the LORD' (i.e. 'before his face') that characterizes the worship events at the chosen place (12:7). The topic of his 'anger' recalls Deut. 29; indeed, these verses are an abbreviated repetition of the themes of that chapter (cf. 29:25-28[24-27]). Verse 17 makes an express link with the curses of chs. 28 – 29.

19-23. Yahweh's speech now introduces the Song, which will follow in ch. 32, by telling Moses and Joshua to write it. The plural command, echoed in 32:44, attributes responsibility to both, even though the chain of commands continues in the singular and Moses alone writes it (22; and see 'Notes on the text'; see there also on 'for yourselves', v. 19). The Song is conceived as a witness against the people. In Deut. 4:26; 30:19; 31:28, the heavens and earth are called as witnesses to the covenant, and this is echoed in the opening words of the Song itself (32:1). The Song is thus an additional element drawn into this important aspect of covenant verification.

Because it is introduced suddenly and without warning to Deuteronomy, and because the Book of the Law is the primary means of securing future generations' knowledge of the covenant and their obedience to it, the role of the Song is not easy to define and has often been thought to represent an independent tradition that has been built into Deuteronomy. Sonnet (1997: 164–165) makes the interesting suggestion, however, that the Song is interpolated into the Book of the Law. The two 'entrustings' of the Book, therefore, in v. 9 and vv. 25–26, correspond to two separate purposes of the law: 1. that of communication, secured by its public reading, and 2. that of witness, secured by its placing with the ark.

The Song derives from the Book of the Law in its prophetic tone, its perception of the unfolding history of the people, and its enshrining of the premiss that Israel will break the covenant. The inevitability of their failure is signalled by the word 'inclination' (yēṣer, 21) used only here in Deuteronomy. The word has the connotation of 'forming' something, and it is used elsewhere to characterize the tendency of humans beings to do evil (Gen. 6:5; 8:21). This introduction to the Song bears only on the announcement of Israel's apostasy and consequent punishment. In fact, the Song will look beyond these things to Yahweh's renewed salvation (32:36–43), just as Deut. 30:1–10 did, and this is also ultimately part of its witness (Sonnet 1997: 177). However, the passage finishes on an up beat, by recording Yahweh's commission to Joshua to take the people into the land (23; see 'Notes on the text'), his exhortation to him to be strong, and his promise of his presence (cf. Josh. 1:6). The command to be strong was given first to the whole people (6), but is now focused on Joshua. And the promise of presence, 'I will be with you', echoes the commission to Moses in Exod. 3:12 (the prelude to the giving of the name 'Yahweh', Exod. 3:14). This commission relates only to the military task of taking the land; the command to distribute it comes later at Josh. 13:1–7 (N. Lohfink 1990b).

31:24–30

The addressees in these verses seem to fluctuate. The passage opens with a plural address to the Levites (26; see 'Notes on the text'), resumed in v. 28, when they are told to assemble the elders and officers for the declamation of the Song. This is interrupted in vv. 26c–27 with words in singular address that are best understood in relation to the people as a whole, an address that in turn is resumed in v. 29, though now in the plural. The passage thus mingles instructions to the leaders in Israel to prepare for future readings of the law (as in vv. 10–13), and to hear the Song imminently, with motivations whose real hearers are the people as a whole.

The passage splices together the themes of the Book of the Law and the Song (cf. the juxtaposition in 32:44–47). The instruction regarding the book continues from vv. 9–13. There Moses wrote the law; now he does so 'to the very end' (24). This is not a second 'finishing' of the job; rather, the narrative is resumed with an emphasis on the completeness of the work (cf. 4:2; it must be entirely heeded, and not added to). In vv. 9–13 the Levites and elders were commanded to read the law every seven years at the chosen place; this is now augmented by a further command to the Levites to place the book of the law *beside* the ark of the covenant (not *in* it, as with the tablets of the Horeb covenant). The document of the covenant is thus placed in a specially designed, 'sacred' place, as were treaty documents (Baltzer 1971: 88 n. 34). By the same token, the book participates in the theme of 'witness' (26). This command is followed by the motif of Israel's congenital rebelliousness, drawn from the passage about the Song (26–29; cf. vv. 16–20).

Finally (30), Moses is said to recite the Song. If the book is the document of the covenant, the Song may be said to correspond to formal accusations made by overlords against vassals (J. A. Thompson 1974: 295).

Explanation

The narrative framework resumes in this chapter, centring themes from Deut. 1 – 3, namely the progress towards full occupation of the land after the initial conquests in Transjordan (31:3–5), Moses' imminent death (2, 16) and the need for Joshua to succeed him as military leader (7–8, 14–23). Yahweh's guidance of Israel and his pre-eminence in the victories ahead are at the heart of the scenario (3–5; cf. 1:30–33). Yet his sovereignty in these matters does not diminish the responsibility of Israel and its leaders to embrace the task, showing faith and courage (6). The issue aired in ch. 1, therefore, is raised again here, though without doubting at this stage that the task would be done.

Joshua, already known in the tradition as one of the two faithful spies who believed, against the common report, that the land could be taken with Yahweh's help (1:36–38; cf. Num. 14:4–10), is brought forward as the one who will accomplish what Moses could not do. In this way God's power to carry out his will is brought together with the need for active human trust in him. This continues to be a theme of the narrative of the people's history, symbolized famously in the taking of Jericho (Josh. 6), and in the exploration of trusting action in the story of Gideon (Judg. 6 – 8).

The chapter is crucial for an understanding of the divine presence. To the concept of Yahweh 'going before' his people is added that of his appearing to them in a cultic setting. Motifs of ark, chosen place and Tent of Meeting are brought together. These have often been wrongly set at odds with each other in OT scholarship. An essay of G. von Rad (1966: 103–124) made popular the view that Tent and ark represented quite different concepts of presence. The former was thought to symbolize mobility and transcendence, and therefore to be a place of occasional meetings between God and people. The texts concerning the Tent in the wilderness narratives, together with passages such as 2 Sam. 7:5–7, were cited in evidence. The ark, in contrast, with imagery that reminded of enthronement, symbolized God's permanent dwelling presence. In von Rad's view, these two concepts represented opposed theological traditions, which were not assimilated in Deuteronomy (since he thought the Tent tradition was not properly at home there), but only later in the priestly concept of the tabernacle, which had the ark at its centre. This approach to the OT texts corresponds to a theological issue, namely the relationship between God's immanence (his presence within the world) and his transcendence (his cosmic freedom, separateness from the world).

However, the different symbols of presence do not neatly match these different concepts. In the OT, no incompatibility is felt between the ideas of God's 'dwelling' with his people and his 'coming to meet' them. (See Jenson's remarks: 1992: 112–114. In important studies, Blum [1990: 297–299], who cites Exod. 29:42–46, rejects the polarizing interpretation of von Rad and others, and argues that in the priestly parts of the Pentateuch the terms for God's presence – tent, ark, glory, meeting, tabernacling [škn] – belong together in a complex structure; and Janowski [1993: 299–301] rightly insists that the theology of presence must emerge from the narrative [he refers to the priestly narrative], rather than supposing that the symbols themselves have permanent fixed meanings.)

Deuteronomy, far from campaigning for transcendence in contrast to dwelling presence (see 'Explanation', on ch. 12), brings the two kinds of idea together quite naturally here. I have argued earlier that the typical deuteronomic phrase for the place of worship ('the place the LORD your God will choose, to put his name there') is consistent with the book's insistence on the need for Israel perpetually to renew the covenant at different times and places (this corresponds to Yahweh's freedom, or transcendence). At the same time, it pictures Israel actually meeting Yahweh ('before the LORD'; corresponding to his immmanence). Both the ark and the Tent of Meeting can be drawn naturally into this theology. The ark's significance in the context is, in any case, not divine immanence as such, but rather the permanent location of the tokens of the covenant. And the Tent is the suitable location, on the plains of Moab, for a special meeting with Yahweh for the purpose of the charge to Joshua and for the declamation of the Song. It has echoes of the encounter at Horeb (4:10; cf. the command to 'assemble' the people/elders, as at 31:28).

Finally, the present chapter is the place where provision is made for the realization of the covenant within the regular life of the community for all time. As we saw in 'Form and structure', the divine encounter with Moses and Joshua is structurally at the centre of the chapter. The charge to Joshua at the Tent is flanked by sections concerning the Book of the Law. The recipe for possessing the land in perpetuity therefore includes 1. persons who are willing and able to keep the covenant, and 2. institutional fixed points that have the function of recalling people constantly to their commitment.

DEUTERONOMY 32:1–52

Translation

> [1]Hear, O heavens, and I will speak;
>> let the earth hear the words of my mouth.
> [2]Let my teaching fall like the rain,
>> my speech distil like the dew;
> like fine rain on new grass,
>> like drenching showers on green growth.
> [3]I will proclaim the name of the LORD;
>> give greatness to our God!
>
> [4]The Rock, his work is perfect;
>> all his ways are justice;
> a God of faithfulness, without guile;
>> righteous and true is he.
> [5]Their flaw has made them false to him,
>> so that they are no longer his children;
> Perverse and crooked generation!
> [6]Should you requite the LORD like this?
>> A people not wise, but foolish!
> Is he not your father who created you?
>> Did he not form you, and make you stand?
> [7]Remember the days long past;
>> consider the ancestral times;
> ask your father and he will tell you;
>> your elders will relate them to you.
> [8]When the Most High brought nations to their lands,
>> apportioning the human race,
> he set the peoples' boundaries
>> according to the number of the sons of God.
> [9]For the LORD's portion is his people,
>> Jacob his special inheritance.

¹⁰He found him in a wasteland,
    in a place unformed, a howling desert;
  he encircled him, cared for him,
    guarded him as the apple of his eye;
¹¹as an eagle stirs up its nest
    and hovers over its young,
  spreads his wings to catch them,
    and bears them up on his pinions,
¹²the Lord alone led his people;
    no strange god was with him.
¹³He made them soar on the high places of the land;
    they ate the good yield of the fields;
  he fed them with fruit from rock,
    and with oil from flinty rock;
¹⁴with curds from the herd and milk from the flock,
    with the fat of lambs,
  with rams and goats of Bashan,
    and with choicest grains of wheat;
  you drank wine from the blood of the grape.

¹⁵But Jacob ate his fill; Jeshurun grew fat and kicked;
    full and overfed, you became unruly;
  they forsook God, who made them,
    and scorned the Rock of their salvation.
¹⁶They stirred his jealousy with foreign gods,
    they angered him with abominations;
¹⁷they sacrificed to demons – no gods at all!
    They turned to gods they had not known,
    to new ones recently arrived, which their forefathers had not
        worshipped.
¹⁸You forsook the Rock, who begot you,
    you forgot God, who gave you birth.

¹⁹The Lord looked and recoiled,
    because of the provocation of his sons and daughters,
²⁰and he said, 'I will hide my Presence from them,
    and see what their end will be;
  for they are a fickle brood,
    children in whom there is no faithfulness.
²¹As they have roused my jealousy with what is no god,
    and angered me with their empty idols,
  so I will make them jealous with what is no people,
    and provoke them with a foolish nation.
²²For a fire is kindled by my anger
    which will blaze to the depths of Sheol;

it will devour both land and produce,
   and ignite the mountains' roots.
²³I will heap disasters on them,
   shoot all my bolts against them.
²⁴They will be weak with hunger,
   consumed by pestilence and bitter plague;
I shall pursue them with the teeth of savage beasts,
   and the venom of creatures that crawl in the dust.
²⁵In the street the sword shall bereave,
   and terror shall be within;
neither youth nor maiden shall escape,
   neither infant nor aged.

²⁶I would have swept them away,
   rooted them out of human memory,
²⁷were it not that I feared the provocation of the enemy,
   lest their foes distort the truth
and say, 'Our great strength, not the LORD, accomplished all this.'
²⁸They are a nation that lacks good counsel;
   there is no discernment in them.
²⁹If only they had wisdom to see these things,
   they would understand what their end must be!
³⁰How can one man chase a thousand,
   or two see off a host,
unless their Rock had sold them,
   unless the LORD had given them up?
³¹For their rock is not like our Rock,
   as even our enemies concede.
³²Their vine is from the vine of Sodom,
   and the vineyards of Gomorrah;
their grapes are poisonous grapes,
   and clusters bitter to taste.
³³Their wine is the venom of serpents,
   the cruel poison of asps.
³⁴Am I not holding all this back,
   sealed up in my storehouses,
³⁵till the day of vengeance and recompense,
   the time when their foot slips?
For the day of their calamity is near;
   their destiny hastens on.

³⁶The LORD will judge his people;
   he will have compassion on his servants,
for he will see that their strength has gone,
   and none remains, bond or free.

³⁷Then he will say: 'Where now are their gods,
    the rock to which they fled,
³⁸the gods that ate the fat of their sacrifices
    and drank the wine they offered?
  Let them rise and help you!
  Let them be your shelter now!
³⁹See now that I, I am He;
    there is no other god beside me.
  It is I who bring death and give life;
    I crush, but it is I who heal;
    no-one escapes from my hand!
⁴⁰For I raise my hand to heaven and declare:
    As I live for ever,
⁴¹when I whet my flashing sword,
    and my hand takes hold on judgment,
  I will take vengeance on my enemies,
    and requite my foes.
⁴²I will make my arrows drunk with blood,
    while my sword gorges flesh,
  – the blood of slain and captive,
    the heads of enemy princes.
⁴³Praise his people, O nations,
    for he will avenge the blood of his
        servants;
  he will repay his enemies,
    and atone for the land of his people.

⁴⁴So Moses, together with Joshua the son of Nun, proclaimed all the words of this Song in the hearing of the people. ⁴⁵When he had finished proclaiming all these words to all Israel, ⁴⁶he said to them: 'Take to heart all the words I use in witness against you this day; charge your children with them, so that they observe carefully all the commands this law. ⁴⁷For these are no empty words for you; they are your life; and by virtue of them you will have long life in the land you are crossing the Jordan to possess.'

⁴⁸On that same day the LORD said to Moses: ⁴⁹'Go up this mountain of the Abarim, that is, Mt Nebo in Moab opposite Jericho; and look upon the land of Canaan, which I am giving to the Israelites as their possession. ⁵⁰There on that mountain that you ascend, you will die, and be taken to your forefathers, just as Aaron your brother died on Mt Hor, and was taken to be with his ancestors. ⁵¹This is because you both broke faith with me, there among the Israelites, by the waters of Meribah-Kadesh in the wilderness of Zin, failing to proclaim my holiness in the presence of the Israelites. ⁵²You shall indeed see the land from outside it; but you shall not go over there, to the land I am giving to the Israelites.'

Notes on the text

4. 'The Rock': the term is regularly in parallelism with names of God in the chapter (cf. vv. 15, 18, 30); LXX simply translates *theos* here and throughout (avoiding the strong physical metaphor for theological reasons). The translation adopted here (cf. NRSV) takes the syntax as a case of *casus pendens*, which makes it unnecessary to fill the word out into a clause: 'He is the Rock' (NIV); but see GKC 126c; cf. Ps. 18:30[31].
5. The translation offered is an attempt to make sense of MT, taking *mûmām* as subject of *šiḥēt*, and *lō' bānāyw* as complement. However, the line is difficult and has been variously reconstructed. The ancient versions take the verb as plural. This makes it possible to take 'not his children' (in an idiom like Hos. 1:6, 9; cf. GKC 152e) as subject, giving, for example, 'those who are not his children have dealt falsely with him', perhaps taking *mûmām* as 'by their fault'; see S. R. Driver 1895: 352 for a fuller note.
6. The interrogative particle (*hᵃ*) has been separated in MT from the following preposition *lᵉ* and divine name, perhaps to make clear that the reading is not *hal*, which may be an older form of the particle (GKC 100i and n.).
The verb *qānâ*, meaning 'create', is known also from Ugarit in the phrase *'el qn' arṣ* (Cross 1973: 50–51). The *dagesh* in *qānekā* ('who created you') is *dagesh euphonicum* (i.e. to help the reading).
7. 'days' (*yᵉmôṯ*): this form of the plural of *yôm* is found only here and at Ps. 90:15, both times in the construct.
8. *bᵉhanḥēl*, 'when he brought (to inherit)', and *yaṣṣēḇ*, 'he set', appear instead of the expected *bᵉhanḥîl*, *yaṣṣîb*. As the two forms are grammatically different, they may have been chosen for euphonic reasons (GKC 109k).
The imperfect (*yaṣṣēḇ*) is the first of a series, continuing in vv. 10–14, which refer to actions in the past.
MT has 'sons of Israel', while LXX, QL have 'sons of God' (*bᵉnê 'ᵉlōhîm*, 4QDeutʲ; 4QDeutᵠ has *bᵉnê 'ēl*, but is only partly legible, and may also have had the fuller *'ᵉlōhîm*; van der Kooij 1994: 93–94 n. 2). The terms *bᵉnê 'ēlîm* and *'ēlîm* are known at Ugarit, and refer to the lesser gods that surround the high god El. *bᵉnê 'ēlîm* (Ps. 29:1), *bᵉnê (hā)'ᵉlōhîm* (Gen. 6:2) and *bᵉnê 'elyôn* (Ps. 82:6) are known in the OT, as reflections of the more overtly polytheistic Canaanite forms. The textual question here is whether MT alters an original reading preserved by LXX, or LXX altered the MT version. If the former is the case, MT presumably altered the text it found because it regarded it as dangerously polytheistic. If the latter, an original 'sons of Israel' has been changed to 'sons of God', a move which is probably harder to account for. (If MT's 'sons of Israel' is original, it might be read simply as a statement that Yahweh apportioned land to Israel, in the context of the creator's distribution of land to all nations, according to their size and need; so S. R. Driver 1895: 355–356.) (See also on v. 43.)

10. 'he found': see on v. 8c. SamP has *y^e'amm^esēhû*, 'he strengthened, sustained' (NRSV) instead of *yimṣā'ēhû*, 'he found'. The difference involves only the transposition of an *'alep*. Either makes good sense.

The *-enhû* endings in *y^esōb^ebenhû, yiṣṣ^erenhû*, are cases of the *nun energicum*, which more usually appears in a double *nun* (*-ennu*); the point of the *nun energicum* is to lay stress on the verb (GKC 58i, k).

11. 'stirs up' is MT *yā'îr*. LXX *skepasai* implies *yiṣṣōr* (*nṣr*), 'he watches over', but MT can be followed.

15. 'But Jacob ate his fill': this follows SamP, LXX (*wayyō'kal ya'^aqōb wayyiśba'*); the phrase echoes 31:20, and therefore is probably authentic (Braulik 1992a: 230).

The *dagesh* in *kāśîṯâ*, 'you became unruly', is *dagesh euphonicum*; cf. v. 6.

19. *ka'as* is taken here as 'provocation', as in v. 27, where it is said of Yahweh's enemies.

23. *'aspeh*, as pointed in MT, is *sph*, hiph., '(cause to) sweep away'; it is usually repointed to *'ôsîp̄â*, *ysp*, hiph., 'to add', or, as here, 'to heap' (*HALAT* 3:721).

26. *'ap̄'êhem*: if the form is correct, it is a unique occurrence of this suffix form, normally possessive, as a verbal suffix; hence the variations in the ancient versions, and the proposed alterations in *BHS*. The verb itself (*p'h*, hiph., by inference 'sweep away'), again if the reading is right, is a *hapax legomenon*. The best alternative proposal is perhaps *'ep̄es hēm*, 'an end of them' (*HALAT* 3:858).

27. 'were it not that' (*lûlê*), the following imperfect probably denoting something habitual (GKC 159y).

On the archaic suffix *ṣārêmô*, 'their foes', see GKC 91l. The reference is to *Israel's* enemies; it is not necessary to read 'our enemies' (*ṣārênû*, SamP and LXX). Cf. vv. 32, 37, 38.

28. *'ōbaḏ*, 'that lacks', 'lacking in': the construct (of *'ōbeḏ*) is unusually pointed with *pathaḥ*.

31. 'as even our enemies concede': lit. 'our enemies are judges' (*HALAT* 3:880); the *waw* gives a sequence that produces emphasis (GKC 156b, n. 1, opposing the view that the clause is circumstantial, thus contrary to S. R. Driver 1895: 372).

32. See on v. 27b.

The *dagesh* in *'inn^ebê*, 'grapes of (poison)', is *dagesh forte dirimens*, intended to make the *shewa* more audible (GKC 20h).

35. SamP and LXX read *l^eyôm*, 'till the day of', instead of MT's 'to me (*lî*) (belong)'. Analogies in Hos. 9:7; Is. 34:8 favour this, as does the syntax in the present line. The same texts also make it preferable to read *šillûm*, 'recompense' (noun) instead of MT's verbal form *šillēm*, which follows badly from the noun *nāqām*, 'vengeance' (cf. Hos. 9:7; Is. 34:8); otherwise *šillēm* may itself be a rare noun form (GKC 52o).

For the masculine singular verb followed by a feminine plural noun see

GKC 145o. The plural noun is perhaps felt to convey a singular idea (cf. GKC 145a).

37-38. See on v. 27.

37. Note the reappearance of the original *yod* of the stem of the 3-*he* verb *ḥsh*, perhaps a poetic feature.

41. 'When I whet ... I will take vengeance': for the sequence of tenses see GKC 159n; also 159l, on '*im* as introducing a conditional sentence in which the condition is regarded as fulfilled or likely to be fulfilled. The second verb in the protasis ('and ... takes hold') is simple *waw* + impf. in MT; *BHS* advises reading *waw*-consecutive, which may be the best explanation for the tense.

42. 'princes' (*pera'*, pl. *p*^{e}*rā'ôt*): otherwise 'long-haired ones', perhaps signifying wildness.

43. LXX and QL attest to longer forms of v. 43. 4QDeut^q has (instead of 'Rejoice [with] his people...'), 'Rejoice, O heavens, with him, and bow down to him, all you gods'; it has *bānāyw*, 'his sons', instead of '^{a}*ḇaḏāyw*, 'his servants'; it adds (after 'he will repay his enemies') 'and requite those who hate him'; and it has 'he will atone for the land of his people', instead of 'his people will atone for his/its land'. LXX also has these phrases, and, in addition (after 'sons of God'), 'rejoice, O nations, with his people, and let all the angels of God be strengthened in him'. LXX is probably expansive, so the issue lies between MT and QL. As in v. 8, it is a moot point whether MT alters an original represented by QL or *vice versa*. The echo of v. 1, 'heavens', produced by QL's 'Rejoice, O heavens' might as well be a secondary invention (*pace* van der Kooij 1994: 97). While QL's six lines may represent a better poetic balance than MT's four (van der Kooij 1994: 98-99), it is not certainly so (MT's four lines show the chiasmus: '*am – nāqām – nāqām – 'am*). The difference between the two versions is that QL places the praise of God's justice in heaven, while MT locates it on earth. MT has a stronger doctrine of the place of Israel in Yahweh's plans. In the translation, MT is followed, except in the final line, where QL's 'land of his people' is better than MT's difficult 'his land, his people', and has extra support from SamP. (For Bogaert's [1985] understanding of QL's 'blood of his sons', see 'Comment'.)

Form and structure

Together with the Blessing of Moses (ch. 33), the Song forms a climax to the book of Deuteronomy in poetic form. (See Watts 1992 for this as a feature of literature designed to be read aloud.) The fact that the form is strikingly different from that of the greater part of the book has led to the view that these sections are not strictly deuteronomic. Noth (1981: 35) thought they were post-Dtr additions made as part of the attempt to relate Deuteronomy to the Tetrateuch. Others point to similarities in thought and content to Deuteronomy, Carlson (1964: 236–237), for example, noting the correspondence in the book between: 1. the Song as witness and the idea of oral transmission, and 2. the elders' responsibility for it (5:23; 19:12; 27:1; 31:9; Carlson 1964: 230–232). The pessimism about Israel's covenantal performance in the Song also echoes elements in Deut. 8 – 9 (cf. Judg. 3:7; 1 Sam. 12:9; 2 Kgs. 17:7ff.; Carlson 1964: 233).

The Song has a coherent development, but it can be divided into seven stanzas as follows:

1–3	Opening declaration, call of witnesses
4–9	Yahweh's faithfulness, Israel's unfaithfulness
10–14	Elaboration of Yahweh's care for Israel
15–18	Israel's apostasy
19–25	Yahweh's decision to judge them
26–35	He relents, because of their folly
36–43	He will finally vindicate himself, and save his people

The structure of the Song partially resembles the well-known ANE lawsuit pattern; that is, an overlord's accusation that a vassal has infringed the conditions of the treaty between them (Huffmon 1959). The form is attested in several prophetic books (Hos. 4:1–6; Mic. 6:1–5; Jer. 2:4–13). It involves the call of witnesses, an accusation, an account of the overlord's benevolence, an affirmation that the covenant has been broken, and an announcement of punishment. These elements correspond to items 1–5 in the outline above. The Song has encompassed this pattern without merely conforming to it (Luyten 1985: 347). Most notably, it continues after the declaration of intent to judge Israel, with two further sections, in which Yahweh decides not to judge them finally after all, but rather to turn his anger against their oppressors, and to bring about a restoration of his people.

The Song has been assigned widely varying dates, from pre-monarchical to post-exilic, on formal, linguistic, traditio-historical and theological criteria. The formal analogy with the lawsuit pattern is not conclusive for an early date, as the same pattern was used by the prophets, including Jeremiah. The language of the poem shows freedom and individuality on the one hand, and strong similarities to other parts of the OT on the other, and is probably inconclusive for dating. Traditio-historically, it has been thought that the exodus from Egypt is not clearly present, and therefore that the poem might come from a time before that tradition had become important in Israel (before Hosea). Neither does the exile appear explicitly, since the divine decision to punish is apparently reversed without a specific announcement of exile (26–35), and this has been taken as a sign of pre-exilic composition. The idea of Yahweh's wrath turning against Israel's oppressors because of their self-glorification (27) also occurs in Is. 10:5–19, and is a major theme in Jeremiah (chs. 25; 50 – 51). Finally, there are specific analogies of style and thought with Is. 40 – 55 (normally dated to the exile), and also with wisdom literature. The numerous affinities with prophetic literature led to its being called by an older critic 'a compendium of prophetical theology' (Cornill 1891: 13.5; cited in S. R. Driver 1895: 346). It does not follow, however, that the Song is derivative from the prophets (Mendenhall 1993: 171).

There are also similarities with several Psalms, including 50, 78, 95 and 105 – 106. Of these, the most interesting analogy is with Ps. 78, with which it shares not only a similar opening, but also the theme of the people's chronic unfaithfulness to faithful Yahweh, and the name 'Most High' (Elyon) for God, as well as the metaphor of the 'Rock' (Ps. 78:35). Ps. 78 can be dated to the time before the fall of the northern kingdom, because its ending appears not to know of that event (Day 1986b). Deut. 32 mentions neither monarchy nor exile, and for that reason has been thought early (eleventh cent., according to Mendenhall 1993: 171). However, these criteria are not cogent in themselves, and need to await the detailed interpretation. (Linguistic criteria have also been taken to prove the early date of the Song [Robertson 1972], though his arguments have been challenged by Young [1993].)

Comment

32:1–3

1–2. Moses' call to the heavens and earth to witness his words has echoes of both wisdom (cf. Ps. 49:1–4[2–5]; 78:1–3; Job 43:2) and prophecy (Is. 1:2). Witness is an indispensable part of any proof, and specifically of the lawsuit pattern that the Song reflects. Here, the arena of witness is the whole created order. The theme of the Song is closer to prophecy than to other forms, and Moses is the archetypal prophet (cf. 18:15–18). Yet the call to obedience runs through virtually all OT literature, and here the prophetic message is announced as 'my teaching' (*liqḥî*, lit. 'what I have acquired'; cf. Prov. 1:5), making Moses a wisdom teacher too, bringing a message of life (Deut. 32:2).

3. He will at the same time 'proclaim the name of the LORD', in an echo of the Shema (6:4). Deuteronomy has rooted all its teaching in this affirmation that Yahweh is Israel's God. To proclaim his name means both to affirm his faithfulness (cf. Exod. 3:14–15) and to call the people to obedience to his covenant.

32:4–9

4. The proclamation of Yahweh's name is now followed by the attribution

of another name, 'the Rock' (4). It is sometimes thought that the sense of
v. 3 is that Moses will now pronounce this new name for Yahweh (Braulik
1992a: 228). I think this unlikely because the term is also used, scathingly,
of a hypothetical other god in vv. 31, 37, suggesting a generic usage.
However, 'the Rock' is an important epithet for Yahweh throughout the
Song (cf. vv. 4, 15, 18, 30, 31; cf. v. 13, and also 'Notes on the text'). Rock
is a natural metaphor in a hot and dangerous land, offering both shade and
hiding. It stands as a symbol of Yahweh's strength and trustworthiness.
His perfect 'work', which will be elaborated in the Song, is his care for his
people Israel; 'his ways are justice' means that all he does is right.
Faithfulness, truth and justice are in his character.

5–6. The accusation that Israel has been false is all the more telling for
Yahweh's truth and trustworthiness. These 'children' (or 'sons') have
become 'false' (or 'corrupt'), so that they are 'not children' (like Hosea's
'not my people', Hos. 1:9; for a similar thought see also Is. 1:2–4; and
'Notes on the text'). The accusation paints the people as having a strong
tendency to be unfaithful ('their flaw ... perverse ... crooked'). Their
rebellion is also folly (a concept from the 'wisdom' realm), that is, moral
as well as intellectual. This rebellion flies in the face of Yahweh's strong
attachment to them.

The idea of Yahweh as 'father' and Israel as 'son' is embedded in the
narrative of his making them his people (Exod. 4:22), and echoed in Hos.
11:1. (For the king as a son of the god, esp. in Egypt, see Keel 1997: 247–
268.) Sonship of God (or the god) is a status conferred (cf. Ps. 2:7). His
'creation' of Israel echoes the epithet in Gen. 14:19, 22, where God (El
Elyon) is 'creator of heaven and earth'. (The same epithet was applied in
Canaan to El; Cross 1973: 50–51.) Here, Israel's becoming Yahweh's
people is pictured as a creation (cf. Exod. 15:16 [where the verb *qānâ* is
translated 'bought', NIV]; and for a similar idea, Is. 43:21 [*yṣr*]). The
following verb ('make you stand', *kûn*, polel) can also connote creation of
the world (Ps. 8:3[4]; 24:2), and can be applied to the 'establishment' of
Zion as Yahweh's chosen city (Ps. 48:8[9]). The sense here is 'sustaining'.
Both the election and establishing of Israel as such are in view here, with
creation language brought to bear.

7–9. Yahweh's election of Israel is now elaborated. The hearers are
directed to the distant past, by way of ancient memories handed down (7),
a theme related to fathers' instruction of children, common to Deuteronomy (e.g. 6:20–21) and wisdom. The election of Israel, uniquely in the
OT (Luyten 1985: 342–343), is thus put in the context of divine plans
going back to the dawn of time (but cf. 4:32). Those plans also involved all
the nations (8), so that the vast sweep of the panorama takes in not only
past ages but also the whole world. In this context the 'Most High' (El
Elyon) established each nation within its allotted boundaries. Israel's
election and establishment in Canaan are therefore only a part of a bigger
picture. (A similar concept is found in the narrative of Israel's approach to

its land, in which it is forbidden to make war on certain nations on the ground that Yahweh has given them their lands also; 2:5, 9, 19.) The vision here is not narrow; the election of Israel is set within a purpose of God for the whole world (see 'Explanation').

The second line of v. 8, however, focuses on Israel in this universal work. (On whether to read 'sons of God' or 'sons of Israel', NIV, see 'Notes on the text'). Adopting the reading 'sons of God', the line matches the theme of a primeval election of Israel with an echo of a decision in the divine council. The term 'sons of God' did not necessarily imply a genealogical relationship between the gods. The biblical form of the divine-council idea is probably closer to the Syro-Phoenician cult of Baalsamem than to that of Ugaritic El, the former merely having pre-eminence over the gods rather than a biological relationship with them (Niehr 1990: ch. 4). In any case, when the Canaanite divine council idea was mediated into the mono-Yahwistic environment of pre-exilic Israel, the gods were de-divinized, and became simply heavenly beings attending Yahweh.

Assuming that MT's 'sons of Israel' is due to a post-exilic adjustment, the motive for the change may not have been mere defensiveness against polytheism, since the divine-council idea was well known and understood non-mythologically. It may rather reflect an idea that entered Jewish interpretation, that the seventy descendants of Jacob (Gen. 46:27) matched the seventy nations catalogued in Gen. 10, and also that each nation had its own angel (Dan. 10:13, 20, 21; M. Barker 1992: 5–6). This in turn may have had mythological origins.

The passage closes with a statement of Yahweh's special love for Israel, an important deuteronomic theme (9; cf. 7:6; 10:15). The issue for interpretation here is how 'Yahweh' in v. 9 related to 'Elyon' in v. 8. Commentators sometimes see in these verses an echo of a belief that the high god (Elyon) delegated nations and territories to the 'sons of God', and that in this schema Yahweh was included along with other national gods, such as Chemosh of Moab or Milcom of Ammon (M. Barker 1992: 6). Ps. 82:6 knows a tradition that makes the 'gods' (*'elōhîm*) 'sons of Elyon' (though in that place *'elōhîm* is applied to earthly judges).

However, the Song shares with other parts of the OT a readiness to apply the name Elyon (or El Elyon) to Yahweh. A number of Psalms do so (e.g. 7:17[18]; 9:1–2[2–3]; 21:7[8]), among them certain 'Zion' and 'kingship' psalms (46:4[5], 7[8]; 47:2[3]; 78:21, [35]). The connection with Jerusalem is strengthened by Gen. 14:18–22, in which Melchizedek is king of Salem (Jerusalem) and priest of El Elyon. In Gen. 14:21 (MT) Elyon is identified with Yahweh. Probably, therefore, the name El Elyon was used in worship in Canaanite Jerusalem before the arrival of Israel there. The adoption of the name for Yahweh was part of a theological process that is also visible in the patriarchal narratives of the Pentateuch (note Exod. 6:3, and see Moberly 1992; Wenham 1980). This was part of the same process in early Israel, noticed above, in which the polytheism of Canaan was domesticated to Yahwistic theology. The present passage is best interpreted in the context of that process. It is the one God, Elyon-Yahweh, who has primeval purposes for the whole world as well as a special attachment to his people Israel. This fits with the strong mono-Yahwistic theology of Deuteronomy. The thought is close to 4:19, and the language of 'inheritance' echoes 4:20–21 (cf. 18:2, which illustrates the intimacy of the idea).

32:10–14

10. The thought of 32:8–9 continues into the next stanza, which focuses on Yahweh's care for the fledgling Israel. The allusion is recognizably to the time in the wilderness following the exodus from Egypt, although there is no express reference to that event itself. The chaotic nature of the wilderness is stressed ('a place unformed' is *tōhû*, as in Gen. 1:2), giving a connection with the primeval context of Israel's election in vv. 8–9. The metaphor of Yahweh's 'finding' Israel is echoed in Hos. 9:10 (where, incidentally, it does not imply that the exodus from Egypt is unknown to Hosea; cf. Hos. 2:14–15[16–17]; see also 'Notes on the text'). The 'finding' conveys joy and ownership (cf. Luke 15:8–10).

11. The act of creation is also evoked in the image of the eagle 'hovering' over its young, like the spirit of God (Gen. 1:2). The idea of birds caring for their young in wild places (10b–11) corresponds eloquently to the topic of protection in a dangerous place. The 'stirring up' of the nest (see 'Notes on the text') perhaps refers to the mother eagle's encouragement of the young to fly, along with her care that they do not fall. Creation and sustaining are bound together in these intimate images of the birth of a people.

12. In the middle of this stanza comes an assertion that Yahweh alone guided the people, in an echo of the pervasive deuteronomic claim that he alone is Israel's God (6:4). The phrase 'foreign god' is also found in Pss. 44:20[21]; 81:9[10], in echoes of the First Commandment (Deut. 5:6–7). Is. 43:12 closely echoes the present text.

13–14. Leading in the wilderness merges easily with leading into the land. The 'high places of the land' are best understood in an ordinary topographical sense, rather than the cultic sense of the noun *bāmôṯ* that is common elsewhere in the OT (esp. in Kings), and the phrase implies conquest or supremacy. It is followed by pictures of the land's natural wealth (cf. 8:7–9; 11:11–12). 'Fruit from rock' may be either honey or the juice of dates or grapes, thickened by cooking (*HALAT* 1:204). The latter makes a better parallelism with '(olive) oil from flinty rock', each signifying the capacity of Israel's land to produce richly from unlikely places.

Verse 14 has several terms that denote plenty deriving from domestic-ated animals (*kārîm*, 'lambs', can also be rams, but here apparently refers to specially fattened or select lambs, as in Amos 6:4). Bashan, in northern Transjordan, is paradigmatic for rich herds (cf. Amos 4:1). Animal and vegetable wealth are fused together in this evocative language: the 'choicest grains [lit. kidney-fat] of wheat' (cf. Ps. 81:16[17]; 147:14); 'the blood of the grape'.

32:15–18

The incongruous rejection of Yahweh by Israel in favour of other gods, despite the riches he provided, is a topic both of Deuteronomy (8:11–20) and of Hosea (2:2–5[4–17]; 9:10). Here it is sudden and full of irony. Poetic names for Israel (Jacob, Jeshurun; cf. 33:5, 26; Is. 44:2; the latter two texts emphasize in turn Yahweh's uniqueness and Israel's chosenness) are used alongside poetic names for God (the Rock, Eloah, the latter an unusual name outside Job). Yet, curiously, this all reinforces the point that Yahweh alone is Israel's God.

15. 'Jeshurun grew fat' (15) echoes the 'fat' or 'oil' (*šemen*) that Yahweh himself had extracted for them from flinty rock (13). The verb is repeated in the next line to suggest gorging. The people reject Yahweh even as they over-indulge in his gifts. They reject him as both provider and creator ('God who made them'); they have no faith in the Rock, the one who could be completely trusted. They 'scorned' him, literally 'regarded him as foolish' (see the echo of this in v. 21).

16–18. The rebellion is now characterized as a choice of other gods, in defiance of the fundamental command of Yahweh. The turning to 'foreign gods' (lit. 'foreign ones', v. 16) flies in the face of his declaration in v. 12. His 'jealousy' is the obverse of his special love (cf. 4:24; 5:9; 6:15). The 'abominations' are the trappings of foreign worship, whose repugnance to Yahweh is frequently recalled in Deuteronomy (cf. 7:25–26). Other gods are now exposed, in succession, as 'demons' and no gods at all, gods they had not known (with all the implications of love, delight and care predicated of Yahweh in vv. 10–14), and as *nouveaux*, usurping Yahweh's rights (17). The stanza finishes (18) with sharp accusations of ingratitude, using birth images, and words for 'forgetting' that have personal and moral overtones rather than suggesting mere neglect (cf. 8:11, 14).

32:19–25

19–21. This stanza matches Yahweh's strong reaction to Israel's rebellion. The 'looking' and being provoked, the withdrawing and waiting to see what will happen, depict his role in vivid, anthropomorphic ways. The issue is joined between closely related parties (Yahweh and 'his sons and daughters', v. 19; cf. v. 5). Within that relationship, the thought of

vv. 19–21 turns on the two corresponding ideas of 'jealousy' and 'provocation' (see also 'Notes on the text'). 'Provocation', or 'anger', was a major theme in 29:22–28[21–27], and recurs at the introduction to the Song (31:29). Yahweh's rejection of his people is described as 'hiding his presence [lit. face]', a common ANE idiom meaning withholding of favour (Balentine 1983). This also echoes the announcement of the Song (31:18–19).

Israel's provocation of Yahweh is now repeated from v. 16 (21ab), in order to introduce the powerful and ironic mirror images in v. 21cd. His 'provoking' them and 'making them jealous' is a bold reversal, the application of the same ideas paradoxically underlining that this is no equal relationship. The making Israel 'jealous' will in fact take the form of a judgment on them. Equally, the mirror image of 'no god' with 'no people' is devastatingly unbalanced, since, while the 'no god' really is no god, the 'no people' will have a terrible reality as the agent of the judgment. The phrase has the added effect of designating this agent of judgment as a people that did not enjoy the chosen status of Israel, yet one that, even so, would now overcome Israel in this rejection of the chosen. The 'foolishness' of this destroying nation echoes the 'scorning' (lit. 'making foolish') of Yahweh by Israel (16). It also recalls that Israel was given the 'wisdom' of Yahweh's tôrâ (4:6), which should have distinguished them from other nations.

22–25. The rejection of Israel is now cast in terms reminiscent of the covenantal curses. The wrath of Yahweh will penetrate the earth, the reference to Sheol making the context universal (22). The point of this is probably to say that a judgment on Israel has universal effects. Yahweh, who loved Israel, has become its enemy (23; cf. Jer. 21; see 'Notes on the text'). Hunger, pestilence and war (24–25) are a well-known triad in the language of cursing (cf. 28:21–25; Jer. 21:7). The catalogue forms a striking antithesis to the pictures of bounty and delight in vv. 13–14.

32:26–35

26–28. The change to words of salvation for Israel and judgment on their enemies begins in this section, with a rationale based on Yahweh's defence of his reputation, a strong motive used also in prophetic intercession and exhortation (27; cf. 9:28; Ezek. 20:22). The enemy is characterized as lacking wisdom when it imagines that it has defeated Israel by its own strength (27–28), in an echo of Israel's own self-delusion (cf. 8:17).

29. It is not clear in this verse which nation (Israel or the enemy) is in view, or who is speaking. There is in fact a subtle interplay between the accusation of the enemy and that of Israel in vv. 28–35. This seems to be a deliberate effect of the poetic expression here. If the enemy is foolish because of its inadequate gods, it must not be forgotten that Israel, too, is foolish because it has spurned Yahweh. As a continuation of vv. 27–28, v. 29 refers to the enemy; yet in its formulation as a wish of Yahweh it reminds one of his desire for Israel.

30. A change of speaker occurs between v. 27, where it is clearly Yahweh, and v. 31, where 'our Rock' and 'our enemies' can hardly be his words. The change may be at v. 30, which goes closely with v. 31 because of the opening 'for' (*kî*) in that verse. It could come earlier, at v. 28, however, since vv. 28–29 could be spoken either by Yahweh or by the new speaker. In either case, the new speaker's contribution probably runs to v. 33, since the line of thought continues naturally to that point, and the voice of Yahweh resumes in v. 34. The new speaker is the narrator of the Song (in the first place Moses).

The nub of the wisdom that the enemy (and implicitly Israel) lacks is contained in v. 30. It means that the fortunes of war, especially where they fly in the face of normal expectations, can be understood only as the result of Yahweh's decree. The closest analogy to the expression here is in Is. 30:17. In both places the implication is that Israel, as the strong party, is inexplicably overcome by a weaker. This can only be explained because 'their Rock' (Yahweh) decided to give them up. An important corollary of this is that Israel's misfortunes may not be put down to weakness on Yahweh's part.

31. The train of thought continues in v. 31, which completes it by saying that the enemies' god ('rock') could not be responsible for the defeat of Israel, as even they admit (see 'Notes on the text'). The thought is rhetorical; that is, it does not represent a particular historical event (such as the exile, in which the Babylonians were the stronger party, and would hardly have regarded Israel's God as more powerful than their own).

32–33. The depiction of the enemies concludes with a reflection on the false basis of the plenty they enjoy; their wine does not represent the blessing that comes from knowing the true God, but is the bitter fruit of falsehood and cruelty.

34–35. When Yahweh speaks again, he declares that the ruin of the enemy is a certainty, merely held back until the time that he should decree. The text adopted here in the translation ('till the day of vengeance', v. 35) is not essentially different from MT's 'Vengeance is mine' (followed in Rom. 12:19; see 'Notes on the text'). The essential point is that restitution is in Yahweh's power and will therefore happen in his time. Vengeance itself is not arbitrary, but is given meaning by the parallel 'recompense', implying a just righting of wrongs. The thought is similar to that in Is. 10:5–12; the scourge of Israel meets its own judgment in due course, and therefore should not be arrogant. Rhetorically speaking, however, v. 35 might also be heard by Israel as reinforcing the warning to them, too, that is the chief theme of the Song.

32:36–43

36–38. The final stanza of the Song asserts Yahweh's unique power in matters of life and death. Vindication of his people is one corollary of this. Yet there is no triumphalism here, for when Yahweh 'judges' (*dîn*), it may be for vindication; but the term can have the more general sense of acting in the capacity of judge, to weigh right and wrong, as in Ps. 96:10; Is. 3:13–14; in the latter case, there are negative overtones. The parallel in v. 36, 'he will have compassion', has as objects 'his servants', who remain to be identified. When he sees that Israel's 'strength has gone, and none remains, bond or free', his response is not immediately to deliver them, but to reinforce their folly in trusting gods who could not give life (37–38). Again, there is mockery in the depiction of other gods as feebly mimicking what only Yahweh can truly do, as gobblers of sacrifices, and as a 'rock' pretending to be the Rock – and Israel was deceived.

39–42. The declaration of uniqueness ('I, I am he', v. 39) stands at the centre of the stanza (Luyten 1985: 346). It closely resembles Is. 41:4; 43:10, 13; 48:12 (cf. 44:6; 45:6–7, 21–22), in the context of that book's argument that Yahweh has no rival among Babylonian gods. In the emphasis there on Yahweh as sole governor of history, and on the insight that can apprehend this (Is. 43:10), there are close similarities to the Song. In the Song, however, the implication, spelt out in vv. 39–42, is couched in general terms. That is, it does not specify a particular act of deliverance for Israel, but rather only that Yahweh alone can do such things. Just as his 'servants' are unspecified in v. 36, so now are his 'enemies' (41), in words that recall v. 35. Yahweh as warrior reappears in v. 42 (cf. v. 23), acting against his own enemies.

43. The stanza closes with a call to the nations to 'Praise his people'. This is in contrast to those texts that have the nations despise Israel because of the evils inflicted upon them by Yahweh (cf. 29:24–28[23–27]), and meets Yahweh's own concern in v. 27. The 'people' here is plainly Israel and the land is Israel's land. The vengeance in this peroration, therefore, puts the agents of Yahweh's acts against his people firmly in their place. Even so, the qualification of the vindicated ones as 'his servants', and of the enemies as '*his* enemies', leaves here, too, a certain openness.

Finally, 'atone for the land of his people' focuses again on Israel's sin. Atonement was also found in 21:8, in the ritual performed to cleanse the people from guilt in the case of the unknown murderer. The thought is not far, either, from Is. 40:1–2 (though the term *kipper* is not used there), where the deliverance of Israel can only follow a period in which it has paid for its sins. In this way, the sin of Israel, and judgment on them, is kept to the fore in the Song, even in this final section in which Yahweh's judgment is put in a larger perspective, in which others may be punished and Israel finally saved. This perspective has been called 'eschatological' (Luyten 1985: 344–345). It is better to think of it as setting out fundamental principles on which Yahweh governs all of history. In this way, the whole thrust of the Song depends on the basis of the election of Israel, set up in 32:8–9. (For a similar view, though differently argued, see Bogaert 1985.)

32:44–52

44–47. The involvement of Joshua with Moses in proclaiming the Song (44) points to its intended function in Israel's future, since its context is the ceremonial handing over of leadership in Israel from Moses to him (31:7, 14–15, 23). It is not necessary to think of the two leaders reciting it in tandem; the speaker, strictly, is Moses (31:22, 30). His final charge to Israel (46–47) returns to basic deuteronomic concepts: taking Yahweh's words to heart, passing them on to future generations, and the basis in them of Israel's long life in the land.

48–50. The story of Moses in relation to the promised land began in 1:34–40; 3:21–25, in which he was shown that he would not enter it, despite his plea to Yahweh, and where the succession of Joshua was already adumbrated. That larger trajectory now comes to its closure, as does the smaller one in chs. 31 – 32, in which Moses recalls that condition laid upon his life (31:1–3). The end of Moses' life is similarly recalled in Num. 27:12–14. He will see the land from Mt Nebo, in the Abarim range (cf. Num. 33:47–48; Deut. 34:1). (The mountain was called Pisgah in 3:27; both names occur in 34:1.) But, like Aaron, he will not enter it (cf. Num. 20:22–29; Deut. 10:6).

51–52. The reason for Moses' exclusion, not specified in the early chapters, is now given, in terms similar to Num. 12:14. The reference is to the event recorded in Num. 20:1–13, where, indeed, the sentence on Moses together with Aaron was first pronounced (12). The precise reason, even in that place, is somewhat elusive, but perhaps bore upon the manner in which Moses and Aaron carried out Yahweh's command. The substance of their sin, in any case, was that they 'broke faith' with Yahweh, a strong term denoting an act tantamount to apostasy (cf. the condemnation of Saul in 1 Chr. 10:13), and did not 'proclaim [his] holiness' (lit. 'sanctify' him). This term is more at home in the language of sacrifice and ritual, and occurs in Deuteronomy only here and in the Sabbath commandment (5:12). The combination characterizes the two great leaders of Israel, the prophet and the priest, in stylized fashion, as capable of the worst rebellion. The point is well embedded in the history as regards Aaron (Exod. 32; Deut. 9 – 10). It is more jarring in Moses' case. But it is striking, especially in the immediate echoes of the Song, that even the greatest may fall.

Explanation

The Song of Moses recapitulates a number of important themes of Deuteronomy, yet does so in a highly individual way. As in the book generally, Yahweh is at its centre, the only God, powerful to rule over all nations and all history. Similarly, Israel is at the heart of his purposes, and its election finds a profound new expression here, being traced to decisions made in the divine council in primeval time (8–9), and set in the context of his governance of the creation, earthly and heavenly. The chosen people, furthermore, are cast as Yahweh's 'sons' or 'sons and daughters' several times (5, 19, 20, 43). This status is conferred; Yahweh has made them his people by his decision. But this is conveyed not in legal language, but rather in terms that are creational and personal. Motifs of creation flow into those of sustaining. The Song is a witness, first of all, to the deep and abiding love of Yahweh for his people.

The depiction of the salvation history differs in important ways from Deuteronomy in general, however. There is no express reference to Israel's deliverance from Egypt, or to Yahweh's bringing them to the promised land. The twin covenants of Horeb and Moab are passed over, as are the comprehensive temporal panorama (patriarchs to return from exile), the journey through time and place, the vision of a nation governed by Yahweh's law as mediated by a diffused administration, and the people most truly itself when worshipping Yahweh at his chosen place. Instead of all this, there is a generalized memory of guidance in the wilderness and provision from the land's wealth (10–15; 'land', however, is not specified in the usual deuteronomic ways). These themes follow seamlessly from the language of primeval creation and election in vv. 6–9.

Just as the past perspective of the Song does not specify exodus and Horeb, so its future vision departs from Deuteronomy's threat of exile followed by restoration to land (chs. 28 – 30). The motifs of powerful foreign nations brought against Israel by Yahweh himself in order to punish it, and turning the tables in a final equalizing of judgment, are familiar enough from prophetic analogies. These motifs certainly have historical reference points. Yet it is not possible to identify them, as it is in the prophetic books. Israel reaches a very low ebb (23–25, 36), but it is not said how or when. Its fortunes are restored, but the topic of restoration is not reducible to a particular event (such as return from Babylonian exile).

One way of accounting for these features is to trace the Song to a different theological tradition from the deuteronomic mainstream (Mayes 1979: 380). Another is to suggest that deuteronomic themes have been deliberately eschatologized, with the playing down of Egypt, desert, exile and return, and the adoption of certain concepts familiar in prophetic visions of the future. This includes a future action of Yahweh stored up for the right time (34; cf. Mal. 3:16; Dan. 12:9), a day of vengeance and the requital of Yahweh's enemies (35; cf. Is. 2:12; 34:8; 61:2), atonement for the land of Israel (43; cf. Zech. 13:1–2; Joel 3:21[4:21]; Luyten 1985: 344–345).

This latter view has strength. The lineaments of Israel's history have been partially obscured in order to highlight certain essential realities. In this context, Yahweh's relationship with the whole created order is in view. Israel's election becomes the canvas on which his deepest and eternal purposes are painted. His love for them is matched only by the treachery of their rejection, and by his jealousy in response, the obverse of his love. This scenario is made to reveal the workings of Yahweh's mind. Any who have wisdom may see it. The distinction between Israel and the nations is blurred in vv. 28–43, as we saw. This was effected partly by the use of the terms 'my servants' and 'my enemies' in a way that carefully did not specify these as Israel as such, partly because it was simply not always possible to know whether certain statements were applied to Israel or to the nations (e.g. vv. 28–29, 37). This had the effect of showing that the judgment of Yahweh is due to all who fail to trust him, and also that the election of Israel was no licence given once for all to that historical nation. The implication that chosen Israel must be or become his servants in reality parallels, for example, the movement in the book of Isaiah (note 'servants' in Is. 63:17; 65:8, 15; 66:14). The subjection of all nations to the same standards as those applied to Israel resembles the movement in Amos (Amos 1 – 2; 9:7, 12), and correspondingly bears hope of salvation for all.

DEUTERONOMY 33:1–29

Translation

[1]This is the blessing with which Moses, the man of God, blessed the Israelites before he died. [2]He said:

> 'The LORD came from Sinai;
>> he dawned upon them from Seir;
>> he shone forth from Mt Paran,
> and with him myriads of holy ones,
>> angels at his right hand.
> [3]O you who cherish peoples,
>> all holy ones are in your hand;
> they submit at your feet,
>> and receive your instruction.
> [4]Moses charged us with a law,
>> as a possession for the assembly of Jacob.
> [5]The LORD became king in Jeshurun,
>> when the heads of the people gathered,
>> the tribes of Israel as a unity.

⁶Let Reuben live and not die out;
　　but let his men be few.'

⁷And this he said of Judah:

　　'Hear, O LORD, the voice of Judah;
　　　　bring him to his people.
　　With his own hands he contended for himself;
　　　　be a help against his foes!'

⁸Of Levi he said:

　　'You gave your Thummim and Urim to your loyal man,
　　　　whom you tested at Massah,
　　　　with whom you contended at the waters of Meribah.
　　⁹He said of father and mother,
　　　　"I have not seen them!"
　　Nor did he show partiality to his brothers,
　　　　or acknowledge his children.
　　Rather, they kept your word,
　　　　and guarded your covenant.
　　¹⁰They teach your precepts to Jacob,
　　　　your law to Israel.
　　They put incense before you,
　　　　the whole burnt offering on your altar.
　　¹¹Bless, O LORD, his strength;
　　　　accept the work of his hands.
　　Crush the loins of his adversaries;
　　　　and his enemies, may they not rise again!'

¹²Of Benjamin he said:

　　'The beloved of the LORD dwells in security;
　　　　the Most High watches over him all day long,
　　　　and he dwells between his shoulders.'

¹³And of Joseph he said:

　　'May his land be blessed by the LORD,
　　　　with the bounty from heaven above,
　　　　and of the deep that lies beneath;
　　¹⁴with the bounty of the produce of the sun,
　　　　the bounty of the yield of the months,
　　¹⁵of the peaks of the ancient mountains,
　　　　and the bounty of the everlasting hills;

¹⁶the bounty of the land and its fullness,
   the favour of the one who dwells in the thorn bush.
  Let these come on the head of Joseph;
   on the brow of the prince among his brothers.
¹⁷Like a firstborn bull in majesty,
   his horns are the horns of a wild ox.
  With them he gores the peoples,
   even those at the ends of the earth.
  Such are the myriads of Ephraim;
   such are the thousands of Manasseh.'

¹⁸And of Zebulun he said:

'Rejoice, Zebulun, when you set forth;
   and Issachar, in your dwellings.
¹⁹They call peoples to the mountain;
   there they offer right sacrifices.
  They suck from the abundance of the seas,
   and the concealed treasures of the sand.'

²⁰And of Gad he said:

'Blessed be he who makes space for Gad;
   he dwells like a lion;
   he tears at arm or head.
²¹He chose the best for himself,
   for there a commander's portion was reserved for him.
  When the leaders of the people assembled,
   he executed the justice of the LORD,
   and his judgments concerning Israel.'

²²And of Dan he said:

'Dan is a lion's cub,
   springing out from Bashan.'

²³And of Naphtali he said:

'Naphtali is rich in favour,
   full of the blessing of the LORD;
   he will inherit the west and south.'

²⁴And of Asher he said:

'Most blessed of sons is Asher!

May he be the favourite of his brothers;
  may he dip his foot in oil.
²⁵May your bolts be of iron and bronze,
  and may you be strong as long as you live!

²⁶'There is none like the God of Jeshurun,
  who rides through the heavens to your help,
  and on the clouds in his majesty.
²⁷The eternal God is a dwelling-place,
  and underneath are the arms of the everlasting one.
 He has driven out the enemy before you,
  and said: "Destroy!"
²⁸So Israel dwelt in peace;
  Jacob dwells alone
 in a land of grain and new wine,
  where the heavens drop down dew.
²⁹How blessed are you, Israel!
  Who is like you,
  a people saved by the Lord!
 Your help is a shield,
  his sword is your triumph!
 Your enemies shall come cringing to you
  and you shall tread upon their backs!'

Notes on the text

2. 'upon them' (*lāmô*, lit. 'upon him', where the singular refers collectively to Israel; GKC 103f, n. 3); LXX has *hēmin*, 'to us', presupposing Hebr. *lānû*. But there is no obvious reason to prefer this.
  'and with him': Hebr. has *we'ātâ*, 'and he came' (as NIV); the translation follows Syr, and assumes *we'ittô*. LXX has 'with myriads [of/from] Kadesh', which observes the echo in *mērib^ebōt qōḏeš* of the place name Meribat Kadesh (32:51; cf. Num. 27:14).
  'marching at his right hand': MT's *'ēšdāṯ* is probably corrupt; the Q, *'ēš dāṯ*, 'fire of a law', makes poor sense, and *dāṯ* in that sense is virtually confined to Esther (and one occurrence in Ezra). The translation follows LXX, 'angels with him', though this is admittedly conjectural.
  3. 'you who cherish peoples' (*'ap ḥōbēb 'ammîm*): this takes *'ap* as a reinforcing particle (LXX has *kai*, 'also'). The next two words then address Yahweh. Instead of *'ammîm*, 'peoples', LXX reads *'ammô*, 'his people', but this probably rationalizes a perceived difficulty.
  'all holy ones' follows LXX *hoi hēgiasmenoi*, rather than Hebr. '*his* holy ones'.
  'they submit': *tukkû* can hardly be *nkh*, hoph. ('to be struck down',

HALAT 3:659; the sense is too strong for the context, and the feminine difficult after *hēm*); it is taken variously from a root *twk*, 'to submit' (*HALAT*, ibid.), *mkk*, 'sink', 'lower oneself' (*BHS*, reading *himtākû*), *tkk*, 'crowd together' (van der Woude 1994: 284).

'they ... receive your instruction' involves reading a plural verb (*yiśś'û[m]*).

5. 'The LORD became king': the words can be translated 'there arose a king in Jeshurun' (NRSV), which would most naturally refer to Saul or David. This would be an unexpected continuation of vv. 1–3, however.

6. Ancient versions and modern translations hesitate over whether this second line is a wish for great numbers or for few (cf. LXX, 'may he be great in number'; NIV). Hebr. is lit. 'may his men be a number', which is opaque, but which echoes the expression 'men of number', meaning 'men of small number' (e.g. Gen. 34:30).

9. LXX and QL have sg. 'he kept ... he guarded', as the reference is to Levi. The following context continues the plural, however, as it envisages the priestly tribe.

10. 'before you' is lit. 'in your nostrils', hence 'before your face'.

11. The use of *min* with the jussive for the negative wish is unusual. Craigie defends it as an interrogative particle also known in Ugaritic (1976a: 395). But QL has *bal* ('let not'), and SamP renders the phrase *mî yᵉqîmennû* ('who will arouse him?'). It seems as if these two are rationalizing a text they did not understand. The translation follows the lead of QL, echoed also in LXX.

12. 'the Most High' reads *'elyôn* instead of MT *'ālāyw*; LXX has *theos*, 'God'.

13. 'above', reading *mē'al* for *miṭṭal* ('from the dew'), for a smoother reading, and a better parallel with the next line.

16. 'in the thorn bush' (*sᵉneh*); an emendation to 'Sinai' (*sᵉnay*) is sometimes accepted (NRSV), but MT is intelligible (cf. Exod. 3:1–6).

17. 'Let these come': reading *tābō'nā* for the anomalous *tābôtâ*. MT has 'his bull' (*šôrô*); the suffix is omitted by QL, SamP, LXX.

21. The translation of v. 21a follows LXX, as MT is difficult. 'assembled': this accepts a change of MT's *wayyēte* ('*th*, 'come') to '*sp*, hith., as v. 5, and cf. LXX.

23. 'he will inherit', reading *yîraš*, with LXX, SamP, instead of MT's imperative: 'possess!'

26. 'the God of Jeshurun' reads *kᵉ'ēl yᵉšurûn*, with LXX, rather than MT's *kā'ēl yᵉšurûn* (= 'like God, O Jeshurun', NRSV).

27. *zᵉrō'ōt 'ôlām* might also be 'the everlasting arms'. The translation is chosen for internal balance.

28. 'dwells alone' reads *'ān*, or *yā'ôn* ('dwells', *BHS*), instead of MT's *'ên*, 'spring of' (van der Woude 1994: 284). 'the heavens' (Syr) for MT's 'his heavens'.

29. *bāmôtêmô* is taken here as 'their backs', not 'their high places', for better sense. The possessive suffix is singular (cf. *pānêmô*, Ps. 11:7; *kappêmô*, Job 27:23), but the sense requires a plural (cf. LXX, and note on v. 2, above).

Form and structure

After the Song of Moses comes the Blessing of Moses. For a similar pairing of songs forming the climax to a long work, 2 Sam. 22; 23:1–7 may be compared (Watts 1992). If the Song had a somewhat ambiguous turning-point in Israel's favour, the chosen status of Israel is now celebrated openly. In the context of Deuteronomy, the blessings of the covenant (28:1–15) gain some elaboration here (Merrill 1994: 32).

The Blessing is in the form of a father's dying blessing upon his children, similar to Isaac's on Jacob and Esau (Gen. 27:1–40) and Jacob's on his sons in Gen. 49. The genre of the father's blessing is extended here to Moses in keeping with his special role in Israel, as the covenant mediator who, in a sense, brought Israel to birth. The pronouncement of the Blessing is situated between Yahweh's command to him to ascend Mt Nebo to see the land and die (32:48–52) and the account of his doing so (ch. 34). The whole of chapter 33 is characterized as Moses' blessing on the tribes (1), though the beginning and ending comprise praises that fall outside the blessings proper.

Moses' Blessing has essentially the same subjects as Jacob's, but the names of the sons are now applied to the tribes that constitute Israel. The blessings themselves are framed by an opening (1–5) and a concluding praise (26–29), which share the themes of the uniqueness of Yahweh and of Israel, his chosen people. These two sections can be read as a single unit into which the blessings have been set, vv. 5 and 26 being linked by the idea of Yahweh as king in 'Jeshurun' (van der Woude 1994: 282–282; Christensen 1984).

The tribal lists in the OT vary in content, while normally preserving the number twelve. Num. 1:5–15 (cf. Deut. 33:20–43) omits Levi but divides Joseph into two, Manasseh and Ephraim (Gen. 48:8–20 gives the basis for this). Num. 26 counts Joseph as one, and keeps Levi, in this respect like Gen. 49. In Deut. 33 Simeon is missing, and consequently only eleven blessings are pronounced, though there is a hint of the compensating division of Joseph into Manasseh and Ephraim (17cd). The omission of Simeon (as in Judg. 5, though Judah and Levi are absent there too) reflects its early disappearance in Israel's history. The order of the tribes in Deut. 33 is unique. Judah is relatively prominent by position, second after Reuben, but somewhat overshadowed by both Levi and Joseph in the weight given to these. Because there is little sign of the Davidic kingship that would emerge in Judah, the Blessing is often dated to the pre-monarchic time.

The function of the father's blessing was more specific than parting good wishes. It could signal preferences (cf. Gen. 27), and, indeed, there is great variation among the sayings in Deut. 33, both in length and in nature. Some are observations about the tribe or its land, rather than explicit wishes for blessing. The perspective, indeed, is often from within the tribe's life in their land, rather than pointing expressly to the future (e.g. Benjamin, Dan, Naphtali, Asher). The Blessing differs from Jacob's dying words (Gen. 49) in that it apportions no blame, and in every case but one (Dan, v. 22) makes a clear comment on or wish for the tribes' blessing, frequently naming Yahweh as the source of it (Braulik 1992a: 237).

Comment

33:1–5

1. Moses is described as 'the man of God', a term for a 'prophet' applied most frequently in the OT to Elisha (29×, V. P. Hamilton 1997: 390), and also to Elijah, Samuel and Moses himself, though only here in Deuteronomy. It marks the person out as carrying the authority of God. In the case of Elisha, it often implies powers to heal. Used of Moses in Deuteronomy, it recalls his special position in Yahweh's deliverance of Israel, and in the giving of the law.

2–3. The march of Yahweh from Sinai (2) is a topic in several OT songs that celebrate the foundation of Israel as his people, his powerful possession of the land of Canaan, and his assumption of the kingship there (Judg. 5:4–5; Ps. 68:7–8[8–9], 17–18[18–19]; Hab. 3:3–7; cf. Exod. 15:17). The locations Sinai and Seir are found together in Judg. 5:4–5, and Paran in Hab. 3:3. All three occur in Deut. 1:1–2 (though only in the present text in Deuteronomy is Sinai/Horeb called Sinai). As in 1:1–2, they do not appear in a systematic way (see notes there), but seem to refer together to the desert area to the south. (Seir may denote a broader area than strictly Edom, including territory directly south of Judah; Bartlett 1987: 41–44; but see 2:1–6.)

However, the origin of Yahweh's progression with Israel is clearly a theophany because of the terms used. The most recognizable 'theophanic' term is 'he shone forth', but 'he came' and 'he dawned' may also echo the Zion theophany in Ps. 50:2. This helps to explain the oddity that the 'shining forth' is associated with Paran, not Sinai; that is, the whole movement from the desert region is portrayed as a theophany. The opening of the Blessing thus resumes the deuteronomic theme, initiated in 1:1–8, of Yahweh's progress from the theophany and law-giving at Sinai to the land he would give to Israel.

The thought in vv. 2–3 is hard to penetrate because of textual difficulties (see 'Notes on the text'). The main problem is to know whether the picture has a broad focus (embracing both heaven and earth), or the narrower theme of Yahweh's love for Israel; and this problem explains widely divergent translations. The interpretation offered here favours the former option. The key textual decisions relate to the meaning of 'peoples' and 'holy ones' (see 'Notes on the text'). Is it Israel who submits in vv. 2–3, or the heavenly host? In my interpretation, 'peoples' is taken in its plainest sense, that is, to refer to the nations in general (cf. v. 19a), though it is often supposed to mean Israel, either by assuming that the 'peoples' are the tribes, in view of the separate blessings to come, or by following LXX, 'his people'. And 'holy ones', though the term can refer to the people of Israel (Lev. 19:2; Num. 16:3), are best seen as divine beings (cf. Job 5:1; 15:15; Ps. 89:5[6], 7[8]; Zech. 14:5; Dan. 8:13; Naudé 1997: 883).

The translation adopted not only produces a natural balance between the heavenly and earthly realms of God, but also echoes a theme in the Song. The divine-council idea was also found in 32:8–9, there too in connection with the nations. My interpretation maintains a continuity in thought with 32:8–9, Yahweh's rule in heaven corresponding to his universal rule on earth. By the same token, the origin of Yahweh's choice of Israel is placed in a cosmic context, in which he 'cherishes' all nations, and his love for these is part of a plan that involves the heavenly beings with them (see also 'Explanation').

4–5. There is then a progression in the thought between v. 3 and vv. 4–5. Yahweh, as supreme in heaven and on earth, now distinguishes Israel in the presence of the divine coucil by giving them the law, and by assuming the status of 'king' in Jeshurun. His kingship by right in heaven is echoed by a kingship chosen on earth, and corresponds to the constitution of the people by the assembling of its leaders. This interpretation resolves some of the difficulties felt by the sudden transition in theme to the lawgiving and the naming of Moses in the third person (Mayes 1979: 400).

Similarly, the translation 'the LORD [Yahweh] became king' is intelligible on this view. This rendering has been doubted on the grounds that the kingship of Yahweh is elsewhere conceived as kingship in heaven (von Rad 1966a: 205). Grammatically, the phrase might mean 'there arose a king' (NRSV; the name 'Yahweh' is not expressed in Hebrew). This has been advocated on the grounds that the appointment of a human king by the assembly of Israel is a likelier topic than that Yahweh should 'become' king there (van der Woude 1994). However, that would be a sudden and isolated change of theme. In spite of von Rad, Yahweh is indeed portrayed as Israel's king (e.g. 1 Sam. 12:12; Is. 44:6). The line is best taken, not as a description of a specific historical event in the assembly, but rather as an assertion that Yahweh's kingship in Israel arose out of his age-old heavenly kingship.

33:6–25

6. Reuben, the eldest son (Gen. 29:32), is the first to receive a blessing, as in Gen. 49:3 and most tribal lists. His blessing, however, is terse and promises little (see 'Notes on the text'), perhaps reflecting his misdemeanour (Gen. 35:22; 49:4). Historically, too, the tribe struggled to survive (cf. 2 Kgs. 10:32–33).

7. Differently from Gen. 49, the Blessing now departs from birth order (Reuben, Simeon, Levi, Judah; Gen. 28:32–35). Simeon has disappeared from the list, presumably in line with its early disappearance as a tribe, absorbed into Judah (cf. Josh. 19:1–9 and 15:26–32, 42; the Simeonite towns appear also in the Judah list; Josh. 19:9 already signals a fragile independence for the tribe). The order of the blessings now follows a rough south–north geographical progression.

The blessing of Judah is surprisingly short, compared with Gen. 49:8–12, and the lengthy description of its territory in Josh. 15.

The prayer for Judah assumes some isolation from the rest of Israel. It would, indeed, be separate from the northern tribes for much of the shared history of Israel and Judah, until the north collapsed as a political entity in 722 BC. But some particular difficulty seems to be in mind, in which Judah has to fight for its survival. The prayer has no messianic hint, unlike Gen. 49:8–12.

8–11. The relatively lengthy blessing of Levi is quite different from Gen. 49:5–7. The form of the Urim and Thummim (normally in that order) is unknown, but they were a means of ascertaining the divine will (Exod. 28:30). The allusion to a testing of Levi at Massah and Meribah is unique, these being the places where Israel tested Yahweh (Exod. 17:1–7), as did Moses and Aaron (Deut. 32:51). Both Exod. 15:25 (Mayes 1979: 403) and Ps. 81:7[8] (Merrill 1994: 439) have possible echoes of the incident in view, but without express reference to Levi. The zeal of Levi for the covenant (9) could recall the incident recorded in Exod. 32:25–29. The responsibility of Levi, as the priestly tribe, for instruction in the *tôrâ* (10a), is known in Hos. 4:6; Mic. 3:11; Mal. 2:1–9. Finally, they are responsible for making Israel's sacrifices.

It is odd, after these various aspects of Levi's priestly vocation, to return to the idea of it as a tribe that might have to fight battles, harking back to the idea of it as warlike (Gen. 49:5). The blessing unfolds a gamut of the tribe's experience over time, and is sometimes regarded as a composition from different periods (Mayes 1979: 402). The consistent thrust, however, portrays a tribe that enjoys a special status and the favour of Yahweh, because of its zeal and priestly calling. The absence of any allusion to territory is in line with its portrayal in Deuteronomy as a tribe without its own land (10:9).

12. Bejamin's blessing (quite different from Gen. 49:27) is a picture of intimacy and security. 'The beloved of the LORD' probably alludes to Gen.

44:20, where Benjamin, as the youngest son of Jacob, is specially loved. The Most High is Elyon, one of the patriarchal names for God (see 'Notes on the text'). The last line means either that Benjamin dwells between the shoulders of God, following the transfer of the father–son image (Jacob and Benjamin) to God and Benjamin, or that God dwells in the territory of Benjamin, where 'dwells' (*šāḵēn*) means the divine presence in a sanctuary (cf. 12:5). The sanctuary would be either Bethel or Jerusalem, which is counted as Benjaminite according to the border descriptions in Josh. 15:8; 18:16; and the 'shoulders' in that case refer to hills (cf. Josh. 15:8, 10–11; 18:12–19). The former meaning is probably preferable on the grounds of correspondence between the two halves of the verse.

13–17. Joseph's blessing lays great emphasis on the fruitfulness of the tribe's land, by accumulating phrases on the theme, and the repeated use of the term 'bounty' (*meḡeḏ*). Joseph's blessing mirrors more than any other the deuteronomic theme of the rich land (cf. 8:7–9; cf. Gen. 49:22, 25–26). It goes beyond the other deuteronomic descriptions, reaching for cosmic language ('heaven above … the deep', v. 13), as in Gen. 49:25.

The tribe's allotted territory covered a large central expanse of Canaan, from just north of Bethel as far as Mt Carmel and the Mediterranean coast in the west, and embracing part of Transjordan (Josh. 16 – 17). As well as mountains in the central ridge, therefore, it took in lush areas such as parts of the Jordan valley and the coastal plain, as well as rich valleys that crossed the ridge. The blessing treats Joseph essentially as a unity. The allusion to Ephraim and Manasseh (17) suggests that this division was well known from an early time, but it is almost an afterthought. The portrayal of Joseph as a 'prince among his brothers' (16) reflects a time when the people of the large central area had primacy in Israel. Its strength is likened to that of a 'firstborn bull', which is familiar in ANE texts and iconography about the gods El and Baal. There is probably no specifically religious connotation here, however. The 'goring of peoples' may refer to the tribe's warlike occupation of the land, 'the ends of the earth' being hyperbolic. The account of their occupation in Joshua depicts a numerous and powerful people that was allocated more than one share and was given permission to expand its land (Josh. 17:14–18).

The supremacy of Joseph also corresponds to the absence of a messianic thrust in the saying about Judah, and adds strength to the view that the Blessing pictures a pre-monarchic situation. Finally, Joseph enjoys the favour of 'the one who dwells in the thorn bush', an allusion to Yahweh's appearing to Moses in the bush at Horeb (Exod. 3:1–6). (The reading is preferable to the emendation to 'Sinai', NRSV; see 'Notes on the text'.)

18–19. Zebulun and Issachar are often bracketed together, as they are here (cf. Gen. 30:17–20; 49:13–14; Judg. 5:14–15). They occupied bordering territories in southern Galilee, north of Manasseh, extending from the Jordan just south of the Sea of Galilee as far as the Mediterranean. The descriptions in Joshua do not permit precise borders to be drawn for these tribes (Josh. 19:10–23), but Gen. 49:13 regards Zebulun as a seafaring people (the allusion to Sidon makes it clear that the seashore in that case means the Mediterranean), and the present saying associates them both with maritime trade. The blessing, 'when you set forth … in your dwellings', may be a variation on the 'going out' and 'coming in' that together embrace all of life (cf. Ps. 121:8; Deut. 28:6; cf. S. R. Driver 1895: 408).

The intriguing v. 19a apparently refers to a worship sanctuary in their territory, probably Tabor,which was on the border between the two tribes (Josh. 19:12, 22). The saying suggests that Tabor was a well-known worship centre whose influence extended beyond the land of the two tribes. It is not clear whether 'peoples' refers to other Israelite tribes (*pace* Mayes 1979: 407), or to other nations whose borders lay not far away (such as Sidon and Tyre). In Hosea's time the cult at Tabor had become idolatrous (Hos. 5:1).

20–21. The warrior character of Gad (20bc–21) is alluded to also in Gen. 49:19. The lands of Gad and Reuben in Transjordan are not clearly distinguished in Deut. 3:12, and, as Judah absorbed Simeon, Gad appears to have absorbed Reuben. The Moabite Stone (ninth cent.) mentions only Gad where one would expect Reuben. This may explain the point that 'he chose the best [of the land] for himself'. 'He who makes space for Gad' is sometimes taken as Yahweh (Braulik 1992a: 242), but need only mean anyone who helps or encourages him. The allusion in v. 21ab is to his military exploits in the taking of the land in Transjordan. Finally (21de) he is cast as a judge in Israel, with a combination ('justice … judgments') deriving from the lawcourt (cf. 16:18–20).

22. The name of Dan, meaning one who 'judges', is made the basis of his blessing in Gen. 49:16, but there is nothing of that explanation here. The 'lion's cub' metaphor is applied to Judah in Gen. 49:8, where it leads into the saying about Judah as leader in Israel. In the world of the Blessing, it is not in itself a negative image, but fits with a vigorous possession and defence of territory. Against this may be set the fact that Dan's ultimate position in the north of the land was not its original apportionment (cf. Josh. 19:40–48). Neither, in fact, was Bashan, in northern Transjordan, which was given to the Transjordanian part of Manasseh (Deut. 3:12). The Danite Samson's struggle against the Philistines was unsuccessful in the end (Judg. 13 – 16), and the tribe's migration north is represented as infamous (Judg. 18). This may lie behind the cryptic nature of the blessing here.

23. Naphtali's possession was in the far north, in Upper Galilee (Josh. 19:32–39). The 'west' is literally 'sea' (*yām*), which in the context could mean the Sea of Galilee, but more probably means 'west' because of the corresponding 'south' (the meaning of *yām* as 'west' arises because the Mediterranean lay in that direction). In either case, the saying, applied to a tribe in the north, is conceived from a localized perspective; that is, it should spread 'west and south' from its core territory. As well as its mountainous centre, with fertile valleys running westward, it embraced the lush plain around Lake Huleh.

24. Asher's land was a mainly fertile plain lying on the coast north of Mt Carmel, stretching as far as Tyre (Josh. 19:24–31). This excellent situation may be in mind when Asher is called 'the favourite of his brothers'. The name itself means 'happy, blessed'. The 'oil' is, of course, olive oil, a symbol of natural wealth. The blessing of Jacob also celebrates Asher's great wealth (Gen. 49:20).

33:26–29

26–27. The final stanza continues the theme of vv. 1–5, namely the favour shown to Israel (Jeshurun) by its unique God. The imagery of riding through the clouds evokes his mastery of the forces of nature (cf. Ps. 18:10[11] and usage in Canaanite literature of Baal), and thus takes up one of the pervading themes of the preceding blessings. It is the 'everlasting' and 'eternal' God who has attached himself to this nation in this time and place, making space for them by victories in battle (27). His 'arms' signify his strength to save and to bring justice, both in familiar deuteronomic language (Deut. 4:34) and elsewhere (Is. 51:5).

28–29. The image of Israel dwelling in peace and plenty corresponds to the deuteronomic ideal of a land held secure, bearing fruit richly, and watered naturally (28; cf. 7:13; 11:10–12). The final picture, of a people supreme over others because of their God's greatness (29), recalls the promises associated with its election and the covenant (7:6; 26:19).

Explanation

The Blessing of Moses fittingly forms part of the climax to the book of Deuteronomy. The specification of blessings for the tribes is not definitive, but imaginative and poetic. Even so, it puts flesh on the theme of covenant blessing. The enumeration of the tribes is unusual in Deuteronomy, which generally treats the people as a unity, and pays attention to tribal distinctions only tangentially (as when it explains the status of Levi as having no tribal inheritance [10:9; 18:2], or in the description of the occupation of Transjordan as part of the thesis that Israel is a unity even though two and a half of its tribes are physically separated from the rest by the River Jordan [3:12–20]).

The tribal enumeration, however, organized according to a geographical sweep from south to north, is a vivid picture of the possession and filling of the land, a land that Moses is about to view in the vast panorama afforded from the summit of Mt Nebo (34:1–3). The great deuteronomic theme of the gift of the land means that Israel in its various parts will have to settle the land systematically. The grand descriptions of its extent (1:7; 11:24) now come down to specific mountain ranges and cross-valleys, both the easy places and the hard, with more and less natural borders and the need to co-exist, and supremely the need to fulfil Yahweh's command to possess. We know, since Deut. 1, that this involves courage and faith. In this vision lie enfolded and latent all the contingencies that attend the occupation and possession of a land. These remain to be developed in the narratives to come, when there is no Moses, but rather Joshua at Israel's head, confronting the peoples of Canaan who hold the lands here ascribed to Israel.

The Blessing is nevertheless full of promise. It is the dying Moses' gift to his 'children' in the covenant. Moses, who cannot enter the land, here relishes it in poetry and image, as he bequeaths what he has secured by Yahweh's strength and guidance. All that he has taught Israel has its culmination in the permission and opportunity to enter this rich arena of their life in the coming generations.

The gift is theirs by the decree of all-powerful Yahweh. The Blessing resumes from the Song the concept of the election of Israel by the God who is king for ever in heaven. His specific, historical kingship in Israel derives from his everlasting cosmic kingship (2–5). The events that constituted Israel a people at Sinai/Horeb and *en route* to Canaan are cast in a framework that allows an insight into heaven itself, where Yahweh is attended by the heavenly beings. Consistently with the vision of the whole book, the specific events reviewed in its great sweep are part of a reality that goes beyond their limits.

Similarly, while the Blessing focuses very much on the special status of Israel, there is a hint of the larger purposes of Yahweh in v. 3, and perhaps also in v. 19, if 'peoples' refers there to nations other than Israel. The term invites an opening out of the vision. The deuteronomic themes of the nations as 'witnesses' (4:6–8), and of Yahweh as the giver of possessions to all (2:1–23), already pointed to his universal interest in the world. Against this background it is quite possible to think of Yahweh as the one who 'cherishes peoples' (3). The remarkable idea of Zebulun and Issachar summoning 'peoples' to worship (19) goes further. In this case, if 'peoples' is not limited to tribes of Israel, there is a curious echo of the invitation to the nations to come and seek Yahweh and his *tôrâ* in Is. 2:2–4.

The invitation has another dimension. The mountain here is plainly not Zion, but an unnamed mountain in the north (Tabor, perhaps, but unidentified nevertheless). This is an interesting echo of the unnamed 'place the LORD your God will choose to put his name and make his habitation there' (Deut. 12:5 and related texts). The inclusion of the Zebulun-Issachar mountain in the Song is one more evidence (along with 16:21; 27:1–8) that the book of Deuteronomy is no apologia for exclusive worship in Jerusalem. Rather, it takes the changing history of Israel seriously. The blessings, indeed, readily accommodate this changing history, with their passing over of Simeon, their scant regard for Reuben and Dan, their dynamic portraits of Naphtali and Gad still expanding, their envisioning Judah in some unnamed crisis, and most importantly their foregrounding of Joseph at the expense of Judah. This is a picture of history unfolding, with shifting centres of gravity. There is no 'end' of history in any cultic establishment here. The ruling spirit is the instruction of Yahweh in his covenant, guarded by Levi (9–10). The Blessing thus fits entirely with the concept of Israel on a 'journey' with Yahweh, ever standing before the covenant's requirements. And the horizon of their life with him is his rule over the whole earth.

DEUTERONOMY 34:1–12

Translation

[1]From the plains of Moab, Moses went up Mt Nebo, to the top of Pisgah, opposite Jericho. And the LORD showed him the whole land: Gilead as far as Dan, [2]all the territory of Naphtali, the land of Ephraim and Manasseh, and the whole land of Judah as far as the Mediterranean; [3]the Negeb and the plain, the valley of Jericho, city of palms, as far as Zoar. [4]And the LORD said to him, 'This is the land I promised on oath to Abraham, Isaac and Jacob that I would give to their descendants. I have let you see it for yourself; but you cannot go into it.'

[5]So Moses, the servant of the LORD, died there in the land of Moab, as the LORD had said. [6]They buried him in a valley in Moab opposite Beth-Peor. But no-one knows his actual burial place even today. [7]Moses was 120 years old when he died. His sight had not dimmed, or his strength failed. [8]The people of Israel mourned Moses in the plains of Moab for thirty days, and they completed the time of mourning for him.

[9]Joshua the son of Nun was filled with the spirit of wisdom, for Moses had laid his hands on him. The people of Israel listened to him, and they did all that the LORD had commanded Moses.

[10]But never again did a prophet like Moses arise in Israel, whom the LORD knew face to face, [11]because of all the signs and wonderful deeds the LORD sent him to do in Egypt, to Pharaoh and to all his servants and his whole land; [12]and because of his strong hand and awesome deeds which he did in the sight of all Israel.

Notes on the text

6. MT has strictly, 'He buried'; SamP, LXX have plural.

9. 'Joshua ... was filled': the clause is circumstantial, with 'Joshua' in the initial position and a participle following, indicating a situation that already exists.

Form and structure

Moses stands at the centre of this short closing narrative in Deuteronomy.
It consists of five parts, each featuring Moses, but putting him in the
context of the larger span of the narrative.

A   Moses is shown the land (1–3)
B   the land shown to Moses is the one promised
     to the patriarchs (4)
C   death of Moses (5–8)
B'   Joshua succeeds Moses (9)
A'   none like Moses arose after him (10–12)

The death of Moses is at the centre of the structure, but the chapter
portrays the whole span of Israel's history as embodied in the book at
large, from the promise of the land to the patriarchs (4; cf. 1:8), and the
exodus from Egypt (11) to an unspecified future (represented by 'even
today', v. 6, and 'never again', v. 10).

Comment

34:1–12

1–3. Moses has been speaking to Israel in 'the plains of Moab', a term
used several times in Numbers and Joshua (e.g. Num. 22:1; 36:13; Josh.
13:22), but here for the first time in Deuteronomy (contrast 1:5). It refers
to the broad plain opposite Jericho going towards the mountains of Moab.
The relationship between Nebo and Pisgah is unclear. The phrase in 3:27
is simply 'the top of Pisgah', and in 32:49, 'Mt Nebo'. Either the two
names are simple alternatives (cf. Horeb and Sinai), preserved in different
lines of tradition, or one of them identifies the place more precisely.
The latter option fits better with the naming of both together here. The
meaning might then be, 'Nebo, the summit of Pisgah' (as Craigie 1976a:
404; Merrill 1994: 451–452).

From Nebo, Moses views the land in a great circle, first looking north
through Transjordan (Gilead) as far as Dan, then west to Galilee,
represented by Naphtali, down the central part of the land (Ephraim and
Manasseh), to Judah and the Negeb in the south, and back up the Dead
Sea basin to the valley of Jericho, and Zoar (respectively at the northern
and southern ends of the Dead Sea), close to where he stood. (The 'plain'
[*hakkikkār*] can apparently designate the Dead Sea basin both north and
south of the Dead Sea; cf. Gen. 19:17–29; 2 Sam. 18:23.) The description
has adopted the viewpoint of the fuller picture in Deut. 33 by using

Israelite tribal and territorial names, in contrast to the generalized geographical descriptions in 1:7; 11:24.

4. The land has everywhere dominated Moses' own discourse in Deuteronomy, yet it was always future and unknown, a land rich only to the eye of faith. Now he sees it for the first time. It is a poignant moment, at the same time fulfilling the ancient promise of which he has been the bearer, and forbidding him to have what is given. A circle has come round fully, from the first intimation of the patriarchal promise (1:8) and the first embargo on Moses' entry (1:37), to this point of near fulfilment.

5–8. Moses was called 'the man of God' in 33:1, and now 'the servant of the LORD' (5). The climax of the book attributes names of honour to him. This name is applied to Moses also in Josh. 1:1, 7, 13, and elsewhere, suggesting that it belongs specially to him (cf. 1 Kgs. 8:53, 56; Ps. 105:26), though it is also used of others (Exod. 32:13; Josh. 24:29; 1 Sam. 23:10; and see 'Explanation'). At 120 years old (cf. 31:2) he had reached an exceptionally great age. Joseph's 110 (Gen. 50:26) is often cited as a perfect age according to Egyptian tradition, and Moses exceeds this (cf. Gen. 6:3, but also Ps. 90:10). The reference to his vigour to the end (in spite of 31:2) stresses his full capacity to lead until the moment when God appointed that he should cease.

'They buried him' (6) is strictly a singular verb, which could mean that Yahweh buried him, the second half of the verse then implying that he did so secretly. But it is likelier that it should be taken impersonally (see 'Notes on the text'), the unknown location of the grave simply being due to the passing of time. The unknown grave outside the land adds further poignancy to Moses' exclusion. There is no possibility here of a later ceremonial transfer of the remains to an honoured resting-place in the land (contrast Joseph; Josh. 24:32).

9. The death of Moses is closely connected with the theme of Joshua's succession, which was prominent also in the Song of Moses section (31:14, 23; 32:44). The reference here is to the narrative in Num. 27:18–23, where Moses commissioned Joshua by laying hands on him. That commissioning had the effect of transferring Moses' wisdom to him, as well as his authority among the people. Wisdom is cited as a necessary quality to lead Israel in 1:13, and may be assumed of Moses as the lawgiver, the law itself being Israel's 'wisdom' (4:6). (Joshua's filling with wisdom, incidentally, is not something that now happens, but rather is already true; see 'Notes on the text'.)

10–12. The book closes with an affirmation of Moses' incomparability as a prophet. 'Prophet' thus becomes the most characteristic description of him. The saying should be set alongside 18:15, which promised that 'one like him' would be raised up afterwards. The incomparability clause has something conventional about it (notice how similar clauses are applied to both Hezekiah and Josiah [2 Kgs. 18:5; 23:25] in a way that is strictly inconsistent). However, Moses remains the ultimate measure of faithfulness to Yahweh (as in the last-named text). His relationship with him was uniquely intimate (cf. Exod. 33:11). And remarkably, the language typically used of Yahweh himself in Deuteronomy to describe the defeat of Pharaoh and the powerful feats of the exodus from Egypt (4:34) is now used of Moses, in this last extravagant tribute.

Explanation

Two great themes of Deuteronomy converge in this narrative and tribute: the gift of the land and the sacrificial life of God's prophet and servant Moses. Moses' view of the land is a symbolic fulfilment of the promise, the naming of the regions in Israelite terms signifying ownership. The scope of this goes far beyond Deuteronomy itself, reaching back to the beginning of the Pentateuchal narrative (Gen. 12:3; 15:1–6, 7; 17:3–8). The ending of Deuteronomy, therefore, is in an important way the ending of the Pentateuch also. Even that is only a relative ending, however, since the land has not actually been entered at this point. The story of that will be told in Joshua, and will stretch even further, to take in the story of Israel's life in the land (Judges–Kings), which has been so strong a theme in Deuteronomy.

For this reason, interpretation of the first books of the Bible has hesitated over whether to speak of a 'Pentateuch' (five books) or a 'Hexateuch' (six books) as the first major unit of the biblical story (and, indeed, other names have been used to take in subsequent books). Such names have only a relative and provisional status, of course. The tradition of the Pentateuch, equivalent to the Jewish Torah (in the stricter sense of the term), is ancient, and owes much to its being (largely) coextensive with the life of Moses. However, it has considerable theological force also. For its final scene leaves Israel outside the land, its lawgiver deceased, having bequeathed to them in his instruction the means to live in covenant with Yahweh. The scene therefore encapsulates Israel's permanent situation, poised to receive the blessings of Yahweh, and at the same time obliged to keep entering into covenant with him.

The death of Moses is therefore an essential theme of the book. The challenge to Israel is to live in the land without him, but with the statutes and laws that he has given, which are able to lead to life (30:11–20; see also Olson 1994). His greatness lies in the fact that he has brought them to this point. In doing so, he has exhibited the great prophetic characteristics, not only of faithfully proclaiming the word of God, but of investing his own life totally in the servant role. This is why he is the servant *par excellence*. His life is lived on behalf of others; he himself is denied precisely that which is promised to them, into which he has led them. The topic of Yahweh's anger with Moses is (oddly) never fully explained, least of all in Deuteronomy. This only strengthens the impression that the punishment of Moses has something vicarious about it.

The lines from here to the Servant of Isaiah's Servant Songs will be clear. At least part of the background to that Servant figure is Moses. The Servant now brings 'justice' not just to Israel but to the nations of the world (Is. 42:3–4; 49:5–6), and there are even echoes of the Servant's death, his bearing of others' sins, and his intercessory role elaborated in 52:13 – 53:12.

BIBLIOGRAPHY

COMMENTARIES ON DEUTERONOMY

Buis, P., and J. Leclerq (1963), *Le Deutéronome*, SB, Paris: Gabalda.

Braulik, G. (1986a, 1992a), *Deuteronomium*, 2 vols., NEchtB, Würzburg: Echter Verlag.

Christensen, D. L. (1991), *Deuteronomy 1 – 11*, WBC, Dallas, TX: Word.

—— (2001a), *Deuteronomy 1 – 17*, WBC, Dallas, TX: Word.

—— (2001b), *Deuteronomy 18 – 34*, WBC, Dallas, TX: Word.

Craigie, P. C. (1976a), *The Book of Deuteronomy*, NICOT, Grand Rapids, MI: Eerdmans.

Driver, S. R. (1895), *A Critical and Exegetical Commentary on Deuteronomy*, ICC, Edinburgh: T. & T. Clark.

Mayes, A. D. H. (1979), *Deuteronomy*, NCB, London: Oliphants; Grand Rapids, MI: Eerdmans, 1981.

Merrill, E. H. (1994), *Deuteronomy*, NAC, Nashville, TN: Broadman & Holman.

Miller, P. D. (1990), *Deuteronomy*, Interpretation, Louisville, KY: John Knox.

Payne, D. (1985), *Deuteronomy*, DSB, Edinburgh: St Andrew Press; Philadelphia, PA: Westminster.

Rad, G. von (1966a), *Deuteronomy*, OTL, London: SCM; Philadelphia, PA: Westminster.

Rose, M. (1994), *5 Mose*, vols. 1, 2, ZBK, Zürich: Theologischer Verlag.

Thompson, J. A. (1974), *Deuteronomy*, TOTC, London: IVP; Downers Grove, IL: IVP, 1975.

Tigay, J. H. (1996), *Deuteronomy, Debarim*, JPSTC, Philadelphia, PA, and Jerusalem: Jewish Publication Society.

Weinfeld, M. (1991), *Deuteronomy 1 – 11*, AB, New York: Doubleday.

Wright, C. J. H. (1996), *Deuteronomy*, NIBC, Peabody, MA: Hendrickson; Carlisle: Paternoster.

OTHER WORKS

Abba, R. (1977a), 'Priests and Levites in Deuteronomy', *VT* 27:257–267.

—— (1977b), 'The Origin and Significance of Hebrew Sacrifice', *BTB* 7:257–267.

Aejmelaeus, A. (1986), 'Function and Interpretation of *kî* in Biblical Hebrew', *JBL* 105:193–209.

Aharoni, Y. (1968), 'Arad: Its Inscriptions and Temple', *BA* 31:26.

——— (1979), *The Land of the Bible*, Philadelphia, PA: Westminster.

Ahlström, G. (1982), *Royal Administration and National Religion in Ancient Palestine*, SHANE 1, Leiden: Brill.

Albertz, R. (1994), *A History of Israelite Religion in the Old Testament Period 1: From the Beginnings to the End of the Exile*, London: SCM; Louisville, KY: Westminster John Knox.

Albright, W. F. (1959), 'Some Remarks on the Song of Moses in Deuteronomy XXXII', in M. Noth (ed.), *Essays in Honour of Millar Burrows*, 343–344, Leiden: Brill.

——— (1968), *Yahweh and the Gods of Canaan*, New York: Doubleday.

Alt, A. (1959), 'Die Heimat des Deuteronomiums', in *Kleine Schriften zur Geschichte des Volkes Israel*, 250–275, Munich: Beck.

——— (1989), *Essays on Old Testament History and Religion*, Sheffield: JSOT.

Anbar, M. (1985), 'The Story about the Building of an Altar on Mt Ebal: The History of its Composition and the Question of the Centralization of the Cult', in N. Lohfink (ed.) 1985: 304–309.

Andersen, F. I. (1974), *The Sentence in Biblical Hebrew*, Janua Linguarum, Series practica 231, The Hague: Mouton.

Andersen, F. I., and D. N. Freedman (1980), *Hosea*, AB, New York: Doubleday.

Anderson, G. A., and S. M. Olyan (eds.) (1991), *Priesthood and Cult in Ancient Israel*, JSOTSup 125, Sheffield: JSOT.

Arnold, B. T. (1999), 'Religion in Ancient Israel', in D. W. Baker and B. T. Arnold (eds.), *The Face of Old Testament Studies: A Survey of Contemporary Approaches*, 391–420, Grand Rapids, MI: Baker; Leicester: Apollos.

Aurelius, E. (1988), *Der Fürbitter Israels: Eine Studie zum Mosebild im Alten Testament*, ConBOT 27, Stockholm: Almqvist & Wiksell.

Austin, J. L. (1975), *How to Do Things with Words*, 2nd ed., Cambridge, MA: Harvard University Press.

Balentine, S. E. (1983), *The Hidden God: The Hiding of the Face of God in the Old Testament*, Oxford: Oxford University Press.

——— (1985), 'Prayer in the Wilderness: In Pursuit of Divine Justice', *HAR* 9:53–74.

Baltzer, K. (1971), *The Covenant Formulary*, Oxford: Oxford University Press.

Barker, M. (1992), *The Great Angel: A Study of Israel's Second God*, London: SPCK; Louisville, KY: Westminster John Knox.

Barker, P. (1995), 'Faithless Israel, Faithful Yahweh in Deuteronomy', PhD dissertation, Bristol University.

——— (1998), 'The Theology of Deuteronomy 27', *TynB* 49:277–303.

Barthélemy, D. (1982), *Critique textuelle de l'Ancient Testament 1*, OBO 50.1, Fribourg, Switzerland: Universitaires.

Bartlett, J. R. (1969), 'The Use of the Word *rō'š* as a Title in the OT', *VT* 19:1–10.

——— (1987), *Edom and the Edomites*, JSOTSup 77, Sheffield: JSOT.

Barton, J. (1978), 'Understanding Old Testament Ethics', *JSOT* 9:44–64.

——— (1998), 'Approaches to Ethics in the Old Testament', in J. Rogerson (ed.), *Beginning Old Testament Study*, 2nd ed., 113–130, St Louis, MO: Chalice. (First published Louisville, KY: Westminster John Knox, 1982; London: SPCK, 1983.)

Bauckham, R. (1998), *God Crucified*, Carlisle: Paternoster; Grand Rapids, MI: Eerdmans, 1999.

Baumgarten, J. M. (1985), 'The First and Second Tithes in the Temple Scroll', in A. Kort and S. Morschauser (eds.), *Biblical and Related Studies Presented to Samuel Iwry*, 5–15, Winona Lake, IN: Eisenbrauns.

Begg, C. T. (1982), 'The Reading *sbty(km)* in Deut 29,9 and 2 Sam 7,7', *ETL* 58:87–105.

——— (1983), 'The Tables and the Lawbook', *VT* 33:96–97.

Bellefontaine, E. (1975), 'The Curses of Deuteronomy 27: Their Relationship to the Prohibitions', in J. W. Flanagan and A. W. Robinson (eds.), *No Famine in the Land: Studies in Honor of John L. McKenzie*, 49–61, Missoula, MT: Scholars.

——— (1979), 'Reviewing the Case of the Rebellious Son', *JSOT* 13:13–39.

Benichou-Safar, H. (1988), 'Sur l'incinération des enfants aux tophets de Carthage et de Sousse', *RHR* 205:57–67.

Ben-Tor, A. (1992), *Archaeology of Ancient Israel*, New Haven, CT: Yale University Press; Tel Aviv: Open University.

Birch, B. C., W. Brueggemann, T. E. Fretheim and D. L. Petersen (1999), *A Theological Introduction to the Old Testament*, Nashville, TN: Abingdon.

Blenkinsopp, J. (1992), *The Pentateuch: An Introduction to the First Five Books of the Bible*, London: SCM; New York: Doubleday.

——— (1995), 'Deuteronomy and the Politics of Post-Mortem Existence', *VT* 45:1–16.

Block, D. (2000), *The Gods of the Nations*, 2nd ed., Grand Rapids, MI: Baker.

Blum, E. (1990), *Studien zur Komposition des Pentateuch*, BZAW 189, Berlin: de Gruyter.

Boecker, H. J. (1969), *Die Beurteilung der Anfänge des Königtums in den deuteronomistischen Abschnitten des 1. Samuelbuches*, WMANT 31, Neukirchen-Vluyn: Neukirchener Verlag.

——— (1980), *Law and the Administration of Justice in the Old Testament and Ancient East*, London: SPCK; Minneapolis, MN: Augsburg.

Bogaert, P.-M. (1985), 'Les Trois rédactions conservées et la forme originale de l'envoi du Cantique de Moïse, Dt 32,43', in N. Lohfink (ed.) 1985: 329–340.

Boorer, S. (1992), *The Promise of the Land as Oath: A Key to the Formation of the Pentateuch*, BZAW 205, Berlin: de Gruyter.

Braulik, G. (1970), 'Die Ausdrücke für Gesetz im Buch Deuteronomium', *Biblica* 51:39–66.

—— (1984), 'Law as Gospel', *Int* 38:5–14; ET of 'Gesetz als Evangelium: Rechtfertigung und Begnadigung nach der deuteronomischen Tora', *ZThK* 79 (1982): 127–160.

—— (1986b), 'Das Deuteronomium und die Menschenrechte', *ThQ* 166:15–16.

—— (1989), 'Besprechung von Knapp', *RB* 96:266–286.

—— (1991a), 'Die Ablehnung der Göttin Aschera in Israel: War sie erst deuteronomistisch, diente sie zur Unterdrückung der Frauen?', in Wacker & Zenger (eds.) 1991: 106–136 (also in Braulik 1997: 81–118).

—— (1991b), *Die deuteronomischen Gesetze und der Dekalog*, Stuttgart: Katholisches Bibelwerk.

—— (1992b), 'Haben in Israel auch Frauen Geopfert? Beobachtungen am Deuteronomium', in S. Kreuzer and K. Lüthi (eds.), *Zur Aktualität des Alten Testament: Festschrift für Georg Sauer zum 65. Geburtstag*, 19–28, Frankfurt-am-Main: Peter Lang.

—— (1993), 'The Sequence of the Laws in Deuteronomy 12 – 26', in Christensen (ed.) 1993: 313–335; ET of 'Die Abfolge der Gesetze in Deuteronomium 12 – 26 und der Dekalog', in N. Lohfink (ed.) 1985: 252–272.

—— (1995a), 'Die dekalogische Redaktion der deuteronomischen Gesetze: Ihre Abhängigkeit von Levitikus 19 am Beispiel von Deuteronomium 22:1–12; 24:10–22 und 25:13–16', in Braulik (ed.) 1995b: 1–25 (also in Braulik 1997: 147–182).

—— (ed.) (1995b), *Bundesdokument und Gesetz: Studien zum Deuteronomium*, HBS 4; Freiburg: Herder.

—— (1996), 'Weitere Beobachtungen zur Beziehung zwischen dem Heligkeitsgesetz und Deuteronomium 19 – 25', in Veijola (ed.) 1996: 23–55 (also in Braulik 1997: 183–223).

—— (1997a), *Studien zum Deuteronomium*, SBAB 24, Stuttgart: Katholisches Bibelwerk.

—— (1997b), 'Die Funktion von Siebenergruppierungen im Endtext des Deuteronomiums', in Braulik 1997a: 63–79.

Brekelmans, C., and J. Lust (eds.) (1990), *Pentateuchal and Deuteronomistic Studies: Papers Read at the XIIIth IOSOT Congress, Leuven, 1989*, BETL 94, Leuven: Leuven University Press.

Brenner, A. (1994a), 'An Afterword: The Decalogue – Am I an Addressee?', in Brenner (ed.) 1994b: 255–258.

—— (ed.) (1994b), *A Feminist Companion to Exodus to Deuteronomy*, Sheffield: Sheffield Academic Press.

Brett, M. (1978), 'Biblical Studies and Theology: Negotiating the Intersections', *BibInt* 6:131–141.

Brettler, M. Z. (1995), *The Creation of History in Ancient Israel*, London: Routledge.

Brichto, H. C. (1973), 'Kin, Cult, Land and Afterlife', *HUCA* 44:1–54.

—— (1974), 'On Slaughter and Sacrifice, Blood and Atonement', *HUCA* 47:19–55.

Brin, G. (1994), *Studies in Biblical Law: From the Hebrew Bible to the Dead Sea Scrolls*, JSOTSup 176, Sheffield: JSOT.

Brown, M. L. (1997), '$r^e p\bar{a}'\hat{\imath}m$', *NIDOTTE* 3:1173–1180.

Brueggemann, W. (1968), 'Is 55 and Deuteronomic Theology', *ZAW* 80:191–203.

—— (1977), *The Land*, OBT 1, Philadelphia, PA: Fortress.

—— (1979), 'Trajectories in Old Testament Literature and the Sociology of Ancient Israel', *JBL* 98:161–185.

—— (1997), *Theology of the Old Testament*, Minneapolis, MN: Augsburg.

Bruin, W. M. de (1999), 'Die Freistellung vom Militärdienst in Deut. xx 5–7', *VT* 49:21–33.

Budd, P. J. (1984), *Numbers*, WBC, Waco, TX: Word.

Budde, K. (1926), 'Das Deuteronomium und die Reform des König Josias', *ZAW* 44:177–224.

Buis, P. (1967), 'Deutéronome xxvii 15–26: Malédictions ou exigences de l'alliance', *VT* 17:478–479.

Cansdale, G. S. (1970), *Animals of Bible Lands*, Exeter: Paternoster. = *All Animals of Bible Lands*, Grand Rapids, MI: Zondervan.

Carlson, R. A. (1964), *David, the Chosen King: A Traditio-Historical Approach to the Second Book of Samuel*, Uppsala: Almqvist & Wiksell.

Carmichael, C. M. (1967), 'Deuteronomic Laws, Wisdom and Historical Traditions', *JSS* 12:198–206.

—— (1974), *The Laws of Deuteronomy*, Ithaca, NY: Cornell University Press.

—— (1977), 'A Ceremonial Crux: Removing a Man's Sandal as a Female Gesture of Contempt', *JBL* 96:321–336.

—— (1982), 'Forbidden Mixtures', *VT* 32:394–415.

—— (1985), *Law and Narrative in the Bible: The Evidence of the Deuteronomic Laws and the Decalogue*, Ithaca, NY: Cornell University Press.

—— (1992), *The Origins of Biblical Law*, Ithaca, NY: Cornell University Press.

—— (1996), *The Spirit of Biblical Law*, Athens, GA: University of Georgia Press.

Carrire, J.-M. (1992), 'L'Organisation des lois en *Dt 19 – 26*: Les lois sur le mariage', *NRTh* 114:519–532.

Cassuto, U. (1967), *A Commentary on the Book of Exodus*, Jerusalem: Magnes.

Cazelles, H. (1948), 'Sur un rituel du Deutéronome, Deut xxvi, 14', *RB* 55:54–71.

—— (1985), 'Droit public dans le Deutéronome', in N. Lohfink (ed.) 1985: 99–106.

Chaney, M. L. (1991), 'Debt Easement in Israelite History and Tradition', in D. Jobling et al. (eds.) 1991: 127–139.

Childs, B. S. (1967), 'Deuteronomic Formulae of the Exodus Tradition', in
B. Hartmann, E. Jenni, E. Y. Kutscher, V. Maag, R. Smend and I. L.
Seeligmann (eds.), *Hebräische Wortforschung*, VTSup 16:30–39, Leiden:
Brill.

Chirichigno, G. C. (1993), *Debt-Slavery in Israel and the Ancient Near East*,
JSOTSup 141, Sheffield: JSOT.

Cholewinski, A. (1976), *Heiligkeitsgesetz und Deuteronomium*, AnBib 66,
Rome: Pontifical Biblical Institute.

Christ, H. (1977), *Blutvergiessen im alten Testament*, Basel: Friedrich Reinhardt.

Christensen, D. L. (1984), 'Two Stanzas of a Hymn in Deuteronomy 33', *Biblica*
65:382–389.

—— (ed.) (1993), *A Song of Power and the Power of Song*, SBTS 3, Winona
Lake, IN: Eisenbrauns.

Clark, G. R. (1992), *The Word Ḥesed in the Hebrew Bible*, JSOTSup 157,
Sheffield: Sheffield Academic Press.

Clements, R. E. (1965a), 'Deuteronomy and the Jerusalem Cult Tradition', *VT*
15:300–312.

—— (1965b), *God and Temple*, Oxford: Basil Blackwell; Philadelphia, PA:
Fortress.

—— (1975), *Prophecy and Tradition*, Oxford: Basil Blackwell; Atlanta, GA:
John Knox.

—— (1989), *Deuteronomy*, OTG, Sheffield: JSOT.

Clines, D. J. A. (1989), *The Theme of the Pentateuch*, JSOTSup 10, 2nd ed.,
Sheffield: Sheffield Academic Press.

Coats, G. W. (1988), *Moses*, JSOTSup 57, Sheffield: Sheffield Academic Press.

Cody, A. (1969), *A History of Old Testament Priesthood*, AnBib 35, Rome:
Pontifical Biblical Institute.

Cogan, M. (1993), 'Judah under Assyrian Hegemony: A Reexamination of
Imperialism and Religion', *JBL* 112:403–414.

Cole, A. (1973), *Exodus*, TOTC, London: Tyndale; Downers Grove: IVP.

Cooper, A., and B. R. Goldstein (1992), 'Exodus and *Massôt* in History and
Tradition', *Maarav* 8:15–37.

Cornill, C. H. (1891), *Einleitung in das Alte Testament*, Tübingen: Mohr.

Cragg, K. (1995), *The Lively Credentials of God*, London: Darton, Longman &
Todd.

Craigie, P. C. (1976b), *The Problem of War in the Old Testament*, Grand
Rapids, MI: Eerdmans.

Cross, F. M. (1973), *Canaanite Myth and Hebrew Epic*, Cambridge, MA:
Harvard University Press.

Crüsemann, F. (1985), 'Der Zehnte in der israelitischen Königszeit', in H.-P.
Stähli (ed.), *Wort und Dienst*, Jahrbuch der Kirchlichen Hochschule,
Bethel 18:21–47, Bielefeld: Kirchliche Hochschule, Bethel.

—— (1996), *The Torah: Theology and Social History of Old Testament Law*,
Minneapolis, MN: Fortress.

Dandamayev, M. A. (1991), 'Neo-Babylonian Society and Economy', in
    J. Boardman et al. (eds.), *The Cambridge Ancient History*, 2nd ed.,
    3.2:252–275, Cambridge: Cambridge University Press.

Daube, D. (1947), *Studies in Biblical Law*, Cambridge: Cambridge University
    Press.

—— (1961), 'Direct and Indirect Causation in Biblical Law', *VT* 11:246–269.

—— (1969), 'The Culture of Deuteronomy', *Orita* 3:27–52.

—— (1971), 'To Be Found Doing Wrong', in *Studi in onore di E. Volterra*,
    Pubblicazioni della Facultà di Giurisprudenza dell' Universita di Roma
    41:2:1–13, Milan: Guiffr.

—— (1973), 'The Self-Understood in Legal History', *Juridical Review*
    85:26–34.

Davies, E. W. (1981), 'Inheritance Rights and the Hebrew Levirate Marriage',
    VT 31:138–144, 257–268.

Davies, P. R. (1993), *In Search of 'Ancient Israel'*, JSOTSup 148, Sheffield:
    Sheffield Academic Press.

Day, J. (1986a), 'Asherah in the Hebrew Bible and Northwest Semitic
    Literature', *JBL* 105:385–408.

—— (1986b), 'Pre-Deuteronomistic Allusions to the Covenant in Hosea and
    Psalm lxxviii', *VT* 36:1–12.

—— (1989), *Molech: A God of Human Sacrifice in the Old Testament*,
    University of Cambridge Oriental Publications 41, Cambridge:
    Cambridge University Press.

—— (1990), *The Psalms*, OTG, Sheffield: JSOT.

—— (ed.) (1998), *King and Messiah in Israel and the Ancient Near East*,
    JSOTSup 270, Sheffield: Sheffield Academic Press.

Dearman, J. A. (1992), *Religion and Culture in Ancient Israel*, Peabody, MA:
    Hendrickson.

Deist, F. (1994), 'The Dangers of Deuteronomy: A Page from the Reception
    History of the Book', in García Martínez et al. (eds.) 1994: 13–29.

Deurloo, K. A. (1994), 'The One God and All Israel in its Generations', in
    García Martínez et al. (eds.) 1994: 31–46.

Diepold, P. (1972), *Israels Land*, BWANT 15; Stuttgart: Kohlhammer.

Dietrich, W. (1972), *Prophetie und Geschichte: Eine redaktionsgeschichtliche
    Untersuchung zum deuteronomistischen Geschichtswerk*, FRLANT 108,
    Göttingen: Vandenhoeck & Ruprecht.

Dion, P. (1980), 'Tu feras disparaître le mal du milieu de toi', *RB* 78:321–349.

—— (1991), 'The Suppression of Alien Religious Propaganda in Israel during
    the Late Monarchical Era', in Halpern & Hobson (eds.) 1991: 147–216.

—— (1997), review of Steymans 1995a, *Biblica* 78:271–275.

Dogniez, C., and M. Harl (1992), *Le Deutéronome*, La Bible d'Alexandrie 5;
    Paris: Cerf.

Donner, H., R. Hanhart and R. Smend (eds.) (1977), *Beiträge zur
    alttestamentlichen Theologie: Festschrift für Walther Zimmerli zum 70.
    Geburtstag*, Göttingen: Vandenhoek & Ruprecht.

Douglas, M. (1966), *Purity and Danger: An Analysis of Concepts of Pollution and Taboo*, London: Routledge & Kegan Paul; New York: Praeger.

Driver, G. R. (1955), 'Birds in the Old Testament', *PEQ* 87:5–20, 129–140.

Driver, G. R., and J. C. Miles (1952, 1955), *The Babylonian Laws*, 2 vols., Oxford: Clarendon.

——— (1975), *The Assyrian Laws*, rev. ed., Aalen: Scientia. (First published Oxford: Clarendon, 1935.)

Dumermuth, F. (1958), 'Zur deuteronomischen Kulttheologie und ihren Voraussetzungen', *ZAW* 70:59–98.

Ehrlich, A. B. (1909–14), *Randglossen zur hebräischen Bible*, Leipzig: J. C. Hinrichs.

Eichler, B. L. (1987), 'Literary Structure in the Laws of Eshnunna', in F. Rochberg-Halton (ed.), *Language, Literature and History* (*FS* Erica Reiner), AOS 67, 71–84, New Haven, CT: American Oriental Society.

Eissfeldt, O. (1917), *Erstlinge und Zehnten im alten Testament: Ein Beitrag zur Geschichte des israelitisch-jüdischen Kultus*, BWAT 22, Leipzig: J. C. Hinrichs.

——— (1958), *Das Lied Moses Deuteronomium 32:1–43 und Das Lehrgedicht Asaphs Psalm 78 samt einer Analyse der Umgebung des Mose-Liedes*, BVSAWL, Philologisch-historische Klasse B and 104, part 5; Berlin: Akademie.

——— (1970), 'Gilgal or Shechem?' in J. I. Durham and J. R. Porter (eds.), *Proclamation and Presence: OT Essays in Honour of Gwynne Henton Davies*, 90–101, London: SCM.

Elwolde, J. (1994), 'The Use of *'ĒT* in Non-Biblical Hebrew Texts', *VT* 44:170–182.

Emerton, J. A. (1962), 'Priests and Levites in Deuteronomy', *VT* 12:129–138.

——— (1982), 'New Light on Israelite Religion: The Implications of the Inscriptions from Kuntillet "Ajrud" ', *ZAW* 94:2–20.

——— (ed.) (1990), *Studies in the Pentateuch*, VTSup 41, Leiden: Brill.

Epzstein, L. (1986), *Social Justice in the Ancient Near East and the People of the Bible*, London: SCM.

Erling, B. (1986), 'First-Born and Firstlings in the Covenant Code', SBLSP 25:470–478.

Eslinger, L. (1981), 'The Case of an Immodest Lady Wrestler in Deuteronomy 25:11–12', *VT* 31:269–281.

——— (1984), 'More Drafting Techniques in Deuteronomic Laws', *VT* 34:221–226.

Eynakel, E. (1996), *The Reform of King Josiah and the Composition of the Deuteronomistic History*, OTS 33, Leiden: Brill.

Fenton, T. T. (1989), '*bᵉkol 'awat napšô* – Phraseological Criteria for the Study of Deuteronomic Cult-Restriction', *Aram* 1:21–35.

Firmage, E. (1990), 'The Biblical Dietary Laws and the Concept of Holiness', in Emerton (ed.) 1990: 177–208.

Fishbane, M. (1985), *Biblical Interpretation in Ancient Israel*, Oxford: Clarendon.

Fowler, M. D. (1987), 'The Meaning of *lipnê YHWH* in the Old Testament', *ZAW* 99:384–390.

Frankel, D. (1996), 'The Deuteronomic Portrayal of Balaam', *VT* 46:30–42.

Frankena, R. (1965), 'The Vassal Treaties of Esarhaddon and the Dating of Deuteronomy', *OtSt* 14:122–154.

Fretheim, T. E. (1968), 'The Ark in Deuteronomy', *CBQ* 30:1–14.

———(1991), *Exodus*, Interpretation, Louisville, KY: Westminster John Knox.

Frick, F. (1994), 'Widows in the Hebrew Bible', in Brenner (ed.) 1994a: 139–151.

Gammie, J. G., and L. Perdue (eds.) (1990), *The Sage in Israel and the ANE*, Winona Lake, IN: Eisenbrauns.

García López, F. (1978), 'Analyse littéraire de Deutéronome V–XI', *RB* 85:5–49 (also in *RB* 84 [1977]: 481–522).

———(1982), 'Un peuple consacré: Analyse critique de Deutéronome 7', *VT* 32:43–63.

———(1985), 'Le roi d'Israël: Dt 17,14–20', in N. Lohfink (ed.) 1985: 277–297.

García Martínez, F., A. Hilhorst, J. T. A. G. M. van Ruiten and A. S. van der Woude (eds.) (1994), *Studies in Deuteronomy in Honour of C. J. Labuschagne on the Occasion of his 65th Birthday*, VTSup 53, Leiden: Brill.

Gemser, B. (1953), 'The Importance of the Motive Clause in Old Testament Law', in G. W. Anderson et al. (eds.), Congress Volume, Copenhagen 1953, VTSup 1:51–66, Leiden: Brill.

Gertz, J. C. (1994), *Die Gerichtsorganisation Israels im deuteronomischen Gesetz*, FRLANT 165, Göttingen: Vandenhoeck & Ruprecht.

Gibson, J. C. L. (1961), 'Observations on Some Important Ethnic Terms in the Pentateuch', *JNES* 20:217–238.

Glatt-Giladi, David A. (1997), 'The Re-interpretation of the Edomite–Israelite Encounter in Deuteronomy II', *VT* 47:441–455.

Goldberg, M. L. (1984), 'Gifts or Bribes in Deuteronomy', *Int* 38:15–25.

Goldingay, J. E. (1987), *Theological Diversity and the Authority of the Old Testament*, Grand Rapids, MI: Eerdmans.

———(1990), *Approaches to Old Testament Interpretation*, 2nd ed., Leicester: IVP.

Gordon, C. H. (1970), 'His name is "One": [Zech:14:9]', *JNES* 29:198–199.

Gordon, R. P. (1997a), '*'rr*: curse', *NIDOTTE* 1:524–526.

———(1997b), 'Curse, Malediction', *NIDOTTE* 4:491–493.

Görg, M. (1993), 'Die "Astarte des Kleinviehs', *BN* 69:9–11.

Gosse, B. (1995), 'Les rédactions liées à la mention de sabbat dans le Deutéronome et dans le livre d'Esaïe', *ETR* 70:581–585.

Goudoever, J. van (1985), 'The Liturgical Significance of the Date in Dt 1,3', in N. Lohfink (ed.) 1985: 145–148.

Green, R. M. (1984), 'Ethics and Taxation: A Theoretical Framework', *JRE* 12:146–161.

Greenberg, M. (1951), 'Hebrew *segulla*: Akkadian *sikiltu*', *JAOS* 71:172–174.

———(1959), 'The Biblical Conception of Asylum', *JBL* 78:125–132.

Grintz, J. M. (1970–1), 'Do Not Eat on the Blood', *ASTI* 8:78–105.

Gunneweg, A. H. J. (1965), *Leviten und Priester*, FRLANT 89, Göttingen: Vandenhoeck & Ruprecht.

Gunton, C. (1993), *The One, the Three and the Many: God, Creation and the Culture of Modernity*, Cambridge: Cambridge University Press.

Gurewicz, S. B. (1958), 'The Deuteronomic Provisions for Exemption from Military Service', *ABR* 6:111–121.

Hadley, J. M. (1997), 'Asherah', *NIDOTTE* 1:569–170.

Hahn, J. (1981), *Das "Goldene Kalb": Die Jahwe-Verehrung bei Stierbildern in der Geschichte Israels*, Europäische Hochschulschriften 23.154:217–266, Frankfurt-am-Main: Peter Lang.

Halbe, J. (1975a), 'Erwägungen zu Ursprung und Wesen des Massotfestes', *ZAW* 87:324–345.

———(1975b), 'Passa-Massot im deuteronomischen Festkalendar: Komposition, Entstehung und Programm von Dtn. 16:1–8', *ZAW* 87:147–168.

———(1985), 'Gemeinschaft, die Welt unterbricht', in N. Lohfink (ed.) 1985: 55–75.

Halpern, B. (1981a), 'The Centralisation Formula in Deuteronomy', *VT* 31:20–38.

———(1981b), *The Constitution of the Monarchy in Israel*, HSM 25; Chico, CA: Scholars.

———(1991), 'Jerusalem and the Lineages in the Seventh Century BCE: Kinship and the Rise of Individual Moral Liability', in Halpern & Hobson (eds.) 1991: 11–107.

Halpern, B., and D. Hobson (eds.) (1991), *Law and Ideology in Monarchic Israel*, JSOTSup 124, Sheffield: Sheffield Academic Press.

Hamilton, J. M. (1992), *Social Justice and Deuteronomy: The Case of Deuteronomy 15*, Atlanta, GA: Scholars.

Hamilton, V. P. (1992), 'Marriage: Old Testament and Ancient Near East', *ABD* 4:559–569.

———(1997), '*'îš*', *NIDOTTE* 1:388–390.

Han, D.-G. (1993), 'Das Deuteronomium und seine soziale Konstellation', PhD dissertation, Frankfurt University.

Handy, L. K. (1994), *Among the Host of Heaven: The Syro-Palestinian Pantheon as Bureaucracy*, Winona Lake, IN: Eisenbrauns.

Haran, M. (1959), 'The Ark and the Cherubim', *IEJ* 9:30–38, 89–94.

———(1969), 'The Divine Presence in the Israelite Cult and Cultic Institutions', *Biblica* 50:251–267.

———(1978), *Temples and Temple Service: An Enquiry into the Character of Cult Phenomena and the Historical Setting of the Priestly School*, Oxford: Clarendon.

────(1979), 'Seething a Kid in its Mother's Milk', *JJS* 30:24–35.

Harl, M. (1995), 'L'Originalité lexicale de la version grecque du Deutéronome (LXX) et la "Paraphrase" de Flavius Josephus (A. J. IV, 176–331)', in L. Greenspoon and O. Muich (eds.), *VIII Congress of the IOSCS, Paris 1992*, SBLSCS 41:1–20, Atlanta, GA: Scholars.

Hays, R. B. (1996), *The Moral Vision of the New Testament: Community, Cross, New Creation: A Contemporary Introduction to New Testament Ethics*, Edinburgh: T. & T. Clark; San Francisco CA: HarperSanFrancisco.

Heider, G. C. (1985), *The Cult of Molek: A Reassessment*, JSOTSup 43, JSOT.

Heltzer, M. (1975), 'On Tithe Paid in Grain at Ugarit', *IEJ* 25:124–128.

Hempel, J. (1914), *Die Schichten des Deuteronomiums*, Leipzig: R. Voigtländer.

Herman, M. (1991), *Tithe as Gift: The Institution in the Pentateuch and in Light of Mauss's Presentation Theory*, Distinguished Dissertation Series 20; San Francisco, CA: Mellen Research University Press.

Herrmann, S. (2000), 'The Royal Novella in Egypt and Israel', in McConville & Knoppers (eds.) 2000: 493–515; ET of 'Die Königsnovelle in Ägypten und in Israel', *WZUL* 3 (1953–4): 51–62.

Hess, R. (1991), 'Yahweh and his Asherah? Epigraphic Evidence for Religious Pluralism in Old Testament Times', in A. D. Clarke and B. W. Winter (eds.), *One God, One Lord in a World of Religious Pluralism*, 11–13, Cambridge: Tyndale House.

Hilhorst, A. (1994), 'Deuteronomy's Monotheism and the Christians – the Case of Deut 6:13 and 10:20', in García Martínez et al. (eds.) 1994: 83–91.

Hillers, D. R. (1964), *Treaty Curses and the Old Testament Prophets*, BibOr 16, Rome: Pontifical Biblical Institute.

Hobbs, T. R. (1985), *2 Kings*, WBC; Waco, TX: Word.

Hoffmann, H.-D. (1980), *Reform und Reformen: Untersuchungen zu einem Grundthema der deuteronomistischen Geschischtsschreibung*, Zürich: Theologischer Verlag.

Hoffner, H. A. (1969), 'Some Contributions of Hittitology to OT Study', *TynB* 20:48–51.

Holladay, J. S. (1987), 'Religion in Israel and Judah under the Monarchy: An Explicitly Archaeological Approach', in P. D. Miller, P. D. Hanson and S. D. McBride (eds.), *Ancient Israelite Religion: Essays in Honor of Frank Moore Cross*, 249–299, Philadelphia, PA: Fortress.

Holladay, W. L. (1958), *The Root Šûbh in the Old Testament (With Particular Reference to its Usages in Covenantal Contexts)*, Leiden: Brill.

────(1989), *Jeremiah 2*, Hermeneia, Minneapolis, MN: Fortress.

Hölscher, G. (1922), 'Komposition und Ursprung des Deuteronomiums', *ZAW* 40:161–255.

Horst, F. (1930), *Das Privilegrecht Jahves: Rechtsgeschichtliche Untersuchungen zur Deuteronomium*, FRLANT 28, Göttingen: Vandenhoeck & Ruprecht.

Hossfeld, F.-L. (1983), 'Wahre und falsche Propheten in Israel', *BK* 38:139–144.

Hostetter, E. H. (1995), *Nations Mightier and More Numerous: The Biblical View of Palestine's Pre-Israelite Peoples*, BIBAL Dissertation Series 3, North Richmond Hills, TX: BIBAL Press.

Houston, W. (1993), *Purity and Monotheism: Clean and Unclean Animals in Biblical Law*, JSOTSup 140, Sheffield: JSOT.

Houten, C. van (1991), *The Alien in Israelite Law*, JSOTSup 107, Sheffield: JSOT.

Houtman, C. (1984), 'Another Look at Forbidden Mixtures', *VT* 34:226–228.

———— (1993), *Der Himmel im Alten Testament: Israels Weltbild und Weltanschauung*, OTS 30, Leiden: Brill.

———— (1996), 'Säkularisation im alten Israel', *ZAW* 108:408–425.

Huffmon, H. B. (1959), 'The Covenant Lawsuit in the Prophets', *JBL* 78:285–295.

Ishida, T. (1979), 'The Structure and Historical Implications of the Lists of the Pre-Israelite Nations', *Biblica* 60:461–490.

Jackson, B. S. (1975), 'From Dharma to Law', *AJCL* 23:490–512.

Jagersma, H. (1981), 'The Tithes in the Old Testament', in B. Albrektson et al. (eds.), *Remembering All the Way: A Collection of Old Testament Studies Published on the Occasion of the Fortieth Anniversary of the Oudtestamentisch Werkgezelschap in Nederland*, OTS 21:116–128, Leiden: Brill.

Jamieson-Drake, D. W. (1991), *Scribes and Schools in Monarchic Judah: A Socio-Archaeological Approach*, JSOTSup 109, Sheffield: Sheffield Academic Press.

Janowski, B. (1982), *Sühne als Heilsgeschehen: Studien zur Sühnetheologie der Priesterschrift und der Wurzel KPR im Alten Orient und im Alten Testament*, WMANT 55, Neukirchen-Vluyn: Neukirchener Verlag.

———— (1993), *Gottes Gegenwart in Israel*, BTAT, Neukirchen: Neukirchener Verlag.

Janzen, J. G. (1987), 'On the Most Important Word in the Shema (Deuteronomy vi 4–5)', *VT* 37:280–300.

———— (1994), 'The "Wandering Aramean" Reconsidered', *VT* 44:359–375.

Japhet, S. (1986), 'The Relationship between the Legal Corpora in the Old Testament in the Light of the Manumission Laws', in Japhet (ed.) 1986: 63–89. First published in Hebrew, 1978.

———— (ed.) (1986) *Studies in Bible 1986*, ScrHier 31, Jerusalem: Magnes.

Jenson, P. P. (1992), *Graded Holiness: A Key to the Priestly Conception of the World*, JSOTSup 106, Sheffield; Sheffield Academic Press.

———— (1997), '*'eḥād*', *NIDOTTE* 1:349–351.

Jeremias, J., and L. Perlitt (eds.) (1981), *Die Botschaft und die Boten: für Hans Walter Wolff zum 70. Geburtstag*, Neukirchen-Vluyn: Neukirchener Verlag.

Jobling, D., P. L. Day and G. T. Sheppard (eds.) (1991), *The Bible and the Politics of Exegesis: Essays in Honor of Norman K. Gottwald on his Sixty-fifth Birthday*, Cleveland, OH: Pilgrim.

Jobling, J. (1986), *The Sense of Biblical Narrative 2: Structural Analyses in the Hebrew Bible*, JSOTSup 39, Sheffield: JSOT.

Johnston, R. M. (1982), ' "The Least of the Commandments": Deuteronomy 22:6–7 in Rabbinic Judaism and Early Christianity', *AUSS* 20:202–215.

Joosten, J. (1996), *People and Land in the Holiness Code: An Exegetical Study of the Ideational Framework of the Law in Leviticus 17 – 26*, VTSup 67, Leiden: Brill.

—— (1998), 'The *Numeruswechsel* in the Holiness Code (Lev. XVII–XXVI)', in K.-D. Schunk and M. Augustin (eds.), *"Lasset uns Brücken bauen..."*: *Collected Communications to the XVth Congress of the Organization for the Study of the Old Testament, Cambridge, 1995*, BEATAJ 42:67–71, Frankfurt-am-Main: Peter Lang.

Joyce, P. (1989), *Divine Initiative and Human Response in Ezekiel*, JSOTS 51, Sheffield: Sheffield Academic Press.

Kaufman, S. (1978–9), 'The Structure of the Deuteronomic Law', *Maarav* 1.2:105–158.

—— (1984), 'A Reconstruction of the Social Welfare Systems of Ancient Israel', in W. B. Barrick and J. R. Spencer (eds.), *In the Shelter of Elyon: Essays on Ancient Palestinian Life and Literature in Honor of G. W. Ahlström*, JSOTSup 31, Sheffield: JSOT.

—— (1985), 'Deuteronomy 15 and Recent Research on the Dating of P', in N. Lohfink (ed.) 1985: 273–276.

Keel, O. (1980), *Das Böcklein in der Milch seiner Mutter und Verwandtes im Lichte eines altorientalischen Bildmotivs*, OBO 33, Freiburg: Universitätsverlag.

—— (1995), 'Conceptions religieuses dominantes en Palestine/Israël entre 1750 et 900', VTSup 61:119–144.

—— (1997), *Symbolism of the Biblical World*, Winona Lake, IN: Eisenbrauns.

Keller, M. (1996), *Untersuchungen zur deuteronomisch-deuteronomistischen Namenstheologie*, BBB 105, Weinheim: Beltz Athenäum.

Kirk, A. (ed.) (1988), *Handling Problems of Peace and War: A Debate with John Stott, Jerram Barrs, Alan Kreider*, Basingstoke: Marshall Pickering.

Kitchen, K. A. (1966), *Ancient Orient and Old Testament*, London: Tyndale; Chicago, IL: IVP.

—— (1989), 'The Fall and Rise of Covenant, Law and Treaty', *TynB* 40:118–135.

Kline, M. G. (1963), *The Treaty of the Great King*, Grand Rapids, MI: Eerdmans.

—— (1972), *The Structure of Biblical Authority*, Grand Rapids, MI: Eerdmans.

Knapp, D. (1987), *Deuteronomium 4: Literarische Analyse und theologische Interpretation*, Göttingen: Vandenhoeck & Ruprecht.

Knauf, E. A. (1988), 'Zur Herkunft und Sozialgeschichte Israels: "Das Böckchen in der Milch seiner Mutter" ', *Biblica* 69:153–169.

Knierim, R. (1961), 'Exodus 18 und die Neuordnung der mosaiachen
    Gerichtsbarkeit', *ZAW* 32:146–171.
———(1995), *The Task of Old Testament Theology*, Grand Rapids, MI:
    Eerdmans.
Knohl, I. (1995), *The Sanctuary of Silence: The Priestly Torah and the Holiness
    School*, Minneapolis, MN: Fortress.
Knoppers, G. N. (1993), *Two Nations under God: The Deuteronomistic History
    of Solomon and the Dual Monarchies*, 2 vols., HSM 52, Atlanta, GA:
    Scholars.
———(1994), 'Sex, Religion, and Politics: The Deuteronomist on Intermarriage',
    HAR 14:121–141.
———(1996), 'Deuteronomy and the Law of the King', *ZAW* 108:329–346.
Knowles, M. P. (1989), ' "The Rock, His Work is Perfect": Unusual Imagery for
    God in Deuteronomy 32', *VT* 39:307–322.
Kooij, A. van der (1994), 'The Ending of the Song of Moses: On the Pre-
    Masoretic Version of Deut 32:43', in García Martínez et al. (eds.) 1994:
    93–100.
Koorevaar, H. J. (1992), 'The Structure of the Ten Words in Exodus 20:1–17', in
    M. W. Pretorius (ed.), *The Secret of the Faith: In Your Heart – In Your
    Mouth* (*FS* Donald Moreland), 91–99, Leuven-Heverlee: Evangelische
    Theologische Faculteit.
Kreider, A. (1988), 'Following Jesus Implies Unconditional Pacifism', in Kirk
    (ed.) 1988: 22–40.
Kreuzer, S. (1995), 'Die Verbindung von Gottesherrschaft und Königtum Gottes
    im Alten Testament', VTSup 61:145–162.
Laberge, L. (1985), 'Le lieu que YHWH a choisi pour y mettre son Nom (TM,
    Vg et Targums): Contribution à la critique textuelle d'une formule
    deutéronomiste', *EstBíb* 43:209–236.
Lambert, W. G. (1997–8), review of Steymans 1995a, *AfO* 44:396–399.
Lang, B. (1982), 'The Social Organization of Peasant Poverty in Ancient Israel',
    JSOT 24:47–63.
———(1998), 'The Decalogue in the Light of a Newly Published Palaeo-Hebrew
    Inscription', *JSOT* 77:21–25.
Langer, G. (1989), *Von Gott Erwählt*, ÖBS, Klosterneuberg: Katholisches
    Bibelwerk.
Lasserre, G. (1995), 'Lutter contre la paupérisation et ses conséquences: Lecture
    rhétorique de Dt 15/12–18', *ETR* 70:481–492.
Leggett, D. A. (1974), *The Levirate and Goel Institutions in the Old Testament*,
    Cherry Hill, NJ: Mack.
Lemche, N. P. (1988), *Ancient Israel: A New History of Israelite Society*, Biblical
    Seminar; Sheffield: JSOT.
Lenchak, T. (1993), *'Choose Life': A Rhetorical-Critical Investigation of Deut
    28,69 – 30,20*, AnBib 129, Rome: Pontifical Biblical Institute.
Levenson, J. D. (1975), 'Who Inserted the Book of the Torah?', *HTR*
    68:203–233.

Levin, C. (1985), *Die Verheissung des Neuen Bundes in ihrem theologiegeschichtlichen Zusammenhang ausgelegt*, FRLANT 137, Göttingen: Vandenhoeck & Ruprecht.

Levinson, B. M. (1990a), 'Calum Carmichael's Approach to the Laws of Deuteronomy', *HTR* 83.3:227–257.

——— (1990b), 'McConville's Law and Theology in Deuteronomy', *JQR* 80:396–404.

——— (ed.) (1994), *Theory and Method in Biblical and Cuneiform Law: Revision, Interpolation and Development*, JSOTSup 181, Sheffield: Sheffield Academic Press.

——— (1995), 'But you Shall Surely Kill him!' in Braulik (ed.) 1995b: 37–63.

——— (1997), *Deuteronomy and the Hermeneutics of Legal Innovation*, New York: Oxford University Press.

L'Hour, J. (1963), 'Une code criminelle dans le Deutéronome', *Biblica* 44:1–28.

Lichtheim, M. (1975), *Ancient Egyptian Literature* 1, Berkeley, CA: University of California Press.

Lilley, J. P. (1993),'Understanding the Herem', *TynB* 44:170–177.

Lind, M. C. (1980), *Yahweh Is a Warrior: The Theology of Warfare in Ancient Israel*, Scottdale, PA: Herald.

Lindenberger, J. M. (1991), 'How Much for a Hebrew Slave? The Meaning of Mišneh in Deut 15:18', *JBL* 110:479–482.

Lipiński, E. (1979), *State and Temple Economy in the Ancient Near East*, 1–2, OLA 5–6, Leuven: Department Oriëntalistiek.

Loader, J. A. (1994), 'Of Barley, Bulls and Levirate', in García Martínez et al. (eds.) 1994: 123–138.

Locher, C. (1986), *Die Ehre einer Frau in Israel: Exegetische und Rechtsvergleichende Studien zu Deuteronomium 22,13–21*, OBO 70, Freiburg: Universitätsverlag.

Lohfink, G. (1975), *Die Sammlung Israels: Eine Untersuchung zur lukanischen Ekklesiologie*, SANT 34, Munich: Kosel.

Lohfink, N. (1960), 'Darstellungskunst und Theologie in Dtn 1,6 – 3,29', *Biblica* 41:105–134.

——— (1962), 'Der Bundesschluss im Land Moab: Redaktionsgeschichtliches zu Dt 28:69 – 32:47', *BZ* 6:32–56.

——— (1963), *Das Hauptgebot: Eine Untersuchung literarischer Einleitungsfragen zu Dtn 5 – 11*, AnBib 20, Rome: Pontifical Biblical Institute.

——— (1965a), *'Höre Israel!' Auslegung von Texten aus dem Buch Deuteronomium*, Die Welt der Bibel 18; Düsseldorf: Patmos.

——— (1965b), 'Zur Dekalogfassung von Dt 5', *BZ* 9:17–32.

——— (1970–), '*ḥrm*', *ThWAT* 3:192–213.

——— (1976), 'Deuteronomy', *IDBSup*, 229–232.

——— (1977), 'Culture Shock and Theology: A Discussion of Theology as a Cultural and a Sociological Phenomenon Based on the Example of a Deuteronomic Law', *BTB* 7:12–21.

—— (1981), 'Kerygmata des Deuteronomistischen Geschichtswerks', in Jeremias & Perlitt (eds.): 87–100.

—— (ed.) (1985), *Das Deuteronomium: Entstehung, Gestalt und Botschaft*, BETL 68, Leuven: Leuven University Press.

—— (1987), 'The Cult Reform of Josiah of Judah: II Kings 22 – 23 as a Source for the History of Israelite Religion', in P. D. Hanson (ed.), *Ancient Israelite Religion: Essays in Honor of Frank Moore Cross*, 459–475, Philadelphia, PA: Fortress. = 'Die Kultreform Joschijas von Juda: 2 Kön 22 – 23 als religions-geschichtliche Quelle', in N. Lohfink 1991d: 209–227.

—— (1989), 'Die "*huqqîm umispātîm*" im Buch Deuteronomium und ihre Neubegrenzung durch Dtn 12,1', *Biblica* 70:1–27.

—— (1990a), 'Das deuteronomische Gesetz in der Endgestalt – Entwurf einer Gesellschaft ohne marginale Gruppen', *BN* 51:25–40.

—— (1990b), 'Die deuteronomische Darstellung des Übergangs der Führung Israels von Mose auf Josue', *Schol* 37:32–44; repr. in N. Lohfink 1990e: 83–97.

—— (1990c), 'Dt 26,17–19 und die Bundesformel', *ZKT* 91 (1969): 517–553; repr. in N. Lohfink 1990e: 211–262.

—— (1990d), 'Gibt es eine deuteronomische Bearbeitung im Bundesbuch?', in Brekelmans & Lust 1990: 91–113.

—— (1990e), *Studien zum Deuteronomium und zur deuteronomistischen Literatur* 1, SBAB 8, Stuttgart: Katholisches Bibelwerk.

—— (1990f), 'Zum "kleinen geschichtlichen Credo", Dtn 2,5–9', in N. Lohfink 1990e: 263–290. (First published in *TP* 46 [1971]: 19–30.)

—— (1991a), '*'ed(w)t* im Deuteronomium und in den Königsbüchern', *BZ* 35:86–93.

—— (1991b), *Die Väter Israels im Deuteronomium: Mit einer Stellungnahme von Thomas Römer*, OBO 111, Freiburg: Universitätsverlag; Göttingen: Vandenhoeck & Ruprecht.

—— (1991c), 'Poverty in the Laws of the Ancient Near East and of the Bible', *TS* 52:34–50.

—— (1991d), *Studien zum Deuteronomium und zur deuteronomistischen Literatur* 2, SBAB 12, Stuttgart: Katholisches Bibelwerk.

—— (1991e), 'Zur deuteronomischen Zentralisationsformel', in N. Lohfink 1991d: 147–177. (First published in *Biblica* 65 [1984]: 297–328.)

—— (1993a) 'Die ältesten Israels und der Bund: Zum Zusammenhang von Dtn 5,13; 26,17–19; 27,1.9f und 31,9', *BN* 67:26–42.

—— (1993b), 'Distribution of the Functions of Power: The Laws Concerning Public Offices in Deuteronomy 16:18 – 18:22', in Christensen (ed.) 1993: 336–352; ET of 'Die Sicherung der Wirksamkeit des Gotteswortes durch das Prinzip der Schriftlichkeit der Tora und durch das Prinzip der Gewaltenteilung nach den Ämtergesetzen des Buches Deuteronomium (Dt 16,18–18,22)', in H. Wolter (ed.), *Testimonium Veritati* (*FS* W. Kempf), 143–155, Frankfurt-am-Main: Knecht, 1971.

——— (1994), 'Moab oder Sichem – Wo Wurde Dtn 28 nach der Fabel des Deuteronomiums Proklamiert?', in García Martínez et al. (eds.) 1994: 139–153.

——— (1995a), 'Bund als Vertrag im Deuteronomium', ZAW 107:215–239.

——— (1995b), 'Kultzentralisation und Deuteronomium: Zu einem Buch von Eleonore Reuter', ZABR 1:117–148.

——— (1995c), Studien zum Deuteronomium und zur deuteronomistischen Literatur 3, SBAB 20, Stuttgart: Katholisches Bibelwerk.

——— (1995d), 'Opferzentralisation, Säkularierungsthese und mimetische Theorie', in Lohfink 1995c: 219–260.

——— (1995e), 'The Destruction of the Seven Nations in Deuteronomy and the Mimetic Theory', Contagion 2:103–117.

——— (1995f), 'The Laws of Deuteronomy: A Utopian Project for a World Without Any Poor?' Lattey Lecture, St Edmund's College, Cambridge: Von Hügel Institute.

——— (1995g), 'Zur Fabel des Deuteronomiums', in Braulik (ed.) 1995b: 65–78.

——— (1996), 'Fortschreibung? Zur Technik von Rechtsrevisionen im deuteronomischen Bereich, erörtert an Deuteronomium 12, Ex 21,2–11 und Dtn 15,12–18', in Veijola (ed.) 1996: 126–171.

——— (1997a), 'Geschichtstypologisch Orientierte Textstrukturen in den Büchern Deuteronomium und Josua', in Vervenne & Lust (eds.) 1997: 133–160, Leuven University Press.

——— (1997b), 'Landeroberung und Heimkehr: Hermeneutisches zum Heutigen Umgang mit dem Josuabuch', JBT 12:3–24.

——— (1998), 'Der Neue Bund im Buch Deuteronomium', ZABR 4:100–125.

Longman, T., and D. G. Reid (1995), God is a Warrior, Grand Rapids, MI: Zondervan; Carlisle: Paternoster.

Lundbom, J. R. (1996), 'The Inclusio and Other Framing Devices in Deuteronomy', VT 46:296–315, 302–304.

Lust, J. (1994), 'For I Lift up my Hand to Heaven and Swear: Deut 32:40', in García Martínez et al. (eds.) 1994: 155–164.

Luyten, J. (1985), 'Primeval and Eschatological Overtones in the Song of Moses (Dt 32,1–43)', in N. Lohfink (ed.) 1985: 341–347.

Maarsingh, B. (1961), Onderzoek naar de ethiek van de wetten in Deuteronomium, Winterswijk: Van Amstel.

McBride, S. D. (1973), 'The Yoke of the Kingdom: An Exposition of Deuteronomy 6:4–5', Int 27:273–306.

——— (1993), 'Polity of the Covenant People: The Book of Deuteronomy', in Christensen (ed.) 1993: 62–77. (First published in Int 41 [1987]: 229–244.)

McCann, C. (1993), A Theological Introduction to the Book of Psalms: The Psalms as Torah, Nashville, TN: Abingdon.

McCarthy, D. J. (1965), 'Notes on the Love of God in Deuteronomy and the Father–Son Relationship between Yahweh and Israel', CBQ 27:144–147.

——— (1981), *Treaty and Covenant*, rev. ed., AnBib 21a; Rome: Pontifical Biblical Institute.

McConville, J. G. (1984), *Law and Theology in Deuteronomy*, JSOTSup 33, Sheffield: JSOT.

——— (1989), 'Narrative and Meaning in the Books of Kings', *Biblica* 70:31–49.

——— (1993a), *Grace in the End: A Study in Deuteronomic Theology*, Grand Rapids, MI: Zondervan; Carlisle: Paternoster.

——— (1993b), *Judgment and Promise: An Interpretation of the Book of Jeremiah*, Leicester: Apollos; Winona Lake, IN: Eisenbrauns.

——— (1993c), 'Yahweh and the Gods in the Old Testament', *EJT* 2:107–117.

——— (1994), 'Jerusalem in the Old Testament', in P. W. L. Walker (ed.), *Jerusalem Past and Present in the Purposes of God*, 2nd ed., 21–51, Carlisle: Paternoster; Grand Rapids, MI: Baker.

——— (1997a), 'Deuteronomic/-istic Theology', *NIDOTTE* 4.528–537.

——— (1997b), 'The Old Testament Historical Books', *Them* 22:3–13.

——— (1998), 'King and Messiah in Deuteronomy and the Deuteronomistic History', in J. Day (ed.), *King and Messiah in the Old Testament*, 271–295, Sheffield; Sheffield Academic Press.

——— (1999a), 'Faces of Exile in Old Testament Historiography', in V. P. Long (ed.), *Israel's Past in Present Research: Essays on Ancient Israelite Historiography*, 519–534, Winona Lake, IN: Eisenbrauns. (First published in J. Barton and D. J. Reimer [eds.], *After the Exile: Essays in Honor of Rex Mason*, 27–44, Macon, GA: Mercer University Press, 1996.)

——— (1999b), 'Priesthood in Joshua to Kings', *VT* 49:73–87.

——— (2000a), '1 Kings viii 46–53 and the Deuteronomic Hope', in McConville & Knoppers (eds.) 2000: 358–369. (First published in *VT* 42 (1992): 67–79.)

——— (2000b), 'Deuteronomy: Torah for the Church of Christ', *EJT* 9:33–47.

——— (2000c), 'Deuteronomy's Unification of Passover and Massot – A Response to B. M. Levinson', *JBL* 119:47–58.

——— (2000d), 'The Old Testament and the Enjoyment of Wealth', in C. Bartholomew and T. Moritz (eds.), *Christ and Consumerism*, 34–53, Carlisle: Paternoster.

——— (2002a), 'Divine Speech and the Book of Jeremiah', in C. R. Trueman (ed.), *The Trustworthiness of Our God*, Leicester: Apollos.

——— (2002b), 'Singular Address in the Deuteronomic Law and the Politics of Legal Administration', *JSOT* 97:19–36.

McConville, J. G., and G. N. Knoppers (eds.) (2000), *Reconsidering Israel and Judah: Recent Studies on the Deuteronomistic History*, SBTS, Winona Lake, IN: Eisenbrauns.

McConville, J. G., and J. G. Millar (1994), *Time and Place in Deuteronomy*, JSOTSup 179, Sheffield: Sheffield Academic Press.

McKeating, H. (1979), 'Sanctions against Adultery in Ancient Israelite Society, with Some Reflections on Methodology in the Study of Old Testament Ethics', *JSOT* 11:57–62.

Malbon, E. S. (1993), 'Texts and Contexts: Interpreting the Disciples in Mark', *Semeia* 62:81–102.

Malchow, B. V. (1996), *Social Justice in the Hebrew Bible: What Is New and What Is Old?* Collegeville, MN: Liturgical.

Maloney, R. P. (1974), 'Usury and Restrictions on Interest Taking in the ANE', *CBQ* 36:1–20.

Manor, D. W. (1992), 'Beersheba', *ABD* 1:641–645.

Manor, D. W., and G. W. Herion (1992), 'Arad', *ABD* 1:331–336.

Matthews, V. H. (1994), 'The Anthropology of Slavery in the Covenant Code', in B. M. Levinson (ed.), *Theory and Method in Biblical and Cuneiform Law: Revision, Interpretation and Development*, JSOTSup 181:119–135, Sheffield: Sheffield Academic Press.

Mayes, A. D. H. (1994), 'Deuteronomy 14 and the Deuteronomic World View', in García Martínez et al. (eds.) 1994: 165–181.

Mendenhall, G. E. (1993), 'Samuel's "Broken *Rîb*": Deuteronomy 32', in Christenson (ed.) 1993: 169–180. (First published in J. W. Flanagan and A. W. Robinson [eds.], *No Famine in the Land: Studies in Honor of J. L. McKenzie*, 63–74, Missoula, MT: Scholars.)

Merendino, R. P. (1969), *Das deuteronomische Grundgesetz: eine literarkritische, gattungs- und überlieferungsgeschichtliche Untersuchung zu Dt 12 – 26*, BBB 31, Bonn: Peter Hanstein.

——— (1980), 'Dt 27:1–8: Eine literarkritische und überlieferungsgeschichtliche Untersuchung', *BZ* 24:194–207.

Mettinger, T. (1982), *The Dethronement of Sabaoth: Studies in the Shem and Kabod Theologies*, ConBOT 18, Lund: Gleerup.

Milgrom, J. (1963), 'The Biblical Diet Laws as an Ethical System: Food and Faith', *Int* 17:288–301.

——— (1973), 'The Alleged "Demythologization" and "Secularization" in Deuteronomy', *IEJ* 23:151–156.

——— (1976), 'Profane Slaughter and a Formulaic Key to the Composition of Deuteronomy', *HUCA* 47:1–17.

——— (1981), 'Sancta Contagion and Altar/City Asylum', in J. A. Emerton (ed.), *Congress Volume, Vienna 1980*, VTSup 32:278–310, Leiden: Brill.

——— (1991), *Leviticus 1 – 16*, AB, New York: Doubleday.

Millar, J. G. (1998), *Now Choose Life: Theology and Ethics in Deuteronomy*, Leicester: Apollos; Grand Rapids, MI: Eerdmans.

———, see McConville & Millar 1994.

Millard, A. R. (1972), 'The Practice of Writing in Ancient Israel', *BA* 35:98–111.

——— (1988), 'King Og's Bed and Other Ancient Ironmongery', in L. Eslinger and G. Taylor (eds.), *Ascribe to the LORD: Biblical and other Studies in Memory of Peter C. Craigie*, JSOTSup, 67:481–492, Sheffield: JSOT.

Miller, P. D. (1969), 'The Gift of God: The Deuteronomic Theology of the Land', *Int* 23:451–465.

Minette de Tillesse, G. (1962), 'Sections "tu" et sections "vous" dans le Deutéronome', *VT* 12:29–87.

Mitchell, G. (1993), *Together in the Land*, JSOTSup 134, Sheffield: JSOT

Mittmann, S. (1975), *Deuteronomium 1:1 – 6:3 literarkritisch und traditionsgeschichtlich untersucht*, BZAW 39; Berlin: Alfred Töpelman.

Moberly, R. W. L. (1983), *At the Mountain of God*, JSOTSup 22, Sheffield: JSOT.

——— (1990), '"Yahweh Is One": The Translation of the Shema', in Emerton (ed.) 1990: 209–216.

——— (1992), *The Old Testament of the Old Testament*, OBT, Philadelphia, PA: Augsburg-Fortress.

——— (1999), 'Toward an Interpretation of the Shema', in Seitz & Greene-McCreight (eds.) 1999: 124–144.

Moor, J. C. de (1994), 'Poetic Fragments in Deuteronomy and the Deuteronomistic History', in García Martínez et al. (eds.) 1994: 183–196.

——— (ed.) (1995), *Synchronic or Diachronic? A Debate on Method in Old Testament Exegesis*, OTS 34, Leiden: Brill.

Moore, M. S. (1996), 'Role Pre-emption in the Israelite Priesthood', *VT* 46:316–329.

Moran, W. L. (1963a), 'The Ancient Near Eastern Background of the Love of God in Deuteronomy', *CBQ* 25:77–87.

——— (1963b), 'The End of the Unholy War and the Anti-Exodus', *Biblica* 44:333–342.

——— (1966), 'The Literary Connection between Lev 11:13–19 and Deut 14:12–28', *CBQ* 28:271–277.

Morrow, W. S. (1995), *Scribing the Center: Organization and Redaction in Deuteronomy 14:1 – 17:3*, SBLMS 49, Atlanta, GA: Scholars.

Myers, J. M. (1961), 'The Requisites for Response: On the Theology of Deuteronomy', *Int* 15:14–31.

Nakanose, S. (1993), *Josiah's Passover: Sociology and the Liberating Bible*, New York: Orbis.

Naudé, J. A. (1997), '*qdš*', *NIDOTTE* 3:877–887.

Nelson, R. D., (1981), *The Double Redaction of the Deuteronomistic History*, JSOTSup 18, Sheffield: JSOT.

——— (1991), 'The Role of the Priesthood in the Deuteronomistic History', VTSup 43:132–147.

——— (1997), '*ḤEREM* and the Deuteronomic Social Conscience', in Vervenne & Lust (eds.) 1997: 39–54.

Nicholson, E. W. (1967), *Deuteronomy and Tradition*, Oxford: Basil Blackwell; Philadelphia, PA: Fortress.

——— (1986), *God and His People*, Oxford: Clarendon; New York: Oxford University Press.

Niehaus, J. (1992), 'The Central Sanctuary: Where and When?', *TynB* 43:3–30.

Niehr, H. (1990), *Der höchste Gott: Alttestamentlicher JHWH-Glaube im Kontext syrisch-kanaanäischer Religion des 1. Jahrtausends v. Chr*, BZAW 190, Berlin: de Gruyter.

Nigosian, S. (1997), 'Linguistic Patterns in Deuteronomy 32', *Biblica* 78:206–224.

Norin, S. (1994), 'Ein Aramäer dem Umkommen nahe – ein Kerntext der Forschung und Tradition', *SJOT* 8:87–104.

North, R. G. (1954), '*Yâd* in the Shemitta Law', *VT* 4:196–199.

Noth, M. (1930), *Das System der zwölf Stämme Israels*, BWANT 4.1, Stuttgart: Kohlhammer.

——— (1960), *The History of Israel*, 2nd ed., New York: Harper & Row.

——— (1966), *The Laws in the Pentateuch*, London: Oliver & Boyd; Philadelphia, PA: Fortress, 1967.

——— (1981), *The Deuteronomistic History*, JSOTSup 15, Sheffield: JSOT.

O'Connell, R. (1992a), 'Deuteronomy ix 7 – x 7,10–11: Panelled Structure, Double Rehearsal and the Rhetoric of Covenant Rebuke', *VT* 42:492–509.

——— (1992b), 'Deuteronomy VII 1–26: Asymmetrical Concentricity and the Rhetoric of Conquest', *VT* 42:248–265.

O'Connor, D. (1995), 'The Social and Economic Organization of Ancient Egyptian Temples', in J. M. Sasson (ed.), *Civilizations of the Ancient Near East*, 1:319–329, 4 vols., New York: Charles Scribner's Sons.

Oden, R. A. (1984), 'Taxation in Biblical Israel', *JRE* 12.2:162–181.

O'Donovan, O. (1996), *The Desire of the Nations: Rediscovering the Roots of Political Theology*, Cambridge: Cambridge University Press.

Ollenburger, B. C. (1987), *Zion, City of the Great King: A Theological Symbol of the Jerusalem Cult*, JSOTSup 41, Sheffield: JSOT.

Olson, D. (1994), *Deuteronomy and the Death of Moses*, Minneapolis, MN: Fortress.

Olyan, S. M. (1988), *Asherah and the Cult of Yahweh in Israel*, SBLMS 34, Atlanta, GA: Scholars.

Otto, E. (1988), *Wandel der Rechtsbegründungen in der Gesellschaftsgeschichte des antiken Israel: Eine Rechtsgeschichte des 'Bundesbuches' Ex XX 22 – XXIII 13*, Studia Biblica 3, Leiden: Brill.

——— (1992), 'Das Verbot der Wiederherstellung einer geschiedenen Ehe: Deuteronomium 24:1–4 im Kontext des israelitischen und judäischen Eherechts', *UF* 24:301–310.

——— (1993a), 'Town and Rural Countryside in Ancient Israelite Law', *JSOT* 57:3–22.

——— (1993b), 'Vom Bundesbuch zum Deuteronomium: Die deuteronomische Redaktion in Dtn 12 – 26', in G. Braulik, W. Gross and S. E. McEvenue (eds.), *Biblische Theologie und gesellschaftlicher Wandel: Für Norbert Lohfink, SJ*, 260–278, Freiburg: Herder.

——— (1994), 'Aspects of Legal Reforms and Reformulations in Ancient Cuneiform and Israelite Law', in Levinson (ed.) 1994: 160–196.

——— (1995a), 'Rechtsreformen in Deuteronomium XII – XXVI und im Mittelassyrischen Kodex der Tafel A, KAV 1', VTSup 61:239–273.

——— (1995b), 'Von der Programmschrift einer Rechtsreform zum Verfassungsentwurf des neuen Israel: Die Stellung des Deuteronomiums in der Rechtsgeschichte Israels', in Braulik (ed.) 1995b: 93–104.

——— (1996), 'Deuteronomium 4: Die Pentateuchredaktion im Deuteronomiumsrahmen', in Veijola (ed.) 1996: 196–222.

——— (1998), 'False Weights in the Scales of Biblical Justice? Different Views of Women from Patriarchal Hierarchy to Religious Equality in the Book of Deuteronomy', in V. H. Matthews, B. M. Levinson and T. Frymer-Kensky (eds.), *Gender and Law in the Hebrew Bible and the Ancient Near East*, JSOTSup 262:128–146, Sheffield: Sheffield Academic Press.

Oyen, H. van (1967), *Die Ethik des Alten Testaments*, Gütersloh: Gerd Mohn.

Parpola, S. (1987), 'Neo-Assyrian Treaties from the Royal Archives of Nineveh', *JCS* 39:161–189.

Patrick, D. (1985), *Old Testament Law*, Atlanta, GA: John Knox; London: SCM, 1986.

——— (1995), 'The Rhetoric of Collective Responsibility in Deuteronomic Law', in D. P. Wright et al. (eds.) 1995: 421–436.

Paul, S. M. (1970), *Studies in the Book of the Covenant in the Light of Cuneiform and Biblical Law*, VTSup 18, Leiden: Brill.

Peckham, B. (1975), 'The Composition of Deut 9:1 – 10:11', in J. Plevnik (ed.), *Word and Spirit: Essays in Honor of David Michael Stanley on his 60th Birthday*, 3–59, Willowdale, ON: Regis College Press.

Perlitt, L. (1969), *Bundestheologie im Alten Testament*, WMANT 36, Neukirchen-Vluyn: Neukirchener Verlag.

——— (1977), 'Sinai und Horeb', in Donner et al. (eds.) 1977: 302–322.

——— (1981), ' "Wovon der Mensch lebt" (Dtn 8,3b)', in Jeremias & Perlitt (eds.) 1981: 403–426.

——— (1983), 'Motive und Schichten der Landtheologie im Deuteronomium', in G. Strecker (ed.), *Das Land Israels in biblischer Zeit*, Symposium 1981 der Hebr. Universität und der Georg-August Universität; GTA 25:46–58, Göttingen.

——— (1990–), *Deuteronomium*, BKAT 5, Neukirchen-Vluyn: Neukirchener Verlag.

——— (1994), 'Der Staatsgedanke im Deuteronomium', in S. E. Balentine and J. Barton (eds.), *Language, Theology and the Bible: Essays in Honour of James Barr*, 182–198, Oxford: Clarendon.

Petschow, H. (1965), 'Zur Systematik und Gesetzestechnik im Codex Hammurabi', *ZA* 57:146–172.

Phillips, A. (1970), *Ancient Israel's Criminal Law: A New Approach to the Decalogue*, Oxford: Basil Blackwell; New York: Schocken.

——— (1981), 'Another Look at Adultery', *JSOT* 20:3–25.

Plöger, J. G. (1967), *Literarkritische, formgeschichtliche und stilkritische Untersuchungen zum Deuteronomium*, BBB 26, Bonn: Peter Hanstein.

Polzin, R. (1980), *Moses and the Deuteronomist*, New York: Seabury.

Porter, J. R. (1994), 'The Interpretation of Deuteronomy xxxiii 24–5', *VT* 44:267–270.

Poulter, A. J. (1989), 'Rhetoric and Redaction in Deuteronomy 8: Linguistic Criticism of a Biblical Text', PhD dissertation, Cambridge University.

Pressler, C. (1993), *The View of Women Found in Deuteronomic Family Law*, BZAW 216, Berlin: de Gruyter.

——— (1994), 'Sexual Violence and Deuteronomic Law', in Brenner (ed.) 1994: 102–112.

Preuss, H. D. (1968), ' "...ich will mit dir sein" ', *ZAW* 80:139–173.

Provan, I. (1995), 'Ideologies, Literary and Critical: Reflections on Recent Writing on the History of Israel', *JBL* 114:585–606.

Rad, G. von (1929), *Das Gottesvolk im Deuteronomium*, BWANT 47, Stuttgart: Kohlhammer.

——— (1953), *Studies in Deuteronomy*, SBT 9, London: SCM.

——— (1966), *The Problem of the Hexateuch and Other Essays*, London: SCM; New York: McGraw-Hill.

Raitt, T. M. (1977), *A Theology of Exile: Judgment/Deliverance in the Theology of Jeremiah and Ezekiel*, Philadelphia, PA: Fortress.

Redford, D. B. (1972), 'Studies in the Relations between Palestine and Egypt during the First Millennium BC: The Taxation System of Solomon', in J. W. Wevers and D. B. Redford (eds.), *Studies in the Ancient Palestinian World: Presented to F. V. Winnett*, 141–156, Toronto: University of Toronto Press.

Reif, S. C. (1972), 'Dedicated to ḥnk', *VT* 22:495–501.

Reimer, D. J. (1990), 'Concerning Return to Egypt: Deut xvii 16 and xxviii 68 Reconsidered', in Emerton (ed.) 1990: 217–229.

——— (1997), 'ṣdq', *NIDOTTE* 3:744–769.

Reindl, J. (1970), *Das Angesicht Gottes im Sprachgebrauch des alten Testaments*, ETS 25, Leipzig: St Benno.

Rendtorff, R. (1981), 'Die Erwählung Israels als Thema deuteronomischen Theologie', in Jeremias & Perlitt (eds.) 1981: 75–86.

——— (1993), *Canon and Theology*, OBT, Minneapolis, MN: Fortress.

Reuter, E. (1993), *Kultzentralisation: Entstehung und Theologie von Dtn 12*, BBB 87, Frankfurt-am-Main: Hain.

Reventlow, H. G., Y. Hoffmann and B. Uffenheimer (eds.) (1994), *Politics and Theopolitics in the Bible and Postbiblical Literature*, JSOTSup 171, Sheffield: JSOT.

Reviv, H. (1989), *The Elders in Ancient Israel: A Study of a Biblical Institution*, Jerusalem: Magnes.

Robertson, D. (1972), *Linguistic Evidence in Dating Early Hebrew Poetry*, SBLDS 3, Missoula, MT: Scholars.

Rofé, A. (1985a), 'The Covenant in the Land of Moab (Deuteronomy 28:69 – 30:20): Historico-Literary, Comparative and Formcritical Considerations', in N. Lohfink (ed.) 1985: 310–320.

——— (1985b), 'The Laws of Warfare in the Old Testament: Their Origins, Intent and Positivity', *JSOT* 32:23–44.

——— (1987), 'Family and Sex Laws in Deuteronomy and the Book of the Covenant', *Henoch* 9: 131–159.

——— (1988), 'The Arrangement of the Laws in Deuteronomy', *ETL* 64:265–287.

——— (1990), 'The Tenth Commandment in the Light of Four Deuteronomic Laws', in Segal & Levi (eds.) 1990: 45–65.

Rogerson, J. (1985), *The New Atlas of the Bible*, London: Macdonald.

Römer, T. (1990), *Israels Väter: Untersuchungen zum Väterthematik im Deuteronomium und in der deuteronomistischen Tradition*, OBO 99, Freiburg: Universitätsverlag; Göttingen: Vandenhoeck & Ruprecht.

——— (2000), 'Deuteronomy in Search of Origins', in McConville & Knoppers (eds.) 2000: 112–138; ET of 'Le Deutéronome à la quête des origines', in P. Haudebert (ed.), *Le Pentateuque: Débats et recherches*, LD 151:65–98, Paris: Cerf, 1992.

Römer, W. H. P. (1974), 'Randbemerkungen zur Travestie von Deut 22,5', in M. S. H. G. Heerma van Voss, P. H. J. Houwink ten Caate and N. A. van Ochelen, *Travels in the World of the Old Testament: Studies Presented to Professor M. A. Beek on the Occasion of his 65th Birthday*, SSN 16, 217–222, Assen: van Gorcum.

Rose, M. (1975), *Der Ausschliesslichkeitsanspruch Jahwes*, BWANT 106, Stuttgart: Kohlhammer.

Rosenberg, J. (1986), *King and Kin: Political Allegory in the Hebrew Bible*, Bloomington, IN: Indiana University Press.

Rowley, H. H. (1967), *Worship in Ancient Israel: Its Forms and Meaning*, London: SPCK; Phildelphia, PA: Fortress.

Ruiten, J. T. A. G. M. van (1994), 'The Use of Deut 32:39 in Monotheistic Controversies in Rabbinic Literature', in García Martínez et al. (eds.) 1994: 223–241.

Rüterswörden, U. (1987), *Von der politischen Gemeinschaft zur Gemeinde: Studien zu Dt 16,18 – 18,22*, BBB 65, Frankfurt-am-Main: Athenäum.

Sailhamer, J. (1992), *The Pentateuch as Narrative: A Biblical-Theological Commentary*, Grand Rapids, MI: Zondervan.

Sanders, P. (1996), *The Provenance of Deuteronomy 32*, OTS 37, Leiden: Brill.

Schäfer-Lichtenberger, C. (1985), 'Exodus 18 – Zur Begründung königlicher Gerichtsbarkeit in Israel-Juda', *DBAT* 21:61–85.

——— (1990), 'Göttliche und Menschliche Autorität im Deuteronomium', in Brekelmans & Lust (eds.) 1990: 125–142.

——— (1994), 'Bedeutung und Funktion von Herem in biblisch-hebräischen Texten', *BZ* 38:270–275.

——— (1995), *Josua und Salomo: Eine Studie zu Autorität und Legitimität des Nachfolgers im Alten Testament*, VTSup 58, Leiden: Brill.

——— (1996), 'JHWH, Israel und die Völker aus der Perspektive von Dtn 7', *BZ* 40:194–218.

Scharbert, J. (1981), 'Die Fürbitte im Alten Testament', in R. Beer, *Diener in Eurer Mitte* (*FS* A. Hofmann), 91–109, Passau: Katholisch-Theologische Fakultät, Universität Passau.

Schenker, A. (1980), 'Unwiderrufliche Umkehr und Neuer Bund: Vergleich zwischen Dt 4:25–31; 30:1–14; Jer 31:31–34', *FZPhTh* 27:93–106.

Schmid, H. H. (1968a), *Gerechtigkeit also Weltordnung: Hintergrund und Geschichte der alttestamentlichen Gerechtigkeitsbegriffes*, BHT 40, Tübingen: Mohr.

——— (1968b), *Mose: Überlieferung und Geschichte*, BZAW 110, Berlin: Alfred Töpelmann.

——— (1976), 'Rechtfertigung als Schöpfungsgeschehen: Notizen zur alttestamentlichen Vorgeschichte eines neutestamentlichen Themas', in J. Friedrich (ed.), *Rechtfertigung* (*FS* E. Käsemann), 403–414, Tübingen: Mohr; Göttingen: Vandenhoeck & Ruprecht.

Schreiner, J. (1963), *Sion-Jerusalem: Jahwehs Königssitz: Theologie der Heiligen Stadt im Alten Testament*, SANT 9, Munich: Kosel.

Schulz, H. (1969), *Das Todesrecht im Alten Testament*, BZAW 114, Berlin: Alfred Töpelmann.

Schwartz, B. J. (1991), 'The Prohibitions concerning the "Eating" of Blood in Leviticus 17', in Anderson & Olyan (eds.) 1991: 34–66.

Searle, J. (1970), *Speech Acts: An Essay on the Philosophy of Language*, Cambridge: Cambridge University Press.

Seccombe, D. P. (1983), *Possessions and the Poor in Luke–Acts*, Linz: Fuchs.

Seebass, H. (1982), 'Garizim und Ebal als Symbole von Segen und Fluch', *Biblica* 63:22–31.

Seeligmann, L. (1977), 'Erkenntnis Gottes und historisches Bewusstsein im alten Israel', in Donner et al. (eds.) 1977: 414–445.

Segal, B.-Z., and G. Levi (eds.) (1990), *The Ten Commandments in History and Tradition*, Jerusalem: Magnes.

Segal, J. B. (1963), *The Hebrew Passover: From the Earliest Times to* AD *70*, London: Oxford University Press.

Seifert, B. (1996), *Metaphorisches Reden von Gott im Hoseabuch*, FRLANT 166, Göttingen: Vandenhoeck & Ruprecht.

Seitz, C. (1998), *Word Without End: The Old Testament as Abiding Theological Witness*, Grand Rapids, MI: Eerdmans.

——— (1999), 'The Call of Moses and the "Revelation" of the Divine Name: Source-critical Logic and its Legacy', in Seitz & Greene-McCreight (eds.) 1999: 145–161; also in Seitz 1998: 229–247.

Seitz, C., and K. Greene-McCreight (eds.) (1999), *Theological Exegesis: Essays in Honor of Brevard S. Childs*, Grand Rapids, MI: Eerdmans.

Seitz, G. (1971), *Redaktionsgeschichtliche Studien zum Deuteronomium*, BWANT 93, Stuttgart: Kohlhammer.

Skehan, P. W. (1951), 'The Structure of the Song of Moses in Deuteronomy (32:1–43)', *CBQ* 13:153–163; repr. in Christensen (ed.) 1993: 156–168.

Sklba, R. J. (1981), 'The Call to New Beginnings: A Biblical Theology of Conversion', *BTB* 11:67–73.

Smend, R. (2000), 'The Law and the Nations: A Contribution to Deuteronomistic Tradition History', in McConville & Knoppers (ed.) 2000: 95–110; ET of 'Das Gesetz und die Völker: Ein Beitrag zur deuteronomistischen Redaktionsgeschichte', in H. W. Wolff (ed.), *Probleme biblischer Theologie: Gerhard von Rad zum 70. Geburtstag*, 494–509, Munich: Kaiser, 1971.

Sollamo, R. (1985), 'Den bibliska formeln "Inför Herren/Inför Gud" ', *SEÅ* 50:21–32.

Sonnet, J.-P. (1997), *The Book within the Book: Writing in Deuteronomy*, Biblical Interpretation Series 14; Leiden: Brill.

Spieckermann, H. (1982), *Juda unter Assur in der Sargonidenzeit*, FRLANT 129, Göttingen: Vandenhoeck & Ruprecht.

Sprinkle, J. M. (1994), *The Book of the Covenant: A Literary Approach*, JSOTSup 174, Sheffield: JSOT.

Stamm, J. J., and M. E. Andrew (1967), *The Ten Commandments in Recent Research*, SBT 2.2, London: SCM; Naperville, IL: Allenson.

Steck, J. D. (1990), 'A History of the Interpretation of Genesis 49 and Deuteronomy 33', *BSac* 147:16–31.

Steinbert, N. (1991), 'The Deuteronomic Law Code and the Politics of State Centralization', in D. Jobling et al. (eds.) 1991: 161–170.

Steuernagel, C. A. (1900), *Deuteronomium, Josua, Einleitung zum Hexateuch*, HAT, Göttingen: Vandenhoeck & Ruprecht.

Steymans, H. U. (1994), 'Die Opfer im Buch Deuteronomium: Ihre Funktion im Leben des Gottesvolkes', *BK* 49:126–131.

—— (1995a), *Deuteronomium 28 und die adê zur Thronfolgeregelung Asarhaddons: Segen und Fluch im Alten Orient und in Israel*, OBO 145, Göttingen: Vandenhoeck & Ruprecht.

—— (1995b), 'Eine assyrische Vorlage für Deuteronomium 28,20–44', in Braulik (ed.) 1995b: 118–141.

Stulman, L. (1990), 'Encroachment in Deuteronomy: An Analysis of the Social World of the D Code', *JBL* 109:613–632.

—— (1992), 'Sex and Familial Crimes in the D Code: A Witness to Mores in Transition', *JSOT* 53:47–64.

Sumner, W. A. (1968), 'Israel's Encounters with Edom, Moab, Ammon, Sihon and Og According to the Deuteronomist', *VT* 18:216–228.

Talstra, E. (1995), 'Deuteronomy 9 and 10: Synchronic and Diachronic Observations', in de Moor (ed.) 1995: 187–210.

Terrien, S. (1970), 'The Omphalos Myth and Hebrew Religion', *VT* 20:315–338.

—— (1978), *The Elusive Presence: Toward a New Biblical Theology*, San Francisco, CA: Harper & Row.

Tertel, H. J. (1994), *Text and Transmission: An Empirical Model for the Literary Development of the OT-Narratives*, BZAW 221, Berlin: de Gruyter.

Thompson, T. L. and D. (1968), 'Some Legal Problems in the Book of Ruth', *VT* 18:79–99.

Thompson, T. L. (1992), *The Early History of the Israelite People: From the Written and Archaeological Sources*, SHANE 4, Leiden: Brill.

Tigay, J. H. (1986), *You Shall Have No Other Gods: Israelite Religion in the Light of Hebrew Inscriptions*, HSS 31, Atlanta, GA: Scholars.

—— (1995), 'Some Archaeological Notes on Deuteronomy', in D. P. Wright et al. (eds.) 1995: 373–380.

Torrance, T. F. (1956), 'The Israel of God', *Interpretation* 10:305–322.

Tsevat, M. (1994), 'The Hebrew Slave According to Deut 15:12–18', *JBL* 113:587–595.

Turner, H. W. (1979), *From Temple to Meeting House: The Phenomenology and Theology of Places to Worship*, The Hague: Mouton.

Unterman, J. (1987), *From Repentance to Redemption: Jeremiah's Thought in Transition*, JSOTSup 54, Sheffield: JSOT.

Vanhoozer, K. (1994), 'God's Mighty Speech-Acts: The Doctrine of Scripture Today', in P. E. Satterthwaite and D. F. Wright (eds.), *A Pathway into Holy Scripture*, 143–181, Grand Rapids, MI: Eerdmans.

—— (1995), 'The Semantics of Biblical Literature: Truth and Scripture's Diverse Literary Forms', in D. A. Carson and J. D. Woodbridge (eds.), *Hermeneutics, Authority and Canon*, 49–104, Grand Rapids, MI: Baker; Carlisle: Paternoster.

—— (1998), *Is There a Meaning in This Text?* Grand Rapids, MI: Zondervan.

Van Leeuwen, R. C. (1985), 'What Comes out of God's Mouth: Theological Wordplay in Deuteronomy 8', *CBQ* 47:55–57.

Vanoni, G. (1981), 'Der Geist und der Buchstabe: Überlegungen zum Verhältnis der Testamente und Beobachtungen zu Dtn 30,1–10', *BN* 14:65–98.

Vaughan, P. H. (1974), *The Meaning of Bama in the Old Testament*, SOTSMS 3, Cambridge: Cambridge University Press.

Vaux, R. de (1961), *Ancient Israel: Its Life and Institutions*, London: Darton, Longman & Todd; New York: McGraw-Hill.

—— (1967), 'Le lieu que Yahvé a choisi pour y établir son nom', in F. Maass (ed.), *Das Ferne und Nahe Wort: Festschrift Leonhard Rost zur seines 70. Lebensjahres am 30. November 1966 gewidmet*, BZAW 105:219–228, Berlin: Alfred Töpelmann.

Veijola, T. (1992), 'Höre Israel! Der Sinn und Hintergrund von Deuteronomium VI 4–9', *VT* 42:528–541.

—— (1993), 'Principle Observations on the Basic Story in Deuteronomy 1 – 3', in Christensen (ed.) 1993: 137–146.

—— (ed.) (1996), *Das Deuteronomium und Seine Querbeziehungen*, SFEG 62, Göttingen: Vandenhoeck & Ruprecht.

Vermeylen, J. M. (1985a), 'L'Affaire du veau d'or (Ex 32 – 34): Une clé pour la "question deutéronomiste" ', *ZAW* 97:1–23.

—— (1985b), 'Les sections narratives du Deut 5 – 11', in N. Lohfink (ed.) 1985: 174–207.

Vervenne, M. (1994), 'The Question of "Deuteronomic" Elements in Genesis to Numbers', in García Martínez et al. (eds.) 1994: 243–268.

Vervenne, M., and J. Lust (eds.) (1997), *Deuteronomy and the Deuteronomic Social Conscience* (*FS* C. Brekelmans), BETL 133, Leuven University Press.

Vriezen, T. C. (1953), *Die Erwählung Israels nach dem Alten Testament*, ATANT 24, Zurich: Zwingli.

Wacker, M.-T. (1991), 'Aschera oder die Ambivalenz des Weiblichen: Anmerkungen zum Beitrag von Georg Braulik', in Wacker & Zenger (eds.) 1991: 137–150.

Wacker, M.-T., and E. Zenger (eds.) (1991), *Der Eine Gott und die Göttin: Gottesvorstellungen des biblischen Israel im Horizont feministischer Theologie*, Freiburg: Herder.

Wakely, R. (1997), '*ndr*', *NIDOTTE* 3:37–42.

Waldow, H. E. von (1970), 'Social Responsibility and Social Structure in Early Israel', *CBQ* 32:182–204.

———— (1974), 'Israel and her Land: Some Theological Considerations', in H. Bream (ed.), *A Light unto My Path: Old Testament Studies in Honor of J. M. Myers*, 493–508, Philadelphia, PA: Temple University Press.

Wall, R. W. (1987), 'The Finger of God: Deuteronomy 9:10 and Luke 11:20', *NTS* 33:144–150.

Walton, J. H. (1991), 'The Place of the *hutqattel* within the D-Stem, and its Implications in Deuteronomy 24:4', *HS* 32:7–17.

Warren, A. (1998), 'Did Moses Permit Divorce?' *TynB* 49.1:39–56.

Watson, F. B. (1997), *Text and Truth: Redefining Biblical Theology*, Edinburgh: T. & T. Clark; Grand Rapids, MI: Eerdmans.

Watts, J. W. (1992), *Psalm and Story*, JSOTSup 139, Sheffield: Sheffield Academic Press.

———— (1995), 'Rhetorical Strategy in the Composition of the Pentateuch', *JSOT* 68:3–22.

———— (1998), 'The Legal Characterization of Moses in the Rhetoric of the Pentateuch', *JBL* 117:415–426.

Weinfeld, M. (1961), 'The Origin of Humanism in Deuteronomy', *JBL* 80:241–247.

———— (1970), 'The Covenant of Grant in the Old Testament and in the ANE', *JAOS* 90:184–203; *JAOS* 92 (1972): 468–469.

———— (1972), *Deuteronomy and the Deuteronomic School*, Oxford: Clarendon.

———— (1976a), 'Jeremiah and the Spiritual Metamorphosis of Israel', *ZAW* 88:18–56.

———— (1976b), 'The Loyalty Oath in the ANE', *UF* 8:379–414.

———— (1977), 'Judge and Officer in the Ancient Near East', *IOS* 7:65–88.

Weippert, H. (1980), 'Der Ort, den Jahwe erwählen wird', *BZ* 24:76–94.

Welch, A. C. (1924), *The Code of Deuteronomy: A New Theory of its Origin*, London: James Clarke.

Wellhausen, J. (1889), *Die Composition des Hexateuchs und der historischen Bücher des Alten Testaments*, Berlin: Georg Reimer.

—— (1957), *Prolegomena to the History of Ancient Israel*, Cleveland, OH: World. (German original 1878; ET 1885.)

Wenham, G. J. (1971a), 'Deuteronomy and the Central Sanctuary', *TynB* 22:103–118.

—— (1971b), 'The Deuteronomic Theology of the Book of Joshua', *JBL* 90:140–148.

—— (1971c), 'The Structure and Date of Deuteronomy', PhD dissertation, London University.

—— (1972), 'Betulah, a Girl of Marriageable Age', *VT* 22:326–348.

—— (1978), 'Law and the Legal System in the Old Testament', in B. N. Kaye and G. J. Wenham (eds.), *Law, Morality and the Bible*, 24–52, Leicester: IVP.

—— (1979a), *Leviticus*, NICOT, Grand Rapids, MI: Eerdmans.

—— (1979b), 'The Restoration of Marriage Reconsidered', *JJS* 30:36–40.

—— (1980), 'The Religion of the Patriarchs', in A. R. Millard and D. J. Wiseman (eds.), *Essays on the Patriarchal Narratives*, 157–188, Leicester: IVP; Winona Lake, IN: Eisenbrauns, 1983.

—— (1981), *Numbers*, TOTC, Leicester and Downers Grove, IL: IVP.

—— (1987), *Genesis 1 – 15*, WBC, Waco, TX: Word.

—— (2000), *Story as Torah: Reading the Old Testament Ethically*, Edinburgh: T. & T. Clark.

Wenham, G. J., and W. Heth (1997), *Jesus and Divorce*, 2nd ed., Carlisle: Paternoster.

Wenham, G. J., and J. G. McConville (1980), 'Drafting Techniques in Some Deuteronomic Laws', *VT* 30:248–252.

Westbrook, R. (1986), 'The Prohibition on Restoration of Marriage in Deuteronomy 24:1–4', in Japhet (ed.) 1986: 387–405.

—— (1991), *Property and the Family in Biblical Law*, JSOTSup 113, Sheffield: JSOT.

Westermann, C. (1984), *Genesis 1 – 11*, London: SPCK; Minneapolis, MN: Augsburg.

—— (1993), *Die Geschichtsbücher des Alten Testaments: Gab es ein deuteronomistisches Geschichtsbuch?* TB 87 AT, Munich: Chr. Kaiser.

Wette, W. M. L. de (1805), *Dissertatio critico-exegetica qua Deuteronomium a prioribus Pentateuchi libris diversum, alius cuiusdam recentioris auctoris opus esse monstratur*, Jena.

Wevers, J. W. (1995), *Notes on the Greek Text of Deuteronomy*, SCSS 39, Atlanta, GA: Scholars.

Whitelam, K. W. (1996), *The Invention of Ancient Israel: The Silencing of Palestinian History*, London: Routledge.

Wiebe, J. M. (1989), 'The Form, Setting and Meaning of the Song of Moses', *Studia Biblica et Theologica*, 17:119–163.

Wiener, H. M. (1926), 'The Arrangement of Deuteronomy 26', *JPOS* 6:185–195.

Williamson, H. G. M. (1998), 'The Messianic Texts in Isaiah 1 – 39', in Day (ed.) 1998: 238–270.

Wilson, I. (1995), *Out of the Midst of the Fire: Divine Presence in Deuteronomy*, SBLDS 151, Atlanta, GA: Scholars.

Wilson, P. E. (1997), 'Deuteronomy XXV 11–12: One for the Books', *VT* 47:220–235.

Wiseman, D. J. (1958), *The Vassal Treaties of Esarhaddon*, London: British School of Archaeology in Iraq.

Wolff, H. (1976), 'The Kerygma of the Deuteronomic Historical Work', in W. Brueggemann and H. Wolff (eds.), *The Vitality of the Old Testament Traditions*, 83–100, Atlanta, GA: John Knox.

Wolterstorff, N. (1995), *Divine Discourse: Philosophical Reflections on the Claim that God Speaks*, Cambridge: Cambridge University Press.

Woude, A. S. van der (1994), 'Erwägungen zum Rahmenpsalm von Deuteronomium 33', in García Martínez et al. (eds.) 1994: 281–288.

Wright, C. J. H. (1984), 'What Happened Every Seven Years in Israel? Old Testament Sabbatical Institutions for Debt, Land and Slaves', *EvQ* 56:387–403.

——— (1988), 'The Ten Commandments', *ISBE* 4:786–790.

——— (1990), *God's People in God's Land*, Grand Rapids, MI: Eerdmans.

Wright, D. P. (1987), 'Deuteronomy 21:1–9 as a Rite of Elimination', *CBQ* 49:387–403.

——— (1991), 'The Spectrum of Priestly Impurity', in Anderson & Olyan (eds.) 1991: 150–181.

——— (1992), 'Clean and Unclean', *ABD* 6:739–741.

Wright, D. P., D. N. Freedman and A. Hurvitz (eds.) (1995), *Pomegranates and Golden Bells: Studies in Biblical, Jewish and Near Eastern Ritual, Law and Literature in Honor of Jacob Milgrom*, Winona Lake, IN: Eisenbrauns.

Wright, G. E. (1954), 'The Levites in Deuteronomy', *VT* 4:325–330.

Wright, L. S. (1989), '*MKR* in 2 Kings 12:5–17 and Deuteronomy 18:8', *VT* 39:438–448.

Wright, N. T. (1991), *The Climax of the Covenant: Christ and the Law in Pauline Theology*, Edinburgh: T. & T. Clark; Minneapolis, MN: Fortress.

——— (1992), *The New Testament and the People of God*, London: SPCK; Minneapolis, MN: Fortress.

——— (1996), *Jesus and the Victory of God*, London: SPCK.

Wright, N. T., and M. Borg (1999), *The Meaning of Jesus: Two Visions*, San Francisco, CA: HarperCollins.

Yaron, R. (1966), 'The Restoration of Marriage', *JJS* 17:1–11.

Yoder, H. (1994), *The Politics of Jesus*, 2nd ed., Grand Rapids, MI: Eerdmans; Carlisle: Paternoster.

Young, I. (1993), *Diversity in Pre-exilic Hebrew*, FAT 5, Tübingen: Mohr.

Zevit, Z. (1976), 'The 'Egla Ritual of Deuteronomy 21:1–9', *JBL* 95:377–390.

Zimmerli, W. (1978), *Old Testament Theology in Outline*, Edinburgh: T. & T. Clark.

Zobel, K. (1992), *Prophetie und Deuteronomium: Die Rezeption prophetischer Theologie durch das Deuteronomium*, BZAW 199, Berlin: de Gruyter.

Zwickel, W. (1994), 'Wirtschaftliche Grundlagen in Zentraljuda gegen Ende des 8. Jh.s. aus archäologischer Sicht – Mit einem Ausblick auf die wirtschaftliche Situation im 7. Jh.', *UF* 26:557–592.

INDEX OF SCRIPTURE REFERENCES

INDEX OF AUTHORS

INDEX OF SUBJECTS

This is a selected index. It omits certain terms very frequent in Deuteronomy, notably 'gift' and 'land'.